ANOKA COUNTY LIBRARY

P9-DEH-822

2/07

A FIELD GUIDE TO

MAMMALS

OF NORTH AMERICA

A FIELD GUIDE TO

MAMMALS

OF NORTH AMERICA
NORTH OF MEXICO

·

FOURTH EDITION

❧

FIONA A. REID

SPONSORED BY THE NATIONAL AUDUBON SOCIETY,
THE NATIONAL WILDLIFE FEDERATION, AND
THE ROGER TORY PETERSON INSTITUTE

HOUGHTON MIFFLIN COMPANY
BOSTON   NEW YORK   2006

Copyright © 2006 by Fiona A. Reid
Maps copyright © 2006 by Fiona A. Reid and Larry Rosche
Skull photographs copyright © 2006 by James Knowles

All rights reserved

For information about permission to reproduce selections from this
book, write to Permissions, Houghton Mifflin Company,
215 Park Avenue, New York, New York 10003.

Visit our Web site: www.houghtonmifflinbooks.com.

PETERSON FIELD GUIDES and PETERSON FIELD GUIDE SERIES
are registered trademarks of Houghton Mifflin Company.

Library of Congress Cataloging-in-Publication Data
Reid, Fiona.
    A field guide to mammals of North America / Fiona A. Reid — 4th ed.
        p. cm. — (The Peterson field guide series.)
    Includes bibliographical references and index.
    ISBN-13: 978-0-395-93596-5 (alk. paper)
    ISBN-10: 0-395-93596-2 (alk. paper)
    1. Mammals — United States — Identification.   2. Mammals —
Canada — Identification.   I. Title.   II. Series.
    QL717.R45   2006
599.097 — dc22   2005037897

Book design by Anne Chalmers
Typeface: Fairfield, Futura Condensed

Printed in Singapore

TWP 10 9 8 7 6 5 4 3 2 1

The Roger Tory Peterson Institute, Jamestown, New York

The legacy of America's great naturalist and creator of this field guide series, Roger Tory Peterson, is preserved through the programs and work of the Roger Tory Peterson Institute of Natural History (RTPI), located in his birthplace of Jamestown, New York. RTPI is a national nature education organization with a mission to continue the legacy of Roger Tory Peterson by promoting the teaching and study of nature and to thereby create knowledge of and appreciation and responsibility for the natural world. RTPI also preserves and exhibits Dr. Peterson's extraordinary collection of artwork, photography, and writing.

You can become a part of this worthy effort by joining RTPI. Simply call RTPI's membership department at 800-758-6841 ext. 226, fax 716-665-3794, or e-mail members@rtpi.org for a free one-year membership with the purchase of this Peterson Field Guide. Check out our award-winning Web site at www.enaturalist.org. You can link to all our programs and activities from there.

CONTENTS

LIST OF PLATES

ACKNOWLEDGMENTS

Many people have helped with the development and production of this book. It has been many years in the making, and I can only hope that most of the people who contributed are mentioned below. I send my regrets to anyone I have forgotten to list.

I visited a variety of areas in the United States and Canada to study, catch, and draw mammals from life. In some states I worked under my own permits, in others permits were granted to some of the people listed below. I would like to thank everyone on the following list, arranged by state or province, for help with fieldwork. Arizona: Janet Tyburek, Cullen Geiselman, Michael Nachman, Wade Sherbrook, Fred and Nancy Gehlbach, Bryan Milstead, Ami Pate, Katy Hinman, Bat Conservation International, Southwestern Research Station, Arizona Department of Game and Fish (special thanks to the incredible efficiency of Melissa Swain), U.S. Forest Service–Williams District (Sheila Sandusky), Grand Canyon National Park permit office (Della Snyder). California: Jim Patton, Karen Carter, Matina Kalcounis-Ruppell, Sophie Webb, Tim Lawlor, Brian Arbogast, Michael King, Simpson Timber Company (Keith Hamm and Joel Thompson). Oregon: Tom Manning, Oregon Department of Fish and Wildlife. Washington: Dale Herter, Dean Rofkar, Jim Kenagy, Patricia Otto, and David Wisner. Missouri: Sybill and Joe Amelon. Florida: Jeff Gore, Cindy Marks, Terry Doonan, Florida Fish and Wildlife Conservation Commission, The Lubee Foundation. Texas: Bob and Paula Dowler, Loren Ammerman, Terry and Ann Maxwell, Jana Higginbotham. Ontario, Canada: Mark Engstrom, Mary Gartshore, Peter Carson, Yemisi Dare, Bev and Read Whatmough, Bill and Irene McIlveen, Ray Blower, Don Scallen, John Pisapio, and last but not least, one of the great small mammal collectors on my street, the Forsyth cat.

I visited a number of museums to study mammals. My home

base at the Royal Ontario Museum was invaluable; here I was aided by Mark Engstrom, Judith Eger, Burton Lim, Susan Woodward, and Jim Borack. I also used the extensive collections at the U.S. National Museum, with help from Linda Gordon, Bob Fisher, Michael Carleton, Louise Emmons, and others. At the American Museum of Natural History, N.Y., Rob Voss and Nancy Simmons provided help and hospitality. At the Museum of Vertebrate Zoology in Berkeley, Jim Patton and Chris Conroy provided much-needed assistance and loaned specimens to me. John Koprowski and Yar Petryszn facilitated a visit to the University of Arizona mammal collection. I also examined mammal collections at the Burke Museum and the Vertebrate Museum at Humboldt State University. Bob Timm kindly provided data and loaned specimens from the University of Kansas Museum. Phil Myers and Steve Hinshaw sent me information on specimens in their care at the University of Michigan Museum of Zoology.

In addition to extensive fieldwork and museum research, I also used photo collections to compose realistic renderings of some species. Guy Tudor loaned numerous photos and provided much input on design and layouts of the color plates; he was always ready to discuss aspects of field guide production. Michael Patrikeev sent me a number of his excellent slides and prints of small mammals. Mark Riegner, George Smiley, and Andy Jones also provided images.

Several biologists read and commented on parts of the book. Their input greatly improved the final product. The reviewers are ordered by arrangement of text in the book: Mark Engstrom (rodents, rabbits, and many other accounts), Jim Patton (selected rodents and lagomorphs), Daniel Williams (kangaroo rat range maps), Robert Dowler (pocket gophers), Jerry Choate (shrews and moles), Janet Tyburek (bats), Steven Gehman and Andrea Bixler (carnivores), Robert Stewart and David Lavigne (seals and sea lions), Thomas Jefferson (selected cetaceans), Robert Pitman (beaked whales, whale maps, and whale taxonomy), Pierre Richard (Arctic cetaceans), and Philip Clapham (rorqual whales).

James Knowles provided the beautiful skull photographs, with technical assistance from Mark Engstrom. James Knowles and I designed the skull plates from his digital images.

Larry Rosche carefully digitized range maps and was extremely patient with endless changes and modifications as new information became available to me.

Paul Cryan provided useful data for range maps of bats, and Keith Geluso improved the accuracy of many of the small mammal range maps. Many other biologists answered questions about the distribution of a species or other details. I thank all of those who responded to my requests for information. Here is an undoubtedly incomplete list of contributors: Robert Baker, Brian Bartels, Floyd Connor, Rita Dixon, Bill Gannon, Mark Hafner, Dave Johnston, William Kilpatrick, Marjorie Matocq, Tom Owens, John Radcliffe, Brett Riddle, Dave Wyatt, and Bill Zielinski.

I thank my friends and family for support and encouragement, and particularly my husband, Mark Engstrom, for living through the production of yet another field guide. My children, Holly and Ian, cheerfully suffered through my many absences and accompanied us on some field trips. Special thanks to Stephen Linsley for financial support of some of my fieldwork. Queen's University Biological Station funded some fieldwork in Ontario.

Staff at Houghton Mifflin, in particular Lisa White, provided much-needed editorial input during the development and production of this guide. This book replaces the third edition of the Peterson Field Guide to mammals, by William H. Burt and Richard P. Grossenheider, a work that inspired several generations of mammalogists. Grossenheider was one of the first artists to really do justice to the small mammals. I can only hope to live up to his precedent.

Thanks in advance also to all the readers who will, I hope, send in their corrections and comments on range maps and species accounts.

INTRODUCTION

HOW TO USE THIS BOOK

The primary purpose of this book is to enable the reader to identify mammals seen in the wild. Many mammals are shy and retiring, allowing only a glimpse before disappearing from view. For some of the small mammals, successful identification to species might be possible only from a dead specimen. The identification process for dead, live, well-viewed, or glimpsed animals should be the same: Look through the color plates and determine what type of animal you saw. Turn to the text page for the species that most resembles your sighting and look at the range map. If the map is not shaded for your area, then return to the color plates and try another similar species. Keep in mind that many species vary in color from one region to another and that not all color morphs can be illustrated in a portable field guide. When you find a species that resembles your sighting and occurs in the correct geographic area, read the text to see if the description fits the habitat that you are in and any behavior you may have observed. Also check the "Similar species" section for other possibilities in your area.

PLATES

Species are shown to scale on the plates unless indicated. Related species are generally grouped on the same plate, but in some cases unrelated species are placed together, either because they look similar or for practical or design purposes. Within families, species are usually arranged by similarity rather than by taxonomic relatedness. Note that certain species vary considerably in size or color throughout their range as well as with age or season. Some of these variants are portrayed on the same plate, while others are discussed in the text. Most of the color illustrations of small mammals were painted directly from live animals caught in the wild.

Skull Plates

If you find the skull of a mammal, turn to the Skull Plates on p. 134. Be sure to examine the teeth and compare them with the dental formula given (see p. 135 for an explanation of how to use the formula to count and characterize teeth).

Species Accounts

The main text of this book consists of individual species accounts that are designed to aid in identification and also to provide some general information on the species seen. The accounts are arranged as follows.

MEASUREMENTS. The identification section begins with a list of external measurements in English and metric units. Head and body measurements are taken with the subject laid flat on its back, from the tip of the nose to the base of the tail. The tail is measured from its base to the tip of the tailbone (excluding tufts of hair). The hind foot is measured from the heel to the tip of the longest claw. The ear is measured from the basal notch inside the ear to the tip. For bats, the forearm is measured from the elbow to the base of the thumb, with the wing in the closed position. Measurements for hind feet and ears are given for the smaller, more easily confused species when these measurements can help confirm identification. Nonmetric measurements for the small mammals are given mostly as averages to aid in comparing between species seen in the wild. Metric measurements are given as a range to provide a more precise guide for animals in the hand. I have given the usual range of variation, which does not include unusually large or small adults, young animals, or pregnant females.

DESCRIPTION. The external characteristics are described, along with variation among populations and between sexes and age classes. Features that are most important for identification are shown in italics.

SIMILAR SPECIES. This section lists those species — primarily ones that occur in the same geographic area — that might be confused with the species discussed.

SOUNDS. In addition to barks and cries made by the animal, sounds that it sometimes makes when foraging are also listed.

HABITS. The habits section does not include everything that is known about the behavior and ecology of a species, but focuses on information that may be relevant to identification: whether it is nocturnal or diurnal, solitary or social; the way it moves; and what type of den or nest it uses. A brief description of its breeding biology is also given.

HABITAT. The main types of terrain or environment that the animal occupies (forest, field, desert, etc.) are indicated. Elevational range is included for many species.

RANGE. The geographic range (both within and beyond the U.S. and Canada) is briefly described.

STATUS. This section indicates the species's relative abundance and lists its conservation status in cases where the species is threatened or endangered. Organizations that list the status of a species are abbreviated as outlined below.

USFWS: U.S. Fish and Wildlife Service

US-ESA: U.S. Endangered Species Act

CITES: Convention on International Trade in Endangered Species of Wild Flora and Fauna (categories used include Appendix I, for the most endangered species, those threatened with extinction; and Appendix II, for endangered species that may be threatened with extinction in the near future)

COSEWIC: Committee on the Status of Endangered Wildlife in Canada

IUCN: International Union for Conservation of Nature and Natural Resources

GEOGRAPHIC SCOPE

This book includes all wild mammals that occur in the continental U.S. and Canada and their adjacent islands. Marine mammals of the waters of the U.S. (excluding Hawaii) and Canada are also included. Nonnative land mammals that have established sustained breeding populations in the wild are also described, although some species that occur only on private lands (primarily ranches in Texas or California) are not listed.

RANGE MAPS

Maps are given for all species. In some cases two or more species may be shown on one map to aid in delimiting the border or area of overlap of similar species. The shaded area is the region where the species occurs at present, although within this area it will not be found in unsuitable habitat. For some species the historical range is marked with a green dashed line, and introduced or reintroduced populations are indicated in blue. The wild range of nonnative species is also marked in blue. Extralimital range points are marked in gold.

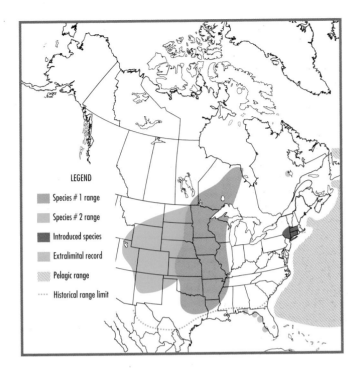

LEGEND

- Species # 1 range
- Species # 2 range
- Introduced species
- Extralimital record
- Pelagic range
- Historical range limit

COMMON AND SCIENTIFIC NAMES

Common names used in this field guide are, in general, the names that have been in use for the longest period and have the widest acceptance. For some groups there have been attempts to standardize common names. The bat names used in this book follow a listing that was developed by a committee of mammal book authors. For some of the rodents I have selected common names that have been used for many years, often following the earlier edition of this field guide. For these common names and many others in this book, I closely follow the "Revised checklist of North American mammals north of Mexico, 2003," by Baker et al., as well as authors such as Whitaker and Hamilton (1998).

More important for identification purposes are the scientific names. These formal names follow the listings in Wilson and Reeder (2005) with few exceptions. Many species are currently being renamed or split into two or more species based on new genetic or molecular data. I hesitate to include all of the most recent information, as in some cases further work may not back up the initial study, rendering any changes unstable. For the general reader, new names may cause unnecessary confusion. Where they arise, taxonomic issues are outlined in a section titled "Note" at the end of the species account.

TAXONOMIC RELATIONSHIPS AND ORDER OF ACCOUNTS

The relationships among the orders of mammals have been the subject of considerable interest and study in recent years. Systematists (scientists who study the diversity of life) have made more progress in understanding these relationships in the past 30 years than in the previous 300. Many of our earlier assumptions about alliances among orders and evolutionary lineages have changed, most recently with the advent of DNA sequencing and other kinds of molecular genetics evidence. For the general reader it may be confusing to see the order Rodentia (rodents) appear in the middle of some books (Hall, 1981), as the final accounts in others (Wilson and Ruff, 1999), and near the beginning of this book. None of these approaches is necessarily right or wrong. Relationships among orders of mammals should be viewed as a branching tree, with higher, short-tipped branches indicating closer alliances among orders and lower branchings signifying deeper relationships among individual orders and groups of orders.

One order of mammals in our region, the Didelphimorphia (opossums), can be truly considered an early divergent branch of living mammals. Opossums are metatherians (marsupials), with a rudimentary placenta, short-term pregnancy, and relatively undeveloped young at birth. They are the sister group to all other living North American mammals, the eutherian mammals (with an intrusive placenta, extended pregnancy, and relatively well-developed young at birth). Among the eutherians, xenarthrans (armadillos, anteaters, and sloths) are one of the earliest and most divergent groups. Opossums and armadillos therefore appear first in this book, representing some of the earliest branches of the evolutionary tree in North America. Likewise, Sirenia (manatees) are the only North American representatives of another deep branch in the tree, the Afrotheria, which includes such exotic mammals as elephants, hyraxes, golden moles, elephant shrews, and aardvarks. The text account for manatee thus appears near the beginning of the book. Traditionally, the Soricimorpha (true shrews and moles — often grouped together with other shrewlike or hedgehoglike animals in the Insectivora) were considered to be a primitive eutherian group, but they are now thought to be allied to a related group of orders that form the third deep branch of the eutherian tree, the Laurasiatheria, that includes carnivores, bats, whales, and hoofed mammals. Inclusion of bats within this group has been a revelation: previously bats had been thought most closely related to primates, tree shrews, and flying lemurs (groups that do not occur in the area covered by this book). Seals and sea lions were once grouped into a separate order, Pinnipedia, but are now known to be members of the order Carnivora (carnivores).

Some North American orders are closely allied: for example, rodents and rabbits are each other's nearest relatives and therefore appear together in this guide. Cetacea (whales, dolphins, and porpoises) are closely related to Artiodactyla (even-toed hoofed mammals), although the two groups could hardly appear to be more distinct in form.

The text is arranged following known systematic relationships, described above. Within each order, families are arranged by taxonomic relationship. Genera and species are arranged similarly. Recently, many books on mammals have arranged the species accounts alphabetically, a system that is practical for listing all known species. In my opinion, however, an alphabetic listing has little merit in a field guide, where the majority of readers will not know the scientific names of the species. I chose to list species by relationship, where known. This allowed me to place closely related species on the same range map because the text accounts for these species are adjacent. It also enables readers to easily find the texts for similar, related species for comparative purposes.

The plates are arranged roughly systematically but with some concessions to design, scale, convenience, and ecological relationships. Marine mammals form a distinct geographic and ecological unit and appear together in the plate section. To this end, the artiodactyls are separated from their closest relatives, the cetaceans, and placed before the carnivores; and the manatee is depicted with the dolphins. The carnivore plates show the aquatic mustelids (the otters), followed by the seals and sea lions. The seal plates are followed by the manatee and cetacean plates, so that seals, manatees, whales, and sea otters can be viewed in a single section, even though these groups are not closely related. Within some families of mammals, plates are arranged by geography rather than systematic relationships (for example, chipmunks, kangaroo rats, and voles). Other groups may be split by relative size (for example, shrew plates and some cetacean plates). These arrangements were made to aid in identification of very similar species and to avoid issues of pronounced differences in scale on the same plate. Images on the plates are shown to scale except when indicated by a scale bar (also flight studies of bats). Images on legend pages are not to scale with the plate, but where more than one image is given, they are to scale with one another.

A FIELD GUIDE TO

MAMMALS

OF NORTH AMERICA

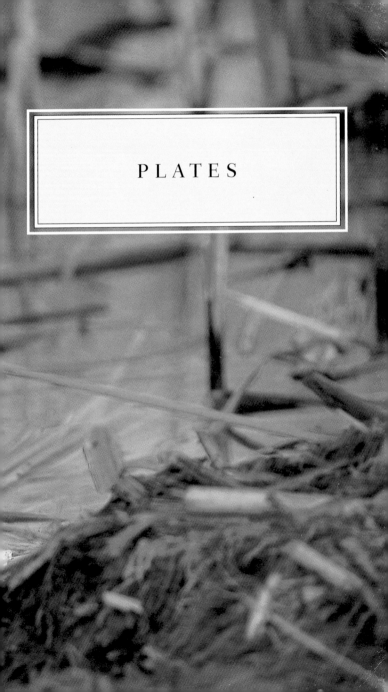

PLATES

PLATE 1

OPOSSUM AND ARMORED MAMMALS

These unrelated mammals could be called "invaders from the south," as all are sole North American representatives of families that are found in South America.

VIRGINIA OPOSSUM   *Didelphis virginiana*   **P. 171**
Scruffy, ratlike appearance; body grizzled gray contrasting with white head; tail naked, scaly, black at base, tip white.

NINE-BANDED ARMADILLO   *Dasypus novemcinctus*   **P. 173**
Our only armor-plated mammal.

NORTH AMERICAN PORCUPINE   *Erethizon dorsatum*   **P. 338**
Body covered with sharp quills, partially concealed in long fur.

TRACKS

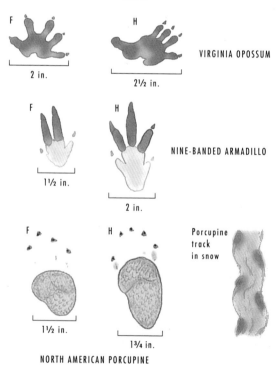

F   H   VIRGINIA OPOSSUM
2 in.   2½ in.

F   H   NINE-BANDED ARMADILLO
1½ in.   2 in.

F   H   Porcupine track in snow
1½ in.   1¾ in.

NORTH AMERICAN PORCUPINE

PLATE 1

VIRGINIA OPOSSUM

NINE-BANDED ARMADILLO

NORTH AMERICAN PORCUPINE

PLATE 2

LARGE SEMIAQUATIC RODENTS

These large rodents are nearly always found in or near water.

COMMON MUSKRAT *Ondatra zibethicus*   **P. 326**
Glossy brown fur, tail flattened on sides; found near water; swims
with part of head, back, and tail exposed (3 humps).

ROUND-TAILED MUSKRAT *Neofiber alleni*   **P. 325**
Glossy brown or blackish fur, tail rounded; smaller than Common
Muskrat. SE.

AMERICAN BEAVER *Castor canadensis*   **P. 179**
Scaly, paddle-shaped tail; webbed hind feet; swims with only head
or head, neck, and upper back exposed (1 hump).

COYPU *Myocastor coypus*   **P. 339**
Larger than Common Muskrat, with coarser fur and rounded tail;
head "squared-off," with white whiskers; swimming profile similar
to Beaver.

TRACKS

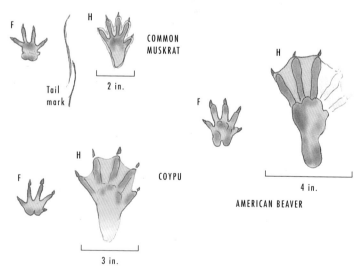

F

H

COMMON
MUSKRAT

2 in.

Tail
mark

F

H

F

H

COYPU

3 in.

AMERICAN BEAVER

4 in.

PLATE 2

COMMON MUSKRAT

ROUND-TAILED MUSKRAT

Muskrat swimming

Beaver swimming

AMERICAN BEAVER

COYPU

PLATE 3

SEWELLEL AND MARMOTS

SEWELLEL   *Aplodontia rufa*   **P. 178**
   Dark brown or black; tiny tail usually obscured; small ears, long claws. Local, NW.

Marmots are large stocky rodents with short brushy tails. They are usually seen near burrows.

WOODCHUCK   *Marmota monax*   **P. 181**
   Grizzled brown with dark legs and tail; can be blackish (melanistic).

YELLOW-BELLIED MARMOT   *Marmota flaviventris*   **P. 182**
   Belly yellow-orange contrasting with grizzled brown back; white marks between eyes. W.

OLYMPIC MARMOT   *Marmota olympus*   **P. 184**
   Blond or orange-brown. Local, NW.

VANCOUVER ISLAND MARMOT   *Marmota vancouverensis*   **P. 185**
   Dark chocolate brown to black with white muzzle. Vancouver I. only.

ALASKA MARMOT   *Marmota broweri*   **P. 184**
   Very similar to Hoary Marmot but top of head black. Local, n. Alaska.

HOARY MARMOT   *Marmota caligata*   **P. 183**
   Forequarters silvery, rump and tail orange-brown; black-and-white markings on face. NW.

TRACKS

F

H

WOODCHUCK

1¾ in.

2 in.

PLATE 3

SEWELLEL

melanistic phase

WOODCHUCK

YELLOW-
BELLIED
MARMOT

OLYMPIC
MARMOT

VANCOUVER
ISLAND
MARMOT

ALASKA
MARMOT

HOARY
MARMOT

PLATE 4

PRAIRIE DOGS

Live in large "towns" in open grassland habitats throughout the prairies.

BLACK-TAILED PRAIRIE DOG   *Cynomys ludovicianus*   **P. 186**
Body yellowish or pinkish brown; tail relatively long, tipped black.

WHITE-TAILED PRAIRIE DOG   *Cynomys leucurus*   **P. 187**
Body yellow-gray; black markings above and below eyes; tail short, pure white at tip.

UTAH PRAIRIE DOG   *Cynomys parvidens*   **P. 188**
Body usually rich cinnamon orange; black markings above and below eyes; tail white at tip.

GUNNISON'S PRAIRIE DOG   *Cynomys gunnisoni*   **P. 188**
Body yellowish; faint black markings above and below eyes; short tail edged with white.

PLATE 4

BLACK-TAILED PRAIRIE DOG

WHITE-TAILED PRAIRIE DOG

UTAH PRAIRIE DOG

GUNNISON'S PRAIRIE DOG

PLATE 5

LARGE GROUND SQUIRRELS

Mostly seen on the ground but Rock and California Ground Squirrels climb well. Same size or larger than gray squirrels.

FRANKLIN'S GROUND SQUIRREL   *Spermophilus franklinii*   **P. 200**
Dark gray or brown, finely grizzled; head usually grayer than back; prairies. N Central.

ARCTIC GROUND SQUIRREL   *Spermophilus parryii*   **P. 196**
Large; color variable, may have distinct cream flecks or fine grizzle on back; top of head, belly, and legs orange; tail tipped black.

COLUMBIAN GROUND SQUIRREL   *Spermophilus columbianus*   **P. 195**
Similar to Arctic Ground Squirrel but more finely flecked on back, tail tipped cream, and white blaze on sides of neck and shoulder.

ROCK SQUIRREL   *Spermophilus variegatus*   **P. 201**
Grizzled gray-brown (more coarsely grizzled than tree squirrels); tail long and thick. Variable in color: may be all-black or with blackish forequarters and grizzled rump (shown).

CALIFORNIA GROUND SQUIRREL   *Spermophilus beecheyi*   **P. 201**
Grizzled gray-brown to blackish, white blaze on neck and shoulders; tail long and thick.

PLATE 5

FRANKLIN'S GROUND SQUIRREL

ARCTIC GROUND SQUIRREL

COLUMBIAN GROUND SQUIRREL

melanistic phase

ROCK SQUIRREL

gray phase

CALIFORNIA GROUND SQUIRREL

PLATE 6

MEDIUM-SIZED GROUND SQUIRRELS

Found in grasslands of the prairies and Great Plains, also in the Great Basin.

GREAT BASIN GROUND SQUIRREL   *Spermophilus mollis*   P. 191
Small, very pale; tail very short. See Columbia Plateau Ground Squirrel (*S. canus*), p. 191, almost identical.

TOWNSEND'S GROUND SQUIRREL   *Spermophilus townsendii*   P. 189
Very similar to above but slightly darker.

IDAHO GROUND SQUIRREL   *Spermophilus brunneus*   P. 192
Small, relatively short tail; reddish brown with distinct flecks of white on back; red-orange nose and rump. *S. b. brunneus* is brown (illustrated); *S. b. endemicus* is grayish.

WASHINGTON GROUND SQUIRREL   *Spermophilus washingtoni*   P. 191
Small; back dark brown flecked with white, sharply delineated from whitish sides and belly; tail short.

BELDING'S GROUND SQUIRREL   *Spermophilus beldingi*   P. 194
Medium sized; upper back orange-brown contrasting with grayish sides; tail reddish with a dark tip.

WYOMING GROUND SQUIRREL   *Spermophilus elegans*   P. 193
Medium sized, yellow-gray; tail grizzled, black near tip and edged with cream.

UINTA GROUND SQUIRREL   *Spermophilus armatus*   P. 194
Body gray or gray-brown, top of head orangish; tail grayish.

RICHARDSON'S GROUND SQUIRREL   *Spermophilus richardsonii*   P. 192
Very similar to Wyoming Ground Squirrel; yellow often extends onto head around ears; tail has less black at tip than in Wyoming.

GREAT BASIN
GROUND SQUIRREL

PLATE 6

TOWNSEND'S
GROUND
SQUIRREL

WASHINGTON
GROUND SQUIRREL

IDAHO
GROUND SQUIRREL

BELDING'S
GROUND
SQUIRREL

WYOMING GROUND SQUIRREL

UINTA GROUND
SQUIRREL

RICHARDSON'S
GROUND
SQUIRREL

PLATE 7

SMALL GROUND SQUIRRELS

Mostly found in deserts of the Southwest.

Antelope Squirrels superficially resemble chipmunks but do not have stripes on head.

HARRIS'S ANTELOPE SQUIRREL *Ammospermophilus harrisii* **P. 205**
White stripe on sides, reddish limbs; tail gray above and below.

WHITE-TAILED ANTELOPE SQUIRREL *Ammospermophilus leucurus* **P. 206**
Similar to Harris's but tail white below.

TEXAS ANTELOPE SQUIRREL *Ammospermophilus interpres* **P. 207**
Very similar to White-tailed but tail has 2 bars of black at tip on underside (ranges do not overlap).

NELSON'S ANTELOPE SQUIRREL *Ammospermophilus nelsoni* **P. 208**
Larger and more yellowish than other antelope squirrels; tail white below. Calif.

MOHAVE GROUND SQUIRREL *Spermophilus mohavensis* **P. 202**
Very pale, pinkish brown; tail blackish near tip, underside white or cream.

ROUND-TAILED GROUND SQUIRREL *Spermophilus tereticaudus* **P. 203**
Similar to Mohave but usually slightly darker with whitish on cheeks and around ears; tail longer, brown below, little black near tip.

SPOTTED GROUND SQUIRREL *Spermophilus spilosoma* **P. 199**
Pale pinkish gray, with small white spots (not arranged in rows) on back.

THIRTEEN-LINED GROUND SQUIRREL *Spermophilus tridecemlineatus* **P. 197**
Distinct alternating pattern of stripes and rows of spots on back.

MEXICAN GROUND SQUIRREL *Spermophilus mexicanus* **P. 198**
Distinct spots arranged in rows but rarely forming stripes; background color paler than in Thirteen-lined; tail long and bushy, edged with cream.

PLATE 7

HARRIS'S ANTELOPE SQUIRREL

WHITE-TAILED ANTELOPE SQUIRREL

TEXAS ANTELOPE SQUIRREL

NELSON'S ANTELOPE SQUIRREL

MOHAVE GROUND SQUIRREL

ROUND-TAILED GROUND SQUIRREL

SPOTTED GROUND SQUIRREL

THIRTEEN-LINED GROUND SQUIRREL

MEXICAN GROUND SQUIRREL

PLATE 8

NORTHERN CHIPMUNKS AND GOLDEN-MANTLED GROUND SQUIRRELS

Mostly found in forest and forest gaps, but some occur in drier regions.

EASTERN CHIPMUNK   *Tamias striatus*   **P. 209**
Indistinct facial stripes; short stripes on sides, rump reddish.

LEAST CHIPMUNK   *Tamias minimus*   **P. 211**
Small; color variable (see Pl. 10). Facial and back stripes usually prominent; tail noticeably long and narrow.

YELLOW-PINE CHIPMUNK   *Tamias amoenus*   **P. 212**
Fairly small; usually bright yellow or orange on shoulders and sides; tail slightly shorter than in Least.

TOWNSEND'S CHIPMUNK   *Tamias townsendii*   **P. 213**
Large and dark; facial stripes whitish, back stripes gray (inland) or cream (coastal). See Pl. 9 for related species.

RED-TAILED CHIPMUNK   *Tamias ruficaudus*   **P. 220**
Brightly colored; orange rust on sides; underside of long tail bright orange-red.

GOLDEN-MANTLED GROUND SQUIRREL   *Spermophilus lateralis*   **P. 204**
No facial stripes; very bold cream white stripe on sides bordered with black, lower sides usually cream; mantle bright red-orange.

CASCADE GROUND SQUIRREL   *Spermophilus saturatus*   **P. 205**
Very similar to above, but gray (not white) on lower sides; mantle usually orange.

PLATE 8

EASTERN CHIPMUNK

LEAST CHIPMUNK

Northeast

West

YELLOW-PINE CHIPMUNK

TOWNSEND'S CHIPMUNK

inland

coastal

RED-TAILED CHIPMUNK

GOLDEN-MANTLED GROUND SQUIRREL

CASCADE GROUND SQUIRREL

PLATE 9

CALIFORNIA CHIPMUNKS

These species are endemic or near endemic to California. Also see Least, Uinta, and Panamint Chipmunks (Pl. 10), which enter e. or n. California.

ALPINE CHIPMUNK   *Tamias alpinus*   **P. 210**
Very small, pale in color; relatively short tail with blackish tip.

LODGEPOLE CHIPMUNK   *Tamias speciosus*   **P. 222**
Brightly colored, with large white spots behind ears and distinct stripes, but no dark stripe below white side stripe.

LONG-EARED CHIPMUNK   *Tamias quadrimaculatus*   **P. 222**
Very distinct stripes, with large white spots behind long ears.

YELLOW-CHEEKED CHIPMUNK   *Tamias ochrogenys*   **P. 215**
Large; dark brown, with indistinct stripes on back; cheeks yellow-orange.

SISKIYOU CHIPMUNK   *Tamias siskiyou*   **P. 215**
Very similar to Yellow-cheeked but cheeks usually pale gray.

ALLEN'S CHIPMUNK   *Tamias senex*   **P. 214**
Very similar to Siskiyou but grayer, with grayish spots behind ears. Inland form usually brighter, orange-brown.

SONOMA CHIPMUNK   *Tamias sonomae*   **P. 216**
Large; white facial stripes and ear spots; tail long, edged with white.

MERRIAM'S CHIPMUNK   *Tamias merriami*   **P. 216**
Large; facial stripes white, back stripes gray and brown, usually indistinct.

CALIFORNIA CHIPMUNK   *Tamias obscurus*   **P. 217**
Very similar to Merriam's, can be duller in color. Separated mostly by range and habitat.

PLATE 9

ALPINE CHIPMUNK

LODGEPOLE CHIPMUNK

LONG-EARED CHIPMUNK

YELLOW-CHEEKED CHIPMUNK

SISKIYOU CHIPMUNK

ALLEN'S CHIPMUNK

MERRIAM'S CHIPMUNK

CALIFORNIA CHIPMUNK

SONOMA CHIPMUNK

PLATE 10

SOUTHERN AND SOUTHWESTERN CHIPMUNKS

Chipmunks mostly of dry or highland areas.

PALMER'S CHIPMUNK   *Tamias palmeri*   **P. 225**
Cheeks and ear spots pale gray; no dark stripe below pale stripe on sides.

UINTA CHIPMUNK   *Tamias umbrinus*   **P. 224**
Back stripes brown, not black; no dark stripe below pale stripe on sides; ear spots white.

PANAMINT CHIPMUNK   *Tamias panamintinus*   **P. 223**
Cheeks and spots behind ears whitish; no dark stripe below white stripe on sides.

COLORADO CHIPMUNK   *Tamias quadrivittatus*   **P. 218**
Very similar to Uinta but dark stripes on back blackish, rump reddish brown.

HOPI CHIPMUNK   *Tamias rufus*   **P. 219**
Small, much brighter orange than other species, with dark stripes of orange-brown on back.

LEAST CHIPMUNK   *Tamias minimus*   **P. 211**
Small; can be pale gray with no orange in dry regions (see Pl. 8 for other color variants).

CLIFF CHIPMUNK   *Tamias dorsalis*   **P. 218**
Body gray with almost no stripes on sides.

GRAY-COLLARED CHIPMUNK   *Tamias cinereicollis*   **P. 221**
Distinct stripes on face and back, hind feet usually pale orange; neck grayish.

GRAY-FOOTED CHIPMUNK   *Tamias canipes*   **P. 221**
Very similar to Gray-collared but usually less stripy; some pale orange on neck; hind feet pale gray.

PLATE 10

UINTA CHIPMUNK

PALMER'S CHIPMUNK

PANAMINT CHIPMUNK

COLORADO CHIPMUNK

HOPI CHIPMUNK

LEAST CHIPMUNK

CLIFF CHIPMUNK

GRAY-COLLARED CHIPMUNK

GRAY-FOOTED CHIPMUNK

PLATE 11

LARGE EASTERN SQUIRRELS

Our most familiar and widespread tree squirrels.

EASTERN GRAY SQUIRREL *Sciurus carolinensis*   **P. 225**
Usually gray with some orange-brown on lower sides and face, tail clearly frosted white. Can be all-black in some areas, or dark brown with pale brown tail. Southern forms much smaller, gray or brown, belly usually white but can be rusty; tail almost always frosted white.

EASTERN FOX SQUIRREL *Sciurus niger*   **P. 227**
Large; typically gray-brown above, orange below and on edge of tail, but highly variable. Delmarva Fox Squirrel pale gray above, no rust in body or tail, ears very small. Southern and southeastern forms with variable amounts of black on head and foreparts.

EASTERN FOX SQUIRREL: color variants

S. n. niger
(New Orleans,
La.)

S. n. avicennia
(Collier
Co., Fla.)

S. n. niger
(Charleston,
S.C.)

PLATE 11

black form (Ont.)

EASTERN
GRAY SQUIRREL

typical northern
form

Southeast
S. c. fuliginosus
(La.)

EASTERN
FOX SQUIRREL

northern form

Delmarva
Fox Squirrel
S. n. cinereus
(Md.)

Sherman's
Fox Squirrel
S. n. shermani
(Fla.)

PLATE 12

LARGE WESTERN SQUIRRELS

TASSEL-EARED SQUIRREL *Sciurus aberti* **P. 230**
Long ears with pronounced tufts of fur in winter. *South of Grand Canyon:* Abert's race is dark gray with white belly and tail gray above, white below. *North of Grand Canyon:* Kaibab race similar but belly blackish, tail all-white. Color all-black or all-brown in N.

MEXICAN FOX SQUIRREL *Sciurus nayaritensis* **P. 228**
Very long-tailed; bright orange limbs and underparts. Chiricahua Mts.

WESTERN GRAY SQUIRREL *Sciurus griseus* **P. 229**
Large; dark gray on back, tail gray edged with white; no rust at center of tail; feet black or pale gray.

ARIZONA GRAY SQUIRREL *Sciurus arizonensis* **P. 228**
Upper back yellow-brown in summer (gray in winter); center of tail brownish. Local, SW.

TRACKS

WESTERN GRAY SQUIRREL

1¼ in.

1½ in.

PLATE 12

northern form
(winter)

TASSEL-EARED SQUIRREL

Abert's
(summer)

Kaibab
(winter)

MEXICAN FOX
SQUIRREL

WESTERN GRAY
SQUIRREL

ARIZONA GRAY SQUIRREL
(summer)

PLATE 13

FLYING SQUIRRELS AND SMALL TREE SQUIRRELS

SOUTHERN FLYING SQUIRREL *Glaucomys volans*   **P. 234**
Small, usually grayish; white fur below eyes, belly pure white to base of fur; tail flat, paler below.

NORTHERN FLYING SQUIRREL *Glaucomys sabrinus*   **P. 233**
Larger than Southern; fur gray below eyes, belly fur gray at base; tail flat, bushy, usually darker at tip, underside brown. In Pacific NW dark brown with buff belly.

RED SQUIRREL *Tamiasciurus hudsonicus*   **P. 231**
Small; typical form orange to gray-brown above, white below. *Winter:* tufts of fur on ears, no black line on sides. *Summer:* black line on sides, ears not tufted. SW mts. (Spruce Squirrel): dark brown above, gray-white below.

DOUGLAS'S SQUIRREL *Tamiasciurus douglasii*   **P. 232**
Dark brown above, pale orange on belly; black line on sides in summer only; ears tufted in winter.

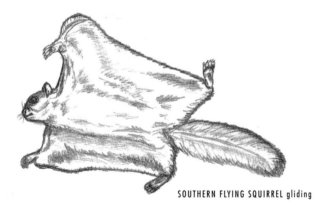

SOUTHERN FLYING SQUIRREL gliding

PLATE 13

SOUTHERN FLYING SQUIRREL

Pacific Northwest

NORTHERN FLYING SQUIRREL

widespread form

winter

RED SQUIRREL

summer

Spruce Squirrel (Southwest mts.)

summer

DOUGLAS'S SQUIRREL

PLATE 14

POCKET GOPHERS

Not all species of pocket gophers are illustrated. Many are more easily separated based on distribution (see range maps).

Geomys: Two grooves on upper incisors (Fig. 5).

SOUTHEASTERN POCKET GOPHER *Geomys pinetis* **P. 236**
Medium sized; usually brown; large forelegs and claws; small eyes and ears. Only pocket gopher in SE.

PLAINS POCKET GOPHER *Geomys bursarius* **P. 237**
Similar to Southeastern; color variable.

Thomomys: Upper incisors not grooved (Fig. 5).

IDAHO POCKET GOPHER *Thomomys idahoensis* **P. 244**
Very small, pale yellow; local. Wyoming Pocket Gopher (*T. clusius*), p. 244, is very similar, but ranges do not overlap.

NORTHERN POCKET GOPHER *Thomomys talpoides* **P. 241**
Long dull fur, usually grayish, can be reddish brown; tail lightly haired; small but distinct black ear spots.

WESTERN POCKET GOPHER *Thomomys mazama* **P. 242**
Fur usually orange-brown; large black ear spots.

TOWNSEND'S POCKET GOPHER *Thomomys townsendii* **P. 245**
Large, usually pale yellow-gray; inconspicuous ear spots; may have white patches on head.

BOTTA'S POCKET GOPHER *Thomomys bottae* **P. 242**
Highly variable in size and color; usually with little or no ear spots; upper incisor teeth procumbent.

Cratogeomys: Single groove on upper incisors (Fig.5).

YELLOW-FACED POCKET GOPHER *Cratogeomys castanops* **P. 240**
Large; yellowish, especially on cheeks; large eyes.

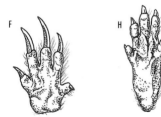

PLAINS POCKET GOPHER feet: undersides

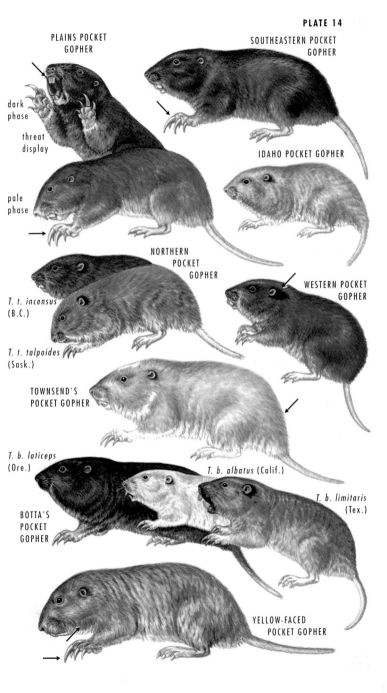

PLATE 14

PLAINS POCKET
GOPHER

SOUTHEASTERN POCKET
GOPHER

dark
phase

threat
display

pale
phase

IDAHO POCKET GOPHER

NORTHERN
POCKET
GOPHER

T. t. incensus
(B.C.)

WESTERN POCKET
GOPHER

T. t. talpoides
(Sask.)

TOWNSEND'S
POCKET GOPHER

T. b. laticeps
(Ore.)

T. b. albatus (Calif.)

T. b. limitaris
(Tex.)

BOTTA'S
POCKET
GOPHER

YELLOW-FACED
POCKET GOPHER

PLATE 15

SPINY AND CRESTED-TAILED POCKET MICE

Small to medium-sized mice with external fur-lined cheek pouches; most have coarse or spiny fur and/or long crested tails.

CALIFORNIA POCKET MOUSE *Chaetodipus californicus* **P. 251**
Distinct white spiny hairs on rump; orange line on sides; ears long, project above crown; tail longer than head and body. Calif.

SAN DIEGO POCKET MOUSE *Chaetodipus fallax* **P. 250**
Similar to California but ears much smaller, tail relatively shorter, indistinct orange line on sides. S. Calif.

SPINY POCKET MOUSE *Chaetodipus spinatus* **P. 251**
Distinct white spiny hairs on rump and flanks to shoulders; no orange line on sides; ears rather small. Se. Calif.

NELSON'S POCKET MOUSE *Chaetodipus nelsoni* **P. 250**
Distinct white spiny hairs on rump; white spot at base of ear; soles of hind feet black. Sw. Tex., se. N.M.

DESERT POCKET MOUSE *Chaetodipus penicillatus* **P. 248**
Fur coarse and shiny but not spiny; sandy soils. See Chihuahuan Pocket Mouse (p. 249), almost identical.

ROCK POCKET MOUSE *Chaetodipus intermedius* **P. 249**
Similar to Desert, usually smaller with some thin black spines on rump; color varies with soil type, can be all-black; gravel soils and rocky areas. SW.

BAILEY'S POCKET MOUSE *Chaetodipus baileyi* **P. 247**
Largest crested-tailed pocket mouse; fur coarse but not spiny, yellow-gray. SW.

LONG-TAILED POCKET MOUSE *Chaetodipus formosus* **P. 252**
Fur not spiny, often with pronounced sheen; ears prominent, project above crown; tail long with well-developed crest. W.

HISPID POCKET MOUSE *Chaetodipus hispidus* **P. 248**
Large; distinct orange line on sides and around eyes; tail not crested. W, Central.

MEXICAN SPINY POCKET MOUSE *Liomys irroratus* **P. 272**
Large; narrow orange line on sides; ears broad and rounded; small crest on tail. S. Tex.

External cheek pouches of
DESERT POCKET MOUSE: left
side closed, right side open

PLATE 15

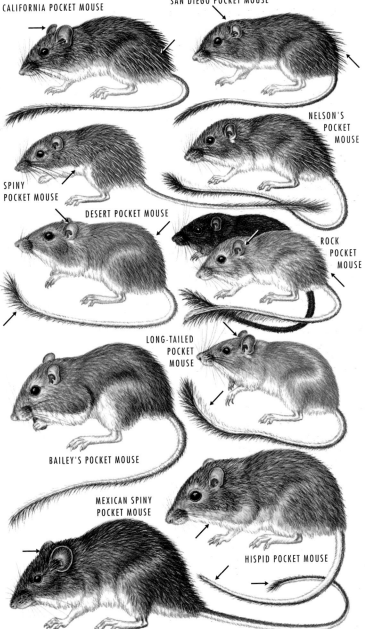

CALIFORNIA POCKET MOUSE

SAN DIEGO POCKET MOUSE

NELSON'S POCKET MOUSE

SPINY POCKET MOUSE

DESERT POCKET MOUSE

ROCK POCKET MOUSE

LONG-TAILED POCKET MOUSE

BAILEY'S POCKET MOUSE

MEXICAN SPINY POCKET MOUSE

HISPID POCKET MOUSE

PLATE 16

SOFT-FURRED POCKET MICE AND KANGAROO MICE

Small mice with external fur-lined cheek pouches and silky fur; most have little fur on the tail.

WHITE-EARED POCKET MOUSE *Perognathus alticola*   **P. 255**
Rather large; small flap of skin inside ear; tail haired at tip. S. Calif.

SAN JOAQUIN POCKET MOUSE *Perognathus inornatus*   **P. 258**
Yellow spot behind ear and around eye; tail short. Calif.

ARIZONA POCKET MOUSE *Perognathus amplus*   **P. 257**
Similar to San Joaquin but larger and with a longer tail. SW.

LITTLE POCKET MOUSE *Perognathus longimembris*   **P. 256**
Small, usually pale, relatively short tail. W.

SILKY POCKET MOUSE *Perognathus flavus*   **P. 255**
Very small; distinct yellow spot behind ear; tail short, nearly naked. W Central.

MERRIAM'S POCKET MOUSE *Perognathus merriami*   **P. 256**
Almost identical to Silky but spot behind ear smaller. Tex., e. N.M.

GREAT BASIN POCKET MOUSE *Perognathus parvus*   **P. 254**
Rather large; usually grayish but can be brown; small flap of skin inside ear; tail haired at tip.

PLAINS POCKET MOUSE *Perognathus flavescens*   **P. 254**
Fairly small, tail almost naked. Color variable: whitish (*P. f. gypsi*), orange-brown (*P. f. apache* and others), or dark brown (*P. f. perniger*); other intermediate colors known.

OLIVE-BACKED POCKET MOUSE *Perognathus fasciatus*   **P. 253**
Back olive brown, almost greenish; otherwise similar to Plains Pocket Mouse. N. Great Plains.

DARK KANGAROO MOUSE *Microdipodops megacephalus*   **P. 259**
Large head; tail thickened in center; hind feet very long, furred below; back usually sprinkled with black, tip of tail black above. Great Basin.

PALE KANGAROO MOUSE *Microdipodops pallidus*   **P. 259**
Similar to Dark Kangaroo Mouse but paler with no black fur on tail. Nev., e. Calif.

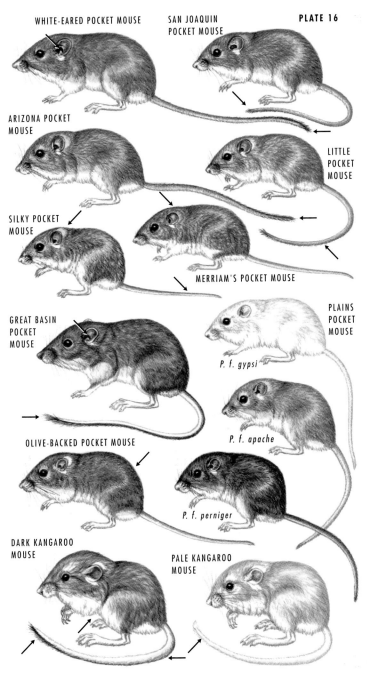

PLATE 16

WHITE-EARED POCKET MOUSE

SAN JOAQUIN POCKET MOUSE

ARIZONA POCKET MOUSE

LITTLE POCKET MOUSE

SILKY POCKET MOUSE

MERRIAM'S POCKET MOUSE

GREAT BASIN POCKET MOUSE

PLAINS POCKET MOUSE

P. f. gypsi

P. f. apache

OLIVE-BACKED POCKET MOUSE

P. f. perniger

DARK KANGAROO MOUSE

PALE KANGAROO MOUSE

PLATE 17

KANGAROO RATS OF THE SOUTHWEST

ORD'S KANGAROO RAT *Dipodomys ordii* **P. 261**
Fairly small, tail relatively short; color varies with soil type; 5 toes on hind foot; usually on sandy soil.

MERRIAM'S KANGAROO RAT *Dipodomys merriami* **P. 270**
Similar to Ord's but tail averages longer; 4 toes on hind foot; can occur on clay or gravel soil.

GULF COAST KANGAROO RAT *Dipodomys compactus* **P. 262**
Similar to Ord's (5-toed) but has a shorter tail; island form (shown here) very pale. S. Tex.

CHISEL-TOOTHED KANGAROO RAT *Dipodomys microps* **P. 263**
Medium sized, with bold markings on face; 5 toes on hind foot; lower incisors chisel-shaped.

PANAMINT KANGAROO RAT *Dipodomys panamintinus* **P. 264**
Medium sized, markings on face indistinct; 5 toes on hind foot; tail long with dark stripes grayish, mixed black and white at tip.

BANNER-TAILED KANGAROO RAT *Dipodomys spectabilis* **P. 268**
Large; 4 toes on hind foot; tail boldly marked with a long white tip.

TEXAS KANGAROO RAT *Dipodomys elator* **P. 269**
Very similar to Banner-tailed but smaller. Very local, n. Tex.

DESERT KANGAROO RAT *Dipodomys deserti* **P. 270**
Very large, pale to very pale; 4 toes on hind foot; no dark stripe on underside of tail, tip white.

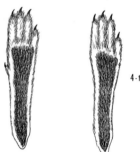

5-toed kangaroo rat: sole of hind foot

4-toed kangaroo rat

PLATE 17

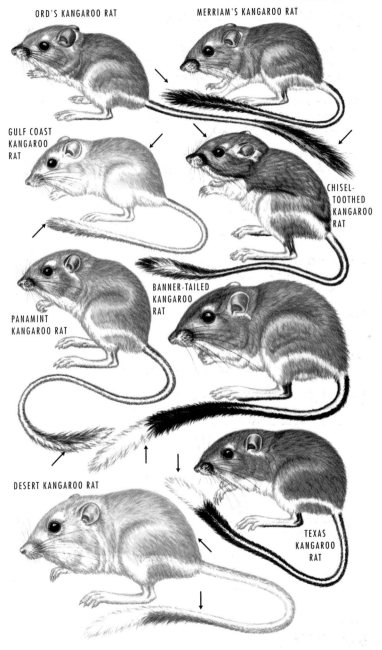

ORD'S KANGAROO RAT

MERRIAM'S KANGAROO RAT

GULF COAST KANGAROO RAT

CHISEL-TOOTHED KANGAROO RAT

PANAMINT KANGAROO RAT

BANNER-TAILED KANGAROO RAT

DESERT KANGAROO RAT

TEXAS KANGAROO RAT

PLATE 18

KANGAROO RATS OF CALIFORNIA

These species are endemic or near endemic to California. Other widespread species that occur in California (Merriam's, Ord's, Chisel-toothed, Panamint, and Desert) are shown on Pl. 17.

SAN JOAQUIN KANGAROO RAT *Dipodomys nitratoides* **P. 271**
Small; 4 toes on hind foot; tail tipped brown mixed with white hairs.

CALIFORNIA KANGAROO RAT *Dipodomys californicus* **P. 266**
Dark; 4 toes on hind foot; prominent white tail tip.

AGILE KANGAROO RAT *Dipodomys agilis* **P. 265**
Relatively large ears; 5 toes on hind foot; long white stripes on sides of tail. See similar Dulzura Kangaroo Rat (p. 266).

STEPHENS'S KANGAROO RAT *Dipodomys stephensi* **P. 264**
Medium sized, dark back; small ears; 5 toes on hind foot; pronounced black tip on tail.

HEERMANN'S KANGAROO RAT *Dipodomys heermanni* **P. 267**
Similar to Stephens's (compare range) but tail tip dusky (or white in some races).

NARROW-FACED KANGAROO RAT *Dipodomys venustus* **P. 265**
Large and dark with prominent facial markings and very large ears; 5 toes on hind foot.

GIANT KANGAROO RAT *Dipodomys ingens* **P. 268**
Largest kangaroo rat; 5 toes on hind foot.

SAN BERNARDINO KANGAROO RAT
(*Dipodomys merriami parvus*), p. 271

PLATE 18

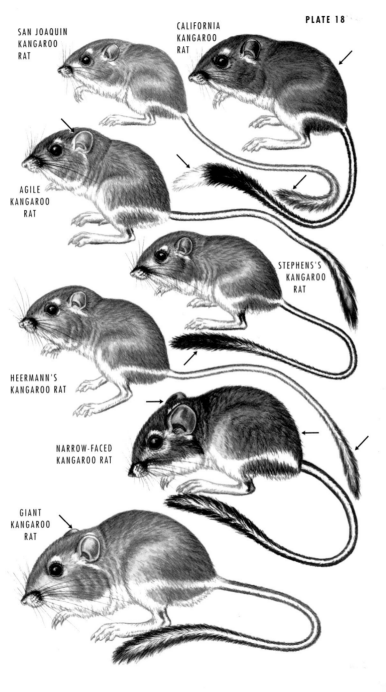

SAN JOAQUIN
KANGAROO
RAT

CALIFORNIA
KANGAROO
RAT

AGILE
KANGAROO
RAT

STEPHENS'S
KANGAROO
RAT

HEERMANN'S
KANGAROO RAT

NARROW-FACED
KANGAROO RAT

GIANT
KANGAROO
RAT

PLATE 19

HARVEST, PYGMY, AND HOUSE MICE

These are very small mice. Harvest mice have grooved upper incisor teeth; Pygmy and House Mice have ungrooved incisors.

SALT-MARSH HARVEST MOUSE *Reithrodontomys raviventris* **P. 290**
Large dark ears; long, nearly naked tail. Southern subspecies (*R. r. raviventris*) orangish below; northern subspecies (*R. r. halicoetes*) white below. Very local, cen. Calif.

WESTERN HARVEST MOUSE *Reithrodontomys megalotis* **P. 289**
Long, lightly haired, clearly bicolor tail. W, Central.

PLAINS HARVEST MOUSE *Reithrodontomys montanus* **P. 288**
Similar to Western but upper back dark, contrasting with paler sides; thin dark line on rather short tail. SW, Central.

FULVOUS HARVEST MOUSE *Reithrodontomys fulvescens* **P. 291**
Orangish; ears lined with orange fur; tail relatively long. SW, S Central.

EASTERN HARVEST MOUSE *Reithrodontomys humulis* **P. 288**
Smallest harvest mouse, rather short tail. SE.

NORTHERN PYGMY MOUSE *Baiomys taylori* **P. 292**
Tiny; tail much shorter than body; eyes small, ears rounded. SW, S Central.

HOUSE MOUSE *Mus musculus* **P. 331**
Belly off-white; tops of feet gray; tail nearly naked, not clearly bicolor.

SOLES OF FEET

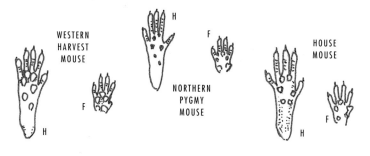

WESTERN HARVEST MOUSE

NORTHERN PYGMY MOUSE

HOUSE MOUSE

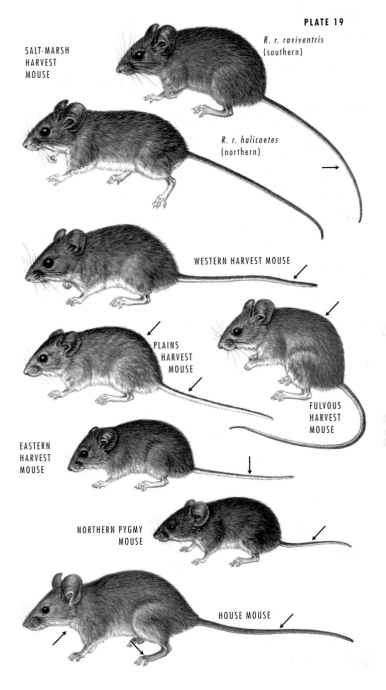

PLATE 19

SALT-MARSH
HARVEST
MOUSE

R. r. raviventris
(southern)

R. r. halicoetes
(northern)

WESTERN HARVEST MOUSE

PLAINS
HARVEST
MOUSE

FULVOUS
HARVEST
MOUSE

EASTERN
HARVEST
MOUSE

NORTHERN PYGMY
MOUSE

HOUSE MOUSE

PLATE 20

EASTERN AND CENTRAL DEER MICE

AMERICAN DEER MOUSE *Peromyscus maniculatus*   **P. 277**
Woodland form: large ears; long, bicolor, furred tail. Prairie form (*P. m. bairdii*): smaller; blackish ears; short, very bicolor and well-furred tail (see Pl. 21 for western form).

WHITE-FOOTED MOUSE *Peromyscus leucopus*   **P. 278**
Very similar to Woodland Deer Mouse, but tail lightly haired and less bicolor (see text for additional differences).

COTTON MOUSE *Peromyscus gossypinus*   **P. 279**
Larger and darker than above species. SE.

OLDFIELD MOUSE *Peromyscus polionotus*   **P. 276**
Very small and short-tailed; coastal subspecies (Beach Mouse) almost white. SE.

FLORIDA MOUSE *Podomys floridanus*   **P. 284**
Larger than eastern *Peromyscus*, with longer feet and ears; hind feet have 5 (not 6) pads on soles. Fla.

GOLDEN MOUSE *Ochrotomys nuttalli*   **P. 291**
Orange-brown, semi-arboreal. SE.

WHITE-ANKLED MOUSE *Peromyscus pectoralis*   **P. 280**
Ankles white; tail lightly haired with short fur at tip. Mostly Tex.

TEXAS MOUSE *Peromyscus attwateri*   **P. 282**
Ankles dusky; tail well haired with a small brush at tip. W Central. Compare with Brush Mouse (Pl. 21).

FLORIDA MOUSE
5 pads on hind foot

COTTON MOUSE
6 pads on hind foot

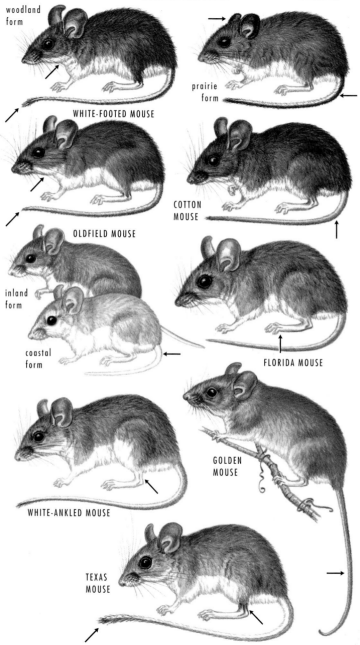

AMERICAN DEER MOUSE

PLATE 20

woodland
form

prairie
form

WHITE-FOOTED MOUSE

COTTON
MOUSE

OLDFIELD MOUSE

inland
form

coastal
form

FLORIDA MOUSE

GOLDEN
MOUSE

WHITE-ANKLED MOUSE

TEXAS
MOUSE

PLATE 21

WESTERN DEER MICE

AMERICAN DEER MOUSE *Peromyscus maniculatus* **P. 277**
Western desert form: tail clearly bicolor, shorter than head and body; back gray-brown to bright orange-brown.

KEEN'S MOUSE *Peromyscus keeni* **P. 276**
Dark brown; tail long, bicolor; only deer mouse in most of its range.

WHITE-FOOTED MOUSE *Peromyscus leucopus* **P. 278**
Western form: usually gray or pale brown; tail shorter than head and body, narrow, somewhat bicolor.

BRUSH MOUSE *Peromyscus boylii* **P. 281**
Back grayish, orange line on sides; tail longer than head and body, tufted.

CACTUS MOUSE *Peromyscus eremicus* **P. 274**
Head grayer than body; lower sides usually orange; tail nearly naked, not strongly bicolor.

NORTHERN ROCK MOUSE *Peromyscus nasutus* **P. 284**
Similer to Brush Mouse but darker and slightly larger.

CANYON MOUSE *Peromyscus crinitus* **P. 280**
Small with big ears; color variable; tail thickly haired and tufted.

PIÑON MOUSE *Peromyscus truei* **P. 282**
Very large ears; color variable; tail usually relatively short, bicolor, with a small tuft.

CALIFORNIA MOUSE *Peromyscus californicus* **P. 275**
Largest species; dark, with long hind feet and large ears; tail bicolor, tufted.

PIÑON MOUSE: ears curled back

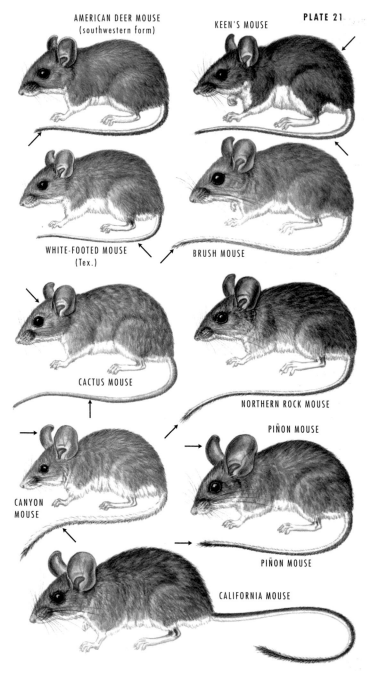

AMERICAN DEER MOUSE
(southwestern form)

KEEN'S MOUSE

PLATE 21

WHITE-FOOTED MOUSE
(Tex.)

BRUSH MOUSE

CACTUS MOUSE

NORTHERN ROCK MOUSE

PIÑON MOUSE

CANYON
MOUSE

PIÑON MOUSE

CALIFORNIA MOUSE

PLATE 22

JUMPING AND GRASSHOPPER MICE

Jumping Mice are not closely related to other mice. They belong to the family Dipodidae. They have extremely long tails and long narrow hind feet. Jumping mice are found in forests and wet areas.

MEADOW JUMPING MOUSE *Zapus hudsonius*   **P. 335**
   Dark back contrasts with yellow-brown sides; tail dark to tip.

WOODLAND JUMPING MOUSE *Napaeozapus insignis*   **P. 334**
   Dark back contrasts strongly with orange sides; tip of tail white.

WESTERN JUMPING MOUSE *Zapus princeps*   **P. 336**
   Similar to Meadow but larger and sides usually brighter yellow; ears thinly edged with white. Tip of tail lightly haired.

PACIFIC JUMPING MOUSE *Zapus trinotatus*   **P. 337**
   Sides orange, ears edged with brown. Tail nearly naked at top.

Grasshopper Mice are murid rodents. They are stocky with short white-tipped tails. They occur in deserts and dry grassy areas and eat insects in addition to seeds.

SOUTHERN GRASSHOPPER MOUSE *Onychomys torridus*   **P. 286**
   Color varies from gray to sandy brown; no white fur at base of ears; tail relatively long.

MEARNS'S GRASSHOPPER MOUSE *Onychomys arenicola*   **P. 287**
   Similar to Southern but has a shorter snout and more grizzled fur; white tufts at base of ears.

NORTHERN GRASSHOPPER MOUSE *Onychomys leucogaster*   **P. 285**
   Largest and most variable species; back dark to pale gray, or sandy brown to pale orange; often has white tufts at base of ears; tail relatively short.

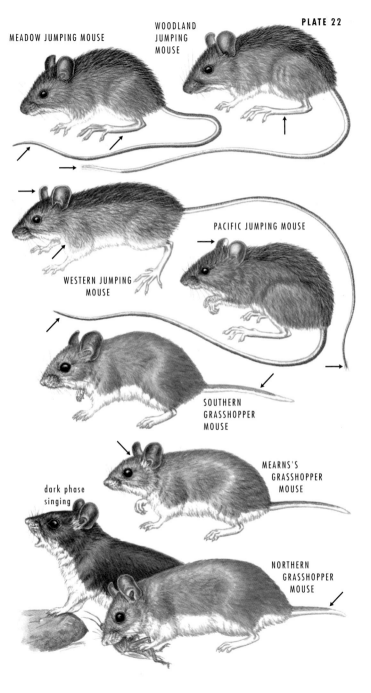

PLATE 22

MEADOW JUMPING MOUSE

WOODLAND JUMPING MOUSE

PACIFIC JUMPING MOUSE

WESTERN JUMPING MOUSE

SOUTHERN GRASSHOPPER MOUSE

MEARNS'S GRASSHOPPER MOUSE

dark phase singing

NORTHERN GRASSHOPPER MOUSE

PLATE 23

WOODRATS

Large attractive rats, mostly with hairy bicolor tails. Some species recently described based on genetic data are not illustrated.

BUSHY-TAILED WOODRAT *Neotoma cinerea*   **P. 301**
Large; very thickly haired tail.

STEPHENS'S WOODRAT *Neotoma stephensi*   **P. 298**
Tail well haired, does not appear to taper.

EASTERN WOODRAT *Neotoma floridana*   **P. 293**
Large; tail not strongly bicolor. See Allegheny Woodrat (p. 294).

DESERT WOODRAT *Neotoma lepida*   **P. 297**
Rather small; ears large. See Arizona Woodrat (p. 298).

SOUTHERN PLAINS WOODRAT *Neotoma micropus*   **P. 295**
Very large; steel gray.

MEXICAN WOODRAT *Neotoma mexicana*   **P. 299**
Medium sized; gray-brown or orangish.

WESTERN WHITE-THROATED WOODRAT *Neotoma albigula*   **P. 296**
Large; throat and chest white to base of hairs (gray at base in other species). See Eastern White-throated Woodrat (p. 297).

DUSKY-FOOTED WOODRAT *Neotoma fuscipes*   **P. 300**
Very large, dark brown; tops of hind feet brown; tail entirely dark or very faintly bicolor. See Big-eared Woodrat (p. 301).

PLATE 23

STEPHENS'S WOODRAT

BUSHY-TAILED WOODRAT

EASTERN WOODRAT

DESERT WOODRAT

SOUTHERN PLAINS WOODRAT

MEXICAN WOODRAT

WESTERN WHITE-THROATED WOODRAT

DUSKY-FOOTED WOODRAT

PLATE 24

RICE, COTTON, AND HOUSE RATS

Rice Rats have long, nearly naked tails and long slim feet. They are found near water.

COUES'S RICE RAT   *Oryzomys couesi*   P. 302
    Belly pale buff.

MARSH RICE RAT   *Oryzomys palustris*   P. 303
    Smaller than Coues's, with a gray-white belly.

Cotton Rats have short tails and thick grizzled fur. The soles of the hind feet are blackish. They occur in grassy areas.

HISPID COTTON RAT   *Sigmodon hispidus*   P. 304
    Belly whitish, tail almost unicolor. See Arizona Cotton Rat (similar but larger), p. 305.

YELLOW-NOSED COTTON RAT   *Sigmodon ochrognathus*   P. 306
    Yellow-orange nose and eye-ring; tail bicolor.

TAWNY-BELLIED COTTON RAT   *Sigmodon fulviventer*   P. 305
    Belly pale orange, tail all-black.

House Rats have thick, scaly, nearly naked tails. They occur near human dwellings.

ROOF RAT   *Rattus rattus*   P. 332
    Black or brown; belly slightly paler than back; tail longer than head and body.

NORWAY RAT   *Rattus norvegicus*   P. 333
    Brown, stocky; ears and tail relatively short.

HIND FEET

RICE RAT   COTTON RAT   HOUSE RAT

PLATE 24

MARSH RICE RAT

COUES'S RICE RAT

YELLOW-NOSED COTTON RAT

HISPID COTTON RAT

TAWNY-BELLIED COTTON RAT

brown phase

ROOF RAT

black phase

NORWAY RAT

PLATE 25

VOLES OF EASTERN, CENTRAL, AND SOUTHWESTERN U.S.

Voles are stocky, short-tailed rodents usually found in grassy areas. Unlike most rodents, they may be active by day.

SOUTHERN RED-BACKED VOLE *Clethrionomys gapperi* **P. 308**
Typical red-backed form more common than gray-backed; relatively long tail and large ears. N. See Pls. 26 and 27 for related species.

EASTERN HEATHER VOLE *Phenacomys ungava* **P. 310**
Nose and hair inside ears orange; tops of feet whitish. N. See Pl. 26 for Western.

SOUTHERN BOG LEMMING *Synaptomys cooperi* **P. 328**
Big-headed; very short tail. NE. See Pl. 27 for Northern.

MEADOW VOLE *Microtus pennsylvanicus* **P. 313**
Usually dark brown; tail faintly bicolor and relatively long.

PRAIRIE VOLE *Microtus ochrogaster* **P. 320**
Similar to Meadow but belly usually pale buff, tail shorter and more bicolor. Central.

ROCK VOLE *Microtus chrotorrhinus* **P. 319**
More mouselike than other voles; snout orange; tail long. NE.

MEXICAN VOLE *Microtus mexicanus* **P. 321**
Belly buff or cream; tail rather short.

WOODLAND VOLE *Microtus pinetorum* **P. 322**
Velvety, molelike fur; small eyes and very short tail. E.

MONTANE VOLE *Microtus montanus* **P. 315**
Color of back variable, can be dark brown; belly and feet usually silvery; tail moderately long. W.

SAGEBRUSH VOLE *Lemmiscus curtatus* **P. 325**
Pale gray; very short tail; soles of hind feet hairy. NW.

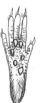

MEADOW VOLE
6 pads on
hind foot

PRAIRIE VOLE
5 pads on
hind foot

PLATE 25

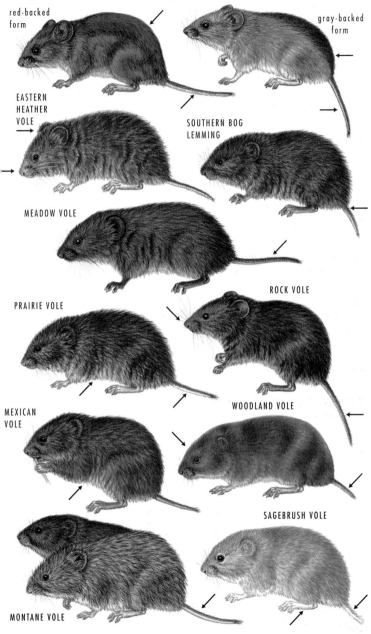

SOUTHERN RED-BACKED VOLE

red-backed form

gray-backed form

EASTERN HEATHER VOLE

SOUTHERN BOG LEMMING

MEADOW VOLE

PRAIRIE VOLE

ROCK VOLE

MEXICAN VOLE

WOODLAND VOLE

SAGEBRUSH VOLE

MONTANE VOLE

PLATE 26

VOLES OF THE PACIFIC NORTHWEST

Species of the humid coastal forests and mountains of the Northwest states. Montane Vole (Pl. 25) overlaps in range with some of
these species.

WESTERN RED-BACKED VOLE   *Clethrionomys californicus*   P. 307
Dark gray with dark red-brown stripe on back; small eyes.

RED TREE VOLE   *Arborimus longicaudus*   P. 312
Reddish brown; long brown tail; arboreal.

SONOMA TREE VOLE   *Arborimus pomo*   P. 313
Similar to Red Tree Vole but brighter orange.

WHITE-FOOTED VOLE   *Arborimus albipes*   P. 311
Reddish brown; long bicolor tail.

CREEPING VOLE   *Microtus oregoni*   P. 319
Smallest western vole; small eyes and short tail.

CALIFORNIA VOLE   *Microtus californicus*   P. 316
Stocky; relatively short tail; grassy areas.

TOWNSEND'S VOLE   *Microtus townsendii*   P. 317
Large; back, feet, and tail dark; belly silvery.

LONG-TAILED VOLE   *Microtus longicaudus*   P. 318
Slim-bodied; relatively long tail.

GRAY-TAILED VOLE   *Microtus canicaudus*   P. 316
Belly and underside of tail silvery. Local, Ore.

WESTERN HEATHER VOLE   *Phenacomys intermedius*   P. 310
Short tail; high mts.

WATER VOLE   *Microtus richardsoni*   P. 324
Large; relatively long tail; mountain streams.

PLATE 26

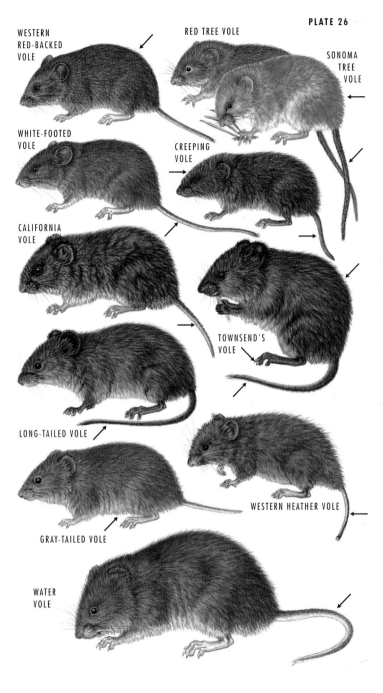

WESTERN
RED-BACKED
VOLE

RED TREE VOLE

SONOMA
TREE
VOLE

WHITE-FOOTED
VOLE

CREEPING
VOLE

CALIFORNIA
VOLE

TOWNSEND'S
VOLE

LONG-TAILED VOLE

GRAY-TAILED VOLE

WESTERN HEATHER VOLE

WATER
VOLE

PLATE 27

TUNDRA VOLES AND LEMMINGS

These species are mostly found in Alaska and the Far North. Meadow Vole (Pl. 25) also occurs in the tundra.

TUNDRA VOLE *Microtus oeconomus*   P. 318
Large; relatively long, bicolor tail.

NORTHERN RED-BACKED VOLE *Clethrionomys rutilus*   P. 309
Brightly colored; large ears and hairy, bicolor tail; belly whitish.

TAIGA VOLE *Microtus xanthognathus*   P. 320
Very large and dark; nose bright orange.

INSULAR VOLE *Microtus abbreviatus*   P. 324
Bright orange on sides. Hall and St. Matthew Is. only.

NORTHERN BOG LEMMING *Synaptomys borealis*   P. 328
Dark fur; big head; very short tail (indistinguishable from Southern Bog Lemming, Pl. 25, except by range).

SINGING VOLE *Microtus miurus*   P. 323
Rather small, yellowish; tail hairy, cream below.

BROWN LEMMING *Lemmus trimucronatus*   P. 327
Stocky; midback bright orange-brown; tiny tail.

UNGAVA COLLARED LEMMING *Dicrostonyx hudsonius*   P. 330
Stocky and short-tailed; usually dull brown; young and some adults have dark brown line down midback.

RICHARDSON'S COLLARED LEMMING *Dicrostonyx richardsoni*   P. 331
Similar to Ungava but brighter orange on chest and sides.

NORTHERN COLLARED LEMMING *Dicrostonyx groenlandicus*   P. 329
Similar to other collared lemmings but usually more silvery on back and head. *Winter* (all 3 collared lemmings): pure white.

winter

Front feet and claws
of collared lemmings

summer

PLATE 27

TUNDRA VOLE

NORTHERN RED-BACKED VOLE

TAIGA VOLE

INSULAR VOLE

NORTHERN BOG LEMMING

SINGING VOLE

BROWN LEMMING

UNGAVA COLLARED LEMMING

winter

RICHARDSON'S COLLARED LEMMING

NORTHERN COLLARED LEMMING

summer

PLATE 28

PIKAS AND WESTERN RABBITS

Pikas are small and have rounded ears. They are almost tailless.

AMERICAN PIKA *Ochotona princeps*   P. 342
 Gray, orange-brown, or dark brown; indistinct collar patch.

COLLARED PIKA *Ochotona collaris*   P. 341
 Gray with a buff collar from ear to throat.

Rabbits have long prominent ears and often have cottony tails.

PYGMY RABBIT *Brachylagus idahoensis*   P. 343
 Smallest rabbit; white-edged, fur-lined ears; tiny gray tail. *Summer:* dark steely gray. *Winter:* pale gray-brown.

BRUSH RABBIT *Sylvilagus bachmani*   P. 344
 Rather small; uniformly dark brown or gray-brown; ears naked inside, not black-tipped; tail small, grayish below.

DESERT COTTONTAIL *Sylvilagus audubonii*   P. 351
 Pale, grayish; black-tipped ears longer than hind feet.

MOUNTAIN COTTONTAIL *Sylvilagus nuttallii*   P. 350
 Gray-brown; ears rather short and lined with white hair.

EASTERN COTTONTAIL *Sylvilagus floridanus*   P. 347
 Back grizzled; ears variable but always shorter than hind feet.

PLATE 28

AMERICAN PIKA

O. p. cuppes (B.C.)

O. p. lutescens (Alta.)

COLLARED PIKA

O. p. brunnescens (B.C.)

PYGMY RABBIT

summer

winter

BRUSH RABBIT

DESERT COTTONTAIL

MOUNTAIN COTTONTAIL

EASTERN COTTONTAIL

PLATE 29

EASTERN RABBITS

MARSH RABBIT   *Sylvilagus palustris*   **P. 346**
Dark brown; ears short and rather broad, naked inside; very small gray tail.

SWAMP RABBIT   *Sylvilagus aquaticus*   **P. 345**
Largest native rabbit; similar to Marsh Rabbit but larger, with tail white below.

NEW ENGLAND COTTONTAIL   *Sylvilagus transitionalis*   **P. 349**
Heavily grizzled fur; ears short; black spot between ears. Also see Appalachian Cottontail (almost identical, found farther south), p. 349.

EASTERN COTTONTAIL   *Sylvilagus floridanus*   **P. 347**
Medium-sized; grizzled fur with an orange band on back, sides grayer; often has white blaze on forehead; narrow ears.

EUROPEAN RABBIT   *Oryctolagus cuniculus*   **P. 351**
Large and stocky; color highly variable: wild form (shown) gray-brown, fur finely grizzled. Introduced.

Tracks of EASTERN COTTONTAIL running:
hind feet paired, front feet offset

PLATE 29

swimming

MARSH RABBIT

SWAMP RABBIT

NEW ENGLAND
COTTONTAIL

EASTERN
COTTONTAIL

EUROPEAN RABBIT

PLATE 30

NORTHERN HARES AND JACKRABBITS

SNOWSHOE HARE *Lepus americanus* **P. 352**

Smallest hare; ears shorter than head; tail short; hind feet very long. *Summer:* dark brown or reddish brown. *Winter:* white; fur dark at roots.

EUROPEAN HARE *Lepus capensis* **P. 358**

Very large; ears longer than head; long tail black above, white below. Introduced.

WHITE-TAILED JACKRABBIT *Lepus townsendii* **P. 355**

Ears longer than head; tail pure white year-round. See Pl. 31 for summer form. *Winter:* white; fur white at roots, buff in middle, and tipped white. *Molting:* brown patches on face and upper back; ears brown.

ARCTIC HARE *Lepus arcticus* **P. 354**

Very large; ears shorter than head. *Summer (southern part of range):* brown or gray-brown; legs and tail white. *Summer (northern part of range):* white with some brown on face and ears only. *Winter:* all-white, fur white to roots (very similar to Alaskan Hare).

ALASKAN HARE *Lepus othus* **P. 353**

Very large; ears shorter than head. *Summer:* brown or gray-brown (very similar to Arctic Hare). *Winter:* all-white, fur white to roots.

PLATE 30

SNOWSHOE HARE

winter

summer

EUROPEAN HARE

WHITE-TAILED JACKRABBIT

winter

molting

summer far north

ARCTIC HARE

ALASKAN HARE

winter

summer north

PLATE 31

SOUTHWESTERN AND WESTERN JACKRABBITS

WHITE-TAILED JACKRABBIT   *Lepus townsendii*   **P. 355**
Large; ears longer than head but not as long as in other jack-rabbits; all-white tail. *Summer and year-round in S:* brown or gray-brown. *Winter in N:* all-white; see Pl. 30.

BLACK-TAILED JACKRABBIT   *Lepus californicus*   **P. 355**
Very long, black-tipped ears; sides of body gray-brown; lower rump and upper side of tail black.

WHITE-SIDED JACKRABBIT   *Lepus callotis*   **P. 356**
Very long, white-tipped ears; sides pure white. Very local, N.M.

ANTELOPE JACKRABBIT   *Lepus alleni*   **P. 357**
Largest southwestern jackrabbit; very long, white-tipped ears; sides gray, rump whitish. Long-legged.

PLATE 31

WHITE-TAILED
JACKRABBIT

summer

BLACK-TAILED
JACKRABBIT

WHITE-SIDED
JACKRABBIT

ANTELOPE
JACKRABBIT

PLATE 32

SMALL SHREWS

MERRIAM'S SHREW   *Sorex merriami*   **P. 379**
   Pale gray-brown; white belly; dry areas. W. See similar Arizona
   Shrew (*S. arizonae*), p. 379.

DESERT SHREW   *Notiosorex crawfordi*   **P. 383**
   Pale gray; short tail; prominent ears; patch on flank is a scent
   gland. SW.

PREBLE'S SHREW   *Sorex preblei*   **P. 372**
   Very small; gray-brown; tail short. W.

DWARF SHREW   *Sorex nanus*   **P. 377**
   Very small; relatively long tail; dry areas. W Central. See similar
   Inyo Shrew (*S. tenellus*), p. 377.

VAGRANT SHREW   *Sorex vagrans*   **P. 375**
   Brownish; wet areas. W.

ORNATE SHREW   *Sorex ornatus*   **P. 376**
   Gray-brown or blackish; fairly short, naked-looking tail. Calif.

MONTANE SHREW   *Sorex monticolus*   **P. 374**
   Brown; relatively long tail. W, NW.

SMOKY SHREW   *Sorex fumeus*   **P. 365**
   Gray-brown in summer, dark gray in winter; feet pale; larger than
   most eastern shrews. NE.

ROCK SHREW   *Sorex dispar*   **P. 366**
   Dark gray; slim-bodied and long-tailed. NE. See Gaspé Shrew (*S.
   gaspensis*), p. 367.

MASKED SHREW   *Sorex cinereus*   **P. 369**
   Dark brown; tail clearly bicolor, dark at tip. Widespread. See
   Mount Lyell Shrew (*S. lyelli*), p. 371.

SOUTHEASTERN SHREW   *Sorex longirostris*   **P. 371**
   Reddish brown; fairly short tail, pale feet. SE.

HAYDEN'S SHREW   *Sorex haydeni*   **P. 370**
   Very similar to Masked Shrew; tail tip brown; prairies.

PYGMY SHREW   *Sorex hoyi*   **P. 378**
   Brown or gray-brown; very small in S, larger in N; relatively short
   tail. Widespread.

BARREN GROUND SHREW   *Sorex ugyunak*   **P. 368**
   Distinctive pale sides and darker back. Nw. Canada. See Pribilof
   Island Shrew (*S. hydrodromus*), p. 369.

SAINT LAWRENCE ISLAND SHREW   *Sorex jacksoni*   **P. 368**
   Striking dark back and pale sides. Arctic Is. only.

PLATE 32

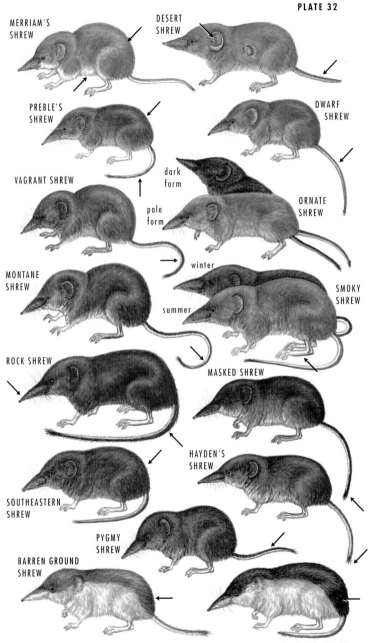

MERRIAM'S SHREW

DESERT SHREW

PREBLE'S SHREW

DWARF SHREW

VAGRANT SHREW

dark form

pale form

ORNATE SHREW

MONTANE SHREW

winter

summer

SMOKY SHREW

ROCK SHREW

MASKED SHREW

SOUTHEASTERN SHREW

HAYDEN'S SHREW

PYGMY SHREW

BARREN GROUND SHREW

SAINT LAWRENCE ISLAND SHREW

PLATE 33

LARGER SHREWS

ARCTIC SHREW   *Sorex arcticus*   **P. 361**
Back dark brown, sides pale brown. N. See Maritime Shrew (*S. maritimensis*), p. 362.

TUNDRA SHREW   *Sorex tundrensis*   **P. 363**
Back dark brown, sides whitish; much larger than white-sided shrews on Pl. 32. Alaska, Yukon.

TROWBRIDGE'S SHREW   *Sorex trowbridgii*   **P. 380**
Dark gray; belly same color as back; tail long, clearly bicolor. Pacific NW.

PACIFIC SHREW   *Sorex pacificus*   **P. 372**
Reddish brown; long tail. W. Ore. See very similar Fog Shrew (*S. sonomae*), p. 373.

BAIRD'S SHREW   *Sorex bairdi*   **P. 373**
Dark red-brown; larger than Montane Shrew (Pl. 32). Nw. Ore.

AMERICAN WATER SHREW   *Sorex palustris*   **P. 364**
Gray with white belly or entirely blackish; tail long, bicolor; hind feet fringed with fur; streams and lakes. Widespread.

MARSH SHREW   *Sorex bendirii*   **P. 364**
Blackish; tail long, all-dark; feet not fringed. NW.

SOUTHERN SHORT-TAILED SHREW   *Blarina carolinensis*   **P. 381**
Stocky; bare skin around eye; very short tail. SE. See Elliot's Short-tailed Shrew (*B. hylophaga*), p. 382.

NORTHERN SHORT-TAILED SHREW   *Blarina brevicauda*   **P. 380**
Very similar to Southern but larger. NE.

LEAST SHREW   *Cryptotis parva*   **P. 383**
Dull brown or grayish; similar to short-tailed shrews but much smaller. E.

NORTHERN
SHORT-TAILED
SHREW

AMERICAN DEER
MOUSE (for
comparison)

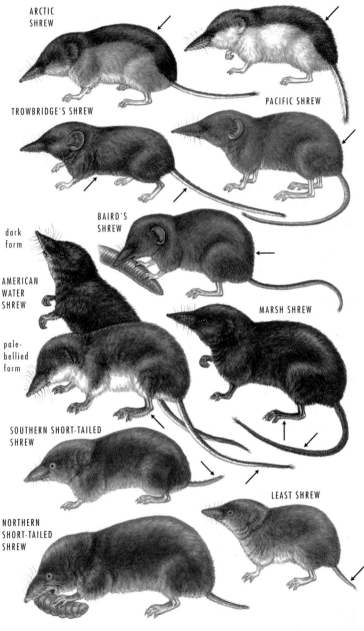

PLATE 33

TUNDRA SHREW

ARCTIC
SHREW

TROWBRIDGE'S SHREW

PACIFIC SHREW

BAIRD'S
SHREW

dark
form

AMERICAN
WATER
SHREW

MARSH SHREW

pale-
bellied
form

SOUTHERN SHORT-TAILED
SHREW

LEAST SHREW

NORTHERN
SHORT-TAILED
SHREW

PLATE 34

MOLES

EASTERN MOLE *Scalopus aquaticus*   P. 388
Tail very short and naked. Large, dull brown in N. Small and blond in SW.

HAIRY-TAILED MOLE *Parascalops breweri*   P. 387
Dark gray; tail short and hairy; winter coat thick and woolly (shown), summer coat more velvety. NE.

STAR-NOSED MOLE *Condylura cristata*   P. 389
Unique starlike ring of tentacles on nose; tail long and hairy. NE.

BROAD-FOOTED MOLE *Scapanus latimanus*   P. 386
Gray-brown or blackish; tail short and lightly haired. W.

AMERICAN SHREW MOLE *Neurotrichus gibbsii*   P. 385
Smallest mole; broad forefeet and long, thick tail, unlike similar-sized shrews. NW.

COAST MOLE *Scapanus orarius*   P. 386
Similar to Broad-footed Mole but darker; tail nearly naked. NW.

TOWNSEND'S MOLE *Scapanus townsendii*   P. 387
Largest mole; tail nearly naked. NW.

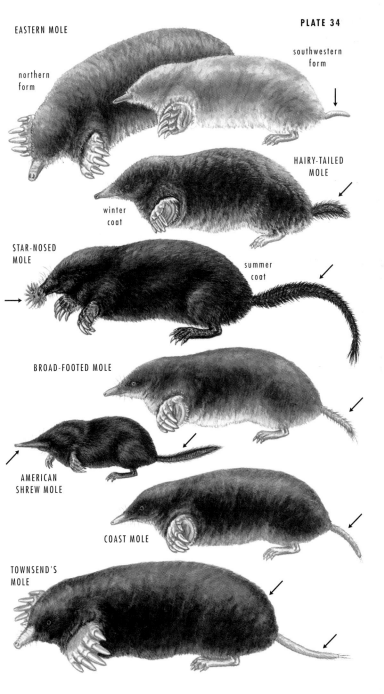

PLATE 34

EASTERN MOLE

northern form

southwestern form

winter coat

HAIRY-TAILED MOLE

STAR-NOSED MOLE

summer coat

BROAD-FOOTED MOLE

AMERICAN SHREW MOLE

COAST MOLE

TOWNSEND'S MOLE

PLATE 35

LEAF-CHINNED AND LEAF-NOSED BATS

Medium-sized to large bats, most with a triangular flap of skin on the nose (noseleaf). Leaf-chinned bats have small flaps of skin on the chin. These are tropical bats that enter the southern and southwestern U.S. only.

PETERS'S GHOST-FACED BAT *Mormoops megalophylla* **P. 392**
Peculiar face, flaps of skin on chin; rounded ears; tail sticks out of membrane at rest. S. Tex.

CALIFORNIA LEAF-NOSED BAT *Macrotus californicus* **P. 394**
Our only big-eared bat with a noseleaf. SW.

HAIRY-LEGGED VAMPIRE *Diphylla ecaudata* **P. 398**
Flattened nosepads; no tail and almost no tail membrane. Vagrant, Tex.

JAMAICAN FRUIT-EATING BAT *Artibeus jamaicensis* **P. 397**
Large and stocky; broad noseleaf and short, striped muzzle are distinctive; no tail. Fla. Keys.

MEXICAN LONG-NOSED BAT *Leptonycteris nivalis* **P. 396**
Long tapered muzzle and small noseleaf; no tail; small fringe on tail membrane and fur on elbows. Extreme sw. Tex. and N.M.

LESSER LONG-NOSED BAT *Leptonycteris yerbabuenae* **P. 395**
Fur gray or orange; similar to Mexican Long-nosed Bat but smaller, with nearly naked tail membrane and almost no fur on elbows. S. Ariz., N.M.

MEXICAN LONG-TONGUED BAT *Choeronycteris mexicana* **P. 397**
Very long, tapered muzzle and small noseleaf; short tail. SW.

ACCIDENTAL BATS FROM THE FLORIDA KEYS

CUBAN FIG-EATING BAT
(*Phyllops falcatus*), p. 398

CUBAN FLOWER BAT
(*Phyllonycteris poeyi*), p. 395

BUFFY FLOWER BAT
(*Erophylla sezekorni*),
p. 395

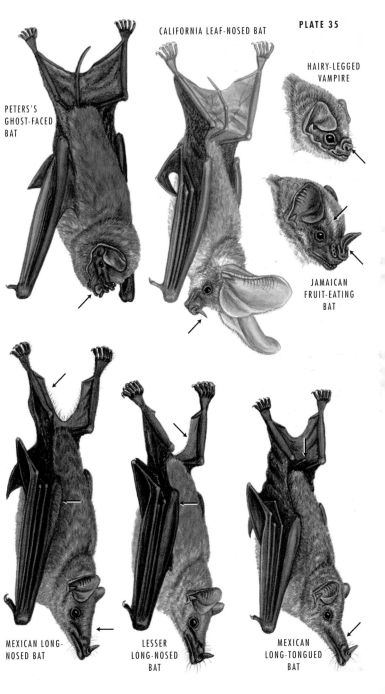

PLATE 35

PETERS'S GHOST-FACED BAT

CALIFORNIA LEAF-NOSED BAT

HAIRY-LEGGED VAMPIRE

JAMAICAN FRUIT-EATING BAT

MEXICAN LONG-NOSED BAT

LESSER LONG-NOSED BAT

MEXICAN LONG-TONGUED BAT

PLATE 36

EASTERN VESPER BATS

Very small to fairly large bats with plain noses and medium-sized ears. Tragus (lobe inside ear) shape may be useful for identification.

EASTERN PIPISTRELLE *Pipistrellus subflavus* **P. 413**
Very small; fur tricolor (dark at roots, pale in middle, tipped brown); pinkish skin on face, ears, and forearms; tragus broad.

EASTERN SMALL-FOOTED MYOTIS *Myotis leibii* **P. 401**
Very small; fur fluffy, yellowish; face and wings black; calcar keeled.

SOUTHEASTERN MYOTIS *Myotis austroriparius* **P. 405**
Gray-brown or orange; belly distinctly paler than back; facial skin pinkish. Calcar unkeeled.

GRAY MYOTIS *Myotis grisescens* **P. 407**
Larger than other eastern *Myotis*; wings attach to ankle (base of toe in all others).

INDIANA MYOTIS *Myotis sodalis* **P. 404**
Dull brown fur; pinkish skin around eyes; short hair on claws.

LITTLE BROWN MYOTIS *Myotis lucifugus* **P. 403**
Glossy yellow-brown fur; dark facial skin; long hair on claws; relatively large feet. See p. 74 for NW form.

NORTHERN MYOTIS *Myotis septentrionalis* **P. 408**
Fluffy; yellow or brown; long ears and long narrow tragus; facial skin pinkish brown.

EVENING BAT *Nycticeius humeralis* **P. 419**
Velvety brown fur; rounded ears and broad tragus.

BIG BROWN BAT *Eptesicus fuscus* **P. 414**
Large; glossy yellow-brown fur; rounded ears and broad tragus; muzzle dark, inflated; tip of tail sticks out beyond tail membrane (tail reaches tip of membrane in other species).

Tragus

Tail tip
Calcar
Keel
Wing attached to base of toe
No keel on calcar
Wing attached to ankle

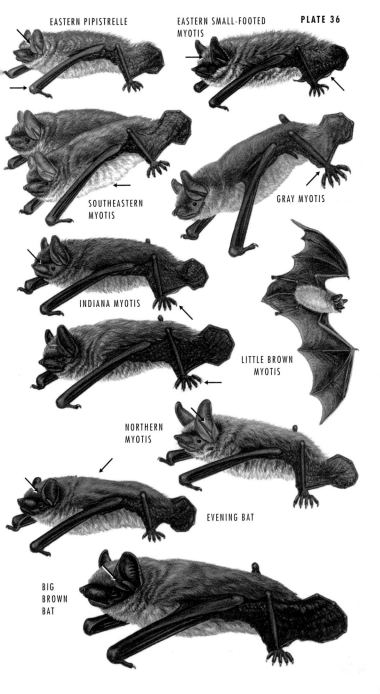

EASTERN PIPISTRELLE

EASTERN SMALL-FOOTED MYOTIS

PLATE 36

SOUTHEASTERN MYOTIS

GRAY MYOTIS

INDIANA MYOTIS

LITTLE BROWN MYOTIS

NORTHERN MYOTIS

EVENING BAT

BIG BROWN BAT

PLATE 37

WESTERN VESPER BATS

Tiny to medium-sized, plain-nosed bats. Big Brown Bat and Little Brown Myotis (Pl. 36) also occur in this region.

WESTERN PIPISTRELLE *Pipistrellus hesperus* **P. 412**
Tiny; fur pale blond, membranes black; tragus broad, eyes large.

YUMA MYOTIS *Myotis yumanensis* **P. 402**
Color variable, dark to pale brown; belly often whitish; feet relatively large. Desert form opposite, NW form below.

WESTERN SMALL-FOOTED MYOTIS *Myotis ciliolabrum* **P. 401**
Fur yellow or yellow-gray; membranes black; tail tip sticks out slightly beyond tail membrane.

CALIFORNIA MYOTIS *Myotis californicus* **P. 400**
Fur yellow or orange, dull; membranes blackish; tail extends to tip of tail membrane. Dark NW form below.

LONG-LEGGED MYOTIS *Myotis volans* **P. 407**
Fur dark brown, pale brown, or blond; membranes brown; ears rounded at tips; calcar keeled; inside edge of wing thickly furred.

CAVE MYOTIS *Myotis velifer* **P. 406**
Relatively large; fur usually grayish, short; facial skin pinkish around eye; calcar not keeled.

FRINGED MYOTIS *Myotis thysanodes* **P. 411**
Fur yellowish or brown; facial skin black on nose, paler around eye; ears long; edge of tail membrane fringed with short hair.

SOUTHWESTERN MYOTIS *Myotis auriculus* **P. 409**
Usually yellow-brown; facial skin pink; ears long.

KEEN'S MYOTIS *Myotis keenii* **P. 410**
Dark brown fur; facial skin blackish with some pink inside ears and around eyes; ears long and narrow. Local, NW.

LONG-EARED MYOTIS *Myotis evotis* **P. 410**
Fur dark brown to yellowish; very similar to Keen's, but ears slightly longer and facial skin usually darker.

CALIFORNIA MYOTIS Northwest

ARIZONA MYOTIS (*Myotis occultus*), p. 404

YUMA MYOTIS Northwest

LITTLE BROWN MYOTIS Northwest, p. 403

PLATE 37

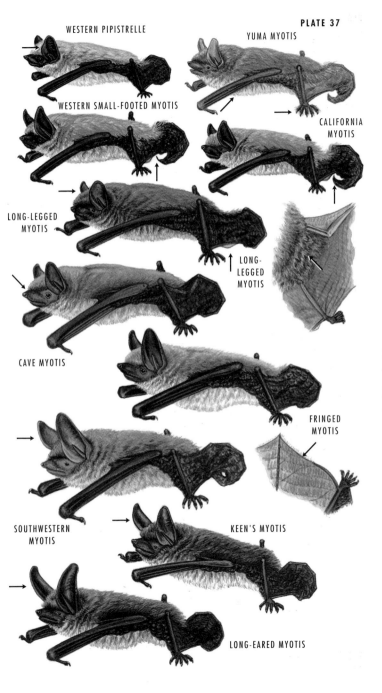

WESTERN PIPISTRELLE

YUMA MYOTIS

WESTERN SMALL-FOOTED MYOTIS

CALIFORNIA MYOTIS

LONG-LEGGED MYOTIS

LONG-LEGGED MYOTIS

CAVE MYOTIS

FRINGED MYOTIS

SOUTHWESTERN MYOTIS

KEEN'S MYOTIS

LONG-EARED MYOTIS

PLATE 38

TREE BATS

These attractive bats have thickly haired tail membranes.

SILVER-HAIRED BAT   *Lasionycteris noctivagans*   **P. 411**
Fur black, well frosted with white; edge of ear yellowish.

SEMINOLE BAT   *Lasiurus seminolus*   **P. 418**
Fur mahogany; white spots on shoulders and around thumbs; female similar to Eastern Red Bat female but slightly darker.

WESTERN RED BAT   *Lasiurus blossevillii*   **P. 417**
Fur yellow-orange to reddish, usually duller than Eastern Red Bat.

EASTERN RED BAT   *Lasiurus borealis*   **P. 416**
Male deep orange-red, female pinkish brown; white spots on shoulders and around thumbs.

HOARY BAT   *Lasiurus cinereus*   **P. 418**
Large; fur dark brown, heavily frosted with white; band of yellow around face.

SOUTHERN YELLOW BAT   *Lasiurus ega*   **P. 415**
Fur yellowish; ears pinkish with a broad curved tragus; tail membrane furred for about half its length.

NORTHERN YELLOW BAT   *Lasiurus intermedius*   **P. 416**
Very similar to Southern Yellow Bat but larger, can be grayer.

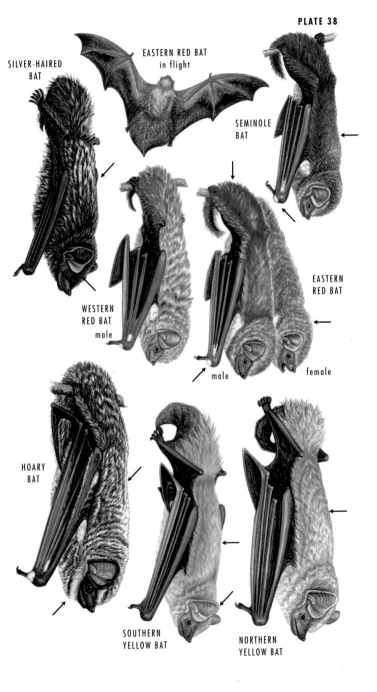

PLATE 38

SILVER-HAIRED BAT

EASTERN RED BAT
in flight

SEMINOLE BAT

WESTERN RED BAT
male

EASTERN RED BAT

male

female

HOARY BAT

SOUTHERN YELLOW BAT

NORTHERN YELLOW BAT

PLATE 39

LONG-EARED VESPER BATS

Plain-nosed bats with exceptionally long ears. Most have broad wings for slow, agile flight.

RAFINESQUE'S BIG-EARED BAT   *Corynorhinus rafinesquii*   P. 422
Lumps on either side of muzzle; back brown, belly whitish (fur dark at roots); long hairs on hind toes.

TOWNSEND'S BIG-EARED BAT   *Corynorhinus townsendii*   P. 422
Similar to Rafinesque's but belly buff, fur not dark at roots; no long hairs on hind toes.

ALLEN'S BIG-EARED BAT   *Idionycteris phyllotis*   P. 421
No lumps on muzzle; flaps of skin on forehead (lappets) from base of each ear.

SPOTTED BAT   *Euderma maculatum*   P. 420
Spectacular black-and-white fur and enormous pink ears.

PALLID BAT   *Antrozous pallidus*   P. 423
Pale fur; long, forward-pointing ears; piglike nostrils open forward.

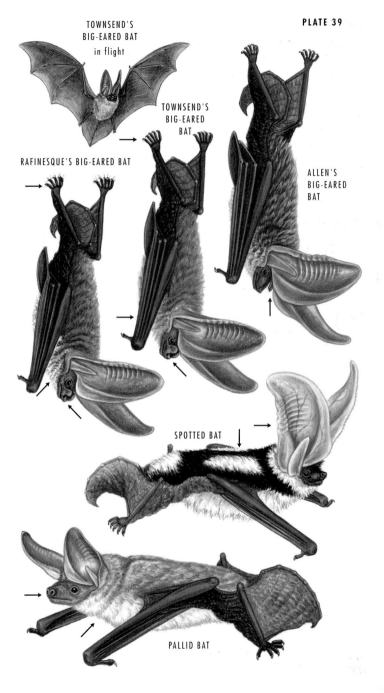

PLATE 39

TOWNSEND'S
BIG-EARED BAT
in flight

TOWNSEND'S
BIG-EARED
BAT

RAFINESQUE'S BIG-EARED BAT

ALLEN'S
BIG-EARED
BAT

SPOTTED BAT

PALLID BAT

PLATE 40

FREE-TAILED BATS

These high-flying bats have long narrow wings and their tail sticks out beyond the tail membrane. Compare lips (smooth or wrinkled) and shape of antitragus (lobe of skin in front of ear).

BRAZILIAN FREE-TAILED BAT *Tadarida brasiliensis* **P. 425**
Fairly small; deep wrinkles on upper lips; ears meet on forehead, but not joined; stiff whiskers on top of snout; no long hairs on rump.

LITTLE MASTIFF BAT *Molossus molossus* **P. 430**
Small; lips not wrinkled; ears separate; narrow, steeply ridged muzzle. Fla. Keys.

POCKETED FREE-TAILED BAT *Nyctinomops femorosaccus* **P. 426**
Similar to Brazilian Free-tail but larger, with long hairs on rump; ears joined above forehead; no stiff bristles on top of snout.

BIG FREE-TAILED BAT *Nyctinomops macrotis* **P. 427**
Large; dark brown; similar to Pocketed but larger, with no long rump hairs.

FLORIDA BONNETED BAT *Eumops floridanus* **P. 428**
Broad head and thick nostrils; ears meet on forehead; low broad antitragus; long hairs on rump. S. Fla.

UNDERWOOD'S BONNETED BAT *Eumops underwoodi* **P. 429**
Similar to Florida but larger and paler; long hairs on rump. Local, s. Ariz.

WESTERN BONNETED BAT *Eumops perotis* **P. 428**
Our largest bat; darker than Underwood's; no long hairs on rump.

BRAZILIAN FREE-TAILED BAT in flight

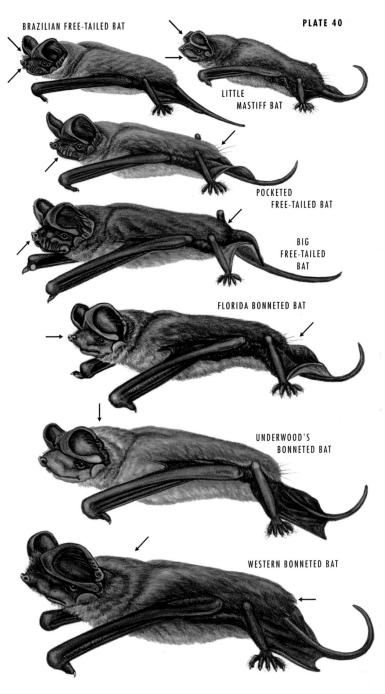

BRAZILIAN FREE-TAILED BAT

PLATE 40

LITTLE
MASTIFF BAT

POCKETED
FREE-TAILED BAT

BIG
FREE-TAILED
BAT

FLORIDA BONNETED BAT

UNDERWOOD'S
BONNETED BAT

WESTERN BONNETED BAT

PLATE 41

WHITE-TAILED AND MULE DEER

WHITE-TAILED DEER *Odocoileus virginianus*   **P. 494**
Long tail brown above, white below. *Winter:* grayish in North. *Summer:* reddish brown. Some southern populations gray-brown year-round. *Male:* antlers have several forks off main branch. *Young:* reddish with white spots. Key Deer: very small, orange-brown year-round.

MULE DEER *Odocoileus hemionus*   **P. 496**
Tail narrow, whitish with a black tip; large ears. *Winter:* grayish. *Summer:* gray-brown. *Male:* antlers divide into 2 main branches that both fork. *Young:* dark gray-brown with white spots. Black-tailed Deer: tail black above (shorter than in White-tail), summer coat orange-brown.

TRACKS

2½ in.
WHITE-TAILED or MULE DEER
(toes sometimes splayed)

3½ in.
ELK

PLATE 41

tail raised in alarm

female summer

WHITE-TAILED DEER

male winter

Key Deer

fawn

MULE DEER

female summer

male winter

male summer

antlers in velvet

fawn

Black-Tailed Deer

PLATE 42

ELK AND INTRODUCED DEER

SIKA DEER *Cervus nippon*   **P. 491**
   Winter: dark brown, unspotted. *Summer:* orange-brown, spotted, with dark line on midback. *Rump pattern:* short tail mostly white, ringed by black semicircle. Introduced.

ELK *Cervus elaphus*   **P. 490**
   Large; dark brown head and neck, paler body; cream white rump. *Male:* antlers have several forks off main branch; shaggy neck. *Female:* no antlers, shorter fur on neck. *Young:* spotted.

FALLOW DEER *Dama dama*   **P. 493**
   Usually spotted in summer, dark brown in winter; can be blond. *Rump pattern:* long black tail bordered white, with 2 black lines on sides of rump. Male has large palmate antlers and tuft of hair on penis sheath. Introduced.

AXIS DEER *Axis axis*   **P. 492**
   Spotted year-round; no black on rump. Male has simple antlers forked at tip. Introduced.

female winter

FALLOW DEER

AXIS DEER

male summer

male year-round

PLATE 42

FALLOW DEER

AXIS DEER

SIKA DEER
female
summer

SIKA DEER

SIKA DEER
male
winter

ELK
male

young

PLATE 43

CARIBOU AND MOOSE

CARIBOU *Rangifer tarandus* **P. 498**
Pale neck contrasts with dark head and body. Woodland Caribou (*R. t. caribou*) male has long, partially flattened antlers that project forward and back. Peary Caribou (*R. t. pearyi*) is small and whitish; male has spindly antlers. All female Caribou have smaller, thinner antlers without flat sections (see Skull Pl. 11).

MOOSE *Alces alces* **P. 497**
Huge, with long "Roman nose." Adults blackish with pale legs; young reddish brown. Male has broad palmate antlers; female lacks antlers.

TRACKS

5 in.
CARIBOU

5 in.
MOOSE

PLATE 43

Barren Ground Caribou

male

Peary Caribou

male

CARIBOU

male

MOOSE

young

PLATE 44

PIGS AND PRONGHORN

COLLARED PECCARY   *Tayassu tajacu*   **P. 488**
  Piglike; large head with pale collar; no tail. Young pinkish brown.

WILD BOAR   *Sus scrofa*   **P. 487**
  Larger than Collared Peccary; long tail and prominent furry ears.
  Young striped.

PRONGHORN   *Antilocapra americana*   **P. 500**
  White markings on neck, sides, and rump; thin black mane. *Male:*
  dark horns with small forward fork, blackish nose. *Female:* stubby
  horns barely visible.

BLACKBUCK   *Antilope cervicapra*   **P. 504**
  Male very distinctive, black-and-white with long spiraled horns.
  Female similar to Pronghorn female but with no white markings
  on head, neck, and rump. Introduced (Tex.)

TRACKS

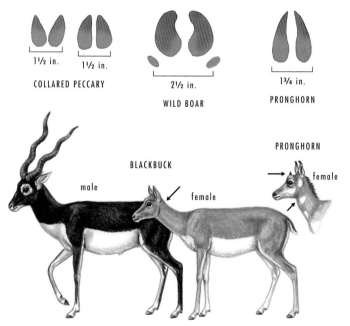

1½ in.   1½ in.

COLLARED PECCARY

2½ in.

WILD BOAR

1¾ in.

PRONGHORN

PRONGHORN

female

BLACKBUCK

male   female

PLATE 44

COLLARED PECCARY

young

WILD BOAR

young

PRONGHORN

male

PLATE 45

COWLIKE BOVIDS

AMERICAN BISON   *Bos bison*   **P. 502**
　　Massive; head very broad, large hump on shoulder of male. Female has horns but smaller shoulders. Young orange-brown.

MUSKOX   *Ovibos moschatus*   **P. 505**
　　Stocky and dark, with very long fur and downturned horns. Arctic.

NILGAI   *Boselaphus tragocamelus*   **P. 502**
　　Lanky with a small head; distinctive white bands on ankles. Male dark gray, female sandy brown. Introduced (s. Tex.).

TRACKS

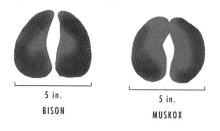

5 in.
BISON

5 in.
MUSKOX

NILGAI

male

female

PLATE 45

AMERICAN BISON

male

young

MUSKOX

PLATE 46

SHEEP AND GOATS

MOUNTAIN GOAT *Oreamnos americanus* **P. 504**
Long white fur; slim, upright black horns (both sexes).

DALL'S SHEEP *Ovis dalli* **P. 508**
Typical form white; coiled yellowish horns (narrower and more upright on female). Stone Sheep is dark gray to blackish, head paler, rump white. Intermediate gray forms not illustrated.

BIGHORN SHEEP *Ovis canadensis* **P. 507**
Yellow-brown to gray-brown fur with contrasting white rump; male has massive, coiled yellowish horns. Narrow, nearly upright horns on female.

BARBARY SHEEP *Ammotragus lervia* **P. 506**
Sandy brown; long fur on neck and forelegs; backward curved horns in both sexes (larger in male). Introduced.

EUROPEAN MOUFLON *Ovis musimon* **P. 509**
Whitish saddle and "Roman nose" on male. Female lacks horns. Introduced (Tex.).

TRACKS

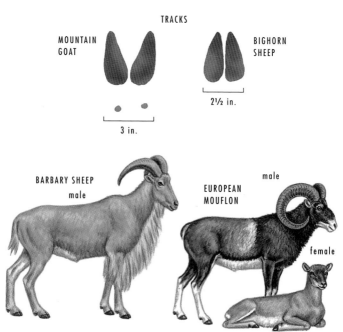

MOUNTAIN GOAT

BIGHORN SHEEP

2½ in.

3 in.

BARBARY SHEEP
male

EUROPEAN MOUFLON

male

female

PLATE 46

MOUNTAIN GOAT

DALL'S
SHEEP

northern
male

STONE SHEEP
male

northern
female

BIGHORN
SHEEP

male

female

PLATE 47

SHORT-TAILED CATS

BOBCAT *Lynx rufus*   **P. 435**
Short tufts on ears; short tail, tip black above, white below; coat
color varies from gray to reddish brown, with or without distinct
spots.

CANADA LYNX *Lynx canadensis*   **P. 436**
Long tufts on ears; very short tail entirely black at tip; huge feet
and long legs. *Winter:* grayish, fur very thick; spots on legs and
belly indistinct. *Summer:* gray-brown, distinct spots on legs and
belly; fur shorter, appears rangier and very leggy. N.

TRACKS

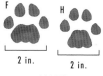

BOBCAT

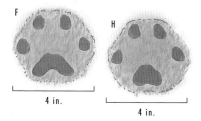

CANADA LYNX

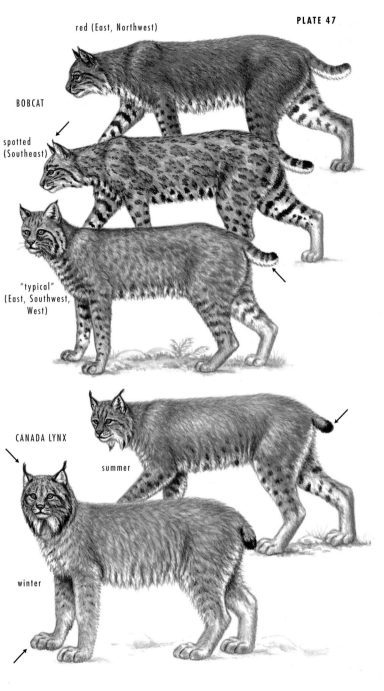

PLATE 47

red (East, Northwest)

BOBCAT

spotted (Southeast)

"typical" (East, Southwest, West)

CANADA LYNX

summer

winter

PLATE 48

LONG-TAILED CATS

Most of these cats are found near our southern border as they are tropical species that only just enter the U.S. or stray in on occasion.

OCELOT *Leopardus pardalis*   **P. 434**
Distinct spots forming splotches and stripes on body. Rare, SW.

JAGUARUNDI *Herpailurus yagouaroundi*   **P. 435**
Long-bodied and short-legged; dark gray-brown, gray, or reddish color; long tail not tipped black. Rare, SW.

COUGAR *Puma concolor*   **P. 433**
Very large, with a relatively small head; tail tipped black; young spotted. W, SE.

JAGUAR *Panthera onca*   **P. 437**
Massive and stocky, with very large head and feet; tail relatively short; spots form rosettes. Rare, SW.

TRACKS

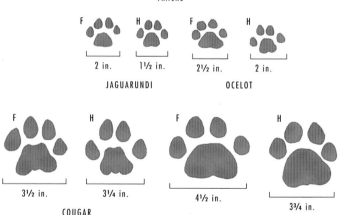

F H F H
2 in. 1½ in. 2½ in. 2 in.
JAGUARUNDI OCELOT

F H F H
3½ in. 3¼ in. 4½ in. 3¾ in.
COUGAR JAGUAR

PLATE 48

OCELOT

JAGUARUNDI

red phase

gray phase

COUGAR

young

JAGUAR

PLATE 49

COYOTE AND WOLVES

COYOTE *Canis latrans* **P. 439**
Narrow pointed muzzle; long rusty ears and rusty legs.

RED WOLF *Canis rufus* **P. 443**
Narrow muzzle and long ears; reddish with a pale saddle; belly buff or white; well-defined white throat and upper neck contrast with orange lower neck. Rare, SE.

EASTERN TIMBER WOLF *Canis lycaon* **P. 442**
Very similar to Red Wolf but usually grayer on back, muzzle a little heavier; belly and neck gray-white; dark line on inner forelegs. NE.

GRAY WOLF *Canis lupus* **P. 441**
Largest canid; muzzle stocky, ears relatively short; color gray, black, or white. Mainly NW.

TRACKS

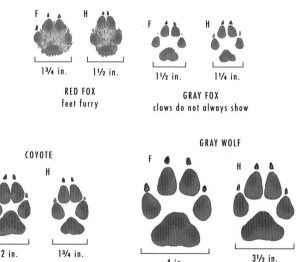

F H
1¾ in. 1½ in.
RED FOX
feet furry

F H
1½ in. 1¼ in.
GRAY FOX
claws do not always show

COYOTE
F H
2 in. 1¾ in.

GRAY WOLF
F H
4 in. 3½ in.

PLATE 49

COYOTE

RED WOLF

EASTERN
TIMBER
WOLF

GRAY WOLF

PLATE 50

FOXES

KIT FOX   *Vulpes macrotis*   P. 446
Small and slim-bodied; large ears and long, black-tipped tail. SW.

SWIFT FOX   *Vulpes velox*   P. 445
Similar to Kit Fox but slightly larger, with smaller ears and a shorter tail. W.

COMMON GRAY FOX   *Urocyon cinereoargenteus*   P. 448
Tail black on upper side and at tip; ears and sides of neck orange. See Island Gray Fox (very similar but much smaller), p. 449.

RED FOX   *Vulpes vulpes*   P. 447
Long, white-tipped tail; legs and ears blackish; body usually orange-brown. *Summer:* rangy, long-legged. *Winter:* coat thick, appears more stocky. Cross phase summer coat and silver phase winter coat shown below.

ARCTIC FOX   *Alopex lagopus*   P. 444
Short legs and small ears. Two color phases, each with different winter and summer coats. *Mainland form:* pure white in winter, brown with pale underparts in summer. *Island/coastal form (rare):* pale blue-gray in winter, blue-black in summer (below).

RED FOX   cross phase summer

RED FOX   silver phase winter

ARCTIC FOX   island form summer

PLATE 50

KIT FOX

SWIFT FOX

COMMON
GRAY FOX

RED FOX

ARCTIC FOX

island
winter

mainland
winter

mainland
summer

PLATE 51

BEARS

BLACK BEAR *Ursus americanus* **P. 450**
   Rump higher than shoulder; ears prominent, muzzle straight or convex in profile; usually black with a brown muzzle but can be cinnamon, dark brown, or blond (mostly western forms). Kermode Bear white (coastal B.C., rare); Glacier Bear bluish gray (coastal Alaska, rare).

BROWN OR GRIZZLY BEAR *Ursus arctos* **P. 451**
   Shoulder humped, as high or higher than rump; facial profile concave; coat dark brown to blond, grizzled or uniformly colored; claws very long and powerful.

POLAR BEAR *Ursus maritimus* **P. 453**
   White; small head and relatively long neck. Arctic.

TRACKS

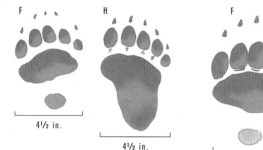

F   H

4½ in.

4½ in.

BLACK BEAR

F

6½ in.

BROWN BEAR

PLATE 51

cinnamon phase

BLACK
BEAR

black
(typical)
phase

Glacier or
Blue Bear

Kermode
Bear

GRIZZLY BEAR

POLAR BEAR

PLATE 52

"PATTERNED" CARNIVORES

RINGTAIL   *Bassariscus astutus*   **P. 454**
   Catlike form; very long, bushy, banded tail. W.

NORTHERN RACCOON   *Procyon lotor*   **P. 455**
   Black mask; short banded tail.

WHITE-NOSED COATI   *Nasua narica*   **P. 456**
   Long white snout and white markings on head; tail very long,
   faintly banded. Local, SW.

AMERICAN BADGER   *Taxidea taxus*   **P. 470**
   Long low profile; black-and-white facial markings.

TRACKS

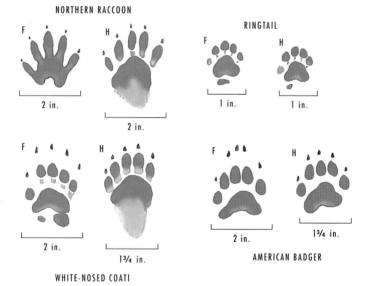

NORTHERN RACCOON

RINGTAIL

F   H

F   H

2 in.

2 in.

1 in.   1 in.

F   H

F   H

2 in.

1¾ in.

2 in.

1¾ in.

AMERICAN BADGER

WHITE-NOSED COATI

PLATE 52

RINGTAIL

NORTHERN
RACCOON

WHITE-NOSED
COATI

AMERICAN
BADGER

PLATE 53

SKUNKS

EASTERN SPOTTED SKUNK   *Spilogale putorius*   **P. 459**
 Small; distinctive pattern of stripes and spots; narrow black line
 below ear; tail mostly black.

WESTERN SPOTTED SKUNK   *Spilogale gracilis*   **P. 457**
 Very similar to Eastern Spotted Skunk but broader line below ear,
 tail mostly white.

STRIPED SKUNK   *Mephitis mephitis*   **P. 459**
 Striping pattern variable, typically with 2 white stripes that meet
 on nape; sometimes 1 broad stripe down back or mostly blackish
 with white nape.

HOODED SKUNK   *Mephitis macroura*   **P. 460**
 Smaller and longer-tailed than Striped Skunk; pattern variable,
 often has thick white "hood." White-backed form usually shows
 some grizzle on back; striped forms have stripes low on sides; 3-
 striped form (back stripe and low side stripes) not illustrated. SW.

WHITE-BACKED HOG-NOSED SKUNK   *Conepatus leuconotus*   **P. 460**
 Largest skunk, with relatively short tail; bare pink snout; no white
 blaze on forehead; back pure white; tail white with some black on
 underside near base. Local, SW.

TRACKS

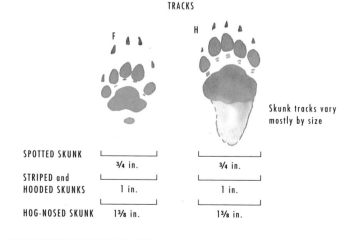

Skunk tracks vary
mostly by size

	F	H
SPOTTED SKUNK	³/₄ in.	³/₄ in.
STRIPED and HOODED SKUNKS	1 in.	1 in.
HOG-NOSED SKUNK	1³/₈ in.	1³/₈ in.

PLATE 53

EASTERN
SPOTTED
SKUNK

WESTERN
SPOTTED
SKUNK

STRIPED SKUNK

HOODED
SKUNK

HOODED SKUNK

WHITE-BACKED
HOG-NOSED SKUNK

PLATE 54

WEASELS AND FERRET

Long, slim-bodied carnivores. Females are much smaller than males. Northern species turn white in winter.

LEAST WEASEL *Mustela nivalis*   **P. 464**
Very small; tail very short, not tipped black. *Winter:* white. *Summer:* brown with white toes.

ERMINE *Mustela erminea*   **P. 465**
Tail medium sized with distinct black tip. *Winter:* white. *Summer:* dark brown with white belly and toes.

LONG-TAILED WEASEL *Mustela frenata*   **P. 466**
Tail relatively long, tipped black. *Winter (northern forms):* white. *Summer:* brown, underparts cream or orange. "Bridled" race (SW) has distinct black-and-white markings on face, orange underparts. Intermediate western races (below).

BLACK-FOOTED FERRET *Mustela nigripes*   **P. 468**
Black mask and tip of tail; yellowish body contrasts with dark legs. Very rare, W.

TRACKS

F   H

1 in.   1 in.

LONG-TAILED WEASEL

LONG-TAILED WEASEL

Sask.

S. Calif.

PLATE 54

LEAST WEASEL

winter female

summer male

ERMINE

summer male

winter female

"bridled" form (Southwest)

winter female

LONG-TAILED WEASEL

summer male (eastern form)

winter female

BLACK-FOOTED FERRET

PLATE 55

MEDIUM-SIZED MUSTELIDS

AMERICAN MINK   *Mustela vison*   **P. 467**
  Dark brown with white on chin and chest; larger and darker than
  other brown weasels (See Pl. 54); usually near water.

AMERICAN MARTEN   *Martes americana*   **P. 462**
  Usually dark brown, head paler than body, chest orange; tail thickly
  furred. Color varies from blond or straw-colored to blackish brown.
  Variation in some animals from Ontario (below). N.

FISHER   *Martes pennanti*   **P. 463**
  Large and dark; head and shoulders grizzled with cream; very
  bushy, long tail. N.

TRACKS

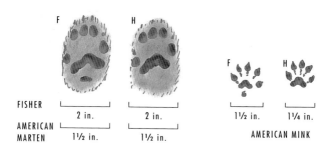

FISHER
            2 in.   2 in.
AMERICAN
MARTEN   1½ in.   1½ in.

F   H
1½ in.   1¼ in.
AMERICAN MINK

AMERICAN MARTEN: color variations

Nipissing,
Ont.

Algoma,
Ont.

Sudbury,
Ont.

PLATE 55

AMERICAN MINK

AMERICAN
MARTEN

FISHER

PLATE 56

WOLVERINE AND OTTERS

WOLVERINE *Gulo gulo*   P. 469
Stocky; dark brown with pale band on forehead and blond band on sides. N.

NORTHERN RIVER OTTER *Lontra canadensis*   P. 471
Long low profile; thick tapering tail; dark chocolate brown, paler below; feet webbed; near water.

SEA OTTER *Enhydra lutris*   P. 472
Head paler than body; relatively short tail; floats on back. West Coast.

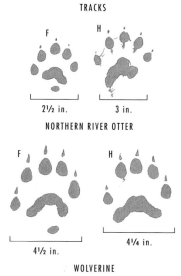

TRACKS

F   H

2½ in.   3 in.

NORTHERN RIVER OTTER

F   H

4½ in.   4¼ in.

WOLVERINE

PLATE 56

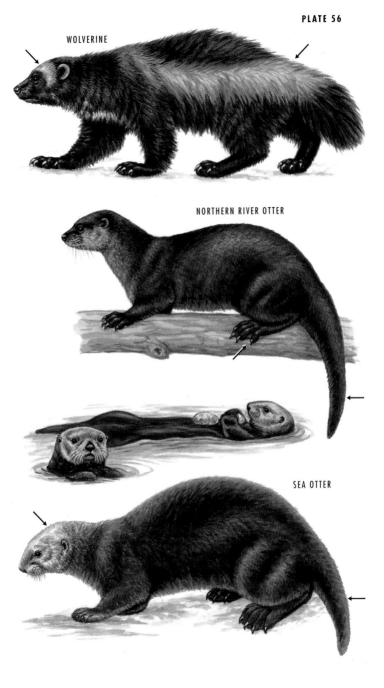

WOLVERINE

NORTHERN RIVER OTTER

SEA OTTER

PLATE 57

FUR SEALS AND SEA LIONS

Eared seals with well-developed front flippers that support part of the animal's weight on land. Females are much smaller than males and can be very difficult to distinguish at sea.

GUADALUPE FUR SEAL *Arctocephalus townsendi*   P. 476
Muzzle medium sized, straight in profile. *Male:* blackish grizzled silver on neck. *Female:* brown. Rare, SW.

NORTHERN FUR SEAL *Callorhinus ursinus*   P. 475
Muzzle short, convex in profile. *Male:* blackish brown, very thick neck, small head. *Female:* dark brown. *Young:* black. NW.

CALIFORNIA SEA LION *Zalophus californianus*   P. 477
Rather long muzzle. *Male:* dark brown with bulbous forehead. *Female:* pale brown (but may appear dark when wet). W.

STELLER'S SEA LION *Eumetopias jubatus*   P. 476
Largest eared seal; golden brown. *Male:* broad muzzle, very thick neck. *Female:* very similar to California Sea Lion female but slightly broader muzzle (appears blond when wet). NW.

PLATE 57

NORTHERN FUR SEAL

GUADALUPE FUR SEAL

male

male

female

female

young

STELLER'S SEA LION

CALIFORNIA SEA LION

male

male

female

female

PLATE 58

EARLESS SEALS

Earless or phocid seals have small front flippers that do not support their weight on land.

RIBBON SEAL *Histriophoca fasciata*   **P. 482**
Unique pattern of pale bands in male that encircle head, flippers, and lower body. Female similar but background color paler, rings not as pronounced.

RINGED SEAL *Pusa hispida*   **P. 480**
Small; marked with pale rings on a dark background. Pup white at birth; young gray without ring pattern.

HARBOR SEAL *Phoca vitulina*   **P. 478**
Variable color: often pale brown with dark spots, but may be dark brown with pale rings (similar to smaller Ringed Seal); muzzle usually pale. Young dark at birth.

LARGHA SEAL *Phoca largha*   **P. 480**
Similar to dark spotted form of Harbor Seal but muzzle usually dark. Young white at birth.

GRAY SEAL *Halichoerus grypus*   **P. 482**
Large; long muzzle, especially in male (appears "Roman-nosed"). Male dark gray to blackish with paler spots. Female pale gray with dark blotches. Young white at birth.

HARP SEAL *Pagophilus groenlandicus*   **P. 481**
Adult has distinctive black head and harp-shaped pattern on back. Pup white at birth; young pale gray with scattered black spots.

HOODED SEAL *Cystophora cristata*   **P. 483**
Silvery with blackish markings. Male can inflate black hood on head into 2-lobed sac; may also extrude and inflate nasal membrane into red "balloon." Female is similar to Gray Seal but muzzle shorter and markings more prominent. Young steel gray above, white below.

BEARDED SEAL *Erignathus barbatus*   **P. 485**
Large, with a small head and prominent whiskers; flippers small, rectangular. Young dark brown with pale markings on head.

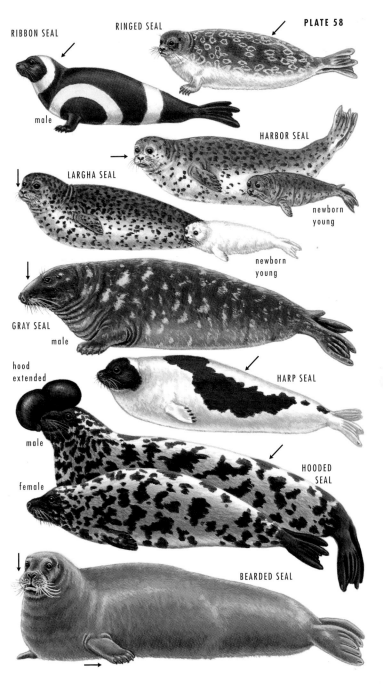

RIBBON SEAL

RINGED SEAL

PLATE 58

male

HARBOR SEAL

LARGHA SEAL

newborn
young

newborn
young

GRAY SEAL
male

hood
extended

HARP SEAL

male

HOODED
SEAL

female

BEARDED SEAL

PLATE 59

ELEPHANT SEAL AND WALRUS

These unrelated species are much larger than any other seals or sea lions.

NORTHERN ELEPHANT SEAL   *Mirounga angustirostris*   **P. 485**
Male massive, thick-necked, with bulging pendulous nose; gray-brown. Female much smaller, yellow-brown, with slightly elongated nose. No external ears. Young blackish.

WALRUS   *Odobenus rosmarus*   **P. 473**
Long whitish tusks (longer in male than female); wrinkled pinkish skin (goes blue-gray in water).

PLATE 59

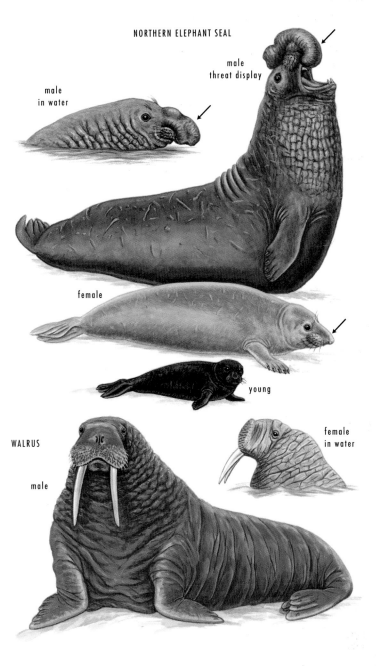

NORTHERN ELEPHANT SEAL

male
threat display

male
in water

female

young

WALRUS

male

female
in water

PLATE 60

MANATEE AND SHORT-BEAKED DOLPHINS

WEST INDIAN MANATEE   *Trichechus manatus*   **P. 175**
Rotund body and blunt muzzle; rounded tail, no dorsal fin; nails on flippers. SE.

WHITE-BEAKED DOLPHIN   *Lagenorhynchus albirostris*   **P. 520**
Short beak usually white; dark gray saddle; diffuse gray and black markings on sides. NE.

ATLANTIC WHITE-SIDED DOLPHIN   *Lagenorhynchus acutus*   **P. 521**
Short beak white below, black above; sides boldly marked with yellow and white patches; white area above flipper. NE.

PACIFIC WHITE-SIDED DOLPHIN   *Lagenorhynchus obliquidens*   **P. 521**
Short dark beak; bicolor dorsal fin; pale gray "suspenders" and pale gray patch above flipper. W.

FRASER'S DOLPHIN   *Lagenodelphis hosei*   **P. 518**
Short thick beak and very stubby appendages; bold black line from beak to anus.

NORTHERN RIGHT WHALE DOLPHIN   *Lissodelphis borealis*   **P. 522**
No dorsal fin; very long, slim body; mainly black.

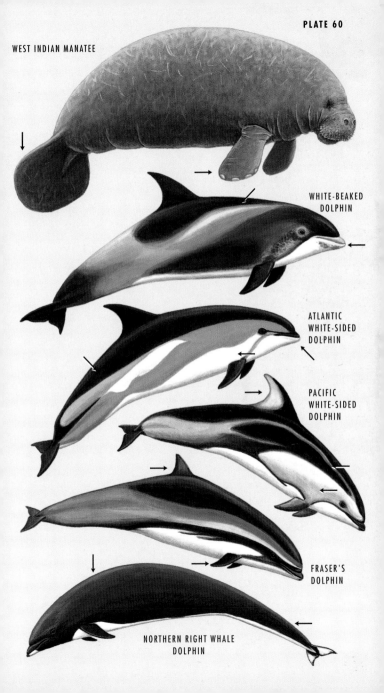

WEST INDIAN MANATEE

WHITE-BEAKED
DOLPHIN

ATLANTIC
WHITE-SIDED
DOLPHIN

PACIFIC
WHITE-SIDED
DOLPHIN

FRASER'S
DOLPHIN

NORTHERN RIGHT WHALE
DOLPHIN

PLATE 61

"TYPICAL" BEAKED DOLPHINS

PANTROPICAL SPOTTED DOLPHIN *Stenella attenuata* **P. 515**
Slim body with small white spots; dark lines extend from beak to eye and flipper; dark cape dips down below dorsal fin. Young unspotted.

ATLANTIC SPOTTED DOLPHIN *Stenella frontalis* **P. 516**
Stockier than Pantropical, black spots on belly. No dark line to flipper. Pale gray blaze under dorsal fin. Young unspotted

SPINNER DOLPHIN *Stenella longirostris* **P. 516**
Very slim and long-beaked; dark line from eye to flipper; parallel bands of color on sides.

STRIPED DOLPHIN *Stenella coeruleoalba* **P. 518**
Dark stripes from eye to flipper and eye to anus; beak black; pale blaze below dorsal fin.

CLYMENE DOLPHIN *Stenella clymene* **P. 517**
Fairly stocky; dark shadow from eye to flipper; top of beak marked with black and white; dark cape dips down below dorsal fin. SE.

LONG-BEAKED COMMON DOLPHIN *Delphinus capensis* **P. 520**
Very similar to Short-beaked but beak longer and narrower; black line from beak to flipper and grayish line above flipper. Coastal, SW.

SHORT-BEAKED COMMON DOLPHIN *Delphinus delphis* **P. 519**
Hourglass pattern with yellowish patch on sides; thin black line from below mouth to flipper; white above flipper. Mainly offshore.

COMMON BOTTLENOSE DOLPHIN *Tursiops truncatus* **P. 514**
Large, grayish, without well-defined patterning; beak rather short and stocky. Tall dorsal fin.

ROUGH-TOOTHED DOLPHIN *Steno bredanensis* **P. 514**
Whitish lips and belly, with some white spots on sides; head cone-shaped without crease between beak and melon.

PLATE 61

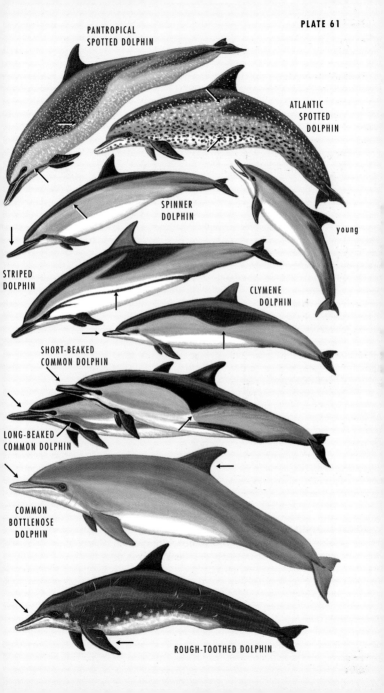

PANTROPICAL SPOTTED DOLPHIN

ATLANTIC SPOTTED DOLPHIN

SPINNER DOLPHIN

young

STRIPED DOLPHIN

CLYMENE DOLPHIN

SHORT-BEAKED COMMON DOLPHIN

LONG-BEAKED COMMON DOLPHIN

COMMON BOTTLENOSE DOLPHIN

ROUGH-TOOTHED DOLPHIN

PLATE 62

SMALL BLUNT-HEADED CETACEANS

Porpoises are small beakless cetaceans with small heads and stocky
bodies.

HARBOR PORPOISE *Phocoena phocoena*   P. 527
Very small; low triangular dorsal fin.

DALL'S PORPOISE *Phocoenoides dalli*   P. 527
Dorsal fin black and white, erect; bold white belly patch; tail
flukes fan-shaped.

PYGMY KILLER WHALE *Feresa attenuata*   P. 523
Prominent erect dorsal fin; very blunt head; tips of flippers
rounded.

MELON-HEADED WHALE *Peponocephala electra*   P. 523
Prominent dorsal fin; slightly elongated head; tips of flippers
pointed.

RISSO'S DOLPHIN *Grampus griseus*   P. 522
Tall narrow dorsal fin; crease on forehead; body grayish, often
scarred.

Small Sperm Whales have an underslung jaw and a fold of skin on the
side of the head that forms a false gill. The dorsal fin is relatively
low and set further down the back than in other cetaceans of similar size.

DWARF SPERM WHALE *Kogia simus*   P. 537
Medium-sized dorsal fin positioned about halfway down back.

PYGMY SPERM WHALE *Kogia breviceps*   P. 536
Very small dorsal fin positioned more than halfway down back.

HARBOR PORPOISE

PLATE 62

DALL'S PORPOISE

PYGMY KILLER WHALE

MELON-HEADED WHALE

RISSO'S DOLPHIN

DWARF SPERM WHALE

PYGMY SPERM WHALE

PLATE 63

MEDIUM-SIZED BLUNT-HEADED CETACEANS

Pilot Whales are stocky-bodied with a bulbous forehead and a thick tail stock. The dorsal fin is broad at the base and low, positioned well forward on the body.

SHORT-FINNED PILOT WHALE *Globicephala macrorhynchus*   **P. 525**
Relatively short, pointed flippers.

LONG-FINNED PILOT WHALE *Globicephala melas*   **P. 526**
Long pointed flippers.

FALSE KILLER WHALE *Pseudorca crassidens*   **P. 524**
Slim-bodied; upper lip overhangs lower lip; narrow erect dorsal fin; hump on leading edge of flippers.

KILLER WHALE *Orcinus orca*   **P. 524**
Large and strikingly marked; broad rounded flippers. *Male:* very tall, erect dorsal fin. *Female:* smaller, curved dorsal fin.

NARWHAL *Monodon monoceros*   **P. 511**
Spindle-shaped body; no dorsal fin; pattern of brown spots on white background, variable in extent; tail fan-shaped. *Male:* very long single tusk ("unicorn horn"). *Female:* usually no tusk, though some may have one. Arctic.

BELUGA *Delphinapterus leucas*   **P. 512**
Stocky, with a bulbous melon; white color is unmistakable. Young grayish. Mainly Arctic.

PLATE 63

SHORT-FINNED PILOT WHALE

LONG-FINNED PILOT WHALE

FALSE KILLER WHALE

female dorsal fin

male

KILLER WHALE

NARWHAL

male

BELUGA

PLATE 64

BEAKED WHALES

Beaked whales have cigar-shaped bodies with small flippers and small dorsal fins set low on the back. Most are poorly known; information is mainly from stranded animals. Males have 2 large teeth on the lower jaw. The shape and position of the teeth are important in identification. Females are very difficult to distinguish. All figures on plate are males.

TRUE'S BEAKED WHALE   *Mesoplodon mirus*   P. 532
Small tooth at tip of jaw; mouthline almost straight. E.

GERVAIS'S BEAKED WHALE   *Mesoplodon europaeus*   P. 532
Tooth near tip of jaw; head rather flat. E.

SOWERBY'S BEAKED WHALE   *Mesoplodon bidens*   P. 532
Tooth about halfway down long narrow beak. NE.

PERRIN'S BEAKED WHALE   *Mesoplodon perrini*   P. 531
Tooth low and broad, very near tip of beak. Rare, SW.

HUBBS'S BEAKED WHALE   *Mesoplodon carlhubbsi*   P. 533
Tooth large and broad, located at midpoint of arched jaw; rounded white cap on head. W.

GINKGO-TOOTHED BEAKED WHALE   *Mesoplodon ginkgodens*   P. 534
Tooth broad, located at midpoint of arched jaw; head slightly rounded; color uniformly gray. SW.

PYGMY BEAKED WHALE   *Mesoplodon peruvianus*   P. 533
Smaller than other species; jaw arched; small tooth located at midpoint, may not be visible above gum. Rare, SW.

BLAINVILLE'S BEAKED WHALE   *Mesoplodon densirostris*   P. 534
Tooth large, angled forward on highly arched jaw; body covered with white spots and scratches. E, W.

STEJNEGER'S BEAKED WHALE   *Mesoplodon stejnegeri*   P. 534
Tooth large and broad, located on midpoint of arched jaw; body mainly blackish. W.

LONGMAN'S BEAKED WHALE   *Indopacetus pacificus*   P. 531
Bulbous melon and short, well-defined beak; body shape similar to Northern Bottlenose Whale. Rare, SE, possibly SW.

CUVIER'S BEAKED WHALE   *Ziphius cavirostris*   P. 529
Small tooth at tip of jaw; beak short and thick. *Male:* head white. *Female:* beak and throat whitish.

BAIRD'S BEAKED WHALE   *Berardius bairdii*   P. 530
Large and dark; prominent melon; small tooth at tip of long narrow beak; small dorsal fin.

NORTHERN BOTTLENOSE WHALE   *Hyperoodon ampullatus*   P. 530
Bulbous melon and short, well-defined beak; beak and forehead white in some males.

PLATE 64

TRUE'S BEAKED WHALE

GERVAIS'S BEAKED WHALE

SOWERBY'S BEAKED WHALE

PERRIN'S BEAKED WHALE

HUBBS'S BEAKED WHALE

GINKGO-TOOTHED BEAKED WHALE

PYGMY BEAKED WHALE

BLAINVILLE'S BEAKED WHALE

STEJNEGER'S BEAKED WHALE

BLAINVILLE'S BEAKED WHALE

STEJNEGER'S BEAKED WHALE

CUVIER'S BEAKED WHALE

LONGMAN'S BEAKED WHALE

BAIRD'S BEAKED WHALE

NORTHERN BOTTLENOSE WHALE

PLATE 65

TYPICAL RORQUALS

Long slim baleen whales with small dorsal fins and grooves on throat and chest. Seen in coastal and deep waters.

SEI WHALE *Balaenoptera borealis* **P. 544**
Dark gray, marked with oval scars; dorsal fin (relatively large, rises sharply from back) usually seen at same time as blow; one ridge on rostrum, snout pointed.

FIN WHALE *Balaenoptera physalus* **P. 543**
Larger than Sei, with asymmetrical color pattern: right lower jaw white, left lower jaw dark gray; dorsal fin (small, gently sloping) seen 1–2 seconds after blow; tip of snout pointed.

BLUE WHALE *Balaenoptera musculus* **P. 542**
Huge, uniformly blue-gray; dorsal fin small, set well back, appears 3–4 seconds after blow; tip of snout rounded when viewed from above.

MINKE WHALE *Balaenoptera acutorostrata* **P. 545**
Smallest baleen whale; blow seldom seen; back and relatively tall, upright dorsal fin appear at surface simultaneously; white bands on flippers; tip of snout pointed.

BRYDE'S WHALE *Balaenoptera brydei* **P. 545**
Very similar to Sei Whale but has 3 ridges on rostrum; often arches back steeply when surfacing.

PLATE 65

SEI WHALE

FIN WHALE

BLUE
WHALE

MINKE
WHALE

BRYDE'S
WHALE

PLATE 66

OTHER VERY LARGE WHALES

HUMPBACK WHALE   *Megaptera novaeangliae*   **P. 546**
Baleen whale with unusually long flippers that are bumpy on their leading edge; small dorsal fin often positioned on a low hump; trailing edge of tail flukes serrated, often exposed before a dive; small protuberances on head and lower jaw.

NORTH ATLANTIC RIGHT WHALE   *Eubalaena glacialis*   **P. 538**
Stocky baleen whale; head very large, marked with irregular whitish patches (callosities); no dorsal fin; flippers very broad. See North Pacific Right Whale (*Eubalaena japonica*), p. 539.

BOWHEAD WHALE   *Balaena mysticetus*   **P. 539**
Very stocky baleen whale; similar to right whales but tip of lower jaw white; massive head is ⅓ body length.

GRAY WHALE   *Eschrichtius robustus*   **P. 540**
Long-bodied baleen whale; mottled grayish color with rough patches of barnacles on head and upper back; no dorsal fin; small hump on lower back and series of ridges on tail stock.

SPERM WHALE   *Physeter macrocephalus*   **P. 535**
Largest toothed whale; unique squared-off head with small, underslung lower jaw; wrinkled skin on body; trailing edge of tail straight. Blowhole off-center: blow angles forward and left.

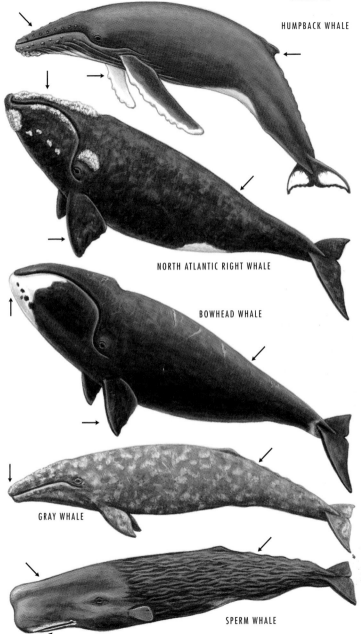

PLATE 66

HUMPBACK WHALE

NORTH ATLANTIC RIGHT WHALE

BOWHEAD WHALE

GRAY WHALE

SPERM WHALE

SKULL PLATES

The skull plates are arranged by size (small to large) and then grouped by taxonomic relationship.

Approximate skull lengths are given, measured from base to tip when placed on a flat tape measure.

It is often very helpful to know the number and arrangement of teeth when trying to identify skulls. The dental formulae are given for all terrestrial North American genera (in most cases species within the same genus have the same dental formula). The dental formula is for one side of the jaw and gives the number of upper/lower teeth with the following abbreviations: i = incisors, c = canines, p = premolars, m = molars. To calculate the total number of teeth in a skull add all the upper and lower numbers and multiply by 2.

BATS

Vesper bats have a characteristic U-shaped gap in the nasals.

1. EASTERN PIPISTRELLE *Pipistrellus subflavus*   **P. 413**
Length ½ in. (13 mm). Dental formula: i 2/3, c 1/1, p 2/2, m 3/3 (formula the same in *Euderma*).

2. LITTLE BROWN MYOTIS *Myotis lucifugus*   **P. 403**
Length ⅝ in. (15 mm). Dental formula: i 2/3, c 1/1, p 3/3, m 3/3.

3. PALLID BAT *Antrozous pallidus*   **P. 423**
Length ¾ in. (20 mm). Dental formula: i 1/2, c 1/1, p 1/2, m 3/3.

4. EVENING BAT *Nycticeius humeralis*   **P. 419**
Length ⅝ in. (16 mm). Dental formula (for 4, 5, and 6): i 1/3, c 1/1, p 1/2, m 3/3.

5. EASTERN RED BAT *Lasiurus borealis*   **P. 416**
Length ⅝ in. (15 mm).

6. HOARY BAT *Lasiurus cinereus*   **P. 418**
Length ¾ in. (19 mm).

7. BIG BROWN BAT *Eptesicus fuscus*   **P. 414**
Length ¾ in. (20 mm). Molars W-shaped. Dental formula: i 2/3, c 1/1, p 1/2, m 3/3.

8. SILVER-HAIRED BAT *Lasionycteris noctivagans*   **P. 411**
Length ⅝ in. (16 mm). Dental formula: i 2/3, c 1/1, p 2/3, m 3/3 (*Corynorhinus* and *Idionycteris* have the same dental formula).

9. BRAZILIAN FREE-TAILED BAT *Tadarida brasiliensis*   **P. 425**
Length ⅝ in. (17 mm). Skull flat in profile. Dental formula: i 1/3, c 1/1, p 1/2, m 3/3.

10. MEXICAN LONG-TONGUED BAT *Choeronycteris mexicana*   **P. 397**
Length 1¼ in. (30 mm). Very elongate skull. Dental formula: i 2/0, c 1/1, p 2/3, m 3/3.

Dental formulae of bats not illustrated:
Leptonycteris i 2/2, c 1/1, p 2/3, m 2/2.
Macrotus, Mormoops i 2/2, c 1/1, p 2/3, m 3/3.
Eumops, Nyctinomops i 1/2, c 1/1, p 2/2, m 3/3.

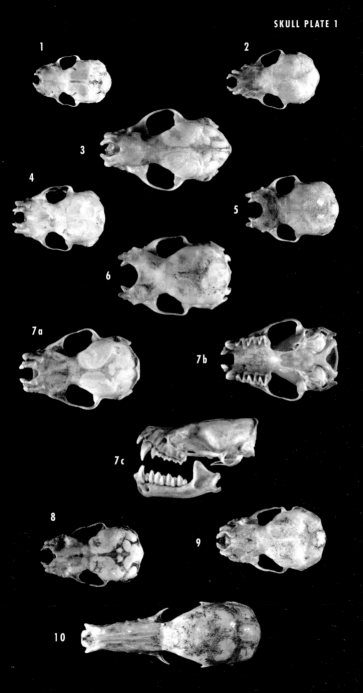

SHREWS AND MOLES

Skulls long and narrow, very small to moderate in size. In shrews, some of the incisors, premolars, and canines are undifferentiated, single-cusped teeth called unicuspids. The middle incisor is well developed and pincerlike. See Fig. 2.

1. MASKED SHREW *Sorex cinereus* **P. 369**
Length ⅝ in. (17 mm). Dental formula (1 and 2): i 3/1, c 1/1, p 3/1, m 3/3 (5 upper unicuspids).

2. NORTHERN SHORT-TAILED SHREW *Blarina brevicauda* **P. 380**
Length 1 in. (25 mm).

3. LEAST SHREW *Cryptotis parva* **P. 383**
Length ⅝ in. (16 mm). Dental formula: i 3/1, c 1/1, p 2/1, m 3/3 (4 upper unicuspids).

4. AMERICAN SHREW MOLE *Neurotrichus gibbsii* **P. 385**
Length 1 in. (24 mm). Dental formula: i 2/1, c 1/1, p 3/4, m 3/3.

5. HAIRY-TAILED MOLE *Parascalops breweri* **P. 387**
Length 1¼ in. (33 mm). Dental formula (5, 6, 7, and 8): i 3/3, c 1/1, p 4/4, m 3/3.

6. STAR-NOSED MOLE *Condylura cristata* **P. 389**
Length 1¼ in. (33 mm).

7. COAST MOLE *Scapanus orarius* **P. 386**
Length 1⅜ in. (34 mm).

8. TOWNSEND'S MOLE *Scapanus townsendii* **P. 387**
Length 1¾ in. (45 mm).

9. EASTERN MOLE *Scalopus aquaticus* **P. 388**
Length 1⅝ in. (40 mm). Dental formula: i 3/2, c 1/0, p 3/3, m 3/3.

Dental formula of desert shrew, *Notiosorex* (not illustrated): i 3/1, c 1/1, p 1/1, m 3/3 (3 upper unicuspids).

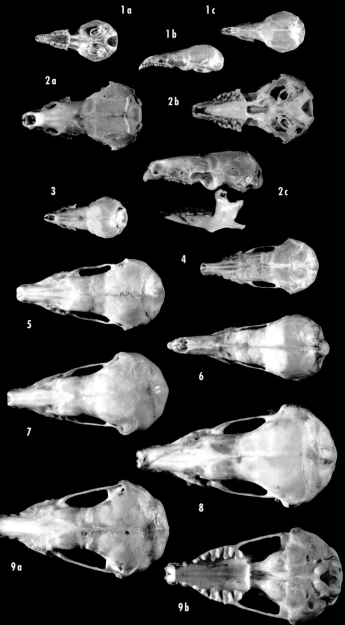

MICE AND VOLES

Rodent skulls can be recognized by the arrangement of the teeth: there is a pronounced gap (diastema) between a single pair of large incisors and the molar teeth (there are no canines and usually no premolars). Almost all small murid rodents and voles have the same dental formula: i 1/1, c 0/0, p 0/0, m 3/3. Exceptions to this are noted below. See Figs. 3 and 4 for teeth.

1. MEADOW JUMPING MOUSE *Zapus hudsonius* **P. 335**
Length ⅞ in. (24 mm). All jumping mice have grooved upper incisors. Dental formula (*Zapus*): i 1/1, c 0/0, p 1/0, m 3/3. Woodland Jumping Mouse, *Napaeozapus,* lacks upper premolars and has the typical rodent dental formula given above.

2. WESTERN HARVEST MOUSE *Reithrodontomys megalotis* **P. 289**
Length ¾ in. (20 mm). Upper incisors grooved.

3. NORTHERN PYGMY MOUSE *Baiomys taylori* **P. 292**
Length ⅝ in. (17 mm).

4. HOUSE MOUSE *Mus musculus* **P. 331**
Length ⅞ in. (22 mm).

5. NORTHERN GRASSHOPPER MOUSE *Onychomys leucogaster* **P. 285**
Length 1⅛ in. (30 mm).

6. AMERICAN DEER MOUSE *Peromyscus maniculatus* **P. 277**
Length 1 in. (25 mm).

7. GOLDEN MOUSE *Ochrotomys nuttalli* **P. 291**
Length 1 in. (26 mm). Short rostrum.

8. MEADOW VOLE *Microtus pennsylvanicus* **P. 313**
Length 1⅛ in. (28 mm). Very short rostrum.

9. NORTHERN COLLARED LEMMING *Dicrostonyx groenlandicus* **P. 329**
Length 1¼ in. (30 mm). Broad, stocky skull.

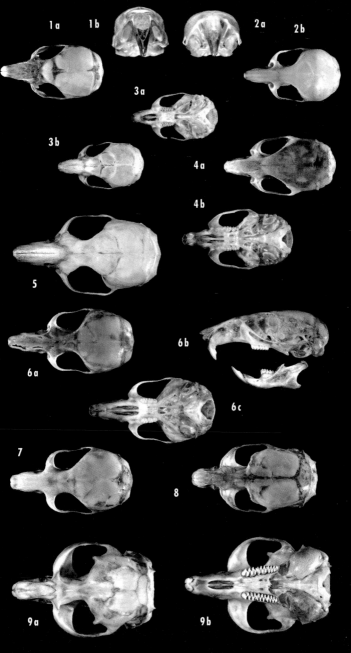

POCKET MICE, KANGAROO RATS, AND MURID RATS

The heteromyid rodents (*Chaetodipus, Perognathus, Microdipodops, Dipodomys,* and *Liomys*) have the following dental formula: i 1/1, c 0/0, p 1/1, m 3/3. These mice have large auditory capsules and a large opening on the side of the rostrum. The murids (*Neotoma, Rattus, Sigmodon,* and *Oryzomys*) have the same dental formula as for the small rodents on Skull Pl. 3 (i 1/1, c 0/0, p 0/0, m 3/3). See Fig. 3 for close-ups of molars.

1. HISPID POCKET MOUSE *Chaetodipus hispidus* **P. 248**
Length 1⅛ in. (30 mm).

2. SILKY POCKET MOUSE *Perognathus flavus* **P. 255**
Length ¾ in. (21 mm).

3. DARK KANGAROO MOUSE *Microdipodops megacephalus* **P. 259**
Length 1 in. (28 mm).

4. MERRIAM'S KANGAROO RAT *Dipodomys merriami* **P. 270**
Length 1⅜ in. (35 mm).

5. WESTERN WHITE-THROATED WOODRAT *Neotoma albigula* **P. 296**
Length 1⅝ in. (43 mm).

6. NORWAY RAT *Rattus norvegicus* **P. 333**
Length 1½ in. (40 mm).

7. MARSH RICE RAT *Oryzomys palustris* **P. 303**
Length 1¼ in. (33 mm).

8. HISPID COTTON RAT *Sigmodon hispidus* **P. 304**
Length 1⅜ in. (35 mm).

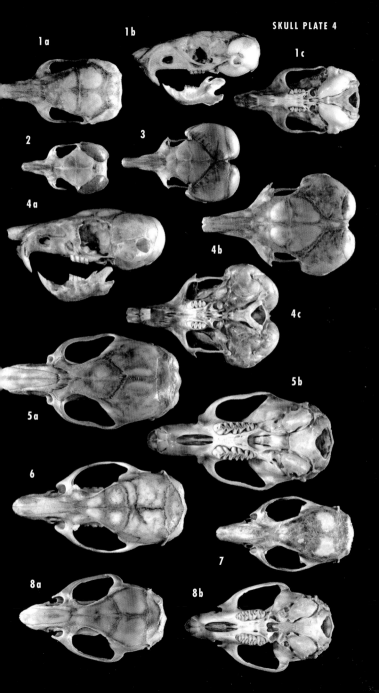

SCIURIDS AND POCKET GOPHERS

Most sciurids have the following dental formula: i 1/1, c 0/0, p 2/1, m 3/3. *Sciurus nayaritensis, S. niger, S. arizonensis, Tamias striatus* (but not other *Tamias*), and some *Tamiasciurus hudsonicus* have the same dental formula as the pocket gophers and kangaroo rats: i 1/1, c 0/0, p 1/1, m 3/3.

1. EASTERN CHIPMUNK *Tamias striatus* **P. 209**
Length 1⅝ in. (42 mm).

2. THIRTEEN-LINED GROUND SQUIRREL *Spermophilus tridecemlineatus* **P. 197**
Length 1⅝ in. (42 mm).

3. BLACK-TAILED PRAIRIE DOG *Cynomys ludovicianus* **P. 186**
Length 2⅜ in. (62 mm). Large projections over eye sockets.

4. EASTERN GRAY SQUIRREL *Sciurus carolinensis* **P. 225**
Length 2¼ in. (60 mm).

5. NORTHERN FLYING SQUIRREL *Glaucomys sabrinus* **P. 233**
Length 1½ in. (40 mm).

6. RED SQUIRREL *Tamiasciurus hudsonicus* **P. 231**
Length 1¾ in. (45 mm).

7. WOODCHUCK *Marmota monax* **P. 181**
Length 3¼ in. (82 mm).

8. YELLOW-FACED POCKET GOPHER *Cratogeomys castanops* **P. 240**
Length 2 in. (50 mm). All pocket gophers have wide, robust, flat skulls.

9. PLAINS POCKET GOPHER *Geomys bursarius* **P. 237**
Length 2 in. (50 mm).

10. BOTTA'S POCKET GOPHER *Thomomys bottae* **P. 242**
Length 1½ in. (40 mm).

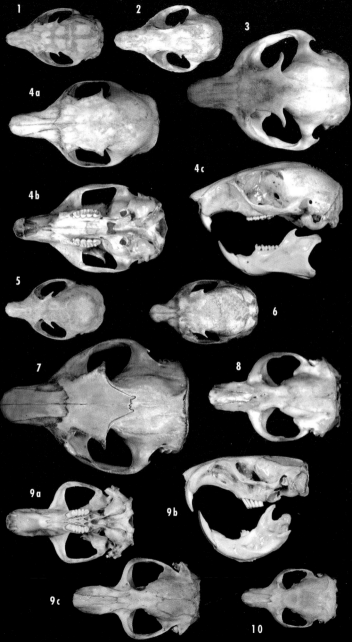

LAGOMORPHS AND LARGE RODENTS

1. AMERICAN PIKA *Ochotona princeps*   **P. 342**
Length 1¾ in. (40 mm). Dental formula: i 2/1, c 0/0, p 3/2, m 2/3.

2. EASTERN COTTONTAIL *Sylvilagus floridanus*   **P. 347**
Length 3 in. (75 mm). Dental formula (2, 3, and 4): i 2/1, c 0/0,
p 3/2, m 3/3.

3. SNOWSHOE HARE *Lepus americanus*   **P. 352**
Length 3 in. (75 mm). Sides of rostrum fenestrated (all rabbits);
small peglike incisors behind middle upper incisors.

4. BLACK-TAILED JACKRABBIT *Lepus californicus*   **P. 355**
Length 3½ in. (90 mm).

5. SEWELLEL *Aplodontia rufa*   **P. 178**
Length 3 in. (75 mm). Very short, broad braincase. Dental formula: i 1/1, c 0/0, p 2/1, m 3/3.

6. ROUND-TAILED MUSKRAT *Neofiber alleni*   **P. 325**
Length 1¾ in. (45 mm). Dental formula (6 and 7): i 1/1, c 0/0, p 0/0,
m 3/3.

7. COMMON MUSKRAT *Ondatra zibethicus*   **P. 326**
Length 2½ in. (60 mm).

8. AMERICAN BEAVER *Castor canadensis*   **P. 179**
Length 5 in. (130 mm). Dental formula (8, 9, and 10): i 1/1, c 0/0,
p 1/1, m 3/3.

9. COYPU *Myocastor coypus*   **P. 339**
Length 4½ in. (115 mm).

10. NORTH AMERICAN PORCUPINE *Erethizon dorsatum*   **P. 338**
Length 4 in. (100 mm).

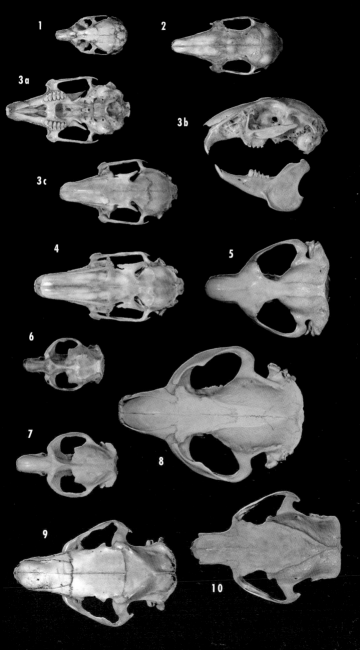

OPOSSUM, ARMADILLO, PROCYONIDS, AND CATS

1. VIRGINIA OPOSSUM *Didelphis virginiana*   P. 171
Length 5 in. (13 cm). More teeth than any other mammal; small braincase. Dental formula: i 5/4, c 1/1, p 3/3, m 4/4.

2. NINE-BANDED ARMADILLO *Dasypus novemcinctus*   P. 173
Length 4 in. (10 cm). Narrow skull; few, conical, peglike teeth. Dental formula: i 0/0, c 0/0, p-m 7/7.

3. NORTHERN RACCOON *Procyon lotor*   P. 455
Length 5 in. (13 cm). Broader than canid skull. Dental formula (3, 4, and 5): i 3/3, c 1/1, p 4/4, m 2/2.

4. WHITE-NOSED COATI *Nasua narica*   P. 456
Length 5 in. (13 cm). Long narrow skull.

5. RINGTAIL *Bassariscus astutus*   P. 454
Length 3¾ in. (9.5 cm).

6. DOMESTIC CAT *Felis domesticus*
Length 4 in. (10 cm). Dental formula (6 and 8): i 3/3, c 1/1, p 3/2, m 1/1.

7. BOBCAT *Lynx rufus*   P. 435
Length 5½ in. (14 cm). Dental formula: i 3/3, c 1/1, p 2/2, m 1/1.

8. COUGAR *Puma concolor*   P. 433
Length 9 in. (23 cm). Projection over eye sockets; few, bladelike teeth (all cats).

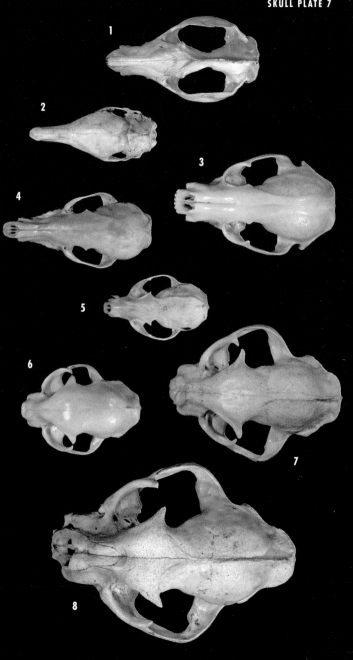

MUSTELIDS

Skulls small to quite large; short, flattened in profile. In most species, skulls of males are larger than female skulls by ½–1 in. (1.3–2.5 cm). Lengths given are for males.

1. EASTERN SPOTTED SKUNK *Spilogale putorius* **P. 459**
Length 2¼ in. (5.5 cm). Dental formula (1, 2, 4, 5, and 8): i 3/3, c 1/1, p 3/3, m 1/2.

2. STRIPED SKUNK *Mephitis mephitis* **P. 459**
Length 3¼ in. (8.5 cm).

3. WHITE-BACKED HOG-NOSED SKUNK *Conepatus leuconotus* **P. 460**
Length 3¼ in. (8.5 cm). Dental formula: i 3/3, c 1/1, p 2/3, m 1/2.

4. AMERICAN MINK *Mustela vison* **P. 467**
Length 2¾ in. (6.5 cm).

5. LONG-TAILED WEASEL *Mustela frenata* **P. 466**
Length 1¾ in. (4.5 cm).

6. AMERICAN MARTEN *Martes americana* **P. 462**
Female
Length 3 in. (8 cm). Dental formula (6, 7, and 10): i 3/3, c 1/1, p 4/4, m 1/2.

7. FISHER *Martes pennanti* **P. 463**
Male (female skull lacks high ridge)
Length 4–5 in. (10–13 cm).

8. AMERICAN BADGER *Taxidea taxus* **P. 470**
Length 5 in. (13 cm).

9. NORTHERN RIVER OTTER *Lontra canadensis* **P. 471**
Length 4¼ in. (11 cm). Dental formula: i 3/3, c 1/1, p 4/3, m 1/2.

10. WOLVERINE *Gulo gulo* **P. 469**
Length 6–7 in. (15–18 cm).

Dental formula of *Enhydra* (not illustrated): i 3/2, c 1/1, p 3/3, m 1/2 (this formula is unique to the genus).

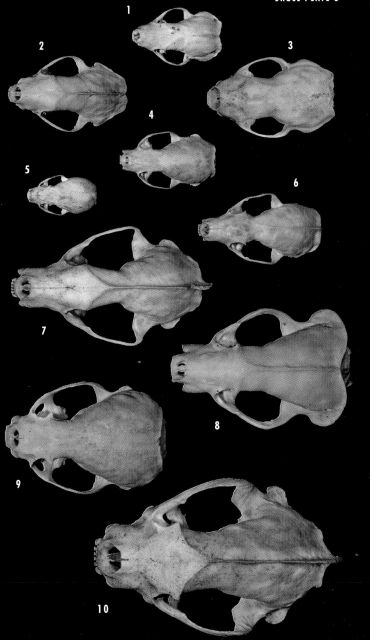

CANIDS AND BEARS

Medium-sized to very large skulls. Dental formula of all canids and bears is: i 3/3, c 1/1, p 4/4, m 2/3.

1. COMMON GRAY FOX   *Urocyon cinereoargenteus*   P. 448
   Length 5 in. (13 cm). Broad parallel ridges on braincase.

2. ARCTIC FOX   *Alopex lagopus*   P. 444
   Length 5½ in. (14 cm).

3. RED FOX   *Vulpes vulpes*   P. 447
   Length 6 in. (15 cm). Single ridge (sagittal crest) on braincase.

4. CHESAPEAKE RETRIEVER   *Canis domesticus*

5. BULLDOG   *Canis domesticus*

6. COYOTE   *Canis latrans*   P. 439
   Length 8 in. (20 cm).

7. EASTERN TIMBER WOLF   *Canis lycaon*   P. 442
   Length 9 in. (23 cm).

8. GRAY WOLF   *Canis lupus*   P. 441
   Length 11 in. (28 cm).

9. BLACK BEAR   *Ursus americanus*   P. 450
   Length 11–13 in. (28–33 cm).

10. BROWN BEAR   *Ursus arctos*   P. 451
   Length 15 in. (38 cm).

11. POLAR BEAR   *Ursus maritimus*   P. 453
   Length 16 in. (41 cm).

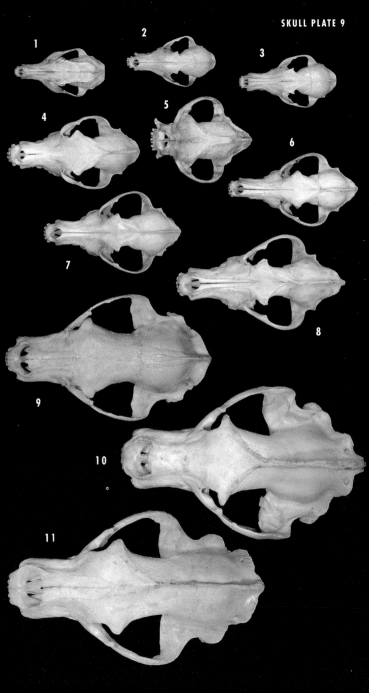

DEER

Some skulls are females and lack antlers; for males, the antlers are either shed or removed. Dental formula of most deer: i 0/3, c 0/1, p 3/3, m 3/3. Exceptions are noted below.

1. FALLOW DEER *Dama dama*   **P. 493**
Male
Length 10 in. (25.5 cm).

2. SIKA DEER *Cervus nippon*   **P. 491**
Female
Length 12 in. (30.5 cm).

3. WHITE-TAILED DEER *Odocoileus virginianus*   **P. 494**
Male
Length 9–13 in. (23–33 cm). Mule Deer is very similar.

4. CARIBOU *Rangifer tarandus*   **P. 498**
Male
Length 13–14 in. (33–36 cm). Upper canines can be present (dental formula as for Elk) or absent (formula as above).

5. ELK *Cervus elaphus*   **P. 490**
Female
Length 18 in. (46 cm). Dental formula: i 0/3, c 1/1, p 3/3, m 3/3.

6. MOOSE *Alces alces*   **P. 497**
Female
Length 22–24 in. (56–61 cm). Short nasal bones forming open cavity in rostrum.

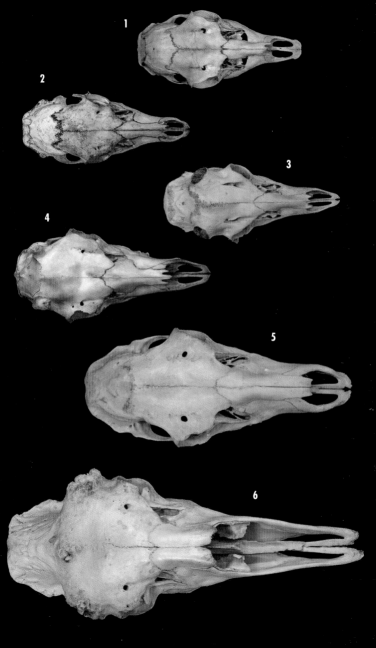

ANTLERS

1. SIKA DEER   *Cervus nippon*   P. 491

2. PEARY CARIBOU   *Rangifer tarandus pearyi*
    Male   P. 498

3. CARIBOU   *Rangifer tarandus*   P. 498
    3a male, 3b female
    Barren Ground or tundra form shown; woodland caribou has
    long, narrower antlers.

4. ELK   *Cervus elaphus*   P. 490

5. MOOSE   *Alces alces*   P. 497

6. WHITE-TAILED DEER   *Odocoileus virginianus*   P. 494
    6a and 6b both males (different angle)
    Note tines branching off main beam.

7. MULE DEER   *Odocoileus hemionus*   P. 496
    Main beam of antler divides and each section branches again.

PECCARIES AND HOOFED DOMESTIC MAMMALS (HORNS REMOVED)

Skulls of these animals are large.

1. COLLARED PECCARY *Tayassu tajacu*   **P. 488**
Length 10 in. (25 cm). Dental formula: i 2/3, c 1/1, p 3/3, m 3/3.

2. WILD BOAR *Sus scrofa*   **P. 487**
Female
Length 13 in. (33 cm). Dental formula (2 and 3): i 3/3, c 1/1, p 4/4, m 3/3.

3. DOMESTIC PIG *Sus scrofa*
Male
Length 14 in. (36 cm). Huge canine teeth in male.

4. GOAT *Capra hircus*
• Length 10 in. (25 cm). Dental formula (4 and 5): i 0/3, c 0/1, p 3/3, m 3/3.

5. SHEEP *Ovis aries*
Length 10 in. (25 cm).

6. COW *Bos taurus*
Length 20–24 in. (51–61 cm). Dental formula: i 0/4, c 0/0, p 3/3, m 3/3.

7. HORSE *Equus caballus*
Length 20–26 in. (51–66 cm). Dental formula: i 3/3, c 1/1, p 3/3 or 4/3, m 3/3.

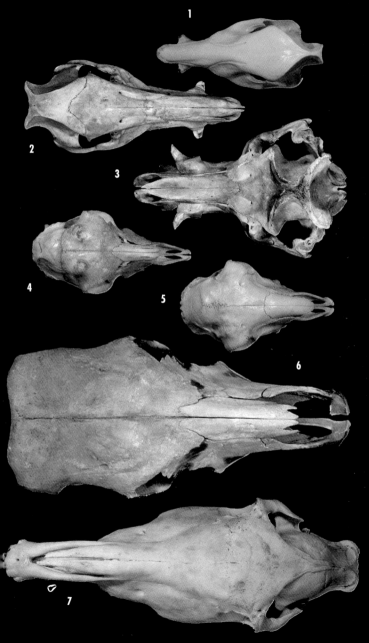

BOVIDS AND PRONGHORN

Dental formula of all genera shown here is: i 0/3, c 0/1, p 3/3, m 3/3.

1. PRONGHORN *Antilocapra americana*   **P. 500**
Length 11 in. (28 cm).

2. AMERICAN BISON *Bos bison*   **P. 502**
Horn sheaths removed. Length 23 in. (59 cm).

3. MUSKOX *Ovibos moschatus*   **P. 505**
Length 20 in. (51 cm).

4. MOUNTAIN GOAT *Oreamnos americanus*   **P. 504**
Narrow spiked horns. Length 12 in. (31 cm).

5. BIGHORN SHEEP *Ovis canadensis*   **P. 507**
Length 11 in. (28 cm). Subadult male shown; in adult, horns spiral
in a full circle.

6. BARBARY SHEEP *Ammotragus lervia*   **P. 506**
Length 14 in. (35 cm).

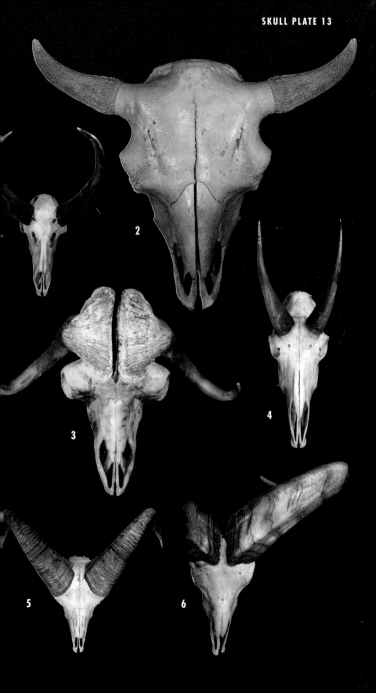

MARINE MAMMALS

These skulls are not to scale; the Minke is much larger than it appears here in comparison to the others.

1. WEST INDIAN MANATEE *Trichechus manatus* **P. 175**
Length 13–16 in. (33–41 cm). Stocky, heavy skull. Skull usually has 24 undifferentiated teeth in use at any one time (dental formula: 6/6).

2. HARBOR SEAL *Phoca vitulina* **P. 478**
Length 7 in. (18 cm). Dental formula: i 3/2, c 1/1, p 4/4, m 1/1 (= 34 teeth). Most earless seals have 34–36 teeth; Hooded Seals and Elephant Seals have 26–34 teeth.

3. WALRUS *Odobenus rosmarus* **P. 473**
3a dorsal view, 3b frontal view
Tusks in both sexes. Length 15 in. (38 cm). Dental formula: i 1/0, c 1/1, p 3/3, m 0/0.

4. CALIFORNIA SEA LION *Zalophus californianus* **P. 477**
Length 10 in. (25 cm). Dental formula: i 3/2, c 1/1, p 4/4, m 2/1 or 1/1. Teeth number varies between individuals from 34 to 38 in all eared seals.

5. BELUGA *Delphinapterus leucas* **P. 512**
Length about 18 in. (46 cm). Teeth: 8/8 to 10/10.

6. COMMON BOTTLENOSE DOLPHIN *Tursiops truncatus* **P. 514**
Length about 19 in. (49 cm). Many peglike teeth. Teeth: 20/18 to 26/24.

7. MINKE WHALE *Balaenoptera acutorostrata* **P. 546**
Length about 6 ft. (183 cm). No teeth.

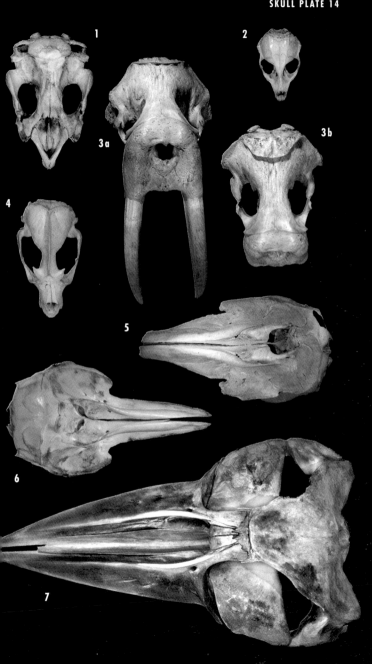

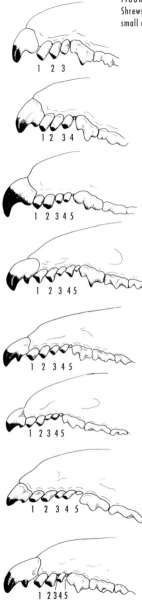

FIGURE 2: SHREW TEETH

Shrews have pincerlike incisors and a series of small unicuspid teeth arranged in a set pattern.

DESERT SHREWS (*Notiosorex*) have only 3 upper unicuspids.

LEAST SHREWS (*Cryptotis*) have 4 upper unicuspids, but the 4th is tiny.

SHORT-TAILED SHREWS (*Blarina*) have 5 upper unicuspids, but the 5th is tiny and often not seen in profile.

LONG-TAILED SHREWS (*Sorex*) have 5 upper unicuspids. Many western species (*S. monticolus, S. vagrans, S. bairdi, S. pacificus,* etc.) have 3rd and 5th unicuspid smaller than 4th.

MASKED SHREW (*S. cinereus*) and others (*S. haydeni, S. merriami, S. preblei,* etc.) have 4 upper unicuspids about the same size, with the 5th much smaller.

SOUTHEASTERN SHREW (*S. longirostris*) has 4th unicuspid slightly bigger than 3rd.

DWARF and INYO SHREWS (*S. nanus* and *S. tenellus*) have 3rd unicuspid smaller than 2nd and 4th.

PYGMY SHREW (*S. hoyi*) has tiny 3rd and 5th unicuspids, not visible in profile or with a hand lens; appears to have only 3 unicuspids.

Some shrews have small projections or tines on the median edge of the incisors. In *Sorex monticolus* (left), these are within the pigmented area. In *Sorex vagrans* (right), the tines are above the pigmented area but are themselves pigmented.

Sorex bairdi (left) has almost no tines, but the incisor teeth diverge from each other. *Sorex pacificus* (right) lacks tines and the incisors remain in contact to the tip.

In *Sorex ornatus*, the tines are just within the pigmented area.

FIGURE 3: MOLAR TEETH OF SMALL RODENTS

Most small rodents have 3 upper and lower molars (upper molars are illustrated). All the murid rodents have this arrangement. The following two (nonmurid) small rodents have 4 upper cheek teeth.

JUMPING MICE (*Zapus*) have a small premolar and flat molar surfaces with an intricate surface pattern.

HETEROMYID RODENTS (e.g., *Perognathus*) have a large premolar and a simple pattern of dentine pools across the teeth.

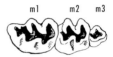

DEER MICE (*Peromyscus*) and relatives have alternating cusps and ill-defined dentine pools.

GRASSHOPPER MICE (*Onychomys*) teeth are similar to deer mice but the 3rd molar is small.

RICE RATS (*Oryzomys*) have alternating cusps and a wavy pattern of dentine.

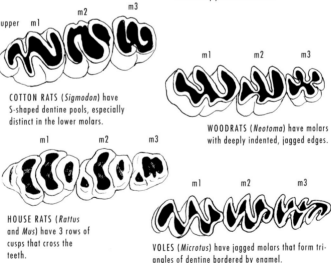

COTTON RATS (*Sigmodon*) have S-shaped dentine pools, especially distinct in the lower molars.

WOODRATS (*Neotoma*) have molars with deeply indented, jagged edges.

HOUSE RATS (*Rattus* and *Mus*) have 3 rows of cusps that cross the teeth.

VOLES (*Microtus*) have jagged molars that form triangles of dentine bordered by enamel.

FIGURE 4: VOLE TEETH

Voles have characteristic patterns on the molar teeth, with well-defined islands of dentine surrounded by enamel.

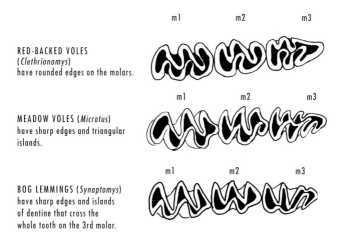

m1   m2   m3

RED-BACKED VOLES
(*Clethrionomys*)
have rounded edges on the molars.

m1   m2   m3

MEADOW VOLES (*Microtus*)
have sharp edges and triangular
islands.

m1   m2   m3

BOG LEMMINGS (*Synaptomys*)
have sharp edges and islands
of dentine that cross the
whole tooth on the 3rd molar.

Upper teeth and partial skulls of some confusing *Microtus* species

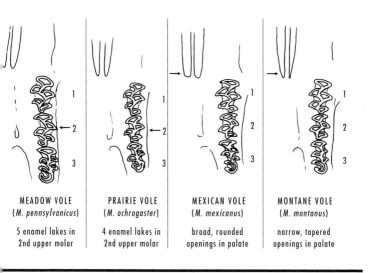

MEADOW VOLE	PRAIRIE VOLE	MEXICAN VOLE	MONTANE VOLE
(*M. pennsylvanicus*)	(*M. ochrogaster*)	(*M. mexicanus*)	(*M. montanus*)
5 enamel lakes in 2nd upper molar	4 enamel lakes in 2nd upper molar	broad, rounded openings in palate	narrow, tapered openings in palate

BOTTA'S POCKET GOPHER
(*T. bottae*)
Thomomys — small
ungrooved incisors.

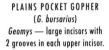

PLAINS POCKET GOPHER
(*G. bursarius*)
Geomys — large incisors with
2 grooves in each upper incisor.

YELLOW-FACED POCKET GOPHER
(*C. castanops*)
Cratogeomys — very large
incisors with single groove
in each upper incisor.

SPECIES
ACCOUNTS

AMERICAN OPOSSUMS:
DIDELPHIMORPHIA, DIDELPHIDAE

The large group of pouched mammals formerly considered as a single order, Marsupialia, has been split into 7 orders, 3 of which occur in the Americas. The largest New World order, Didelphimorphia, contains a single family, Didelphidae. The Virginia Opossum is the only species in the Didelphidae that ranges north into the U.S.; all other New World opossums are found in South and Central America.

RGINIA OPOSSUM   *Didelphis virginiana*   **Pl. 1, Skull Pl. 7**
Head and body 14–20 in. (37–45 cm); tail 9–15 in. (28–37 cm); wt. 2–15 lb. (1–7 kg). *Long-haired and scruffy,* with a naked nose and ears and a *ratlike tail.* Body grizzled gray-white, fur a mix of long

Virginia Opossum demonstrating the use of its prehensile tail. Note the contrasting black feet and pink toes, and naked tail.

VIRGINIA OPOSSUM
Didelphis virginiana

black and white guard hairs, usually with white hairs longer than black. Belly white or yellowish. Head white with narrow black eye-rings and a black line down middle of forehead. Ears all-black or black with white tips. Tail fully furred at base, then naked and black near base, with a long white tip. Tops of feet black with contrasting pink toes. Five toes on each foot, thumb of hind foot opposable. Eyeshine bright red. **SIMILAR SPECIES:** House rats are much smaller with shorter fur and do not have fur on base of tail. **SOUNDS:** Usually silent but may hiss, growl, or clash teeth in defense. Male makes a clicking sound when courting female. **HABITS:** Nocturnal, but sometimes active by day in winter. Walks with a clumsy waddling gait, tail held slightly above body level; climbs well, using prehensile tail for balance. Often climbs trees if pursued. If alarmed, cornered, or attacked, may "play dead," lying on side, drooling, with tongue out and eyes open or closed. Omnivorous; will eat a wide range of plant and animal foods, often foraging along small streams; also raids henhouses and eats human garbage, carrion, and almost anything remotely edible. Usually dens in hollow logs or rocks or in burrows made by other animals. Transports leaves and other nest materials in coiled-up tail. Solitary and seminomadic in habits; uses a series of dens in a shifting home range. Female has litter of 8–16 tiny (2 g) young that crawl to the pouch and attach to one of 13 nipples for about 2 months. Young leave the pouch to crawl onto the mother's back for a short period and remain with her for their third month of life. Breeds Feb.–Oct. and may have 2 or 3 litters per year. Lifespan is usually under 2 years. **HABITAT:** Oldfields, forests, agricultural areas, roadsides, suburbs, and urban regions. **RANGE:** E. and cen. U.S. north to s. Ont.; introduced widely on West Coast. **STATUS:** Common to abundant. Many are killed on roads and occasionally hunted for meat in South.

ARMADILLOS:
CINGULATA, DASYPODIDAE

The armadillos were formerly placed in the Order Xenarthra, with anteaters and sloths. Armadillos are now in a separate order, Cingulata, while anteaters and sloths are in the Order Pilosa. All xenarthrans have extra articulations in the lumbar vertebrae, a condition found only in members of this group. These mammals are found in South and Central America, with only one species ranging into the U.S.

INE-BANDED ARMADILLO   Pl. 1, Skull Pl. 7
asypus novemcinctus

Head and body 15–22 in. (38–57 cm); tail 10–16 in. (28–43 cm); wt. 6–16 lb. (3–7 kg). Familiar and very distinctive "Texas Armadillo." Body scaly with 8–9 moveable, overlapping bands on back. Tail long and fully armored. Four toes on front foot, 5 toes on hind foot. Tracks often birdlike, showing only 2 large front claw marks

Nine-banded Armadillo pauses from digging to stand up and sniff for danger. When startled, this inveterate burrower will jump straight in the air and then run off with a rapid, waddling gate.

and 3 hind claws. No eyeshine. **SIMILAR SPECIES:** None in the U.S. **SOUNDS:** Rummages noisily in leaf litter and may snuffle or snort in alarm. **HABITS:** Mostly nocturnal in summer, active by day or night in winter. Shortsighted and often seemingly oblivious, it can run quickly, with a stiff-legged gait, if alarmed, often beginning with a vertical jump. Does not roll into a ball but will curl to protect soft underparts if cornered. Swims well, gulping air to increase buoyancy or sinking to the bottom and walking across the bed of small streams or ponds. Digs very well and can disappear quickly into loose soil. Burrow entrances are semicircular with well-worn paths radiating out from them. Usually makes nests in burrows but will nest aboveground in areas subject to flooding. Aboveground nests resemble small haystacks. Feeds mostly on invertebrates dug from the soil, also takes some small vertebrates, fruit, and carrion. Solitary but not territorial. Female lies on back to mate. Gives birth to identical quadruplets, born well advanced but with soft armor. Usually has only 1 litter per year. **HABITAT:** Woodland, fields, scrub, and brushy areas. **RANGE:** Okla. and Tex. to S.C. and Fla., south through Central and South America to Uruguay and Argentina. **STATUS:** Common and widespread. Range expanding in U.S. Many are killed on roads; hunted in some areas. Identical young are used in medical research in studies of leprosy and other diseases.

NINE-BANDED ARMADILLO
Dasypus novemcinctus

MANATEES AND DUGONGS:
SIRENIA, TRICHECHIDAE

This order of mammals contains two families. One family and a single species occurs in waters of the U.S. These mammals are more closely related to elephants and hyraxes than to any other marine mammal.

EST INDIAN MANATEE   **Pl. 60, Skull Pl. 14**
ichechus manatus
Florida Manatee, Caribbean Manatee, Antillean Manatee

Length 8–15 ft. (2.5–4.5 m); wt. 1,100–2,200 lb. (500–1,000 kg). Bulky, *aquatic mammal*. Head blunt with split upper lips and short bristles on the muzzle. Rounded flippers have 3–4 vestigial nails. *No dorsal fin; paddle-shaped tail*. **SIMILAR SPECIES:** Unmistakable at close range. Coastal dolphins have dorsal fins and pointed tails; other whales and dolphins are found in deeper water. **SOUNDS:** Sharp exhalation of air when surfacing. Usually quiet, but may grunt or squeak. **HABITS:** A placid herbivore that browses on aquatic vegeta-

Female West Indian Manatee with large young. Note the rounded flippers and tail fin, and blunt, stubbly snout.

tion in shallow water. Usually surfaces to breathe every 3–5 minutes, but can remain underwater for 16 minutes. May travel alone or in small groups. Widely dispersed in summer but congregates in warm waters in winter. Single young born after 12-month gestation; remains with the mother for 1–2 years. Lifespan is 60–70 years. **HABITAT:** Slow-moving rivers, estuaries, and shallow coastal water. Tolerates salt water but needs access to freshwater plants. **RANGE:** *Summer* — Atlantic Coast from Beaufort, N.C., along both coasts of Fla. to La. and Miss. Occasional wanderers reported from Va. and R.I. in north and westward to mouth of Rio Grande. *Winter* — Fla., mainly in Crystal R., Homosassa R., Tampa Bay, Port Everglades, Titusville, Port Myers, and Blue Spring. Also found throughout Caribbean region, e. coast of Central America, and ne. South America. **STATUS:** Endangered (USFWS). Many are killed by motorboats and entanglement in fishing nets; also suffer from habitat alteration and pesticide use. Population in the U.S. is about 3,200 (2001 count).

WEST INDIAN MANATEE
Trichechus manatus

RODENTS: RODENTIA

The rodents are the largest order of mammals worldwide, with nearly 2,000 species, about 40 percent of all the living mammals. They occur on all landmasses except polar regions. Most species are small and ratlike, but some are very large. They range in weight from ¼ oz. to 132 lb. (4g–60 kg). Most rodents have 4 toes on the front foot and 5 on the hind foot. All rodents have similar teeth: 1 pair of upper and 1 pair of lower incisors, then a large gap, or diastema, and several pairs of chewing teeth (molars only in typical mice, premolars and molars in squirrels and allies, jumping mice, and cavylike rodents). The incisor teeth grow continuously throughout life and have chisel-like cutting edges.

There are 2 major groups of rodents in North America — the Sciurognathi (squirrels, rats, mice, voles, jumping mice, pocket gophers and pocket mice, American Beaver, and Sewellel) and the Hystricognathi (in our area represented only by the porcupine and Coypu). Small mouselike rodents are not all closely related. The pocket mice and kangaroo rats are much more closely related to pocket gophers than to deer mice, for example. Jumping mice, with their exceptionally long hind feet and tails, are in the same family as gerbils and other Old World desert-dwelling species. Voles, on the other hand, previously classified in a separate family (Arvicolidae), are now treated as a subfamily of the Muridae (rats and mice). Distinct groups of small rodents may appear superficially similar but are often easily distinguished by their teeth (see figure 3, p. 166), and an understanding of the relationships can help considerably in identification.

Some rodents are serious crop pests and carriers of disease, but the majority of species have little or no impact on human activities, and many are beneficial. They consume large numbers of insects and also eat weed seeds. Many rodents are also important food sources for larger predators, and some aid in seed dispersal or soil aeration or perform other ecological functions. Even the most damaging rodents, the house rats and mice, are indispensable tools of scientific and medical research.

SEWELLELS OR MOUNTAIN BEAVERS: Aplodontiidae

There is a single species in this family, and it is considered to be the most primitive living rodent. "Mountain Beaver" is an inappropriate name for this animal, as it is not restricted to mountains and it is not related to beavers in any way. Sewellels eat plants that other mammals find toxic or unpalatable, such as ferns, fir, and rhododendron. To increase nutrient extraction from these plants, they re-ingest soft fecal pellets. When defecating, they sit on their rump with their short tail protruding up between the hind legs and grab the fecal pellets as they emerge. Hard pellets are flicked off to a latrine area, soft ones are swallowed.

SEWELLEL *Aplodontia rufa* Pl. 3, Skull Pl. 6
Mountain Beaver, Aplodontia

Head and body 13 in. (27–40 cm); tail 1 in. (1–5 cm); hind foot 2 in. (5–6 cm); wt. 2 lb. (0.6–1.2 kg). Stocky. Upperparts dark brown or black, belly gray-brown or blackish. White spot at base of ear. Small eyes and ears. *Very short tail.* **SIMILAR SPECIES:** Muskrat is similar in size and color but has a long tail. Pocket gophers are much smaller. **SOUNDS:** Usually silent, sometimes makes soft whines or sobs, also may squeal or grind teeth. Probably does not "boom" despite the old vernacular name "boomer." **HABITS:** More active by night than day, but can be seen by day especially in late summer. Does not hibernate but may remain underground in bad weather. Semi-fossorial; climbs low shrubs when foraging. Feeds on ferns

The Sewellel is an odd-looking, almost tailless rodent. It ranges in color from brown to blackish. It is a living relic of an ancient rodent lineage.

and other herbaceous plants. Collects and dries some plants that may be used for nesting or winter consumption. Makes an extensive tunnel system with multiple burrow entrances (about 6 in./15 cm in diameter) marked with large piles of dirt. Burrows are usually located in dense vegetation on a slope near a stream or other water source. Home ranges (each about ½ acre/0.2 ha) overlap, but each animal uses separate burrows and nests. Breeds in winter; 1–6 young are born March–April. Females have 1 litter per year. **HABITAT:** Moist forest, thickets, or clearcuts with dense vegetation, usually on sloping ground near water. Sea level to about 6,000 ft. (2,000 m). **RANGE:** Pacific Northwest from s. B.C. to n. Calif. **STATUS:** Locally common.

BEAVERS: Castoridae

Second only to the Capybara in size, beavers are among the world's largest rodents. There are 2 species of beavers in the Northern Hemisphere — an Old World species and our American Beaver. The genus name *Castor* refers to castor glands located at the base of the tail.

AMERICAN BEAVER *Castor canadensis* **Pl. 2, Skull Pl. 6**
Head and body 2–3 ft. (60–90 cm); tail 1 ft. (30–40 cm); wt. 35–70 lb. (16–30 kg). Our *largest rodent.* Semiaquatic. Fur glossy red-brown; small eyes and ears; large orange incisors. *Tail vertically flattened, paddle-shaped,* scaly. Hind feet webbed. In water swims with forehead, eyes, and nose exposed, usually has body and tail below water. When swimming with back exposed, nape is also above water so that a single hump is visible. **SIMILAR SPECIES:** Unmistakable when seen on land. Muskrat swims with top of head, back, and sometimes tail exposed, but nape usually submerged (2 or 3 humps visible). Coypu swims with top of head and upper back

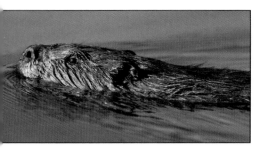

The American Beaver typically swims with only head and upper back exposed; the lower back and tail are submerged.

AMERICAN BEAVER
Castor canadensis

exposed, shoulders underwater. **SOUNDS:** Loud slaps on water surface given as warning. Occasionally growls, hisses, or screams. **HABITS:** One of the most distinctive and conspicuous mammals, well known for its ability to fell trees and alter the landscape by damming lakes and streams. Mainly nocturnal or crepuscular, but sometimes seen by day. Active year-round. Swims well and can remain underwater for 15 minutes. Eats mostly bark in winter (aspen is a staple), roots and green vegetation in summer. Cuts small trees in summer and stores them underwater for winter use. Freshly cut trees (cut wood is pale yellow) indicate presence of beaver. If ice is not too thick, will travel over snow to fell trees in midwinter. Makes dams to keep water levels high enough to maintain open water below the ice in winter. Dams and houses are made of sticks and mud. Along rivers, does not make a house or dam but dens in bank burrows ("bank beavers"). Sometimes digs canals to feeding areas or makes deeply worn trails, neatly chopping any branch that falls across the path. Lives in family groups consisting of a monogamous pair with yearlings and young of the year. Piles mud and sticks at edges of territory and marks them with secretions from anal and castor glands. Breeds in winter; young are born April–June. Litter size is 1–9, usually 3–4; females reproduce once annually. Young are furred at birth, stay in the lodge for a month, and remain with the parents for 2 years. Lifespan is 10–20 years. **HABITAT:** Swamps, lakes, rivers, and streams in wooded areas. Also in ponds in tundra. **RANGE:** Alaska through mainland Canada and U.S. into ne. Mexico. **STATUS:** Widespread, common to abundant. Formerly heavily exploited for fur, some populations were eliminated, but have now recovered; considered a pest in many areas.

QUIRRELS AND ALLIES: Sciuridae

The squirrel family is one of the most conspicuous groups of mammals in North America. Sciurids include prairie dogs, marmots, ground squirrels, tree squirrels, chipmunks, and flying squirrels. All but the flying squirrels are diurnal, and many are easily seen.

The major groups in this large family are considered separately.

ARMOTS: *Marmota*

Marmots are large stocky sciurids that are mostly terrestrial and semi-fossorial. Most species are found at higher elevations. They dig extensive burrows and hibernate for long periods, after gaining a considerable amount of fat in the fall.

OODCHUCK *Marmota monax*   Pl. 3, Skull Pl. 5
Groundhog

Head and body 18 in. (35–50 cm); tail 6 in. (12–18 cm); wt. 5–13 lb. (2.2–5.9 kg). *Large and stocky.* Back grizzled blackish brown and cream; belly rusty brown. Top of *head dark brown,* sides of muzzle whitish, cheeks pale cream-brown. Legs blackish. Tail black edged with cream. Color variable within populations — can be almost entirely black, dark or pale brown, or albino. **SIMILAR SPECIES:** Hoary Marmot has paler shoulders and black-and-white markings on the head. Yellow-bellied Marmot (usually found farther south) has yellow-orange underparts, white spots between eyes, and a

Young Woodchucks. In the East this species typically emerges from hibernation while snow is still on the ground, on or around Groundhog Day (Feb. 2). Mating takes place soon after emergence.

reddish tail. **SOUNDS:** Occasionally makes a sharp whistle or soft chucks, but is less vocal than other marmots. **HABITS:** Active in the early morning and late afternoon, may be seen out sunning at other times of day. Usually seen on the ground, standing up on hind legs at burrow entrance. Climbs well and will climb high up a tree to forage or view its surroundings. Eats mostly green vegetation, including some crops, and will take fruit, twigs, and bark on occasion. Unlike other marmots, this species is solitary and will aggressively defend its burrow area, although it is not territorial. Makes an extensive burrow with several openings. Cleans burrow regularly in summer, leaving a fresh mound of soil at main entrance (unlike burrows of other mammals). Winter dens are often separate from the summer burrow and have a single entrance. Puts on a layer of fat in fall and will hibernate for 3 to 6 months, depending on latitude. Mates soon after spring emergence; litters of 2–9 (usually about 5) young are born April–May. Lifespan is 5–6 years in the wild. **HABITAT:** Fields and brush at forest edge, grassy banks along highways and roadsides. Prefers dry sloping ground. Sometimes found in heavily wooded areas. **RANGE:** Cen. Alaska, s. Canada, and much of e. U.S. **STATUS:** Widespread and common.

WOODCHUCK
Marmota monax

YELLOW-BELLIED MARMOT *Marmota flaviventris* **Pl. 3**
Rockchuck

Head and body 16 in. (33–48 cm); tail 7 in. (13–22 cm); wt. 3–11½ lb. (1.5–5.2 kg). Stocky. Back grizzled gray-brown; *underparts and lower legs pale to bright orange.* Top of head brown with *pale patches between eyes;* sides of neck yellow-buff. Tail reddish brown to dark brown. Forefeet red-brown, hind feet dark brown. **SIMILAR SPECIES:** Woodchuck has a darker belly and no white spots on forehead. **SOUNDS:** Loud whistles, undulating screams, and tooth chatters. **HABITS:** Most active in the early morning and late afternoon. Lives in small family groups, though some lone individuals may be

Yellow-bellied Marmot mother and young. Note the contrasting white muzzle and white spots over the eyes.

encountered. In cold climates hibernates Sept.–May; in warmer regions becomes active as early as Feb. but goes into summer estivation in June and may remain belowground until the next year. Litter size is 3–8, usually 4 or 5. **HABITAT:** Meadows near rocky outcrops and talus slopes, at low elevations in northern part of range, usually above 6,500 ft. (2,000 m) farther south. **RANGE:** Mts. of w. U.S. and sw. Canada. **STATUS:** Southern populations small and isolated, elsewhere common.

HOARY MARMOT *Marmota caligata* Pl. 3

Head and body 22 in. (45–60 cm); tail 9 in. (17–25 cm); wt. 8–20 lb. (3.6–9 kg). Largest of the marmots, stocky. *Shoulders, upper back, forelegs, and chest whitish;* lower back, rump, and tail yellow-brown to russet. *Head pale,* marked with black on crown, snout, and base of whiskers. Feet blackish. **SIMILAR SPECIES:** See Woodchuck and Alaska Marmot. Yellow-bellied Marmot is grizzled gray-brown on back. **SOUNDS:** Piercing, high-pitched whistles used in alarm and as contact calls, also barks, yips, and yells. **HABITS:** Eats a variety of leaves and flowers of alpine plants. Social, lives in family groups of

YELLOW-BELLIED MARMOT
Marmota flaviventris

HOARY MARMOT
Marmota caligata

ALASKA MARMOT
Marmota broweri

Hoary Marmot sunning on a rock. This highly social species uses a shrill whistle to warn other family members of danger.

1 male, 2–3 females, and offspring; several families may feed together. Hibernates Sept.–May, mates soon after emergence. Litters of 2–5 young are active aboveground in late July. Females reproduce every other year. **HABITAT:** Alpine and subalpine meadows near rocky outcrops or talus slopes. **RANGE:** Alaska, Yukon, and B.C. to mts. of n. Wash., n. Idaho, and nw. Mont. **STATUS:** Common.

ALASKA MARMOT *Marmota broweri*   Pl. 3

Head and body 18 in. (43–47 cm); tail 6 in. (13–18 cm); wt. 5½ –9 lb. (2.5–4 kg). Similar in color to Hoary Marmot (formerly considered a subspecies of Hoary Marmot), but *top of head and mouth entirely black,* cheeks gray. Ears very small and well concealed in fur. Feet gray-brown. **SIMILAR SPECIES:** No other marmots occur in its range. **SOUNDS:** Loud whistle in alarm. Other calls as for Hoary Marmot. **HABITS:** Most active in summer on windy days that provide relief from mosquitoes. Ingests large amounts of low-energy tundra vegetation. Dens in deep burrows dug below rocks and may use different den sites in summer and winter. Lives in family groups that probably hibernate together in one den. **HABITAT:** Boulder fields and talus slopes bordering tundra vegetation. **RANGE:** Brooks Range, n. Alaska. **STATUS:** Generally uncommon and patchily distributed. Hunted by Inuit.

OLYMPIC MARMOT *Marmota olympus*   Pl. 3

Head and body 20 in. (47–54 m); tail 9 in. (20–25 cm); wt. 11–15½ lb. (5–7 kg). Large and stocky. Back *blond* to *yellow-brown,* palest on rump and tail; sides, belly, and head red-brown. Muzzle white, cheeks and throat grayish. Feet dark brown. **SIMILAR SPECIES:** No other marmots occur on the Olympic Pen. **SOUNDS:** Several kinds of whistled alarm calls: ascending *wheep,* descending *peeah,* flat *eeeee,* and trilled *chi-chi-chi-chi.* **HABITS:** Spends the day feeding, sunning, and grooming. Several families may feed at the same site, and individuals greet by touching nose to cheek. Makes deep

The Vancouver Island Marmot is highly endangered. It has been the subject of captive breeding programs to save the species from extinction.

OLYMPIC MARMOT
Marmota olympus

VANCOUVER ISLAND MARMOT
Marmota vancouverensis

burrows under rocks. Hibernates Oct.–May. **HABITAT:** Alpine and subalpine meadows and talus slopes. **RANGE:** Olympic Pen., Wash. **STATUS:** Population is very restricted in range, but fully protected.

VANCOUVER ISLAND MARMOT   Pl. 3
Marmota vancouverensis
Head and body 18 in. (43–47 cm); tail 9 in. (16–30 cm); wt. 6–14 lb. (3–6.5 kg). Large and stocky. *Dark brown* or *black,* with a white muzzle and white patches on forehead, chest, and belly. **SIMILAR SPECIES:** No other marmots occur on Vancouver I. **SOUNDS:** High-pitched whistles in alarm. **HABITS:** Similar to Hoary Marmot. **HABITAT:** Alpine and subalpine meadows and rocky slopes, at 3,300–5,000 ft. (1,000–1,500 m). **RANGE:** Se. Vancouver I., B.C. **STATUS:** Endangered (COSEWIC). Population is about 100–200.

PRAIRIE DOGS: *Cynomys*

Prairie dogs are stocky, yellow-brown sciurids with short tails, often seen sitting bolt upright, scanning for danger. They are colonial burrowers that live in grasslands and open plains. They are diurnal and are most active after dawn or before dusk in warm weather, but may be seen aboveground at any time of day. Prairie dogs eat green plant material and roots. They make extensive burrows with conspicuous entrances surrounded by large mounds of bare soil. Prairie dogs live in large colonies known as "towns" that formerly extended for miles and contained millions of individuals. One of the largest towns in Texas covered 25,000 sq. mi. (65,000 km²) and was estimated to house 400,000,000 individuals. Because these rodents are considered to be range and agricultural pests, they have been the target of intensive eradication campaigns by ranchers, farmers, and government agencies. At one time as many as 125,000 people worked to eliminate prairie dogs. They have also suffered great losses due to bubonic plague. All species of prairie dogs are now quite rare and their current distributions are patchy. Although the range limits of the most widespread species, the Black-tailed Prairie Dog, have not changed greatly, it presently occupies only about 2 percent of the lands within its former range.

BLACK-TAILED PRAIRIE DOG Pl. 4, Skull Pl. 5
Cynomys ludovicianus

Head and body 13 in. (28–34 cm); tail 3 in. (6–9 cm); wt. 1½–3¼ lb. (0.6–1.5 kg). Back orange-brown flecked with white, sides and belly pale to deep orange. Diffuse dark patch over eye. *Tail relatively long and narrow, tipped black.* SIMILAR SPECIES: Larger and longer-tailed than other prairie dogs, this is the only species with a black-tipped tail. SOUNDS: Gives repeated series of barks or "chuckles" in alarm. Also tooth chatters, snarls, and growls. Territorial call (may also function as an "all-clear signal") is a characteristic *wee-oo* given from a standing position. In this "jump-yip" the

Black-tailed Prairie Dog jump-yipping. This display is used as an all-clear signal for other members of its coterie.

BLACK-TAILED PRAIRIE DOG
Cynomys ludovicianus

····· historical range limit

head is thrown back for the first syllable and then forward for the second. Numerous colony members may jump-yip at the same time. **HABITS:** Eats green matter and roots of grasses, sedges, and other forbs. Also clips tall vegetation that may not be eaten, probably to allow better visibility of the colony and predators. This species has the most complex and advanced social system and forms the largest colonies of all the prairie dogs. Large towns are divided by topography or vegetation into wards, within each of which the animals form coteries consisting of 1 adult male, 3–4 females, subadults, and young. The members of a coterie defend their territory against neighbors. They make complex, extensive burrows that have dome-shaped or craterlike mounds around the entrance. Burrows are multichambered and have numerous entrances. Crater mounds are made when soils are moist and can be gathered and tamped into place. Raised mounds are important vantage points for scanning for predators, calling, and displaying. Does not hibernate but may stay in burrow for several days in bad weather. Breeds Feb. or March; litter size is 1–8, usually 4–5. **HABITAT:** Shortgrass prairies and well-grazed grasslands at lower elevations. **RANGE:** Great Plains, from extreme s. Sask., Mont., and N.D. to N.M. and Tex. **STATUS:** Locally common, but numbers greatly reduced by human persecution and habitat alteration. Extirpated from e. Arizona and w. New Mexico.

WHITE-TAILED PRAIRIE DOG *Cynomys leucurus* Pl. 4

Head and body 12 in. (26–32 cm); tail 2 in. (4–6 cm); wt. 1½–3¾ lb. (0.7–1.7 kg). Back grayish yellow, sides yellowish, belly and legs pale orange-buff. *Dark spots above and below eyes;* nose and throat cream. Tail short, colored like back at base, with a *pronounced white tip.* **SIMILAR SPECIES:** Gunnison's Prairie Dog has center of tail gray-brown, not all-white. Black-tailed Prairie Dog has a long, black-tipped tail. **SOUNDS:** Territorial call is a "laughing bark." Makes a variety of other calls that are similar to those of Blacktails. **HABITS:** Feeds on grasses, sedges, forbs, and woody plants. Does not clip tall vegetation. Most burrows are marked by raised mounds, but mounds are not tamped down. Less social than Blacktailed Prairie Dog, occurs in loose colonies. Groups of females and young defend their burrows against intruders. Males allow females to enter their territory only during breeding season. Hibernates for 3–6 months, sometimes becoming dormant as early as Aug. Breeds in March or April. Litter size is usually 4–6. **HABITAT:** Sagebrush plains, dry grasslands, and mountain valleys. Usually at 4,000–8,000 ft. (1,200–2,600 m), sometimes up to 10,000 ft. (3,050 m). **RANGE:** W. Wyo., ne. Utah, and nw. Colo. **STATUS:** Locally common. Numbers formerly reduced by pest control programs, but may be stable or increasing now in some areas.

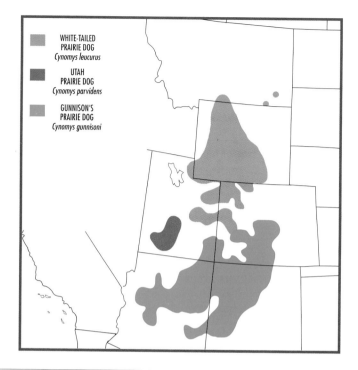

UTAH PRAIRIE DOG   *Cynomys parvidens*   Pl. 4

Head and body 11½ in. (27–31 cm); tail 2 in. (5–6 cm); wt. 1–2½ lb. (0.4–1.2 kg). Brightly colored. Back *pale orange stippled with black;* sides yellow-orange, belly pale orange. Black spot over eye, diffuse mark below eye. Tail short, orange or pale yellow at base, *white at tip.* Legs and feet orange. **SIMILAR SPECIES:** Range does not overlap with other prairie dogs. **SOUNDS:** Very similar to calls of White-tailed Prairie Dog. **HABITS:** Similar to White-tailed Prairie Dog. Burrows usually have single entrances marked by small mounds, but some have multiple entrances and larger mounds. Litters of 3–6 are born in early spring. **HABITAT:** Short-grass prairies. About 5,000–8,500 ft. (1,500–2,600 m). **RANGE:** Sw. Utah only. **STATUS:** Threatened (USFWS). Range and populations greatly reduced due to human persecution.

GUNNISON'S PRAIRIE DOG   *Cynomys gunnisoni*   Pl. 4

Head and body 11 in. (22–33 cm); tail 2 in. (4–7 cm); wt. 1–3 lb. (0.5–1.3 kg). Back and sides yellow-brown grizzled with black; belly, legs, and feet pale orange. Diffuse dark markings above and below eye. *Tail short, yellow-gray at base and center, edge and tip white.* **SIMILAR SPECIES:** White-tailed Prairie Dog (range approaches in Colorado) has an all-white tail. Wyoming Ground Squirrel has a longer tail and less stocky body. **SOUNDS:** Alarm call consists of a long series of 2-syllable barks, the first note at a higher pitch than the second. The call rate speeds up as danger approaches. Territorial call is a raspy chatter. Mating calls, barks, growls, and screams are given between group members. **HABITS:** Feeds mainly on grasses and sedges, also eats leaves and flowers of various forbs and shrubs. Unlike other prairie dogs, does not clip tall vegetation, and parts of the colony may be visually isolated from others. The least specialized of the prairie dogs, this species has social habits that are more similar to colonial ground squirrels. Makes rather shallow burrows with a single nest in each burrow. Lives in loose colonies of 50–100. Females and young remain in a fixed area, but males may wander and are not strongly territorial. Hibernates Oct.–April at higher elevations. Mates soon after emergence; young are born about a month later. Litter size is 3–8, usually 3–4. **HABITAT:** Grassy areas in mountain valleys and plateaus. Usually found at 6,000–12,000 ft. (1,800–3,700 m). **RANGE:** Four Corners regions of ne. Ariz., nw. N.M., se. Utah, and sw. Colo. **STATUS:** Locally common in a limited range. Range limits and many populations reduced by control campaigns. Also suffers from mass die-offs from bubonic plague.

GROUND SQUIRRELS: *Spermophilus*

This large group of sciurids is quite variable in size, color, and habits, but all are terrestrial and semi-fossorial. Ground squirrels spend a considerable amount of time belowground. Most species gain weight in fall for a winter hibernation that may last 6 months or more, and many species also spend much of the summer estivating (sleeping) to avoid hot dry weather. Ground squirrels eat green vegetation and seeds and will also take insects, berries, and carrion. Ground squirrels are usually seen in colonies, but each adult maintains and defends its burrow and a feeding area from other group members.

TOWNSEND'S GROUND SQUIRREL   PL. 6
Spermophilus townsendii

Head and body 7 in. (160–205 mm); tail 1¾ in. (33–53 mm); wt. 4½–12 oz. (129–357 g). Small and *short-tailed.* Upperparts *pale gray-brown or pinkish brown;* limbs, underparts, and lower sides cream white. Ears small. Tail narrow, edged whitish. **SIMILAR SPECIES:**

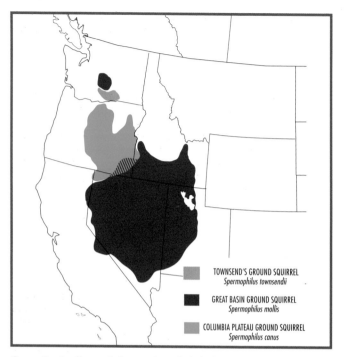

TOWNSEND'S GROUND SQUIRREL
Spermophilus townsendii

GREAT BASIN GROUND SQUIRREL
Spermophilus mollis

COLUMBIA PLATEAU GROUND SQUIRREL
Spermophilus canus

Great Basin Ground Squirrel is slightly larger and can be paler, but the two species are probably externally indistinguishable in Washington (ranges do not overlap — Great Basin Ground Squirrel occurs north of the Yakima R.). Washington Ground Squirrel is about the same size but has white spots or speckles on back and is usually darker (ranges approach but do not overlap). Other ground squirrels in Washington have longer tails. Columbia Plateau Ground Squirrel does not occur in Washington. **SOUNDS:** Makes a single-note whistle and multinote call. Also makes a high-pitched call from inside burrow. **HABITS:** Most active in the early morning. Eats green vegetation and seeds along with some animal matter. Somewhat social; occurs in groups but adults live separately. Spends much of the year belowground; active from late Jan. or Feb. to May or June. Litter size is 4–16 (usually about 8). Young are born in March and emerge in late March or April. **HABITAT:** High sagebrush desert and arid farmland. **RANGE:** Se. Wash., south of Yakima R. and north of Columbia R. **STATUS:** Very local; status not reported. **NOTE:** Formerly considered to be a more widespread species with several subspecies, *S. townsendii* is now limited to Washington

State. Columbia Plateau and Great Basin Ground Squirrels (*S. canus* and *S. mollis*) were separated based on DNA and biochemical differences.

GREAT BASIN GROUND SQUIRREL
PL. 6

Spermophilus mollis

Head and body 6½ in. (144–183 mm); tail 2 in. (40–60 mm); wt. 4½–11 oz. (130–313 g). Small and *short-tailed*. Upperparts gray-brown or *very pale pinkish brown* (almost white in parts of Nevada); limbs, underparts, and lower sides cream white. Ears small. Tail narrow, edged whitish. **SIMILAR SPECIES:** See Townsend's Ground Squirrel. Washington Ground Squirrel is spotted (range does not overlap). Other ground squirrels in its range are larger and longer-tailed. **HABITS:** Similar to Townsend's Ground Squirrel. **HABITAT:** Sagebrush desert and other arid lands. **RANGE:** S. Idaho, w. Utah, Nev., ne. Calif., and s. Ore. Also disjunct population in se. Wash. **STATUS:** Locally common.

COLUMBIA PLATEAU GROUND SQUIRREL

Spermophilus canus

Head and body 6¾ in. (155–190 mm); tail 1¾ in. (36–57 mm); wt. 5–10½ oz. (144–300 g). Small and *short-tailed*. Upperparts gray-brown or *pale pinkish brown*; limbs, underparts, and lower sides cream white. Ears small. Tail narrow, edged whitish. **SIMILAR SPECIES:** Distinguished from Townsend's and Great Basin Ground Squirrels by range and biochemical differences. Other ground squirrels in its range are larger and longer-tailed. **HABITS:** Similar to Townsend's Ground Squirrel. Active aboveground from March to Aug. **HABITAT:** Dry areas with big sagebrush or greasewood, also agricultural land. **RANGE:** E. Ore. into extreme sw. Idaho and nw. Nev. **STATUS:** Fairly common.

WASHINGTON GROUND SQUIRREL
PL. 6

Spermophilus washingtoni

Head and body 7 in. (153–195 mm); tail 1½ in. (32–50 mm); wt. 4–10 oz. (107–300 g). Back *gray-brown marked with conspicuous cream white spots*. Belly and lower sides cream, throat white. Top of snout orange. Ears short and rounded. *Tail short*, grizzled, edged with cream. **SIMILAR SPECIES:** See Townsend's Ground Squirrel. Other ground squirrels in its range are larger with longer tails. **SOUNDS:** Soft lisping whistle in alarm. **HABITS:** During summer it is mainly active in the morning. Stands erect when calling, before dashing into burrow. Eats green vegetation, roots, seeds, and insects. Sometimes raids vegetable or grain crops. Active period is short: emerges from burrow late Jan. to March, adults reenter dormancy in May or June; young of the year remain aboveground until late June or July. Litters of 5–11 young are born in Feb. or March. **HABITAT:** Dry grasslands and sagebrush, mainly in areas with sandy soil. **RANGE:** Se. Wash. and ne. Ore. **STATUS:** Threatened (IUCN). Species of concern (Washington State). Many colonies eliminated by control programs (poisoning); also suffers from loss of habitat to agriculture.

IDAHO GROUND SQUIRREL   *Spermophilus brunneus*   PL. 6

Head and body 7 in. (170–195 mm); tail 2 in. (40–62 mm); wt. 4–10 oz. (120–290 g). Back deep red-brown with white spots, sides pale brown (*S. b. brunneus*); back gray with diffuse spots, sides yellow-gray (*S. b. endemicus*); belly (both subspecies) grizzled gray-brown. Nose orange, eye-ring whitish. Ears relatively large. Forelegs pale yellow, *hind legs deep rufous.* Tail grayish above, reddish below. **SIMILAR SPECIES:** Great Basin Ground Squirrel is much paler and has gray hind legs. Columbian Ground Squirrel is much larger with a longer, bushier tail. **SOUNDS:** Makes a high-pitched ventriloquial whistle in response to predators. **HABITS:** Active by day. Feeds on grasses and forbs. Makes 3 types of burrow: a deep, single-chambered burrow for hibernation; a multichambered, multiple-entrance burrow for rearing young; and auxiliary burrows near the surface. Burrow entrances are usually under rocks or logs. Populations are active for 4–5 months each year, but each individual may be aboveground for only 3 months. *S. b. endemicus* lives at lower elevations and emerges late Jan.–Feb. to June or July; *S. b. brunneus* is active from late March–April to July or Aug. Mates soon after emergence; a female may mate with several males. Litter size is 2–10. Young emerge from the burrow about 50 days after mating. **HABITAT:** Mountain meadows surrounded by conifers, or rangelands in the foothills. **RANGE:** W. Idaho only. **STATUS:** Northern subspecies (*S. b. brunneus*) is threatened (USFWS) and numbered under 500 in 1998. IUCN considers *S. b. brunneus* critically endangered and *S. b. endemicus* vulnerable. Fire suppression has caused loss of meadow habitat for the northern subspecies.

RICHARDSON'S GROUND SQUIRREL   PL. 6
Spermophilus richardsonii

Picket Pin, Flickertail, Prairie Gopher

Head and body 8 in. (137–240 mm); tail 2¾ in. (55–83 mm); wt. 6–26 oz. (175–740 g). Rather large and stocky, *yellowish.* Crown of head and back coarsely grizzled yellow-brown; *cheeks, nape, lower sides, and limbs buffy yellow*; belly cream. Tail grizzled yellow, narrow band of black near tip, edged with cream. **SIMILAR SPECIES:** Wyoming Ground Squirrel (previously considered a subspecies of Richardson's) is slightly smaller and *usually* browner on nape and

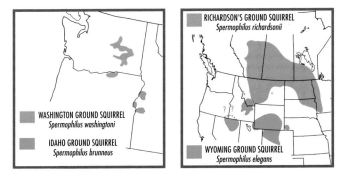

WASHINGTON GROUND SQUIRREL
Spermophilus washingtoni

IDAHO GROUND SQUIRREL
Spermophilus brunneus

RICHARDSON'S GROUND SQUIRREL
Spermophilus richardsonii

WYOMING GROUND SQUIRREL
Spermophilus elegans

cheeks, but color variation occurs in both species. Columbian Ground Squirrel is larger and more brightly colored. **SOUNDS:** Long, high-pitched whistle in response to terrestrial predators; short piercing chirp in response to birds of prey. Recently shown to use echolocation in communication. **HABITS:** Often stands bolt upright to survey for danger, hence the name "Picket Pin," and flicks tail when whistling in alarm. Eats green vegetation, seeds, and insects. Males store large quantities of seeds in their burrow and feed on this supply when they arouse from hibernation in early spring. This species may be seen aboveground from March to Sept., but each individual is active for only a few months. Mating occurs soon after females emerge; males fight vigorously for females and are often injured. Litter size is usually 6–8. Female lifespan is 2–6 years, males rarely live more than 2 years. **HABITAT:** Prairies and open grassland. Favors heavily grazed vegetation. **RANGE:** Alta., s. Sask., and s. Man. to Mont., S.D., and w. Minn. **STATUS:** Locally common.

WYOMING GROUND SQUIRREL

PL. 6

Spermophilus elegans

Head and body 8 in. (185–225 mm); tail 2½ in. (60–80 mm); wt. 7–14 oz. (200–410 g). Medium sized, yellowish. Crown, nape, and back coarsely grizzled yellow-brown; *lower sides, legs, and feet buffy yellow*; belly whitish or cream. Top of snout pale orange, *cheeks brown*. Tail grizzled yellow-brown, *broad band of black near tip*, edged with cream. **SIMILAR SPECIES:** Richardson's Ground Squirrel is slightly larger but almost indistinguishable; it usually has less black in the tail and has yellowish cheeks (hind foot in Richardson's is over 43 mm, in Wyoming hind foot is 42 mm or less). Belding's Ground Squirrel is grayish with a red-brown back. See Uinta Ground Squirrel. **SOUNDS:** Low-volume cricketlike chirps and churrs, often given from burrow entrance. Does not give different calls in response to aerial and terrestrial predators. **HABITS:** Most active midmorning and before dusk. Feeds on green vegetation and seeds but will also take carrion. Like most ground squirrels, this species forms colonies, with each individual occupying its own burrow system. Remains belowground from Aug. or Sept. to late March or April; males emerge before females. Males are territorial during the spring breeding season. Litters of 5–7 young are born in late April or May. **HABITAT:** Plains, sagebrush, talus slopes, montane meadows, and grasslands. Usually found in areas with deep soils. **RANGE:** Isolated populations in sw. Mont. and e. Idaho; ne. Nev., se. Ore., and sw. Idaho; s. Wyo., n. Colo., and sw. Neb. **STATUS:** Locally common in its restricted range.

UINTA GROUND SQUIRREL   *Spermophilus armatus*   **Pl. 6**
Head and body 8½ in. (190–240 mm); tail 2½ in. (44–80 mm); wt. 7–21 oz. (200–600 g). Medium sized, *grayish*. Back dull yellow-brown grading to gray on sides; belly buff. Top of snout orange; *neck and cheeks gray,* throat white. *Ears relatively large.* Legs and feet dull, pale orange. Tail grayish edged with cream. **SIMILAR SPECIES:** Belding's Ground Squirrel has red-brown back and tail reddish below. Wyoming Ground Squirrel is yellowish. Great Basin Ground Squirrel is smaller with lower sides and belly whitish. **SOUNDS:** Chirps, teeth chatters, squawks, growls, and churrs. **HABITS:** Eats green vegetation in spring, seeds in summer. Also takes some insects. Males are nonterritorial, but females defend a territory for raising young. Adults are active from late March or April to mid-July; young of the year may remain aboveground until Sept. Breeds soon after emergence; litter size is 4–7. **HABITAT:** Sagebrush, meadows, and pastures in foothills and mountains. **RANGE:** Rocky Mts. of e. Idaho, sw. Mont., w. Wyo., and n. Utah. **STATUS:** Patchily distributed in a small range, but can be locally abundant.

BELDING'S GROUND SQUIRREL   **Pl. 6**
Spermophilus beldingi
Head and body 6 in. (132–167 mm); tail 2½ in. (48–74 mm); wt. 4–12 oz. (125–340 g). *Crown and upper back orange-brown, usually contrasting with grayish sides,* neck, and cheeks (in Nevada and Idaho back is duller and sides are yellowish). Underparts grayish white or buff. Top of snout orange. Legs and feet cream or buff. Tail grizzled gray-brown above, *reddish orange below.* **SIMILAR SPECIES:** Columbia Plateau and Great Basin Ground Squirrels are smaller with short tails and whitish lower sides. **SOUNDS:** Trills (a series of short whistles given in succession) in response to terrestrial danger; short whistles in response to birds of prey. **HABITS:** Eats green vegetation, seeds, and some insects and carrion. This species is

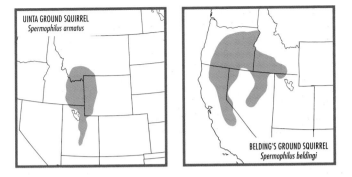

UINTA GROUND SQUIRREL
Spermophilus armatus

BELDING'S GROUND SQUIRREL
Spermophilus beldingi

known to practice infanticide: young are killed and eaten mainly by unrelated yearling males. Piles of dirt mark burrow entrances. Groups are active from March–May (depending on elevation) to July–Sept., with most individuals spending only 3–4 months per year aboveground. During this brief period of activity, each animal doubles its body weight. Sometimes seen carrying grass to burrow, but this is for nesting only — no food is stored for winter use. After emergence, males compete for females and fight fiercely: all adult males are scarred and some are fatally injured. Litter size is 3–8. Harsh weather, during hibernation or after emergence in spring, may account for losses of 50 percent or more of a population. **HABITAT:** Mountain meadows, sagebrush flats, cultivated fields, and roadsides. Seldom far from water. Elevation 1,800–12,000 ft. (550–3,600 m). **RANGE:** E. Ore., sw. Idaho, ne. Calif., n. Nev., and nw. Utah. **STATUS:** Common to abundant.

OLUMBIAN GROUND SQUIRREL   PL. 5
permophilus columbianus
Red Digger (Oregon)

Head and body 9½ in. (195–288 mm); tail 4 in. (91–114 mm); wt. 12–28 oz. (340–800 g). Large. Back coarsely grizzled gray-brown; whitish blaze on side of chest; *underparts and limbs bright orange. Top of snout deep orange*, eye-ring whitish. Ears small. Tail grizzled brownish, edged with white or cream. **SIMILAR SPECIES:** Other ground squirrels in its range are smaller and do not have orange limbs and belly. **SOUNDS:** Loud, rapid series of chirps in response to aerial predators; few, well-spaced chirps in response to terrestrial predators. Chatters teeth in threat. Also squawks, squeals, or growls. **HABITS:** Often seen in an alert posture, standing bolt upright or partially upright. Also sprawls on piles of dirt to dust-bathe or bask in the early morning. Eats flowering plants such as lupine and clover, also seeds, insects, and carrion. Makes a variety of burrows, some with narrow openings and others with wide, funnel-shaped openings. Entrances to nesting burrows are well hidden and are plugged at night. Each year, 13–22 ft. (4–7 m) of burrow are added to the system. This species is more social than most ground squirrels: groups have a complex dominance hierarchy and greet each other by "kissing." Adults are active from March or April to July or Aug. In winter, sleeps in a hibernation chamber with a dome-shaped nest and a drain to keep the nest dry. Litters of 2–7 are born in May or June. **HABITAT:** Wet mountain meadows and clearcuts in coniferous forest, agricultural areas, and rangeland. From about 4,000–8,500 ft. (1,200–2,600 m). **RANGE:** E. B.C. and w. Alta. to Mont., Idaho, and e. Ore. **STATUS:** Fairly common.

COLUMBIAN GROUND SQUIRREL
Spermophilus columbianus

ARCTIC GROUND SQUIRREL   *Spermophilus parryii*   **PL. 5**
Sik-sik

Head and body 10 in. (222–299 mm); tail 4 in. (78–118 mm); wt. 13–36 oz. (385–1,025 g). Large and colorful. Back dark red-brown with *whitish spots* (spots can be small, giving a more grizzled appearance). *Top of snout, chin, limbs, and belly bright tawny orange* (or less commonly limbs and belly yellow-gray). Cream eye-ring. Ears very small. Tail bushy, brownish above, orange below, *tipped black.* **SIMILAR SPECIES:** Other ground squirrels do not occur as far north. Red Squirrel is smaller with a proportionally longer tail. Hoary Marmot has whitish chest and forelimbs. **SOUNDS:** Shrill whistle in response to aerial predator; *sik-sik* or *cheek-chick* in response to humans or other terrestrial danger. **HABITS:** Often stands bolt upright to watch for predators. Active on a diurnal rhythm even during Arctic summer of 24-hour daylight. Eats mostly seeds, berries, and leaves, also takes insects and carrion on occasion. Burrows in well-drained areas where permafrost is well below surface. Fairly

Arctic Ground Squirrel standing up to scan for predators. It gives different whistling calls in response to aerial or terrestrial predators.

ARCTIC GROUND SQUIRREL
Spermophilus parryii

social; forms colonies of females and a dominant male that share a burrow system. Uses several types of burrow including small pits and duck-holes for avoiding predators, more complex double burrows with nest chambers for raising young, and hibernation burrows with hidden entrances and nest chambers lined with woven vegetation. Stores seeds in the hibernation burrow, but is not thought to wake and feed during the winter. These supplies are probably used after emergence when there may not be sufficient new growth available outside. Hibernates from Sept. or Oct. to about mid-April. Litters of 5–10 are born in late June. Naked and helpless at birth, young grow rapidly and reach adult size and weight by Sept. **HABITAT:** Arctic tundra, subalpine meadows, riverbanks, and low ridges. Not found in areas where the permafrost is within 3 ft. (1 m) of the surface. **RANGE:** Alaska and nw. Canada. **STATUS:** Common.

HIRTEEN-LINED GROUND SQUIRREL Pl. 7, Skull Pl. 5
ermophilus tridecemlineatus
Striped Gopher
Head and body 7 in. (148–204 mm); tail 3¼ in. (64–107 mm); wt. 5–8 oz. (150–220 g). *Back strikingly marked with rows of pale stripes and spots* (usually 13 in total) on a dark brown background. Cheeks, lower sides, and legs pale orange, belly white or cream. Tail long, edged with cream, underside tawny near base. **SIMILAR SPECIES:** Mexi-

The Thirteen-lined Ground Squirrel is sometimes called a gopher; the Minnesota Gophers sports teams are in fact named after this distinctive species.

can Ground Squirrel is larger and paler, with rows of spots, but few or no pale stripes. **SOUNDS:** Soft trilling whistle given (mostly by mothers with young) when alarmed. **HABITS:** This is the ground squirrel or "gopher" most often seen standing up by the side of the road or on lawns or golf courses in the Plains States. Eats mostly seeds of grass and herbs, also takes some insects and small vertebrates. Adults in a colony are not social and defend an area around their nest burrow. In addition to a nest burrow, shallow escape burrows are used. Hibernation dates vary with latitude: activity starts Feb.–April, adults may retire in July or Aug., but young of the year stay aboveground until about Oct. Mating takes place aboveground, usually in April or May, and litters of 6–13 are born 4 weeks later. In the southern part of their range, larger females may have a second litter in late summer. **HABITAT:** Grasslands: short-grass prairies, high plains, montane meadows, roadsides, pastures, and agricultural areas. Prefers short grass and avoids wet, low-lying areas. **RANGE:** S.-cen. Canada and e. Ohio to Ariz. and e. Tex. **STATUS:** Common to abundant and widespread. Isolated populations in mts. of Colo., Ariz., and N.M. may be declining.

MEXICAN GROUND SQUIRREL   PL. 7
Spermophilus mexicanus

Head and body 7 in. (140–210 mm); tail 5¼ in. (100–165 mm); wt. 5–10 oz. (140–300 g). Back orange-brown or *dull brown* marked with *rows of pale spots*; spots usually discrete, sometimes fused on lower sides to form a stripe. Limbs pale orange. Tail long and rather bushy, edged with cream. **SIMILAR SPECIES:** See Thirteen-lined Ground Squirrel. Spotted Ground Squirrel is paler, with indistinct spots and a shorter, less bushy tail. **SOUNDS:** Trilling whistle sometimes given in alarm. **HABITS:** Rather timid, will retreat quietly to a

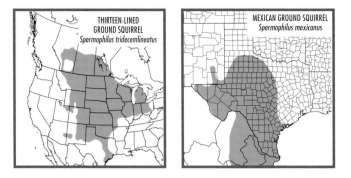

burrow if alarmed. Feeds on mesquite leaves and beans, seeds, and insects, also carrion and small vertebrates. Makes burrows with multiple entrances and also uses pocket gopher burrows. May be active year-round in s. Texas; hibernates in n. Texas from about Sept. to March. Litters of 3–10 are born in March or April. **HABITAT:** Grassy areas or mixed grass and brush, in mesquite and cactus deserts, roadsides and agricultural areas. Prefers areas with sandy soils. **RANGE:** Tex. and se. N.M. to cen. Mexico. **STATUS:** Locally common.

?OTTED GROUND SQUIRREL
PL. 7
‌ermophilus spilosoma

Head and body 6 in. (130–167 mm); tail 2¾ in. (55–80 mm); wt. 3½–7 oz. (100–200 g). Back pale pinkish brown, marked with *small, irregular pale spots* (spots obscure or absent in some individuals). Lower sides, limbs, and belly cream white. Tail long and narrow with a bushy tip. **SIMILAR SPECIES:** Thirteen-lined and Mexican Ground Squirrels have more pronounced spots or stripes arranged in rows. **SOUNDS:** High trill, sometimes given from burrow entrance. **HABITS:** Shy and secretive, often overlooked. Retreats to burrow if disturbed, running with body and tail held low. Active early and late in the day in hot weather, spending midday in its burrow. It also remains in burrow if temperatures are low. Eats mostly grasses and forbs, with some insects and small vertebrates. Burrow entrances are often located under bushes. Lives in small groups with individuals remaining well spaced from each other, so it is unusual to see more than one at a time. In Colorado, adults hibernate from late July or Aug. to April or May. Young may be active until Oct. In Texas some activity occurs year-round, but most adults probably hibernate from about Nov. to March. Litter size is 5–8; young are born about a month after emergence. Females

SPOTTED GROUND SQUIRREL
Spermophilus spilosoma

may have 2 litters per year in s. Texas. **HABITAT:** Dry grassland and deserts. Prefers areas with sparse vegetation and deep sandy soils. **RANGE:** S. S.D. and s. Utah to w. Tex. and n. Mexico. **STATUS:** Fairly common.

FRANKLIN'S GROUND SQUIRREL
PL. 5
Spermophilus franklinii

Head and body 8½ in. (181–252 mm); tail 5½ in. (116–168 mm); wt. 8–19 oz. (231–536 g). Medium sized. Back *finely grizzled yellow-brown contrasting with gray head.* Belly gray-brown or whitish. Pale eye-ring. *Ears small,* not projecting above crown of head. Legs grayish; feet cream or gray. Tail long and bushy, gray with white edging. Some have more uniform coloration with head and back entirely dark gray or brownish. **SIMILAR SPECIES:** Tree squirrels have longer ears that project above crown and longer, thicker tails. Richardson's Ground Squirrel is smaller, shorter-tailed, and more yellowish in color. **SOUNDS:** Loud musical trill given in alarm and during the breeding season. **HABITS:** Usually heard before it is seen, except where habituated to people in parks and picnic areas. Mostly active on the ground, but can climb well. More carnivorous than other ground squirrels: in addition to seeds and green vegetation it raids birds' nests and hunts small mammals, toads, birds, and insects. It is most easily trapped using meat or sardines as bait. Burrow entrances are often concealed in tall grass, sometimes marked with a mound of soil. Mainly solitary, but may form loose colonies. Adults hibernate from July or Aug. to April or May. Young of the year may be active until Oct. Litters of 2–13 (usually 7–9) young are born late May or June. **HABITAT:** Tall grass or shrubby areas, often near marshland or at forest edge. **RANGE:** N.-cen. States and s. prairies of Canada. **STATUS:** Locally common but patchily distributed within its range.

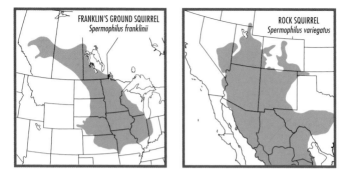

FRANKLIN'S GROUND SQUIRREL
Spermophilus franklinii

ROCK SQUIRREL
Spermophilus variegatus

ROCK SQUIRREL   *Spermophilus variegatus*   PL. 5

Head and body 11 in. (203–360 mm); tail 8½ in. (192–236 mm); wt.
17–35 oz. (490–1,000 g). Large. Upperparts *coarsely grizzled cream
and brown*, underparts off-white, cream, or orange. *Ears prominent. Tail long and bushy.* Varying degrees of melanism seen mostly
in Texas: most commonly head and shoulders blackish, forelegs
dark brown or cream; can be almost entirely black with a pale eye-
ring and yellowish belly. **SIMILAR SPECIES:** Larger than other ground
squirrels in its range. Arizona Gray Squirrel is slate gray with
finely grizzled fur, a thicker tail, and whitish underparts. **SOUNDS:**
Chucks and long clear whistles, short ventriloquial whistles, and
squeals. **HABITS:** Mostly seen on the ground, but can climb well
and sometimes nests in trees. Eats fruit, seeds, green plant material, roots, cacti, and invertebrates. Occasionally kills and eats
young birds and small vertebrates. Semisocial; usually seen in
loose groups consisting of a dominant male with several females
and their young. Each female defends a burrow entrance against
other adults. Hibernates in cold weather and at high altitudes,
elsewhere may be active year-round. Breeds twice a year; litters of
1–7 born April–June and Aug.–Sept. **HABITAT:** Rocky canyons, cliffs,
and hillsides in arid areas. Lowlands to 9,500 ft. (2,900 m). **RANGE:**
Sw. U.S. to cen. Mexico. **STATUS:** Locally common.

CALIFORNIA GROUND SQUIRREL   PL. 5
Spermophilus beecheyi

Head and body 10 in. (225–295 mm); tail 7 in. (152–204 mm); wt.
17–35 oz. (350–850 g). Large. Upperparts orange-brown speckled
with cream; *whitish mantle on shoulders,* sometimes with black triangle or diamond from nape to shoulder. Underparts, legs, and
feet whitish to pale orange. *Ears prominent. Tail long and bushy,*
grizzled cream and black. **SIMILAR SPECIES:** Much larger than other
ground squirrels in its range. Tree squirrels have longer, thicker

tails and more finely grizzled fur on back. **SOUNDS:** Whistles in alarm; chatters given between adults. **HABITS:** Usually seen on the ground, but may climb onto a rock or fencepost to view its surroundings. Feeds on green plant material, seeds, nuts, fruit, and insects. Also eats carrion and birds' eggs, raids crops and garbage, and exploits roadside picnic areas. Individuals are not very social and have separate entrances to a complex, shared burrow system. Makes burrows in well-drained areas, each entrance usually marked by a raised pile of dirt that is used as a lookout point. Adults hibernate in winter and may estivate in summer; young are often active year-round. Litters of 3–9 are born in spring. **HABITAT:** Fields, pastures, agricultural areas, and semiarid lands. Avoids areas with dense vegetation or long grass. Lowlands to 7,200 ft. (2,200 m). **RANGE:** S.-cen. Wash. through w. Ore. and Calif. to n. Baja Calif. **STATUS:** Common to abundant.

MOHAVE GROUND SQUIRREL

PL. 7

Spermophilus mohavensis

Head and body 6 in. (128–165 mm); tail 2½ in. (50–72 mm); wt. 3–10 oz. (70–300 g). Small. *Back pale pinkish brown* finely flecked with white; belly, lower sides, and feet whitish or cream. Ears very small. Tail narrow at base, tufted and somewhat banded near tip; *edge and underside of tail white.* **SIMILAR SPECIES:** Round-tailed Ground Squirrel is very similar (and closely related) but has a longer tail that is pale brown below and a slightly darker back. **SOUNDS:** Usually silent. Low or shrill whistles and high-pitched peeps are given occasionally. **HABITS:** Active throughout the day, keeping to shaded areas at midday. Runs with tail curled up over back. Mostly active on or under the ground, but also climbs high into Joshua trees to feed. Eats seeds, fruit, green plant material, and small amounts of insects. Makes 3 types of burrows: a hibernation burrow, a home burrow for nighttime use, and accessory burrows for thermoregu-

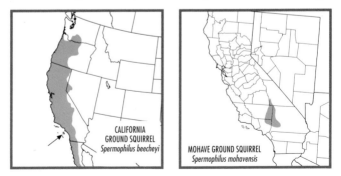

CALIFORNIA
GROUND SQUIRREL
Spermophilus beecheyi

MOHAVE GROUND SQUIRREL
Spermophilus mohavensis

lation and escape during the day. Burrow entrances are usually under desert willow or other plants and are not marked by piles of dirt. Active aboveground from Feb. or March to Aug. Solitary except when breeding. Mates in early spring; litter size is 4–9. **HABITAT:** Shrubby desert, on sand or mixed sand and gravel soils. **RANGE:** Nw. Mohave Desert, Calif. **STATUS:** Threatened (Calif. Dept. of Fish and Game). Suffers from loss of habitat to agriculture and urban development.

ROUND-TAILED GROUND SQUIRREL PL. 7
Spermophilus tereticaudus

Head and body 6 in. (130–181 mm); tail 3½ in. (70–112 mm); wt. 4–7 oz. (110–200 g). Small and *plain*. Back dull gray-brown or pale cinnamon; lower sides, belly, and legs white or cream. Ears very small. Tail *long and narrow,* edge and *underside pale brown.* **SIMILAR SPECIES:** Spotted Ground Squirrel is usually marked with pale spots and is slimmer with a longer muzzle. See Mohave Ground Squirrel. **SOUNDS:** High-pitched single-tone whistle given in alarm; peeps and short sharp cries given between group members. **HABITS:** Active by day, mostly in the morning or late afternoon in hot climates. Feeds on the ground or in bushes and low trees. Eats green plant material and seeds, occasionally eats small birds, insects, or carrion. Although it is inactive from about Aug. to Jan., this species does not hibernate as deeply as other ground squirrels. Periods of torpor are followed by short periods of activity in winter, and in the southern part of its range it may be active year-round. Semicolonial; usually seen in groups with a shared burrow system; females occupy separate burrows during pregnancy and when rearing young. Litter size is 1–12. **HABITAT:** Deserts, mainly on sandy soils in dunes or washes, often near mesquite or

Lactating female Round-tailed Ground Squirrel. This species is more social than most ground squirrels, and large groups may share a burrow system.

ROUND-TAILED
GROUND SQUIRREL
Spermophilus tereticaudus

GOLDEN-MANTLED
GROUND SQUIRREL
Spermophilus lateralis

CASCADE
GROUND SQUIRREL
Spermophilus saturatus

creosote bush. **RANGE:** Extreme s. Nev., s. Calif., and sw. Ariz. to nw. Mexico. **STATUS:** Common.

GOLDEN-MANTLED GROUND SQUIRREL   Pl. 8
Spermophilus lateralis

Head and body 7 in. (145–218 mm); tail 4 in. (70–132 mm); wt. 6–12 oz. (175–350 g). Very colorful. Back gray-brown, *pale stripe on sides thickly edged with two black stripes*. Belly and *lower sides cream white*. Head and nape deep orange, cheeks and neck golden orange. Pale eye-ring. Legs pale orange or yellowish. Tail grizzled black and cream above, bright orange below. **SIMILAR SPECIES:** Western chipmunks have stripes on head and are smaller. Antelope ground squirrels have small ears and occur in deserts. See Cascade Ground Squirrel. **SOUNDS:** Mostly silent, sometimes makes ticking calls, high-pitched cries, and chucks. **HABITS:** Mainly terrestrial, but sometimes climbs and is usually seen sitting on a log or stump. A rather conspicuous resident of campgrounds and wooded picnic areas, where it may become quite tame. Omnivorous in

The Golden-mantled Ground Squirrel is one of the most attractive ground squirrels; it is often seen in campgrounds and picnic areas.

diet, eats fungi, conifer and grass seeds, nuts, green vegetation, insects, birds and birds' eggs, carrion, and a variety of human foods. Uses burrows with multiple entrances for sleeping, hibernation, escape, and raising young. Entrances are located at the base of rocks or stumps or under bushes. Usually solitary, but may congregate where food is abundant. Hibernation period varies with elevation and latitude: sleeps Aug.–May in cold regions, Nov.–March in warmer areas. Young are born June–Aug. and litter size is 2–8. **HABITAT:** Coniferous forest, open mixed woods, edges of alpine meadows, talus slopes, chaparral, and brushy ground. Favors recently logged areas and rocky terrain. **RANGE:** Alta. and B.C. south through mts. to Calif., Ariz., and Colo. **STATUS:** Common.

ASCADE GROUND SQUIRREL PL. 8
ermophilus saturatus

Head and body 7 in. (155–198 mm); tail 4 in. (80–119 mm); wt. 7–12 oz. (200–350 g). Top of head, nape, and back gray-brown, *pale stripe on sides edged with black below, gray above.* Lower sides buff; belly cream. *Cheeks, sides of chest, and limbs orange.* Pale eye-ring. Tail grizzled black and cream above, orange below. **SIMILAR SPECIES:** Golden-mantled Ground Squirrel has a more defined orange mantle and a black stripe above the white side stripe (ranges do not overlap). Western chipmunks have stripes on head and are smaller. **SOUNDS:** Mostly silent, sometimes makes ticking calls, high-pitched cries, and chucks. **HABITS:** Similar to Golden-mantled Ground Squirrel. Hibernates from Aug. or Sept. to April or May. Young are born late May and emerge about a month later. Litter size is 1–5. **HABITAT:** Talus slopes and alpine meadows, yellow pine forest, clear-cuts, and sagebrush with scattered pines, mostly on eastern side of Cascade Mts. **RANGE:** Cascade Mts. of s. B.C. and Wash., north of Columbia R. **STATUS:** Common.

NTELOPE SQUIRRELS: *Ammospermophilus*

Antelope squirrels are desert-dwelling ground squirrels. They bear a very superficial resemblance to chipmunks but lack stripes on the face and have shorter ears and tails. These ground squirrels are remarkably adept at clambering among spiny cacti such as cholla and prickly pear.

ARRIS'S ANTELOPE SQUIRREL PL. 7
mmospermophilus harrisii

Head and body 6¼ in. (137–178 mm); tail 3¼ in. (67–92 mm); wt. 4½ oz. (113–150 g). Back and crown *gray-brown, white stripe on sides.* Belly and lower sides cream white. Top of snout and limbs

Harris's Antelope Squirrel is similar to a chipmunk, but it has much smaller ears and lacks facial stripes.

dull orange-brown. Ears short and rounded. *Tail grizzled black-and-white above and below.* **SIMILAR SPECIES:** Other antelope squirrels have tails white below (ranges do not overlap). Chipmunks have striped faces and longer ears. **SOUNDS:** Long, high-pitched trills in alarm. Also chitters when running off. **HABITS:** Active at any time of day, even in hot weather, but most conspicuous in early morning or late afternoon, surveying the area from an exposed perch on a rock or post. If alarmed, runs with tail held straight up and may trill or stomp forefeet before dashing into a burrow. Often climbs cacti to feed on fruit. Eats fruit and seeds of cactus, mesquite beans, and insects. Stores beans and seeds in burrow. Burrow entrances are usually under a shrub such as creosote bush. Seen singly or in small groups. Does not hibernate. Usually breeds once a year; litters of 4–9 are born in early spring. **HABITAT:** Deserts; in canyons, dry plains, and river valleys. Low desert to about 4,250 ft. (1,300 m). **RANGE:** Ariz. and sw. N.M. to nw. Mexico. **STATUS:** Common.

WHITE-TAILED ANTELOPE SQUIRREL PL. 7
Ammospermophilus leucurus

Head and body 6¼ in. (132–167 mm); tail 2¾ in. (48–87 mm); wt. 3¾ oz. (96–117 g). Back and crown *dark gray or pale gray-brown, white stripe on sides.* Belly and lower sides white. Top of snout and legs pale to bright orange. Ears short and rounded. Tail grizzled above, *underside white with a single band of black near tip.* **SIMILAR SPECIES:** Nelson's Antelope Squirrel is larger and yellowish. Texas Antelope Squirrel is usually darker and has 2 bands of black on underside of tail tip (ranges approach but are separated by the Rio Grande in New Mexico). **SOUNDS:** Long, high-pitched trills in alarm, similar to those of Harris's Antelope Squirrel (duration of call 2.2 seconds). Also chitters and chirps when disturbed. **HABITS:** Most ac-

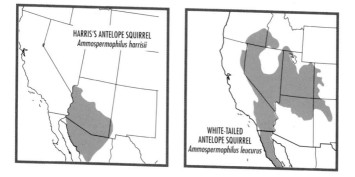

HARRIS'S ANTELOPE SQUIRREL
Ammospermophilus harrisii

WHITE-TAILED ANTELOPE SQUIRREL
Ammospermophilus leucurus

tive early or late in the day in hot weather, all day long in winter. Runs on the ground from one shady area to another when feeding. Feeds on green vegetation, seeds, insects, and small vertebrates. Each individual has several burrows; also often uses kangaroo rat dens. This species is more social than Harris's Antelope Squirrel, forming a dominance hierarchy in summer and sharing burrows in winter. It does not hibernate but may be inactive during bad weather. Litters of 5–14 are born Feb.–June. **HABITAT:** Deserts with mixed shrubs and sandy or rocky soil. Low deserts to juniper belt, up to 6,500 ft. (2,000 m). **RANGE:** Se. Ore. and sw. Idaho to w. N.M., n. Ariz., and s. Calif., south to Baja Calif. **STATUS:** Widespread and fairly common.

TEXAS ANTELOPE SQUIRREL   Pl. 7
Ammospermophilus interpres

Head and body 6 in. (145–155 mm); tail 3 in. (68–84 mm); wt. 4 oz. (99–122 g). Back and crown dark gray, *white stripe on sides.* Belly and lower sides white. Top of snout and legs dull orange. Ears short and rounded. Tail grizzled above, *underside white with 2 bands of black near tip.* **SIMILAR SPECIES:** See White-tailed Antelope Squirrel (ranges do not overlap). **SOUNDS:** Short, harsh trill, lower in pitch than other antelope squirrels (duration of call 1 second). **HABITS:** A good climber, it may be seen in low trees or shrubs or at the top of a rocky outcrop. Most active in early afternoon but easily overlooked; will rush for cover with little provocation. Feeds on seeds, fruit, beans, green vegetation, and insects. Burrows under rocks or dens in rock crevices. This species puts on a layer of fat in fall and may be inactive in bad weather, but probably does not hibernate. Litters of 5–14 are born Feb.–April. Some females may have a second litter later in the summer. **HABITAT:** Rocky slopes, canyons, piñon-juniper woodlands, and foothills at middle elevations, 1,600–6,000 ft. (500–1,800 m). Avoids desert plains and open areas

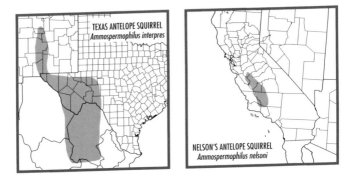

with few rocks. **RANGE:** N.M. and w. Tex. to n. Mexico. **STATUS:** Uncommon and patchily distributed in a limited range.

NELSON'S ANTELOPE SQUIRREL   PL. 7
Ammospermophilus nelsoni

Head and body 6¾ in. (151–194 mm); tail 2¾ in. (57–80 mm); wt. 4¾ oz. (114–158 g). Largest antelope squirrel. Back dull *yellow-brown*, pale stripe on sides. Belly cream, legs pale orange. *Tail relatively short*, grizzled above, underside *white* with a blackish band at tip. **SIMILAR SPECIES:** See White-tailed Antelope Squirrel. **SOUNDS:** Short, harsh trill in alarm (duration 1 second) **HABITS:** Activity times correlate with temperature: emerges late on cool mornings, then is inactive in the heat of the day and reappears in the afternoon. Emerges slowly and cautiously from burrow. Often uses burrows dug by kangaroo rats, with entrances under shrubs. Feeds on green vegetation and seeds in winter, and mostly on insects in summer and fall. Colonies number 6–8 in suitable habitat. Does not hibernate, but may remain in the burrow during cold weather. Breeds once a year; litters of 6–11 are born in March. **HABITAT:** Open deserts with rolling hills or sandy washes, with or without shrub cover. Prefers areas with fine-textured soils. Found from low elevations to 3,600 ft. (1,100 m). **RANGE:** San Joaquin and adjacent valleys of s. Calif. **STATUS:** Threatened (Calif. Dept. of Fish and Game). Does not occupy cultivated land and suffers from habitat loss due to intensive agricultural development in much of its range.

CHIPMUNKS: *Tamias*

Chipmunks are attractive and conspicuous mammals, easily seen at numerous picnic areas and campsites in much of the U.S. and Canada. Species in the West are often difficult to identify, and some can only be reliably identified by examination of the baculum (penis bone). In the field some species can also be separated by call. Chipmunks give a range of calls, including low repeated chucks, trills, chatters, and a repeated high-pitched chip. The chip calls are most useful for species identification and are described in the species accounts. Range and habitat preferences are also useful in identifying chipmunks.

Chipmunks are omnivorous, eating large amounts of seeds and, at various times of year, fungi, green plant material, fruit, or insects. They are semi-arboreal and also semi-fossorial. Most species collect and store large quantities of seeds for winter use. Although chipmunks do not accumulate large amounts of body fat and do rouse occasionally in winter to feed, sometimes leaving the burrow on warm days, they are true hibernators, as they allow their body temperature and respiration rate to drop significantly during sleep periods.

Formerly, all the western chipmunks were placed in the genus *Eutamias,* with Eurasian chipmunks. The Eastern Chipmunk was placed in the genus *Tamias* based mainly on morphological differences. Subsequently, based mainly on biochemical evidence, all chipmunks in North America were placed in the single genus *Tamias.* The most recent work (using both ectoparasite and biochemical data) indicates that the western chipmunks should be placed in the genus *Neotamias,* with only the Eastern Chipmunk in *Tamias,* although this is not accepted by all authors. In these accounts all chipmunks are placed in *Tamias.*

EASTERN CHIPMUNK *Tamias striatus*   Pl. 8, Skull Pl. 5

Head and body 5½ in. (115–160 mm); tail 4 in. (70–115 mm); hind foot 1½ in. (28–44 mm); ear ⅝ in. (12–20 mm); wt. 3½ oz. (80–150 g). *The only chipmunk in the East.* Black mid-dorsal stripe; upper pale stripe broad, gray; lower dark stripes short, blackish; lower pale stripe short, cream. Lower sides pale orange, shoulders yellow-gray; *rump deep orange;* belly white. Top of head grayish; cream eye-ring, cheeks orange-brown. Tail grizzled black and cream, underside orange. **SIMILAR SPECIES:** Least Chipmunk is smaller with a longer tail and more extensive stripes on the back and face (extending to rump and ear, respectively). **SOUNDS:** Low chucks, high chips (given at about 2 notes per second), trills, and chatters. **HABITS:** Commonly seen or heard calling from a raised vantage point on a log, stump, or fencepost. Climbs well and will forage in trees or on the ground. Eats a variety of seeds, fruit, fungi, and animal foods, and is a common visitor to bird feeders and picnic areas. Makes elaborate burrow systems with up to 100 ft. (30 m) of tunnels and multiple entrances; also uses short escape burrows. Gathers and stores large quantities of acorns, nuts, and other seeds in the burrow in fall. Hibernates from Oct.–Dec. to Feb.–

The familiar Eastern Chipmunk with fully stuffed cheek pouches. Although chipmunks are ground squirrels, this species readily climbs shrubs and small trees.

EASTERN CHIPMUNK
Tamias striatus

April, depending on latitude. Mating takes place in early spring, soon after emergence. Litters of 3–5 young are born a month later. In the South, females may have a second litter in late summer. Lifespan is usually about 2 years but has been known to live 13 years in the wild. **HABITAT:** Deciduous forest, brushy forest edge, gardens, and suburban areas. **RANGE:** Se. Canada and e. U.S. west to Minn. **STATUS:** Common to abundant.

ALPINE CHIPMUNK *Tamias alpinus* **Pl. 9**

Head and body 4 in. (96–111 mm); tail 3 in. (65–85 mm); hind foot 1⅛ in. (28–32 mm); ear ½ in. (10–14 mm); wt. 1¼ oz. (31–41 g). *Small, pale, and grayish.* Dark stripes on back are brown, lower dark stripe reddish brown; upper pale stripe gray, lower pale stripe white; sides washed with pale orange; belly whitish. Head gray with brown and white stripes; cheeks whitish. Ears relatively long and *pointed.* White spots behind ears. *Tops of feet whitish. Tail relatively short and bushy,* edged with cream; underside pale orange. **SIMILAR SPECIES:** Yellow-pine Chipmunk is larger and darker in color, with tops of feet buff or orange. Least Chipmunk is about the same size but has a longer and less bushy tail and darker stripes on the back that extend onto the rump. Lodgepole Chipmunk has an orange neck. **SOUNDS:** Chip alarm call a high-pitched, evenly spaced, repeated *tseet-tseet-tseet*. Call rate about 2–3 notes per second. **HABITS:** Very fast and agile on rocky terrain, may be seen dashing about at any time of day. Eats seeds of grasses and other alpine plants, and may take fungi and birds' eggs occasionally. Probably makes nests in burrows under rocks, but the nests have not been described. Hibernates from mid-Oct. to June. Litters of 4–5 young are born in June or July. **HABITAT:** Rocky areas at or above tree line, in alpine meadows, boulder fields, and talus slopes. Elevation 7,550–12,800 ft. (2,300–3,900 m). **RANGE:** Sierra Nevada Mts., Calif. **STATUS:** Common in a limited range.

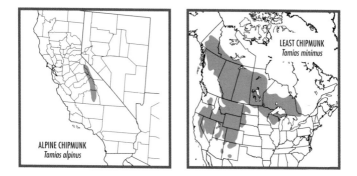

ALPINE CHIPMUNK
Tamias alpinus

LEAST CHIPMUNK
Tamias minimus

EAST CHIPMUNK   *Tamias minimus*   Pls. 8, 10

Head and body 4¼ in. (98–118 mm); tail 3½ in. (80–101 mm); hind foot 1⅛ in. (28–33 mm), ear ⅝ in. (14–18 mm); wt. 1¼ oz. (25–48 g). *Small and long-tailed,* color variable. *Dorsal stripes usually bold and long,* extend from neck to tail; dark stripes black; upper pale stripes gray, lower pale stripes white. Sides usually bright rusty orange from shoulder to hip, rump gray or gray-brown. Bold stripes on head; cheeks pale orange or gray-white. *Ears relatively short,* all-brown or bicolor. Tail edged with cream, dull orange or yellowish below. Feet pale yellow-gray. **GEOGRAPHIC VARIATION:** Least Chipmunks from dry areas (e.g., Nevada, Utah, parts of Idaho) are usually gray with little or no orange on sides; some are very pale, almost white, with pale brown stripes (e.g., s. South Dakota), while others are darker gray with dark brown stripes. Eastern forms are usually reddish brown and strongly marked. Northwestern races are pale to dark gray with pale to deep orange sides. **SIMILAR SPECIES:** Most other chipmunks are larger and have relatively shorter tails; only the Least has a tail that appears to be as long as head and body (above measurements do not include the tuft of fur at tip). The Least is also the only small species that typically runs with the tail held straight up. See other accounts for additional differences. **SOUNDS:** Alarm call a rapidly repeated, evenly spaced, high-pitched *chip-chip-chip*. Call rate about 3–4 notes per second. **HABITS:** A small chipmunk seen dashing across an open area with long tail held up vertically, or pausing to flick its tail up and down (not side to side), is likely to be this widespread species. Climbs well but is more often seen on the ground than other species. Eats a variety of seeds, including some conifers, along with other plant parts, fungi, and some animal foods such as insects, carrion, and birds' eggs. Makes nests in burrows and hibernates in special underground chambers. Hibernation is from Sept.–Nov. to Feb.–April, depending on latitude and elevation. Breeding takes place soon after emergence; litter size is 3–8, with young born in May or June. Lifespan is up to 6 years. **HABITAT:** Prefers montane coniferous forest, but also occurs in sagebrush desert, dry scrub and sand dunes, meadows, alpine tundra, and aspen groves. Found in more open areas than other chipmunks. Low elevations to 12,000 ft. (3,650 m). Usually occurs above 7,000 ft. (2,100 m) in the Southwest. **RANGE:** Yukon and n. B.C. to w. Quebec, south to N.M. and Calif. **STATUS:** Widespread and common.

YELLOW-PINE CHIPMUNK *Tamias amoenus* **Pl. 8**

Head and body 4¾ in. (109–136 mm); tail 3¾ in. (84–113 mm); hind foot 1¼ in. (30–34 mm); ear ⅝ in. (16–22 mm); wt. 2 oz. (35–77 g). Fairly small and long-tailed. Dorsal stripes prominent, including a *dark stripe below lower white stripe*. Sides bright yellow-orange from neck to hip (sometimes with a dusky patch on shoulder). Rump gray or brown; belly cream white. Facial stripes prominent; cheeks whitish; ears bicolor, black in front, white behind. Large white spot behind ear. Tail edged with cream, underside orange. Hind feet buff, orange, or whitish. **GEOGRAPHIC VARIATION:** Yellow-pines from more humid areas usually darker and browner, those from drier areas grayer and paler. Nw. California: dark brown on back, rump dark gray. N. Nevada and parts of Colorado: pale, grayish. Alberta: very dark brown. **SIMILAR SPECIES:** Least Chipmunk is slightly smaller and has a proportionally longer tail that is held straight up when running. See Townsend's, Alpine, Lodgepole, and Allen's Chipmunks. **SOUNDS:** Alarm call a rapidly repeated, evenly spaced, high-pitched *chip-chip-chip*. Call rate about 3–4 notes per second. Call similar to call of Least Chipmunk. **HABITS:** Usually seen on the ground, but climbs well. Runs with tail horizontal or held slightly up but not vertical (unlike Least Chipmunk). Eats a variety of plant and animal foods including seeds, tubers, fungi, and insects. Stores food in underground chambers for winter use. Makes nests in underground burrows and on tree branches. Hi-

YELLOW-PINE CHIPMUNK
Tamias amoenus

bernates Nov.–March. Litters of 4–5 are born in May or June. Young reach adult size by Sept. **HABITAT:** Open pine and juniper forest, also chaparral. Favors rocky areas with dense brush. Usually found at 3,300–9,500 ft. (1,000–2,900 m). **RANGE:** S. B.C. and sw. Alta. to w. Wyo., n. Nev., and e.-cen. Calif. **STATUS:** Common.

OWNSEND'S CHIPMUNK *Tamias townsendii*   PL. 8

Head and body 5½ in. (125–155 mm); tail 4½ in. (91–123 mm); hind foot 1⅜ in. (34–37 mm); ear ⅞ in. (19–24 mm); wt. 3 oz. (60–111 g). *Large and dark.* Pale stripes on back inconspicuous, gray or dull orange, *not white.* Sides ocher or orange-brown, belly gray-white. Facial stripes grayish white, not strongly marked. Ears large, blackish in front, gray behind, with gray or whitish ear spots. Tail dark, lightly edged with white, orange below. Forefeet gray-orange, hind feet orange-brown. **GEOGRAPHIC VARIATION:** Coastal form (*T. t. townsendii*) reddish brown with orange and black stripes on back; inland subspecies (*T. t. cooperi*) grayer, ocher brown with gray and black stripes on back. **SIMILAR SPECIES:** Least and Yellow-pine Chipmunks are smaller and have more prominent white stripes on sides. Range probably does not overlap with very similar Allen's or Yellow-cheeked Chipmunks. Siskiyou Chipmunk may overlap (with *T. t. cooperi*) in s. Oregon; Siskiyou is darker and browner than this subspecies of *T. townsendii,* but they may be indistinguishable (except by call) in the field. **SOUNDS:** Alarm call is a low-frequency, 2- or 3-note *chip-chip, chip-chip-chip.* **HABITS:** Mainly arboreal, rather shy. On the ground, runs with tail held straight up. Eats a variety of fruits, fungi, lichens, seeds, and insects. Hibernates in northern or high-elevation parts of range; active year-round in warmer regions. Litters of 3–5 young are born in May or June. **HABITAT:** Prefers mature humid forest with numerous snags and fallen logs. Also found in brushy clear-cuts and secondary for-

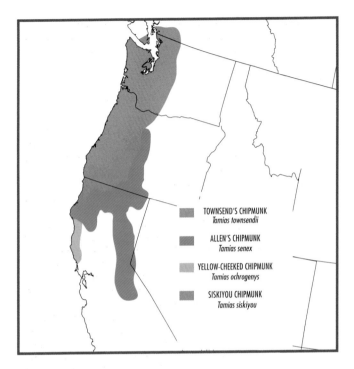

TOWNSEND'S CHIPMUNK
Tamias townsendii

ALLEN'S CHIPMUNK
Tamias senex

YELLOW-CHEEKED CHIPMUNK
Tamias ochrogenys

SISKIYOU CHIPMUNK
Tamias siskiyou

est. Near sea level to 6,600 ft. (2,000 m). **RANGE:** Sw. B.C., w. Wash. and Ore., south to Rogue R. in sw. Ore. **STATUS:** Common.

ALLEN'S CHIPMUNK *Tamias senex*   Pl. 9

Head and body 5½ in. (126–147 mm); tail 4 in. (88–104 mm); hind foot 1⅜ in. (33–37 mm); ear ⅞ in. (20–22 mm); wt. 2¾ oz. (70–92 g). *Large, dark brown or grayish.* Upper dark dorsal stripe black, other dark stripes dark brown, *pale stripes gray.* Sides brown washed with orange. Belly whitish. Facial stripes white, cheeks pale. Ears long, bicolor with pale gray or whitish ear spots. Tail edged with white, underside orange. Feet pale grayish orange. **GEOGRAPHIC VARIATION:** Inland form grayish (illustrated); coastal form darker and browner, very similar to Yellow-cheeked and Siskiyou Chipmunks. In both forms coat is brighter in summer than winter. **SIMILAR SPECIES:** See Townsend's, Long-eared, Sonoma, and Lodgepole Chipmunks. Least and Yellow-pine Chipmunks are smaller and have more prominent white stripes on sides. Siskiyou and Yellow-cheeked Chipmunks probably do not overlap in range; these 3 species are not distinguishable externally in coastal areas. Yellow-cheeked and Allen's Chipmunks may hybridize at Rio Dell, Humboldt Co., California. **SOUNDS:** Alarm call is a series of 3–5 notes of medium frequency (6–12 kHz), with 2–3 seconds between series. It has been described as an "excitable bark." **HABITS:** More arboreal than other chipmunks; often nests and stores food high in trees. Feeds mainly on fungi, also takes insects and seeds. Inland animals hibernate Nov.–April, coastal animals do not hibernate. Young are born in May or June; litter size is 3–5. **HABITAT:** Dense humid forest. Favors old-growth, closed-canopy redwood and Douglas fir forests, also occurs in brushy, cutover areas. Sea level to 9,500 ft. (2,900 m). **RANGE:** Cen. Ore. and n. Calif.; in w. Calif. it is found between Klamath R. and Eel R. **STATUS:** Common.

ELLOW-CHEEKED CHIPMUNK *Tamias ochrogenys* **Pl. 9**

Head and body 5¾ in. (128–161 mm); tail 4½ in. (105–124 mm); hind foot 1½ in. (35–39 mm); ear ⅞ in. (19–23 mm); wt. 3¼ oz. (64–116 g). Large, dark brown. Dark stripes blackish; *upper pale stripe brown, lower pale stripe gray.* Shoulder and rump brown. Sides tinged with rust. Belly buff. Facial stripes cream, *cheeks orange-brown.* Ears long, bicolor, with prominent white ear spots. Tail narrow, blackish, thinly edged with buff or white, orange below. Forefeet orange-gray, hind feet orange-buff. **SIMILAR SPECIES:** See Allen's Chipmunk. Sonoma Chipmunk has a thick tail edged with white and thickly lined with orange; it is usually more brightly colored, but can be dark brown in area of overlap. **SOUNDS:** Alarm call is a low-frequency (ca. 6 kHz) 2-note *chip-chip* unlike the call of any other chipmunk. **HABITS:** Mainly arboreal, more often seen than heard. Litters of 3–4 young are born in April or May. **HABITAT:** Humid coastal forests of redwood and Douglas fir. Occurs in mature and secondary forest but disappears from extensively altered areas. Sea level to 4,200 ft. (1,300 m). **RANGE:** Nw. Calif. north and east to Eel R. **STATUS:** Locally common.

ISKIYOU CHIPMUNK *Tamias siskiyou* **Pl. 9**

Head and body 5½ in. (127–154 mm); tail 4¼ in. (93–124 mm); hind foot 1½ in. (34–39 mm); ear ⅞ in. (20–26 mm); wt. 3 oz. (68–106 g). Large and dark. Dark stripes blackish, *pale stripes gray or brownish*, sides red-brown. Belly buff or white. Facial stripes prominent, blackish above and below eye, bordering white stripes. *Cheeks grayish.* Ears bicolor, with whitish ear spots. Tail edged with buff, orange below. Feet orange-brown. **SIMILAR SPECIES:** See Townsend's Chipmunk. Yellow-pine Chipmunk, the only other chipmunk in its range, is smaller and distinctly striped on back. **SOUNDS:** Alarm call is a single, loud, high-frequency note that rises (to 15 kHz) and falls in pitch (an inverted "V"). Notes are given at intervals of about 4 seconds. **HABITS:** Similar to Allen's Chipmunk. **HABITAT:** Dense humid forest and brushy clearings in forest. Mainly found at 3,300–6,600 ft. (1,000–2,000 m). **RANGE:** Extreme nw. Calif. and w. Ore., between Klamath R. and Rogue R. **STATUS:** Common in a limited range.

SONOMA CHIPMUNK   *Tamias sonomae*   Pl. 9

Head and body 5 in. (115–136 mm); tail 4½ in. (93–125 mm); hind foot 1½ in. (34–38 mm); ear ⅞ in. (20–27 mm); wt. 2¼ oz. (47–82 g). Medium sized. Dark stripes black; upper pale stripe gray, lower pale stripe white or pale gray. *Lower dark stripe inconspicuous or absent.* Side bright orange, shoulder and rump yellow-gray. Belly cream buff. Prominent stripes on head. Ears long, usually bicolor, with small but prominent white ear spots. *Tail long and thick; conspicuous broad band of orange at center* and on underside with a narrow white edge. Feet pale orange. **VARIATION:** Summer: ears not bicolor, sparsely haired, small white ear spot; lower body stripe white, sides bright orange. Winter: ears bicolor, prominent white ear spot; lower body stripe gray, sides orange-brown. *T. s. alleni* (Marin Co., California) very dark brown (similar to Allen's Chipmunk). **SIMILAR SPECIES:** Yellow-pine Chipmunk is smaller with tail edged yellow. Siskiyou, Yellow-cheeked, and Allen's Chipmunks are usually darker and duller in color, with a dark stripe below lower pale stripe and with narrower tails that have a narrow central band of orange. **SOUNDS:** Alarm call is high and birdlike, usually given in bursts of 3–5 notes, but sometimes as an evenly spaced, repeated single note. Each note forms a "V" pattern (high-low-high frequency), unlike inverted "V" notes of Siskiyou Chipmunk. **HABITS:** Shy, mainly arboreal. Makes nests in trees. Those from lower elevations may breed twice per year. **HABITAT:** Dry open forest, chaparral, brushy clearings, and thickets along streams. Sea level to 5,900 ft. (1,800 m). **RANGE:** Nw. Calif. **STATUS:** Common.

MERRIAM'S CHIPMUNK   *Tamias merriami*   Pl. 9

Head and body 5¼ in. (114–145 mm); tail 4½ in. (90–122 mm); hind foot 1⅜ in. (33–37 mm); ear ⅞ in. (20–23 mm); wt. 2½ oz. (52–87 g). Large, *with indistinct back stripes. Dark stripes reddish brown or black, pale stripes gray* (lower pale stripe occasionally whitish); lower sides brown washed with orange. Belly grayish white or cream. Head gray, with dark brown and off-white stripes. Ears long, grayish, with pale gray ear spots. Tail blackish at tip, thinly dusted with cream on sides, deep orange below. Forefeet gray or cream, hind feet pale orange. **SIMILAR SPECIES:** See California Chipmunk. Allen's Chipmunk is darker with white frosting on tail. Lodgepole and Long-eared Chipmunks are more boldly striped.

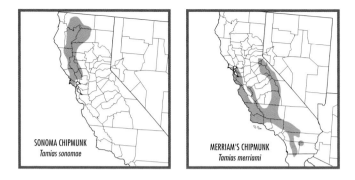

SONOMA CHIPMUNK
Tamias sonomae

MERRIAM'S CHIPMUNK
Tamias merriami

SOUNDS: Alarm call is a medium-frequency, evenly spaced, repeated series of chips. Call rate is 2–3 notes per second. In area of overlap with California Chipmunk, Merriam's Chipmunk calls have a "terminal pulse" after the chip: *CHIP-urr*. **HABITS:** Travels mainly on low branches of shrubs or on fallen logs. When resting, sways tail slowly. Eats acorns, seeds, buds, and insects. Caches seeds and acorns and stores each acorn in a separate pit for future use. Raids supplies of acorns stored by Acorn Woodpeckers. Nests in holes in trees, often using woodpecker holes; also may enter gopher burrows or woodrat nests. Usually does not hibernate, but those living at high elevations may hibernate in bad weather. Raises litters of 3–6 young in tree holes. **HABITAT:** Chaparral and brushy areas, oak-pine woodland, and piñon-juniper associations. Sea level (usually above 3,300 ft./1,000 m) to 9,700 ft. (2,950 m). **RANGE:** S. Calif. **STATUS:** Common in a limited range.

CALIFORNIA CHIPMUNK *Tamias obscurus* Pl. 9

Head and body 5 in. (110–140 mm); tail 3¾ in. (85–102 mm); hind foot 1⅜ in. (32–35 mm); ear ¾ in. (20–21 mm); wt. 2¼ oz. (55–77 g). *Large, with indistinct back stripes.* Dark stripes reddish brown or dark brown, pale stripes gray; lower sides brown washed with orange. Belly grayish white or cream. Head gray, with dark brown and off-white stripes. Ears long, somewhat bicolor, with pale gray ear spots. Tail thick and bushy, blackish at tip, dusted with cream or buff on sides, *deep orange below.* Forefeet gray or cream, hind feet pale orange. **SIMILAR SPECIES:** Merriam's Chipmunk is almost identical, especially in area of overlap (in other areas California Chipmunk is duller than Merriam's). **SOUNDS:** Alarm call is a repeated series of loud chips. Calls are slightly higher in frequency and lack the terminal buzz of Merriam's Chipmunk calls. **HABITS:** Mainly seen on the ground, but climbs well. Eats piñon seeds, acorns, and fruit. Nests in burrows under rocks or in holes

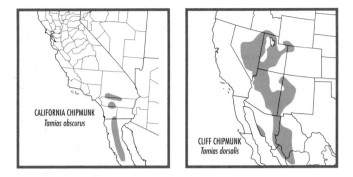

CALIFORNIA CHIPMUNK
Tamias obscurus

CLIFF CHIPMUNK
Tamias dorsalis

in cardon cactus. Active year-round and may have more than 1 litter per year. **HABITAT:** Dry rocky areas in piñon-juniper woodlands and pine-oak woods. Favors granite outcrops and single-leaf piñons. Occurs in drier areas than Merriam's Chipmunk. Elevation 1,000–10,000 ft. (300–3,000 m). **RANGE:** S. Calif. and Baja Calif. **STATUS:** Locally common in California.

CLIFF CHIPMUNK *Tamias dorsalis*   Pl. 10
Head and body 5 in. (113–140 mm); tail 4 in. (87–110 mm); hind foot 1¼ in. (30–35 mm); ear ¾ in. (18–22 mm); wt. 2 oz. (48–96 g). *Grayish.* Mid-dorsal stripe black, other *dark stripes barely visible, pale stripes absent.* Body gray, limbs and lower sides deep orange. Prominent white stripes on face. Ears long, bicolor, brown in front, white behind; large white spot behind ear. Tail edged with buff, deep orange below. Feet pale orange. **SIMILAR SPECIES:** All other chipmunks have distinct stripes on sides of body. **SOUNDS:** Alarm call is a series of single high chirps, given at a rate of 2–3 notes per second. **HABITS:** Usually seen on the ground; hides under rocks if alarmed. Can be shy and retiring, but becomes tame in campsites and picnic areas. Eats a variety of plant and animal foods. Nests under rocks; may occasionally use hollow trees. Hibernates Nov.–April in more northern parts of range, but may be active year-round farther south. This species has a long breeding season, from early spring to fall, but females produce only 1 litter per year. Litter size is 2–8, usually about 4. **HABITAT:** Sagebrush hills, juniper woodlands, and montane forests. Favors canyon walls and rocky areas. Sea level to 12,150 ft. (3,700 m). **RANGE:** S. Idaho to Ariz., N.M., and n. Mexico. **STATUS:** Common.

COLORADO CHIPMUNK *Tamias quadrivittatus*   Pl. 10
Head and body 5 in. (110–140 mm); tail 3¾ in. (85–105 mm); hind foot 1¼ in. (30–35 mm); ear ¾ in. (18–22 mm); wt. 2½ oz. (50–

87 g). *Brownish, strongly marked.* Dark dorsal stripes brown or black, including faint dark line below lower white stripe. Shoulders rusty, sides rust or orange, rump gray. Belly buff or cream. Facial stripes prominent, lower dark stripe brown. Ears medium sized with a moderate white ear spot. Tail thick and bushy, edged with orange-buff, underside rusty orange. Feet buff. SIMILAR SPECIES: Least Chipmunk is smaller and has a proportionally longer tail that is held straight up. Gray-collared Chipmunk is gray on neck and rump. See Uinta and Hopi Chipmunk. SOUNDS: Alarm call is a repeated single note; call rate is 2–3 notes per second. HABITS: When calling sways tail from side to side; runs with tail held horizontally. Climbs well but usually nests in underground burrows. Hibernates in winter and may be inactive during hottest part of summer also. HABITAT: Ponderosa pine forest and juniper woodland, usually on rocky terrain. Foothills to 7,000 ft. (2,135 m) in area of overlap with Uinta Chipmunk in Colorado; up to 12,000 ft. (3,660 m) in New Mexico. RANGE: Ne. Ariz., Colo., and N.M. to w. Okla. STATUS: Fairly common.

COLORADO CHIPMUNK
Tamias quadrivittatus

HOPI CHIPMUNK
Tamias rufus

OPI CHIPMUNK *Tamias rufus* PI. 10

Head and body 4½ in. (107–130 mm); tail 3½ in. (78–96 mm); hind foot 1¼ in. (30–34 mm); ear ¾ in. (18–20 mm); wt. 2 oz. (44–65 g). *Small and brightly colored.* Mid-dorsal stripe black, side stripe black or brown, no lower dark stripe. Upper pale stripe gray-white, lower pale stripe white. *Sides bright orange from neck to rump;* rump gray. Belly white. Facial stripes brown, dark stripe present below eye. Ears medium, bicolor, small white ear spots. Tail edged with pale orange, bright orange below. Feet orange. SIMILAR SPECIES: Least Chipmunk is duller in color and has darker stripes on back, also has a dark stripe below the lower white stripe. Colorado Chipmunk is larger with blackish stripes on head and back. SOUNDS: Probably similar to Colorado Chipmunk. HABITS: Runs with tail

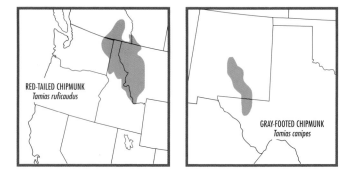

RED-TAILED CHIPMUNK
Tamias ruficaudus

GRAY-FOOTED CHIPMUNK
Tamias canipes

held horizontally. Eats a variety of foods and caches a supply of seeds for winter use. Nests under rocks. Does not hibernate, but stays in burrow during bad weather. Breeds in early spring. **HABITAT:** Juniper and piñon, also yellow pine woods. Favors rocky slopes with abundant brush. Elevation 4,600–9,500 ft. (1,400–2,900 m). **RANGE:** E. Utah, n. Ariz., and w. Colo. **STATUS:** Common in a limited range.

RED-TAILED CHIPMUNK *Tamias ruficaudus* PL. 8

Head and body 5 in. (112–140 mm); tail 4 in. (80–120 mm); hind foot 1⅜ in. (30–36 mm); ear ½ in. (13–15 mm); wt. 2 oz. (50–62 g). *Colorful and long-tailed.* Dark stripes black, including a thin dark line below lower white stripe. *Shoulders and sides usually bright orange* (yellow-gray in some), rump yellow-brown. Belly cream white. Pronounced white stripes above and below eye. *Cheeks usually pale orange.* Ears relatively small, bicolor, with large white ear spots. *Tail long and thick,* edged with cream, *underside bright orange.* Feet pale orange. **SIMILAR SPECIES:** Almost all chipmunks have orange on the underside of the tail, but in this species the orange lining is broad and conspicuous. Yellow-pine Chipmunk is smaller and has a shorter, less colorful tail and whitish cheeks. Least Chipmunk is much smaller and less brightly colored. **SOUNDS:** Alarm chip is a repeated single note (spacing of notes not reported). **HABITS:** Mainly arboreal; usually forages in trees, seldom on the ground. Eats a variety of seeds and fruit. Hibernates in an underground burrow from about Nov. to April. Litters of 4–6 young are born in May or June and are raised in nests in trees. **HABITAT:** Dense coniferous forest and brushy clearings in forest. Elevation 2,300–8,200 ft. (700–2,500 m). **RANGE:** Se. B.C., sw. Alta., w. Mont., n. Idaho, and ne. Wash. **STATUS:** Common.

GRAY-FOOTED CHIPMUNK *Tamias canipes* **Pl. 10**

Head and body 5 in. (121–138 mm); tail 3¾ in. (83–112 mm); hind foot 1¼ in. (31–35 mm); ear ¾ in. (16–23 mm); wt. 2 oz. (50–70 g). Mid-dorsal stripe black, dark side stripes brown; upper pale stripe gray, lower pale stripe white. Faint brown stripe below lower white stripe. *Rump and shoulders grayish,* with some yellow on neck; sides dull orange. Belly whitish. Facial stripes white bordered by dark brown. *Ears long,* small white patch behind ear. Tail edged with cream, underside orange. *Feet usually pale gray,* hind foot sometimes washed with yellow. **SIMILAR SPECIES:** Least Chipmunk is the only other chipmunk in its range; it is smaller with long black (not brown) side stripes on the back. **SOUNDS:** Chips and low, repeated chucks. Calling pattern not reported. **HABITS:** Most active in the early morning. Rather shy and difficult to see. Feeds mainly on acorns. **HABITAT:** Forested slopes, clearings with abundant cover, and rocky areas. Elevation 5,250–11,800 ft. (1,600–3,600 m). **RANGE:** S.-cen. N.M. and w. Tex. **STATUS:** Common.

GRAY-COLLARED CHIPMUNK *Tamias cinereicollis* **Pl. 10**

Head and body 5 in. (112–144 mm); tail 3½ in. (82–101 mm); hind foot 1¼ in. (31–35 mm); ear ¾ in. (17–20 mm); wt. 2 oz. (42–82 g). Dark stripes blackish, well defined; upper pale stripe gray, lower pale stripe white. Orange-brown stripe below lower white stripe. Rump, *neck, and shoulders gray,* contrasting with *orange sides.* Belly whitish. Facial stripes white bordered by dark brown above, red-brown below. Ears medium sized; small white patch behind ear. Tail edged with cream or buff, underside orange. Legs and feet pale buff, hind foot sometimes washed with orange. Some from New Mexico are grayer with little orange on sides. **SIMILAR SPECIES:** Cliff Chipmunk has a gray back with very indistinct stripes. Least Chipmunk is smaller and (in e. Arizona) yellowish on neck

GRAY-COLLARED CHIPMUNK
Tamias cinereicollis

and rump, with long back stripes and a long tail. **SOUNDS:** Alarm call is a repeated series of single, low-frequency notes. **HABITS:** Active on the ground and in trees. If alarmed, rushes up into dense foliage. May sit on a branch and call, waving tail slowly from side to side. Stores acorns and other seeds for winter use. Nests in woodpecker holes, hollow logs, or belowground. Usually hibernates from about Nov. to March. Breeds once a year; litter size is 4–6. **HABITAT:** Ponderosa pine and spruce-fir forests. Elevation 6,400–11,150 ft. (1,950–3,400 m). **RANGE:** Ariz. and w. N.M. **STATUS:** Common.

LONG-EARED CHIPMUNK *Tamias quadrimaculatus* PL. 9

Head and body 5½ in. (115–181 mm); tail 3¾ in. (80–108 mm); hind foot 1⅜ in. (32–37 mm); ear ⅞ in. (21–26 mm); wt. 2¾ oz. (54–95 g). *Strikingly marked.* Dark stripes narrow but prominent, indistinct dark stripe below lower white stripe. Sides orange, rump grayish. Belly white. *Facial stripes very prominent,* black and white; stripe below eye ends in *large dark spot below ear. Ears large, clearly bicolor, large white spots behind ears.* Tail edged with white or buff, underside bright orange. Feet pale orange. **SIMILAR SPECIES:** Long ears and large white ear spots usually diagnostic. Allen's Chipmunk can be similar but has less distinct stripes and lacks a black patch below ear. **SOUNDS:** Alarm call is a loud sharp note usually given singly, with long intervals (about 5 seconds) between notes. Sometimes makes trills of up to 8 notes. **HABITS:** Mostly active on the ground or on logs or low vegetation, but may climb to harvest pinecones. Eats seeds (mainly of conifers), fungi, fruit, and insects. Hibernates Nov.–March. Females have 1 litter of 2–6 young each year; young are born May–July. Females give birth in underground burrows and later move the young to a tree nest. **HABITAT:** Mixed coniferous forest and chaparral. Found in mature forest and second growth. Elevation 3,300–7,550 ft. (1,000–2,300 m). **RANGE:** Sierra Nevada Mts. of Calif. and w. Nev. **STATUS:** Common in a limited range.

LODGEPOLE CHIPMUNK *Tamias speciosus* PL. 9

Head and body 4¾ in. (107–136 mm); tail 3½ in. (76–106 mm); hind foot 1¼ in. (31–35 mm); ear ⅞ in. (18–23 mm); wt. 2 oz. (43–68 g). *Colorful.* Dark dorsal stripes black; upper pale stripe pale gray, lower pale stripe white. No dark stripe below lower white stripe. *Sides bright orange,* shoulders grayish or orange, rump gray. Belly gray-white. *Prominent white facial stripes,* cheeks whitish. Ears bicolor, with large white ear spots. Tail edged with buff, orange below, tip black. Feet whitish or pale yellow. **SIMILAR SPECIES:** Yellow-pine Chipmunk has a distinct dark stripe below lower pale side stripe. Long-eared Chipmunk has longer ears with a black

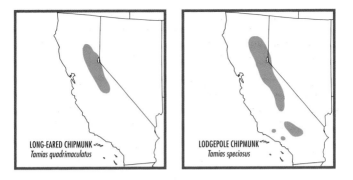

LONG-EARED CHIPMUNK 🐿
Tamias quadrimaculatus

LODGEPOLE CHIPMUNK 🐿
Tamias speciosus

patch below ear. Allen's Chipmunk is larger and grayer with a white-edged tail. **SOUNDS:** Alarm call is a repeated, evenly spaced series of single clear notes. Call rate is about 1.5 notes per second. **HABITS:** Travels and forages on the ground or in low bushes, but will climb into a tree if alarmed and call from a high branch, flipping its tail up and down. Eats conifer seeds, fungi, fruit, insects, and occasionally birds' eggs. Hibernates Nov.–April, but may be seen aboveground on sunny days in midwinter. Litters of 3–6 young are born in June or July. **HABITAT:** Coniferous forest, especially lodgepole pine woods with brushy openings and large boulders. Elevation 5,250–11,000 ft. (1,600–3,350 m). **RANGE:** Mts. of Calif. and w. Nev. **STATUS:** Common.

PANAMINT CHIPMUNK *Tamias panamintinus* PL. 10

Head and body 4¾ in. (111–135 mm); tail 3½ in. (78–104 mm); hind foot 1¼ in. (29–33 mm); ear ⅝ in. (15–20 mm); wt. 2 oz. (46–62 g). Dark dorsal stripes brown or black; upper pale stripe gray, lower pale stripe white. *No dark stripe below lower white stripe.* Shoulders *yellow-gray*, sides *pale to deep orange*; rump gray. Belly white. Head gray with dark stripes above and through eye and a *very faint dark stripe below eye that fades out below ear;* cheeks white. Ears orange in front; prominent white spots behind ears. Tail thick and bushy, thickly edged with buff; broad band of deep orange below. Feet pale buff. Some from s. California are grayer with indistinct brown stripes. **SIMILAR SPECIES:** See Palmer's Chipmunk. Alpine and Least Chipmunks are smaller and have a dark stripe below lower pale stripe on sides. These and other chipmunks in its range (Uinta, Lodgepole, and Yellow-pine) have well-marked dark stripes below eye. **SOUNDS:** Alarm call is a loud note, often with a secondary pulse of sound, usually given as a single note, sometimes in a series of 2–3 notes. Calls are widely spaced, with

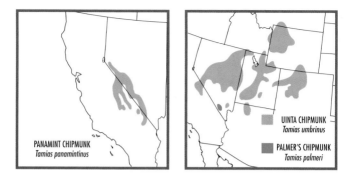

PANAMINT CHIPMUNK
Tamias panamintinus

UINTA CHIPMUNK
Tamias umbrinus

PALMER'S CHIPMUNK
Tamias palmeri

3–5 seconds between each note or short series. **HABITS:** Less arboreal than other chipmunks; uses rocks for cover and escape. Eats fruit and seeds of juniper and piñons, green plant material, and insects. May be active year-round or may hibernate for short periods, depending on elevation. Litters of 3–7 young are born in May or June. **HABITAT:** Piñon-juniper woodland, on dry rocky slopes and ledges. Elevation 4,100–10,500 ft. (1,250–3,200 m). Usually found below 8,500 ft. (2,600 m). **RANGE:** Desert slopes of mts. in se. Calif. and w. Nev. **STATUS:** Common in a limited range.

UINTA CHIPMUNK *Tamias umbrinus*   PL. 10
Head and body 5 in. (119–135 mm); tail 3¾ in. (84–109 mm); hind foot 1⅜ in. (32–35 mm); ear ¾ in. (18–23 mm); wt. 2 oz. (46–77 g). *Brownish.* Dark dorsal stripes usually *dark brown;* upper pale stripe gray, lower stripe white. Stripe below white side stripe is indistinct or absent. Sides orange-brown. Shoulders orange, rump gray. Belly gray-white. Facial stripes prominent, cheeks whitish or pale gray. Ears fairly large, bicolor, with distinct white ear spots. Tail thickly edged with orange, buff, or cream; underside orange. Feet orange. May be grayer or browner, depending on time of year and location. **SIMILAR SPECIES:** Colorado Chipmunk can be very difficult to distinguish but is usually more brightly colored with darker stripes (Colorado Chipmunk occupies lower elevations in Colorado). Least and Yellow-pine Chipmunks are smaller and have a dark stripe below lower pale stripe on sides. See Panamint Chipmunk. **SOUNDS:** Alarm call is a repeated, evenly spaced series of single clear notes. Call rate is about 1.5 notes per second. Sometimes gives short trills, spaced about 5 seconds apart. **HABITS:** Mainly arboreal; forages and travels in trees and may use tree nests, but usually sleeps in dens under rocks. Eats seeds, fungi, and insects. Hibernates from about Nov. to April. **HABITAT:** Prefers ponderosa

pine forest, also found in drier piñon-juniper woods, lodgepole pine forest, and montane coniferous forest. Elevation 5,750–12,000 ft. (1,750–3,650 m); usually found above 7,000 ft. (2,150 m) in Colorado. **RANGE:** Scattered populations in mts. from Idaho and Mont. to Calif., Ariz., and Colo. **STATUS:** Common.

PALMER'S CHIPMUNK   *Tamias palmeri*   Pl. 10

Head and body 5 in. (111–140 mm); tail 3½ in. (75–97 mm); hind foot 1¼ in. (30–35 mm); ear ¾ in. (17–23 mm); wt. 2¼ oz. (53–75 g). Three dark brown dorsal stripes; upper pale stripe gray, lower pale stripe white. No dark stripe below lower pale stripe. Sides orange. *Upper neck and shoulder gray.* Belly white. Head gray with brown and white stripes through eye; very faint dark stripe below eye, fades out below ear. *Cheeks grayish.* Ears bicolor, ear spots pale gray. Tail dark, edged with buff, orange below. Forefeet gray-white, hind feet pale buff. **SIMILAR SPECIES:** Panamint Chipmunk is very similar but is orangish on upper neck and shoulders and has whitish cheeks. **SOUNDS:** Alarm call is a repeated, evenly spaced series of single notes. Call rate is about 1 note per second when animal is stationary, but increases to 3–4 per second when moving. **HABITS:** Shy and retiring; remains close to cover. Mostly seen on the ground or on logs. Hibernates Oct.–March; males emerge earlier than females. Litters of 3–6 young are born in late May or June. **HABITAT:** Prefers white fir–ponderosa pine forest, also found in other coniferous forests and chaparral. Elevation 6,900–11,800 ft. (2,100–3,600 m). **RANGE:** Spring Mts., sw. Nev. **STATUS:** Common but very local.

TREE SQUIRRELS: *Sciurus* and *Tamiasciurus*

The tree squirrels are diurnal in habits, often common, and most species adapt well to human presence. City parks, roadside picnic areas, and tree-lined suburban streets are among the many haunts of these very familiar and conspicuous mammals.

EASTERN GRAY SQUIRREL   Pl. 11, Skull Pl. 5
Sciurus carolinensis

Head and body 9–11¼ in. (230–284 mm); tail 6¼–10¼ in. (160–260 mm); wt. ¾–1½ lb. (340–700 g). The most familiar mammal in the East. *Upperparts gray with a yellow-brown wash on upper back and head* (grayer in winter); eye-ring white or pale orange; ears gray or rusty brown, sometimes white and slightly tufted in winter. *Belly white* (rarely rusty in gray phase). Legs and feet gray or rusty. Tail *yellow-orange at center,* mixed with black and *edged with white.* **GEOGRAPHIC VARIATION:** Variable in size and color. Animals in

Florida are about ⅔ size of those in New York. Some Southeast races are dark brown with gray or buff belly. Melanistic animals (common in North, especially in Ottawa and Toronto, Ontario) can be all-black, black with reddish brown tail, all–dark brown, or brown with pale brown tail. Albinos are less common — mostly in Olney, Ill., Trenton, N.J., and Greenwood, S.C. **SIMILAR SPECIES:** Eastern Fox Squirrel usually has longer tail edged with orange or cream. Where the species co-occur, Fox Squirrels are larger. Delmarva Fox Squirrel (a subspecies of Eastern Fox) has a white-edged tail but lacks rusty wash on back and has pale cheeks and very short ears. Western Gray Squirrel has no rust on back or in tail. **SOUNDS:** Harsh chirr or whicker in alarm; repeated barks of *chuck, chuck,* or *quay, quay;* catlike mews, screeches, and tooth-chattering. Rasping sounds when gnawing on hard nuts or cones. **HABITS:** Mainly arboreal, but also spends time on the ground, especially in fall and winter. Feeds on nuts, acorns, buds, flowers, fungi, fruit, and seeds, and occasionally takes insects or young birds. Often exploits bird feeders and can outwit most "anti-squirrel" devices. Caches nuts and acorns for winter, burying each nut individually, just below the surface. Caches are relocated in spring mainly by odor, not by memory. Makes nests of leaves, twigs, and plant material on branches or inside hollow trees. Each squirrel uses more than one nest. Usually solitary in summer, but may den in groups in winter. Remains active year-round, but may stay in the nest for several days in bad weather. Breeds twice a year, in Jan.–Feb. and June–July. Groups of males chase a receptive female, and she may mate with more than one male. Litter size is usually 2–4, but litters of up to 8 have been recorded. Young become independent at about 2½ months but may stay with the mother until the next litter arrives. Lifespan is seldom more than 6 years. **HABITAT:** Widespread. Favors oak-hickory forests, also found

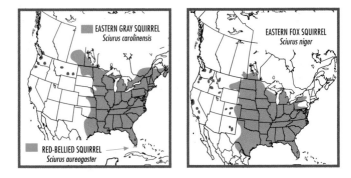

EASTERN GRAY SQUIRREL
Sciurus carolinensis

RED-BELLIED SQUIRREL
Sciurus aureogaster

EASTERN FOX SQUIRREL
Sciurus niger

in other hardwoods and mixed forests as well as in cities and suburbs with scattered large trees. **RANGE:** E. and cen. U.S. and se. Canada. Introduced in B.C., Wash., Ore., and Calif. **STATUS.** Common. This familiar squirrel is an important game animal in some areas; it also plays a role in forest regeneration by caching nuts.

ED-BELLIED SQUIRREL *Sciurus aureogaster* (introduced)
Head and body 10½ in. (232–310 mm); tail 10 in. (215–284 mm); wt. 1 lb. (375–680 g). Head, lower back, and rump grizzled gray; *shoulders, sides, forelegs, and belly mahogany red.* Tail grizzled gray-brown edged with white. About half the Florida population is *all-black.* **SIMILAR SPECIES:** No other squirrels occur on Elliot Key. Eastern Gray Squirrel occurs on Key Largo and on mainland. **SOUNDS:** Usually silent; sometimes makes rasping trills and harsh chatters. **HABITS:** Mainly arboreal and rather shy. Does not frequent picnic areas. Feeds on fruit, seeds, or leaves of mastic, gumbo-limbo, mahogany, sea grape, coconut, papaya, and thatch palm. Dens in hollow trees or makes leaf nests. Breeds year-round. Litter size is 1–2. Young may be gray or black in the same litter. **HABITAT:** Dense tropical forest. **RANGE:** Introduced to Elliot Key, Fla. Native to Mexico and Guatemala. **STATUS:** Appears to be well established in very limited range.

ASTERN FOX SQUIRREL *Sciurus niger*   Pl. 11
Head and body 10¼–14½ in. (260–370 mm); tail 8–13 in. (205–330 mm); wt. 1–3 lb. (500–1,350 g). Largest squirrel in East. Most widespread form (includes all introduced populations): grizzled yellow-brown above; *belly, cheeks, eye-ring, and feet pale orange to rusty brown;* tail strongly *edged orange-brown.* **GEOGRAPHIC VARIATION:** Highly variable in color, both geographically and within populations. Delmarva Fox Squirrel (Delmarva Peninsula, Md.): gray above; belly white; cheeks and eye-ring cream; ears very small; lower legs and feet whitish; tail gray with white frosting. Southeast: back grizzled grayish buff; belly white or pale orange; head and nape *black contrasting with white nose and ears;* tail edged with pale orange. These forms are often partially melanistic, with black extending to forelimbs and sides. Completely black squirrels seen mostly in southern populations. **SIMILAR SPECIES:** Eastern Gray Squirrel is smaller where range overlaps, with tail frosted whitish. See Western Gray Squirrel. **SOUNDS:** Series of barks or chatters (similar to those of Eastern Gray Squirrel) when alarmed. Loud chewing sounds when feeding. Whines and screams during courtship. **HABITS:** Travels and rests in trees, but may feed extensively on the ground, especially in fall. Feeds on nuts, acorns, pinecones, seeds, fungi, and fruit, and may raid cornfields. Eats tree buds and flowers in

winter and spring. Stores nuts in fall, in small underground caches or in large piles in hollow trees. Makes leaf nests on branches or in hollow trees; each squirrel uses 3–6 nests and favors cavity nests in winter. Mates Jan.–Feb. and May–June; groups of males follow a receptive female, sometimes for several days before mating. Two-year-old females may have more than 1 litter per year. Litter size is usually 2–4. Maximum lifespan is 12 years. **HABITAT:** Open stands of woodland, mostly oaks with hickory or pine. Also in suburbs and golf courses with some large trees. Seldom found in woods with dense underbrush or closed canopy. **RANGE:** East and Midwest to Mont., se. Sask., and cen. Tex. Introduced in Calif., Ore., Wash., N.M., Colo., Idaho, N.D., and Ont. **STATUS:** Common in most of its range. Delmarva Fox Squirrel (*S. n. cinereus*) is endangered (USFWS). Sherman's and Big Cypress Fox Squirrels (Florida) are threatened.

MEXICAN FOX SQUIRREL   *Sciurus nayaritensis*   Pl. 12
Apache Fox Squirrel, Nayarit Squirrel, Chiricahua Mountain Squirrel

Head and body 11 in. (240–300 mm); tail 10½ in. (250–280 mm); wt. 1½ lb. (628–814 g). Large and long-tailed. Back grizzled black and ocher; *underparts, eye-ring, lower legs, and feet deep orange.* Tail blackish *edged with creamy orange;* underside bright orange at center. **SIMILAR SPECIES:** No other tree squirrels occur in the Chiricahua Mts. Other large squirrels in Arizona have white-edged tails. **SOUNDS:** Usually silent; may bark or chuck in alarm, occasionally screeches. Sometimes located by rasping sounds made when chewing on pinecones. **HABITS:** This handsome squirrel may be seen on the ground but will take to the trees if disturbed. A prominent visitor at some picnic areas, it can be shy and secretive, especially in early summer. Remains motionless when threatened and is less likely to bark or tail-flick than other squirrels. Feeds on seeds of pines and Douglas fir, acorns, nuts, and some roots or bulbs. Does not bury food for winter. Makes nests of leaves and needles in oaks or pines; nests may be on branches or inside tree cavities. Usually solitary but may congregate at feeding areas and sometimes nests communally. Litters of 2, rarely 3, young are born April–May. **HABITAT:** Open stands of Apache pine and oak, from canyon bottoms to upper limit of oak woodlands. Elevation 5,120–8,900 ft. (1,560–2,700 m). **RANGE:** Chiricahua Mts., Ariz., to s. Jalisco, Mexico. **STATUS:** Uncommon and very local in U.S.

ARIZONA GRAY SQUIRREL   *Sciurus arizonensis*   Pl. 12
Head and body 11 in. (230–342 mm); tail 10 in. (207–270 mm); wt. 1½ lb. (550–875 g). Large. *Back finely grizzled gray,* upper back ocher brown in summer, gray in winter; *underparts and eye-ring*

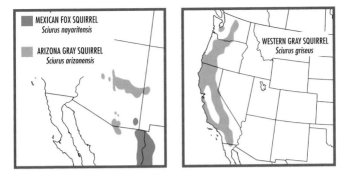

MEXICAN FOX SQUIRREL
Sciurus nayaritensis

ARIZONA GRAY SQUIRREL
Sciurus arizonensis

WESTERN GRAY SQUIRREL
Sciurus griseus

white (underparts can be stained orange-brown). Feet pale gray. *Tail yellow-orange overlaid with black and edged with white.* **SIMILAR SPECIES:** Tassel-eared Squirrel has longer ears and underside of tail pure white. Rock Squirrel has a shorter tail and back coarsely grizzled and washed with buff. **SOUNDS:** Usually silent, but may bark or chuck in alarm. **HABITS:** Mainly arboreal, but will feed and travel on the ground. Remains motionless if disturbed and can be easily overlooked. Feeds heavily on walnuts (and may be stained by walnut juice); also eats acorns, pine seeds, flowers, buds, and fungi. Occasionally stores acorns in leaf litter. Dens in tree cavities or in leaf nests on branches. Leaf nests may be flat platforms used for summer resting areas or large rounded structures used year-round. Several squirrels may share a nest in winter. Litters of 2–4 are born in June or July. **HABITAT:** Deciduous and mixed forest of canyon bottoms. Usually associated with walnut, oak, or alder. Elevation 3,700–8,900 ft. (1,120–2,700 m). **RANGE:** Mts. of cen. and s. Ariz. and w. N.M.; also n. Sonora, Mexico. **STATUS:** Uncommon and local.

WESTERN GRAY SQUIRREL *Sciurus griseus*   PL. 12

Head and body 11½ in. (265–323 mm); tail 11½ in. (240–340 mm); wt. 1¾ lb. (600–950 g). Large and long-tailed. *Upperparts dark steel gray.* Underparts and eye-ring white. Feet pale gray (n. California to Washington) or dark gray (s. California). *Tail dark gray* (mixed black and white hairs) thinly edged with white. **SIMILAR SPECIES:** Introduced Eastern Fox and Eastern Gray Squirrels have rust on sides or belly and have some yellowish hairs in tail. **SOUNDS:** Chirring and chucking calls given in alarm. Loud tearing sounds when stripping pinecones. **HABITS:** Most active early in the day. Travels through trees but often feeds on the ground. More wary and secretive than introduced squirrels in its range. Eats acorns, conifer seeds, fungi, berries, and green vegetation. Stores acorns in many small holes in the ground in fall. Dens in hollow trees or makes stick nests on branches. Adults do not share nests. Litters of 2–5 young are born from Jan. to Aug. Females breed once a year. **HABITAT:** Mostly oak and mixed oak and coniferous forest. Also found in stands of sycamore, cottonwood, or walnut. To 8,500 ft. (2,590 m). **RANGE:** S. Calif. to cen. Wash. **STATUS:** Uncommon. Threatened by habitat loss and competition with introduced Eastern Gray and Eastern Fox Squirrels. Western Grays are less tolerant of humans than eastern species and seldom occur in suburbs or cities.

TASSEL-EARED SQUIRREL *Sciurus aberti* Pl. 12

Head and body 10 in. (206–298 mm); tail 8½ in. (191–243 mm); wt. 1½ lb. (487–899 g). *Long ears tufted with black fur* (tufts longest in winter). Color variable: Kaibab Squirrel (north of Grand Canyon) mainly dark gray with deep reddish stripe on back; lower sides black, belly gray or black; tail pure white. Abert's Squirrel (south of Grand Canyon) dark gray on back with reddish dorsal stripe; black line on lower sides; belly, feet, and eye-ring white; tail gray above, white below and on sides. In e. Arizona, New Mexico, and s. Colorado similar to typical Abert's but reddish dorsal stripe reduced or absent (belly black on some individuals). Melanistic forms (solid black or solid brown) increasingly common north and eastward in Colorado. Population in n. Colorado is 100 percent melanistic. **SIMILAR SPECIES:** Other large squirrels have shorter ears and lack long ear tufts. **SOUNDS:** Clucks, barks, screeches, and squeals. Calls are higher in pitch than in other western squirrels. **HABITS:** Striking in appearance, but can be secretive and difficult to observe. Occupies ponderosa pines and feeds on bark, flowers, and cones of these trees. Cuts twigs, strips off outer bark, and eats

This dark-phase Tassel-eared Squirrel is easily distinguished from other melanistic squirrels by its very long, tufted ears.

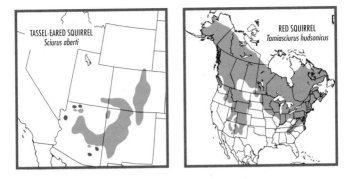

TASSEL-EARED SQUIRREL
Sciurus aberti

RED SQUIRREL
Tamiasciurus hudsonicus

inner bark. Piles of bare twigs under pines are signs of its activity. Descends to feed on truffles and other fungi in the summer. Makes twig nests in large pines or excavates a nest in "witches' brooms" (growths of small twigs caused by mistletoe infection). From Feb. to May, groups of males pursue a female in heat. The female may mate with more than one male. Females give birth once a year to litters of 2–4 young. **HABITAT:** Ponderosa pine forests, sometimes in other conifers. Elevation 5,900–9,850 ft. (1,800–3,000 m). **RANGE:** Mts. of Ariz., N.M., Colo., and extreme s. Wyo.; small population in sw. Utah. Also n. Sonora and Chihuahua to s. Durango, Mexico. **STATUS:** Rare to locally common.

ED SQUIRREL *Tamiasciurus hudsonicus* Pl. 13, Skull Pl. 5
Pine Squirrel

Head and body 7 in. (172–200 mm); tail 5 in. (105–144 mm); wt. 6 oz. (111–237 g). Small with a short tail. *Upper back deep orange, sides brownish* (entire back deep olive brown in parts of sw. U.S., where sometimes known as Spruce Squirrel); black lateral line on lower sides in summer. *Belly and eye-ring white.* Ears tufted in winter. Feet usually orange. Tail orange above, sides and underside grizzled black and yellow. **SIMILAR SPECIES:** Douglas's Squirrel has belly and eye-ring orange, tail edged with white. Other tree squirrels are larger and longer-tailed. **SOUNDS:** Very vocal; makes a sharp bark in alarm that may be repeated for an hour or more, also a trilling chirr and various chirps, rattles, and squeaks. **HABITS:** Conspicuous and noisy resident of coniferous forests. Active year-round. Feeds mainly on pine seeds, hoarding the cones and leaving large piles of stripped cones or middens. The middens are later used as storage areas for new cones. Also eats nuts, fungi, fruit, tree sap, and young birds or birds' eggs. Makes nests of shredded bark, lichen, grass, leaves, and twigs. Nests may be lined with fur or feathers. Prefers to nest in tree cavities but also makes ball

DOUGLAS'S SQUIRREL
Tamiasciurus douglasii

nests on branches or in underground burrows. Solitary in habits, each individual defending an exclusive territory. Males enter a female's territory when she is in heat and engage in noisy chases. Litters of 3–5 are born in spring or summer. Breeds once a year in the North, but may have 2 litters annually in the southern part of its range. **HABITAT:** Favors boreal coniferous forest, also found in mixed deciduous-coniferous forest, orchards, parks, and hedgerows. **RANGE:** Most of Canada, Alaska, and the Northeast, also Rocky and Appalachian Mts. **STATUS:** Widespread and generally common. Mount Graham Red Squirrel (*T. h. grahamensis*) of se. Arizona is endangered (USFWS).

DOUGLAS'S SQUIRREL *Tamiasciurus douglasii*   **PL. 13**
Chickaree

Head and body 7 in. (153–200 mm); tail 5 in. (100–135 mm); wt. 8 oz. (140–300 g). Back dark brown with deep reddish midline and black line on lower sides in summer; back uniformly gray-brown in winter. *Belly and eye-ring pale to deep orange.* Ears tufted in winter. Feet pale to deep orange. Tail mixed buff and black, *tipped with white or cream.* **SIMILAR SPECIES:** See Red Squirrel. Other tree squirrels are much larger. **SOUNDS:** Very vocal. Calls similar to those of Red Squirrel. **HABITS:** Similar to Red Squirrel. Breeds once or twice annually; litter size is 4–6. **HABITAT:** Coniferous and mixed forests. **RANGE:** Pacific Northwest, from s. B.C. to mts. of s. Calif. **STATUS:** Common.

FLYING SQUIRRELS: *Glaucomys*

These attractive small squirrels do not fly but rather glide, using membranes stretched from front to hind feet as a parachute. Flying squirrels are able to glide for long distances and steer. They launch from high up in a tree and normally land within a few feet of the ground on another tree trunk. When gliding, the skin between the legs is stretched out and the body is nearly horizontal. Before landing the squirrel angles to an upright position to slow down and uses the tail as a rudder. Unlike all other sciurids, flying squirrels are strictly nocturnal.

NORTHERN FLYING SQUIRREL Pl. 13, Skull Pl. 5
Glaucomys sabrinus

Head and body 6½ in. (134–199 mm); tail 5½ in. (122–153 mm); wt. 4 oz. (70–155 g). Medium sized. Furred membranes on sides of body, from front to hind feet. Upperparts warm brown or gray-brown, upper edge of membranes blackish; *belly fur whitish at tip, dark gray at base. Cheeks gray.* Ears naked. Tail flattened, brown above, usually with a *dark tip*; underside buff. Fur long and dense. **GEOGRAPHIC VARIATION:** The subspecies in the Pacific Northwest (*G. s. oregonensis*) is very dark gray-brown above, buff below, with an almost black tail. It may prove to be a separate species. **SIMILAR SPECIES:** See Southern Flying Squirrel. **SOUNDS:** Soft chucking notes, audible only at close range; chitters when running away. Generally quieter than Southern Flying Squirrel. **HABITS:** Nocturnal. Active for a few hours after sunset and again before dawn. Remains active year-round. Mainly arboreal, sometimes descends to the ground, but travels mainly by gliding from tree to tree. This species averages about 65 ft. (20 m) in each glide, but has been seen to glide 300 ft. (90 m) on a downhill slope. Eats nuts and seeds, tree sap, fungi, and lichens. More carnivorous than other squirrels: eats birds' eggs and nestlings, mice, insects, and carrion. Usually nests in tree cavities such as woodpecker holes; also makes nests on branches or builds roofs over birds' nests. Uses leaves and twigs in the outer layer of the nest and lines it with shredded bark, grass, lichens, feathers, or pine needles. Usually solitary, but may share a nest in winter and sometimes aggregates

NORTHERN FLYING SQUIRREL
Glaucomys sabrinus

at good sources of food. Litters of 2–4 are born in late spring and often remain with the mother over winter. **HABITAT:** Mainly coniferous forest, also in mixed woods and stands of hardwoods with snags and woodpecker holes. **RANGE:** Canada north to tree line, also cen. Alaska, Pacific Northwest, and Northeast; south in higher mts. to s. Calif., Utah, and Tenn. **STATUS:** Widespread and generally common. Virginia and Carolina Northern Flying Squirrels (*G. s. fuscus* and *G. s. coloratus*) in the Appalachian Mts. are endangered (USFWS).

SOUTHERN FLYING SQUIRREL *Glaucomys volans* Pl. 13

Head and body 5 in. (100–145 mm); tail 4 in. (80–120 mm); wt. 2½ oz. (45–87 g). Small. Furred membranes on sides, from front to hind feet. Upperparts pale gray-brown, upper edge of membranes blackish; *belly fur white to base. Cheeks white,* including fur below eye. Ears naked. Tail flattened, pale brown above, cream or buff below. Fur short and smooth. **SIMILAR SPECIES:** Northern Flying Squirrel is larger with fur on belly dark at base; fur is less sharply contrasting from back to belly. Northern is fluffier, often with a gray face contrasting with brown body, and frequently has tail darker at tip. At a feeder, Southern Flying Squirrel is more aggressive and more skittish, Northern is more inclined to feed quietly for long periods. **SOUNDS:** Birdlike chirps and twitters: *tsepp* or *tseet* given in alarm; also chitters, squeals, and squawks. Young and adults may make ultrasonic calls but have not been shown to echolocate. **HABITS:** Nocturnal. Gliding and nests similar to Northern Flying Squirrel. Diet is similar, but Southern Flying Squirrel eats more nuts and less fungi than Northern, and it stores nuts for winter use. In winter, groups of 3–8, sometimes as many as 50, may share a nest. Becomes torpid in very cold weather. This species may breed once or twice each year. Litter size is 2–4, oc-

Southern Flying Squirrel. Flying squirrels are our only gliding mammals. They are more closely related to Asian flying squirrels than to North American tree squirrels.

casionally up to 6. **HABITAT:** Mainly deciduous forests of oak-hickory or beech-maple. In South, also in pine woodland and live oaks. **RANGE:** S. Ont. and s. New England through e. U.S., west to Minn. and Tex. Also mts. of Mexico and Central America to Honduras. **STATUS:** Generally common. Species of special concern in Ontario (COSEWIC).

SOUTHERN
FLYING SQUIRREL
Glaucomys volans

OCKET GOPHERS: Geomyidae

Pocket gophers occur in Canada, the U.S., Mexico, and Central America, with 1 species barely entering northern South America. There are 3 genera in the U.S. and Canada that can be distinguished as follows:

Geomys: Large strong foreclaws; small eyes; 2 grooves on upper incisors.

Thomomys: Relatively small forelegs and claws; small eyes; no grooves on upper incisors. Incisors strongly procumbent (stick out).

Cratogeomys: Large strong foreclaws; medium-sized eyes; 1 groove on upper incisors. Very large upper and lower incisors.

See figure 5, p. 168.

Species within the genera can be very hard to distinguish, as they all share the same highly conserved morphology and vary considerably in size and color depending on soil color and food source. *Geomys* species in Texas were recently divided based on chromosomal and biochemical differences. Field identification of these species may not be possible, but many can be identified by range, therefore a detailed range map of Texas *Geomys* is given in place of color illustrations.

All pocket gophers share the same modifications for a subterranean life, and many of their physical characteristics are also shared with unrelated fossorial mammals. They have stocky tubular bodies with big heads, no distinct neck, and short naked tails. Their powerful forelegs are equipped with long broad claws. The fur is usually short and velvety, allowing the animal to move in either direction inside its tunnel. The eyes and ears are small. The "pockets" refer to external, fur-lined cheek pouches that are used for transporting food to storage areas in the burrow. The large incisors protrude from the mouth, and gophers can close their lips behind these teeth. This allows them to chew through roots and other obstructions in the tunnel without dirt entering the mouth.

Pocket gophers are seldom seen aboveground, but mounds of loose earth deposited over burrow entrances betray their underground activities. Sometimes the head and shoulders of a pocket gopher may be seen at a mound with damp soil, as the animal pushes a load of dirt to the surface and tamps it into place before closing up the tunnel entrance. Each individual has a complex burrow system that usually includes a central nest, excrement chambers, food storage chambers, and radiating tunnels to feeding areas. Pocket gophers are solitary; burrow systems of different individuals rarely overlap. They resent disturbance and will rear up and threaten with the foreclaws, gnash their teeth, or make wheezy calls if encountered aboveground. They may be active at any time of day or night, and also remain active year-round.

Pocket gophers are vegetarians, eating a variety of roots, tubers, green vegetation, and occasionally bark or wood. They cut green plants at ground level and drag the stems into the burrow. These animals thrive in agricultural areas and can cause considerable damage to crops and orchards as well as to irrigation canals. Their tunneling activities are also unpopular with ranchers, as mounds and burrows are potential hazards for livestock and horses. Pocket gophers have considerable impact on soil mixing and aeration, and their droppings and mounds can promote growth of some native plants.

SOUTHEASTERN POCKET GOPHER   Pl. 14
Geomys pinetis
Salamander, Sandy Mounder

Head and body 6½ in. (145–200 mm); tail 3½ in. (70–105 mm); hind foot 1½ in. (30–36 mm); wt. 5–7 oz. (135–208 g). Medium sized. Upperparts dark seal brown or reddish brown. Belly gray-buff, throat white. SIMILAR SPECIES: No other pocket gophers occur in its range. HABITS: Feeds on roots and tubers, including sweet potatoes; also raids peanuts and other crops. Stores food in burrow. Leaves characteristic mounds of sandy soil at burrow entrances. May breed twice a year, in Feb. or March and again in July or Aug.

Has relatively small litters of 1–3 young. **HABITAT:** Deep sandy soils, in longleaf pine and oak woods and coastal plains. **RANGE:** S. Ala., s. Ga., and Fla. **STATUS:** Fairly common to abundant in a limited range. One subspecies (*G. p. goffi*) from e. Florida is thought to be extinct.

SOUTHEASTERN POCKET GOPHER
Geomys pinetis

ESERT POCKET GOPHER   *Geomys arenarius*

Head and body 6½ in. (143–190 mm); tail 3 in. (63–95 mm); hind foot 1¼ in. (29–34 mm); wt. 3½–9 oz. (101–253 g). Medium sized. Back pale sandy brown, yellow-orange, or yellowish; sides dull yellow; belly white or cream. Tail lightly haired, blotchy. **SIMILAR SPECIES:** Range does not overlap with other *Geomys*. *Thomomys* have smaller claws and ungrooved upper incisors. Yellow-faced Pocket Gophers (*Cratogeomys*) have a single groove in upper incisors. **HABITS:** Makes large and conspicuous mounds. Breeds mostly in summer (June–Aug.); litter size is 4–6 and females may have 2 litters per year. **HABITAT:** Sand dunes and sandy soils along riverbanks and irrigation ditches. **RANGE:** S. N.M., extreme w. Tex., and n. Chihuahua, Mexico. **STATUS:** Locally common in a small range.

LAINS POCKET GOPHER   Pl. 14, Skull Pl. 5, Fig. 5

eomys bursarius

Head and body 7½ in. (160–225 mm); tail 3½ in. (50–121 mm); hind foot 1½ in. (28–38 mm); wt. 4½–13½ oz. (128–380 g). Medium sized, variable in color. Upperparts black, dark brown, gray, chestnut, or pale brown. Belly slightly paler than back. Tail nearly naked, hairs on tail dark near base, pale at tip. Two grooves in upper incisors. **SIMILAR SPECIES:** The only *Geomys* in the North. *Thomomys* have smaller claws and ungrooved upper incisors. Yellow-faced Pocket Gophers (*Cratogeomys*) have a single groove in upper incisors. Other *Geomys* in Texas may be indistinguishable

Plains Pocket Gopher emerging from its burrow. Note the large, powerful front claws and grooved upper incisors.

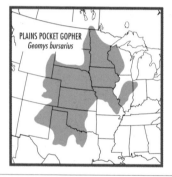

PLAINS POCKET GOPHER
Geomys bursarius

(but probably do not overlap in range). **HABITS:** Eats roots, tubers, and green vegetation. Gives birth to litters of 1–8 young from March to Aug. **HABITAT:** Sandy or deep loam soils in prairies, roadsides, and agricultural areas. **RANGE:** Extreme s.-cen. Man. through cen. U.S. to Tex. **STATUS:** Widespread and locally common but patchily distributed.

JONES'S POCKET GOPHER   *Geomys knoxjonesi*

Head and body 6½ in. (150–180 mm); tail 3¼ in. (60–104 mm); hind foot 1¼ in. (25–32 mm); wt. 6 oz. (160–190 g). Small with a relatively long tail. Back pale sandy brown, sides paler; belly white. **SIMILAR SPECIES:** Range closely approaches range of Plains Pocket Gopher (*G. bursarius*), which is sometimes darker in color but may be indistinguishable except by chromosomal or molecular characters. **HABITS:** Breeds once a year. Litter size is 2–4. **HABITAT:** Found only in deep, light sandy soils that are wind-deposited. Found in grassy areas and yucca grasslands. **RANGE:** Se. N.M. and w. Tex. **STATUS:** Locally common.

TEXAS POCKET GOPHER   *Geomys personatus*

Head and body 7½ in. (157–222 mm); tail 3¾ in. (70–125 mm); hind foot 1½ in. (31–43 mm); wt. 6–14 oz. (160–400 g). Relatively large and long-tailed. Back sandy gray-brown (less commonly dark brown), sides pale gray-brown; belly fur pure cream white to base along midline, gray at base on sides of belly, producing a splotched pattern. **SIMILAR SPECIES:** Range approaches but may not overlap with neighboring Attwater's and Llano Pocket Gophers (*G. attwateri* and *G. texensis*). Both these species are usually slightly smaller, but may be indistinguishable externally. **HABITS:** May breed year-round. Litter size is 1–5. **HABITAT:** Requires deep sandy soils free of silt and clay. Sand must be moist enough to allow tunneling. **RANGE:** S. Tex. (including Padre and Mustang Is.) and extreme ne. Tamaulipas, Mexico. **STATUS:** Some populations very restricted and vulnerable.

AIRD'S POCKET GOPHER   *Geomys breviceps*

Head and body 6½ in. (138–182 mm); tail 2½ in. (54–74 mm); hind foot 1 in. (25–30 mm); wt. 3–5 oz. (80–150 g). Small. Back black or dark brown, sides *paler* with an orange lateral line; belly buff (dark brown in the darkest forms). **SIMILAR SPECIES:** Range borders ranges of Attwater's and Plains Pocket Gophers (*G. attwateri* and *G. bursarius*), both of which may only be distinguished by chromosomal or molecular characters. **HABITS:** Breeds Jan.–Sept.; females

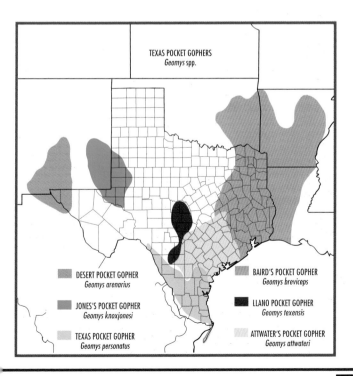

TEXAS POCKET GOPHERS
Geomys spp.

DESERT POCKET GOPHER
Geomys arenarius

JONES'S POCKET GOPHER
Geomys knoxjonesi

TEXAS POCKET GOPHER
Geomys personatus

BAIRD'S POCKET GOPHER
Geomys breviceps

LLANO POCKET GOPHER
Geomys texensis

ATTWATER'S POCKET GOPHER
Geomys attwateri

may have 2 litters per year of 1–4 young. **HABITAT:** Grasslands and prairies with sandy loam soils. **RANGE:** E. Tex., w. La., Ark., and se. Okla. **STATUS:** Locally common.

LLANO POCKET GOPHER   *Geomys texensis*

Head and body 6¼ in. (135–181 mm); tail 3 in. (55–92 mm); hind foot 1 in. (25–31 mm); wt. 4–7 oz. (105–215 g). Fairly small. Back dark brown or dull sandy brown, sides paler, underparts whitish. **SIMILAR SPECIES:** Other *Geomys* are usually larger, and ranges probably do not overlap. **HABITS:** Breeds in spring and early summer. **HABITAT:** Deep sandy loam or gravel and sand in Texas Hill Country. **RANGE:** S.-cen. Tex. **STATUS:** Locally common in a very small range.

ATTWATER'S POCKET GOPHER   *Geomys attwateri*

Head and body 6 in. (131–181 mm); tail 2½ in. (51–77 mm); hind foot 1 in. (24–31 mm); wt. 4–6 oz. (104–167 g). Back orange-brown, gray-brown, or dark brown, sides paler; underparts cream white or buff. Fur pale to base on throat, gray at base on belly. **SIMILAR SPECIES:** See Baird's and Plains Pocket Gophers (*G. breviceps* and *G. bursarius*). **HABITS:** Makes long meandering burrows unlike the short linear or radiating burrows made by other pocket gophers. Breeds Oct.–June. Females may have 2 or more litters per year of 2–3 young. **HABITAT:** Sandy or sand and loam soils in grasslands and coastal prairies. **RANGE:** S. Tex. **STATUS:** Locally common.

YELLOW-FACED POCKET GOPHER   Pl. 14, Skull Pl. 5, Fig. 5
Cratogeomys castanops

Head and body 8 in. (174–223 mm); tail 3 in. (65–93 mm); hind foot 1½ in. (32–40 mm); wt. 7–14 oz. (205–409 g). Large. *Back yellowish with dark brown streaks; sides yellow-brown; belly cream white. Cheeks yellow.* Incisors very large; *upper incisors have a single median groove.* **SIMILAR SPECIES:** *Thomomys* have smaller claws and

YELLOW-FACED POCKET GOPHER
Cratogeomys castanops

NORTHERN POCKET GOPHER
Thomomys talpoides

Yellow-faced Pocket Gopher tamping down a mound of soil at its burrow entrance.

eyes, and smaller incisors that are not grooved. *Geomys* have two grooves on the upper incisors. **HABITS:** Feeds on tubers of desert shrubs, also eats leaves of forbs. Makes one nest per burrow system. Embeds grass and feces in burrow mounds. Breeds Jan.–Oct. in w. Texas; litter size is usually 2–3 and females may have 3 litters per year. **HABITAT:** Favors deep sandy soils, sometimes found in rocky areas. Can tolerate drier regions than other pocket gophers. **RANGE:** Se. Colo. and sw. Kans. to ne. Mexico. **STATUS:** Locally common.

NORTHERN POCKET GOPHER   Pl. 14
Thomomys talpoides

Head and body 6¼ in. (125–200 mm); tail 2¼ in. (40–75 mm); hind foot 1 in. (24–30 mm); wt. 2–5½ oz. (60–160 g). Medium sized. Back dull brown, grayish, orange, yellow, or rusty; belly whitish. Ears small with a *small* but *well-defined black patch* behind ear. Tail short and moderately hairy. Fur long and dull. Female has 3 pairs of pectoral mammae. **SIMILAR SPECIES:** Most pocket gophers have shorter, shiny fur. Mountain Pocket Gopher (*T. monticola*) has longer, pointed ears and female has 2 pairs of pectoral mammae. See Western Pocket Gopher (*T. mazama*). Botta's Pocket Gopher (*T. bottae*) often has inconspicuous black patches behind ears; female has 2 pairs of pectoral mammae. **HABITS:** Eats mostly forbs, taking more green vegetation than roots. Long-term digging activities of this species are thought to have formed mima mounds (circular areas about 6 ft. [2 m] high and 60–160 ft. [20–50 m] in diameter). These are prominent features in western landscapes. Breeds March–April. Litter size is 3–9; females have 1 or 2 litters per year. **HABITAT:** Found in a variety of soil types from deep and soft to shallow with much gravel, in prairies, mountain meadows, sagebrush, agricultural fields, and disturbed forests. Elevation 3,000–

12,300 ft. (900–3,700 m). **RANGE:** S. B.C. to Man., south to Calif. and N.M. **STATUS:** Common and widespread.

WESTERN POCKET GOPHER   *Thomomys mazama*   **Pl. 14**
Head and body 5½ in. (120–166 mm); tail 2½ in. (40–90 mm); hind foot 1 in. (25–30 mm); wt. 2–5 oz. (60–135 g). Medium sized. Back chestnut brown or dull brown (sometimes almost entirely black), sides orange; belly buff or pale orange. White patches on chin and inside cheek pouches. *Ears large and erect with a large black patch behind ear* (patch is about 5 times the area of the ear). **SIMILAR SPECIES:** Northern Pocket Gopher (*T. talpoides*) has smaller black ear patches and is usually grayer in color with longer fur, but the species can be difficult to separate without examining skull or baculum (penis bone). **HABITS:** Eats mostly forbs and grasses. Litter size is 1–7. **HABITAT:** Deep, soft volcanic soils of alpine meadows, prairies, and young or open forest stands. **RANGE:** W. Wash., w. Ore., and nw. Calif. **STATUS:** Populations in Washington may be endangered. Some subspecies presumed extinct.

BOTTA'S POCKET GOPHER   **Pl. 14, Skull Pl. 5, Fig. 5**
Thomomys bottae
Head and body 5–8 in. (132–205 mm); tail 2–3½ in. (43–92 mm); hind foot 1 in. (22–34 mm); wt. 2½–7 oz. (70–181 g). Highly variable in size and color, from pale blond to reddish to black, and from very small to large. Males are larger than females. Ears small and rounded, usually with little or no black patch behind ear. Female has 2 pairs of pectoral mammae. **SIMILAR SPECIES:** See Southern, Mountain, and Northern Pocket Gophers (*T. umbrinus, T. monticola,* and *T. talpoides*). **HABITS:** Color usually matches soil color; size smallest in desert and largest in agricultural areas. The degree of sexual dimorphism also varies with overall size, being

WESTERN POCKET GOPHER
Thomomys mazama

BOTTA'S POCKET GOPHER
Thomomys bottae

Botta's Pocket Gopher is a wide-spread and extremely variable species. Note the slender front claws that typify members of the genus Thomomys.

SOUTHERN POCKET GOPHER
Thomomys umbrinus

greatest in the larger animals. Breeding season depends on habitat: usually breeds when vegetation is green and growing, producing 1–2 litters per year in desert and montane areas, but in irrigated fields may breed almost year-round and have 5 or more litters annually. Litter size varies from 2–10. **HABITAT:** Found in a wide range of soil types and vegetation zones, from below sea level to above timberline. **RANGE:** Ore. and Colo. to w. Tex., south to Baja Calif., Nuevo León, and Sinaloa, Mexico. **STATUS:** Widespread, often common.

SOUTHERN POCKET GOPHER *Thomomys umbrinus*

Head and body 5¼ in. (112–155 mm); tail 2½ in. (43–76 mm); hind foot 1 in. (23–29 mm); wt. 3–6 oz. (80–175 g). Small. Back usually *dark brown,* blackish stripe down midback and an iridescent blue-purple sheen on sides; underparts buff. Female has 1 pair of pectoral mammae. **SIMILAR SPECIES:** Botta's Pocket Gopher (*T. bottae*) is usually larger and paler in region of overlap (where it prefers deeper, less rocky soils), and female has 2 pairs of pectoral mammae. **HABITS:** Breeds Feb.–April in Arizona. Litter size is 2–8. **HABITAT:** Rocky shallow soil in oak woodland. Elevation 3,000–9,000 ft. (1,000–2,700 m) in U.S. **RANGE:** Animas Mts. of sw. N.M.; mts. of s.-cen. Ariz.; also w. Mexico. **STATUS:** Threatened in New Mexico (New Mexico Dept. Game and Fish).

WYOMING POCKET GOPHER *Thomomys clusius*

IDAHO POCKET GOPHER *Thomomys idahoensis*

WYOMING POCKET GOPHER   *Thomomys clusius*

Head and body 5 in. (115–141 mm); tail 2¼ in. (49–67 mm); hind foot 1 in. (23–26 mm); wt. 1½–3 oz. (42–91 g). *Small and pale.* Back dull yellow-gray, sides paler, belly whitish. Top of head washed with orange. Ears small, with small dark patches behind ears. **SIMILAR SPECIES:** Northern Pocket Gopher (*T. talpoides*) is larger and darker. **HABITS:** Not studied. **HABITAT:** Loose gravelly soils on dry ridges. Elevation 8,200–11,000 ft. (2,500–3,350 m). **RANGE:** Sweetwater Co. and Carbon Co., s.-cen. Wyo. **STATUS:** Very local, but may be common within its range.

IDAHO POCKET GOPHER   *Thomomys idahoensis*   Pl. 14

Head and body 5 in. (104–148 mm); tail 3 in. (43–70 mm); hind foot ⅞ in. (21–24 mm); wt. 1¼–3 oz. (36–88 g). *Small to very small.* Back yellow-gray washed with orange on upper back and top of head, sides gray; belly cream (fur gray at base). Ears small and rounded with dark gray patches behind ears. Tail has small tuft of fur at tip. **SIMILAR SPECIES:** Northern Pocket Gopher (*T. talpoides*) is larger and darker and prefers deeper soils. **HABITS:** Not studied. **HABITAT:** Shallow stony soils. **RANGE:** Cen. Idaho, s. and w. Mont.; sw. Wyo., se. Idaho, and ne. Utah. **STATUS:** Locally common.

MOUNTAIN POCKET GOPHER   *Thomomys monticola*

Head and body 5½ in. (123–157 mm); tail 3 in. (60–95 mm); hind foot 1 in. (25–30 mm); wt. 2–4 oz. (58–115 g). Medium sized. Back dark brown, reddish, gray, or yellow-brown; sides paler than back; belly buff or cream. *Ears long* (7–10 mm) and *pointed*, with *large black patches behind ears.* **SIMILAR SPECIES:** Other pocket gophers that approach it in range have rounded ears that are usually less than 7 mm long. See Western Pocket Gopher (*T. mazama*). **HABITS:** Uses snow tunnels in winter for finding food and depositing earth.

Breeds in late spring or summer. Litter size is usually 3–4 and females breed once per year. **HABITAT:** Montane meadows, pastures, and open coniferous forest. Occurs above 5,000 ft. (1,550 m). **RANGE:** Sierra Nevada Mts. of n.-cen. Calif. and w. Nev. **STATUS:** Locally common to abundant.

OWNSEND'S POCKET GOPHER   Pl. 14
Thomomys townsendii

Head and body 7½ in. (161–216 mm); tail 3½ in. (68–113 mm); hind foot 1½ in. (35–42 mm); wt. 6–13½ oz. (170–382 g). Large. Back blond, yellow-gray, or gray; sides paler, belly whitish. Some have white spots on forehead or cheeks. Ears small, rounded, with an inconspicuous black spot behind ear. Tail naked. **SIMILAR SPECIES:** Botta's and Northern Pocket Gophers (*T. bottae* and *T. talpoides*) are usually smaller; Botta's occurs in drier soils and Northern is usually at higher elevations. **HABITS:** Breeds Feb.–June. Litter size is 3–7 and females may have 1 or 2 litters per year. **HABITAT:** Deep moist soils in grasslands and sagebrush. **RANGE:** N. Great Basin: scattered populations in s. Idaho, se. Ore., n. Nev., and ne. Calif. **STATUS:** Common but locally distributed.

CAMAS POCKET GOPHER   *Thomomys bulbivorus*

Head and body 9½ in. (194–289 mm); tail 3 in. (60–99 mm); hind foot 1⅝ in. (36–47 mm); wt. 8–22 oz. (215–629 g). *Very large.* Upperparts *dark red-brown*; belly grayish orange. White on chin and cheek pouches. Fur woolly in winter, short and coarse in summer. Ears small with almost no dark patch behind ear. **SIMILAR SPECIES:** Other pocket gophers in w. Oregon are much smaller. **HABITS:** Eats forbs and grasses, also attacks alfalfa, carrots, potatoes, and roots of fruit and nut trees. Litter size is 2–8; breeds March–Sept.; usually has a single litter per year. **HABITAT:** Fields and agricultural

MOUNTAIN POCKET GOPHER
Thomomys monticola

TOWNSEND'S POCKET GOPHER
Thomomys townsendii

areas, usually with heavy clay soils. **RANGE:** Willamette Valley and area, nw. Ore. **STATUS:** Locally common.

CAMAS POCKET GOPHER
Thomomys bulbivorus

POCKET MICE AND KANGAROO RATS:
HETEROMYIDAE

Heteromyid rodents are characterized by the presence of external, fur-lined cheek pouches, long tails, and forefeet only slightly modified for digging (unlike pocket gophers). They are big-headed, with rather small ears, and most species have long narrow hind feet. These mice have 4 upper cheek teeth (Fig. 3, p. 166).

Pocket mice and kangaroo rats make elaborate multichambered burrows and spend the day, and often much of the winter, underground. Burrow entrances of the smaller species are often located under shrubs or bushes. During the day the mice close the burrow with a plug of soil, helping to maintain humidity in the burrow. These rodents are adapted to desert or semidesert conditions — many species do not need free water and can survive on water obtained as a by-product of seed digestion and other metabolic processes. Heteromyids eat mostly seeds but may take smaller amounts of green vegetable matter and insects. They make large stores of seeds underground; the seeds absorb moisture from the humid air in the tunnels, contributing to these animals' water intake. They can produce highly concentrated urine and dry feces. In winter, northern species enter torpor and remain in the burrow for extended periods. This is not true hibernation, as the animals wake periodically to feed on stored seeds. These mice may also enter torpor on cool summer days.

Heteromyids are nocturnal and solitary. They aggressively defend their territory and seed stores against neighbors. Usually quiet, during disputes these mice make low-pitched growls and high squeals; they also chatter the teeth and drum with the hind feet.

COARSE-FURRED POCKET MICE: *Chaetodipus*

Coarse-furred pocket mice are small to medium-sized heteromyids. Most have long crested tails, but a few lack a tail crest. Most species in this genus have coarse or bristly fur on the rump. The sole of the hind foot is naked, and there is a lobe, or antitragus, at the base of the ear. The upper incisors are grooved.

These mice are usually found on sandy or gravelly soils, although some also occupy rocky desert.

BAILEY'S POCKET MOUSE   *Chaetodipus baileyi*   **Pl. 15**
Head and body 3¾ in. (86–107 mm); tail 4½ in. (109–125 mm); hind foot 1 in. (26–30 mm); ear ⅜ in. (8–11 mm); wt. 1½ oz. (17–42 g). Relatively *large* (male larger than female). Back *gray or yellow-gray, no lateral line*; belly cream white. *Fur coarse but not spiny.* Pale above and below eye. No white spots around ears. Tail long, bicolor, and well haired with a *tuft at tip.* **SIMILAR SPECIES:** Other long-tailed pocket mice are smaller. Hispid Pocket Mouse (*C. hispidus*) has a shorter tail and distinct lateral line. Baja Pocket Mouse (*C. rudinoris*), recently recognized as a distinct species, is separable by range (it is found west of the lower Colorado R.). **HABITS:** Eats a variety of seeds including jojoba (which is normally toxic to mammals). Active year-round. Breeds April–Aug.; litter size is 1–6. Females may have 2 litters each year. **HABITAT:** Deserts with shrubs or cactus and sparse grasses. Unlike most pocket mice, this species does well on stony or gravelly soils and in disturbed and overgrazed areas. **RANGE:** S. Ariz., sw. N.M., and nw. Mexico. **STATUS:** Common.

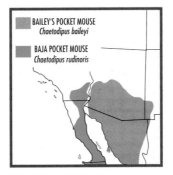

BAILEY'S POCKET MOUSE
Chaetodipus baileyi

BAJA POCKET MOUSE
Chaetodipus rudinoris

BAJA POCKET MOUSE   *Chaetodipus rudinoris*

Externally indistinguishable from Bailey's Pocket Mouse (recently separated from that species). Habits and habitat are probably similar. **RANGE:** Se. Calif. and Baja Calif. **STATUS:** Common.

HISPID POCKET MOUSE   **Pl. 15, Skull Pl. 4**
Chaetodipus hispidus

Head and body 3¾ in. (86–110 mm); tail 4 in. (90–113 mm); hind foot 1 in. (27–30 mm); ear ½ in. (11–12 mm); wt. 1½ oz. (30–47 g). *Large and colorful.* Back brown, grizzled with orange and black; broad orange lateral line on sides; belly white. Fur coarse but not spiny. *Broad orange ring around eye. Tail bicolor, relatively short,* lightly haired and *not tufted.* **SIMILAR SPECIES:** See Bailey's Pocket Mouse (*C. baileyi*) and Mexican Spiny Pocket Mice (*Liomys*). **HABITS:** Does not hop as much as other pocket mice. Active year-round, relying on stored seeds in winter in northern part of range. Breeds once or twice a year in North; may breed year-round in South. Litter size is 2–9. **HABITAT:** Grassy areas in plains and deserts, usually on sandy soils. **RANGE:** S. N.D. to se. Ariz. and w. La.; also n. Mexico. **STATUS:** Common.

DESERT POCKET MOUSE   *Chaetodipus penicillatus*   **Pl. 15**

Head and body 3½ in. (67–105 mm); tail 4 in. (88–116 mm); hind foot 1 in. (20–25 mm); ear ⅜ in. (8–10 mm); wt. ¾ oz. (14–22 g). Back pale pinkish brown, *sandy brown,* or gray-brown; sides paler, usually with no lateral line; belly cream white. Fur smooth and shiny, mostly soft, coarser on rump but *not spiny.* Ears medium sized, usually with *small white spot at base.* Tail long, bicolor, brown tuft at tip (hairs 12–13 mm). **SIMILAR SPECIES:** See Chihuahuan Pocket Mouse (*C. eremicus*). Rock Pocket Mouse (*C. intermedius*) is usually slightly smaller and has inconspicuous spines on the

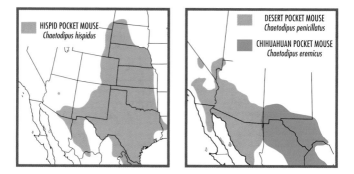

back (also compare habitats). Bailey's Pocket Mouse is larger (hind foot usually over 26 mm). **HABITS:** Eats seeds of mesquite, palo verde, and other plants. Sometimes climbs small trees or shrubs in search of food. Becomes torpid in winter, staying in the burrow and eating stored seeds. Breeds in spring and early summer; litter size is 2–8 and females may have more than 1 litter each year. **HABITAT:** Sandy, open deserts with sparse vegetation. Avoids rocky soils. **RANGE:** Se. Calif to sw. N.M., also nw. Mexico. **STATUS:** Common.

CHIHUAHUAN POCKET MOUSE *Chaetodipus eremicus*

Head and body 3 in. (73–86 mm); tail 3½ in. (85–102 mm); hind foot 1 in. (22–24 mm); ear ⅜ in. (8 mm); wt. ½ oz. (12–19 g). Back pale gray-brown with a *dark brown grizzle*. Sides slightly paler than back, sometimes with a narrow lateral line of orange; belly white. Fur shiny and coarse, but *not spiny*. Ears medium sized with a small white spot at base. Tail long and tufted, dark brown above, white below. **SIMILAR SPECIES:** Desert Pocket Mouse (*C. penicillatus*) is very similar but usually slightly paler in color. Habits and habitat similar to Desert Pocket Mouse. **RANGE:** S. N.M. to sw. Tex., also n. Mexico. **STATUS:** Common.

ROCK POCKET MOUSE *Chaetodipus intermedius* Pl. 15

Head and body 3 in. (72–86 mm); tail 3½ in. (86–103 mm); hind foot ⅞ in. (19–22 mm); ear ⅜ in. (6–9 mm); wt. ½ oz. (10–15 g). Back sandy brown, dark brown, or black, sides paler; in pale form usually with *a narrow pale orange lateral line*; belly cream white (in black form belly is dark gray with a white chest patch). Fur shiny, mostly soft except on rump, where it is slightly coarse with *inconspicuous dark spines*. Ears small, dark at tip, pale at base. Tail bicolor (all dark in black form), tufted at tip (hairs 9–12 mm). Soles of hind feet pinkish. **SIMILAR SPECIES:** See Desert and Nelson's

ROCK POCKET MOUSE
Chaetodipus intermedius

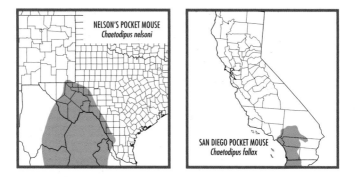

NELSON'S POCKET MOUSE
Chaetodipus nelsoni

SAN DIEGO POCKET MOUSE
Chaetodipus fallax

Pocket Mice (*C. pencillatus* and *C. nelsoni*). **HABITS:** Burrow entrances are usually near or under rocks. Inactive (torpid) Nov.–Feb. Breeds in early spring and summer. Litter size is 1–7. **HABITAT:** Rock ledges, steep rocky ravines, boulders, or gravelly slopes, with sparse, shrubby vegetation. Avoids areas of extensive sand or silt. **RANGE:** S. Utah to Ariz. and sw. Tex.; also nw. Mexico. **STATUS:** Common.

NELSON'S POCKET MOUSE *Chaetodipus nelsoni* Pl. 15

Head and body 3¼ in. (74–95 mm); tail 4 in. (93–110 mm); hind foot 1 in. (21–23 mm); ear ⅜ in. (8–9 mm); wt. ½ oz. (10–20 g). Back yellow-orange grizzled with black, sides paler with a *narrow pale orange lateral line;* belly white or cream. Fur coarse with *distinct blackish spines and white bristles on rump.* Ears medium sized with a *white spot at base.* Tail long and clearly bicolor with a pronounced black tuft at tip (hairs 12–15 mm). *Soles of hind feet blackish.* **SIMILAR SPECIES:** Other pocket mice of similar size in its range have pinkish soles on hind feet and are less spiny. **HABITS:** Active year-round. Breeds in spring and early summer; litter size is 2–4. **HABITAT:** Rocky slopes or gravel flats, with sotol, cactus, and scattered shrubs. **RANGE:** Se. N.M. and sw. Tex. to n. Mexico. **STATUS:** Locally common.

SAN DIEGO POCKET MOUSE *Chaetodipus fallax* Pl. 15

Head and body 3 in. (70–91 mm); tail 4½ in. (105–120 mm); hind foot 1 in. (19–26 mm); ear ⅜ in. (7–10 mm); wt. ⅜ oz. (14–26 g). Back grizzled dark gray or gray-brown, narrow *orange line on sides;* belly white or cream. Fur coarse with distinct *spines on rump.* Ears moderate, do not extend above crown. Tail bicolor, tufted at tip. **SIMILAR SPECIES:** California Pocket Mouse (*C. californicus*) has longer ears. Spiny Pocket Mouse (*C. spinatus*) has spines on flanks and rump and lacks orange lateral line. **HABITS:** Breeds in spring and summer; litter size is 3–6 and females may have more than 1 litter per year. **HABITAT:** Low to high deserts, usually in rocky or gravelly areas. Sea level to 4,600 ft. (1,400 m). **RANGE:** Sw. Calif. to w. Baja Calif. **STATUS:** Common.

ALIFORNIA POCKET MOUSE Pl. 15
haetodipus californicus

Head and body 3¼ in. (73–95 mm); tail 4¾ in. (101–142 mm); hind foot 1 in. (23–27 mm); ear ½ in. (10–14 mm); wt ¾ oz. (15–32 g). Back sandy brown grizzled with black, sides paler with a *distinct orange lateral line*; belly cream white. Fur shiny, coarse, with prominent spines on rump. *Ears long, extend above crown of head.* Tail long and tufted, clearly bicolor. **SIMILAR SPECIES:** See San Diego and Spiny Pocket Mice (*C. fallax* and *C. spinatus*). **HABITS:** Mainly active on the ground, but also climbs shrubs and small trees when feeding. Can become torpid by day at any time of year, and is inactive in cold wet weather. Sea level to 9,200 ft. (2,800 m). **HABITAT:** Prefers dense chaparral; less common in dry grassland and desert scrub. **RANGE:** Calif. and n. Baja Calif. **STATUS:** Common.

fornia Pocket se. Note the acteristic white y hairs on the p and its rela- y long ears.

PINY POCKET MOUSE *Chaetodipus spinatus* Pl. 15
Head and body 3¼ in. (74–91 mm); tail 4½ in. (100–130 mm); hind foot ⅞ in. (21–25 mm); ear ¼ in. (6–9 mm); wt. ½ oz. (11–21 g). Back grizzled gray or gray-brown, sides slightly paler; belly white. Fur coarse with *prominent white spines on rump, back, and flanks. Ears medium sized* with a small white spot at base. Tail long, bicolor, tip tufted. Soles of hind feet black. **SIMILAR SPECIES:** Other spiny pocket mice in California do not have spines on flanks.

HABITS: Poorly known. **HABITAT:** Rocky slopes and boulders with sparse vegetation. Sea level to 3,000 ft. (900 m). **RANGE:** Se. Calif. and Baja Calif. **STATUS:** Common.

LONG-TAILED POCKET MOUSE   Pl. 15
Chaetodipus formosus

Head and body 3 in. (69–88 mm); tail 4½ in. (94–125 mm); hind foot ⅞ in. (22–26 mm); ear ½ in. (10–12 mm); wt. ¾ oz. (16–25 g). Back gray (pale gray, gray-brown, or dark chocolate brown); sides paler, sometimes with a faint narrow orange line in gray forms; belly white or cream. *Fur shiny and soft, not spiny* on back. *Ears relatively long,* project above crown; white ear spots at base of ears small or absent. Tail long, bicolor, *terminal half thickly haired with a pronounced tuft* (fur 15 mm at tip). **SIMILAR SPECIES:** Desert Pocket Mouse (*C. penicillatus*) is usually buffier in color and has shorter ears and a less hairy tail with a slightly shorter tuft. Rock Pocket Mouse (*C. intermedius*) is smaller with shorter ears. **HABITS:** Inac-

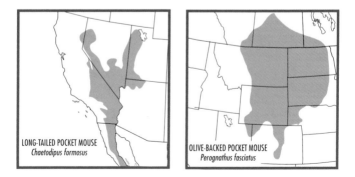

LONG-TAILED POCKET MOUSE
Chaetodipus formosus

OLIVE-BACKED POCKET MOUSE
Perognathus fasciatus

tive in cold weather and for most of the winter. Breeds in spring and summer; litter size is 2–7. **HABITAT:** Usually found among rocks or on gravelly soils in shrubby deserts; occasionally found in sandy soils. Sea level to 6,300 ft. (1,900 m). **RANGE:** Nev., w. Utah, nw. Ariz., and e. Calif. to e. Baja Calif. **STATUS:** Common.

ꓛFT-FURRED POCKET MICE: *Perognathus*

These pocket mice have silky, shiny fur. The ears are rather small and do not project above the crown of the head. There is often a white patch of fur at the base of the ear and sometimes a pale orange or whitish patch behind the ear. The larger species (*P. alticola* and *P. parvus*) have a lobed antitragus — a small flap or projection inside the base of the ear. This lobe is absent in the smaller species. Soft-furred pocket mice have stocky, pinkish tails that are usually not strongly bicolor but tend to be darker at tip than base; the tail is lightly haired and generally not tufted. In the species that have a tuft, hairs at the tip are about 5 mm, shorter than in tufted-tailed pocket mice of the genus *Chaetodipus*. The soles of the hind feet are lightly haired for about half their length from the heel. As in *Chaetodipus*, the upper incisors are grooved. These mice occur mainly in desert regions and are usually found in areas with sandy soil or patches of sand. Soft-furred pocket mice require sand for dust-bathing, and their fur becomes greasy if they are deprived of sand.

ꓡIVE-BACKED POCKET MOUSE   Pl. 16
ꓯrognathus fasciatus

Head and body 2¾ in. (64–75 mm); tail 2½ in. (56–69 mm); hind foot ⅝ in. (16–18 mm); ear ⅜ in. (7–10 mm); wt. ⅜ oz. (7–14 g). Fairly small and short-tailed. Back gray-brown, usually with a greenish cast; narrow to broad pale orange lateral line; belly white. Pale orange patches above and below eye; pale orange or white spots behind ear. White spot at base of ear. Tail faintly bicolor, gray above, white below, and thinly haired with very short fur, almost no hair at tip. **SIMILAR SPECIES:** Plains Pocket Mouse (*P. flavescens*) is very similar, variable in color but not greenish, with slightly longer hair on tail tip (these species best distinguished by skull differences). Silky Pocket Mouse (*P. flavus*) is smaller, Great Basin Pocket Mouse (*P. parvus*) larger. **HABITS:** Active year-round, but may enter torpor in cold weather. Breeds May–Aug.; females have 1 or 2 litters of 2–9 young per year. **HABITAT:** Desert scrub and dry grassland on loose sand or clay soils, mainly in hilly or upland areas with sparse vegetation. To about 8,000 ft. (2,500 m). **RANGE:** S.-cen. Canada to ne. Utah and Colo. **STATUS:** Fairly common.

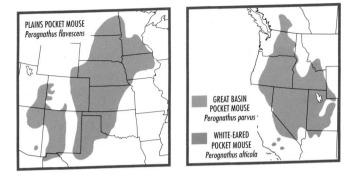

PLAINS POCKET MOUSE   *Perognathus flavescens*   **Pl. 16**

Head and body 2¾ in. (59–76 mm); tail 2¼ in. (50–67 mm); hind foot ⅝ in. (16–19 mm); ear ⅜ in. (6–9 mm); wt. ⅜ oz. (7–13 g). Rather small and short-tailed; color variable. Brown form (widespread, several subspecies): back orange-brown or gray-brown, orange lateral line on sides, belly white. Extensive pale orange patches above and below eye and behind ear; white spot at base of ear. Tail pale, very faintly bicolor at base, darker toward tip; some short hairs at tip (2 mm). **GEOGRAPHIC VARIATION:** White form (*P. f. gypsi*, N.M.): back very pale warm gray, no lateral line; sides white, eye and ear spots white. Dark form (*P. f. relictus*, Colo., n. N.M., and *P. f. perniger*, n. Great Plains): dark gray-brown, orange lateral line; small ear spots, indistinct eye spots. **SIMILAR SPECIES:** See Olivebacked Pocket Mouse (*P. fasciatus*) for comparisons with this and other species. **HABITS:** Eats seeds of grass, sedge, forbs, and corn. Also eats insects and seeds of piñon pine, juniper, and oak. Will climb vegetation when foraging. In the northern part of range, stays belowground Nov.–March. Breeds April–Aug.; litter size is 2–7, females usually breed once per year but may have 2 or more litters if conditions are good. **HABITAT:** Sand dunes and sandy washes in grasslands and sagebrush; also edges of agricultural areas and open stands of conifers. To 7,500 ft. (2,300 m). **RANGE:** N.D. and Minn. to w. Tex., N.M., and ne. Ariz. **STATUS:** Locally common but patchily distributed.

GREAT BASIN POCKET MOUSE   **Pl. 16**
Perognathus parvus

Head and body 3¼ in. (72–94 mm); tail 3½ in. (80–103 mm); hind foot ⅞ in. (21–25 mm); ear ⅜ in. (7–9 mm); wt. ¾ oz. (16–31 g). Back usually *dark gray or gray-brown*, sometimes pale gray-brown; faint pale orange lateral line; belly white. Small pale orange or white spot at base of ear. *Ear has a lobe (antitragus). Tail bicolor, well haired, moderately tufted* (hairs 7–8 mm at tip). **SIMILAR SPECIES:** San Joaquin Pocket Mouse (*P. inornatus*) is slightly smaller with a shorter, less tufted tail and no lobe inside the ear. Other soft-furred pocket mice are smaller. Spiny pocket mice (*Chaetodipus* spp.) usually have coarse or spiny fur and a longer tuft on the tail. **HABITS:** Remains belowground Nov.–March. Breeds April–Oct.; litter size is 2–8 and females have 1–3 litters per year. **HABITAT:** Prefers dry sandy regions dominated by sagebrush, but also occurs in grassland, desert, and open woodlands. To 8,000 ft. (2,450 m). **RANGE:** Great Basin, from s. B.C. and se. Mont. to e. Calif. and nw. Ariz. **STATUS:** Common. **NOTE:** Yellow-eared Pocket Mouse (*P. p. xanthonotus*) is sometimes considered to be a distinct species. It is found in Kern Co., California.

HITE-EARED POCKET MOUSE   Pl. 16
rognathus alticola

Head and body 3¼ in. (68–94 mm); tail 3¼ in. (72–96 mm); hind foot ⅞ in. (20–25 mm); ear ⅜ in. (7–10 mm); wt. ¾ oz. (17–29 g). Relatively large and long-tailed. Back orange-brown with a dark gray wash (*P. a. alticola*), or pale orange lightly grizzled with gray (*P. a. inexpectatus*). Narrow to broad pale orange lateral line on sides. Belly white. Pale race has orange patches above and below eye and behind ear (dark race has smaller, less distinct patches). *Ear has a lobe (antitragus)* and a small white spot at base. Tail pale at base for about ½ its length, then dark above with a dusky tip; hairs 5 mm at tip. **SIMILAR SPECIES:** San Joaquin Pocket Mouse (*P. inornatus*) is slightly smaller with a shorter, less tufted tail and no lobe inside the ear. Little Pocket Mouse (*P. longimembris*) is much smaller. **HABITS:** Poorly known. **HABITAT:** Dry grassland and dry shrub habitats, also open pine forest. Elevation 3,300–6,000 ft. (1,000–1,830 m). **RANGE:** Two populations in s. Calif.: San Bernardino Mts. (San Bernardino Co.) and Transverse Ranges (Kern, Ventura, and Los Angeles Co.). **STATUS:** Rare and local. *P. a. alticola* (San Bernardino Mts.) may be extinct.

LKY POCKET MOUSE   Pl. 16, Skull Pl. 4
rognathus flavus

Head and body 2¼ in. (51–70 mm); tail 1¾ in. (35–60 mm); hind foot ⅝ in. (15–18 mm); ear ¼ in. (6–7 mm); wt. ¼ oz. (5–10 g). *Very small.* Back grizzled orange-brown, *pale orange lateral line,* belly white. Fur very soft and silky. Large pale orange spot behind ear and above and below eye. White spot at base of ear. *Tail short,* nearly naked, faintly bicolor, darker at tip; not tufted. **SIMILAR SPECIES:** Merriam's Pocket Mouse (*P. merriami*) is almost identical externally. It usually has a smaller orange spot behind the ear. Other small pocket mice have longer tails. **HABITS:** Mostly sifts through

The Silky Pocket Mouse, like most members of the genus Perognathus, requires sand for dust-bathing to prevent the fur from becoming matted and greasy.

sand for small seeds, but may climb stalks to harvest green seeds. Breeds March–Oct.; litter size is 1–6. Females may have 1 or more litters per year. **HABITAT:** Dry grasslands and deserts, almost always with some grassy cover and sparse shrubs. Prefers sandy soils but also occurs in rocky areas and on clay soils. **RANGE:** Cen. and s. Great Plains and Mexican Plateau, from Wyo. and Neb. to w. Tex., Ariz., and n. Mexico. **STATUS:** Common.

MERRIAM'S POCKET MOUSE   Pl. 16
Perognathus merriami

Head and body 2¼ in. (53–65 mm); tail 1¾ in. (42–61 mm); hind foot ⅝ in. (16–18 mm); ear ¼ in. (6–7 mm); wt. ¼ oz. (6–9 g). *Very small.* Back grizzled orange-brown, *pale orange lateral line,* belly white. Fur very soft and silky. *Small pale orange spot behind ear and above and below eye.* White spot at base of ear. *Tail short,* nearly naked, faintly bicolor, and darker at tip; not tufted. **SIMILAR SPECIES:** See Silky Pocket Mouse (*P. flavus*). **HABITS:** Similar to Silky Pocket Mouse. Breeds March–Dec.; litter size is 3–6. Females may have 2 or more litters per year. **HABITAT:** Dry grassland and deserts with short sparse vegetation. Found on sand, gravel, and hard-packed soils. **RANGE:** Sw. Okla., w. and s. Tex., se. N.M., and ne. Mexico. **STATUS:** Locally common.

LITTLE POCKET MOUSE   Pl. 16
Perognathus longimembris

Head and body 2¼ in. (50–70 mm); tail 2¾ in. (60–85 mm); hind foot ¾ in. (17–20 mm); ear ¼ in. (5–7 mm); wt. ¼ oz. (6–9 g). Back very pale brown, gray, gray-brown, or dark gray-brown; faint to distinct pale orange line on sides; belly white. Pale orange spots above eye and behind ear. Small white spot at base of ear.

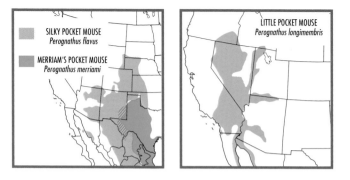

Tail relatively long, somewhat bicolor, lightly haired with some longer hairs at tip (3–4 mm). **SIMILAR SPECIES:** See Arizona Pocket Mouse (*P. amplus*). Other small pocket mice have tails shorter than head and body length. **HABITS:** Stays belowground for up to 9 months in winter, arousing from torpor occasionally to feed on stored seeds. Breeds in spring and early summer; litter size is 2–6. Females have several litters per year if food is plentiful. **HABITAT:** Desert scrub, on sandy or gravelly soils with sparse vegetation. Also found in dry grassland and coastal sage. Sea level to 6,500 ft. (3,000 m). **RANGE:** Se. Ore., Nev., s. Calif., w. Ariz., and nw. Mexico. **STATUS:** Generally common. Pacific Pocket Mouse (*P. l. pacificus*) of coastal s. California is endangered (USFWS).

ARIZONA POCKET MOUSE   *Perognathus amplus*   PL. 16

Head and body 2¾ in. (67–80 mm); tail 3½ in. (84–100 mm); hind foot ⅞ in. (20–24 mm); ear ⅜ in. (7–8 mm); wt. ½ oz. (12–16 g). Back orange-brown with some blackish grizzle (*P. a. rotundus* is very pale orange with no grizzle); distinct broad orange lateral line.

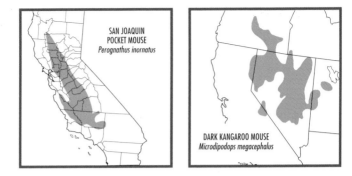

SAN JOAQUIN
POCKET MOUSE
Perognathus inornatus

DARK KANGAROO MOUSE
Microdipodops megacephalus

Belly cream white. Variable amount of orange above and below eye; *large orange patch behind ear*; small white patch at base of ear. Tail slightly bicolor, mostly pale orange, with a small tuft (hairs 4–5 mm at tip). **SIMILAR SPECIES:** Little Pocket Mouse (*P. longimembris*) is usually smaller and shorter-tailed, but can easily be confused. **HABITS:** Feeds on seeds of creosote bush and other plants. Spends winter in burrow in a torpid state. Breeds April–June; litter size is 1–7. Lifespan is up to 10 years. **HABITAT:** Flat desert scrub with sparse vegetation and firm but fine soil. To about 4,000 ft. (1,200 m). **RANGE:** Ariz. and extreme nw. Mexico. **STATUS:** Common.

SAN JOAQUIN POCKET MOUSE   Pl. 16
Perognathus inornatus

Head and body 2¾ in. (63–75 mm); tail 3 in. (70–85 mm); hind foot ¾ in. (18–21 mm); ear ⅜ in. (6–8 mm); wt. ⅜ oz. (8–17 g). Back orange with a heavy grizzle of blackish brown; distinct pale orange lateral line; belly white. Orange patches above and below eye and behind ear; small white spot at base of ear. Tail slightly longer than head and body, bicolor, not tufted. **SIMILAR SPECIES:** Great Basin and White-eared Pocket Mice (*P. parvus* and *P. alticola*) have longer hind feet (over 21 mm). **HABITS:** This species is not a good climber and usually feeds on the ground. Breeds March–July. Litter size is 4–6 and females probably breed twice each year. **HABITAT:** Dry grassland and desert scrub, usually in sandy areas, but sometimes found on rocky slopes. Lowlands to 1,600 ft. (500 m). **RANGE:** W. Calif. **STATUS:** Uncommon and local.

KANGAROO MICE: *Microdipodops*

Similar to kangaroo rats but much smaller, these mice have a thick tail that lacks a terminal crest.

The Dark Kangaroo Mouse looks like a miniature kangaroo rat. Note its proportionally large head (about the same size as the body) and centrally thickened tail.

ARK KANGAROO MOUSE Pl. 16, Skull Pl. 4
icrodipodops megacephalus

Head and body 2¾ in. (61–81 mm); tail 3½ in. (75–97 mm); hind foot 1 in. (23–26 mm); ear ⅜ in. (8–11 mm); wt. ½ oz. (11–16 g). Back dark gray, gray-brown, or pale gray washed with yellow; belly and lower sides white (*fur dark at roots*). Fur very soft and silky. White spots at base of ear and behind ear, at base of whiskers, and above eye. Ears small and rounded. Tail bicolor, *darkest at tip*; tapered at both ends, *thickest in midsection*, with a small tuft at tip. **SIMILAR SPECIES:** Pale Kangaroo Mouse (*M. pallidus*) is usually paler with pinkish roots on belly fur, and it lacks a dark tip to the tail, but the coloration of the two species can be similar. In *M. pallidus* the hind foot is usually more than 25 mm and in *M. megacephalus* it is usually less than 25 mm. Kangaroo rats are larger with crested tails. Pocket mice have smaller hind feet and do not have thickened tails. **HABITS:** Feeds in the open, unlike pocket mice that forage under shrubs. It is most active 1–2 hours after sunset, eating small seeds and insects. Hibernates Nov.–March. Breeds in spring and summer; litter size is 2–7. Females may have 1 or more litters per year. **HABITAT:** Prefers sand dunes and deserts with fine sand soils, but where it overlaps with Pale Kangaroo Mouse it is found on gravelly soil. Elevation 3,900–6,700 ft. (1,200–2,050 m). **RANGE:** Se. Ore., ne. Calif., Nev., s. Idaho, and w. Utah. **STATUS:** Common.

ALE KANGAROO MOUSE *Microdipodops pallidus* Pl. 16
Head and body 2¾ in. (61–74 mm); tail 3½ in. (83–96 mm); hind foot 1 in. (25–28 mm); ear ⅜ in. (9–11 mm); wt. ½ oz. (13–17 g). *Back pale pinkish buff* (sometimes with a dark grizzle); belly and lower sides white (*fur pinkish at roots*). Fur very soft and silky.

White spots at base of whiskers and above eye; prominent white spots behind ear and at base of ear. Ears small and rounded. Tail pinkish above, white below; tapered at both ends, *thickest in midsection,* with a small tuft at tip. **SIMILAR SPECIES:** See Dark Kangaroo Mouse (*M. megacephalus*). **HABITS:** Similar to Dark Kangaroo Mouse. **HABITAT:** Sand dunes and valleys with fine soft sand. Elevation 4,000–5,750 ft. (1,200–1,750 m). **RANGE:** Sw. Nev. and se. Calif. **STATUS:** Common.

PALE KANGAROO MOUSE
Microdipodops pallidus

KANGAROO RATS: *Dipodomys*

Kangaroo rats are among our most attractive and distinctive rodents, with silky golden fur, large eyes, white markings, and long crested tails. Kangaroo rats cannot be confused with any other rodents except perhaps kangaroo mice, but those species lack stripes and crests on the tail and are much smaller.

Kangaroo rats hop bipedally or walk on all fours. They hold the tip of the tail up as they move. When encountered by night they can often be approached closely, but will dip into a burrow if alarmed or escape with a zigzagging series of leaps.

All kangaroo rats are nocturnal, but some species are occasionally seen aboveground by day. Most species are less active on bright moonlit nights, preferring overcast or moonless nights. They usually stay in the burrow during rain or snowstorms and also remain belowground if the weather is very cold or snow cover is deep, but they do not hibernate. Kangaroo rats eat mainly seeds, but they will take a few insects and some green plant material when seed supplies are low. They store seeds in the burrow or in caches near the soil surface. Most kangaroo rats can survive without free water, living on metabolic water from seed digestion, although they usually will drink if water is available.

All kangaroo rats dig burrows that they use by day and to evade predators by night. The larger species generally make large mounds with several entrances into a complex network of burrows. These mounds are occupied by a single rat, but they are the result of generations of digging activity. Most species favor sandy soils for digging, but a few occur on hard-packed clay or gravelly soils. All kangaroo rats need some loose sand or fine silt for dust-bathing. Their fine silky fur becomes greasy and matted if they are deprived of sand.

Kangaroo rats are solitary and most are strongly territorial. They drum with the hind feet to communicate, and it is often possible to find out if a burrow is occupied by tapping on the surface. The occupant will respond by drumming from within the burrow. Although usually silent, calls include low grunts, squeals, and purrs. Kangaroo rats swim well, but they cannot maintain their burrows in heavy rains or irrigated areas. Several species in California have become threatened or endangered as their habitat has been altered for agricultural development or lost to urban sprawl or petroleum exploration.

RD'S KANGAROO RAT *Dipodomys ordii* Pl. 17

Head and body 4 in. (83–120 mm); tail 5¼ in. (114–155 mm); hind foot 1½ in. (34–43 mm); ear ½ in. (11–14 mm); wt. 2 oz. (44–72 g). *Small.* Highly variable in color. Back dark gray, yellow-gray, brown, or bright orange; sides paler than back, usually yellowish or orange; belly white. *White spots* above eyes and below and behind ears *usually diffuse*, sometimes distinct. Dark upper and lower tail stripes; tip of tail blackish, clearly crested for about ⅓ its length from tip. Tail relatively short in northern populations, longer in

*d's Kangaroo Rat,
 common with
 her Dipodomys
 ecies, has attractive
 hite markings and a
 ng furred tail. This
 ecies is relatively
 all and short-
 iled.*

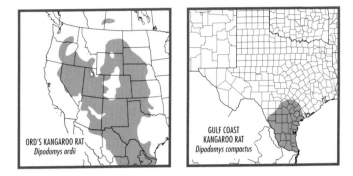

ORD'S KANGAROO RAT
Dipodomys ordii

GULF COAST
KANGAROO RAT
Dipodomys compactus

southern populations. Tops of hind feet white, soles brown; 5 *toes on hind foot.* **SIMILAR SPECIES:** See Chisel-toothed, Panamint, and Gulf Coast Kangaroo Rats (*D. microps, D. panamintinus,* and *D. compactus*). All other kangaroo rats in its range have 4 toes on hind foot. **HABITS:** Most active on dark cloudy nights, seldom aboveground by day or in bad weather. Active year-round but stays in burrow when snow cover is deep or temperatures low. Eats a variety of seeds along with some green plant material and insects. Makes deep burrows, with entrances often under shrubs or on banks. Large mounds seldom develop above burrows. Breeds year-round in some areas, in spring and summer in more northerly regions. Litter size is 1–6. **HABITAT:** Dry grasslands, desert scrub, piñon-juniper, and sagebrush, almost always on fine sandy soils or sand dunes. **RANGE:** S. Alta., s. Sask., and se. Wash. to w. Tex. and Ariz., south to cen. Mexico. **STATUS:** Widespread and common.

GULF COAST KANGAROO RAT   PL. 17
Dipodomys compactus

Head and body 4¼ in. (102–115 mm); tail 4¾ in. (105–130 mm); hind foot 1½ in. (32–41 mm); ear ½ in. (10–14 mm); wt. 2 oz. (44–66 g). Small, with a *relatively short tail.* Five toes on hind foot. **GEOGRAPHIC VARIATION:** Mainland form: upper back dark sandy brown grizzled with black; sides paler, more yellowish; dark upper and lower stripes on tail, lower stripe extends to base of tuft or to tip of tail. Island form: back pale sandy gray washed with pink; sides very pale gray-white; tail pale brown above; lower stripe faint, usually only extends about ⅓ length of tail from base. **SIMILAR SPECIES:** Ord's Kangaroo Rat (*D. ordii*) is very similar to the mainland form, but usually has a longer and bushier tail. **HABITS:** Eats mostly seeds but will also take insects. Females have litters of 2 young in midsummer. **HABITAT:** Sand dunes and deserts with sandy soils and sparse vegetation. Prefers disturbed or overgrazed areas to undisturbed areas with thick vegetation. **RANGE:** Se. Tex. mainland and Mustang and Padre Is., also barrier islands of Tamaulipas, Mexico. **STATUS:** Locally common, but losing habitat to development on some islands.

CHISEL-TOOTHED KANGAROO RAT
Dipodomys microps

Head and body 4¼ in. (100–116 mm); tail 6½ in. (136–190 mm); hind foot 1⅝ in. (40–45 mm); ear ½ in. (11–14 mm); wt. 2 oz. (47–67 g). Back pale sandy brown, pale yellow, or gray-brown, with light to heavy black grizzle; sides yellow or yellow-gray; belly white. *Prominent white spots* at base of whiskers, above eyes, and behind ears. Ears bicolor. *Tail long,* brown above and below, sides white; tip dark brown with some white hairs at the end. Tops of feet white; 5 toes on hind foot. *Lower incisors chisel-like* (face of tooth flat). **SIMILAR SPECIES:** Two other 5-toed kangaroo rats occur in its range: Ord's Kangaroo Rat (*D. ordii*) is usually smaller; Panamint Kangaroo Rat (*D. panamintinus*) is larger (hind foot over 44 mm). Both have awl-shaped lower incisors (face of tooth rounded). **HABITS:** Active for a few hours after dusk, regardless of time of year or lunar cycle. Unlike most kangaroo rats, eats more leaves than seeds and will climb into shrubs to harvest food. Uses flattened incisor teeth to scrape off the salty outer layer of shadscale or saltbush (*Atriplex confertifolia*) leaves and eats the rich, moist inner portion. Makes mounds near or under shrubs, with multiple burrow entrances. Stores food in the burrow. Litter size is 1–4, usually 2; young are born in March or April; females rarely have more than 1 litter per year. **HABITAT:** Prefers desert valleys dominated by saltbush and upland deserts with blackbush; less common in other desert communities and on sand dunes. Usually found on

CHISEL-TOOTHED
KANGAROO RAT
Dipodomys microps

gravelly soils. Usually found at 3,000–5,000 ft. (1,000–1,500 m), but can occur as high as 10,500 ft. (3,200 m). **RANGE:** E. Ore. and sw. Idaho through Nev. and w. Utah to se. Calif. and sw. Ariz. **STATUS:** Common.

PANAMINT KANGAROO RAT Pl. 17
Dipodomys panamintinus

Head and body 4¾ in. (103–142 mm); tail 7 in. (163–200 mm); hind foot 1¾ in. (42–47 mm); ear ½ in. (11–16 mm); wt. 2½ oz. (56–90 g). Medium sized. Back dark brown or gray-brown, sides yellow-orange or gray-yellow, belly white. *Prominent white spots above and below eyes* and behind ears. Ears relatively large and dark, backs of ears bicolor. *Tail long,* upper and lower dark stripes blackish, grizzled with white; *tuft dark brown with some white fur near tip. Hind foot has 5 toes.* **SIMILAR SPECIES:** See Chisel-toothed Kangaroo Rat (*D. microps*). Ord's Kangaroo Rat (*D. ordii*) is usually smaller in area of overlap and has a proportionally shorter tail. Other kangaroo rats in its range have 4 toes on hind foot. **HABITS:** Makes a series of erratic leaps if alarmed. Does not climb but swims well. Active year-round but may stay belowground if snow cover is deep. Eats seeds and green vegetation. Females have litters of 3–4 young in March or April. **HABITAT:** Open desert with scattered shrubs (such as Joshua trees and creosote bush), on sand, gravel, or salt-encrusted soils. Also found in open piñon-juniper desert. Elevation 3,600–8,900 ft. (1,100–2,700 m). **RANGE:** E. Calif. and w. Nev. **STATUS:** Locally common.

STEPHENS'S KANGAROO RAT Pl. 18
Dipodomys stephensi

Head and body 4½ in. (98–129 mm); tail 6½ in. (146–188 mm); hind foot 1⅝ in. (39–44 mm); ear ½ in. (12–15 mm); wt. 3 oz. (45–

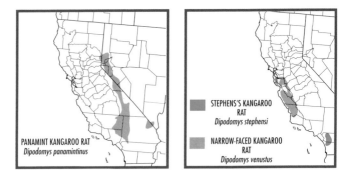

PANAMINT KANGAROO RAT
Dipodomys panamintinus

STEPHENS'S KANGAROO RAT
Dipodomys stephensi

NARROW-FACED KANGAROO RAT
Dipodomys venustus

73 g). Fairly large. *Back dark gray-brown,* sides orange-brown, belly white. Small white spots above eye and at base of ear. Ears relatively small. *Long black crest on long tail.* Hind foot has 5 toes. **SIMILAR SPECIES:** Merriam's Kangaroo Rat (*D. merriami*) has 4 toes on hind foot and is smaller. Dulzura and Agile Kangaroo Rats (*D. simulans* and *D. agilis*) have larger ears (usually over 15 mm). **HABITS:** Uses a network of surface trails linking burrow entrances. Sometimes occupies abandoned pocket gopher or ground squirrel burrows. Breeds in spring or summer; litter size is 2–3. **HABITAT:** Coastal sage scrub and grassland (favors areas with sparse vegetation), on sandy or gravelly soils. Near sea level to 2,800 ft. (850 m). **RANGE:** Sw. Calif. only. **STATUS:** Endangered (USFWS).

ARROW-FACED KANGAROO RAT   Pl. 18
podomys venustus

Head and body 5 in. (113–138 mm); tail 7½ in. (168–206 mm); hind foot 1¾ in. (40–49 mm); ear ¾ in. (17–22 mm); wt. 3 oz. (65–103 g). Large. *Back dark gray-brown* washed with ocher; sides orange-brown, belly white. Diffuse white spots above eyes, small white spots behind ears. *Ears large and dark,* bicolor at back. Tail long, with dark stripes above and below; tip mixed dark brown and white in some, all-dark in others. Hind foot has 5 toes, dark ankles. **SIMILAR SPECIES:** Other kangaroo rats in its range have smaller ears and are usually paler in color. **HABITS:** Eats mostly seeds and some green vegetation. Burrow system is rather simple, consisting of one main tunnel and some side branches to a nest and food storage areas. Separate burrows are used for escape routes. Litter size is 2–4; females may have 1–2 litters per year. **HABITAT:** Chaparral and mixed chaparral and oak or pine on sandy soils. Sea level to 5,800 ft. (1,800 m). **RANGE:** Sw. Calif. **STATUS:** Uncommon and local. **NOTE:** Big-eared Kangaroo Rat (*D. v. elephantinus*) is sometimes considered to be a separate species.

GILE KANGAROO RAT   *Dipodomys agilis*   Pl. 18

Head and body 4¾ in. (98–140 mm); tail 7 in. (153–220 mm); hind foot 1¾ in. (38–47 mm); ear ⅝ in. (14–18 mm); wt. 2½ oz. (63–78 g). Back *dark reddish brown,* sides orange-brown, belly white. White spots above eyes and below and behind ears. *Ears relatively large.* Tail dark above and below, tip blackish with some long white hair visible. Hind foot has 5 toes. **SIMILAR SPECIES:** See Stephens's Kangaroo Rat (*D. stephensi*). Dulzura Kangaroo Rat (*D. simulans*) is very similar but probably does not overlap in range. **HABITS:** Eats seeds of grasses, herbs, and shrubs, as well as acorns, juniper berries, and a few insects. Breeds March–July; litter size is 2–4. **HABITAT:** Coastal sage scrub, chaparral, and piñon-juniper, usually on

AGILE KANGAROO RAT
Dipodomys agilis

DULZURA KANGAROO RAT
Dipodomys simulans

sandy soils. Prefers flat ground and dry washes. Elevation 1,500–7,400 ft. (500–2,300 m). **RANGE:** S. Calif. only. **STATUS:** Common.

DULZURA KANGAROO RAT   *Dipodomys simulans*

Head and body 4¼ in. (85–130 mm); tail 6½ in. (140–200 mm); hind foot 1⅝ in. (39–45 mm); ear ⅝ in. (13–17 mm); wt. 2¼ oz. (55–70 g). Back gray-brown to dark red-brown, sides yellow-gray or orange, belly white. White spots above eyes and below and behind ears. *Ears relatively large* and dark. Tail dark above and below, tip blackish. Hind foot has 5 toes. **SIMILAR SPECIES:** See Agile Kangaroo Rat (*D. agilis*). **HABITS:** Breeds mostly in spring and fall, but can breed year-round. Litter size is 2–4. **HABITAT:** Chaparral and coastal grassland, on gravelly or sandy soils. Sea level to 7,500 ft. (2,300 m). **RANGE:** S. Calif. and Baja Calif. **STATUS:** Common. **NOTE:** Dulzura Kangaroo Rat is closely related to Agile Kangaroo Rat (*D. agilis*) and was considered to be a subspecies of that species until recently. It has a different chromosome number and averages slightly smaller.

CALIFORNIA KANGAROO RAT   PL. 18
Dipodomys californicus

Head and body 5 in. (112–132 mm); tail 7½ in. (163–216 mm); hind foot 1¾ in. (42–46 mm); ear ⅝ in. (15–19 mm); wt. 2½ oz. (50–94 g). Fairly large, dark. *Back dark gray or orange-brown* with a grayish grizzle. Sides slightly paler, orange-brown; belly and rump line white. White spot over eye, cheeks pale but not white. Small white spot below ear but little or no white above ear. Ears bicolor. Tail with broad black stripes and narrow white stripes, *tip white* preceded by black. Hind foot has 4 toes (in rare cases has a very small 5th toe). **SIMILAR SPECIES:** Chisel-toothed Kangaroo Rat (*D. microps*) has 5 toes on hind foot and chisel-like lower incisors. Range does not overlap with other kangaroo rats. **HABITS:** Eats mostly seeds of shrubs and grasses; does not store seeds in burrow but makes small caches in soil. Eats green vegetation when seeds are scarce. Sometimes burrows under boulders. Females have litters of 2–4 young and may breed twice a year. **HABITAT:** Brushy hills and chaparral. Avoids dense vegetation. Found on well-drained rocky or stony soils. Low elevations to 4,300 ft. (1,300 m). **RANGE:** S.-cen. Ore. and n. Calif. **STATUS:** Local, poorly known.

HEERMANN'S KANGAROO RAT
Dipodomys heermanni

PL. 18

Head and body 4½ in. (107–126 mm); tail 7 in. (162–201 mm); hind foot 1⅝ in. (40–44 mm); ear ½ in. (13–15 mm); wt. 2½ oz. (50–90 g). Medium sized. Back yellow-gray, yellow-brown, orange-brown, or blackish brown; sides dull yellow, orange-brown, or deep orange; belly white. Small but distinct white spots above eyes and below and behind ears. *Tail long, with broad upper and lower dark stripes,* narrow white side stripes; tip blackish or mixed black and white. Hind foot has 5 toes. **SIMILAR SPECIES:** Narrow-faced Kangaroo Rat (*D. venustus*) has longer ears. San Joaquin Kangaroo Rat (*D. nitratoides*) is usually smaller and has 4 toes on hind foot. Giant Kangaroo Rat (*D. ingens*) is much larger. **HABITS:** Usually emerges for about 40 minutes soon after dusk, but may remain belowground until moonset on nights with a full moon. Eats seeds and green vegetation and occasionally takes insects. Unlike most kangaroo rats, it cannot survive without free water (obtained from dew, moist food, or puddles). Breeds Feb.–Oct.; litter size is 2–5. **HABITAT:** Coastal plains, valleys, in grassy areas or chaparral and on sparsely vegetated hills. Found on fine, deep sandy soils and shallow rocky areas. Sea level to 3,300 ft. (1,000 m). **RANGE:** S. Calif.

CALIFORNIA KANGAROO RAT
Dipodomys californicus

HEERMANN'S KANGAROO RAT
Dipodomys heermanni

---- historical range limit

GIANT KANGAROO RAT
Dipodomys ingens

only. **STATUS:** Morro Bay Kangaroo Rat (*D. h. morroensis*) is endangered (USFWS, IUCN).

GIANT KANGAROO RAT   *Dipodomys ingens*   **PI. 18**

Head and body 6 in. (139–160 mm); tail 7¼ in. (174–198 mm); hind foot 2 in. (46–51 mm); ear ⅝ in. (14–18 mm); wt. 5 oz. (100–180 g). *Largest kangaroo rat.* Back yellow-gray, sides sandy yellow, belly white. White spots above eyes and below and behind ears. Tail long, tip blackish, with variable amount of white hair near the end. Hind foot has 5 toes, dusky soles. **SIMILAR SPECIES:** Other kangaroo rats in its range are smaller (compare hind foot lengths). **HABITS:** Active for short periods soon after dusk, also occasionally emerges during the day. Eats mostly seeds of grasses and forbs, stockpiling seeds in piles on the surface or in shallow, short-covered pits. Moves seeds underground after they have dried on the surface. Makes simple shallow burrows under small low mounds. Each burrow has a nest chamber and side chambers for food storage. Actively defends its small territory from other kangaroo rats and also from birds or mammals raiding its seed piles. Females give birth to 1–4 young mostly Jan.–Feb.; may have more than 1 litter per year if conditions are good. **HABITAT:** Open desert with scattered shrubs and grasses on sandy loam soils. Usually between 650–2,600 ft. (200–800 m). **RANGE:** Sw. San Joaquin Valley, Calif. **STATUS:** Endangered (USFWS). Losing habitat to agriculture and petroleum development.

BANNER-TAILED KANGAROO RAT   **PI. 17**
Dipodomys spectabilis

Head and body 5¾ in. (130–164 mm); tail 7¾ in. (174–221 mm); hind foot 2 in. (47–55 mm); ear ⅝ in. (13–17 mm); wt. 4½ oz. (97–157 g). *Large, strikingly marked.* Back dark gray-brown, sides

This Banner-tailed Kangaroo Rat has its fur-lined cheek pouches stuffed with seeds that it will take to a storage area in its burrow.

washed with ocher, belly white. Diffuse white spots above eyes and on cheeks, also below and behind ears. Tail long, striped for about ½ length, then all-black, with a *long white tip.* Hind foot has 4 toes, dusky ankles. **SIMILAR SPECIES:** See Desert Kangaroo Rat (*D. deserti*). Other kangaroo rats in its range do not have a white tail tip. **HABITS:** Most active on dark moonless nights. Makes large mounds up to 3 ft. (1 m) high

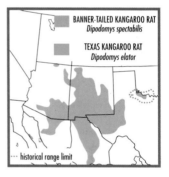

BANNER-TAILED KANGAROO RAT
Dipodomys spectabilis

TEXAS KANGAROO RAT
Dipodomys elator

··· historical range limit

and about 3–12 ft. (1–4 m) wide. Mounds are usually in open areas, sometimes under shrubs. Burrows have multiple entrances and form a complex underground network. Aboveground trails lead to feeding areas. Breeds Jan.–Aug. or year-round; litter size is 1–3. Females may have 2–3 litters per year. **HABITAT:** Desert grasslands with scattered creosote bush and other shrubs. Usually found on hard soils with high gravel content. **RANGE:** S. and e. Ariz., N.M., and sw. Tex. to n. Mexico. **STATUS:** Common.

TEXAS KANGAROO RAT *Dipodomys elator* **Pl. 17**

Head and body 4¾ in. (101–141 mm); tail 7¾ in. (159–197 mm); hind foot 1⅞ in. (44–48 mm); ear ½ in. (12–16 mm); wt. 2¾ oz. (62–90 g). Back dark brown or yellow-brown, sides yellow-orange or gray-yellow; belly white. Small white spots above and below eyes and below ears. Tail striped gray-brown above and below (sides white) for about ⅔ its length from base, then all-black, with a *white tip*. Hind foot has 4 toes. **SIMILAR SPECIES:** Ord's Kangaroo Rat (*D. ordii*) has a dark tail tip. Very similar to Banner-tailed Kangaroo Rat (*D. spectabilis*), but smaller; ranges do not overlap. **HABITS:** Most active on dark moonless nights. Eats mostly grass and forb seeds, also takes some green vegetation and insects. Makes large mounds, usually under mesquites, with complex tunnels and multiple burrow entrances. May breed year-round, but most litters are born in spring and early summer; litter size is 2–4. **HABITAT:** Open mesquite grassland on clay or clay-loam soils. **RANGE:** N. Tex.; formerly in extreme sw. Okla., but may be extinct there. **STATUS:** Rare and local. Threatened (Texas Parks and Wildlife).

DESERT KANGAROO RAT   *Dipodomys deserti*   Pl. 17

Head and body 5¼ in. (104–160 mm); tail 7¾ in. (185–209 mm); hind foot 2 in. (49–55 mm); ear ⅝ in. (15–16 mm); wt. 4 oz. (73–148 g). *Large and very pale.* Back pale sandy brown, belly and lower sides white. White spots around eye and ear. Ears pinkish. Tail long, with pale brown stripe on upper side, *white below and at tip;* dark brown crest precedes white tip. Hind foot has 4 toes. **SIMILAR SPECIES:** Most kangaroo rats in its range are smaller. Banner-tailed Kangaroo Rat (*D. spectabilis*) is darker, with 2 dark stripes on tail and black soles on hind feet. **HABITS:** Mainly nocturnal, but may actively excavate new burrows or remove sand from existing burrows during the day. Eats grass, mesquite, creosote bush seeds, and dried plant material. Makes mounds up to 30 ft. (9 m) across, formed by excavations of deep complex burrows. Burrows have several entrances, often under shrubs, leading to a maze of tunnels with food storage areas and a nest chamber. Uses plugs of sand to close burrow entrances by day to retain moisture. Breeds Jan.–July; litter size is 1–6, and females may have 1 or 2 litters per year. **HABITAT:** Sand dunes and hot dry deserts with loose, deep sandy soils. Below sea level (Death Valley) to 5,600 ft. (1,700 m). **RANGE:** Nev., se. Calif., and Ariz. to nw. Mexico. **STATUS:** Common.

MERRIAM'S KANGAROO RAT   Pl. 17, Skull Pl. 4
Dipodomys merriami

Head and body 4 in. (86–117 mm); tail 5½ in. (123–160 mm); hind foot 1½ in. (35–40 mm); ear ½ in. (10–13 mm); wt. 1½ oz. (28–53 g). Small. Color varies with soil type. Back dark brown, orange-brown, pale yellow-gray, or sand brown; sides paler, washed with yellow or orange; belly white. White spots above eyes and below and behind ears. Dark upper and lower stripes on tail in dark-backed forms, lower stripe absent in pale forms; tip blackish or orange-brown. *Tail extensively crested,* with crest extending for

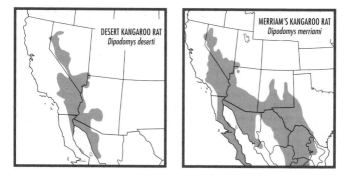

about ½ tail length. Hind foot has 4 toes. **SIMILAR SPECIES:** Ord's Kangaroo Rat (*D. ordii*) has 5 toes on hind foot and has a less pronounced crest on tail. Where the species co-occur, Ord's is found on softer, sandier soils and Merriam's on packed clay or gravelly soils. See San Joaquin Kangaroo Rat (*D. nitratoides*). **HABITS:** Eats a variety of seeds, also green plant material and some insects. Stores food in small caches just below the soil surface throughout its territory, not inside burrow. Makes short simple burrows that do not result in a mound. Burrow entrances are usually under a shrub. Usually breeds in early spring and again in late summer, but may breed year-round in some areas. Litter size is 1–4. **HABITAT:** Open deserts with scattered grasses and shrubs, on sand, clay, or gravelly soils. More tolerant of hard-packed and stony soils than other kangaroo rats. Sea level to 7,000 ft. (2,100 m). **RANGE:** S. Calif. and Nev. to w. Tex., south into n. Mexico. **STATUS:** Generally common and widespread. San Bernardino Kangaroo Rat (*D. m. parvus*), see illustration, p. 36, is endangered (USFWS).

AN JOAQUIN KANGAROO RAT

PL. 18

podomys nitratoides

Fresno Kangaroo Rat

Head and body 4 in. (88–115 mm); tail 5½ in. (125–155 mm); hind foot 1⅜ in. (32–37 mm); ear ½ in. (11–13 mm); wt. 1½ oz. (36–53 g). *Small.* Back gray-brown, dull yellow, or orange-brown; sides dull orange or ocher; belly white. Small white spots above and below eyes and at base of ears. Dark tail stripes slightly grizzled, tip of tail blackish. Crest extends for about ⅓ its tail length. Hind foot has 4 toes. **SIMILAR SPECIES:** Merriam's Kangaroo Rat (*D. merriami*) does not overlap but occurs nearby; it has a more pronounced crest on the tail. See Heermann's Kangaroo Rat (*D. heermanni*). Other kangaroo rats in s. California are much larger.

HABITS: Eats seeds of grass and shrubs such as saltbush. Makes mounds 6–10 ft. (2–3.3 m) wide, usually under shrubs. Stores seeds in pits in the burrow walls. Cannot maintain burrows or keep seed supplies dry in cultivated and irrigated areas, but will exploit abandoned farm fields. Breeds Dec.–Aug. or year-round; litter size is 1–3. **HABITAT:** Dry grassland and desert valleys, often on alkaline soils. Elevation 160–2,600 ft. (50–800 m). **RANGE:** San Joaquin and adjacent valleys, sw. Calif. **STATUS:** Fresno and Tipton's Kangaroo Rats (*D. n. exilis* and *D. n. nitratoides*) are endangered (USFWS). Losing habitat to intensive agricultural development.

SAN JOAQUIN
KANGAROO RAT
Dipodomys nitratoides

SPINY POCKET MICE: *Liomys*

This genus is found mainly in Central America, with one species entering the U.S. in s. Texas. Unlike other heteromyids, the upper incisor teeth are not grooved.

MEXICAN SPINY POCKET MOUSE   Pl. 15
Liomys irroratus

Head and body 4½ in. (104–126 mm); tail 4½ in. (95–127 mm); hind foot 1⅛ in. (28–30 mm); ear ½ in. (13–16 mm); wt. 1¾ oz. (33–65 g). *Large and dark.* Back blackish brown, sides paler with a narrow orange lateral line; belly cream white. Fur coarse and shiny, with *dark spines on rump. Ears large, broad, and rounded*, edges pale. Tail bicolor, lightly furred, with a small tuft at tip. Spoon-shaped claw on hind foot. **SIMILAR SPECIES:** Coarse-furred pocket mice (*Chaetodipus* sp.) are smaller and have narrow ears and grooved upper incisors. **HABITS:** Feeds on seeds of shrubs and weeds; caches seeds in burrows. Entrances to burrow may be covered with leaves by day. Breeds mostly in fall or winter, but may breed year-round if conditions are good. Litter size is 2–8. **HABITAT:**

Palm forest and dense brush along ridges (in Texas). Sea level to 10,000 ft. (3,000 m) in Mexico. **RANGE:** Extreme s. Tex. to s. Mexico. **STATUS:** Common but very local in Texas.

MEXICAN SPINY
POCKET MOUSE
Liomys irroratus

ATS AND MICE: Muridae

The murid rodents, as currently recognized, are a large group of rats, mice, and voles. This family consists of several subgroups: Neotomine-peromyscines (deer mice, harvest mice, grasshopper mice, woodrats, and allies), sigmodontines (rice rats and cotton rats), arvicolines (voles, muskrats, and lemmings), and murines (Old World rats and mice). Although all these rodents have the same dental formula, each group has characteristic patterns on the biting surfaces of the molar teeth. (See figures 3 and 4, pp. 166, 167.)

All of the murid rodents in our area are active year-round, but some may enter torpor for short periods to conserve energy. Most are nocturnal in habits, although many of the voles and cotton rats may be active by day. These rodents occupy a wide diversity of habitats and some have specialized diets.

EER MICE: *Peromyscus*

The deer mice are small to medium-sized mice with rather large eyes and large naked ears. Their tails are relatively thick, usually as long as or longer than head and body length. This group includes the most common and widespread species of native small rodents, and they are represented by one or more species throughout the U.S. and Canada. Deer mice are strictly nocturnal. They are active year-round but may remain in the nest in bad weather. These mice are usually silent, but they may drum with the front or hind feet if alarmed.

CACTUS MOUSE   *Peromyscus eremicus* Pl. 21

Head and body 3½ in. (80–99 mm); tail 4 in. (83–113 mm); hind foot ¾ in. (18–22 mm); ear ¾ in. (17–21 mm); wt. 1 oz. (18–30 g). *Back gray-brown (dark to pale in tone depending on soil color), often contrasting slightly with gray head; lower sides and cheeks orange;* belly white. Ears medium sized, naked; whiskers long and thick. *Tail nearly naked, somewhat bicolor* at base, blotchy or unicolor toward tip. Hairs at tip of tail sparse, about 2 mm long. Feet white, ankles dark, sole of hind foot naked to heel. **SIMILAR SPECIES:** See Mesquite Mouse (*P. merriami*). Most other western *Peromyscus* have haired (often tufted) bicolor tails. White-footed Mouse (*P. leucopus*) has tail shorter than head and body and more uniform coloration of head and body. **HABITS:** Mainly terrestrial, but may climb in low vegetation. Sometimes lives in part of a woodrat den or an abandoned burrow of another mammal. This species is seldom trapped in midsummer and may estivate at that time. Female has litters of 1–4 young year-round. **HABITAT:** Deserts, usually on rocky soil with sparse vegetation, but also occurs on sandy flats and in desert grassland and chaparral. **RANGE:** S. Calif. to sw. Tex., south to San Luis Potosí and Sinaloa, Mexico. **STATUS:** Common.

NORTHERN BAJA MOUSE   *Peromyscus fraterculus*

This species was recently recognized as distinct from Cactus Mouse, *P. eremicus*, based on biochemical and genetic differences. External differences have not been described. The two species are probably similar in habits and habitat. **RANGE:** Sw. Calif. and Baja Calif.

MESQUITE MOUSE   *Peromyscus merriami*

Head and body 3¾ in. (84–107 mm); tail 4¼ in. (94–121 mm); hind foot ⅞ in. (20–24 mm); ear ⅞ in. (19–23 mm); wt. 1 oz. (19–35 g). Back gray-brown or *dark brown*, sides washed with orange; belly

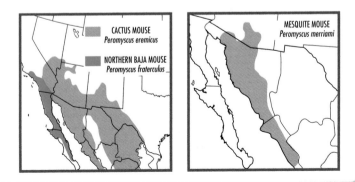

white or cream, sometimes with a rusty spot on the chest. Ears medium sized, naked; whiskers long and thick. *Tail nearly naked, somewhat bicolor* at base, blotchy or unicolor toward tip. Feet white, ankles dark. **SIMILAR SPECIES:** Very similar to Cactus Mouse (*P. eremicus*), but usually slightly larger (hind foot usually 22–23 mm in *merriami*, 20 mm in *eremicus*); upperparts darker, underparts often cream, not white. These mice are best distinguished by comparisons of skull shape and baculum. Cactus Mouse usually occurs in dry rocky areas with sparse vegetation, but sometimes enters mesquite bottomlands. See Cactus Mouse for comparisons with other species. **HABITS:** Mostly terrestrial; usually trapped at the base of trees or under brush. May breed throughout the year, but more young born in early spring than in summer. Litter size is 2–4. **HABITAT:** Closely associated with mesquite, along washes and bottoms in dense vegetation. Sea level to 3,750 ft. (1,150 m). **RANGE:** S. Ariz. to Sinaloa, Mexico. **STATUS:** Locally common but losing habitat where mesquites are cut for firewood and pasture.

CALIFORNIA MOUSE *Peromyscus californicus* PL. 21

Head and body 4½ in. (90–125 mm); tail 5¼ in. (112–156 mm); hind foot 1 in. (23–27 mm); ear ⅞ in. (19–23 mm); wt. 1½ oz. (33–54 g). Back *dark gray-brown*, sides orange-brown, belly gray-white. Ears rather large, naked. Blackish eye-rings. Whiskers long and thick. *Tail long,* somewhat bicolor, *well haired* with a *small tuft* (hairs 7–9 mm). Tops of feet white, heels dusky. **SIMILAR SPECIES:** Other *Peromyscus* in California are smaller. Subadult California Mouse has a shorter tuft on tail than Brush Mouse (*P. boylii*) and usually has a longer hind foot. **HABITS:** Climbs well, but usually encountered on the ground. Eats seeds of laurel and grass, fruit, fungi, and insects. Makes nests on the ground under logs or inside Dusky-footed Woodrat houses. Unlike most small mammals, this mouse forms stable monogamous pairs and lives in small family

CALIFORNIA MOUSE
Peromyscus californicus

groups. Litters of 1–3 are born year-round, and both parents care for the young. **HABITAT:** Chaparral, oak woods, coastal sage scrub, redwood forests, and brushy hills. Sea level to 7,900 ft. (2,400 m). **RANGE:** Calif. and n. Baja Calif. **STATUS:** Locally common.

OLDFIELD MOUSE *Peromyscus polionotus* PL. 20
Beach Mouse

Head and body 3 in. (70–85 mm); tail 2 in. (45–60 mm); hind foot ⅝ in. (16–19 mm); ear ½ in. (13–15 mm); wt. ½ oz. (10–15 g). Small and *short-tailed*. Back *gray-brown* to *very pale fawn*; sides paler, white in pale races; belly white. Tail somewhat bicolor, pale brown above; lightly haired, not tufted. **GEOGRAPHIC VARIATION:** Coastal populations (Beach Mice) very pale, almost white. **SIMILAR SPECIES:** Other eastern *Peromyscus* are larger and darker. Eastern Harvest Mouse is darker, with a grayish belly and grooved upper incisors. **HABITS:** Makes narrow burrows that it may plug from inside during the day. Feeds on grass and weed seeds and some invertebrates. Apparently forms stable monogamous pairs, unlike related species. Litters of 2–4 young are born mainly in fall or winter. **HABITAT:** Sand dunes, open sandy areas, early successional fields (oldfields), and dry scrub. **RANGE:** Se. U.S. to N.C. and e. Miss. **STATUS:** Subspecies on Gulf Coast and islands (Beach Mice) are endangered (*P. p. allophrys, P. p. ammobates, P. p. phasma,* and *P. p. trissyllepsis*) or threatened (*P. p. niveiventris*) (USFWS). These mice suffer from habitat loss due to development, increased predation from house cats, and natural beach erosion. Inland subspecies are locally common.

OLDFIELD MOUSE
Peromyscus polionotus

KEEN'S MOUSE *Peromyscus keeni* PL. 21
Northwestern Deer Mouse

Head and body 4⅜ in. (90–124 mm); tail 4 in. (92–114 mm); hind foot ⅞ in. (20–25 mm); ear ¾ in. (18–22 mm); wt. ¾ oz. (10–30 g).

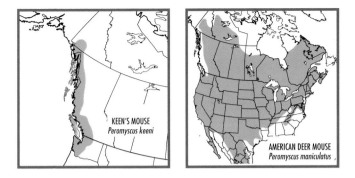

KEEN'S MOUSE
Peromyscus keeni

AMERICAN DEER MOUSE
Peromyscus maniculatus

Back *dark brown* or gray-brown, sides orange-brown, belly gray-white. *Tail almost equal to body length,* lightly haired and bicolor. **SIMILAR SPECIES:** American Deer Mouse (*P. maniculatus*) is usually smaller, paler, and has a shorter tail, but in damp forests near the range of Keen's (*P. keeni*), the two species can be similar in size and color. No other *Peromyscus* occur in its range. **HABITS:** Climbs well, but usually caught on the ground. Often enters buildings. Breeds in spring and early summer; litter size is 4–7. **HABITAT:** Cool, wet coastal forest (favors gaps, cutover areas, and stream banks). Also found in montane forest and at the edge of lakes and streams in alpine meadows. **RANGE:** Sw. Yukon and coastal B.C., including most of Vancouver I., to nw. Wash. **STATUS:** Common. **NOTE:** Previously included as a subspecies of American Deer Mouse (*P. maniculatus*). Includes *P. sitkensis* and *P. oreas*.

MERICAN DEER MOUSE Pls. 20, 21, p. 66, Skull Pl. 3
eromyscus maniculatus
Deer Mouse, North American Deer Mouse

Woodland and desert forms: head and body 3½ in. (80–109 mm); tail 3¼ in. (77–106 mm); hind foot ¾ in. (18–23 mm); ear ¾ in. (16–21 mm); wt. ¾ oz. (15–29 g). Prairie form: head and body 3¼ in. (74–94 mm); tail 2¼ in. (40–68 mm); hind foot ⅝ in. (15–19 mm); ear ⅝ in. (15–19 mm); wt. ⅝ oz. (12–25 g). Highly variable in size and color. Back dark brown, gray-brown, or orange-brown; sides paler but not contrasting with upper back; belly white with *gray underfur visible.* Very small patch of pure white fur on chin. *Tail equal to or shorter than body length, clearly bicolor* and clothed in short hair; *tip tufted* (hairs 4–5 mm at tip). Tops of feet white. **GEOGRAPHIC VARIATION:** Prairie form (*P. m. bairdii*): smaller, ears short and very dark, snout rather blunt; tail strongly bicolor and much shorter than head and body. Woodland form (*P. m. gracilis*): tail relatively long, back usually brown. Desert form (several subspecies): intermediate in size and tail length, back gray-brown fading to orange in older animals; tail stocky, thin line of black on dorsal surface. **SIMILAR SPECIES:** See White-footed Mouse (*P. leucopus*). Other western deer mice have longer tails. **HABITS:** Some forms mainly terrestrial; woodland forms climb very well and are semi-arboreal. Feeds on seeds, fruit, insects, subterranean fungi, and other foods; stores excess in caches. Nests in hollow logs, underground burrows, birds' nests, mattresses, among rocks, and other protected areas. Usually solitary in summer but may huddle together in groups during the winter in the North. Litter size is 1–8, usually about 4. Breeds year-round or seasonally depending on local conditions. **HABITAT:** Occupies almost every habitat type, from boreal forest and tundra to desert, prairies, swamps, and high mountains. Sea level to 11,500 ft. (3,500 m). **RANGE:** Throughout s. Canada and U.S. except Southeast and e. Tex.; also to s. Mexico. **STATUS:** Abundant and widespread. Host species of hantavirus, plague, and Lyme disease.

WHITE-FOOTED MOUSE *Peromyscus leucopus* **Pls. 20, 21**
Head and body 3½ in. (80–100 mm); tail 3 in. (60–95 mm), hind foot ¾ in. (18–23 mm); ear ¾ in. (16–20 mm); wt. ¾ oz. (15–28 g). Upper back dark brown, usually contrasting with orange-brown sides. Belly white; fur gray at roots but only for ¼ length so *appears pure white*. Fur smooth and even. *Chin hair entirely white to roots. Tail narrow, slightly shorter than body*; bicolor, lightly haired; hair at tip of tail 2–3 mm long. Tops of feet white. Young grayish. **GEOGRAPHIC VARIATION:** Southwestern forms paler and grayer, with no dark line on midback. **SIMILAR SPECIES:** Woodland form of American Deer Mouse (*P. maniculatus*) can be very difficult to distinguish. In eastern and northern regions the two can be separated using a combination of features: **1.** Pure white chin patch extends more than 1 cm from mouth (*P. leucopus*) or less than 1 cm from mouth (*P. maniculatus*). **2.** Tail lightly haired (some scales visible) with short hairs (2–3 mm) at tip (*P. leucopus*) or well haired (scales covered) with tuft of fur (hairs 4–5 mm) at tip (*P. maniculatus*). **3.** Back clearly two-tone, with fur smooth and slightly shiny (*P. leucopus*) or more uniform (grading from dark to paler on sides), with fur long and slightly fluffy (*P. maniculatus*). **4.** Fur on belly and sides gray at base for ¼ length, then white for ¾ length (most *P. leucopus*), appearing pure white in life; or fur on belly and sides gray at base for ½ length, then white for ½ length, some gray showing in life (*P. maniculatus*). See Cotton and Oldfield Mice (*P. gossypinus* and *P. polionotus*). Other deer mice have longer tails. **HABITS:** Mainly terrestrial, but climbs well and may forage or nest well above the ground. Swims well and occupies many islands in lakes. Eats insects, seeds, nuts, fruit, and green vegetation.

The White-footed Mouse (photo: southern Ontario) is easily confused with the American Deer Mouse, but note its narrow, lightly haired tail and clean white underparts.

WHITE-FOOTED MOUSE
Peromyscus leucopus

Stores piles of seeds, cherry pits, or other food under logs or near nest site. Often takes up residence in cabins and homes in wooded areas. Makes spherical nests in logs or standing trees, in abandoned burrows or birds' nests, or inside buildings. Breeds mainly in spring and fall; litter size is 3–6. Lifespan is usually less than a year. **HABITAT:** Deciduous and mixed forests, hedgerows, brushy areas, croplands, and dry semidesert regions in Southwest. Usually at low to moderate elevations in North, up to 8,200 ft. (2,700 m) in Southwest. **RANGE:** Se. Canada and e. U.S. west to s. Sask. and Mont. and south to Ariz.; also through e. Mexico to Yucatán Pen. Absent from Fla. **STATUS:** Abundant and widespread.

COTTON MOUSE *Peromyscus gossypinus* **Pl. 20**

Head and body 4 in. (95–110 mm); tail 3¼ in. (65–97 mm); hind foot ⅞ in. (20–26 mm); ear ¾ in. (17–20 mm); wt. 1 oz. (17–46 g). Rather large and dark. Back *dark brown,* almost black on upper back; sides orange-brown or brown; belly gray-white. Ears large, naked, and blackish. Tail bicolor, black above, very *lightly haired.* Feet white with dark heels. **SIMILAR SPECIES:** White-footed Mouse (*P. leucopus*) is very similar but smaller and paler. American Deer Mouse (*P. maniculatus*) has a hairier tail. See Florida Mouse (*Podomys floridanus*). **HABITS:** Climbs and swims well. Eats a variety of plant and animal foods. Makes nests in burrows, under logs, or in brush piles, or may nest well aboveground in trees. Breeds mostly in fall and winter, sometimes year-round. Litter size is 1–7. **HABITAT:** Prefers wet forests, hammocks, and swamps. Also found in pine woods, thickets, and rocky bluffs. **RANGE:** Se. U.S. **STATUS:** Common. One subspecies from Florida Keys (*P. g. allapaticola*) is endangered (USFWS).

COTTON MOUSE
Peromyscus gossypinus

CANYON MOUSE   *Peromyscus crinitus*   **Pl. 21**

Head and body 3 in. (65–89 mm); tail 3¾ in. (83–110 mm); hind foot ¾ in. (18–20 mm); ear ¾ in. (17–21 mm); wt. ½ oz. (10–19 g). *Small.* Back pale to dark gray (sometimes orange-brown) washed with ocher; sides dull brown (or bright orange) with a narrow orange lateral line; belly white. Fur long and very soft. Snout narrow and pointed; *ears large. Tail longer than head and body,* bicolor, *well haired and tufted* (hairs 5–6 mm at tip). Tail sometimes appears thickened. **SIMILAR SPECIES:** Other western *Peromyscus* are usually larger. American Deer Mouse (*P. maniculatus*) has a shorter tail with no tuft at tip. **HABITS:** Climbs with agility on vertical rock faces or overhanging walls and may occupy areas devoid of other small mammals. Uses sand or fine soil for dust-bathing. Does not need to drink water, obtaining sufficient moisture from a diet of insects, seeds, fruits, and green vegetation. Makes nests of shredded plant fibers in rock crevices or in burrows. Litters of 1–5 young are born March–Nov. **HABITAT:** Desolate rocky terrain with very sparse vegetation, on canyon walls, mesas, and talus slopes. Below sea level to over 10,000 ft. (3,200 m). **RANGE:** Idaho and Ore. to Colo., Ariz., s. Calif., and nw. Mexico. **STATUS:** Locally common in suitable habitat.

WHITE-ANKLED MOUSE   *Peromyscus pectoralis*   **Pl. 20**

Head and body 3¾ in. (81–111 mm); tail 3¾ in. (87–105 mm); hind foot ⅞ in. (20–24 mm); ear ¾ in. (17–21 mm); wt. ¾ oz. (16–27 g). Upperparts *gray-brown,* sides brown with a narrow orange lateral

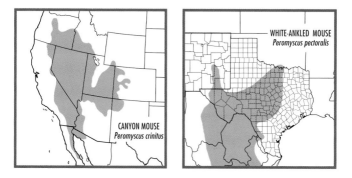

WHITE-ANKLED MOUSE
Peromyscus pectoralis

CANYON MOUSE
Peromyscus crinitus

line, belly white. Ears medium sized, whiskers long and thick. Tail about equal to head and body length, bicolor, lightly haired with a *small tuft* (hairs 3–4 mm at tip). *Ankles* and feet *white,* sole of hind foot haired near heel. **SIMILAR SPECIES:** See Texas Mouse (*P. attwateri*). Cactus Mouse (*P. eremicus*) has no tuft at tip of tail and has naked soles on hind feet. American Deer and White-footed Mice (*P. maniculatus* and *P. leucopus*) have shorter tails. **HABITS:** Mainly terrestrial; usually found on rock ledges or in leaf litter. Feeds on juniper berries, acorns, hackberries, seeds, and insects. Litters of 2–5 are born year-round. **HABITAT:** Rocky outcrops, talus slopes, bluffs, and oak-juniper woodlands. **RANGE:** Tex. and Mexican Plateau. **STATUS:** Common.

***

BRUSH MOUSE   *Peromyscus boylii*   Pl. 21

Head and body 3½ in (85–96 mm); tail 4 in. (95–111 mm); hind foot ⅞ in. (20–23 mm); ear ¾ in. (17–21 mm); wt. ⅞ oz. (22–26 g). Back gray-brown, washed with orange in older animals; *pale orange line on sides;* belly white with gray underfur. Ears large and naked. Narrow black mask around eyes. Whiskers long and thick. *Tail longer than head and body,* bicolor, and *tufted* (hairs 9–10 mm at tip). Feet white, ankles dark. **SIMILAR SPECIES:** Northern Rock, California, and Texas Mice (*P. nasutus, P. californicus,* and *P. attwateri*) usually have longer hind feet (over 23 mm). Piñon Mouse (*P. truei*) has bigger ears. Other deer mice have shorter tails with little or no tuft at tip. **HABITS:** Climbs well, but usually nests in rock crevices or under fallen trees. Probably does not dig its own burrows and requires rocks or other ground cover for shelter. Eats nuts, seeds, acorns, berries, cactus fruits, and insects. Can breed year-round, but most litters are born in spring or summer. Litter size is 2–5. **HABITAT:** Woods and dense brush with rocks, fallen trees, or brush piles. Usually found above 3,000 ft. (900 m) to about 8,500 ft. (2,600 m). **RANGE:** Sw. U.S. from n. Calif and n. Utah to Colo. and

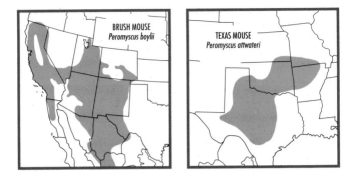

BRUSH MOUSE
Peromyscus boylii

TEXAS MOUSE
Peromyscus attwateri

w. Tex.; also nw. Mexico. **STATUS:** Common and widespread. Readily enters cabins and is the most commonly encountered deer mouse in southwestern mountains.

TEXAS MOUSE *Peromyscus attwateri* **Pl. 20**

Head and body 3¾ in. (83–113 mm); tail 4 in. (90–113 mm); hind foot 1 in. (23–27 mm); ear ¾ in. (17–20 mm); wt. 1 oz. (19–34 g). Upperparts gray-brown or dark brown; sides orange-brown, usually with an orange lateral line; belly white. Ears medium sized, whiskers long and thick. Tail equal to or slightly longer than head and body, strongly bicolor, lightly furred and *tufted at tip* (hairs 6–10 mm at tip). *Ankles dusky,* feet white. **SIMILAR SPECIES:** Brush Mouse (*P. boylii*) is very similar but has shorter hind feet (usually over 24 mm in *attwateri,* under 23 mm in *boylii*). White-ankled Mouse (*P. pectoralis*) has shorter hind feet and white ankles, with hairs at tail tip 3–4 mm long. **HABITS:** Semi-arboreal; climbs high in junipers and other trees, also frequents rocky crevices and fallen logs. Eats seeds, other plant matter, and insects (mostly crickets and beetles). Litters of 1–6 are born from fall to early spring. **HABITAT:** Cliffs and rocky areas dominated by juniper, also oak woodland and cedar glades. **RANGE:** Tex., Okla., Mo., Ark., and Kans. **STATUS:** Common.

PIÑON MOUSE *Peromyscus truei* **Pl. 21**

Head and body 3¾ in. (81–114 mm); tail 3¾ in. (80–117 mm); hind foot ⅞ in. (21–26 mm); ear 1 in. (22–28 mm); wt. 1¼ oz. (20–50 g). Back gray or brown to blackish; sides orange or orange-brown; belly white (fur gray at base). *Ears naked and very large,* usually longer than hind foot. Whiskers long and thick. Tail bicolor, *well haired and tufted* (hairs 6–10 mm at tip). Tops of hind feet white, heels dusky. **GEOGRAPHIC VARIATION:** California: ears about equal to hind foot; tail longer than head and body length. East of California: ears longer than hind foot, tail shorter than head and body length. Fur color varies with soil color. **SIMILAR SPECIES:** See Osgood's Mouse (*P. gratus*). Brush Mouse (*P. boylii*) has shorter ears and is usually smaller. Northern Rock Mouse (*P. nasutus*) can be very similar but usually has a proportionally longer tail. **HABITS:** Hops away when disturbed, may climb a tree or disappear among rocks if pursued. Eats mostly piñon and juniper seeds, also takes insects and fungi. Nests among rocks or in hollow trees. Females have litters of 3–6 young in spring and summer in the northern part of range; may breed year-round farther south. **HABITAT:** Prefers piñon and piñon-juniper stands, usually among rocks. Less common in juniper-sage, chaparral, desert scrub, or pine forest. Elevation 500–10,500 ft. (150–3,200 m), commonly at about 6,500 ft. (2,000 m). **RANGE:** Ore. to Colo., w. Tex. and N.M., south to Calif. and n. Baja Calif.; also extreme s. Baja. **STATUS:** Fairly common.

SGOOD'S MOUSE   *Peromyscus gratus*

Head and body 3¾ in. (86–101 mm); tail 4 in. (92–106 mm); hind foot ⅞ in. (22–23 mm); ear ⅞ in. (20–23 mm); wt. 1 oz. (20–33 g). Back *gray-brown* to *blackish brown;* sides paler, sometimes washed with orange; belly white (fur gray at base). *Ears large* but usually equal to or shorter than hind foot length. Tail slightly longer than head and body, bicolor, lightly haired and tufted at tip (hairs 6–10 mm). Hind feet white, heels dusky. **SIMILAR SPECIES:** Northern Rock Mouse (*P. nasutus*) is slightly larger and usually has a longer tail, but can be difficult to distinguish (ranges approach but may not overlap in N.M.). Brush Mouse (*P. boylii*) is slightly smaller. Piñon Mouse (*P. truei*) is very similar but usually has longer ears and a relatively shorter tail in New Mexico. **HABITS:** Probably similar to Piñon Mouse. **HABITAT:** Rocky areas with a broad range of vegetation types, including piñon-juniper, oak forest, grasslands, and coniferous forest. Elevation 6,000–10,000 ft. (1,800–3,100 m). **RANGE:**

PIÑON MOUSE
Peromyscus truei

OSGOOD'S MOUSE
Peromyscus gratus

Sw. N.M. to s. Mexico. **STATUS:** Uncommon in New Mexico. **NOTE:** Recently separated from Piñon Mouse (*P. truei*) based on genetic differences.

NORTHERN ROCK MOUSE *Peromyscus nasutus* PL. 21

Head and body 3⅞ in. (90–107 mm); tail 4¼ in. (87–125 mm); hind foot ⅞ in. (23–25 mm); ear ⅞ in. (22–26 mm); wt. 1 oz. (23–32 g). Back *dark gray* or gray-brown; sides yellow-brown, usually without a pronounced lateral line; belly pale gray or white. *Ears large. Tail long,* bicolor, well haired, with a terminal tuft (hairs 6–8 mm at tip). Hind feet white, heels dusky. **SIMILAR SPECIES:** Brush Mouse (*P. boylii*) is slightly smaller (hind foot 22 mm or less). Piñon Mouse (*P. truei*) has ears longer than hind foot and a proportionally shorter tail. **HABITS:** Semi-arboreal; climbs well, using its long tail for balance. This mouse can hear frequencies to 100 kHz and may use ultrasonics when navigating through rocky terrain at night. Eats acorns, nuts, juniper berries, and plant material. Litters of 4–6 are born from spring to fall. **HABITAT:** Mainly at higher elevations (7,000 ft. [2,150 m] or more) in rocky outcrops and talus slopes in the piñon-oak-juniper zone. Also found on lava flows in New Mexico. **RANGE:** Colo., N.M., w. Ariz., and w. Tex. into n. Mexico. **STATUS:** Uncommon to rare and local. **NOTE:** Formerly considered a subspecies of the Rock Mouse (*P. difficilis*).

FLORIDA MOUSE *Podomys floridanus* PL. 20
Gopher Mouse

Head and body 4 in. (94–113 mm); tail 3½ in. (78–100 mm); hind foot 1 in. (24–28 mm); ear ⅞ in. (22–25 mm); wt. 1½ oz. (27–45 g). Back *pale gray-brown,* grading to pale or bright orange on sides; belly white. Ears large. *Tail nearly naked,* faintly bicolor. Feet white, *5 small pads on soles of hind foot.* **SIMILAR SPECIES:** Eastern deer mice are smaller and usually darker in color and have 6 prominent

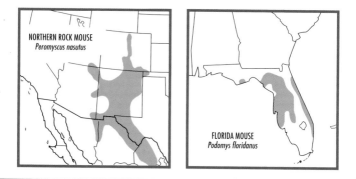

pads on the soles of the hind foot. **HABITS:** More fossorial than deer mice, constructing small tunnels within Gopher Tortoise burrows. Feeds on acorns, insects, seeds, fruit, and other plant material. Litters of 1–5 may be born year-round. **HABITAT:** Dry upland areas with sandy soils dominated by scrub oaks, slash pine, or longleaf pine. **RANGE:** Fla. **STATUS:** Species of special concern (Florida Fish and Wildlife Cons. Comm.). Suffers from habitat loss in its limited range.

RASSHOPPER MICE: *Onychomys*

Grasshopper mice are small, short-tailed rodents that occur in deserts and other dry habitats. These mice are more carnivorous than other small rodents and eat a variety of insects and even other mice. They announce their territory by loud calls, often given from a standing position.

ORTHERN GRASSHOPPER MOUSE   Pl. 22, Skull Pl. 3
nychomys leucogaster

Head and body 4¼ in. (97–122 mm); tail 1½ in. (30–60 mm); hind foot ⅞ in. (22–24 mm); ear ⅝ in. (15–19 mm); wt. 1½ oz. (26–50 g). Largest grasshopper mouse. Back sandy brown, pale gray-brown, bright orange, gray, or very dark gray. In brown forms, color is brighter on rump than shoulder. Belly white or cream. Fur silky. Ears medium sized, usually with a white tuft of fur at base of leading edge. *Tail short, less than half head and body length;* brown above, white below and at tip (in blackish forms, tail is black above to tip). **SIMILAR SPECIES:** Other grasshopper mice are smaller with proportionally longer tails (more than half head and body length). **SOUNDS:** Adults of both sexes stand on hind legs and give a loud,

Northern Grasshopper Mouse with prey. The mouse has bitten off parts of the hind legs of the grasshopper to immobilize it.

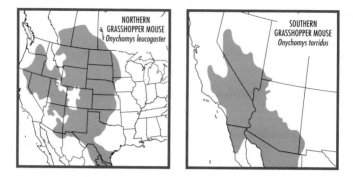

single-note whistle. **HABITS:** Nocturnal; most active on dark moonless nights. As the name suggests, this mouse eats grasshoppers and other insects and is much more carnivorous than most mice, taking large scorpions and beetles and some small vertebrates. The diet also includes seeds and plant material. Travels across open desert floor when hunting and requires sand patches for dust-bathing. Has several burrows within a large territory: a nest burrow, cache burrows for seeds, retreat burrows for escape, defecation burrows, and signpost burrows for scent-marking territorial boundaries. Solitary except when breeding; adults communicate by whistling. Breeds Feb.–Aug.; litter size is 1–6. Parental care is more developed than in other small rodents, and the father assists in raising pups. **HABITAT:** Deserts, grasslands, prairies, and shrub steppe. Favors areas with rather sparse vegetation and sandy soils. **RANGE:** Much of w. North America from Sask. and s. Alta. to ne. Calif., Ariz., and w. Tex.; also n. and ne. Mexico. **STATUS:** Fairly common and widespread.

SOUTHERN GRASSHOPPER MOUSE   PL. 22
Onychomys torridus

Head and body 3½ in. (73–98 mm); tail 2 in. (44–60 mm); hind foot ¾ in. (18–23 mm); ear ⅝ in. (16–18 mm); wt. 1 oz. (16–40 g). Back usually *sandy brown,* can be orange-brown, gray, or dark gray-brown. Belly white or cream. Ears medium sized, with a tuft of brown or white fur at base of leading edge. *Tail more than half head and body length;* brown above, white below and at tip. White tip of tail averages 11 mm. **SIMILAR SPECIES:** See Northern and Mearns's Grasshopper Mice. **HABITS:** Similar to Northern Grasshopper Mouse in habits and calls. Breeds mainly May–July; litter size is 1–5. **HABITAT:** Low desert with scattered shrubs such as creosote bush and mesquite. **RANGE:** S. Calif. and w. Nev. to Ariz; also nw. Mexico. **STATUS:** Fairly common.

Onychomys arenicola

Head and body 3½ in. (82–97 mm); tail 2 in. (35–57 mm); hind foot ¾ in. (20–22 mm); ear ⅝ in. (14–16 mm); wt. 1 oz. (20–35 g). Upperparts dull brown, sandy brown, or pinkish gray; belly white or cream. Fur on back *slightly grizzled.* Ears rather small with a prominent *white tuft of fur at base* of leading edge. Tail slightly more than half head and body length; brown above, white below and at tip. White tip of tail averages 8 mm. **SIMILAR SPECIES:** Northern Grasshopper Mouse (*O. leucogaster*) is larger with a proportionally shorter tail. Southern Grasshopper Mouse (*O. torridus*) is very difficult to distinguish — it is slightly larger and sometimes has brown (not white) tufts of fur at the base of ears (ranges overlap in sw. New Mexico and possibly se. Arizona). **HABITS:** Similar to Northern Grasshopper Mouse in habits and calls. Breeds April–Aug.; litter size is 2–7. **HABITAT:** Low desert with scattered shrubs such as creosote bush, tarbush, and snakeweed, on gravelly or rocky soils. Uncommon in mesquite flats. Mostly between 4,300–5,200 ft. (1,300–1,600 m). **RANGE:** W. Tex., s. N.M., and se. Ariz. into n. Mexico. **STATUS:** Fairly common. **NOTE:** Although this grasshopper mouse is externally most similar to the Southern Grasshopper Mouse (*O. torridus*), it is genetically more closely related to the Northern (*O. leucogaster*).

MEARNS'S
GRASSHOPPER MOUSE
Onychomys arenicola

HARVEST MICE: *Reithrodontomys*

Very small mice with long narrow tails. Upper incisors have a central vertical groove down the front of each tooth. Other small mice (*Baiomys, Mus, Peromyscus*) have ungrooved upper incisors, although the unrelated jumping mice and pocket mice also have grooved incisors. Harvest mice are nocturnal. Most tropical harvest mice produce a high, 2-note call that can be heard, usually soon after dusk, in the wild. Among our more northerly species, only two are known to call.

PLAINS HARVEST MOUSE
PL. 19
Reithrodontomys montanus

Head and body 2⅝ in. (58–77 mm); tail 2¼ in. (48–64 mm); hind foot ⅝ in. (15–16 mm); ear ½ in. (12–15 mm); wt. ¼ oz. (7–9 g). Small. *Narrow dark mid-dorsal stripe*; sides brownish buff; belly white. Ears dark, lined with orange hair. *Whiskers fine and short, not extending to shoulder.* Tail bicolor, *mostly white with narrow dark stripe on upper side*; clothed in short fur. Feet whitish. **SIMILAR SPECIES:** This is the only harvest mouse with a *narrow* dark stripe on back and tail. Western Harvest Mouse (*R. megalotis*) has long dark whiskers that extend to shoulder and a slightly longer tail. Eastern Harvest Mouse (*R. humulis*), usually separable by range, is smaller and more uniformly colored. Fulvous Harvest Mouse (*R. fulvescens*) has a much longer tail. **SOUNDS:** Not reported for this species. **HABITS:** Feeds on flowers and seeds of weeds and grasses, also eats grasshoppers and other insects. Makes a ball-shaped nest on or just above the ground. Breeds year-round in southern part of range, spring to fall in north. Litter size is 1–9. **HABITAT:** Prairies, grasslands, and cultivated fields. Favors open country with short grasses. **RANGE:** Sw. S.D. and se. Mont. to e. Tex., Ariz., and n. Mexico. **STATUS:** Locally common.

EASTERN HARVEST MOUSE
PL. 19
Reithrodontomys humulis

Head and body 2½ in. (60–68 mm); tail 2⅛ in. (47–61 mm); hind foot ⅝ in. (14–6 mm); ear ½ in. (11–12 mm); wt. ¼ oz. (6–12 g). *Very small.* Back dark brown, not grizzled, often with a reddish wash; sides paler; belly grayish white. Ears blackish. Tail nar-

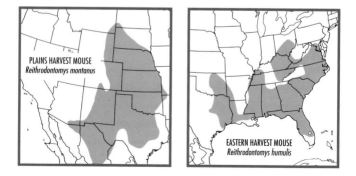

PLAINS HARVEST MOUSE
Reithrodontomys montanus

EASTERN HARVEST MOUSE
Reithrodontomys humulis

row, almost naked, somewhat bicolor; *shorter than head and body* (about 80 percent of body length). Feet pale gray or white. **SIMILAR SPECIES:** Other harvest mice are larger and usually have proportionally longer tails. Fulvous Harvest Mouse (*R. fulvescens*) is orangish with a much longer tail. See Plains Harvest Mouse (*R. montanus*). Northern Pygmy Mouse (*Baiomys*) lacks grooved upper incisors and has a shorter tail. **SOUNDS:** Calling has not been documented in this mouse. **HABITS:** Feeds on small seeds of grasses and weeds, also moth larvae and insects. Makes a ball-shaped nest of grass and plant fibers in low vegetation. Gathers and stores seeds in nest. Young are born late spring to fall, or year-round in Florida. Litter size is 2–7. **HABITAT:** Oldfields, waste ground, and ditches or other wet areas, also broom sedge and brier patches. Seldom found in forests. **RANGE:** Se. U.S. from Va. and s. Ohio to Fla. and e. Tex. **STATUS:** Uncommon to rare.

ESTERN HARVEST MOUSE Pl. 19, Skull Pl. 3
ithrodontomys megalotis

Head and body 2⅝ in. (59–77 mm); tail 3 in. (71–79 mm); hind foot ⅝ in. (16–18 mm); ear ⅝ in. (15–16 mm); wt. ⅜ oz. (6–11 g). Small. Upper back *dark brown with a grizzle of black hairs* (*broad dark stripe*); sides paler, often orange-brown; belly whitish. Ears lined with orange hair. Tail bicolor, rather well haired (scales obscured by fur); equal to or slightly longer than body length. Feet white. **SIMILAR SPECIES:** Plains Harvest Mouse (*R. montanus*) is very similar but has a *narrow* dark stripe on upper back and top of tail (white sides of tail visible when viewed from above) and is slightly smaller. Fulvous and Salt-marsh Harvest Mice (*R. fulvescens* and *R. raviventris*) are larger with proportionally longer tails that appear nearly naked. **SOUNDS:** Makes a high trilling call, loudest midtrill and tapering at each end. **HABITS:** Feeds on small seeds, moth

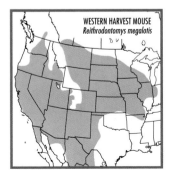

WESTERN HARVEST MOUSE
Reithrodontomys megalotis

larvae, beetles, and other insects. Makes a ball-shaped nest of plant fibers lined with plant down. Nests are usually well concealed on the ground or low in vegetation. Breeds year-round in warmer regions, mainly spring and fall in cool climates. Litter size is 1–9, usually 3–4. **HABITAT:** Prefers wet meadows and overgrown fields; also found in dry areas and clearings in forests. **RANGE:** W. U.S. and sw. Canada east to Ind. and south to cen. Mexico. **STATUS:** Common and widespread. May be locally abundant.

SALT-MARSH HARVEST MOUSE Pl. 19
Reithrodontomys raviventris

Head and body 2¾ in. (56–84 mm); tail 3¼ in. (68–91 mm); hind foot ¾ in. (17–21 mm); ear ⅝ in. (13–16 mm); wt. ⅜ oz. (9–12 g). Relatively large and dark. Back blackish on midline, grading to orange-brown on sides. Belly whitish (*R. r. halicoetes*) or orange (*R. r. raviventris*). Ears blackish, lined with orange hairs. *Tail longer than head and body,* somewhat bicolor but not pure white below; narrow and *nearly naked* (scales visible). Feet white or pale cream. **SIMILAR SPECIES:** Western Harvest Mouse (*R. megalotis*) has a shorter, thicker tail that is clothed in short fur concealing scales. Deer mice are larger with no groove on upper incisors. **SOUNDS:** Calls have not been reported for this species. **HABITS:** Climbs well among marsh vegetation. Adapted to a wet environment, this mouse is a buoyant and strong swimmer; its fur stays dry for a time in water. Moves to upper zone of marsh as tide rises. Can drink salty water. When trapped, this species is docile and seeks cover, unlike the more aggressive Western Harvest Mouse. Makes a ball-shaped nest on the ground or in low vegetation. Sometimes builds a roof over a bird's nest. Young are born from spring to fall; breeds 2–3 times per year. Litter size is 1–7, usually 3–4. **HABITAT:** Middle and upper zone of salt marshes; favors pickleweed (*Salicornia*)

SALT-MARSH HARVEST MOUSE
Reithrodontomys raviventris

and thick damp grass. **RANGE:** San Francisco Bay area, Calif. **STATUS:** Endangered (USFWS, Calif. Dept. of Fish and Game). Loss of habitat and habitat degradation (filling, subsidence, and diking) are primary causes of decline. Needs sufficient cover in upper tidal zone during high tide to avoid predators.

ULVOUS HARVEST MOUSE

ithrodontomys fulvescens

PL. 19

Head and body 2¾ in. (57–82 mm); tail 3⅞ in. (84–118 mm); hind foot ¾ in. (17–20 mm); ear ½ in. (12–16 mm); wt. ½ oz. (9–17 g). Relatively large and long-tailed. *Back rusty brown* peppered with black; *sides orange;* belly white or buff. Ears lined with orange hair. *Tail long and narrow, naked looking,* somewhat bicolor. Feet white. **SIMILAR SPECIES:** Other harvest mice in its range have shorter tails. Deer mice (*Peromyscus*) and Golden Mouse (*Ochrotomys*) have ungrooved upper incisors and thicker tails. **SOUNDS:** Makes a high-pitched, 2-note call, detectable at close range in the wild. **HABITS:** A good climber; more likely to be trapped in a vine tangle or shrub than on the ground. Eats mostly invertebrates in spring and summer, seeds in fall and winter. Constructs baseball-sized nests of shredded plant material in vegetation, up to 3 ft. (1 m) above the ground. Two adults often share a nest and may travel together. Breeds in spring and fall; litter size is 2–4. **HABITAT:** Oldfields, thickets, and mixed brushy grassland. **RANGE:** Mo. to La. and s. Ariz., south through Mexico to Honduras. **STATUS:** Locally common to abundant.

OLDEN MOUSE   *Ochrotomys nuttalli*   PL. 20, Skull Pl. 3

Head and body 3 in. (66–89 mm); tail 3 in. (67–85 mm); hind foot ¾ in. (17–19 mm); ear ⅝ in. (15–16 mm); wt. ¾ oz. (17–27 g). *Upperparts rich orange-brown,* sides paler orange, belly *creamy*

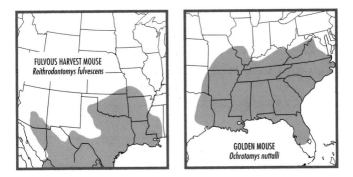

FULVOUS HARVEST MOUSE
Reithrodontomys fulvescens

GOLDEN MOUSE
Ochrotomys nuttalli

The beautiful Golden Mouse is a denizen of the Southeast. Largely arboreal in habits, it has a semi-prehensile tail and rather short, stocky feet.

yellow. Tail bicolor, nearly naked, tip prehensile. Young are reddish at birth. **SIMILAR SPECIES:** White-footed and American Deer Mice (*Peromyscus leucopus* and *P. maniculatus*) can be orange-brown (in older adults) but are very seldom bright orange, and they have white (not yellowish) underparts. **HABITS:** Semi-arboreal; climbs among vines and dense thickets using its semi-prehensile tail for balance. Feeds on seeds, nuts, berries, and invertebrates. Carries its food to a nest or feeding platform well above the ground. Makes globular nests of coarsely shredded vegetation lined with finer material. In addition to baseball-sized nests used by a single adult, sometimes makes larger nests that are occupied by a group of 8 or more. Breeds from early spring to fall; litter size is 2–5. Several litters may be born each year, but breeding activity is reduced in midsummer. **HABITAT:** Forested areas with dense tangles of briars, vines, and brush. Most common in floodplains but also found in upland pine woods. **RANGE:** Se. U.S. to e. Tex., Mo., and W. Va. **STATUS:** Locally common.

NORTHERN PYGMY MOUSE   Pl. 19, Skull Pl. 3
Baiomys taylori

Head and body 2½ in. (57–77 mm); tail 1¾ in. (36–54 mm); hind foot ⅝ in. (13–15 mm); ear ⅜ in. (10–12 mm); wt. ⅜ oz. (8–11 g). *Tiny.* Back dark gray-brown, sides gray, belly grayish white; not clearly demarcated from sides. Eyes small, ears medium sized, *rounded. Tail short,* nearly naked, slightly bicolor. Upper incisors not grooved. **SIMILAR SPECIES:** Other small mice have longer tails. Harvest mice have grooved upper incisors. **SOUNDS:** Makes a variety of high-pitched trills and twitters. **HABITS:** Mainly nocturnal, but sometimes active by day. Makes tiny runways through grass from nest to feeding area. Eats mostly seeds, fruit, and green veg-

The Northern Pygmy Mouse, our smallest rodent, is similar to the House Mouse but has a shorter tail, broader ears, and a whitish belly.

etation. Constructs ball-shaped nests with 1–2 openings. Nests are located under logs or fallen vegetation or in small burrows. Breeds year-round; litter size is 1–5. **HABITAT:** Grassy areas with thick ground cover: roadsides, fields, prairies, desert grasslands, and open woodlands. **RANGE:** S. Okla. and Tex.; se. Ariz. and sw. N.M.; also n. Mexico. **STATUS:** Uncommon to locally common.

NORTHERN PYGMY MOUSE
Baiomys taylori

WOODRATS: *Neotoma*

Large attractive rats that look like overgrown deer mice. Unlike house rats, they have a well-haired, bicolor tail, and most species have white tops of feet. These rats are mainly nocturnal but may be active before dark on overcast days. Woodrats make large houses of sticks and other material and often haul a variety of junk to decorate their nest, hence the vernacular "pack rats." Woodrats are solitary and territorial.

EASTERN WOODRAT *Neotoma floridana* Pl. 23
Head and body 9 in. (170–285 mm); tail 6¼ in. (135–190 mm); hind foot 1½ in. (36–42 mm); ear 1 in. (24–28 mm); wt. 10 oz. (200–375 g). Back *gray-brown*, dark brown, or sandy brown; sides washed with buff; belly grayish white or cream white. Hairs white to base on throat, gray at base on neck and belly. Ears large, whiskers long

and thick. Tops of feet white. *Tail moderately haired* (some scales usually visible), clearly bicolor in northern populations, faintly bicolor in southern populations. **SIMILAR SPECIES:** Allegheny Woodrat (*N. magister*) is very similar, distinguished by skull and biochemical differences. Ranges do not overlap. Southern Plains Woodrat (*N. micropus*) can be similar (and occasionally hybridizes) but is steely gray and has neck and chest pure white to base of hairs. See house rats (*Rattus* spp.). **SOUNDS:** Drums hind feet in alarm; occasionally chatters by grating teeth. **HABITS:** Active year-round, but may stay in its house in bad weather. Climbs well and is semi-arboreal. Eats leaves, fruit, berries, fungi, nuts, and seeds. Relies heavily on acorns in some areas. As with other woodrats, makes large houses of sticks and other materials. Activity is centered around the house. In the fall, stores food in the top of the house for winter use. Houses are typically about 5 ft. (1.5 m) wide and 3 ft. (1 m) high and may be placed under rocks or at the base of trees. In Alabama, builds large nests on tree branches. In e. Texas, uses underground burrows and may not construct a house. Breeds year-round in Georgia and Florida, from spring to fall farther north. Litter size is 1–7, usually 2–4; females may have 2–3 litters per year. **HABITAT:** Variable; includes bluffs and rocky areas (mainly in the Great Plains), swamps and hammocks, forested uplands, and dry scrub pine. **RANGE:** Neb. and e. Colo. to s. N.C. and south to e. Tex. and Fla. Isolated populations on Key Largo, Fla., and in n. Neb. **STATUS:** Generally common and widespread. Key Largo Woodrat (*N. f. smalli*) is endangered (USFWS).

ALLEGHENY WOODRAT   *Neotoma magister*

Head and body 8¾ in. (200–245 mm); tail 6½ in. (141–192 mm); hind foot 1⅝ in. (38–46 mm); ear 1 in. (25–28 mm); wt. 12 oz. (217–455 g). Back *dark brown;* sides brown or washed with buff; belly

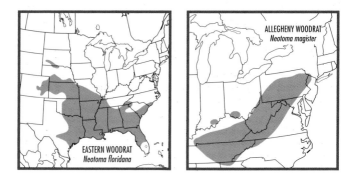

EASTERN WOODRAT
Neotoma floridana

ALLEGHENY WOODRAT
Neotoma magister

SOUTHERN PLAINS WOODRAT
Neotoma micropus

whitish, hairs white to base on throat, gray at base on neck and belly. Midline of belly sometimes stained brown. Ears large, whiskers long and thick. Tops of feet white. *Tail moderately haired, dark brown above, white below.* **SIMILAR SPECIES:** See Eastern Woodrat (*N. floridana*) also house rats (*Rattus* spp.). **SOUNDS:** Similar to Eastern Woodrat. **HABITS:** Unlike most other woodrats, does not make large houses but builds a large, cup-shaped nest on a rock ledge or under boulders. Gathers debris such as sticks, bones, and trash around the openings to den sites and may make separate piles for food storage (middens). Litter size is 1–4; females may have 3–4 litters per year. **HABITAT:** Closely associated with rocky habitats such as cliffs, rockslides, and caves, often near red cedar. **RANGE:** Appalachian Mts. from Pa. and ne. N.J. to n. Ala. and Tenn. **STATUS:** Declining in northern part of range, no longer found in New York. **NOTE:** Formerly considered to be a subspecies of Eastern Woodrat (*N. floridana*).

SOUTHERN PLAINS WOODRAT *Neotoma micropus* **PL. 23**

Head and body 8½ in. (180–245 mm); tail 6 in. (130–175 mm); hind foot 1⅝ in. (36–45 mm); ear 1 in. (25–29 mm); wt. 10 oz. (180–317 g). Large. *Back and sides steely gray* or blue-gray; belly white; *hairs white to base on throat, neck, and chest,* gray at base on belly. *Tail shorter than head and body,* bicolor, moderately haired. **SIMILAR SPECIES:** White-throated Woodrat (*N. albigula*) is brown. See Eastern Woodrat (*N. floridana*). **SOUNDS:** Drums hind feet in alarm. **HABITS:** Eats cactus leaves and fruit, mesquite beans, acorns, and other plant material and can obtain sufficient water from its food. Makes a house under a prickly pear cactus or shrub (seldom uses rocks for shelter) and probably uses the same house for life. Den has 2–5 entrances, each with well-worn trails that radiate out to feeding areas. Litter size is 2–3. Breeding peaks in spring in the northern part of the range, in spring and fall in the southern part. **HABITAT:** Dry grasslands with cactus, mesquite, and other shrubs. Mainly found in flat plains, occasionally on rocky hillsides. **RANGE:** Se. Colo., sw. Kans., N.M., Tex., and ne. Mexico. **STATUS:** Common.

WESTERN WHITE-THROATED WOODRAT *Neotoma albigula*

Pl. 23, Skull Pl. 4

Head and body 7 in. (144–210 mm); tail 6¼ in. (120–193 mm); hind foot 1⅜ in. (31–37 mm); ear 1⅛ in. (25–32 mm); wt. 7 oz. (127–280 g). Back yellow-gray, sides ocher; *throat, chin, and chest pure white to base of hairs,* belly usually white with gray at base of hairs; patch of pure white fur between hind legs. Tail clearly bicolor, well furred with short fur. Smaller-bodied with larger ears in low desert; larger with thick fur and relatively small ears at high elevations. **SIMILAR SPECIES:** Desert and Mexican Woodrats (*N. lepida* and *N. mexicana*) can be very similar but have fur on throat and chest gray at base. See Stephens's and Bushy-tailed Woodrats (*N. stephensi* and *N. cinerea*). **SOUNDS:** Drums hind feet in alarm (e.g., in response to snakes) and before mating. **HABITS:** Mainly nocturnal, but sometimes seen loitering near its house by day in overcast weather. Eats mostly cacti, also juniper leaves and berries, yucca, and other green plant material. Usually builds a large house under a prickly pear cactus, yucca, or cholla, but may den in a rock crevice, cramming the opening with twigs and refuse. Transports and climbs jumping cholla without injury and often uses this cactus in house construction. Breeds in early spring and summer in California, year-round in Arizona. Litter size is 2–3; females may have 2 litters or more per year. **HABITAT:** Low to high deserts with abundant succulents, also piñon-juniper zone. Favors moderately rocky

The Western White-throated Woodrat, with its white belly and bicolored tail, looks like an overgrown White-footed Mouse. It is the same size as a house rat.

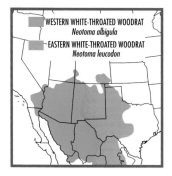

WESTERN WHITE-THROATED WOODRAT
Neotoma albigula

EASTERN WHITE-THROATED WOODRAT
Neotoma leucodon

slopes. Found from near sea level to 8,200 ft. (2,500 m). **RANGE:** Sw. Colo. and s. Utah to s. Calif. and w. N.M., also nw. Mexico. **STATUS:** Very common.

ASTERN WHITE-THROATED WOODRAT
eotoma leucodon

Recent studies of mitochondrial DNA resulted in the recognition of 2 species of White-throated Woodrats, separated by the Rio Grande in New Mexico and Texas. No differences in external morphology have been reported, nor have any differences in habitat or habits of the 2 species been addressed. This species is usually similar in color to *N. albigula,* but it is blackish above where it occurs on lava rock in Texas and New Mexico. See Western White-throated Woodrat for comparisons with other woodrats. **RANGE:** Se. Colo., w. Tex., and e. N.M. west to Rio Grande, also n. Mexico.

ESERT WOODRAT   *Neotoma lepida*   PL. 23

Head and body 6½ in. (146–190 mm); tail 5½ in. (100–180 mm); hind foot 1⅛ in. (28–33 mm); ear 1⅛ in. (28–32 mm); wt. 5 oz. (130–160 g). Back gray or gray-brown; sides pale orange or buff; belly off-white. *Throat hairs gray at base,* patches of pure white fur between forelegs and between hind legs. *Ears large,* protrude well above crown. Tail well haired with short fur, *clearly bicolor.* Tops of hind feet white. **GEOGRAPHIC VARIATION:** Darker and larger in coastal California. **SIMILAR SPECIES:** White-throated Woodrat (*N. albigula*) has a pure white throat and chest. Arizona Woodrat (*N. devia*) separated mainly by range. Dusky-footed Woodrat (*N. fuscipes*) has dark hind feet and an all-dark tail. **SOUNDS:** Drums with hind feet in alarm. **HABITS:** As with other desert-dwelling woodrats, this species requires large amounts of water, which it obtains from fleshy plants such as yucca and prickly pear cactus. It usually makes a

stick house under one of these food plants, or may den among rocks. House materials include cacti, sticks, bones, and a variety of trash. Houses provide insulation against heat as well as protection from predators. Breeds in late winter or spring. Females have 1–2 litters per year, with 2–4 young per litter. **HABITAT:** Deserts and coastal sage scrub. Favors areas with rocky outcrops and plentiful succulents. Near sea level to at least 7,000 ft. (2,300 m). **RANGE:** Se. Wash., sw. Idaho, and Utah to Nev., Calif., and Baja Calif. **STATUS:** Common. **NOTE:** The subspecies *N. l. intermedia,* from coastal California, may be a distinct species.

ARIZONA WOODRAT   *Neotoma devia*

Head and body 6½ in. (145–190 mm); tail 5¼ in. (111–150 mm); hind foot 1⅛ in. (27–33 mm); ear 1⅛ in. (27–32 mm); wt. 4 oz. (100–132 g). Very similar to Desert Woodrat but *slightly smaller* and usually paler in color (although color varies with color of rocks). **SIMILAR SPECIES:** See Desert Woodrat (*N. lepida*). **SOUNDS:** Drums hind feet in alarm. **HABITS:** Makes houses in rock piles or under cacti. Houses are smaller and have fewer cacti around the edges than houses of White-throated Woodrats in the same habitat. Litter size is 1–4; young may be born year-round, although mostly breeds Nov.–July. **HABITAT:** Low and high deserts, in a variety of habitats, often near rock piles and canyons. Near sea level to 7,100 ft. (2,150 m). **RANGE:** W. Colo., Utah, and w. Ariz. to n. Sonora, Mexico. **STATUS:** Common. **NOTE:** Previously considered to be a subspecies of Desert Woodrat. The two are genetically distinct.

STEPHENS'S WOODRAT   *Neotoma stephensi*   PL. 23

Head and body 6½ in. (132–203 mm); tail 5 in. (113–143 mm); hind foot 1¼ in. (31–34 mm); ear 1 in. (21–26 mm); wt. 6 oz. (111–217 g). Fairly *small.* Upperparts usually buffy orange with a dark grizzle (can be dark gray on dark substrates); belly pale orange or cream. Fur on throat usually gray at base, sometimes white to the base. Fur thick and soft. Tail bicolor, *thickly haired, almost bushy, does not appear to taper at tip.* **SIMILAR SPECIES:** Bushy-tailed Woodrat (*N. cinerea*) is much larger (hind foot over 37 mm); other woodrats in its range (*N. lepida, N. mexicana,* and *N. albigula*) have shorter hair on the tail so that the tail appears tapered at tip. **SOUNDS:** Drums hind feet in alarm and may chatter teeth. **HABITS:** Eats mainly juniper and appears to be unaffected by the chemical compounds that make this plant indigestible to most mammals. Probably obtains most of its water from juniper leaves and fruit. Nests are less conspicuous than in most other woodrats and are usually located in rock piles or among the roots of junipers. Occasionally nests above the ground in juniper or yellow pine. Breeds in early spring and summer; females have 1–5 litters per year but normally have only 1 young per litter, rarely twins. **HABITAT:** Rocky areas in the piñon-juniper zone, at 5,000–7,000 ft. (1,650–2,750 m). **RANGE:** Extreme s. Utah, Ariz., and w. N.M. **STATUS:** Locally common in a limited range.

MEXICAN WOODRAT *Neotoma mexicana*   Pl. 23

Head and body 7 in. (147–204 mm); tail 5½ in. (123–157 mm); hind foot 1⅜ in. (32–38 mm); ear ⅞ in. (22–26 mm); wt. 5 oz. (112–194 g). *Relatively small.* Back yellow-gray grizzled with black; sides yellowish or orange; belly white, *fur on throat gray at base* (except for a small patch on chin that is white to base). Tail bicolor, well haired with short fur. **SIMILAR SPECIES:** White-throated Woodrat (*N. albigula*) is usually larger and has fur on throat and chest white to base of hairs. Arizona Woodrat (*N. devia*) has larger ears and shorter hind feet (and usually occurs at lower elevations). Stephens's and Bushy-tailed Woodrats (*N. stephensi* and *N. cinerea*)

MEXICAN WOODRAT
Neotoma mexicana

have longer hair on the tail. **SOUNDS:** Drums hind feet in alarm.
HABITS: Eats a variety of green plant material including some conifers, also seeds, berries, and acorns. Sometimes stores food at the
den. This woodrat seldom makes a large stick house but usually
constructs its nest in a rock crevice. It may also use a hollow tree
or abandoned cabin as a nest site. It drags sticks and other rubbish
to the nest entrance and also leaves large piles of droppings on
nearby ledges. Northern populations breed March–May, in Arizona breeding may continue until Sept. Females have 1–2 litters
per year, with 1–4 young per litter. **HABITAT:** Cliffs, talus slopes, and
rocky outcrops mostly in montane coniferous forest, sometimes in
scrub oak and piñon-juniper woods. Usually found at 5,000–9,500
ft. (1,650–2,750 m) in the U.S. **RANGE:** Colo. and Utah to Ariz. and w.
Tex. Also through Mexico and Central America to w. Honduras.
STATUS: Common.

DUSKY-FOOTED WOODRAT *Neotoma fuscipes* Pl. 23

Head and body 8¼ in. (180–240 mm); tail 7¾ in. (148–240 mm);
hind foot 1½ in. (34–48 mm); ear 1 in. (24–36 mm); wt. 11 oz. (200–
430 g). *Large and dark.* Back dark brown, sides brown or orange-
brown, belly white or buff. Throat usually gray at base of hair, but
patch of fur on chest usually white to base and much of throat and
belly pure white in some animals. *Tail all-dark or very faintly
bicolor, lightly haired* (scales visible). *Tops of hind feet brown near
ankles.* **SIMILAR SPECIES:** Other woodrats in its range have distinctly
bicolor tails and white tops of hind feet. **SOUNDS:** Rattles tip of tail
when disturbed in its house. May chatter teeth when fighting.
HABITS: Eats foliage of live oak and other plants as well as fruit,
seeds, acorns, and fungi. Stores food in the house. Makes large
houses, about 3 ft. (1 m) high, 3–7 ft. (1–2 m) wide, usually placed
on the ground around the trunks of trees or in dense brush. May

DUSKY-FOOTED WOODRAT
Neotoma fuscipes
BIG-EARED WOODRAT
Neotoma macrotis

construct a nest high above the ground in the crotch of a tree. Each rat usually has two houses in its home range. Generations of these woodrats use the same house, increasing the size of the structure and accumulating large mounds of droppings around the periphery. Several other small mammals, amphibians, and reptiles may use parts of the house for refuge. Breeds in spring or summer and usually has 1 litter of 1–4 young per year. **HABITAT:** Dense chaparral, mixed deciduous forest with thick understory, coniferous forest, and coastal sage scrub. **RANGE:** W. Ore. to sw. Calif. **STATUS:** Riparian Woodrat (*N. f. riparia*) is endangered (USFWS). Elsewhere locally common. Disappears if underbrush is cleared or burned.

G-EARED WOODRAT   *Neotoma macrotis*

This species was recently separated from Dusky-footed Woodrat based on skull morphology, molecular characters, and differences in the penis. The penis in *N. macrotis* is "flowerlike" and about 2 mm long, in *N. fuscipes* it is oblong and about 5 mm long. The name suggests that this species should have larger ears than the Dusky-footed Woodrat, and this may be true, but external measurements of the two species overlap and cannot be used to separate them reliably in the field. Information in the account for *N. fuscipes* pertains to both species. **RANGE:** S. and e. Calif. south to n. Baja Calif.

JSHY-TAILED WOODRAT   *Neotoma cinerea*   **Pl. 23**

Head and body 9 in. (175–265 mm); tail 7 in. (150–204 mm); hind foot 1⅞ in. (39–53 mm); ear 1¼ in. (30–36 mm); wt. 14 oz. (200–585 g). *Very large*; males are larger than females. Back usually yellow-gray (can be gray or blackish) grizzled with black; sides orange, yellow-brown, or gray; belly whitish, throat white to base of

BUSHY-TAILED WOODRAT
Neotoma cinerea

hairs. *Tail bushy,* gray to black above, white below. Tops of feet white, soles furred to base of toes. **GEOGRAPHIC VARIATION:** Large, with a very thick, bushy tail in North and on high mountains; upperparts usually dark gray or black in Pacific Northwest; smaller, less bushy-tailed and usually buff or orange-brown farther south. **SIMILAR SPECIES:** See Stephens's Woodrat. Other woodrats do not have bushy tails. **SOUNDS:** Drums hind feet in alarm. **HABITS:** This large woodrat is adapted for cool climates, using its bushy tail as a wrap in cold weather; it cannot survive high temperatures. Active year-round. In fall, collects plants for winter storage at the den. Usually makes nests among rocks or in caves or mine tunnels; may use an abandoned building. Seldom constructs an elaborate house but will accumulate mounds of sticks and other rubbish around the nest site. Piles of droppings, food, and other debris may be preserved by dried urine if conditions are suitable. In the Southwest some middens date back 10,000–40,000 years, providing an important fossil record. Solitary and territorial; marks its territory with urine. In arid areas the urine dries to form white streaks on the tops of rocks. Breeds in spring and summer; females have 2–3 litters per year with 2–5 young per litter. **HABITAT:** Rocky outcrops, talus slopes, caves, and cliffs, in canyons and mountainous areas. Sea level to 14,000 ft. (4,300 m). **RANGE:** S. Yukon and sw. N.W.T. to w. N.D., n. N.M., and n. Calif. **STATUS:** Common.

RICE RATS: *Oryzomys*

Mostly tropical in distribution, only 2 species of rice rats occur in the U.S. These rats have long narrow feet with the outer toes much shorter than inner toes. They can be mistaken for house rats, but they have narrower, bicolor, nearly hairless tails. Our species are semiaquatic and seldom found far from water.

COUES'S RICE RAT *Oryzomys couesi* **Pl. 24**
Head and body 5½ in. (100–164 mm); tail 5½ in. (120–160 mm); hind foot 1¼ in. (27–33 mm); ear ⅝ in. (13–18 mm); wt. 2½ oz. (43–82 g). Back grizzled *warm brown,* sides yellow-brown, *belly pale orange or buff.* Ears relatively small, thickly haired. *Tail long, nearly naked and bicolor,* brown above, white below. Tops of feet white. *Hind feet long and narrow,* outer toes much shorter than inner toes. **SIMILAR SPECIES:** Marsh Rice Rat usually has a white belly, relatively shorter tail, and darker back. House rats have naked ears, thick unicolor tails, and tops of feet dusky. **HABITS:** Semiaquatic; swims well and usually dives into water if disturbed. Sometimes seen at night swimming in deep water at some distance from land. Usually trapped on the ground or on floating veg-

COUES'S RICE RAT
Oryzomys couesi

MARSH RICE RAT
Oryzomys palustris

etation, but can climb reeds and shrubs. Eats insects, snails, green vegetation, and seeds. Makes ball-shaped nests of reeds about 3 ft. (1 m) above the ground or water. Breeds in winter; litter size is 2–7. **HABITAT:** Cattail and bulrush marshes, wet grassy areas near oxbow lakes in Texas; brackish or fresh water. Found in other habitats farther south but is almost always near water. **RANGE:** Extreme s. Tex.; Mexico and Central America to nw. Colombia. **STATUS:** Very local in U.S. and losing habitat. Common elsewhere.

MARSH RICE RAT *Oryzomys palustris* **Pl. 24, Skull Pl. 4**

Head and body 4¾ in. (94–165 mm); tail 4½ in. (100–155 mm); hind foot 1¼ in. (28–32 mm); ear ⅝ in. (15–20 mm); wt. 2 oz. (41–80 g). *Back dark brown* (can be black, gray-brown, or rich deep yellow-brown); sides yellow-brown or tawny; *belly usually grayish white,* occasionally cream. Ears inconspicuous, well haired. *Tail nearly naked and bicolor,* brown above, white below. Tops of feet white. Hind feet long and narrow, outer toes much shorter than inner toes. **SIMILAR SPECIES:** See Coues's Rice Rat. Hispid Cotton Rat (*Sigmodon hispidus*) has a shorter tail and dark feet. House rats are larger, with unicolor tails and stockier, dusky-topped feet. **HABITS:** Semiaquatic; swims well and usually dives into water if disturbed. Can swim 35 ft. (10 m) underwater. Climbs well in low vegetation. Eats invertebrates, small vertebrates, carrion, green vegetation, and seeds. More carnivorous than most small rodents. Makes a ball-shaped nest of reeds or may build a roof over a bird's nest. May breed year-round or from spring to fall. Litter size is 2–7. **HABITAT:** Most common in coastal marshes but also found in inland marshes and waterways, wet grassy areas, and sometimes in wet areas in forest. Sea level to 3,100 ft. (950 m). **RANGE:** S. N.J. to Mo. and s. Tex.; barely enters Mexico at Matamoros. **STATUS:** Common to abundant. Lower Keys Rice Rat (*O. p. natator,* in part) is endangered (USFWS). **NOTE:** The Silvery or Lower Keys Rice Rat is sometimes regarded as a separate species (*O. argentatus*). It is treated here as a population of *O. p. natator,* a subspecies that also occurs on mainland Florida.

COTTON RATS: *Sigmodon*

Cotton rats are stocky-bodied and blunt-nosed, with short tails. They somewhat resemble voles, and like the voles they can be active by day, especially near dawn or dusk. These rats occur in grassy areas.

HISPID COTTON RAT *Sigmodon hispidus* Pl. 24, Skull Pl. 4

Head and body 6 in. (113–179 mm); tail 4 in. (78–130 mm); hind foot 1⅛ in. (27–32 mm); ear ¾ in. (15–21 mm); wt. 3½ oz. (49–143 g). Upperparts *grizzled dark brown and buff* (overall tone varies from yellow-brown to almost black, darkest in the Southeast); belly grayish white. Eye-ring cream. Ears rounded, lightly haired. Tail faintly bicolor, brown above, gray-white below, *shorter than head and body. Skin on feet entirely black,* tops lightly covered with whitish hair, appear gray. **SIMILAR SPECIES:** See Arizona, Tawny-bellied, and Yellow-nosed Cotton Rats. Rice rats and house rats have tails longer than head and body. Voles have shorter tails and smaller eyes and ears. **HABITS:** Mainly crepuscular, but can be active at any time of day or night. Broad distribution, abundance, and daytime activity make this one of our more conspicuous small rodents. Makes wide runways through grass; litters active runways with grass clippings. Eats grass and other plants, also takes some insects and fungi. Makes nests in dense clumps of grass or in short underground burrows. Nests are cup-shaped or spherical and can

Hispid Cotton Rat. Unlike most small rodents, this species is sometimes active by day and may be seen in grassy areas and roadsides.

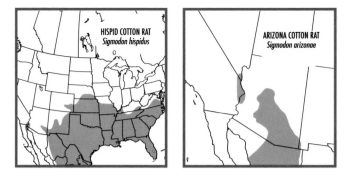

be located by following runways to thick grass. Can breed year-round or in spring and fall. Litter size is 1–14; northern populations have the largest litters. **HABITAT:** Tall-grass prairies, meadows, agricultural areas, and oldfields. Favors areas with dense vegetation but also occurs in mesquite desert with little ground cover. Sea level to 8,500 ft. (2,600 m). **RANGE:** Se. and s.-cen. U.S.; s. Ariz. and se. Calif. Also through Mexico and Central America to cen. Panama. **STATUS:** Abundant.

ARIZONA COTTON RAT   *Sigmodon arizonae*

Head and body 6½ in. (133–193 mm); tail 5 in. (106–142 mm); hind foot 1⅜ in. (32–38 mm); ear ⅞ in. (20–23 mm); wt. 6 oz. (70–310 g). *Largest cotton rat.* Back *grizzled dark brown and buff*; sides paler; belly gray-white. Eye-ring cream. Ears rounded, lightly haired with pale fur. Tail somewhat bicolor, brown above, gray-white below, *shorter than head and body.* Tops of hind feet gray, soles black. **SIMILAR SPECIES:** Hispid Cotton Rat is very similar but smaller (hind foot usually less than 32 mm) and can be darker in color. See Yellow-nosed and Tawny-bellied Cotton Rats. **HABITS:** Similar to Hispid Cotton Rat. Probably breeds year-round; litter size is 5–12. **HABITAT:** Grassy borders of ponds, irrigated fields, and stream banks. Also in mesquite desert with sparse grass. Sea level to at least 6,000 ft. (1,800 m). **RANGE:** S. Ariz. and nw. Mexico. **STATUS:** Locally common.

TAWNY-BELLIED COTTON RAT   Pl. 24
Sigmodon fulviventer

Head and body 5 in. (107–161 mm); tail 3¾ in. (85–106 mm); hind foot 1⅛ in. (27–33 mm); ear ¾ in. (16–20 mm); wt. 3 oz. (45–134 g). *Back black, heavily peppered with cream white hairs*; sides paler; *belly orange.* Eye-ring cream. Ears well haired with whitish fur, small orange spot behind ear. *Tail black above, slightly paler below*

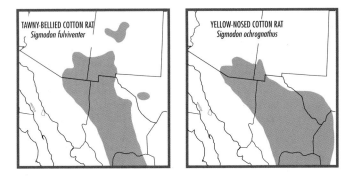

but not bicolor. Tops of feet gray, soles of hind feet black. **SIMILAR SPECIES:** Other cotton rats have whitish bellies and less peppery fur. **HABITS:** Similar to Hispid Cotton Rat. Around the edge of a pond in se. Arizona, Tawny-bellied Cotton Rat was caught among sedges at water's edge, while Hispid was found in the more peripheral grassy areas. **HABITAT:** Dense grass, mesquite grassland, grassy areas in oak and piñon-juniper woodlands. Sea level to about 8,000 ft. (2,400 m). **RANGE:** Se. Ariz., sw. N.M., and sw. Tex.; also w. Mexico. **STATUS:** Locally common.

YELLOW-NOSED COTTON RAT   PL. 24
Sigmodon ochrognathus

Head and body 5 in. (117–152 mm); tail 4 in. (88–133 mm); hind foot 1⅛ in. (26–32 mm); ear ⅝ in. (15–18 mm); wt. 2½ oz. (50–105 g). Back grizzled dark brown and buff, sides paler, belly white. *Snout, base of whiskers, and eye-rings yellow-orange.* Ears rounded, lightly haired. Tail bicolor, dark brown above, white below. Forelegs pale orange. Tops of feet gray, soles of hind feet black. **SIMILAR SPECIES:** Other cotton rats have brown snouts. **HABITS:** Diurnal and fairly easy to observe dashing from one area of cover to another. Makes surface runways and usually nests aboveground, but may use pocket gopher burrows. Breeds March–Oct.; litter size is 2–6. **HABITAT:** Rocky slopes with scattered clumps of grass in foothills and mountains. Occupies drier and more upland terrain than other cotton rats. Usually at 3,000–8,500 ft. (900–2,600 m). **RANGE:** Se. Ariz., sw. N.M., and sw. Tex.; also n. Mexico. **STATUS:** Locally common.

VOLES, MUSKRATS, AND LEMMINGS: ARVICOLINAE

The arvicolines are small to fairly large rodents, mostly stocky-bodied and short-tailed. This group includes the voles and lemmings as well as the muskrats. Muskrats are much larger than typical voles and have a long, naked-looking tail. They are adapted to a semiaquatic existence. Voles are a conspicuous part of the mammalian fauna in almost every corner of the continent, and in most areas at least one species is common. They eat green vegetation and, as this is a low-energy food, they have bouts of activity throughout the day and night. They occur in relatively open areas and leave clear signs of their activities in the form of runways through grass and piles of cut stems along runways. A short-tailed rodent seen dashing across the road by day is most likely to be a vole. Most voles are terrestrial and use surface runways and short underground burrows to enter their nesting chambers. A few are more subterranean in habit, and one group of voles is arboreal. All voles are active year-round; those that live in northern climates remain active under the snow layer in winter.

Populations of voles and lemmings often undergo dramatic boom-bust cycles, particularly in northern climates. Even at times of great abundance, however, North American lemmings do not disperse en masse and do not plunge off cliffs (this is a behavior occasionally observed in Norwegian Lemmings and greatly exaggerated in popular lore). Voles can cause serious damage to crops and orchards, but they are also an important food source for many carnivores, owls, and raptors.

Identifying voles can be very difficult. It may be useful to examine the biting surfaces of the molar teeth, as these have characteristic patterns. (See figures 3 and 4, pp. 166, 167.) Molar teeth of muskrats are similar to other voles but much larger.

WESTERN RED-BACKED VOLE Pl. 26, Fig. 4
Clethrionomys californicus

Head and body 4 in. (94–113 mm); tail 1¾ in. (34–60 mm); hind foot ¾ in. (17–21 mm); ear ½ in. (14–16 mm); wt. 1 oz. (15–34 g).

WESTERN
RED-BACKED VOLE
Clethrionomys californicus

Upper back and crown of head dark chestnut-brown, sides gray or yellow-gray, belly off-white or buff with gray underfur. Fur smooth and even. Ears fairly prominent, nearly naked. Eyes small. Tail less than half head and body length, bicolor, lightly haired. Tops of feet whitish. **SIMILAR SPECIES:** See White-footed Vole (*Arborimus albipes*). Creeping Vole (*Microtus oregoni*) has a shorter tail. Other voles in its range are larger, lack reddish backs, and have shaggy fur. **HABITS:** Active at any time in Coast Range, thought to be diurnal in Cascades. Travels under logs or under leaf litter. Does not climb. Eats mostly fungi and lichens and may store food for winter use. Makes nests under logs or in burrows. Can have 3–4 litters per year, with 1–7 young per litter. **HABITAT:** Moist forest with numerous fallen logs. Prefers old-growth coniferous forest with a closed canopy and little undergrowth. Seldom found in riparian areas. **RANGE:** W. Ore. and nw. Calif. **STATUS:** Fairly common.

SOUTHERN RED-BACKED VOLE   Pl. 25, Fig. 4
Clethrionomys gapperi

Head and body 4 in. (82–112 mm); tail 1½ in. (29–50 mm); hind foot ¾ in. (17–20 mm); ear ½ in. (14–16 mm); wt. 1 oz. (16–36 g). *Upper back and crown dark red-brown* or chestnut (occasionally gray-brown or yellow-brown); sides pale gray or yellow-gray, *contrasting with back;* belly silvery or cream with gray underfur. Fur medium length, smooth. Ears conspicuous, nearly naked. Eyes medium sized. *Tail bicolor, nearly naked,* with a small tuft (hairs 3 mm at tip). Tops of feet off-white or gray. **SIMILAR SPECIES:** Northern Red-backed Vole has a thickly haired tail and brighter orange back. Other voles lack a reddish stripe on back. **HABITS:** Active at any time, but tends to be more diurnal in winter and mainly nocturnal in summer. Travels under leaf litter and fallen logs but does not construct an underground burrow system. Eats fungi, seeds, nuts, berries, lichen, and a few arthropods. Makes globular nests

SOUTHERN RED-BACKED VOLE
Clethrionomys gapperi

in burrows or under logs. Breeds March–Nov. and has 4–8 young per litter. Females breed 2–3 times per year. **HABITAT:** Damp forest with fallen logs, also mountain meadows, clear-cuts, and bogs. **RANGE:** Canada and n. U.S., south in Rocky Mts. to N.M. and in Appalachian Mts. to n. Ala. **STATUS:** Common and widespread.

ORTHERN RED-BACKED VOLE
lethrionomys rutilus

Pl. 27, Fig. 4

Head and body 4 in. (84–111 mm); tail 1¼ in (22–41 mm); hind foot ¾ in. (17–20 mm); ear ½ in. (13–15 mm); wt. 1 oz. (16–33 g). Back *bright rusty orange,* sides yellow-gray or ocher-brown; belly buff with gray underfur. Fur long and soft. *Ears conspicuous,* well haired with orange hair on leading edge. Eyes medium, with cream eye-rings. *Tail bicolor, well haired, and tufted* (hairs 7 mm at tip). Tops of feet whitish. **SIMILAR SPECIES:** See Southern Red-backed Vole. Other tundra voles do not have reddish backs. **HABITS:** Active by day or night. Tunnels under snow in winter. Eats mainly leaves in tundra regions, also takes fungi, fruit, seeds, and berries in northern forests. Populations of this species have irregular cycles of abundance, and can reach densities of 150/acre (60/ha). Breeds in spring and summer; litter size is 4–9. Females may have 2 litters per year. **HABITAT:** Tundra and northern boreal forest (taiga). **RANGE:** Alaska and nw. Canada. **STATUS:** Common.

The Northern Red-backed Vole has much larger ears and a hairier tail than the Southern and Western Red-backed Voles.

NORTHERN RED-BACKED VOLE
Clethrionomys rutilus

WESTERN HEATHER VOLE
Phenacomys intermedius

EASTERN HEATHER VOLE
Phenacomys ungava

WESTERN HEATHER VOLE   Pl. 26
Phenacomys intermedius

Head and body 4¼ in. (95–117 mm); tail 1¼ in. (29–42 mm); hind foot ¾ in. (17–20 mm); ear ½ in. (12–15 mm); wt. 1 oz. (22–37 g). Back dark brown, gray-brown, or reddish brown; sides gray-brown; belly grayish white. Fur thick and dense, slightly woolly. *Whiskers thick and long,* extend to top of ear if laid back. Ears furred on leading edge, lightly lined with yellowish hair. *Tail short and narrow, bicolor,* very lightly haired. Tops of feet white. Long hairs over claws of front feet. **SIMILAR SPECIES:** Most voles have longer tails and do not occur in heather meadows. Montane Vole (*Microtus montanus*) is very similar but usually has a longer tail; its whiskers do not extend to tops of ears if laid back (all *Microtus* have relatively short whiskers), and it has few hairs over claws of front feet. Eastern Heather Vole (*P. ungava*) has an orange nose and is usually larger (ranges do not overlap). See Meadow Vole (*M. pennsylvanicus*). **HABITS:** Mainly crepuscular or nocturnal. Eats bark of dwarf willow, white heather, and other shrubs, also berries and green vegetation. Caches food near burrow entrances. Nests underground in summer, aboveground (but under snow) in winter. Usually solitary but may huddle in communal nests in winter. Breeds May–Sept.; litter size is 2–9, can have 2–3 litters per year. **HABITAT:** Heather meadows, alpine areas, and open coniferous forest with a dense cover of low shrubs. Usually found at 4,000–12,000 ft. (1,200–3,700 m), sometimes at lower elevations. **RANGE:** B.C. and Alta. through Rocky Mts. to Calif. and N.M. **STATUS:** Apparently uncommon or rare, but this may reflect difficulty of capture of this species.

EASTERN HEATHER VOLE   *Phenacomys ungava*   Pl. 25
Head and body 4½ in. (95–126 mm); tail 1¼ in. (28–37 mm); hind foot ¾ in. (19–20 mm); ear ½ in. (12–15 mm); wt. 1 oz. (25–40 g).

Back and sides dull brown, belly grayish white, sometimes washed with buff. Fur thick and soft. *Top of nose and eye-rings dull to bright orange. Whiskers long,* extend to top of ear if laid back. Ears partially concealed in fur, *tuft of stiff orange hair in front of ear. Tail short and narrow, bicolor,* lightly haired with short fur. Tops of feet white. **SIMILAR SPECIES:** See Western Heather Vole (*P. intermedius*). Bog Lemmings (*Synaptomys*) have shorter tails. Other voles (*Microtus*) almost always have longer tails and do not have orange hair in the ears. **HABITS AND HABITAT:** Similar to Western Heather Vole. **RANGE:** Most of mainland Canada. **STATUS:** Uncommon or rare over a wide range. **NOTE:** Several references have stated that Western Heather Vole has orange hair in front of the ears. Heather Voles were formerly considered to be one species, *P. intermedius*, and this character was described for the species complex, but it is the Eastern (not Western) Heather Vole that has the orange ear tufts.

WHITE-FOOTED VOLE *Arborimus albipes*   PL. 26

Head and body 4 in. (91–110 mm); tail 2¾ in. (53–85 mm); hind foot ¾ in. (19–21 mm); ear ½ in. (12–15 mm); wt. ¾ oz. (16–28 g). Back rich *dark red-brown;* sides paler, yellow-brown; belly grayish buff. Eyes small. *Ears naked,* partly concealed in fur. *Tail long, more than half head and body length, clearly bicolor,* thinly covered with short hair. Tops of feet white. **SIMILAR SPECIES.** See Western Red-backed Vole (*Clethrionomys californicus*). Other voles of similar size have shorter tails and/or are not red-brown. **HABITS:** Poorly known. Apparently nocturnal and semi-arboreal, can climb to canopy height. May travel below the leaf litter when on the ground. Feeds on leaves of trees (mainly alder and willow), shrubs, and forbs; also eats hazel catkins and small amounts of fungi and insects. One nest was found on the ground. Litter size is 2–4. **HABITAT:** Forests; favors riparian woodland with high densities of alder and

WHITE-FOOTED VOLE
Arborimus albipes

hazel or salmonberry. **RANGE:** Pacific Northwest, from Ore. to n. Calif. **STATUS:** Thought to be very rare based on specimen records. Extremely difficult to capture in typical rodent live-traps, more often caught in snap-traps or pitfalls.

RED TREE VOLE   *Arborimus longicaudus*   **Pl. 26**

Head and body 4 in. (92–121 mm); tail 3 in. (60–94 mm); hind foot ¾ in. (19–23 mm); ear ½ in. (12–14 mm); wt. 1 oz. (20–44 g). *Back reddish brown peppered with black*; sides paler; *belly grayish buff*, not contrasting with sides. Fur thick and soft. Ears short and rounded, partially concealed in fur. *Tail long and hairy*, bicolor near base, *all-dark at tip*. Feet stocky, tops whitish, soles pinkish. **SIMILAR SPECIES:** Sonoma Tree Vole is more brightly colored (ranges do not overlap). Other voles have shorter tails. Old adult deer mice (*Peromyscus*) can be orange, but they have white bellies and bicolor tails. **HABITS:** Nocturnal and highly arboreal; very rarely descends to the ground. Eats mainly Douglas fir needles, clipping a small branch and carrying it back to the nest. Strips the sides of more than 2,000 young needles per night, discarding their resin ducts; piles of these spines collect under occupied nests. Also eats some bark and occasionally needles of other conifers. Obtains water by licking dew off needles. Makes very large, low nests on high branches. In younger trees, uses the trunk and radiating branches to support the nest; in older trees the nest may sit out on a large branch. Makes nests from twigs, needles, lichen, and droppings. Each nest is occupied by a single individual. When disturbed in the nest, this vole may plummet to the ground from heights of up to 60 ft. (18 m) and then race off to hide. Breeds Dec.–May; litter size is 1–4. **HABITAT:** Coniferous forest; favors old-growth Douglas fir forest. **RANGE:** Endemic to w. Ore. **STATUS:** Locally common but vulnerable to logging and habitat fragmentation due to limited dispersal ability.

RED TREE VOLE
Arborimus longicaudus

SONOMA TREE VOLE
Arborimus pomo

Sonoma Tree Vole nest. Tree voles construct and occupy very large nests. Freshly stripped needles of Douglas fir accumulate below nests that are in active use.

SONOMA TREE VOLE *Arborimus pomo* Pl. 26

Head and body 4 in. (93–110 mm); tail 2¾ in. (59–81 mm); hind foot ¾ in. (18–21 mm); ear ½ in. (13–15 mm); wt. 1 oz. (20–31 g). *Back bright orange,* lightly peppered with black; sides yellow-orange; belly grayish buff. Fur thick and soft. Ears short and rounded, partially concealed in fur. *Tail long and hairy, all-dark.* Feet stocky, tops whitish, soles pinkish. SIMILAR SPECIES: See Red Tree Vole. HABITS: Similar to Red Tree Vole. May breed year-round; litter size is usually 2. HABITAT: Coniferous forest, mostly with Douglas fir. RANGE: Endemic to nw. Calif. STATUS: Locally common but vulnerable to logging and habitat fragmentation.

MEADOW VOLE *Microtus pennsylvanicus* Pl. 25, Skull Pl. 3, Fig. 4

Head and body 4¾ in. (95–138 mm); tail 1¾ in. (32–57 mm); hind foot ⅞ in. (19–23 mm); ear ½ in. (13–16 mm); wt. 1½ oz. (22–66 g). *Back dark brown,* sides brown or gray-brown, *belly gray-white.* Fur thick and coarse but not grizzled. Ears mostly concealed in fur, lined with hair. *Tail relatively long* (usually over 40 mm), somewhat bicolor, lightly haired. Tops of hind feet dark brown or grayish. Soles lightly haired near heel (skin visible), 6 pads on soles of hind feet. Female has 8 mammae. SIMILAR SPECIES: See Prairie Vole (*M. ochrogaster*). Montane Vole (*M. montanus*) is very similar but usually has a slightly shorter tail and has tops of hind feet white, soles of hind feet thickly haired near heel. Heather Voles (*Phenacomys*) have shorter tails, longer whiskers, and tops of feet white. SOUNDS: Chatters by grinding teeth when alarmed; young produce ultrasonic squeaks. HABITS: Active night or day. Swims well but cannot climb. A small, short-tailed rodent seen dashing across a road is most likely this common and widespread species. Other signs of its presence are networks of runways through grass,

The Meadow Vole is the most widespread species of North American vole. It occurs in a variety of habitats but favors moist meadows with dense vegetation.

MEADOW VOLE
Microtus pennsylvanicus

BEACH VOLE
Microtus breweri

marked with piles of clipped grass and greenish droppings. Often clips grass into short sections to bring the maturing seed head into reach. Eats a variety of green plant material, bark, roots, and tubers. Females are solitary and territorial in summer, but occupy shared nests in winter; males move more freely year-round. Makes nests aboveground under clumps of grass, or, less often, in shallow burrows. Highly prolific: breeds March–Nov. or year-round, and litter size is about 6 (range 1–11). One female can have 17 litters per year (in captivity). Populations follow a cyclic pattern, with peaks every 2–5 years. In the hand, this is an aggressive vole that does not hesitate to bite. **HABITAT:** Damp meadows, roadsides, orchards, and other areas with a thick cover of lush grass. **RANGE:** Mainland Canada, Alaska, and much of n. and cen. U.S. **STATUS:** Florida Salt Marsh Vole (*M. p. dukecambelli*) is endangered (USFWS). Elsewhere it is abundant and widespread. May damage orchards by girdling trees in winter; pilfers hay and cereal crops in summer.

BEACH VOLE *Microtus breweri*

Head and body 5¼ in. (112–137 mm); tail 2 in. (41–60 mm); hind foot ⅞ in. (22–23 mm); wt. 2 oz. (45–63 g). Back rich yellow-brown, sides ocher, belly gray-white or cream. Ears almost concealed in fur. Sometimes has a white patch on forehead or on

throat. Tail medium length, bicolor. Feet off-white. **SIMILAR SPECIES:**
No other voles occur on Muskeget I. **HABITS:** Makes surface runways on grassy dunes, also burrows into the sand. Eats mostly
beach grass. Unlike most vole species, Beach Vole populations do
not follow boom-bust cycles but are usually quite stable. Breeds
April–Oct.; litter size is 1–6. **HABITAT:** Sandy, coastal areas with abundant beach grass. **RANGE:** Muskeget I., Mass. **STATUS:** Common in a
very small range. **NOTE:** Formerly considered to be a subspecies of
Meadow Vole.

MONTANE VOLE *Microtus montanus* Pl. 25, Fig. 4

Head and body 4¾ in (93–137 mm); tail 1½ in. (30–62 mm); hind
foot ¾ in. (17–22 mm); ear ¾ in. (12–16 mm); wt. 1½ oz. (25–65 g).
Back dark brown, gray-brown, or pale gray; sides slightly paler and
grayer than back; *belly silvery* (very rarely washed with buff). Ears
lightly haired along edge, partially concealed in fur. *Tail short*
(about ⅓ head and body length), bicolor, and lightly haired. *Tops
of feet whitish.* Female has 8 mammae. Male has oily glands on
flanks. **SIMILAR SPECIES:** See Meadow, Mexican, and Long-tailed Voles
(*M. pennsylvanicus, M. mexicanus,* and *M. longicaudus*). Also see
Sagebrush Vole (*Lemmiscus curtatus*) and Western Heather Vole
(*Phenacomys intermedius*). **HABITS:** Mainly diurnal. Makes surface
runways through grass but may not use runways in other types of
vegetation. Usually nests on the ground under cover of a log or
rock, but may make shallow underground burrows for nesting.
This is a prolific vole that can breed year-round in some areas. Litter size is 1–13, usually 6. **HABITAT:** Damp grassland, often near
streams or marshes, sometimes in low brush or dense woods.
Usually found at 5,000–11,000 ft. (1,500–3,400 m), sometimes at
lower elevations in northern part of range. **RANGE:** S. B.C. to Calif.,
Ariz., and n. N.M. **STATUS:** Common to abundant and widespread.

MONTANE VOLE
Microtus montanus

GRAY-TAILED VOLE *Microtus canicaudus* Pl. 26

Head and body 4¼ in. (95–119 mm); tail 2 in. (32–44 mm); hind foot ¾ in. (18–20 mm); wt. 1¼ oz. (25–52 g). *Back dark brown, sides washed with yellow,* belly gray. Fur smooth and even. Eyes moderately large. Tail bicolor, brown above, pale gray or whitish below, with small tuft at tip. Feet silvery. **SIMILAR SPECIES:** Long-tailed Vole (*M. longicaudus*) has a proportionally longer tail. Townsend's Vole (*M. townsendii*) is darker and usually larger. Creeping Vole (*M. oregoni*) is smaller with tiny eyes. **HABITS:** Makes surface runways and underground tunnels. If tunnels are flooded will swim to dry sections or abandon area and move to higher ground. Makes nests underground or below boards or hay bales. Breeds mainly in spring and fall but can breed year-round. Litter size is 3–7. **HABITAT:** Grasslands and agricultural areas. **RANGE:** Willamette Valley, Ore., and s. Wash. **STATUS:** Locally common. **NOTE:** Montane Vole is closely related and very similar; many specimens of Montane Vole are externally indistinguishable from Gray-tailed Vole, but ranges of the two species do not overlap.

CALIFORNIA VOLE *Microtus californicus* Pl. 26

Head and body 4½ in. (106–128 mm); tail 2 in. (40–64 mm); hind foot ⅞ in. (20–23 mm); ear ½ in. (13–15 mm); wt. 1¾ oz. (33–66 g). *Back dark brown grizzled with cream,* sides yellow-brown, belly grayish buff. Fur long and shaggy. Ears conspicuous and well haired. Tail bicolor, lightly furred. Tops of feet whitish. **SIMILAR SPECIES:** Townsend's Vole (*M. townsendii*) is usually larger and has darker feet and tail. Long-tailed Vole (*M. longicaudus*) has a proportionally longer tail. Montane Vole (*M. montanus*) occurs at higher elevations. **HABITS:** Mainly diurnal; most active in the early morning. Makes runways through grass and also uses shallow underground tunnels. Clips grass to reach seed heads, leaves piles of

GRAY-TAILED VOLE
Microtus canicaudus

CALIFORNIA VOLE
Microtus californicus

clippings in active runways. Eats green vegetation when available, roots and seeds during dry summer months. Makes a nest of shredded grass in the burrow or under a log. May breed year-round or late winter to spring and again in fall. Litter size is 1–10. **HABITAT:** Grassy fields, meadows, marshes, coastal wetlands, and recent clear-cuts. Prefers shorter grass than Townsend's Vole. **RANGE:** Sw. Ore. to n. Baja Calif. **STATUS:** Generally common in suitable habitat. Amargosa Vole (*M. c. scirpensis*) is endangered (USFWS).

TOWNSEND'S VOLE *Microtus townsendii* Pl. 26

Head and body 5 in. (104–145 mm); tail 2½ in. (45–72 mm); hind foot 1 in. (21–29 mm); ear ⅝ in. (14–19 mm); wt. 3 oz. (57–103 g). *Large. Back dark brown,* sides dark yellow-brown, belly gray. Fur long and thick. Ears partially concealed in fur, edges haired. *Tail about half head and body length, somewhat bicolor,* lightly haired with a very short tuft at tip. *Tops of feet brown.* **SIMILAR SPECIES:** Larger than other voles in its range. Subadult and juvenile recognized by relatively long tail (only Long-tailed Vole, *M. longicaudus,* has a proportionally longer tail, all other voles have shorter tails). **HABITS:** Active by day or night. Swims well and can occupy seasonally flooded areas. Makes runways through grass that may be used by generations of voles. In dry areas these runways become deeply worn grooves. Eats grass, clover, and rushes. Makes a nest of grass on a hummock in wet areas, belowground in drier regions. Breeds Feb.–Nov.; litter size is 3–9. **HABITAT:** Wet fields, marshes, stream banks, and other areas with dense grass. Seldom found in forests. Sea level to 6,000 ft. (1,850 m). **RANGE:** Vancouver I. and s. B.C. to nw. Calif. **STATUS:** Common to abundant (this species can reach a higher density than any other vole in U.S.), but difficult to capture in live-traps.

TOWNSEND'S VOLE
Microtus townsendii

TUNDRA VOLE *Microtus oeconomus* Pl. 27

Head and body 4¾ in. (105–140 mm); tail 1½ in. (30–48 mm); hind foot ⅞ in. (19–23 mm); ear ½ in. (13–15 mm); wt. 1¾ oz. (30–67 g). Back *reddish brown* or *yellow-brown*; sides paler, yellowish; belly white or cream with gray underfur. Fur long and thick. Ears partially hidden in fur, lined with hair. *Tail short,* clearly bicolor, thickly haired and *tufted.* Tops of feet white, undersides of hind feet haired near heel. **SIMILAR SPECIES:** See Singing Vole (*M. miurus*). Meadow Vole (*M. pennsylvanicus*) has smoother fur and a less bicolor tail without a tuft at tip. Taiga Vole (*M. xanthognathus*) has a yellow nose. **HABITS:** Active day or night. Uses well-worn runways and sometimes digs shallow burrows. Eats green vegetation in summer; stores seeds and roots for winter use. Breeds May–Sept. and may have 2–3 litters per year. Litter size is 3–11. **HABITAT:** Low-lying tundra, wet meadows, and marshes. **RANGE:** Alaska and nw. Canada. **STATUS:** Common. **NOTE:** The name *oeconomus* or "economic vole" refers to its habit of storing food for winter use. In the past, Inuit women collected the voles' large stores of licorice-root and other tubers for their own use.

LONG-TAILED VOLE *Microtus longicaudus* Pl. 26

Head and body 4¾ in. (97–148 mm); tail 3 in. (58–105 mm); hind foot 1 in. (19–27 mm); ear ½ in. (13–17 mm); wt. 1¾ oz. (27–75 g). Slim-bodied. Back brown, *sides yellow-brown,* belly gray washed with buff. Fur long and shaggy. Ears partly concealed in fur, haired on edge. *Tail more than half head and body length, bicolor,* with a small tuft at tip. Tops of feet pale gray or brownish. **SIMILAR SPECIES:** Other voles have proportionally shorter tails. **HABITS:** Usually does not make runways and leaves little sign of its presence. Eats green plant material, seeds, fruit, fungi, and bark. Breeds May–Nov.; litter size is 2–8. **HABITAT:** Forests, brushy areas, clear-cuts, and sagebrush. Often found along rivers or streams. Sea level to 6,000 ft.

(1,800 m). **RANGE:** E. Alaska and w. Canada to w. S.D., N.M., and Calif. **STATUS:** Generally uncommon but widely distributed.

CREEPING VOLE *Microtus oregoni*   Pl. 26

Head and body 3½ in. (80–108 mm); tail 1¼ in. (26–41 mm); hind foot ¾ in. (16–20 mm); ear ½ in. (10–14 mm); wt. ¾ oz. (13–33 g). *Small.* Back dark brown, sides brown, belly gray with a buff wash. Fur short and wavy. *Eyes very small.* Ears almost concealed in fur. *Tail short, somewhat bicolor,* sparsely haired. Tops of feet pale, 5 pads on soles of hind feet. **SIMILAR SPECIES:** Small size and pinprick eyes separate it from other voles in its range. Other small northwestern voles have 6 pads on soles of hind feet. **HABITS:** Makes tiny tunnels among grass roots and sometimes uses underground burrows. Feeds on green vegetation and fungi. Makes nests under logs or in burrows. Breeds March–Sept.; litter size is 2–6. **HABITAT:** Forested and open areas; favors grassy clearings in forests. **RANGE:** S. B.C. to nw. Calif. **STATUS:** Fairly common.

ROCK VOLE *Microtus chrotorrhinus*   Pl. 25

Head and body 4¼ in. (102–120 mm); tail 1¾ in. (35–50 mm); hind foot ¾ in. (19–21 mm); ear ½ in. (12–15 mm); wt. 1¼ oz. (29–42 g). Back dark brown, sides gray-brown, belly gray. *Snout and eye-rings orange.* Ears rather conspicuous, lightly haired. Tail somewhat bicolor. Feet gray. **SIMILAR SPECIES:** Adult has a distinctive orange nose. Young is similar to Woodland Vole (*M. pinetorum*), but that species has smaller eyes and ears. **HABITS:** Travels around and under mossy rocks. Eats bunchberry and other green plants and may cache food under rocks. Breeds March–Oct.; litter size is 2–5. **HABITAT:** Rocky areas in cool moist hardwood or mixed forests. Often found near streams. **RANGE:** E. Canada and the Northeast south through Appalachian Mts. to N.C. and Tenn. **STATUS:** Uncommon and patchily distributed.

CREEPING VOLE
Microtus oregoni

ROCK VOLE
Microtus chrotorrhinus

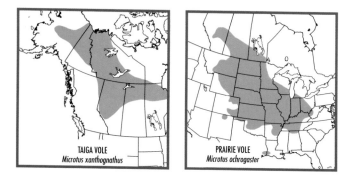

TAIGA VOLE
Microtus xanthognathus

PRAIRIE VOLE
Microtus ochrogaster

TAIGA VOLE   *Microtus xanthognathus*   Pl. 27
Yellow-cheeked Vole, Chestnut-cheeked Vole

Head and body 6 in. (145–160 mm); tail 1¾ in. (38–50 mm); hind foot 1 in. (23–27 mm); ear ¾ in. (17–19 mm); wt. 4 oz. (60–150 g). *Large.* Back dark gray-brown, almost black on upper back; sides dark yellow-brown; belly dark gray, hairs tipped buff. *Snout and base of whiskers bright orange.* Ears almost hidden in fur, orange fur at base of ears. *Tail short, clearly bicolor,* lightly haired and tufted. **SIMILAR SPECIES:** Other northwestern voles are smaller and do not have orange noses. Lemmings have shorter tails. **SOUNDS:** High-pitched, pulsating whistles given in alarm. Male makes low chirps when pursuing a female before mating. **HABITS:** Active day or night. Swims well, looks like a very small muskrat in the water. Uses runways above- and belowground. Underground burrows lead to nest chambers and may be marked by mounds of earth up to 10 ft. (3 m) across. Stores food at burrow entrance and underground. Eats marsh vegetation, grasses, berries, and fungi. Forms dense but transient colonies. During the breeding season, males occupy separate territories that overlap the range of several females. Males mark their territories with scent from glands on the flanks. In fall and winter, groups of up to 10 voles occupy a communal nest and share the same food cache. Breeds May–July; litter size is 7–10, and females usually have 2 litters per year. **HABITAT:** Recently burned or cutover forest, often in riparian areas with mineral soils. **RANGE:** Boreal areas from w. Hudson Bay to cen. Alaska. **STATUS:** Locally common. Habitat is favorable for only a few years, so colonies are patchy and unstable.

PRAIRIE VOLE   *Microtus ochrogaster*   Pl. 25, Fig. 4

Head and body 4½ in. (100–131 mm); tail 1¼ in. (28–43 mm); hind foot ¾ in. (19–22 mm); ear ½ in. (12–15 mm); wt. 1½ oz. (25–55 g).

Back grizzled gray, *gray-brown,* or dark brown; sides paler, often with a thin buff line on lower side. *Belly buff, cream,* or grayish white. Fur long and coarse. Ears partially concealed in fur, lined with hair. *Tail short, clearly bicolor,* haired with a small tuft at tip. Tops of hind feet pale; 5 pads on soles. Female has 6 mammae. **SIMILAR SPECIES:** Meadow Vole (*M. pennsylvanicus*) has a slightly longer tail, a gray belly, and darker feet with 6 pads on soles of hind feet (female has 8 mammae). Woodland Vole (*M. pinetorum*) and Southern Bog Lemming (*Synaptomys cooperi*) have shorter tails. **HABITS:** Most active at dawn or dusk. Makes runways through grass, also burrows belowground. Feeds on a variety of green plants in summer; in winter stores roots and tubers underground. Summer nests are usually in a clump of grass. Unlike most voles, Prairie Voles form monogamous pairs that share a nest. Both parents care for the young and defend their home range. Older offspring may remain with the parents and help tend a new litter. Breeds mainly in summer but can breed year-round if conditions are suitable. Litter size is 1–8, usually 3–5. **HABITAT:** Prairies, grasslands, and agricultural areas, usually on dry sandy soils. Lower elevations, mainly below 3,300 ft. (1,000 m). **RANGE:** S.-cen. Canada and prairie states of U.S. **STATUS:** Common and widespread.

EXICAN VOLE   *Microtus mexicanus*   Pl. 25, Fig. 4
Head and body 4¼ in. (97–120 mm); tail 1 in. (21–33 mm); hind foot ¾ in. (17–21 mm); ear ½ in. (12–14 mm); wt. 1 oz. (24–39 g). Upperparts dark brown or gray-brown, sometimes washed with yellow; *belly buff* with gray underfur. Ears well haired. *Tail very short,* bicolor, and lightly haired. Tops of feet brownish or pale gray. Female has 4 mammae. **SIMILAR SPECIES:** Montane Vole (*M. montanus*) is very similar but usually has a gray belly and a slightly longer tail (female has 8 mammae). Other voles in its range have

MEXICAN VOLE
Microtus mexicanus

proportionally longer tails. **HABITS:** Active day or night, but most active at midday or at dusk in high mountains. Makes surface runways through grass, marked with piles of bright green droppings and grass clippings. Nests in shallow underground burrows or under logs. Breeds April–Aug. Litter size is smaller than in most voles, usually 2–3 (litters of 1–6 have been recorded). **HABITAT:** Grassy areas near ponderosa pine and other conifers. Found in drier habitat than most voles, from 4,000–11,000 ft. (1,200–3,400 m). **RANGE:** Se. Utah and sw. Colo. to Ariz., N.M., and w. Tex., south to s. Mexico. **STATUS:** Most populations are isolated and some are declining. Hualapai Vole (*M. m. hualpaiensis*), Arizona, is endangered (USFWS). **NOTE:** Several authors consider the U.S. populations of *M. mexicanus* to be a separate species, the Mogollon Vole (*M. mogollensis*). Others, however, continue to regard them as a subspecies, as is done here.

WOODLAND VOLE *Microtus pinetorum* PL. 25
Pine Vole

Head and body 4 in. (82–122 mm); tail ¾ in. (16–28 mm); hind foot ¾ in. (15–21 mm); ear ⅜ in. (8–11 mm); wt. 1¼ oz. (23–46 g). Back usually *reddish brown* (ranges from dark brown to pale gray-brown); sides orange-brown; belly gray, hairs tipped buff. *Fur short and velvety,* molelike. *Tail very short,* nearly naked, faintly bicolor. Tops of feet whitish, 5 pads on soles of hind feet. Female has 4 mammae. **SIMILAR SPECIES:** Other voles have longer tails and do not have velvety fur. Southern Bog Lemming (*Synaptomys cooperi*) has long lax fur and occurs in wetter habitats. **HABITS:** Mainly subterranean; makes burrows under leaf litter or in shallow soil, only emerging to race to another burrow. Eats roots year-round, also grass stems in summer, fruits and

Woodland Vole. This vole spends most of its time underground. It has small eyes and a very short tail.

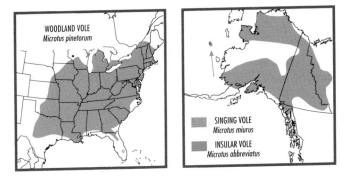

WOODLAND VOLE
Microtus pinetorum

SINGING VOLE
Microtus miurus

INSULAR VOLE
Microtus abbreviatus

seeds in fall, and bark in winter. Lives in small family groups and is usually monogamous. Breeds year-round in the South, March–Nov. in the North. Litter size is 1–5, and females may have up to 4 litters per year. **HABITAT:** Deciduous forest with thick leaf litter, grassy patches in woodlands or orchards, and dense brush. Favors areas with sandy soils. **RANGE:** Throughout the East and Midwest. Barely enters e. Canada. **STATUS:** Locally common or abundant. May raid crops or girdle fruit trees.

NGING VOLE *Microtus miurus*   **Pl. 27**

Head and body 4¾ in. (112–127 mm); tail 1¼ in. (25–36 mm); hind foot ¾ in. (18–21 mm); ear ⅝ in. (14–17 mm); wt. 1½ oz. (28–60 g). Upperparts orange-brown or gray-brown, *often with an orange line on lower sides* (most pronounced on flanks of male); *belly buff* with gray underfur. Fur thick and soft. *Orange patch* at base of whiskers and *around base of ears.* Ears hairy. *Tail short, bicolor, brown above, pale orange* below; thickly haired and tufted (hairs 7 mm at tip). Tops of feet cream. **SIMILAR SPECIES:** Other voles in its range do not have an orange line on sides and usually have longer tails. **SOUNDS:** Makes high-pitched, pulsating squeaks when disturbed. **HABITS:** Active night or day. Makes shallow underground burrows, also shelters under rocks. Eats green plant material and constructs hay piles for winter use. Willow, horsetail, licorice-root, and a variety of forbs are used in the piles. Unlike most voles, it is semicolonial and may squeak to warn others in the colony about approaching danger. A person moving through an active colony elicits squeaks from numerous voles, tracing the path of the intruder. Breeds in late spring and summer; litter size is 4–12. **HABITAT:** Well-drained tundra, usually near running water. Found up to at least 6,000 ft. (1,800 m). **RANGE:** Alaska and nw. Canada. **STATUS:** Generally common.

INSULAR VOLE *Microtus abbreviatus*

Pl. 27

Head and body 5 in. (109–136 mm); tail 1 in. (22–31 mm); hind foot ⅞ in. (23–24 mm); wt. 2 oz. (45–80 g). *Upperparts orange-brown,* orange line on *lower sides, belly pale orange.* Fur thick and soft. Orange fur at base of whiskers and around base of ear. Ears hairy, almost concealed in fur. *Tail very short and hairy,* brown above, pale orange below and at tip. Tops of forefeet gray, hind feet buff. **SIMILAR SPECIES:** Closely related to Singing Vole (*M. miurus*). Insular Vole is slightly larger and more colorful, but otherwise similar in external appearance and habits to Singing Vole. **RANGE:** St. Matthew and Hall Is., Bering Sea. **STATUS:** Common in a small range. Populations follow boom-bust cycles.

WATER VOLE *Microtus richardsoni*

Pl. 26

Head and body 6½ in. (120–199 mm); tail 3 in. (57–107 mm); hind foot 1⅛ in. (25–31 mm); ear ⅝ in. (14–18 mm); wt. 3½ oz. (65–132 g). *Large. Back dark brown,* sides gray-brown or yellow-brown, belly gray. Fur dense and soft, slightly woolly. Ears almost concealed in fur. Eyes small. Whiskers long and dark. Tail bicolor, lightly haired with a small tuft at tip. Tops of feet gray. Long claws on front and hind feet, 5 *pads on soles of hind feet.* Male and female have large flank glands. **SIMILAR SPECIES:** Other voles in its range are smaller and have 6 pads on sole of hind foot. **SOUNDS:** Rubs hind feet on flank glands and stomps feet on ground ("drum-marking") to mark territory. **HABITS:** Mainly nocturnal; spends more than half the year in tunnels under snow. Swims well and can swim against the current. Makes runways that crisscross streams, also burrows into banks above and below water level. Eats green vegetation, roots, and seeds and does not store food for winter use. Breeds May–Sept.; litter size is 2–10, and females usually breed twice a year. **HABITAT:** Along streams and ponds through alpine and subalpine meadows. Elevation 2,300–10,500 ft. (700–3,200 m), usually

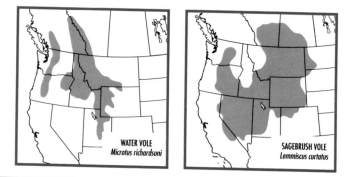

WATER VOLE
Microtus richardsoni

SAGEBRUSH VOLE
Lemmiscus curtatus

above 5,000 ft. (1,500 m). **RANGE:** Two discontinuous bands: Cascade Mts. of w. B.C., Wash., and Ore.; and Rocky Mts. from Alta. to Utah. **STATUS:** Generally uncommon and patchily distributed.

GEBRUSH VOLE *Lemmiscus curtatus* **PL. 25**

Head and body 4 in. (82–113 mm); tail 1 in. (17–32 mm); hind foot ⅝ in. (15–19 mm); ear ⅜ in. (7–12 mm); wt. ¾ oz. (16–35 g). *Upperparts pale gray* or yellow-gray, belly whitish. Ears partially hidden in fur. Eyes small. *Tail very short,* bicolor, lightly haired. Tops of feet whitish, soles of feet and sides of toes hairy. **SIMILAR SPECIES:** Montane Vole (*Microtus montanus*) is usually darker gray or brownish with a proportionally longer tail (prefers wetter habitats). **HABITS:** Mainly crepuscular, but can be active at any time. Eats green vegetation including sagebrush, also some fungi. Lives colonially in a shared burrow system. Burrows are usually built under cover and have multiple entrances. Uses surface runways to connect burrows to feeding areas but, unlike most voles, does not keep runways clear of vegetation. Colonies change burrows when food is depleted and may move back to an abandoned burrow system. Breeds year-round; litter size is 3–11. **HABITAT:** Dry areas with sagebrush or rabbitbrush, on stony soils. **RANGE:** S. Alta. and Sask. to n. Colo., Utah, and e. Calif. **STATUS:** Locally common but difficult to capture in rodent live-traps.

OUND-TAILED MUSKRAT *Neofiber alleni* **PL. 2, Skull Pl. 6**

Head and body 8 in. (18–22 cm); tail 5 in. (10–16 cm); hind foot 1¾ in. (4–5 cm); wt. 10 oz. (200–350 g). *Semiaquatic.* Upperparts dark brown, belly gray tipped with buff. Fur dense, with long shiny guard hairs. Ears small and almost concealed in fur. *Tail rounded, scaly,* nearly naked, and all-dark. Hind feet slightly webbed. **SIMILAR SPECIES:** Common Muskrat is much larger and has a laterally compressed tail. Rice rats are smaller. **HABITS:** Crepuscular or noctur-

ROUND-TAILED MUSKRAT
Neofiber alleni

nal. Less aquatic than Common Muskrat, but swims well and takes to water if alarmed. Eats aquatic grasses and other emergent plants. Makes spherical houses of grass and sedges (much finer than the cattail nests of Common Muskrats). Houses are 1–2 ft. (0.3–0.6 m) wide and have 2 underwater entrances. Also makes feeding platforms near the house. Breeds year-round; litter size is 1–4. **HABITAT:** Grassy marshes, salt savannahs, and wet agricultural areas. **RANGE:** Fla. and se. Ga. **STATUS:** Local, populations fluctuate greatly. Rare in Florida.

COMMON MUSKRAT *Ondatra zibethicus* Pl. 2, Skull Pl. 6

Head and body 12 in. (26–36 cm); tail 9 in. (19–27 cm); hind foot 3 in. (6–9 cm); wt. 2½ lb. (0.7–1.5 kg). *Semiaquatic.* Upperparts rich brown, belly grayish white. Cheeks often white. Fur dense with long glossy guard hairs. Ears almost concealed in fur. *Tail scaly, nearly naked, laterally compressed.* Hind feet partly webbed. **SIMILAR SPECIES:** American Beaver and Coypu are larger; beaver has a paddle-shaped tail and swims with only head exposed. Coypu has a rounded tail and white fur on nose and mouth. See Round-tailed Muskrat. **SOUNDS:** Slaps water when alarmed; occasionally chatters teeth, hums, or squeaks. **HABITS:** Mainly nocturnal, but also active on overcast or rainy days; more likely to be seen by day than other large semiaquatic rodents. Almost always seen in or close to water except when dispersing to a new area (usually in spring). Swims well and is more buoyant than a beaver: top of head, upper back, and (sometimes) part of tail are visible as 2 or 3 separate humps. Eats cattail (roots and stems) and other aquatic emergents. Can close lips behind incisor teeth to harvest food underwater without taking in water. Makes a lodge or house out of cattail or sedges (does not use sticks). Sometimes makes a nest in a bank burrow. Builds lodge in shallow water and accesses it via underwa-

COMMON MUSKRAT
Ondatra zibethicus

ter tunnels. Also makes smaller feeding shelters. These are covered in the North but may be simple uncovered platforms in the South. Usually 2 adults and 2–4 young share a house, although individuals feed alone and are almost always seen singly. Home range is small: 200 ft. (60 m) in diameter. Male Common Muskrat has scent glands on either side of the penis (female has smaller glands); uses scent to mark lodge and other parts of range. Breeds in winter or early spring in the North, year-round in the South. Litter size is 3–8. Young remain with the parents for a year, until they reach maturity. Yearlings are forced out of the house and disperse in spring. **HABITAT:** Shallow marshes with abundant cattails. Less common along streams or in wooded swamps. **RANGE:** Mainland Canada, Alaska, and most of U.S. except Fla. and dry Southwest. **STATUS:** Common and widespread. Displaced by Coypu in parts of Southeast.

BROWN LEMMING   *Lemmus trimucronatus*   Pl. 27

Head and body 5 in. (117–150 mm); tail ½ in. (13–20 mm); hind foot ⅞ in. (18–23 mm); wt. 3 oz. (50–125 g). Upper back and sides yellow-brown; lower back and *rump bright tawny orange;* shoulders and lower sides pale orange; belly gray, fur tipped buff. Fur thick and soft. Ears concealed in fur, marked by orange tufts. *Tail very short, almost concealed in fur.* **SIMILAR SPECIES:** Other lemmings are grayish. Voles and bog lemmings have longer tails. **HABITS:** Active day and night. Makes runways through grass in summer, tunnels under snow in winter. Eats grass and sedges in summer, in winter relies heavily on moss for food. Breeds year-round if conditions are good. Litter size is about 8 in summer, 4 in winter. Populations go through a boom-bust cycle every 3–4 years. **HABITAT:** Low-lying, wet tundra with dense vegetation. **RANGE:** Alaska, w. Canada, and larger Canadian Arctic islands. **STATUS:** Common.

BROWN LEMMING
Lemmus trimucronatus

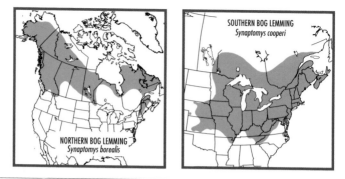

NORTHERN BOG LEMMING
Pl. 27, Fig. 4

Synaptomys borealis

Head and body 4 in. (88–110 mm); tail ¾ in. (14–25 mm); hind foot ¾ in. (16–20 mm); ear ½ in. (13–15 mm); wt. 1 oz. (18–35 g). Almost identical externally to Southern Bog Lemming but usually has *orange hairs in front of ears.* Upper incisors narrow and *grooved.* Female has 8 mammae. **SIMILAR SPECIES:** See Southern Bog Lemming. Heather Voles (*Phenacomys*) have ungrooved upper incisors. Other voles have longer tails. Lemmings have almost no tail. **HABITS:** Probably similar to Southern Bog Lemming. Breeds May–Aug.; litter size is 2–8. **HABITAT:** Mainly bogs, wet meadows, gaps and openings in forest, or alpine tundra. Also found in sagebrush in British Columbia. **RANGE:** Most of Alaska and mainland Canada, n. New England, and near the Canadian border in the western U.S. **STATUS:** Uncommon or rare through a wide range.

SOUTHERN BOG LEMMING
Pl. 25, Fig. 4

Synaptomys cooperi

Head and body 4 in. (85–122 mm); tail ¾ in. (12–24 mm); hind foot ¾ in. (17–20 mm); ear ½ in. (12–14 mm); wt. 1 oz. (20–40 g). Compact and *big-headed. Back dark brown grizzled with buff,* sides dark yellow-brown, belly silvery gray. Fur long and shaggy. Eyes rather small and close to nose. *Tail very short,* bicolor, and lightly haired. Tops of feet brown. *Upper incisors grooved.* Female has 6 mammae. **SIMILAR SPECIES:** Most voles have longer tails. Woodland Vole (*Microtus pinetorum*) has velvety fur and ungrooved upper incisors. Northern Bog Lemming is very similar but has narrower lower incisors and usually has orange fur in front of the ears; female has 8 mammae. **SOUNDS:** Harsh, grating squeaks when fighting. Makes high-pitched notes in series during courtship and short low notes from mother to young. **HABITS:** Mainly nocturnal, sometimes active by day. Makes surface runways through grass or may travel below the surface in mole tunnels. Eats mostly grass and sedges, also some fungi, berries, and moss. Lives in colonies of 3–30. Usually makes nests in underground burrows. Breeds year-round in southern part of range, spring to fall in northern part. Litter size is 1–8, usually 3. **HABITAT:** Variable, but usually in or near green grass and sedge. Found around sphagnum bogs, in dense woodlands, spruce-fir forest, and in dry bluegrass fields. **RANGE:** Eastern U.S. and se. Canada. **STATUS:** Fairly common but patchily distributed, even in suitable habitat.

NORTHERN COLLARED LEMMING   Pl. 27, Skull Pl. 3
Dicrostonyx groenlandicus

Head and body 4¾ in. (96–133 mm); tail ½ in. (10–19 mm); hind foot ¾ in. (16–20 mm); ear ¼ in. (5–8 mm); wt. 1–3 oz. (30–100 g). Back *pale gray to dark gray; line on lower sides and entire throat reddish orange;* belly white, tipped pale orange. Fur thick and soft. Dark stripe on forehead. Ears concealed in orange fur. Tail very short, gray above at base, white below and at tip. Feet white with fully furred soles. Young gray-brown with a black stripe from shoulder to rump. Winter coat *white.* **SIMILAR SPECIES:** Richardson's Collared Lemming is usually brown, not gray (in summer). Brown Lemming has a reddish brown rump. Voles (*Microtus* spp.) have longer tails. **SOUNDS:** Young make shrill, high-pitched cries. **HABITS:** Active night or day. Has several short burrows, also takes refuge under boards or debris. In winter lives in tunnels beneath the snow and makes nests on the soil surface but under the snow layer. Feeds on a variety of tundra vegetation, eating mostly willow in winter. Solitary except when breeding. Female modifies an underground burrow for raising young, adding chambers for a nest and a latrine and additional entrances. Young are born March–Sept. or year-round in good years. Litter size is 1–7. **HABITAT:** Arctic tundra. Dry rocky areas in summer, lower meadows in winter. **RANGE:** N. and w. Alaska, nw. Canada, and High Arctic islands.

Northern Collared Lemming in defensive pose. Collared lemmings are the only North American rodents that turn white in winter, when they look like animated powder puffs.

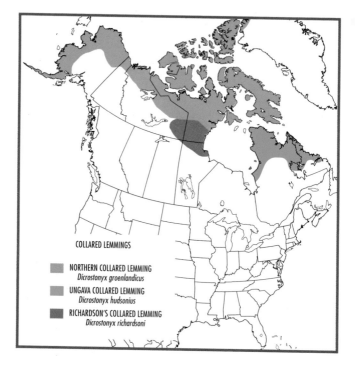

COLLARED LEMMINGS

■ NORTHERN COLLARED LEMMING
Dicrostonyx groenlandicus

■ UNGAVA COLLARED LEMMING
Dicrostonyx hudsonius

■ RICHARDSON'S COLLARED LEMMING
Dicrostonyx richardsoni

STATUS: Common. Populations fluctuate greatly on a 3- to 4-year cycle. **NOTE:** Female *Dicrostonyx* are unusual in having XX or XY sex chromosomes. All males have XY sex chromosomes. This should lead to a bias of females in the population, but in the wild, males appear to be more common than females.

UNGAVA COLLARED LEMMING   Pl. 27
Dicrostonyx hudsonius

Head and body 5 in. (112–150 mm); tail ½ in. (12–17 mm); hind foot ⅞ in. (20–25 mm); wt. 1½–3 oz. (40–90 g). Upperparts *dark gray-brown,* often with a black stripe down spine (this is a feature seen in all young collared lemmings, but seems more pronounced in adults of this species); lower sides dull orange; throat orange, belly gray. In all other respects similar to Northern Collared Lemming. **SIMILAR SPECIES:** Range does not overlap with other lemmings. **HABITS:** Similar to Northern Collared Lemming. **HABITAT:** Rocky tundra, beach terraces, and alpine meadows. **RANGE:** Ungava Pen. in n. Que. and Lab.; also Belcher and King George Is., Nunavut. **STATUS:** Locally common.

CHARDSON'S COLLARED LEMMING

Pl. 27

crostonyx richardsoni

Head and body 5 in. (95–145 mm); tail ½ in. (9–15 mm); hind foot ¾ in. (16–18 mm); wt. 1½–3 oz. (35–90 g). Upperparts *dark gray-brown* or brown, usually with a black stripe down spine; *lower sides deep orange; throat orange,* belly whitish. In all other respects similar to Northern Collared Lemming. **SIMILAR SPECIES:** Northern Collared Lemming is usually grayer, but young and winter individuals best distinguished by teeth or chromosomal differences. **HABITS:** Similar to Northern Collared Lemming. **HABITAT:** Dry open tundra, sand beaches, gravel or rock ridges. **RANGE:** W. of Hudson Bay in Nunavut, ne. Man., and e. N.W.T. **STATUS:** Locally common.

NTRODUCED RATS AND MICE: MURINAE

The 3 species of introduced small rodents originated in Asia but now occur worldwide.

OUSE MOUSE *Mus musculus* (introduced)   Pl. 19, Skull Pl. 3

Head and body 3¼ in. (70–115 mm); tail 3 in. (69–93 mm); hind foot ¾ in. (16–20 mm); ear ½ in. (12–16 mm); wt. ½ oz. (7–24 g). Upperparts gray-brown or yellow-brown; *belly slightly paler or grayer but not sharply demarcated.* Fur short and even. Head rather small; ears large and naked. *Tail robust, uniformly brown, naked-looking.* Tops of feet pale brown or whitish. Female has 10 mammae. Has a distinct and rather unpleasant musky odor. **SIMILAR SPECIES:** Harvest mice have narrow bicolor tails and white or buff bellies, also grooved upper incisor teeth. Northern Pygmy Mouse has a shorter tail. Deer mice have sharply contrasting white bellies. **SOUNDS:** Young twitter and squeak in nest; adult makes a churring song audible at close range. **HABITS:** Nocturnal and mainly terres-

HOUSE MOUSE
Mus musculus

trial, but climbs well. Eats grain, seeds, and insects, also human foodstuffs, soap, and other items. Nests in underground burrows in fields, but may nest in a drawer or other crevice inside a building. Can breed year-round; litter size is 3–11, usually 6. **HABITAT:** Agricultural areas, especially grain fields; roadsides and buildings in rural and urban areas. **RANGE:** Introduced worldwide, found in all U.S. states and s. Canada. Originally from Asia. **STATUS:** Common and widespread. In grain fields eats weed seeds more than crops, but damages and eats much stored grain. Originator of white mouse used in lab research.

ROOF RAT *Rattus rattus* (introduced) **Pl. 24**
Black Rat

Head and body 7 in. (160–210 mm); tail 7½ in. (160–224 mm); hind foot 1½ in. (34–39 mm); ear ⅞ in. (22–24 mm); wt. 7 oz. (100–250 g). Large. Back *dark brown* or *black;* belly gray, buff, or whitish, not sharply defined from sides. Fur long and coarse. Ears large, brown, and naked. Snout long and pointed with long thick whiskers. *Tail slightly longer than head and body,* brown, *nearly naked, scaly.* Feet long and broad, tops brown or gray. Female has 10–12 mammae. **SIMILAR SPECIES:** Norway Rat is larger with relatively shorter tail and ears. Woodrats have contrasting white bellies and hairier tails. Rice rats have narrower, white-topped feet and bicolor tails. **HABITS:** Mainly nocturnal. Climbs well and usually occupies roofs or attics. Where it co-occurs with Norway Rat, Roof Rat nests in trees or attics and Norway Rat nests underground. Eats grain, seeds, fruit, garbage, and other items of dubious edibility. Adults nest alone, although young may remain with the mother long after weaning. Breeds in spring and summer or year-round; litter size is 4–10, usually about 8. **HABITAT:** Buildings in cities and rural areas, ships, wharves, dockside warehouses, coastal forests, and plantations. Usually in association with humans but sometimes in for-

ested areas far from dwellings. **RANGE:** Introduced worldwide, now found in southern (north to Ill.) and coastal U.S., to Me. in East, and on West Coast to B.C. **STATUS:** Common to abundant. Carries plague and typhus fever. Can impact native species and is especially harmful on islands (e.g., Florida Keys).

NORWAY RAT *Rattus norvegicus* (introduced) Pl. 24, Skull Pl. 4
Brown Rat

Head and body 8¾ in. (170–260 mm); tail 7½ in. (150–220 mm); hind foot 1½ in. (37–44 mm); ear ⅝ in. (15–20 mm); wt. 14 oz. (200–540 g). *Very large.* Back *yellow-brown,* belly gray-white or yellowish, not sharply defined from sides. Fur long and coarse. *Ears short,* lightly haired. Snout blunt, with short thick whiskers. *Tail shorter than head and body, robust,* slightly bicolor, *thinly covered with coarse short hairs.* Feet large and broad, tops gray-white or dusky. Female has 10–12 mammae. **SIMILAR SPECIES:** See Roof Rat. Woodrats have contrasting white bellies and hairier tails. Rice rats are smaller with long narrow feet and proportionally longer tails. **HABITS:** Mainly nocturnal, but can be seen by day where common. This is the ugly urban rat seen at bird feeders or in subway systems. Terrestrial, but climbs well on occasion; swims well. Eats grain, fruit, garbage, and any available foods. It is more carnivorous than the Roof Rat and may kill hens or young livestock. Lives in colonies (one male, several females, and young) in a complex burrow system. Breeds year-round; litter size is 2–22. **HABITAT:** Towns, cities, grain fields, and salt marshes. In cities favors sewers and other wet areas. **RANGE:** Introduced worldwide and found in all U.S. states and populated parts of Canada. Originally from se. Siberia and China. **STATUS:** Abundant in many areas. A later arrival, this species takes over nests of Roof Rat and has displaced that species in the North. Our most serious pest mammal, causing enormous damage to stored grains, spreading disease, and damaging structures. On the flip side, Norway Rats have been bred for laboratory use and have played a major role in the advancement of medicine and science.

JUMPING MICE: DIPODIDAE

Jumping mice are not closely related to other New World mice but are in the same family as jerboas and other desert rodents found in the Old World. These mice were formerly placed in the family Zapodidae, but recent taxonomic work indicates that this group is a subfamily within the Dipodidae.

Jumping mice have extremely long and narrow tails (usually about 1½ times the head and body length) and exceptionally long hind feet. They are among our most attractive small rodents, with distinctly marked orange or yellowish sides and contrasting dark backs. The upper incisor teeth are deeply grooved.

As the name suggests, jumping mice are capable of long leaps; some species can leap 10 ft. (3 m) in a single bound. They use the long tail for balance — a mouse with a broken tail somersaults and seldom lands on its feet after a long jump. Jumping mice also swim well and are often found in riparian areas. Although they are mainly nocturnal, they are occasionally seen by day. Jumping mice are deep hibernators. They do not store food for winter use, but accumulate a layer of fat in the fall just before entering hibernation. In northern regions, hibernation lasts 6 months or more, and those mice that have not gained sufficient weight in fall do not survive the winter.

WOODLAND JUMPING MOUSE   Pl. 22
Napaeozapus insignis

Head and body 3 in. (65–95 mm); tail 5¾ in. (126–167 mm); hind foot 1¼ in. (28–34 mm); ear ⅝ in. (15–17 mm); wt. ¾ oz. (17–28 g). Back and top of head *dark brown strongly contrasting with bright yellow-orange or reddish brown sides* and cheeks. Belly pure white. Ears medium sized, haired on outside, rims cream. *Tail very long and narrow*, bicolor (dark brown above, white below) with a *pure white tip*. Hind feet very long and narrow, tops of feet white. Upper incisors grooved, no upper premolars. **SIMILAR SPECIES:** Meadow Jumping Mouse lacks a white tail tip and has a less distinct color change from back to sides. It has a small upper premolar. **SOUNDS:** Usually silent but may drum tail, also makes low clucking sounds and will squeal if disturbed. **HABITS:** Mainly nocturnal, but sometimes seen by day in overcast weather. When encountered, may remain motionless, but if further alarmed can make spectacular leaps of up to 10 ft. (3 m). Eats seeds (of *Impatiens* and other species), berries, subterranean fungi, insects, and insect larvae.

Woodland Jumping Mouse. Note the exceptionally long, narrow hind feet and tail that characterize all jumping mice. This species has a white tail tip.

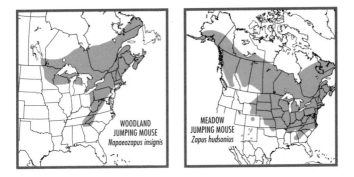

WOODLAND
JUMPING MOUSE
Napaeozapus insignis

MEADOW
JUMPING MOUSE
Zapus hudsonius

Weight just prior to hibernation is about 150 percent of spring weight. Hibernates for 6–8 months (Oct.–May). Litters of 3–6 young are born May–Aug. **HABITAT:** Wet cool woods, often in dense herbaceous vegetation along streams or swamps. Usually found in areas with mixed conifers and hardwoods. Sea level to 6,600 ft. (2,000 m). **RANGE:** Se. Canada and ne. U.S., south through Appalachian Mts. to N.C. **STATUS:** Uncommon to locally common.

MEADOW JUMPING MOUSE
Zapus hudsonius

Head and body 3½ in. (80–100 mm); tail 5½ in. (110–155 mm); hind foot 1¼ in. (28–33 mm); ear ⅝ in. (14–17 mm); wt. ¾ oz. (14–28 g). Back and top of head dark brown contrasting with orange or yellow-brown sides. Belly white or cream. Ears medium sized, haired on outside, rims cream. *Tail very long and narrow,* bicolor (dark brown above, white below). Hind feet very long and narrow, tops of feet white. Upper incisors grooved, 4 upper cheek teeth (3 molars and a small premolar). **SIMILAR SPECIES:** See Woodland Jumping Mouse. Western Jumping Mouse is more grizzled and usually yellow on sides, with a less distinctly bicolor tail. **SOUNDS:** Usually silent but may drum tail, also makes low clucking sounds and birdlike chirps. **HABITS:** Mainly nocturnal, but can be seen by day on the ground or in water. Swims well both above and under the water and may cross bodies of open water. Can leap about 3 ft. (1 m), but usually moves in short hops or crawls. When wet meadows are harvested for hay, these mice concentrate in the unmown areas until these all but disappear and the harvester forces them to erupt like popcorn in all directions. Eats grass seeds, fruit, fungi, and insects, especially moth larvae. Weight just prior to hibernation is about 150 percent of spring weight. Hibernates for 6 to 10 months (Oct.–May in southern part of range). Makes spherical hibernation nests of grass or leaves, usually placed 1–2 ft. (0.5 m) belowground. Litters of 3–7 young are born May–Aug. Females may have 2 litters per year. **HABITAT:** Grassy or weedy fields in both dry and wet areas, also in forest clearings and along streams and bogs at forest edge. Favors areas with dense herbaceous vegetation. Sea level to about 6,600 ft. (2,000 m). **RANGE:** S. Alaska, s. Canada, cen. and e. U.S. Isolated populations in Colo., Ariz., and N.M. **STATUS:** Common. Preble's Meadow Jumping Mouse (*Z. h. preblei*), Colorado, is threatened (USFWS).

WESTERN JUMPING MOUSE *Zapus princeps* Pl. 22

Head and body 3⅜ in. (72–96 mm); tail 5¾ in. (131–158 mm); hind foot 1¼ in. (30–35 mm); ear ⅝ in. (15–18 mm); wt. 1 oz. (18–44 g). Back dark brown contrasting with yellowish sides. Sides heavily grizzled with black. Belly white or cream. Ears yellow edged. Tail long and narrow, somewhat bicolor, with a tuft of fur at tip. Hind feet very long and narrow, tops of feet white. Upper incisors grooved, 4 upper cheek teeth. **SIMILAR SPECIES:** This jumping mouse usually has straw yellow or lemon yellow sides, while other species usually have orange sides. See Meadow and Pacific Jumping Mice. **SOUNDS:** Probably similar to Meadow Jumping Mouse. **HABITS:** Usually walks on all fours or moves with short hops, but may leap 6 ft. (2 m) or more if alarmed. Eats grass seeds, fruit, fungi, and insects. Hibernates for 8 to 10 months (from Aug. or Sept to May or June). Litter size is 3–8; females have 1 litter per year. **HABITAT:** Usually found along streams through mountain meadows and willow-alder associations. Seldom occurs more than 350 ft. (100 m) from water. Elevation 2,000–10,500 ft. (600–3,200 m). **RANGE:** Rocky and Cascade Mts. from Yukon to Calif. and N.M. (previously reported from Ariz. but probably does not occur there), east to N.D and S.D. **STATUS:** Locally common.

WESTERN
JUMPING MOUSE
Zapus princeps

Head and body 3½ in. (77–103 mm); tail 5½ in. (115–160 mm); hind foot 1¼ in. (29–35 mm); ear ⅝ in. (13–18 mm); wt. 1 oz. (18–38 g). Back and top of head dark brown, contrasting strongly with deep orange sides and cheeks; sides lightly grizzled with black. Belly white or cream. Ears edged with white. Tail long and narrow, somewhat bicolor, with a short tuft at tip. Hind feet very long and narrow, tops of feet white. Upper incisors grooved, 4 upper cheek teeth. **SIMILAR SPECIES:** The only jumping mouse in most of its range. Western Jumping Mouse (range overlaps in B.C.) usually has yellow, heavily grizzled sides. Meadow Jumping Mouse is less colorful, with a more strongly bicolor tail. **SOUNDS:** Usually silent but may drum tail, squeals when fighting. **HABITS:** Mainly nocturnal, but sometimes seen abroad by day. If disturbed, makes 3–4 leaps of 3–7 ft. (1–2 m). Eats grass seeds, fruit, fungi, and insects. Also known to eat birds' eggs on occasion. Makes spherical nests of grass and leaves in summer, usually placed on the ground, occasionally on the branch of a tree a few feet above the ground, or in a burrow. Hibernates for 6 to 7 months (Oct.–April), nesting in underground burrows. Litter size is 4–8; females have 1 litter per year. **HABITAT:** Along streams, wetlands, and meadows within coniferous forest, often in association with alder and salmonberry. Sea level to 6,500 ft. (2,000 m). **RANGE:** Sw. B.C. to nw. Calif. **STATUS:** Locally common.

PACIFIC
JUMPING MOUSE
Zapus trinotatus

NEW WORLD PORCUPINES: ERETHIZONTIDAE

This is a South American family, with only one species entering the U.S. and Canada. These large rodents have long sharp spines over most of the body, especially on the rump and tail. Porcupine quills have reversed barbs on the tips that cause the quills to work their way deeper into the flesh and make them very difficult to remove by hand. Porcupines do not throw their quills, but they can spin around and whack a predator with the quilled tail.

NORTH AMERICAN PORCUPINE Pl. 1, Skull Pl. 6
Erethizon dorsatum

Head and body 20 in. (46–100 cm); tail 7 in. (16–23 cm); wt. 7–40 lb. (3–18 kg). Larger in West than East. Large and heavy-bodied. *Prominent yellowish quills on head, rump, and upper surface of tail.* Long guard hairs conceal quills on back and shoulders. Guard hairs mainly blackish in East, mostly yellow in West. Tail short and thick, quilled above, bristly below. Four claws on forefoot, 5 claws on hind foot. Soles of feet naked and pocked. **SIMILAR SPECIES:** No other mammal in our area has quills. **SOUNDS:** Grunts, loud moans, and screams, mainly during fall breeding season. **HABITS:** Mainly nocturnal, but sometimes seen ambling along roadsides by day, especially after spring thaw. Active year-round. In spring eats buds from a variety of trees, in summer eats leaves of trees and herbaceous plants. In fall takes acorns, beechnuts, and apples in addition to leaves. Feeds on inner bark of trees in winter, girdling upper limbs, and will also eat hemlock and other conifer needles. The ground below a tree fed on by a porcupine is often littered

North American Porcupine in defensive pose. If attacked it flicks its tail, driving short, thin quills deep into the body of the predator. It does not throw its quills.

with small clipped branches ("nip-twigs") from which the buds have been removed and eaten. Has a well-known craving for salt and will chew plywood and frequent roadsides in spring in search of salt. Females and young den in rocky outcrops, hollow trees, or outbuildings in winter; males may use a den or may spend the daytime in trees year-round. Mates in the fall; a single young is born in early summer, after a 7-month gestation. Young are weaned at about 4 months. **HABITAT:** Deciduous and coniferous forest. Sometimes found in brushy areas or stands of acacia along washes in desert. **RANGE:** W. and ne. U.S., Alaska, and most of mainland Canada. **STATUS:** Common and widespread. Range has been reduced in the Northeast.

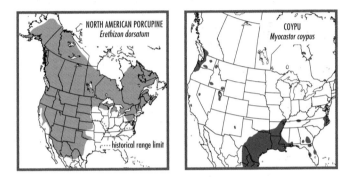

COYPU: Myocastoridae

This family contains a single species, native to South America. It has been introduced widely in North America.

COYPU *Myocastor coypus* (introduced)   **Pl. 2, Skull Pl. 6**
Nutria

Head and body 22 in. (50–65 cm); tail 13 in. (30–45 cm); wt. 10–24 lb. (5–11 kg). *Large and semiaquatic. Square muzzle.* Body dark brown or yellow-brown, cheeks paler, grizzled; fur around nose and mouth white; *long white whiskers. Tail cylindrical,* lightly haired. Feet blackish, hind foot webbed between toes 1–4. Swims with head and back above the water, shoulders underwater. **SIMILAR SPECIES:** American Beaver is larger and has a paddle-shaped tail. Common Muskrat is much smaller with a laterally compressed tail. **SOUNDS:** Loud contact call: *waark.* Hums, growls, and grinds teeth in defense. Slaps tail in water when disturbed. **HABITS:** Mainly nocturnal or crepuscular. Sometimes active by day in cold weather.

PIKAS, RABBITS, AND HARES:
LAGOMORPHA

This order includes the rabbits and hares (Leporidae) and the pikas (Ochotonidae). Lagomorphs are thought by most authors to be closely allied to rodents.

Lagomorphs have 3 pairs of upper incisors at birth, but the outer pair is soon lost. The second, peglike upper incisor is located directly behind the middle incisors. Rodents, by contrast, have a single pair of upper incisors.

Lagomorphs eat vegetation. They produce two types of fecal pellets — dry pellets that are discarded and wet pellets that are re-ingested. This allows food that is broken down by bacterial action in the cecum to be absorbed by the stomach and small intestine when it makes a second pass.

PIKAS: OCHOTONIDAE

Pikas are rat-sized mammals with short but conspicuous rounded ears. They have a very small tail that barely extends beyond the fur. They are found in mountainous regions in association with rockslides or talus slopes. There are 22 species, mostly found in Eurasia. Two species occur in our region.

COLLARED PIKA *Ochotona collaris*   PL. 28
Head and body 7 in. (160–204 mm); tail ½ in. (12–16 mm); hind foot 1¼ in. (29–32 mm); ear 1 in. (22–25 mm); wt. 5 oz. (114–146 g). Back *grayish* or gray-brown, often with some blackish patches (molt line); belly white. *White, cream, or buff-colored collar from throat to ear. Ears broad* and *rounded,* edged with white. Tail very small, only visible in the hand. Feet white, soles thickly furred. **SIMILAR SPECIES:** American Pika is browner and darker, with a less pronounced collar (ranges do not overlap). Rabbits are much larger with longer ears. Voles have visible tails and less conspicuous ears.

Collared Pika gathering food for winter. Pikas collect as much as a bushel of vegetation that they stack outside until dry and then store in the burrow for winter use.

SOUNDS: Short whistled barks given by both sexes in alarm; longer whistles given by males during courtship. **HABITS:** Diurnal; in summer spends most of the day feeding or gathering food for winter storage, with brief periods spent basking or sunning. Does not hibernate, but gathers grass and other vegetation that it piles up into haystacks for winter use (the material is not dried and turned before stacking). Solitary and territorial for most of the year except during the breeding season, when pairs defend a joint territory. Females may have 2 litters of 2–6 young each year. **HABITAT:** Talus slopes and other rocky areas near meadows. **RANGE:** Alaska, Yukon, extreme n. B.C., and w. N.W.T., Canada. Records from the Brooks Range, Alaska, based on sightings only. **STATUS:** Fairly common.

AMERICAN PIKA   *Ochotona princeps*   **Pl. 28, Skull Pl. 6**
Head and body 7 in. (157–203 mm); tail ½ in. (13–18 mm); hind foot 1¼ in. (28–34 mm); ear 1 in. (20–27 mm); wt. 5 oz. (119–176 g). Overall color varies regionally and seasonally from gray-brown to

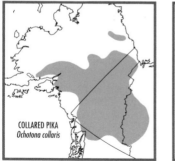

COLLARED PIKA
Ochotona collaris

AMERICAN PIKA
Ochotona princeps

orange-brown to dark brown. Head and shoulders brighter than lower back. *Shoulders, sides of neck, cheeks, and lower sides usually orange.* Belly cream, buff, or deep orange. *Ears broad and rounded,* edged with white. Tail very small, only visible in the hand. Feet pale orange, soles thickly furred. **SIMILAR SPECIES:** See Collared Pika. Rabbits are larger with cottony tails. Voles have inconspicuous ears and short to moderately long tails. **SOUNDS:** Short whistled barks given by both sexes in alarm; longer whistles given by males during courtship. **HABITS:** Similar to Collared Pika. **HABITAT:** Talus slopes and rocky areas near meadows. Usually above 8,000 ft. (2,500 m) in southern part of range. **RANGE:** S. B.C. and sw. Alta. through mts. to Calif., Utah, and N.M. **STATUS:** Declining. Appears to have disappeared from almost 30 percent of the range it occupied in 1900s. It is disappearing from lower elevations, perhaps as a result of increased temperature and decreased humidity due to global warming.

RABBITS AND HARES: LEPORIDAE

Rabbits and hares usually have long ears, long hind feet, and a short cottony tail. Hares, including the jackrabbits, are generally larger than rabbits. There are small hares and large rabbits, however, and they are best distinguished by the early developmental stages and care of young. Rabbits make a fur-lined nest and give birth to altricial young that are blind and nearly naked at birth. Hares never make a nest for their young and have more precocial babies that are fully furred and run about soon after birth.

PYGMY RABBIT *Brachylagus idahoensis*   **Pl. 28**
Head and body 9½ in. (22–28 cm); tail 1 in. (1–3 cm); hind foot 2¾ in. (7–8 cm); ear 1¾ in. (4–5 cm); wt. 15 oz. (335–547 g). *Small, with short rounded ears.* Overall color grayish. Summer: back dark

PYGMY RABBIT
Brachylagus idahoensis

steely gray with a faint wash of brown; belly grayish white. Winter: back pale gray with a buff wash; belly white. *Ears densely haired, white-edged; lined with white fur in winter, gray fur in summer. Small orange nape patch hidden by ears. Short, inconspicuous, grayish tail.* Feet and legs pale orange with dark hairy soles. **SIMILAR SPECIES:** Desert and Mountain Cottontails are much larger with white cotton tails. Brush Rabbit is larger and browner with longer ears (it is not usually found in sagebrush habitats). **SOUNDS:** Buzzy alarm call of 1–7 notes. **HABITS:** Mostly crepuscular, but can be seen by day. Unlike other rabbits, does not hop but rather walks or scurries. This is the only native North American rabbit that constructs underground burrows. Burrows may be simple or complex. In winter may tunnel under snow to feed on snow-covered sagebrush. In summer eats sagebrush and grasses. Lives alone or in groups. Thought to be more social than other rabbits, as exemplified by use of alarm calls. Breeds in early spring and summer; females may have 2–3 litters per year, with 4–8 young per litter. **HABITAT:** Closely associated with tall dense stands of sagebrush, primarily big sagebrush (*Artemisia tridentata*). **RANGE:** Sw. Mont. and s. Ore. south to w. Calif., Nev., Utah, and sw. Wyo. Also isolated population in cen. Wash. **STATUS:** Endangered (USFWS). Range in Washington much reduced in recent years, now present only in Sagebrush Flats, Douglas Co. Elsewhere can be locally common but suffering from habitat loss throughout range.

BRUSH RABBIT *Sylvilagus bachmani*   **Pl. 28**
Head and body 12 in. (27–34 cm); tail 1½ in. (3–5 cm); hind foot 3 in. (7–8 cm); ear 2½ in. (5–7 cm); wt. 21 oz. (499–684 g). Rather small. *Back dark brown or gray-brown,* sides yellow-gray; belly grayish white. Small orange-brown nape patch. Broad cream-colored eye-rings. Ears relatively long, naked inside, *not tipped black.*

BRUSH RABBIT
Sylvilagus bachmani

Tail short and inconspicuous, gray-brown above, pale gray or whitish below. Legs rusty brown, feet pale gray or pale orange. **SIMILAR SPECIES:** Desert and Mountain Cottontails larger and paler with pronounced white cotton tails. See Pygmy Rabbit. **SOUNDS:** Thumps hind feet in alarm; squeals in distress. **HABITS:** Mainly nocturnal, but may emerge to sunbathe by day. Makes tunnels and runways through dense vegetation but does not dig burrows. If pursued, may climb up a shrub or low tree. Eats grass, thistles, clover, and berries, also consumes some woody plants in winter. Seen singly or in groups when feeding; each animal maintains its individual space of 1 ft. (0.3 m) or more. Breeds from midwinter to summer; females produce 3–4 litters of 1–7 young each year. Young are raised in a fur-lined depression; mother covers young with a plug of fur and grass when she leaves to feed. **HABITAT:** Dense brush, forest edge, old clear-cuts and burns in forest. Sea level to 7,000 ft. (2,070 m). **RANGE:** W. Ore. to Calif. and south through Baja Calif. **STATUS:** Generally common. Riparian Brush Rabbit (*S. b. riparius*) of cen. California is endangered (USFWS).

WAMP RABBIT   *Sylvilagus aquaticus*   PL. 29
Cane-cutter

Head and body 17½ in. (40–48 cm); tail 2¼ in. (5–6 cm); hind foot 4 in. (10–11 cm); ear 2¾ in. (6–8 cm); wt. 5 lb. (2.0–2.5 kg). Largest native rabbit. Back orange-brown heavily grizzled with black, sides paler, belly white. Prominent orange eye-ring. *Ears relatively short and broad, insides naked,* pinkish; black line between ears, small orange nape patch. *Tail small and inconspicuous,* brown above, white below. Legs and feet orange. **SIMILAR SPECIES:** Marsh Rabbit is very similar but smaller, with shorter ears and tail usually grayish below. Eastern Cottontail has shorter hind feet and proportionally

The Swamp Rabbit, unlike most rabbits, is an accomplished swimmer and is usually found near water. Note the short, broad ears.

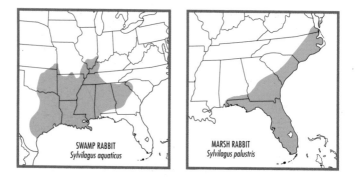

SWAMP RABBIT
Sylvilagus aquaticus

MARSH RABBIT
Sylvilagus palustris

longer, narrower ears. **SOUNDS:** Usually silent, may squeal if disturbed. **HABITS:** Active at dawn and in the late afternoon in spring and summer, mostly nocturnal in winter. Swims well and takes to water more readily than Marsh Rabbit. Walks when traveling slowly. Often leaves piles of droppings on logs or stumps that are probably used as observation sites. Rests in holes or under logs, or hides among tall grass. Feeds on green vegetation, including tree seedlings. This species is more territorial than other rabbits; male marks his territory with scent from a chin gland. Makes a covered nest in a depression, often against a support such as a fencepost or tree. Litter size is 1–6, usually 3; females may produce 2–5 litters per year, from spring to fall. **HABITAT:** Swamps, marshes, and bottomlands. **RANGE:** S.C. to Tex. and north to Mo., Ind., and Tenn. **STATUS:** Diminishing in northern part of its range, locally common in South. **NOTE:** Swamp and Marsh Rabbits are very similar, and some authors have suggested that they represent a single species.

MARSH RABBIT *Sylvilagus palustris*   Pl. 29

Head and body 15 in. (35–40 cm); tail 1½ in. (3–4 cm); hind foot 3½ in. (8–9 cm); ear 2 in. (4–5 cm); wt. 3 lb. (1.0–1.6 kg). Back reddish brown grizzled with black, sides orange-brown, belly buff with white on abdomen. *Ears short and broad,* naked and pink inside. *Tail short and inconspicuous,* brown above, white or gray below. *Legs and feet slender,* reddish brown. Front claws very long, toes and claws conspicuous in tracks. **SIMILAR SPECIES:** See Swamp Rabbit. Eastern Cottontail has larger, narrower ears and a more conspicuous cottony tail. **SOUNDS:** Usually silent but will thump with hind feet; sometimes squeals when disturbed and screams if injured. **HABITS:** Mainly nocturnal, but may be seen at dawn or dusk. When feeding, usually walks rather than hops, and scurries when alarmed. This species can walk on its hind legs. Swims well; readily enters water if pursued and may float almost entirely submerged, only the eyes and nose above water. Makes runways through thick grass that may lead to its "form" (a bare depression) among dense vegetation where it rests during the day. The same form may be used for extended periods. Eats a variety of green plants and emergent marsh vegetation. Makes a covered nest of reeds and grasses lined with fur. Young are born well haired but with their eyes closed. Litter size is 2–4; females may have 6–7 litters per year. **HABITAT:** Brackish and freshwater marshes, edges of lakes and mangroves, and other wet areas. Lowlands and coastal areas to 500 ft. (150 m). **RANGE:** Se. Va. to Fla. and s. Ala. **STATUS:** Generally common; considered a pest of sugar cane in Florida. Lower Keys Marsh Rabbit (*S. p. hefneri*) is endangered (USFWS) mainly due to habitat loss (dredging and filling of marshes for human use). Predation by feral house cats and mortality from highway traffic may also be significant factors.

ASTERN COTTONTAIL
lvilagus floridanus

Pls. 28, 29, Skull Pl. 6

Head and body 14 in. (31–40 cm); tail 2¼ in. (4–8 cm); hind foot 3¾ in. (9–10 cm); ear 3 in. (6–8 cm); wt. 2½ lb. (0.8–1.5 kg). Back *orange grizzled with black, sides paler and grayer;* belly white. Nape usually *deep orange.* Ears short in northern parts of range, longer in warmer regions, edged whitish and tipped black. Sometimes

Eastern Cottontail, our most familiar rabbit, stands up to scan its surroundings. It has numerous predators and seldom survives more than 2 years in the wild.

has *white blaze on forehead*. Eye-rings cream. Tail gray-brown above (fur rusty at base) with a narrow white edge, cottony white below. Legs usually deep orange, sometimes pale orange; feet large, whitish or pale orange. **SIMILAR SPECIES:** See Desert, New England, and Mountain Cottontails. Although these species can often be distinguished by relative ear length, Eastern Cottontail ear size varies with habitat and elevation (larger in western deserts than in Northeast or mountainous regions). Also see Marsh and Swamp Rabbits. **SOUNDS:** Screams when injured, squeals during copulation. Female grunts if nest approached by intruder. **HABITS:** Mainly nocturnal, but may be active at dawn or dusk. Moves by hopping, and when alarmed travels rapidly in a zigzag path to cover. If less disturbed will slink off, moving low to the ground with ears pinned back. Sleeps under brush piles or in thickets or dense grass. In winter may shelter in woodchuck burrows. Eats a variety of herbaceous plants in summer, supplemented by woody plants in winter. Breeds year-round in the South, March–Sept. in the North; males chase each other and perform courtship displays to female, jumping over her or dashing by and urinating on her. Females may have 7 litters per year, with 3–6 young per litter. Young are born in a shallow depression lined with grass and fur. The mother covers the nest when she leaves the young, visiting once or twice a day to nurse. Young are blind and nearly naked at birth but develop quickly and are weaned at about 3 weeks. **HABITAT:** Thickets and oldfields, edges of hardwood forest, farmland, prairies, and swamps. Favors areas with a mosaic of habitats that include grassy areas and cover. **RANGE:** S. Canada, cen. and e. U.S. west to Mont. and Ariz. Also Mexico to Panama and n. South America. Introduced in B.C., Wash., and Ore. **STATUS:** Common. The most widespread cottontail and an important game animal. Can be a pest in gardens, orchards, and agricultural areas. **NOTE:** Some authors consider *S. f. robustus* (w. Texas) to be a distinct species.

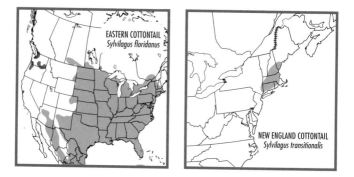

EASTERN COTTONTAIL
Sylvilagus floridanus

NEW ENGLAND COTTONTAIL
Sylvilagus transitionalis

vilagus transitionalis

Head and body 15 in. (33–43 cm); tail 1½ in. (3–5 cm); hind foot 3¾ in. (9–10 cm); ear 2½ in. (6–7 cm); wt. 2½ lb. (0.8–1.4 kg). Back *orange-brown heavily grizzled with black*, sides slightly paler; belly white, chest orange. *Ears short,* marked with *black along leading edge* and tip, fringed with cream, *trailing edge orange.* Nape orange, *black spot on forehead* between ears. Eye-rings orange. Tail brown above, white below. Legs orange-brown, feet pale orange or whitish. **SIMILAR SPECIES:** Appalachian Cottontail is almost identical, separated by range and genetic differences. Eastern Cottontail is usually slightly paler or grayer, with cream eye-rings; it often has a white spot on the forehead (never a black spot), and its longer ears lack strong black edging. **SOUNDS:** Usually silent. Squeals when handled. **HABITS:** Becomes active at dusk, but is more secretive than Eastern Cottontail and seldom ventures far from cover. Eats grass and clover in summer, twigs and forbs in winter. Dens in thickets or may enter woodchuck holes. Breeds March–Sept. Males compete for females with chases, vertical jumps, and face-offs. Female makes a breeding nest in a shallow depression, lines nest with fur and covers it with twigs and leaves. Litter size is 3–8. **HABITAT:** Open woodland, thickets, and brushy areas bordering clearings. **RANGE:** Sw. Me., s. N.H., Mass., Conn., R.I., and se. N.Y. **STATUS:** Uncommon. Formerly more widespread in New England (thought to have disappeared from Vermont and n. New York). Densities declining in areas where it is still known to occur.

PPALACHIAN COTTONTAIL   *Sylvilagus obscurus*

Head and body 14 in. (34–38 cm); tail 1½ in. (2–6 cm); wt. 2 lb. (0.7–1 kg). Externally inseparable from New England Cottontail; see that species for comparisons with other rabbits. **HABITS:** Presumably similar to New England Cottontail. **HABITAT:** Coniferous

APPALACHIAN COTTONTAIL
Sylvilagus obscurus

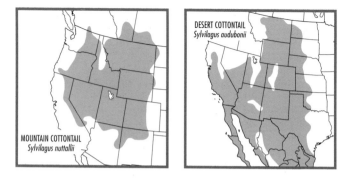

and deciduous woods with dense heaths (mountain laurel and blueberry) at higher elevations. **RANGE:** Appalachian Mts. from Pa. to n. Ala. **STATUS:** Poorly known, local. **NOTE:** This rabbit was recently recognized as distinct from New England Cottontail on the basis of chromosomal differences. In the field it is best distinguished by range.

MOUNTAIN COTTONTAIL *Sylvilagus nuttallii* PL. 28
Nuttall's Cottontail

Head and body 13 in. (29–37 cm); tail 1¾ in. (3–6 cm); hind foot 3½ in. (8–10 cm); ear 2 in. (5–6 cm); wt. 2 lb. (0.7–1.1 kg). Back buff with a dark grizzle (very dark gray in parts of Idaho), rump gray; sides paler and grayer than back; belly white. Nape of neck orange. *Ears short,* edged whitish, black line on leading edge but no black at tip; *well haired on inner surface.* Legs and front feet rusty, hind feet whitish or pale orange. Tail gray above (hairs rusty at base, gray at tips), white below. **SIMILAR SPECIES:** Eastern Cottontail can be very similar but is usually larger with proportionally longer ears that are nearly naked inside. Eastern also has more grizzled fur with an orange wash on the back. Desert Cottontail has longer ears and usually occurs at lower elevations. **SOUNDS:** Usually silent. **HABITS:** Most active at dawn or dusk. Rests by day in "forms" (bare depressions) in dense vegetation, or in burrows or rock crevices in more open areas. Feeds on sagebrush, juniper, and grasses, usually keeping close to cover. Unlike most rabbits, this cottontail sometimes climbs trees. It is most often seen climbing in junipers at dawn during the summer and may obtain water exuded from the leaves at this time. More solitary than other cottontails, it is most often seen singly or in pairs. Breeds Feb.–July; litter size is 4–8, and females may have 5 litters per year. **HABITAT:** Rocky areas in sagebrush flats. Also riparian areas and gullies near ponderosa pines or spruces. **RANGE:** Intermountain West, from sw. Canada to Ariz. and N.M. **STATUS:** Fairly common, declining in some areas.

ESERT COTTONTAIL *Sylvilagus audubonii*   **Pl. 28**

Head and body 12 in. (27–34 cm); tail 1¾ in. (4–6 cm); hind foot 3¼ in. (7–10 cm); ear 3 in. (7–8 cm); wt. 2 lb. (735–946 g). Back yellowish-gray finely grizzled; sides slightly paler but *not contrasting with back*; belly white. *Nape pale orange*; eye-rings cream. *Ears relatively long, finely tipped with black.* Tail gray-brown above (to base of hairs) with a broad white edge, white below. Legs and front feet pale orange, hind feet whitish. **SIMILAR SPECIES:** Eastern Cottontail can be very similar, especially in hot dry regions. In Eastern Cottontail the ears are always shorter than the hind feet, and in Desert Cottontail the ears and hind feet are about the same length. Eastern has a deeper orange and more extensive nape patch, also a more heavily grizzled orange-brown back contrasting with grayish sides. Mountain Cottontail has shorter ears. See Brush Rabbit. **SOUNDS:** Usually silent. May drum hind feet in alarm and will squeal if handled. **HABITS:** Most active soon after dawn or at dusk. Retreats to a burrow made by another species or into a shady thicket to avoid the heat of the day. Leaves piles of droppings on logs and stumps that are probably used as lookout posts. Sometimes climbs on woodpiles or low trees. Feeds on a variety of green vegetation, berries, and acorns. Usually solitary but may gather in small groups at good feeding areas. May breed year-round or from early spring to fall; litter size is 2–4, and females have about 5 litters per year. **HABITAT:** Varied, mainly in dry lowlands including deserts, grasslands, riparian brush, and piñon-juniper woodlands. Sea level to 6,000 ft. (1,800 m). **RANGE:** N.D. and Mont. to Calif. and Tex.; also Baja Calif. and n. Mexico. **STATUS:** Common and widespread.

UROPEAN RABBIT *Oryctolagus cuniculus* (introduced) **Pl. 29**

Head and body 16 in. (35–50 cm); tail 2¾ in. (6–8 cm); hind foot 3¾ in. (8–11 cm); ear 2¾ in. (6–8 cm); wt. 4 lb. (1.2–2.5 kg). Relatively *large and stocky*. Upperparts variable in color, typically *uniform gray-brown or brown* (can be black, white, or mixed colors); fur finely grizzled with black; belly gray or whitish. Ears shorter than head, tipped brown or black. Nape deep orange. Tail blackish above, white below. Front feet orange-brown, hind feet brown. **SIMILAR SPECIES:** Cottontails are smaller and less stocky, with fur more coarsely grizzled on back (cottontails do not dig extensive burrows). **SOUNDS:** Thumps hind feet when alarmed; gives a high-pitched squeal in distress. **HABITS:** Usually crepuscular or nocturnal, but may be active by day. Eats green vegetation in summer,

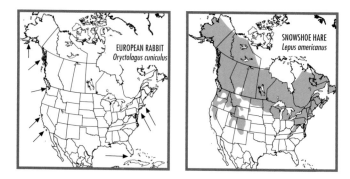

roots and bark in winter. More social than other rabbits; lives in groups of up to 20 with activity centered around extensive burrow systems known as warrens. Burrow entrances are usually on banks, surrounded by close-cropped vegetation. Breeds year-round; may have 6 litters per year of 4–12 young. Young are naked and blind at birth, born in grass-lined nesting chamber within burrow. **HABITAT:** Meadows, fields, and brushy edges of deciduous woods. **RANGE:** Introduced on San Juan Is., Wash.; South Farallon, Santa Barbara, and Anacapa Is., Calif.; Middleton I., Alaska; and Bare and Strongtide Is., B.C. Mainland releases (e.g., in Pa., Wisc., Ind., Ill., and Ont.) and escapees are widespread, but not thought to have established breeding populations. Native to Britain and w. Europe. **STATUS:** Some island populations are large and cause erosion, loss of native plants, and other problems.

SNOWSHOE HARE   *Lepus americanus*   Pl. 30, Skull Pl. 6
Varying Hare

Head and body 16 in. (35–47 cm); tail 1½ in. (3–5 cm); hind foot 5½ in. (12–15 cm); ear 2¾ in. (6–8 cm); wt. 3 lb. (0.9–2.2 kg). Smallest hare, not much larger than a cottontail. Female is slightly larger than male. Summer: upperparts *dark brown* or brown; eyering, cheeks, and sides orange-brown; belly and chin off-white. Ears shorter than head, clearly tipped black. *Tail short,* brown above, *gray or whitish below.* Winter: *entirely white* except for black ear tips. White fur when parted is dark gray at base, midsection brown, tipped white. *Hind feet very long and heavily furred below.* Stays brown year-round in Washington and Oregon; some in Adirondack Mts., New York, are blackish year-round. During molt may be mainly brown with white ears, legs, feet, underparts, and tail, or may be mostly white with some brown on face. **SIMILAR SPECIES:** Other hares are much larger. Cottontails have much shorter hind feet and conspicuous white tails. **SOUNDS:** Usually silent. Gives high-pitched squeals in distress. Thumps hind feet in alarm. **HABITS:** Mostly nocturnal or crepuscular; shelters by day under logs or in thick vegetation. This forest hare relies on cover and usually sneaks off if disturbed, but it can travel at high speed, leaping up to 12 ft. (3.5 m) in a single bound and circling back to its starting point. It makes well-worn pathways between rest sites and feeding areas. Eats grass, green vegetation, and berries in summer, mostly twigs and bark in winter. It will also take carrion and may run hunters' trap lines. Breeds 2–5 times per year; litter size is 1–8. Young born well developed, weaned after 1 month. **HABITAT:** Forests and dense thickets, often associated with low wet areas. In coniferous forest in northern part of range, hardwood forests farther south. **RANGE:** Canada, Alaska, and n. U.S., south in western mts. to Utah and N.M. **STATUS:** Locally common. Populations in North fluctuate greatly on a 10-year cycle. Canada Lynx, a major predator, shows a similar pattern.

ALASKAN HARE *Lepus othus* PI. 30
Tundra Hare

Head and body 22 in. (50–60 cm); tail 3½ in. (6–10 cm); hind foot 7 in. (17–19 cm); ear 3 in. (7–8 cm); wt. 12 lb. (3.5–7.2 kg). *Very large.* Summer (May/June to Sept.): back reddish brown or gray-brown; belly, *legs, feet, tail,* eye-rings, and backs of ears *white.* Ears tipped black. Winter: *entirely white to base of fur,* except for black ear tips. **SIMILAR SPECIES:** Snowshoe Hare is smaller, tail brown above in summer, fur dark at roots in winter. Very similar to Arctic Hare, but ranges do not overlap (easily separated by skull and dental differences: in Alaskan the upper incisors are strongly recurved, in Arctic they are slightly recurved). **SOUNDS:** Usually silent; may puff or hiss. **HABITS:** Eats crowberries and green vegetation in summer, twigs and woody plants in winter. Stout claws enable it to dig through hard-packed snow in winter. Mainly solitary but may be

ALASKAN HARE
Lepus othus

seen in groups in early summer during mating season. Female has litter of 5–7 young in late May or June. Young huddle together in shallow depressions in dense brush or on exposed tundra. Young are precocial but may nurse for 2 months, allowing them to approach adult size by winter. **HABITAT:** Tundra; prefers dense alder thickets, but also found in wet meadows and sedge flats. **RANGE:** W. Alaska. **STATUS:** Generally uncommon; populations fluctuate from year to year.

ARCTIC HARE *Lepus arcticus* PL. 30

Head and body 21 in. (47–58 cm); tail 3 in. (5–10 cm); hind foot 6 in. (14–17 cm); ear 3½ in. (7–10 cm); wt. 10 lb. (2.5–6 kg). *Very large.* Summer: back dark or *pale gray-brown*; belly, legs, *feet, tail,* eye-rings, and backs of ears *white. Ears are shorter than head* and tipped black. Winter: *entirely white* except for black ear tips and yellow-brown soles of feet. *Fur pure white to roots.* In northern part of range it is white year-round, or may be white with some brown on nose and ears only. Young are brown at birth, even if mother is white year-round. **SIMILAR SPECIES:** Snowshoe Hare (seldom found in tundra) is smaller, tail brown above in summer, fur dark at roots in winter. See Alaskan Hare. **SOUNDS:** Usually silent; makes a drumming sound when scraping snow; low growls from female to young; screams in distress. **HABITS:** Rests during midday; seldom digs into snow but uses a rock or shallow depression for shelter. Moves in a series of 4-legged hops, and may keep one foreleg lifted, leaving a 3-legged track. Can also stand and hop on hind legs. Feeds mainly on dwarf willow, especially in winter, eating woody stems and roots. In summer also eats green vegetation and berries. Moves onto windswept slopes in winter, where snow cover is shallow and food easier to find. Mates in April–May. Female gives birth to litters of 2–8 young in fur- and grass-lined nest often situated under rocks. Young are brown at birth but turn white in

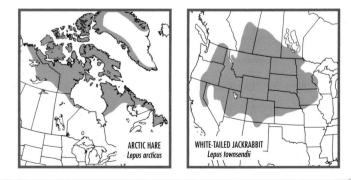

ARCTIC HARE
Lepus arcticus

WHITE-TAILED JACKRABBIT
Lepus townsendii

2–3 weeks. They are weaned at 2 months. **HABITAT:** Tundra, mostly beyond the tree line, on rocky slopes and hills. Avoids wet, low-lying areas. Sea level to 3,000 ft. (900 m). **RANGE:** N. Canada mainland and islands, also coastal Greenland. **STATUS:** Uncommon to locally abundant.

HITE-TAILED JACKRABBIT *Lepus townsendii* Pls. 30, 31

Head and body 21 in. (44–70 cm); tail 4½ in. (8–14 cm); hind foot 5½ in. (13–15 cm); ear 4 in. (10–11 cm); wt. 7½ lb. (2.5–4.3 kg). Summer: *upperparts gray with a yellowish wash;* belly white. *Tail entirely white* or white with a narrow dusky stripe above. Ears fairly long (longer than head), tipped black; back of ear white. Winter (in northern regions): *entirely white* (hair white at roots, brown in midsection, then tipped white) with black ear tips. Brown year-round in southern part of range. **SIMILAR SPECIES:** See Black-tailed Jackrabbit. Snowshoe Hare is smaller and has shorter ears. **SOUNDS:** Usually silent. **HABITS:** Mainly nocturnal, but may be active at dawn or dusk. When pursued, follows a zigzag path, with leaps of up to 16 ft. (5 m) and bursts of speed of 35 mph (55 km/h). Spends the day resting in a shallow depression or "form." Feeds on grasses and forbs in summer, shrubs and woody vegetation in winter. Mainly solitary in habit but may aggregate at a feeding area in winter. Breeds in late winter and produces 1 litter per year in northern part of range, up to 4 litters per year in the southern part. Litter size is 1–11, usually 4–5. Young are raised in fur- or grass-lined nests, well concealed by vegetation. **HABITAT:** Open grassland, meadows, and cultivated areas. Less common in sagebrush flats. Sea level to 14,000 ft. (4,300 m). **RANGE:** Canadian prairies, Wash., and Wisc. to Calif. and n. N.M. **STATUS:** Locally common. Range has expanded north and eastward with conversion of forest to farmland, but has been reduced in Kansas and Colorado where native prairie has been lost to agriculture or pastureland.

LACK-TAILED JACKRABBIT Pl. 31, Skull Pl. 6
pus californicus

Head and body 18½ in. (43–52 cm); tail 3½ in. (6–12 cm); hind foot 5 in. (11–14 cm); ear 4½ in. (10–13 cm); wt. 6 lb. (1.8–3.6 kg). Back buff grizzled with black, sides slightly paler; belly white or pale orange; chest orange-brown. *Ears very long,* with *conspicuous black tips.* Tail black above, with *black usually extending onto rump;* white or buff below. **SIMILAR SPECIES:** See White-sided and Antelope Jackrabbits. White-tailed Jackrabbit has proportionally shorter ears and an all-white tail. **SOUNDS:** Usually silent but may squeal or scream in distress; thumps hind feet when alarmed. **HABITS:** Nocturnal or crepuscular; rests by day in a shallow soil depression or "form," usually in the shade of a bush. Uses speed and

Black-tailed Jackrabbit, its huge ears backlit, showing an abundant supply of blood vessels that are used to dissipate heat.

BLACK-TAILED JACKRABBIT
Lepus californicus

agility to avoid predators and can travel at up to 35 mph (55 km/h) with leaps of 20 ft. (6 m) at a time. By obtaining most or all of its water from food and using a variety of physiological and behavioral methods of thermoregulation, this jackrabbit can exploit hot, dry desert regions and overgrazed barren lands. It eats a wide variety of plants including nutritionally poor foods such as creosote bush. Usually solitary, but may be seen in pairs or occasionally in larger aggregations. Breeds in spring and summer in the northern part of its range, producing 1–4 litters per year. In the southern part, breeds year-round and may have 7 litters per year. Litter size is 1–8, usually 4 in the northern part, 2 in the southern. Young are fully furred at birth and can run within a few hours. The mother places each young in a separate nest, visiting them to nurse at intervals during the night. **HABITAT:** Sagebrush flats, overgrazed pastures and rangelands, deserts, prairies, and agricultural land. Sea level to 12,500 ft. (3,800 m). **RANGE:** S. Wash., S.D., and Mo. to Tex. and n. Mexico. Introduced to Fla. and parts of the Northeast. **STATUS:** Common and widespread.

WHITE-SIDED JACKRABBIT *Lepus callotis* Pl. 31
Head and body 18½ in. (41–52 cm); tail 2½ in. (5–7 cm); hind foot 5 in. (12–13 cm); ear 4¾ in. (11–12 cm); wt. 6 lb. (2.4–2.9 kg). Back

WHITE-SIDED JACKRABBIT
Lepus callotis

buff grizzled with black; *sides white, contrasting with back*; rump very pale gray. Neck and shoulders buff. Ears long, edged with cream; some black along leading edge near tip, but *tip cream white.* Tail black above, with black extending only to base of rump; white below. **SIMILAR SPECIES:** Antelope Jackrabbit has gray sides and longer ears. Black-tailed Jackrabbit is more uniformly colored, with black-tipped ears and a longer tail with black extending onto rump. **SOUNDS:** Usually silent; male may grunt at intruding male; screams in distress. **HABITS:** Nocturnal; most active from 10 P.M. to 5 A.M. on clear moonlit nights. Rests by day in a "form" surrounded by dense clumps of tall grass. Feeds on a variety of grasses. Usually seen in pairs during spring and summer; may be solitary in winter. Litter size is 1–4. **HABITAT:** Flat grasslands with little or no shrub cover. Elevation 4,900–5,250 ft. (1,520–1,600 m) in U.S. **RANGE:** Animas and Playas Valleys, Hidalgo Co., sw. N.M.; also to cen. Mexico. **STATUS:** Rare and local throughout range; threatened in New Mexico (New Mexico Dept. Game and Fish). Much of this jackrabbit's grassland habitat has been degraded or lost. In overgrazed areas, replaced by the more adaptable Black-tailed Jackrabbit.

NTELOPE JACKRABBIT *Lepus alleni*   **Pl. 31**
Head and body 22 in. (52–58 cm); tail 3 in. (5–10 cm); hind foot 5¼ in. (12–14 cm); ear 6 in. (14–17 cm); wt. 6½–9 lb. (3–4 kg). *Very large.* Upper back buff heavily grizzled with black; *sides pale gray;* belly white. Neck pale orange. *Ears very long, tips and edges white.* Tail black above, grayish white below. **SIMILAR SPECIES:** Black-tailed Jackrabbit has tips of ears black. White-sided Jackrabbit has white sides and proportionally smaller ears (ranges do not overlap). **SOUNDS:** Usually silent; sometimes grunts or makes a repeated chuck, may scream in distress. **HABITS:** Crepuscular and nocturnal,

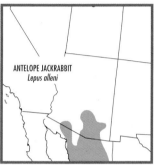

The Antelope Jackrabbit enters the U.S. only in southern Arizona. If undisturbed, it spends much of the day resting in shallow depressions or "forms" with its long ears laid back.

ANTELOPE JACKRABBIT
Lepus alleni

but may be active all day when skies are overcast. Rests by day in the shade of a bush, sitting on flat ground or in a shallow depression, ears held flat against body. When alarmed can run at up to 45 mph (72 km/h) and can cover 23 ft. (7 m) in a single bound. Sometimes hops off on its hind legs, body upright. Also moves on all fours with an occasional vertical jump to view its pursuer. When frightened exposes a large white patch on the rump that is normally concealed when resting or moving quietly. Eats grass, green vegetation such as mesquite leaves, and cacti. Seen singly or in pairs. Breeds 3–4 times per year; litter size is 1–5. **HABITAT:** Grassy slopes in dry areas, often with scattered mesquite, catclaw, and cacti. Sea level to 5,000 ft. (1,500 m). **RANGE:** S. Ariz. and nw. Mexico. **STATUS:** Fairly common in a limited range.

EUROPEAN HARE *Lepus capensis* (introduced)   **PL. 30**
Brown Hare
Head and body 22 in. (51–62 cm); tail 4 in. (6–13 cm); hind foot 6 in. (14–16 cm); ear 4 in. (8–12 cm); wt. 11 lb. (2.5–7 kg). *Very large.* Back yellow-brown grizzled with black; belly white, chest orange-brown. *Ears long, tipped black.* Tail black above (black does not extend onto rump), white below; *tail held down when running.* Legs, feet, and lower sides orange-brown. **SIMILAR SPECIES:** Snowshoe Hare is much smaller, has relatively shorter ears and tail, and is

white in winter. White-tailed Jackrabbit has all-white tail. Black-tailed Jackrabbit (introduced in N.J.) has a longer tail with black extending onto rump. **SOUNDS:** Usually silent; chatters teeth when alarmed and may scream in distress. Female bugles to attract young. **HABITS:** Mainly nocturnal or crepuscular. This hare does not seek cover when hunted but tries to outrun the predator. Extremely fast, it can reach speeds of 45 mph (75 km/h) and follows a zigzag path if pursued. Feeds on green vegetation, seeds, and berries in summer, twigs and bark in winter. Does not make a burrow but rests in a "form" (a scratched-out depression in the ground); holds ears flat to head when resting. This is the "Mad March Hare" that may stand up and box during the breeding season (often an unreceptive female repelling the advances of a male). Breeds mostly in late winter or spring and may produce 3–4 litters per year, usually 3–4 young per litter. Young are precocial at birth and scatter into individual forms where they remain motionless and well camouflaged by day. Mother visits each form nightly to nurse young. **HABITAT:** Meadows, pastures, and cultivated fields. **RANGE:** Introduced in the Northeast and se. Canada. Native to Europe, n. Africa, and much of Asia. **STATUS:** Presently declining in North America. Populations stable in s. Ontario; probably also occurs in Hudson River Valley, New York, and w. Connecticut. Previously found in Vermont, Massachusetts, Maryland, e. Pennsylvania, and n. Wisconsin. These populations thought to be extirpated.

EUROPEAN HARE
Lepus capensis

Shrews and Moles: Soricimorpha

Shrews and moles were previously included in the Insectivora, with tenrecs, hedgehogs, and gymnures. These groups have been split into several orders that do not appear to be closely related (see figure 1, p. xix). Shrews and moles are small and have long, narrow snouts. They have 5 digits on the front and hind feet.

SHREWS: Soricidae

Shrews are small to tiny mouselike mammals with very long, narrow snouts. They are the smallest mammals in North America. Shrews may superficially resemble mice, but they are not closely related and are fairly easy to distinguish. Shrews have a long snout with a continuous row of small teeth. Mice have shorter snouts and have a conspicuous gap between the incisor teeth and the molars. Shrews have 5 toes on each foot, while mice have 4 toes on the front foot and 5 toes on the hind foot. Shrews from northern climates molt in spring and fall. In general, their fur is grayer in winter and browner in summer. Many shrews have a musky odor produced by scent glands on the sides of the body or abdomen. Both sexes may have these scent glands.

Shrews are terrestrial; they often burrow near the surface in the leaf litter or humus layer, or travel through burrows and runways made by moles or voles. They usually do not climb, but some species clamber about in shrubs and a few have been recorded well above the ground. Some shrews swim well and are modified for a semiaquatic life. Shrews are mainly nocturnal, but most species are also active sporadically throughout the day. They are well known for their nervous and high-strung behavior as well as for their legendary consumption of food. In captivity, many species will eat two or more times their own weight in food each day and may die of starvation or stress if food-deprived for a few hours. In the wild, many shrews are exposed to periods of food shortage. They survive these periods by resting or becoming torpid. Even in captivity, short-tailed shrews (*Blarina* spp.) can be maintained for several months on diets of 10 percent of their body weight per day.

Shrews eat earthworms, larval and adult insects, and other invertebrates. They sometimes also eat small vertebrates, such as young mice and salamanders, as well as fungi and seeds. Shrews locate their prey mainly by touch. Many shrews squeak and twitter almost constantly; some calls can be heard at close range, others are ultrasonic. Some shrews are known to use these calls for echolocation.

Shrews are typically solitary in habits and cannot be maintained together in captivity. The Least Shrew is more social and sometimes nests communally. Lifespan is usually a year or less. Shrews are seldom caught in live-traps set for mice. Many species are too small to set off the trigger of the trap, and shrews are seldom attracted to conventional baits. Some may be caught in snap-traps, but the most successful method of trapping shrews is in a pitfall. Pitfall traps are smooth-sided containers sunk in the soil to below ground level. Measures of the abundance of some shrews may reflect the extent of capture efforts more than actual abundance. In many areas, recovery of shrew bones from owl pellets indicate that a species is quite common, while trapping efforts may infer that the same species is rare.

Shrews are often very difficult to identify to species level. Shrews are usually dead when encountered, allowing close inspection. It is often necessary to examine the teeth with a hand lens to confirm identification. Points to look for: On the upper incisors, check the pigmentation (all our shrews have reddish tips to the teeth) and look for the tines (small bumps projecting from the middle of the upper incisors). Behind the large incisor teeth are several small teeth known as unicuspids. There are 3–5 upper unicuspids — note the number visible in profile and the relative size of these teeth (see individual species descriptions below and see figure 2, pp. 164–65). In case of doubt, specimens should be sent to a museum for identification.

RCTIC SHREW   *Sorex arcticus*   PL. 33

Head and body 3 in. (68–89 mm); tail 1¾ in. (36–48 mm); hind foot ⅝ in. (13–16 mm); wt. ⅜ oz. (8–12 g). *Large, with striking three-tone coloration: dark chocolate brown on upper back,* sides pale dusky brown, belly whitish. Juveniles and subadults are dark brown on back and sides with a pale belly. Tail fairly long, bicolor, with a slight tuft. Five upper unicuspids: 3 larger than 4, 5 small but clearly visible in tooth row. **SIMILAR SPECIES:** No other shrew in its

range is tricolored. See Maritime Shrew. **HABITS:** Feeds on pupae of larch sawflies in summer and fall. Has been observed hunting grasshoppers by climbing up nearby vegetation and jumping on prey. Litter size is 5–9. **HABITAT:** Range is limited to boreal coniferous forest. Favors openings in forest and wet areas such as marshes, meadows, and willow-alder copses. **RANGE:** N.W.T. to Gulf of St. Lawrence, Canada. **STATUS:** Common.

MARITIME SHREW   *Sorex maritimensis*

Head and body 2½ in. (60–72 mm); tail 1⅝ in. (37–42 mm); hind foot ½ in. (13–14 mm); wt. ¼ oz. (7–8 g). Tricolor: upper back brown, sides yellow-brown, belly yellow-gray. Tail bicolor. **SIMILAR SPECIES:** Very similar to Arctic Shrew but slightly smaller, upper back paler (ranges do not overlap). **HABITS:** Poorly known. **HABITAT:** Edges of swamps and marshes; wet grassy areas. **RANGE:** Maritime Provinces, e. Canada, N.S., and e. N.B. **STATUS:** Local, apparently uncommon or rare. **NOTE:** Previously considered to be a subspecies of Arctic Shrew (*S. arcticus*). Separated based on biochemical data.

TUNDRA SHREW *Sorex tundrensis*

Pl. 33

Head and body 3 in. (61–86 mm); tail 1¼ in. (28–38 mm); hind foot ½ in. (13–15 mm); wt. ⅜ oz. (6–14 g). Medium sized, distinctively marked, and *short-tailed.* Summer (June–Aug.) coat *tricolor:* upper back brown, sides pale brown, lower sides and belly whitish. Winter coat *bicolor:* back and upper sides deep red-brown, *sharply contrasting with whitish lower sides and belly.* Fur very thick and plush. Tail bicolor, pale brown above, well furred and tufted at tip. Five upper unicuspids: 3 larger than 4, 5 small but clearly visible in tooth row. **SIMILAR SPECIES:** See Barren Ground Shrew (S. *ugyunak*). Other shrews in Alaska — Masked, Montane, and Pygmy (S. *cinereus, S. monticolus,* and S. *hoyi*) — lack contrasting whitish sides and are usually smaller. **HABITS:** Not studied. Litter size is 8–12. **HABITAT:** Slopes and well-drained tundra with dense vegetation. Avoids the wet, low-lying areas favored by Barren Ground Shrew (S. *ugyunak*). **RANGE:** Alaska and extreme nw. Canada. **STATUS:** Common. **NOTE:** Previously considered to be a subspecies of Arctic Shrew (S. *arcticus*).

ALASKA TINY SHREW *Sorex yukonicus*

Head and body 1¾ in. (45–48 mm); tail 1 in. (23–27 mm); hind foot ⅜ in. (8–10 mm); wt. 1⁄16 oz. (1.5–1.7 g). *Tiny. Somewhat tricolor:* back dark brown, sides gray-brown, belly pale gray. Tail bicolor. Five upper unicuspids visible in tooth row. **SIMILAR SPECIES:** Other shrews in Alaska are larger. Pygmy Shrew (S. *hoyi*) is relatively large in northern part of its range (probably separable by size), with 3 unicuspids visible in side view of tooth row. **HABITS:** Unknown. **HABITAT:** The few records are all from riparian areas. **RANGE:** Yukon R. and upper Susitna R., Alaska. **STATUS:** Unknown. **NOTE:** This species is related to *Sorex minutissimus* of Siberia. It was first described in 1997 from seven specimens caught in pitfall traps (its small size probably renders snap-trapping and live-trapping inef-

ALASKA TINY SHREW
Sorex yukonicus

fective). Further deployment of pitfalls in suitable areas may expand its known range and provide some information on abundance.

MARSH SHREW   *Sorex bendirii*   PL. 33
Bendire's Shrew
Head and body 3½ in. (70–101 mm); tail 3 in. (60–80 mm); hind foot ⅞ in. (18–23 mm); wt. ½ oz. (10–21 g). *Large and dark* with a *long tail. Back blackish,* sometimes smattered with pale hairs; *belly usually dark,* about the same color as back. Tail naked-looking and not tufted, usually *all-dark,* occasionally slightly bicolor. Feet large and dark, some hair on sides of hind feet, but not heavily fringed. **GEOGRAPHIC VARIATION:** *S. b. albiventer* (Olympic Pen., Washington) has a white belly. **SIMILAR SPECIES:** American Water Shrew (*S. palustris*) has a clearly bicolor tail and well-fringed hind feet. Other large shrews in its range are brown. **HABITS:** Swims well, both near the surface and underwater, and can run on the water surface for several seconds. About half its diet is aquatic insect larvae; also feeds on soft-bodied land invertebrates. **HABITAT:** Streams, marshes, and other riparian areas in forest and at forest edge. **RANGE:** Pacific Northwest, from s. B.C. to n. Calif. **STATUS:** Uncommon and local.

AMERICAN WATER SHREW   *Sorex palustris*   PL. 33
Head and body 3¼ in. (67–96 mm); tail 2¾ in. (60–76 mm); hind foot ¾ in. (18–20 mm); wt. ½ oz. (9–18 g). Large and dark, with a *long bicolor tail.* Color variable: back blackish, sometimes flecked with white, belly contrasting silvery white or buffy brown; or, less commonly, entirely blackish above and below with no white flecks

American Water Shrew. This is a semiaquatic shrew that feeds on insect larvae and other small prey in fast-flowing streams.

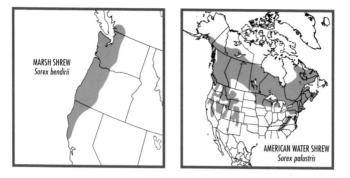

MARSH SHREW
Sorex bendirii

AMERICAN WATER SHREW
Sorex palustris

on back. Throat and chest usually paler than back in dark-bellied form. Tip of tail tufted. *Feet large,* toes on hind foot partially webbed and *fringed on sides with white hair.* **SIMILAR SPECIES:** Larger and longer-tailed than most shrews in its range. Marsh Shrew (*S. bendirii*) is similar in size but lacks fringes on feet and nearly always has a unicolor tail. **HABITS:** Swims well and appears silvery in water because the fur traps air, increasing buoyancy. Hairs on hind feet also trap air and enable it to run across the water surface. Eats aquatic insect larvae, small fish, and terrestrial invertebrates. Females breed after their first winter and may have 2–3 litters per year. Breeds Feb.–July; litter size is 2–10. Maximum lifespan is about 18 months. **HABITAT:** Most common along cold, fast-flowing streams with abundant cover. Also found at edges of lakes, ponds, sluggish streams, marshes, and bogs. **RANGE:** Much of Canada and n. U.S., also Rockies, Appalachians, and Sierra Nevada Mts. **STATUS:** Widespread; uncommon to fairly common in some areas. **NOTE:** Some authors consider the Glacier Bay Water Shrew, *S. p. alaskanus,* to be a distinct species. It is known only from Point Gustavus, Glacier Bay, Alaska, and has not been recorded since 1899.

SMOKY SHREW   *Sorex fumeus*   PL. 32

Head and body 2¾ in. (59–75 mm); tail 1⅞ in. (43–53 mm); hind foot ½ in. (12–15 mm); wt. ¼ oz. (5–9 g). *Medium sized.* Summer coat: *back gray-brown;* belly pale brown. Winter coat: *back dark gray* to blackish, belly pale gray. Ears rather conspicuous. Tail bicolor with a slight tuft at tip. Tops of feet whitish. In southern part of range may have a dark dorsal stripe that extends onto forelimbs; sides paler. Young of the year are gray. Five upper unicuspids: 1 and 2 larger than 3 and 4 (3 slightly larger than 4), 5 very small. **SIMILAR SPECIES:** Masked Shrew (*S. cinereus*) is smaller. See

Smoky Shrew eating an earthworm. In its brown summer coat (shown here) this species is very similar to the smaller Masked Shrew, but note its pale hind feet.

SMOKY SHREW
Sorex fumeus

Rock Shrew (*S. dispar*). American Water Shrew (*S. palustris*) is larger with a longer tail and fringed hind feet. **HABITS:** Travels in tunnels under leaf litter and rotting logs. Mainly nocturnal but may be active by day. Feeds on medium-sized invertebrates, also kills salamanders by biting through the spinal cord. Breeds March–Aug. and may have 2–3 litters per year. Litter size is 2–7; young stay in the nest until they are nearly adult size but do not breed until the next spring. Life expectancy is 14–17 months. **HABITAT:** Moist areas in hardwood or coniferous forest. **RANGE:** E. Canada and ne. U.S. south to n. Ga. and ne. Ala. **STATUS:** Fairly common.

ROCK SHREW *Sorex dispar*   Pl. 32
Long-tailed Shrew

Head and body 2½ in. (48–79 mm); tail 2¼ in. (46–67 mm); hind foot ½ in. (12–15 mm) wt. ⅜ oz. (4–8 g). *Fairly small* with a *very long tail*. Back *slate gray*, belly gray, slightly paler than back. *Muzzle long and slender* with long whiskers. Tail faintly bicolor, dark gray above. Tops of feet pale. Five upper unicuspids: 1 and 2 larger than 3 and 4 (3 slightly larger than 4), 5 very small. Teeth long and narrow compared with other shrews. **SIMILAR SPECIES:** See Gaspé Shrew (*S. gaspensis*). Smoky Shrew (*S. fumeus*) is about the same size and is grayish in winter, but its tail is about 75 percent of body length (tail of Rock Shrew is 90 percent or more of body length). American Water Shrew (*S. palustris*) is larger, with a white belly and fringed hind feet. **HABITS:** Subterranean in habits, travels 2 ft. (0.6 m) or more below the surface in a network of tunnels and crevices between talus rocks or boulders. Diet includes centipedes, insects, and spiders. Litter size is 2–5. **HABITAT:** As the name suggests, this shrew is invariably found in rocky regions. Favors boulder-strewn streams at the base of steep slopes in hardwood or coniferous forest. **RANGE:** N.S. and se. N.B. to N.C. and Tenn. **STATUS:** Apparently uncommon or rare, perhaps because it is seldom taken in pitfall traps set near the surface. If traps are set arm's length below surface rocks, more specimens are obtained.

ROCK SHREW
Sorex dispar

GASPÉ SHREW
Sorex gaspensis

ASPÉ SHREW   *Sorex gaspensis*

Head and body 2¼ in. (51–65 mm); tail 2 in. (47–55 mm); hind foot ½ in. (11–13 mm); wt. ⅛ oz. (2–5 g). *Very small; tail almost as long as body.* Back *slate gray,* belly gray, slightly paler than back. Muzzle long and slender with long whiskers. Tail faintly bicolor, dark gray above. Tops of feet pale. **SIMILAR SPECIES:** Rock Shrew (*S. dispar*) is very similar in color and proportions but averages larger (ranges closely approach on Me./N.B. border but probably do not overlap). Smoky Shrew (*S. fumeus*) is larger with a clearly bicolor and relatively shorter tail (less than 75 percent of head and body length). Masked Shrew (*S. cinereus*) is brown. **HABITS:** Very few specimens have been collected. Stomach contents of two animals consisted of plant material, beetles, and spiders. Three pregnant females had embryo counts of 5–6. **HABITAT:** In common with Rock Shrew, it is restricted to rocky slopes, usually along small streams through coniferous or hardwood forest. **RANGE:** Three disjunct populations: Gaspé Pen., Que.; Cape Breton I., N.S.; nw. N.B. **STATUS:** Apparently uncommon to rare and very limited in distribution.

BARREN GROUND SHREW   *Sorex ugyunak*   Pl. 32

Head and body 2¼ in. (47–70 mm); tail 1¼ in. (26–36 mm); hind foot ⅜ in. (10–12 mm); wt. ⅛ oz. (3–5 g). Small and *short-tailed.* Back brown, *contrasting with whitish lower sides and belly.* Tail bicolor, pale brown above, well haired and tufted at tip. **SIMILAR SPECIES:** Tundra Shrew (*S. tundrensis*) is similar in color but is larger (usually weighs over 8 g). Masked Shrew (*S. cinereus*) does not have contrasting white belly and sides and has a longer tail. **HABITS:** Not described. **HABITAT:** Moist tundra, in thickets of dwarf willow and birch and in low sedge-grass meadows. **RANGE:** Nw. Alaska to w. Hudson Bay. **STATUS:** Locally common. **NOTE:** Formerly considered to be a subspecies of Masked Shrew (*S. cinereus*).

SAINT LAWRENCE ISLAND SHREW   *Sorex jacksoni*   Pl. 32

Head and body 2⅝ in. (62–71 mm); tail 1⅜ in (32–37 mm); hind foot ½ in. (12–14 mm); wt. ⅛ oz. (4–5 g). Medium sized. Strikingly marked: *back dark brown, belly and lower sides white* washed with pinkish orange. Tail bicolor, pale brown above, short hairs at tip.

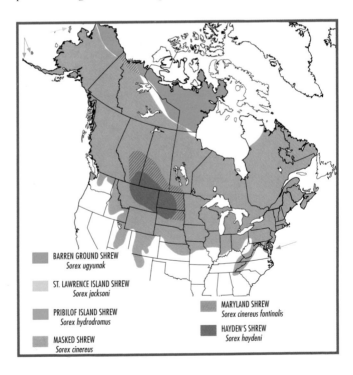

BARREN GROUND SHREW
Sorex ugyunak

ST. LAWRENCE ISLAND SHREW
Sorex jacksoni

PRIBILOF ISLAND SHREW
Sorex hydrodromus

MASKED SHREW
Sorex cinereus

MARYLAND SHREW
Sorex cinereus fontinalis

HAYDEN'S SHREW
Sorex haydeni

Fur short and dense. **SIMILAR SPECIES:** No other shrews occur within its range. **HABITS:** Poorly known. **HABITAT:** Maritime tundra. **RANGE:** Endemic to St. Lawrence I., Bering Sea. **STATUS:** Probably not uncommon in its limited range. **NOTE:** Considered by some authors to be a subspecies of Masked Shrew (*S. cinereus*).

PRIBILOF ISLAND SHREW *Sorex hydrodromus*

Head and body 2½ in. (59–67 mm); tail 1¼ in. (31–32 mm); hind foot ½ in. (13 mm); wt. ⅛ oz. (4–6 g). Medium sized. Back brown with a grayish cast; lower sides and belly off-white or yellowish white. Tail bicolor, well haired and tufted at tip. **SIMILAR SPECIES:** No other shrews occur within its range. It is very similar in size and color to Barren Ground Shrew (*S. ugyunak*). **HABITS:** Not described. **HABITAT:** Maritime tundra. **RANGE:** St. Paul I., Pribilofs, possibly Unalaska I., Alaska. **STATUS:** Probably common on St. Paul I.; may be extinct (or may never have occurred) on Unalaska I.

MASKED SHREW *Sorex cinereus* Pl. 32, Skull Pl. 2, Fig. 2
Cinereous Shrew

Head and body 2⅛ in. (42–67 mm); tail 1½ in. (33–45 mm); hind foot ½ in. (11–13 mm); wt. ⅛ oz. (3–6 g). *Small with a relatively long tail.* Back *brown*, usually uniformly dark brown, occasionally with a darker dorsal line and paler sides (grayer in winter). Belly noticeably paler than back, gray-brown, slightly silvery. *Tail clearly bicolor with a distinct black tuft* (hairs 2–3 mm at tip). Five upper unicuspids: 1–4 about equal in size, 5 smaller but visible in tooth row. **SIMILAR SPECIES:** See Pygmy, Southeastern, Hayden's, Smoky, and Barren Ground Shrews (*S. hoyi, S. longirostris, S. haydeni, S. fumeus,* and *S. ugyunak*). Montane and Vagrant Shrews (*S. monticolus* and *S. vagrans*) have 3rd upper unicuspid smaller than 4th.

The Masked Shrew, although common and widespread, is seldom seen, as it spends much of its time burrowing under leaf litter in search of food.

HABITS: Travels on the surface and under leaf litter, or in tiny runways through moss or wet grass. Feeds on small invertebrates, young mice, salamanders, and carrion. Survives on dormant insects during winter or supplements diet with some plant material. Makes nests of leaves or grasses under logs or in a burrow. May breed 3 times a year; litter size is 4–10. Young are weaned at 3 weeks and breed the following spring. Lifespan is about 15 months. **HABITAT:** Occupies a wide variety of habitats including woods, fields, swamps, and marshes. Usually found in moist areas. **RANGE:** Alaska, most of mainland Canada, and n. U.S. **STATUS:** Widespread, common to abundant. **NOTE:** The Maryland Shrew, *S. c. fontinalis* (n. Maryland, n. Delaware, se. Pennsylvania, and ne. West Virginia), is regarded by many authors as a distinct species. It averages smaller and has a shorter tail than most *S. cinereus*. It is very similar externally to *S. longirostris* but differs cranially and dentally (unicuspids 3 and 4 are same size in *S. c. fontinalis*; 4 is usually larger than 3 in *S. longirostris*).

HAYDEN'S SHREW   *Sorex haydeni*   Pl. 32, Fig. 2

Head and body 2¼ in. (47–67 mm); tail 1⅜ in. (30–41 mm); hind foot ⅜ in. (10–12 mm); wt. ⅛ oz. (2–5 g). *Small.* Back *brown*, sides slightly paler than back; belly off-white, sometimes washed with yellow. Winter coat darker and grayer, with belly color extending higher on sides. *Tail clearly bicolor,* dark brown above, *tuft of brown hair* at tip (hairs 3–4 mm). Unicuspid teeth similar to Masked Shrew. **SIMILAR SPECIES:** Masked Shrew (*S. cinereus*) is very similar (Hayden's was formerly considered to be a subspecies of Masked Shrew) but slightly larger and darker with a black tuft at tip of tail. See Pygmy, Preble's, and Merriam's Shrews (*S. hoyi, S. preblei,* and *S. merriami*). **HABITS:** Similar to Masked Shrew. Where the two species occur together, Masked Shrew occupies woodland and

MOUNT LYELL SHREW
Sorex lyelli

areas with tall vegetation, Hayden's Shrew occupies grassland. **HABITAT:** Favors wet prairies and grasslands, also sometimes found in dry pinewoods. **RANGE:** Northern Great Plains. **STATUS:** Uncommon to locally common.

MOUNT LYELL SHREW *Sorex lyelli*

Head and body 2¼ in. (50–68 mm); tail 1⅝ in. (39–44 mm); hind foot ½ in. (11–12 mm); wt. ⅛ oz. (4–6 g). Small. Back *pale gray-brown*, sides gray; belly grayish white. Fur short and smooth. Tail bicolor, pale brown above, small tuft at tip (hairs about 4 mm). Feet whitish. *Third unicuspid larger than 4th.* **SIMILAR SPECIES:** Other shrews in its range have 3rd unicuspid tooth smaller than 4th. Other external differences: Inyo Shrew (*S. tenellus*) is slightly smaller; Montane and Vagrant Shrews (*S. monticolus* and *S. vagrans*) are usually brown. Ornate Shrew (*S. ornatus*) occurs at lower elevations in Sierra Nevadas. **HABITS:** Unknown. **HABITAT:** Dry sagebrush steppe and wetlands in montane regions. Elevation 6,900–10,500 ft. (2,100–3,200 m). **RANGE:** Cen. Sierra Nevada Mts., Calif. **STATUS:** Very local and apparently rare, known from very few specimens.

SOUTHEASTERN SHREW *Sorex longirostris* Pl. 32, Fig. 2

Head and body 2 in. (44–57 mm); tail 1¼ in. (24–37 mm); hind foot ⅜ in. (9–11 mm); wt. ⅛ oz. (3–4 g). *Small and short-tailed.* Back *reddish brown*, belly pale buffy gray. Tail narrow, bicolor, with a very short tuft (hairs 1.5 mm at tip). Tops of feet pale. Five unicuspids visible in side view: 4th usually larger than 3rd. **SIMILAR SPECIES:** Masked Shrew (*S. cinereus*) is slightly larger (hind foot usually more than 11 mm) and has a longer, thicker tail with a more noticeable tuft at tip. It has unicuspids 3 and 4 about the same size. Pygmy Shrew (*S. hoyi*) is very similar but has only 3 up-

SOUTHEASTERN SHREW
Sorex longirostris

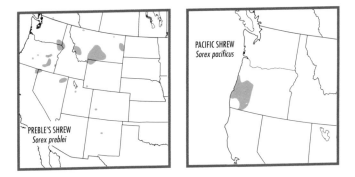

PREBLE'S SHREW
Sorex preblei

PACIFIC SHREW
Sorex pacificus

per unicuspids visible in side view. **HABITS:** Active day or night, feeding on small spiders, insects, and centipedes. Breeds March–Oct.; litter size is 1–6. Raises young in nests of shredded leaf litter located under rotten logs. **HABITAT:** Favors wet areas with dense ground cover but also occurs in dry sandy soils, pine plantations, and oldfields. **RANGE:** Md. to s. Ind. and south to La. and Fla. **STATUS:** Fairly common. One subspecies, *S. l. fisheri* (endemic to Dismal Swamp of Virginia and North Carolina), is threatened (USFWS).

PREBLE'S SHREW *Sorex preblei* Pl. 32, Fig. 2

Head and body 2 in. (44–57 mm), tail 1¼ in. (28–38 mm); hind foot ⅜ in. (9–11 mm); wt. 1/16 oz. (2–4 g). *Very small.* Back deep brown with a slightly reddish tone (grayish in winter), sides paler; belly whitish with an orange wash. Tail bicolor, brown above. Tops of feet pale. **SIMILAR SPECIES:** Masked and Hayden's Shrews (*S. cinereus* and *S. haydeni*) are very similar but average larger (positive identification of intermediate-sized animals requires measurements of skull characters). These shrews do not occur in arid sagebrush. See Merriam's Shrew (*S. merriami*). **HABITS:** Not reported. **HABITAT:** Higher elevations; usually in arid sagebrush and sagebrush steppe, also found in coniferous forest and near marshes and other wet areas. Elevation 4,200–9,000 ft. (1,280–2,750 m). **RANGE:** Scattered records from s. B.C. to Wyo., N.M., and Calif. **STATUS:** Apparently rare; known from very few specimens across a wide area.

PACIFIC SHREW *Sorex pacificus* Pl. 33, Fig. 2

Head and body 3½ in. (76–97 mm); tail 2¼ in. (51–68 mm); hind foot ⅝ in. (15–18 mm); wt. ½ oz. (7–16 g). *Large* and long-tailed. Notably long, slim legs. *Rich rusty brown* to dark brown above, *belly orange-brown,* very slightly paler than back. Tail faintly bicolor, pale brown above, nearly naked. Tops of feet pale brown.

Upper incisors lack tines and have no median gap. **SIMILAR SPECIES:** See Fog and Baird's Shrews (S. *sonomae* and S. *bairdi*). Vagrant Shrew (S. *vagrans*) is smaller with a shorter, bicolor tail. Trowbridge's Shrew (S. *trowbridgii*) is grayish. Marsh Shrew (S. *bendirii*) is blackish. **HABITS:** Eats a variety of invertebrate prey including large, hard-bodied insects. May cache excess food under a log for later consumption. Breeds May–Aug.; litter size is 2–7. **HABITAT:** Alder thickets and moist, brushy areas within forest. Favors small wooded streams with ferns and mossy fallen logs. **RANGE:** Cascade Mts. and Coast Range of Ore. **STATUS:** Local; common in suitable habitat.

FOG SHREW *Sorex sonomae*

Head and body 3¼ in. (67–89 mm); tail 2⅛ in. (49–68 mm); hind foot ⅝ in. (15–17 mm); wt. ½ oz. (7–14 g). *Large* and long-tailed. Back rusty brown, *reddish brown, or dark brown;* belly orange-brown or *reddish brown, very slightly paler than back.* Tail all-dark or faintly bicolor, nearly naked. Tops of feet brownish. **SIMILAR SPECIES:** Pacific Shrew (S. *pacificus*) is externally almost identical, and these species cannot be reliably distinguished in the field (they can be distinguished by subtle differences in the teeth and skull of museum specimens). See Pacific Shrew for comparisons with other shrews. **HABITS:** Eats snails and slugs, amphibians, insect larvae, and other invertebrates. Breeds March–Nov.; litter size is 3–5. **HABITAT:** Marshes, wooded streams, alder thickets, and other moist areas within coniferous forest. **RANGE:** W. Ore. and nw. Calif. **STATUS:** Common in suitable habitat.

FOG SHREW
Sorex sonomae

BAIRD'S SHREW *Sorex bairdi* Pl. 33, Fig. 2

Head and body 2¾ in. (58–81 mm); tail 2 in. (45–61 mm); hind foot ⅝ in. (13–16 mm); wt. ¼ oz. (5–11 g). Relatively large. Back *dark reddish brown* or blackish brown, belly gray-brown. Tail *faintly*

BAIRD'S SHREW
Sorex bairdi

bicolor, nearly naked. Tops of feet pale brown. Upper incisors have very small tines within the pigmented area and have a median gap below the tines. **SIMILAR SPECIES:** Montane Shrew (*S. monticolus*) is difficult to distinguish — it is usually slightly smaller with a distinctly bicolor tail, and it has more conspicuous medial tines on the upper incisors. Trowbridge's Shrew (*S. trowbridgii*) is gray. Pacific and Fog Shrews (*S. pacificus* and *S. sonomae*) are larger and usually a brighter orange-brown. Vagrant Shrew (*S. vagrans*) is smaller with a shorter tail. **HABITS:** One was observed to be active during the day. Litter size is 4–7. **HABITAT:** Douglas fir forest with numerous rotting logs. **RANGE:** Nw. Ore. **STATUS:** Very local; relative abundance poorly known.

MONTANE SHREW *Sorex monticolus*   Pl. 32, Fig. 2
Dusky Shrew

Head and body 2½ in. (53–76 mm); tail 2 in. (42–61 mm); hind foot ½ in. (11–16 mm); wt. ¼ oz. (4–10 g). Small to *medium sized* with a *relatively long tail. Upperparts brown or dark brown,* belly buffy brown or grayish, paler than back. *Tail bicolor,* brown above, with a tuft of fur at tip (hairs 3 mm long). Upper incisors pigmented well above point where the teeth meet and including pigmented tines; 3rd unicuspid smaller than 4th. **SIMILAR SPECIES:** See Vagrant and Baird's Shrews (*S. vagrans* and *S. bairdi*). Masked Shrew (*S. cinereus*) has 3rd unicuspid larger than 4th. Trowbridge's Shrew (*S. trowbridgii*) is gray. American Water Shrew (*S. palustris*) is larger with a longer tail. Other brown highland shrews — Dwarf, Pygmy, and Inyo (*S. nanus, S. hoyi,* and *S. tenellus*) — are smaller. **HABITS:** Eats a wide variety of invertebrate prey, foraging under leaf litter and among dense vegetation. Home range of breeding adults may be as large as 43,000 sq. ft. (4,000 m²). Females may breed twice a year; litter size is 2–9. **HABITAT:** Wet areas; willow and alder thickets, grassy stream banks, moist coniferous forest, and alpine

MONTANE SHREW
Sorex monticolus
NEW MEXICO SHREW
Sorex neomexicanus

tundra. Elevation 4,000–11,000 ft. (1,200–3,400 m). **RANGE:** Alaska and w. Canada south through mts. to Calif., Ariz., N.M., and n. Mexico. **STATUS:** Widespread, often abundant. Usually the most common shrew in an area.

NEW MEXICO SHREW *Sorex neomexicanus*
Very similar to Montane Shrew (formerly included in that species). Ranges do not overlap. **HABITAT:** Canyons in stands of fir, ponderosa pine, and aspen. Elevation 9,000–10,000 ft. (3,000 m). **RANGE:** Capitan, Manzano, and Sandia Mts., s.-cen. N.M.

VAGRANT SHREW *Sorex vagrans*   **Pl. 32, Fig. 2**
Head and body 2½ in. (56–71 mm); tail 1⅝ in. (32–50 mm); hind foot ½ in. (12–14 mm); wt. ¼ oz. (3–9 g). *Small. Dull brown* to dark gray-brown above, belly grayish. Tail rather short, lightly haired; unicolor or somewhat bicolor, brownish above, whitish below. Pigment on upper incisor teeth extends up to the point where the teeth meet, but not above. *Pigmented tines* (usually present) *are positioned above the level of pigment on the incisor;* 3rd unicuspid smaller than 4th. **SIMILAR SPECIES:** Montane Shrew (*S. monticolus*) is usually slightly larger with a noticeably longer tail. In Montane (*S. monticolus*) and other small western shrews — Ornate, Inyo, Preble's, and Mount Lyell (*S. ornatus, S. tenellus, S. preblei,* and *S. lyelli*) — pigment on upper incisors extends above level where the teeth meet and includes pigmented tines. Masked Shrew (*S. cinereus*) has a slightly longer tail and 3rd unicuspid larger than 4th. **HABITS:** Active at the soil surface, darting from open areas to cover and often using vole runways through grass. Eats insect larvae, slugs, snails, earthworms, and spiders, also some fungi and plant material. Female has 2–3 litters per year and breeds Feb.–Nov. Litter size is 1–8. **HABITAT:** Usually in wet grassy areas with scattered trees, marshes, or muddy stream

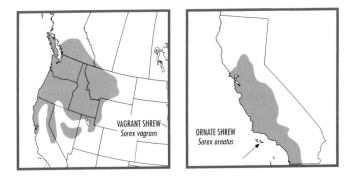

banks. Seldom found in deep forest. Lowlands to at least 8,200 ft. (2,500 m). **RANGE:** S. B.C. and w. U.S. Isolated population in cen. Mexico. **STATUS:** Common to abundant.

ORNATE SHREW *Sorex ornatus* Pl. 32, Fig. 2

Head and body 2¼ in. (45–70 mm); tail 1½ in. (31–40 mm); hind foot ½ in. (11–13 mm); wt. ⅛ oz. (3–7 g). Small. Back *gray-brown or dark brown;* belly silvery gray. Tail rather short, somewhat bicolor, and nearly naked, with very short hair (1 mm) at tip. Third unicuspid smaller than 4th. **GEOGRAPHIC VARIATION:** In salt marshes in the Bay Area and parts of s. California almost *entirely black.* **SIMILAR SPECIES:** Most shrews in its range are larger. Trowbridge's Shrew (*S. trowbridgii*) has a long, clearly bicolor tail. Vagrant Shrew (*S. vagrans*) is similar in size (range overlaps in Bay Area) but has pigment on tines of upper incisors discontinuous with pigment on rest of tooth (in Ornate [*S. ornatus*] the pigmented tines are within the pigmented area of the incisors). **HABITS:** Forages for invertebrates in leaf litter, alternating bursts of activity with periods

of inactivity. Usually breeds in April or in May and gives birth to litters of 4–6. **HABITAT:** Coastal salt marshes, freshwater swamps, streamsides, and upland areas with low, dense vegetation. Lowlands to 7,900 ft. (2,400 m). **RANGE:** West Coast from cen. Calif. to Baja Calif. Small disjunct population on s. tip of Baja. **STATUS:** Buena Vista Lake Shrew (S. o. relictus) is endangered (USFWS). Other populations eliminated or threatened by development and habitat alteration.

DWARF SHREW *Sorex nanus*   Pl. 32, Fig. 2

Head and body 2¼ in. (50–60 mm); tail 1⅜ in. (27–45 mm); hind foot ⅜ in. (10–11 mm); wt. ¹⁄₁₆ oz. (2–4 g). *Very small.* Back dull brown; belly silvery washed with buff. Paler and grayer in winter. Fur short, ears rather conspicuous. *Tail faintly bicolor, pale above, nearly naked* with no hair at tip. Third upper unicuspid smaller than unicuspids 2 and 4. **SIMILAR SPECIES:** Hayden's, Preble's, and Masked Shrews (S. haydeni, S preblei, and S. cinereus) have unicuspids 1–4 about equal in size. Pygmy Shrew (S. hoyi) has only 3 unicuspids visible in side view. Other shrews in its range are larger. **HABITS:** Often associated with rocky hills and talus slopes, presumably feeding on the abundant small invertebrates that dwell among rocks. Litter size is 4–8. **HABITAT:** Alpine tundra, montane forests, rockslides, and dry short-grass prairie. Elevation 2,000–14,100 ft. (600–4,300 m). **RANGE:** Cen. and s. Rocky Mts. and e. Great Plains, south to mts. of Ariz. and N.M. **STATUS:** Uncommon.

INYO SHREW *Sorex tenellus*   Fig. 2

Head and body 2½ in. (48–74 mm); tail 1⅝ in. (36–48 mm); hind foot ½ in. (11–12 mm); wt. ⅛ oz. (3–4 g). Very small. Back pale gray with a brownish wash; belly silvery gray. Tail slightly bicolor, pale brown above with a small blackish tuft at tip. Feet pale. Third upper unicuspid smaller than unicuspids 2 and 4. **SIMILAR SPECIES:**

INYO SHREW
Sorex tenellus

Closely related and very similar to Dwarf Shrew (*S. nanus*) (ranges do not overlap). Merriam's Shrew (*S. merriami*) is similar but has a whiter belly. Preble's Shrew (*S. preblei*) is smaller and has 3rd unicuspid larger than 4th. Vagrant Shrew (*S. vagrans*) has pigmented tines above level of pigment on upper incisors. Other shrews in its range are larger. **HABITS:** Unknown. **HABITAT:** Usually found on the dry side of mountain slopes, but also occurs in moist pockets such as canyon bottoms. Also found in humid red fir forest. Elevation 5,000–9,500 ft. (1,500–2,900 m). **RANGE:** Mts. of e. Calif. and sw. Nev. **STATUS:** Rare and local.

PYGMY SHREW *Sorex hoyi* Pl. 32, Fig. 2

Head and body 2⅜ in. (52–70 mm); tail 1¼ in. (28–37 mm); hind foot ⅜ in. (10–12 mm); wt. ¹⁄₁₆–¼ oz. (1–7 g). *Very small and short-tailed.* Back dull smoky brown to bright copper brown; belly pale gray-brown in summer, whitish in winter. Tail bicolor, dark brown above, with a distinct tuft (hairs about 4 mm at tip). Feet small, tops pale. *Characteristic teeth: only 3 unicuspids are visible in side view* (3rd and 5th unicuspids are tiny). **GEOGRAPHIC VARIATION:** Tiny in southern parts of range (wt. 1–3 g), larger in Alaska and northern regions (wt. 4–7 g). **SIMILAR SPECIES:** Usually the smallest shrew in a region. Masked Shrew (*S. cinereus*) can be very similar but usually has a slightly longer tail. Masked Shrew and all other small *Sorex* have 4–5 unicuspids visible in side view. **HABITS:** Makes tiny burrows under leaf litter and near the soil surface. Feeds on small arthropods, worms, carrion, and some plant material. Females probably breed 2–3 times per year; litter size is 2–8. **HABITAT:** Variable, from open fields to wooded slopes, in both wet and dry soils. **RANGE:** S. Alaska and much of Canada and n. U.S. Disjunct populations in Appalachian Mts. and in Colo. and Wyo. **STATUS:** Generally un-

PYGMY SHREW
Sorex hoyi

common, but sometimes caught in considerable numbers in pit-fall traps.

ARIZONA SHREW   *Sorex arizonae*

Head and body 2¼ in. (50–73 mm); tail 1¾ in. (37–46 mm); hind foot ½ in. (11–13 mm); wt. ⅛ oz. (2–5 g). *Small,* relatively *long-tailed.* Back *pale gray.* Upper incisors have small pigmented tines on the medial edge; 3rd upper unicuspid same size or larger than 4th. **SIMILAR SPECIES:** Merriam's Shrew (*S. merriami*) is very similar but does not have tines on the incisors (ranges not known to over-lap). Montane Shrew (*S. monticolus*) has 3rd upper unicuspid smaller than 4th. See Desert Shrew (*Notiosorex*). **HABITS:** Not de-scribed. **HABITAT:** Wooded slopes and rocky areas with dense ground cover. Often found near water. Elevation 5,150–8,500 ft. (1,570–2,590 m). **RANGE:** Se. Ariz., sw. N.M., and nw. Mexico. **STATUS:** Endan-gered in New Mexico (New Mexico Dept. Game and Fish).

MERRIAM'S SHREW   *Sorex merriami*   Pl. 32, Fig. 2

Head and body 2¼ in. (48–69 mm); tail 1½ in. (30–42 mm); hind foot ½ in. (11–14 mm); wt. ¼ oz. (3–7 g). *Small,* with a medium-length tail. Back pale gray-brown; *belly whitish.* Fur short, ears rather conspicuous. Tail faintly bicolor, pale brown above, short tuft at tip (hairs 2–3 mm). *Feet whitish.* No tines on upper incisors. **SIMILAR SPECIES:** Few shrews occur in dry regions: Preble's and Dwarf Shrews (*S. preblei* and *S. nanus*) are smaller (usually less than 4 g). See Arizona Shrew (*S. arizonae*) and Desert Shrew (*Notio-sorex*). **HABITS:** Uses runways of Sagebrush Vole and other mice. Lit-ter size is 5–7. **HABITAT:** Dry areas, often associated with sagebrush. Also in arid grassland, woodland, and brushy slopes. Lowlands to 9,500 ft. (2,900 m). **RANGE:** S. B.C. and w. U.S. **STATUS:** Apparently un-common, poorly known.

ARIZONA SHREW
Sorex arizonae

MERRIAM'S SHREW
Sorex merriami

TROWBRIDGE'S SHREW
Sorex trowbridgii

TROWBRIDGE'S SHREW   *Sorex trowbridgii*   **Pl. 33**

Head and body 2⅜ in. (57–75 mm); tail 2¼ in. (50–64 mm); hind foot ⅝ in. (13–16 mm); wt. ¼ oz. (4–6 g). *Fairly small, long-tailed.* Upperparts *gray, gray-brown,* or dark charcoal gray; *belly almost the same color as back* (slightly paler and grayer). *Tail very clearly bicolor,* dark gray above, white below; hairy in juvenile, nearly naked in adult. Tops of feet whitish. Many adults have a distinct "skunky" odor. **SIMILAR SPECIES:** The combination of a strongly bicolor tail and lack of contrast between back and belly is usually diagnostic in its range. Montane Shrew (*S. monticolus*) is browner in color. **HABITS:** Burrows deeply into organic soil or leaf litter, more of a "digger" than other shrews. Also has been photographed climbing high into Douglas firs. Has an unspecialized diet that includes insects, spiders, worms, conifer seeds, and fungi. Sometimes hoards and buries seeds. Litter size is 3–6; breeds March–May in Washington, Feb.–June in California. **HABITAT:** Favors mature forest with deep leaf litter, moss, and ferns. Also in drier pine forest or under dense grass and brush. Avoids very wet, marshy soil. To at least 8,500 ft. (2,600 m). **RANGE:** Sw. B.C. to s. Calif. **STATUS:** Usually the most common shrew in forests of the Pacific Northwest.

NORTHERN SHORT-TAILED SHREW   **Pl. 33,**
Blarina brevicauda   **Skull Pl. 2, Fig. 2**

Head and body 4 in. (90–114 mm); tail 1 in. (18–30 mm); hind foot ⅝ in. (13–16 mm); wt. ¾ oz. (12–30 g). *Largest shrew in North America.* Upperparts silvery gray to dark charcoal gray, belly silvery. Bare patch of skin around small eye; ears tiny, concealed in fur. Front feet relatively broad with long claws. Tail short, faintly bicolor, tiny tuft at tip. **SIMILAR SPECIES:** Most shrews in its range are much smaller. American Water Shrew (*Sorex palustris*) has a longer tail. See Southern and Elliot's Short-tailed Shrews

e Northern Short-
led Shrew is a
ficient digger that
s ultrasonic clicks
navigate and locate
y. It is one of very
venomous North
erican mammals.

(*B. carolinensis* and *B. hylophaga*). **HABITS:** Somewhat molelike in appearance and habits, this common shrew makes extensive shallow burrows in soil, under leaf litter, or under snow. Burrows, punctuated with exit holes, may honeycomb an area. Makes nests in burrows and lines them with grass or fur. Active mostly at night or in the early morning. Has poisonous saliva that can paralyze or kill insects or subdue large prey such as mice. Sometimes stores paralyzed prey alive for later consumption. Diet is mainly worms, snails, sowbugs, and other invertebrates. Active year-round; occasionally visits bird feeders in winter and will eat seeds, also attacks small mammals when insects are scarce. Breeds Feb.–Sept. Litter size is 3–7; young are weaned at 25 days and can breed at 7 weeks. Lifespan is usually less than a year. **HABITAT:** Most common in hardwood forests with deep leaf litter and in brushy borders of ponds or streams. Also found in pine forest and grassland. **RANGE:** Ne. to n.-cen. U.S. and s. Canada. **STATUS:** Abundant.

OUTHERN SHORT-TAILED SHREW Pl. 33, Fig. 2
arina carolinensis

Head and body 3 in. (69–80 mm); tail 7⁄8 in. (12–25 mm); hind foot 3⁄8 in. (10–13 mm); wt. 3⁄8 oz. (6–13 g). Very similar to Northern Short-tailed Shrew but smaller. All *Blarina* have 5 upper unicuspid teeth. **SIMILAR SPECIES:** Least Shrew (*Cryptotis*) is nearly always smaller and has a more bicolor tail. It has 4 upper unicuspids, 3 visible in tooth row (4th is very small). Long-tailed shrews (*Sorex*) have more conspicuous ears and longer tails. **HABITS:** Similar to Northern Short-tailed Shrew, but not known to feed on vertebrates. Breeds March–June and Sept.–Nov. Litter size is 2–6. **HABITAT:** Moist hardwood forest, also pine forest, thickets, and fields. **RANGE:** E. Va. south to Fla. and west to e. Tex., also north to s. Ill. **STATUS:** Common to abundant. **NOTE:** Until recently, Southern Short-tailed Shrew (*B. carolinensis*) and Elliot's Short-tailed Shrew

NORTHERN SHORT-TAILED SHREW
Blarina brevicauda

SOUTHERN SHORT-TAILED SHREW
Blarina carolinensis

B. c. shermani

ELLIOT'S SHORT-TAILED SHREW
Blarina hylophaga

(*B. hylophaga*) were considered to be small subspecies of Northern Short-tailed Shrew (*B. brevicauda*). They are now recognized as distinct based on chromosomal differences. *B. carolinensis* is the smallest and is usually distinguishable from *B. brevicauda* by size. It is slightly smaller than *B. hylophaga*. In areas of overlap, these 2 species can be distinguished with certainty only by counting chromosomes. A small subspecies in s. Florida may represent a separate species, *B. c. shermani*.

ELLIOT'S SHORT-TAILED SHREW

Fig. 2

Blarina hylophaga

Head and body 3½ in. (72–96 mm); tail 1 in. (19–25 mm); hind foot ½ in. (10–14 mm); wt. ½ oz. (8–16 g). Very similar to Northern Short-tailed Shrew but slightly smaller. See Northern and Southern Short-tailed Shrews for differences between *Blarina* and other shrews. **HABITS:** Similar to Northern Short-tailed Shrew. It has poisonous saliva and eats small mammals, reptiles, and amphibians in addition to invertebrates. **HABITAT:** Favors moist areas with dense vegetation. **RANGE:** Central Great Plains; also Bastrop and Aransas Co., Tex. **STATUS:** Locally common.

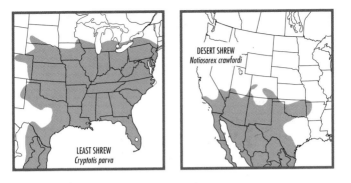

LEAST SHREW
Cryptotis parva

DESERT SHREW
Notiosorex crawfordi

LEAST SHREW *Cryptotis parva* **Pl. 33, Skull Pl. 2, Fig. 2**

Head and body 2¼ in. (52–68 mm); tail ¾ in. (13–23 mm); hind foot ½ in. (10–12 mm); wt. ¼ oz. (3–10 g). Small, with a *very short tail*. Back *dull brown* to nearly black (coat grayer in winter, browner in summer); belly gray-brown to silvery. *Ears very small, concealed in fur*. Tail bicolor, brown above, tiny tuft at tip. Four upper unicuspid teeth. **SIMILAR SPECIES:** Short-tailed shrews (*Blarina* spp.) are almost always bigger (wt. over 8 g, tail over 20 mm) and grayer, with less bicolor tails and 5 upper unicuspids. Long-tailed shrews (*Sorex* spp.) have longer tails and more conspicuous ears. **HABITS:** May dig a burrow or use burrows made by other animals. Eats a variety of invertebrates and may store excess prey in the burrow. Makes nests of leaves and grasses, placed on the ground in a concealed spot. Most shrews appear to be solitary in habits, but this species is fairly social; large numbers of adults (up to 31) may share a nest. Litter size is 2–7; young are born March–Nov. in the North, probably year-round in the South. **HABITAT:** Occupies a variety of habitats, especially in the South. Prefers overgrown fields and brush, also found in marshes, woods, and dry areas. **RANGE:** Midwest and e. U.S.; also e. Mexico and Central America to w. Panama. **STATUS:** Fairly common.

DESERT SHREW *Notiosorex crawfordi* **Pl. 32, Fig. 2**

Head and body 2¼ in. (51–64 mm); tail 1 in. (22–32 mm); hind foot ⅜ in. (10–11 mm); wt. ⅛ oz. (2.5–6 g). Very small with a *short tail and conspicuous ears*. Back pale gray-brown, belly pale gray or whitish. Tail unicolor or faintly bicolor, pale brown above, whitish below. *Three unicuspids in upper tooth row*. **SIMILAR SPECIES:** Few shrews occur in deserts. Other shrews in its range have longer tails and have 4–5 unicuspid teeth visible in the upper tooth row. **HABITS:** Usually occupies areas with fallen vegetation and other ground cover that provides a more humid microhabitat within the

The Desert Shrew does not require free water, obtaining moisture from insect larvae and other prey. It often makes its nest inside a woodrat house.

desert. Makes golf-ball-sized nests of fine plant fibers, often inside woodrat houses. Litters of 3–5 young are born in spring or summer. **HABITAT:** Desert and desert scrub, dry woodland, piñon-juniper, and ponderosa pines. **RANGE:** Cen. Calif. to w. Ark., south to sw. Mexico. **STATUS:** Probably not uncommon in suitable habitat. **NOTE:** A new species of Desert Shrew, *Notiosorex cockrumi,* has recently been described. It is distinguished from *N. crawfordi* based on chromosomal and biochemical differences only. *N. cockrumi* occurs in s. Arizona and Sonora, Mexico. The western and northern limits of its range are not known. I am including *N. cockrumi* in the account for *N. crawfordi* until further information is available on the identity of desert shrews in California, Nevada, and Colorado. Range maps showing only partial and presumed ranges for the 2 species seem premature at this time.

MOLES: Talpidae

Moles are relatively large insectivores that are greatly modified for a burrowing or fossorial life. They have reduced eyes that are covered with thin skin and no external ears. The front feet are very broad and turned outward, equipped with long, scoop-shaped claws. Their fur is velvety and can lie forward or backward, facilitating travel in either direction in the burrow. Their spine is very flexible, allowing the mole to turn on itself inside a narrow burrow. Seldom seen aboveground, their presence is detected by ridges in the soil made by shallow tunnels and by volcano-shaped mounds of dirt (molehills) thrown up from deeper tunnels. Molehills are not marked by an entrance hole.

Moles are found in Eurasia and North America. There are 42 species worldwide and 7 species in Canada and the U.S.

AMERICAN SHREW MOLE
Neurotrichus gibbsii

...IERICAN SHREW MOLE

...urotrichus gibbsii

Pl. 34, Skull Pl. 2

Head and body 3 in. (68–84 mm); tail 1⅝ in. (34–48 mm); hind foot ⅝ in. (13–18 mm); wt. ⅜ oz. (8–14 g). About the size of a large shrew, with a *very long, narrow snout*. Body entirely dark charcoal gray to blackish, sometimes peppered with pale gray. *Tail long, thickened near base*, well haired and *tufted*. *Forefeet well developed, broad*, with long sturdy claws. **SIMILAR SPECIES:** Other moles are much larger. Shrews have smaller front feet and narrow tails. **HABITS:** Active both night and day; alternates short bursts of activity with short rests. Makes a system of runways under leaf litter and near the surface in soft soil but does not form molehills. Also travels on the surface and can climb small shrubs. Swims well. Feeds on earthworms, sowbugs, insects and their larvae, and other invertebrates. Does not hibernate. Appears to be gregarious; several may share a burrow system. Unlike other moles, does not nest underground but makes nests of dry leaves at the surface. May breed

The American Shrew Mole is less specialized for digging and may spend more time aboveground than other moles. Note the extremely long snout.

year-round; litter size is 1–4. **HABITAT:** Willow or alder thickets along streams and other moist, low-lying areas with soft soil. Favors areas with shrub cover and deep leaf litter but also found on bare mud. Avoids grassy sod and hard soils. To 8,000 ft. (2,440 m). **RANGE:** Pacific Northwest, from sw. B.C. to cen. Calif. **STATUS:** Common.

BROAD-FOOTED MOLE *Scapanus latimanus* Pl. 34
California Mole

Head and body 5½ in. (111–165 mm); tail 1½ in. (29–40 mm); hind foot ¾ in. (18–21 mm); wt. 2 oz. (39–78 g). Narrow snout. Upperparts *gray-brown, underparts silvery gray.* Tail short, *lightly haired, with a small tuft at tip.* Forefeet modified, width greater than length, with long, scoop-shaped claws (despite the common name, the feet are no broader than in other moles). **SIMILAR SPECIES:** Coast Mole is darker with a nearly naked tail. See Townsend's Mole. **HABITS:** Makes temporary foraging tunnels just below the soil surface, leaving a visible ridge in the soil. Feeds mainly on earthworms. Deeper tunnels are used for nest-building and resting, marked by molehills. Breeds once a year in Jan. or Feb. Young are born in March or April; litter size is 2–5. Young remain in the mother's tunnel system for about 3 months. **HABITAT:** Favors rich damp soils with little vegetation. Avoids heavy clay or stony soils. Sea level to 9,800 ft. (3,000 m). **RANGE:** Sw. Ore., w. Nev., and Calif; also n. Baja Calif., Mexico. **STATUS:** Common.

COAST MOLE *Scapanus orarius* Pl. 34, Skull Pl. 2

Head and body 5 in. (108–142 mm); tail 1½ in. (28–45 mm); hind foot ⅞ in. (18–23 mm); wt. 2¼ oz. (43–90 g). Narrow snout. Upperparts *blackish,* underparts slightly paler. *Tail short, almost naked, not tufted.* Forefeet modified, width greater than length, with long, scoop-shaped claws. **SIMILAR SPECIES:** Townsend's Mole is larger (compare body and hind foot lengths). In both species,

BROAD-FOOTED MOLE
Scapanus latimanus

TOWNSEND'S MOLE
Scapanus townsendii

males are larger than females; young, if not separable by hind foot length, distinguished by skull and dental characteristics. Broad-footed Mole is paler with a haired tail. **HABITS:** Active by day or night. Digs surface tunnels marked with ridges and deep tunnels marked by small, well-spaced mounds. Adults remain underground but young apparently disperse on the surface and may fall prey to Barn Owls or house cats. Breeds

COAST MOLE
Scapanus orarius

early in the year; litter size is 2–4. **HABITAT:** Well-drained, often sandy soil in open meadows, brush, and woods. Avoids very wet areas. Sea level to 5,600 ft. (1,700 m). **RANGE:** Sw. B.C. to n. Calif. and w. Idaho. **STATUS:** Common.

TOWNSEND'S MOLE *Scapanus townsendii* **Pl. 34, Skull Pl. 2**
Head and body 6 in. (147–174 mm); tail 1¾ in. (35–50 mm); hind foot 1⅛ in. (24–28 mm); wt. 4 oz. (60–150 g). Narrow snout. Entirely *dark chocolate brown or black. Tail short, almost naked, not tufted.* Forefeet modified, width greater than length, with long, scoop-shaped claws. **SIMILAR SPECIES:** See Coast Mole. Broad-footed Mole is paler (ranges meet but do not overlap). **HABITS:** Makes surface ridges and deeper tunnels. The deep tunnels are marked by large mounds that are thrown up 2–3 ft. (0.6–0.9 m) apart (closer than in Coast Mole). Also may make very deep tunnels marked by several large mounds. Makes a large nest chamber 6–8 in. (15–20 cm) below the surface that is lined with green grass with an inner lining of dry grass. Nests are marked by a very large mound or "fortress" of small mounds. Litters of 2–5 are born in early spring. **HABITAT:** Moist to wet meadows, river flood plains, and fir forests. Uncommon in dense brush. Usually below 2,300 ft. (700 m) except on Olympic Pen. where it occurs up to 6,200 ft. (1,900 m). **RANGE:** Pacific Northwest from sw. B.C. to nw. Calif. **STATUS:** Common in U.S. Endangered in Canada (COSEWIC).

HAIRY-TAILED MOLE *Parascalops breweri* **Pl. 34, Skull Pl. 2**
Head and body 5 in. (115–133 mm); tail 1¼ in. (26–37 mm); hind foot ¾ in. (15–20 mm); wt. 1½ oz. (30–59 g). Long narrow snout. *Charcoal gray or blackish* above, silvery gray below; snout sometimes white. *Tail clothed with long coarse hair* (hair usually black near base, black or white at tip). Forefeet modified, width greater than length, with long, scoop-shaped claws. **SIMILAR SPECIES:** Eastern

Hairy-tailed Mole, in its sleek summer coat, digging up an earthworm. Note the short, well-haired tail for which this mole is named.

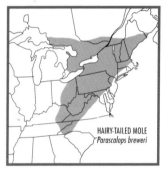

HAIRY-TAILED MOLE
Parascalops breweri

Mole has a nearly naked tail. Star-nosed Mole has tentacles on the snout. **HABITS:** Active by day or night. At night may forage on the surface. Shallow tunnels form inconspicuous ridges in the soil. Remains near the surface in summer, but in fall moves deeper underground, excavating new tunnels and producing numerous small molehills. Eats earthworms and insects, especially beetles. Litters of 4–5 are born in April or May. **HABITAT:** Deciduous and coniferous woods, oldfields, and roadsides with moist but light, well-drained soil. Sea level to 3,000 ft. (900 m). **RANGE:** Ne. U.S. and se. Canada. **STATUS:** Locally common.

EASTERN MOLE *Scalopus aquaticus* Pl. 34, Skull Pl. 2

Head and body 5½ in. (117–162 mm); tail 1¼ in. (20–38 mm); hind foot ¾ in. (17–24 mm); wt. 3¼ oz. (50–130 g). Narrow snout. Usually *gray-brown* above, slightly paler below. *Tail short, nearly naked.* Forefeet modified, width greater than length, with long, scoop-shaped claws. **GEOGRAPHIC VARIATION:** Large and dark gray-brown in North; small and whitish or golden in South. **SIMILAR SPECIES:** Hairy-tailed Mole has a hairy tail. Star-nosed Mole has tentacles on the snout. **HABITS:** Makes shallow burrows for feeding that may be used only once or may be used for several years. These burrows produce prominent ridges on the surface. Uses deep tunnels for nesting and during cold weather. Throws up large mole-

Eastern Mole emerges from its burrow, displaying its huge, shovel-like front feet. It digs with the front feet and also pushes dirt with its head.

EASTERN MOLE
Scalopus aquaticus

hills when excavating deep tunnels. Eats earthworms and other invertebrates, also consumes plant material. Male's home range is about 3 times larger than female's. Litters of 2–5 young are born March–June. Lifespan may be 6 years or more. **HABITAT:** Fields or woods with soft moist soils. Avoids wet areas, heavy clay, and gravelly or rocky soils. **RANGE:** E. U.S. to Midwest. Barely enters e. Canada. **STATUS:** Locally common. An isolated subspecies, *S. a. inflatus*, (w. Texas and n. Tamaulipas, Mexico) is rare, possibly extinct.

STAR-NOSED MOLE *Condylura cristata* **Pl. 34, Skull Pl. 2**
Head and body 4 in. (88–125 mm); tail 3 in. (56–85 mm); hind foot 1 in. (25–30 mm); wt. 2 oz. (34–80 g). *"Star" of 22 fleshy, tentacle-like appendages around tip of snout.* Body entirely chocolate brown to blackish. *Tail long, well haired,* thick at base, tapering to a point at tip. Forefeet modified, width greater than length, skin black and scaly, with long, scoop-shaped claws. **SIMILAR SPECIES:** Unmistakable. **HABITS:** Unlike other moles, swims well and makes tunnels leading into water. Makes shallow burrows that have an undulating path. Also active on or under snow. May travel on the surface, and in some areas leaves little evidence of its presence. Elsewhere makes deep burrows and throws up molehills. Feeds on aquatic invertebrates and small fish caught in the muddy bottoms of streams and

The Star-nosed Mole is named for the unique ring of fleshy tentacles on the tip of its snout that it uses to locate its aquatic invertebrate prey.

STAR-NOSED MOLE
Condylura cristata

ponds. The "star" may be used to detect electric fields of earthworms and other prey in water. It may also function as a tactile organ. This mole appears to be more social than other moles, and several individuals may share a runway. Nests are dug in hillocks or under stumps or logs above high-water level. Litters of 2–7 are born March–Aug. **HABITAT:** Wet areas in meadows, woods, swamps, or streams. Usually in mucky soil, occasionally in drier leaf litter or fields. **RANGE:** E. Canada and e. U.S., west to Minn. and south to Ga. **STATUS:** Locally common, especially in northern part of range.

BATS: CHIROPTERA

Bats are the only mammals capable of powered flight. Some other mammals glide, but they cannot sustain lift. The bat wing is supported by the upper arm, a long forearm, and very long finger bones. The small thumb is not enclosed in the wing. The wing membrane is formed by two very thin, elastic layers of skin stretched over the forearm and hand and attached to the sides of the body and to the foot or leg. Another membrane usually extends from legs to tail and may cover all or part of the tail. This membrane is controlled in part by a bone (the calcar) that extends from the ankle. The calcar may lie on the edge of the membrane and be smooth-edged (unkeeled), or it may have a small projection (keel) that extends outward (see p. 72).

Most bats roost upside down; from this position they can drop, spread their wings, and take flight. Bats with short broad wings can fly slowly, hover, and maneuver in dense vegetation. Bats with long narrow wings can fly at high speeds for long distances, but they are less agile at slow speeds and often need to free-fall to obtain lift. Many of the most agile fliers are also equipped with very long ears. These bats use their excellent hearing to listen for sounds made by an insect walking across a leaf, then glean their prey from the ground or vegetation.

Almost all of our bats are insectivores, and most species hunt flying insects. They emit high-frequency calls that hit nearby objects and send a returning pulse of sound back to the bat, allowing it to locate objects such as small moving moths. This process is called echolocation. Some bats have folds of skin on the snout or chin, others have lumps on the muzzle; some have greatly enlarged ears, and most have a spearlike structure in the ear (the tragus). These features probably all play a part in sending or receiving sounds, enabling bats to feed on the wing at night. The very features that seem oddest to humans — their leathery wings and modified faces — are actually awe-inspiring adaptations to life on the wing in the dark. Bats are not blind; in fact, most species see very well. They use vision in the roost and to locate distant objects in flight, and some may use eyesight to find food.

Bats are a highly successful group, second only to rodents in terms of overall diversity. There are over 1,000 species of bats worldwide; 45 species occur the U.S., and 21 of these species also enter Canada. **BATS AND RABIES:** Bats can carry rabies, and any bat seen on the ground should not be handled without a glove. Bats found by children or pets, and bats that cannot fly away, are likely to be sick. Among these bats, about 10 percent will test positive for rabies. In free-flying populations of bats, however, only about 0.5 to 1 percent will be rabid. Bats roosting in houses do not transmit airborne rabies to the occupants. Bats with rabies are generally not aggressive, unlike rabid dogs or raccoons. Very few human deaths result from bat-related rabies — far fewer than from rabid dogs — but any bite from a wild animal should be reported to a physician. **CONSERVATION OF BATS:** Bats are common inhabitants in much of the U.S. and Canada, and most of our bats are insect eaters. They require large amounts of food and often eat 50 percent or more of their body weight in insects each night. A large colony of bats therefore plays a significant role in insect control. Most bats probably do not eat a lot of mosquitoes; they generally specialize on moths or beetles, the larvae of many of which are significant agricultural pests. Bats provide a natural pest control that farmers are beginning to use and appreciate. Some farmers who have erected bat houses found that once bats became established, they no longer needed to spray their crops. Bats are sometimes unpopular residents in houses: they can be noisy, have a musky odor, and leave droppings. Unwanted bats should be excluded from the roost during the winter; if possible, bat houses should be erected as alternative roosts. For more on the conservation of bats, bat house construction, and harmless exclusion methods, contact Bat Conservation International (www.batcon.org).

LEAF-CHINNED BATS: Mormoopidae

Bats in this family have leaflike flaps of skin on the chin. They echolocate by opening the mouth wide to form a megaphone. Limited to the New World and mainly found in Latin America, one species enters the U.S.

PETERS'S GHOST-FACED BAT   Pl. 35
Mormoops megalophylla
Head and body 2½ in. (57–70 mm); tail 1 in. (20–29 mm); forearm 2⅛ in. (51–58 mm); wt. ½ oz. (12–19 g). Fur orange-brown or

gray-brown. Unusual "pug nose" and *leaflike flaps on chin*; ears rounded, encircle face. Tail projects out of tail membrane at rest but is taken up into extended membrane in flight. **SIMILAR SPECIES:** Strange face with elaborate folds of skin is unlike all other U.S. bats. **HABITS:** Emerges well after dark to feed on insects, sometimes hunting over standing water. Flight is strong and swift. Large groups (up to 500,000) roost in deep hot caves and mines. Individuals do not cluster together when roosting. Young are raised in separate nursery colonies. **HABITAT:** Desert scrub. **RANGE:** Extreme se. Ariz. and s. Tex. Also Mexico to Honduras; n. South America. **STATUS:** Generally uncommon.

PETERS'S GHOST-FACED BAT
Mormoops megalophylla

EAF-NOSED BATS: PHYLLOSTOMIDAE

Leaf-nosed bats have an erect triangular flap of skin (the noseleaf) on the tip of the nose. They are thought to echolocate through the nostrils and may use the noseleaf to direct the sound. They are known as "whispering bats" because their echolocation calls are very low amplitude and are usually not picked up by a bat detector.

This is a large and diverse family of bats with over 100 species. Leaf-nosed bats are restricted to the New World, with greatest diversity in the Neotropics; only 5 species are resident in the U.S. These are the only bats in the U.S. and Canada that are not insectivorous, feeding instead on nectar, fruit, or blood. Vampire bats (subfamily Desmodontinae) are included in the leaf-nosed bat family although they do not have a free noseleaf. Instead of a noseleaf, the nostrils are surrounded by a flattened nosepad, and there is a secondary fold of skin between eyes and nose.

The nectar bats are very important pollinators of a variety of desert plants.

California Leaf-nosed Bat in flight. Note the large round ears, small noseleaf, and long tail, a combination of features that is unique to this species.

CALIFORNIA LEAF-NOSED BAT   PL. 35
Macrotus californicus

Head and body 2¼ in. (55–65 mm); tail 1⅜ in. (30–40 mm); fore-arm 2 in. (47–55 mm); wt. ½ oz. (12–20 g). Fur grayish. Very *large, rounded ears* (over 30 mm); erect *triangular noseleaf* on tip of snout. Tip of tail extends beyond tail membrane. Membranes pinkish brown. **SIMILAR SPECIES:** No other bats in the U.S. have very large ears *and* a noseleaf. **HABITS:** Emerges about a half to one hour after sunset, flying slowly, low to the ground. Feeds mainly on moths, katydids, and butterflies that are gleaned from the ground or vegetation and are often located visually. Roosts in caves and mines by day; at night sometimes roosts under bridges or in buildings. Groups may number 100 or more; each bat hangs separately from the ceiling by one foot or two. This bat can walk "upside down" but cannot crawl on feet and thumbs like most bats. Young are raised in separate maternity colonies. **HABITAT:** Lowland desert scrub. **RANGE:** Extreme s. Nev., s. Calif., and s. Ariz. Also Baja Calif., Sonora and w. Tamaulipas, Mexico. **STATUS:** Locally common.

CALIFORNIA LEAF-NOSED BAT
Macrotus californicus

Head and body 2¾ in. (66–73 mm); tail ⅜ in. (7–13 mm); forearm
1¾ in. (44–50 mm); wt. ½ oz. (10–19 g). Back pale gray or gray-
brown, underparts whitish. Fur very short, frosted with white.
Large pointed ears; long, narrow, but not tapered muzzle with *rudimentary noseleaf* and raised fold of skin around noseleaf. Facial
skin pinkish. Small tail extends beyond tail membrane. Tail membrane very short, attached halfway down hind leg. *No calcar.* Membranes pinkish brown. **SIMILAR SPECIES:** Buffy Flower Bat (*Erophylla*)
has longer fur, a short but distinct calcar, and a small spear on
the noseleaf. Other leaf-nosed bats in Florida lack a tail. **HABITS:**
Feeds on fruit, pollen, nectar, and insects. Roosts in caves in large
groups. Single young are born in June. **HABITAT:** Tropical forest,
plantations, and gardens. **RANGE:** Accidental in Fla. where known
from one record from Stock I., Key West. Not mapped. Native to
Cuba, Isle of Pines, and Hispaniola. **STATUS:** Uncommon to rare.

Head and body 2½ in. (56–68 mm); tail ⅜ in. (7–14 mm); forearm
1¾ in. (44–50 mm); wt. ½ oz. (10–19 g). Back pale yellow-brown
or buff, underparts whitish. Fur relatively long and fluffy. Large
pointed ears. Long, narrow, but not tapered muzzle with a *small
noseleaf* and raised fold of skin around noseleaf. Facial skin brown.
Small tail extends beyond reduced tail membrane. *Small but distinct calcar.* **SIMILAR SPECIES:** See Cuban Flower Bat (*Phyllonycteris*).
HABITS: Feeds on fruit, pollen, nectar, and insects. Roosts in caves
in large groups. Single young, rarely twins, are born May–July. **HAB-
ITAT:** Tropical forest, plantations, and gardens. **RANGE:** Accidental in
Fla. where known from one sight record from Elliot Key and one
specimen from near Key West. Not mapped. Native to Cuba, Ja-
maica, Bahamas, and Cayman Is. **STATUS:** Uncommon to rare.

ptonycteris yerbabuenae

Head and body 3 in. (70–82 mm); tail ⅛ in. (3 mm); forearm 2 in.
(51–56 mm); wt. ¾ oz. (15–25 g). Fur orange-brown or grayish,
short and smooth. *Long narrow snout* with a *small noseleaf and
short ears.* Tail membrane narrow, V-shaped, *edge appears naked*
(indistinctly fringed with short hairs about 1 mm long). *Tiny tail
present* but difficult to detect in life. **SIMILAR SPECIES:** Mexican Long-
tongued Bat (*Choeronycteris*) has a visible tail and a longer, U-
shaped tail membrane; it also has a longer, more tapered snout
with lower jaw extending beyond upper jaw. Mexican Long-nosed
Bat (*L. nivalis*) is slightly larger with longer fur, a fringe on the
edge of the tail membrane, and no tail. **HABITS:** Activity starts about

Lesser Long-nosed Bat approaching an agave. This endangered nectar-feeder has a small noseleaf and a narrow, U-shaped tail membrane.

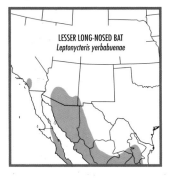

LESSER LONG-NOSED BAT
Leptonycteris yerbabuenae

an hour after sunset; feeds on nectar and pollen of agaves and large cacti. It also takes some insects and fruit and will visit hummingbird feeders. Feeding areas may be 20 mi. (32 km) or more from roosts. Roosts in large caves and deep tunnels in rocky, mountainous areas. Young, born May–June, are raised in huge maternity colonies. Migrates to Mexico Sept.–May. **HABITAT:** Deserts, dry grassland, and canyons, up to the oak-pine zone. **RANGE:** Extreme sw. N.M. and s. Ariz. Also Mexico to s. Guatemala; n. South America. **STATUS:** Endangered (as *L. curasoae yerbabuenae*) (USFWS). Uncommon to locally common in se. Arizona.

MEXICAN LONG-NOSED BAT *Leptonycteris nivalis* **Pl. 35**
Head and body 3¼ in. (78–88 mm); tail 0; forearm 2¼ in. (55–60 mm); wt. ⅞ oz. (18–30 g). Fur gray-brown to dull brown, short on body, longer on head and neck. *Long narrow snout* with a small triangular noseleaf and short ears. Tail membrane narrow, V-shaped, *edge fringed with short hair* (hairs 2–3 mm long); *no tail.* **SIMILAR SPECIES:** Lesser Long-nosed Bat (*L. yerbabuenae*) is smaller, with shorter fur and almost no fringe on the tail membrane. It has a tiny tail that can be more easily felt by hand than seen. Mexican Long-tongued Bat (*Choeronycteris*) has a noticeable tail and a long tapered snout. **HABITS:** Similar to Lesser Long-nosed Bat. After mating in Mexico, females form maternity colonies of about 10,000 in large caves in Texas. The U.S. population may consist

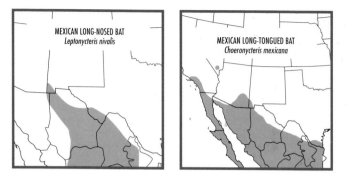

MEXICAN LONG-NOSED BAT
Leptonycteris nivalis

MEXICAN LONG-TONGUED BAT
Choeronycteris mexicana

entirely of females and young. **HABITAT:** Pine-oak forest and high deserts, usually above 3,000 ft. (1,000 m). **RANGE:** Big Bend Natl. Park and adjacent sw. Tex.; Animas Mts., Hidalgo Co., N.M. Also Mexico to s. Guatemala. **STATUS:** Endangered (USFWS). Rare and local, suffers from habitat degradation.

EXICAN LONG-TONGUED BAT   Pl. 35, Skull Pl. 1
oeronycteris mexicana
Mexican Hog-nosed Bat

Head and body 2¾ in. (65–80 mm); tail ⅜ in. (8–12 mm); forearm 1¾ in. (43–48 mm); wt. ⅝ oz. (10–25 g). Fur grayish or gray-brown, hairs pale at roots. Long tapered snout with *lower jaw extending beyond upper jaw*; small triangular noseleaf. Tail membrane *broad, edge U-shaped*; small but conspicuous tail. **SIMILAR SPECIES:** Long-nosed bats (*Leptonycteris*) are larger (forearm over 50 mm) and have less elongated snouts, no visible tail, and reduced tail membranes. **HABITS:** Feeds on nectar, pollen, and fruit, and may take insects. As with other nectar-feeding bats, the tip of the long tubular tongue is covered with brushlike projections, allowing it to lap nectar deep within flowers. This is the bat most likely to be seen raiding hummingbird feeders at night in residential areas. It roosts in caves, mines, and buildings, hanging near the roost entrance. Individuals roost separately, clinging by one foot and spinning around if disturbed. Single young born June–July; well furred at birth. Females form small maternity colonies. **HABITAT:** Desert scrub, canyons, and pine-oak forest. **RANGE:** S. Calif., s. Ariz., and sw. N.M. Also Mexico to Nicaragua. **STATUS:** Generally rare in U.S.

MAICAN FRUIT-EATING BAT   *Artibeus jamaicensis* Pl. 35
Head and body 3 in. (70–85 mm); forearm 2½ in. (55–67 mm); wt. 1¼ oz. (29–51 g). Large and *stocky*; fur usually gray or gray-

brown above, pale gray below. *Pale stripes above and below eye;* short, bulldoglike snout, *broad triangular noseleaf. No tail.* **SIMILAR SPECIES:** No other leaf-nosed bats occur in the East. **HABITS:** Feeds on fruit (mainly figs), often traveling long distances each night. Small harems roost in hollow trees, buildings, caves, or under foliage. Bachelor groups and nonreproductive females roost separately. **HABITAT:** Forests and plantations. **RANGE:** In U.S. only in Fla. Keys (Key West, Cudjoe, and Ramrod). Escapees may occur on mainland Fla. Also Caribbean islands and Mexico through Central America to Ecuador and Venezuela. **STATUS:** Abundant and widespread in most of its range. Known in Florida from specimens from Key West as well as observations from Key West and other keys.

JAMAICAN FRUIT-EATING BAT
Artibeus jamaicensis

HAIRY-LEGGED VAMPIRE
Diphylla ecaudata

CUBAN FIG-EATING BAT   *Phyllops falcatus*   **p. 70**
Head and body 2¼ in. (58–59 mm); forearm 1¾ in. (41–45 mm); wt. ½ oz. (14–16 g). Fur gray-brown. Ears medium sized, rounded. Short muzzle with a well-developed noseleaf. Facial skin brown. *White patches of fur on shoulders. No tail.* Finger bone on leading edge of wing is falcate or sickle-shaped (this bone is straight in most bats). **SIMILAR SPECIES:** Jamaican Fruit-eating Bat (*Artibeus*) is much larger with stripes on face and no white spots on shoulders. **HABITS:** Feeds on fruit, especially figs. Roosts in small groups in hollow trees or among foliage; will use bat houses. **HABITAT:** Tropical forest, plantations, and gardens. **RANGE:** Accidental in Fla. where known from one record from Key West. Not mapped. Native to Cuba, Hispaniola, and Grand Cayman I. **STATUS:** Uncommon to rare.

HAIRY-LEGGED VAMPIRE   *Diphylla ecaudata*   **Pl. 35**
Head and body 3 in. (70–82 mm); forearm 2 in. (49–56 mm); wt. ⅞ oz. (18–33 g). Thick, *M-shaped nosepad* above nostrils; large eyes; short broad ears. Very long thumbs. *No tail and greatly reduced tail*

membrane; robust, hairy hind legs and large feet. *Upper incisors large and pointed.* **SIMILAR SPECIES:** Thickened nosepad, thumbs, and narrow hairy tail membrane unlike any other U.S. bat. **HABITS:** Feeds on blood of birds, may occasionally attack cattle. Scurries on thumbs and feet toward prey, then climbs up to bite the leg or cloaca of a sleeping bird. Roosts alone or in small groups in caves and mines. Single young born at any time of year. This species has never been known to bite a human. **HABITAT:** Forests at low elevations. **RANGE:** Known in U.S. only from Val Verde Co., Tex. Also e. Mexico to n. South America. **STATUS:** Rare vagrant, known in U.S. from a single record in 1967, 435 mi. (700 km) north of nearest Mexican locality. Elsewhere generally uncommon and local.

ESPER BATS: VESPERTILIONIDAE

Vesper or plain-nosed bats usually have unadorned nostrils and mouths. They have long tails that are entirely enclosed in a tail membrane, with no more than a small tail tip projecting beyond the membrane. Most vesper bats are aerial insectivores, using the wing tips or tail membrane as a scoop to capture flying insects. Some species glean insects from vegetation. Loud echolocation calls are given from the mouth and are easily picked up with a bat detector.

Most of the northern vesper bats hibernate in winter. They congregate at cave entrances in large swarms in the fall and usually mate at this time. The female stores sperm, but fertilization is delayed until she awakes from hibernation. Many vesper bats (all the *Myotis* as well as Spotted Bats and the big-eared bats) have single young. Pipistrelles, Silver-haired Bats, Big Brown Bats, Evening Bats, and Pallid Bats commonly give birth to twins. Bats of the genus *Lasiurus* (Hoary, Red, and Seminole Bats and the yellow bats) are unusual in producing litters of 1–4 young. Most bats have 2 teats and cannot raise more than 2 young, but the Lasiurines have an extra pair of teats, located low on the abdomen, and therefore can successfully raise large litters.

Most of our bats belong to the family Vespertilionidae, and all bats found in Canada and the Northeast are vesper bats. This is the largest bat family in the world, with over 320 species. Vesper bats can be difficult to identify, at both the species and genus levels. The following genera of plain brownish bats can be confused with one another:

LITTLE BROWN MYOTIS AND ALLIES (*Myotis*): Small brownish bats with narrow ears that are medium to large in size, with a long, spear-shaped tragus (leaflike projection inside the ear — see Plate 36). The upper tooth row appears to have a *gap* after the large canine tooth (2 small premolars are present but not easily seen). The calcar may be keeled or unkeeled (this can be a useful feature in identifying different species within the genus — see p. 72).

BIG BROWN BAT (*Eptesicus*): A large bat with a blunt and slightly curved tragus. The upper tooth row has a large tooth immediately behind the canine (no apparent gap, unlike *Myotis*). Calcar keeled. Tip of tail free.

EVENING BAT (*Nycticeius*): Small bat; tragus and tooth row as in *Eptesicus*. Calcar unkeeled.

PIPISTRELLES (*Pipistrellus*): Tiny bats with a broad blunt tragus. Calcar not keeled. One small tooth after the canine in the upper tooth row (small gap).

CALIFORNIA MYOTIS *Myotis californicus* PL. 37

Head and body 1¾ in. (38–48 mm); tail 1½ in. (32–45 mm); foot ¼ in. (5–7 mm); ear ½ in. (12–15 mm); forearm 1⅜ in. (31–35 mm); wt. ⅛ oz. (3–5 g). *Very small. Fur dull*, not glossy, blackish at roots. *Black mask and ears contrast with pale fur*; mask paler at base of ears and around eyes. Ears medium sized. Tragus narrow and pointed. Tail tip extends no more than 1–2 mm beyond membrane. Tail membrane haired below knee. *Foot very small*; calcar keeled. **GEOGRAPHIC VARIATION:** Fur on back ranges from pale yellow (Southwest deserts) to chestnut brown (Pacific Northwest). **SIMILAR SPECIES:** Western Pipistrelle (*Pipistrellus hesperus*) is usually smaller with paler fur and a broad blunt tragus. Western Small-footed Myotis (*M. ciliolabrum*) is easily confused: it has a slightly darker mask; when viewed from above the hairless part of the muzzle is 1.5 times longer than the width of the nostrils (in *californicus* it is the same length as the width of the nostrils); *ciliolabrum* has a flatter skull with a smooth slope from nose to ears (the skull of *californicus* feels bumpy where braincase arises sharply from rostrum); and in *ciliolabrum* the tail tip extends 2–3 mm beyond membrane (longer than in *californicus*). Little Brown and Yuma Myotis can be similar in color in the Pacific Northwest, but they have larger feet, unkeeled calcars, and do not have hair below level of knee on tail membrane. **HABITS:** Emerges after dark to feed on flies and small moths. Fluttery flight is slow and erratic, often near to ground. At night, roosts mainly in buildings and man-made structures; by day lone individuals or small groups occupy a variety of crevices — in rocks, under bark, behind shutters, or in buildings. Young, born May–July, are raised in small maternity colonies. May hibernate in mines or caves or may remain active all winter, even at temperatures below freezing. **HABITAT:** Desert scrub, riparian woodland, canyons, and forest. Lowlands to at least 8,000 ft.

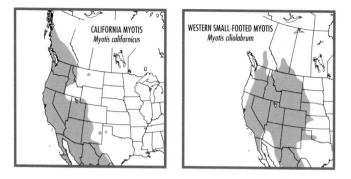

(2,500 m). **RANGE:** Se. Alaska to Calif. and w. Tex. Also Mexico to cen. Guatemala. **STATUS:** Common.

ESTERN SMALL-FOOTED MYOTIS   PL. 37
yotis ciliolabrum

Head and body 1⅞ in. (40–50 mm); tail 1½ in. (35–45 mm); foot ¼ in. (6–8 mm); ear ½ in. (13–16 mm); forearm 1⅜ in. (31–36 mm); wt. ⅛ oz. (3–6 g). *Very small.* Fur pale *yellowish to orange,* slightly glossy, dark at roots. *Black mask and ears contrast with pale fur.* Ears medium sized. Tragus narrow and pointed. Tail tip extends 2–3 mm beyond membrane. Tail membrane haired below knee. *Foot very small;* calcar keeled. **SIMILAR SPECIES:** Easily confused with California Myotis (see that species for differences). Western Pipistrelle is smaller with a broader, blunt tragus. Other *Myotis* are larger or have unkeeled calcars. **HABITS:** Feeds on moths, beetles, and other flying insects, foraging over rocks and cliff faces. Roosts singly or in small groups in crevices in rocks, mines, caves, under bark, or in buildings. Young, born May–July, are raised in small maternity colonies. Young can fly after 1 month. Hibernates in winter in mines and caves. **HABITAT:** Desert, short-grass prairies, riparian areas, and coniferous forests. To about 9,000 ft. (2,750 m). **RANGE:** S. B.C., Alta., and s. Sask. through Dakotas to Tex. Also n. Mexico. **STATUS:** Uncommon.

ASTERN SMALL-FOOTED MYOTIS   *Myotis leibii*   PL. 36

Head and body 1¾ in. (40–50 mm); tail 1½ in. (33–40 mm); foot ¼ in. (6–8 mm); ear ½ in. (12–15 mm); forearm 1¼ in. (30–34 mm); wt. ⅛ oz. (3–6 g). *Very small.* Fur on back pale yellow to *golden brown;* belly cream. Hairs black at roots. *Black mask and ears contrast with pale fur.* Ears medium sized. Tragus narrow and pointed. *Foot very small; calcar keeled.* **SIMILAR SPECIES:** This is the smallest

Myotis in the East. Little Brown Myotis (*M. lucifugus*) has longer forearm and larger hind foot; the calcar is not keeled. Indiana Myotis (*M. sodalis*) has pinkish face and brown fur. Eastern Pipistrelle (*P. subflavus*) has pale face and ears and pinkish forearms. **HABITS:** Emerges at dusk to forage, flight slow and erratic. Roosts singly or in small groups in crevices or under bark. Young born May–July, raised in small maternity colonies. Roosts in caves and mines in winter. Hibernates later than other *Myotis* and tolerates low temperatures during hibernation. **HABITAT:** Deciduous and coniferous forests, often at higher elevations. **RANGE:** S. Ont. and Me. southwest through Appalachians to e. Okla. and Ark. **STATUS:** Thought to be rare; poorly known. **NOTE:** Western and Eastern Small-footed Myotis were formerly considered to be a single species, *Myotis subulatus* or *Myotis leibii*.

EASTERN SMALL-FOOTED MYOTIS
Myotis leibii

YUMA MYOTIS *Myotis yumanensis* PL. 37

Head and body 1¾ in. (38–50 mm); tail 1⅜ in. (30–40 mm); foot ⅜ in. (8–10 mm); ear ½ in. (12–15 mm); forearm 1⅜ in. (32–37 mm); wt. ¼ oz. (5–7 g). Small. *Fur dull*, slightly frizzy, even in length. Ears medium sized. *Feet rather large*, toes haired. Calcar not keeled. **GEOGRAPHIC VARIATION:** Arid areas: fur pale brown on back, *whitish on belly*; facial skin, ears, and membranes pale brown, not contrasting greatly with fur. Pacific Northwest: fur dull brown to very dark brown on back, buff or gray-white on belly; facial skin, ears, and membranes blackish. **SIMILAR SPECIES:** Little Brown Myotis (*M. lucifugus*) is often darker with buff, not white belly. In Pacific Northwest the two species are almost indistinguishable: Yuma is slightly smaller (forearm often under 36 mm) with dull, not glossy fur (fur 4–6 mm long on midback in Yuma, 6–7 mm in Little Brown). Other small western *Myotis* have keeled calcars. **HABITS:** Emerges at dusk to forage over water. Hunts very close to the water surface, feeding mainly on moths and flies. Large groups roost in buildings, under bridges, or in vertical cracks in cliffs. Single young born May–July. Large maternity colonies occupy structures with high temperatures (up to 130°F/55°C). Thought to hibernate in caves or mines in winter. **HABITAT:** Humid forest to desert, always near ponds, lakes, or rivers. **RANGE:** B.C. to Calif. and Tex. Also w. and cen. Mexico. **STATUS:** Fairly common but patchily distributed.

YUMA MYOTIS
Myotis yumanensis

LITTLE BROWN MYOTIS *Myotis lucifugus* p. 74, Pl. 36,
Little Brown Bat Skull Pl. 1

Head and body 2⅛ in. (46–58 mm); tail 1⅜ in. (30–40 mm); foot ⅜ in. (8–10 mm); ear ½ in. (14–16 mm); forearm 1½ in. (34–41 mm); wt. ¼ oz. (4–9 g). Small. *Fur on back glossy,* usually yellow-brown; *belly buff yellow* or gray-white. Fur dark at roots, pale at tips. Snout and ears dark brown to blackish. Ears medium sized. Tragus straight, narrow, not sharply pointed. *Calcar not keeled;* feet relatively large, long hairs on toes. **GEOGRAPHIC VARIATION:** Fur on back dark brown to blackish (Pacific Northwest). **SIMILAR SPECIES:** Big Brown Bat (*Eptesicus*) is much larger, with a blunt curved tragus. Indiana Myotis (*M. sodalis*) has dull brown fur, a pinkish face, and only a few short hairs on tips of toes (hairs extend beyond claws in *lucifugus,* not in *sodalis*). Northern Myotis (*M. septentrionalis*) has longer ears and a long, sharply pointed tragus. See Yuma Myotis (*M. yumanensis*). Southeastern Myotis (*M. austroriparius*) has woolly gray fur. **SOUNDS:** Much squeaking and bickering may be heard at roost, especially near dusk. **HABITS:** Emerges at dusk or later, usually flying to water to forage and drink. May also hunt above trees in relatively open areas. Feeds mainly on emerging aquatic insects, including some mosquitoes. Each bat consumes half its body weight in insects each night (lactating females may eat more than their weight per night). Together with the Big Brown

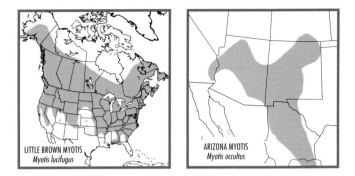

LITTLE BROWN MYOTIS
Myotis lucifugus

ARIZONA MYOTIS
Myotis occultus

Bat, this is the common house bat in much of the U.S. and Canada, as it typically roosts in houses and man-made structures in summer. Females form large maternity colonies, usually in hot attics. Young are left at the roost when the mother hunts. In late summer large numbers swarm around cave and mine entrances, traveling 100–400 mi. (160–650 km). They return to their summer grounds after swarming and eventually fly back to the caves to hibernate in fall. Maximum lifespan is about 40 years. **HABITAT:** Forests and rural areas, usually near streams and lakes. **RANGE:** Widespread from Alaska across Canada to Nfld., throughout U.S. except Southwest and South-Central states. **STATUS:** Very common.

ARIZONA MYOTIS   *Myotis occultus*   p. 74

Very similar to Little Brown Myotis but fur blond, membranes dark. **SIMILAR SPECIES:** California and Western Small-footed Myotis (*M. californicus* and *M. ciliolabrum*) are smaller and have keeled calcars; in Arizona Myotis the calcar is unkeeled. **RANGE:** Se. Calif., Ariz., s. Colo., and N.M. Also n.-cen. Mexico. **NOTE:** Has been treated as a subspecies of Little Brown Myotis (*M. lucifugus*).

INDIANA MYOTIS   *Myotis sodalis*   Pl. 36

Indiana Bat

Head and body 1¾ in. (42–48 mm); tail 1½ in. (28–45 mm); foot ¼ in. (7–9 mm); ear ½ in. (10–15 mm); forearm 1½ in. (35–40 mm); wt. ¼ oz. (5–10 g). Small. Fur on back *dull, pinkish brown or gray-brown* (dark at roots, pale midsection, darker tip); belly buff. Snout pale brown, *skin around eyes pinkish.* Ears brown, medium sized. Tragus narrow, not sharply pointed. Calcar has a slight keel; feet rather small, toes sparsely haired. **SIMILAR SPECIES:** Little Brown Myotis (*M. lucifugus*) has glossy fur, a darker face, no keel on the calcar, and slightly bigger feet with hairs extending over the claws

INDIANA MYOTIS
Myotis sodalis

(toe hairs are shorter than claws in Indiana). Southeastern Myotis (*M. austroriparius*) has larger feet with longer hair over the claws, no keel on the calcar, and woolly gray fur. Northern Myotis (*M. septentrionalis*) has longer ears and a long pointed tragus. **HABITS:** Feeds on moths and other insects in wooded areas. In summer roosts alone or in small groups under loose bark of dead trees. Young, born June–July, are raised in small maternity colonies. In late summer large groups swarm at cave entrances for 2–3 weeks and eventually hibernate in large dense clusters on cave walls or ceilings. Hibernation sites are cooler than those used by other *Myotis*. **HABITAT:** Woods, mainly bottomland forest, sometimes more open areas. **RANGE:** New England to s. Mich. and south to ne. Okla. and n. Fla. **STATUS:** Endangered (USFWS). Almost all Indiana Bats hibernate in only 15 caves. Human disturbance at hibernacula probably caused declines in populations. Most sites are now protected, but loss of summer habitat may also be a problem.

OUTHEASTERN MYOTIS   *Myotis austroriparius*   **Pl. 36**
Head and body 2 in. (45–55 mm); tail 1½ in. (33–44 mm); foot ⅜ in. (10–12 mm); ear ½ in. (14–16 mm); forearm 1½ in. (35–41 mm); wt. ¼ oz. (6–12 g). Small. Back yellow-gray, gray-brown, or bright orange; *belly whitish* (in gray-backed individuals). Fur slightly woolly. Face pinkish brown. Ears medium sized. Calcar not keeled; *feet relatively large.* **SIMILAR SPECIES:** Most small *Myotis* have smaller feet and buff or cream bellies. Gray Bat (*M. grisescens*) is larger with wings attached to ankle (wings attach to base of toes in Southeastern Myotis and all other *Myotis*). **HABITS:** Emerges well after dark and flies directly to water. Forages for insects (mainly mosquitoes and craneflies) close to the water surface. Roosts in caves, buildings, or hollow trees. Unlike other *Myotis*, this species

SOUTHEASTERN MYOTIS
Myotis austroriparius

mates in spring and usually gives birth to twins in late April or May. Nursery colonies are usually in caves that contain water. Very few maternity roosts have been found north of Florida. In the northern part of its range it hibernates, usually in caves, but it may be active all year in Florida. **HABITAT:** Wooded and open areas, usually near water. **RANGE:** Disjunct populations: s. Ill. and s. Ind.; w. Ky.; Ark. and La. to nw. Fla.; N.C. and S.C. **STATUS:** Fairly common but declining. Many important maternity colonies in Florida are no longer in use.

CAVE MYOTIS   *Myotis velifer*   **Pl. 37**

Head and body 2⅛ in. (46–59 mm); tail 1¾ in. (37–47 mm); foot ⅜ in. (9–12 mm); ear ⅝ in. (14–17 mm); forearm 1¾ in. (40–47 mm); wt. ½ oz. (9–15 g). Relatively large. Fur rather short, usually gray-brown, about the *same color from root to tip.* Often has a bare patch between shoulder blades. *Facial skin pinkish.* Ears medium sized, brown, often not contrasting greatly with fur color. *Calcar not keeled.* **GEOGRAPHIC VARIATION:** Fur on back blond to almost white (Kansas to Texas), pale gray to blackish (New Mexico, Arizona, and California). **SIMILAR SPECIES:** Long-legged Myotis (*M. volans*) has a keeled calcar and rounded ears. Little Brown Myotis (*M. lucifugus*) usually smaller, with darker ears and glossy fur. Other *Myotis* of similar size have longer ears. **HABITS:** Emerges soon after sunset; flight is strong and less fluttery than other *Myotis.* Feeds on beetles and moths, flying just above vegetation. Roosts in large groups in caves or mines, seldom in buildings. Single young are born June–July after a 2-month gestation. Nursery colonies may be in the winter roosts or in nearby caves. **HABITAT:** Arid regions, mainly at lower elevations. **RANGE:** S.-cen. Kans. south to w. Tex. and west to Ariz. and se. Calif. Also Mexico to Honduras. **STATUS:** Uncommon to locally common.

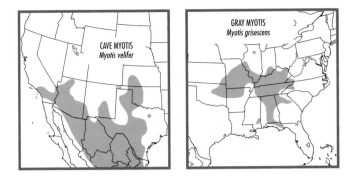

GRAY MYOTIS *Myotis grisescens* Pl. 36

Head and body 2 in. (47–52 mm); tail 1½ in. (33–44 mm); foot ⅜ in. (9–11 mm); ear ⅝ in. (13–16 mm); forearm 1¾ in. (40–46 mm); wt. ⅜ oz. (5–14 g). Relatively large. *Fur short,* same color from root to tip; usually grayish, may be bleached to orange-brown in late summer. Ears medium sized; tragus long and pointed. *Wing attaches to ankle. Feet large;* calcar not keeled. **SIMILAR SPECIES:** All other U.S. *Myotis* have wing attached to base of toe, not ankle, and all eastern species have fur dark at roots. **HABITS:** Usually forages for insects over water. Roosts in caves, favoring ones with streams running through them. Travels 100 mi. (60 km) or more to a few hibernation caves where large clusters form, one on top of another. Young are born May–June. Young are weaned at 3 weeks but do not reproduce until their second year. **HABITAT:** Forested areas close to streams, rivers, or lakes. **RANGE:** Mo. and nw. Okla. east to Ky., Tenn., nw. Fla., and Ga. **STATUS:** Endangered (USFWS). Populations have declined sharply, mainly due to human disturbance at roosts.

LONG-LEGGED MYOTIS *Myotis volans* Pl. 37

Head and body 2⅛ in. (45–63 mm); tail 1¾ in. (40–50 mm); foot ⅜ in. (8–11 mm); ear ½ in. (12–15 mm); forearm 1½ in. (38–42 mm); wt. ¼ oz. (5–10 g). Fur on back usually dark brown or reddish brown, sometimes blond. Brown snout and ears often match fur color. *Snout short,* furred almost to nose; ears medium sized, tips *rounded. Calcar keeled. Underside of wing lightly furred* near body to a line from elbow to knee. **SIMILAR SPECIES:** Cave and Little Brown Myotis (*M. velifer* and *M. lucifugus*) have longer snouts and more pointed ears; they also have unkeeled calcars (as do all western *Myotis* with forearms of over 38 mm). Fur may be present on underside of wing in other species but is usually

Long-legged Myotis. Like most bats, this species drinks on the wing by lowering its head as it passes near the water surface, as beautifully demonstrated in this photo.

LONG-LEGGED MYOTIS
Myotis volans

sparse. **HABITS:** Feeds on moths and other insects, often hunting in forest openings. Flight is swift and direct. Roosts in crevices, snags, caves, and buildings. Hibernates in caves and mines. Young are born May–Aug. One animal lived at least 21 years. **HABITAT:** Coniferous forests and canyons, usually at 6,000–10,000 ft. (1,800–3,000 m). **RANGE:** B.C. to Calif. and w. Tex. Also Baja Calif. and w.-cen. Mexico. **STATUS:** Uncommon.

NORTHERN MYOTIS *Myotis septentrionalis* Pl. 36

Head and body 1¾ in. (40–46 mm); tail 1½ in. (36–43 mm); foot ⅜ in. (7–10 mm); ear ⅝ in. (16–19 mm); forearm 1⅜ in. (35–39 mm); wt. ¼ oz. (5–10 g). Small. Fur on back dark brown, yellow-brown, or blond; scruffy-looking; hairs dark at roots. Facial skin pinkish at base of ears and around eyes. *Ears long,* extend beyond muzzle when laid forward; *tragus very long and narrow with a pointed tip.* Calcar unkeeled or with an indistinct keel. **SIMILAR SPECIES:** Little Brown Myotis (*M. lucifugus*) has shorter ears and shorter tragus with a rounded tip. Long-eared Myotis (*M. evotis*) has longer, darker ears. Gray Bat (*M. grisescens*) has bigger feet and wings attached to ankles, not base of toes. **HABITS:** Forages in upland forest, flying near the understory vegetation. Catches flying insects and also gleans prey from vegetation. In summer, roosts of males or small maternity colonies are located under bark, behind window shutters, or in buildings. Young are born June–July. In winter, hibernates in tight crevices within caves, hanging

Northern Myotis. This species can be distinguished from other Myotis *by its very long, narrow tragus. The tragus is used in echolocation to help direct sound to the ear.*

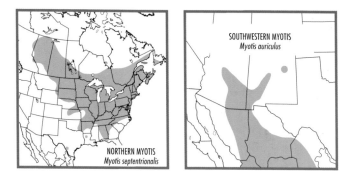

NORTHERN MYOTIS
Myotis septentrionalis

SOUTHWESTERN MYOTIS
Myotis auriculus

singly or in small groups. **HABITAT:** Wooded areas. **RANGE:** Sask. and Nfld. to nw. Fla. **STATUS:** Locally common and widespread. **NOTE:** Formerly included in *Myotis keenii.*

SOUTHWESTERN MYOTIS *Myotis auriculus*   **Pl. 37**
Head and body 2 in. (46–55 mm); tail 1⅝ in. (40–49 mm); foot ⅜ in. (9–11 mm); ear ¾ in. (19–21 mm); forearm 1½ in. (37–40 mm); wt. ¼ oz. (6–8 g). Fur dull, buff to orange-brown on back. Snout long and narrow, large *patch of bare pink skin around small eye. Ears long and brown.* Calcar not keeled. **SIMILAR SPECIES:** Fringed Myotis (*M. thysanodes*) has a fringe on the tail membrane and darker ears. Long-eared Myotis (*M. evotis*) has blackish face and ears. Other southwestern *Myotis* have shorter ears. **HABITS:** As in other long-eared *Myotis*, this species is a gleaner. It has been seen to take insects off buildings and tree trunks and may hover. Its day roosts and hibernation sites are unknown; at night it rests in caves or buildings. Single young are born June–July. **HABITAT:** Desert

grassland, mesquite, chaparral, and oak-pine forests. Favors rocky canyons. **RANGE:** Se. Ariz. and sw. N.M.; also w. and ne. Mexico. **STATUS:** Common.

LONG-EARED MYOTIS *Myotis evotis*   Pl. 37

Head and body 1⅞ in. (43–52 mm); tail 1⅝ in. (36–45 mm); foot ⅜ in. (8–10 mm); ear ⅞ in. (18–24 mm); forearm 1½ in. (37–40 mm); wt. ¼ oz. (4–9 g). Fur rather long and fluffy, back yellowish to dark brown (darkest in Pacific Northwest). *Facial skin and ears black,* contrasting with paler fur. *Ears very long,* extend 5 mm or more beyond muzzle when pushed forward. Calcar not keeled.

SIMILAR SPECIES: Usually recognizable by very long black ears. See Keen's Myotis (*M. keenii*). **HABITS:** Gleans moths and beetles from vegetation and may rely on hearing, not echolocation, to find prey. In summer roosts in various places including under bark, in sinkholes, and in buildings. Young born June–July and are raised in small maternity colonies. Hibernation sites are poorly known. **HABITAT:** Mainly forested regions, up to 10,000 ft. (3,000 m) elevation. **RANGE:** S. B.C. to Sask. and south to Calif. and nw. N.M. **STATUS:** Uncommon to locally common.

LONG-EARED MYOTIS
Myotis evotis

KEEN'S MYOTIS *Myotis keenii*   Pl. 37

Head and body 1¾ in. (40–50 mm); tail 1½ in. (34–44 mm); foot ⅜ in. (8–10 mm); ear ⅝ in. (16–20 mm); forearm 1⅜ in. (34–38 mm); wt. ¼ oz. (4–6 g). Fur on back yellowish brown to dark brown. Snout and ears blackish. *Ears long,* extend beyond nose when laid forward. *Tragus long, narrow, and pointed.* Calcar has an indistinct keel. **SIMILAR SPECIES:** Fringed Myotis (*M. thysanodes*) has a fringe on the tail membrane. Very difficult to distinguish from Long-eared Myotis (*M. evotis*). In *evotis,* ears average larger and darker (can be over 20 mm), and fur on midback is 9–11 mm long with pale tips of 4–5 mm; in *keenii,* fur is 6–9 mm long with pale tips of 2–3 mm. **HABITS:** Flies slowly and hunts well aboveground inside forest or above water. Roosts under rocks, in crevices, and tree cavities. One known hibernation site is a large humid cave. **HABITAT:** Coastal and old-growth forests. **RANGE:** Queen Charlotte I., Vancouver I., and coastal B.C.; Olympic Pen. and w. Wash. Also Wrangell I., Siberia. **STATUS:** Very local and apparently rare. Provin-

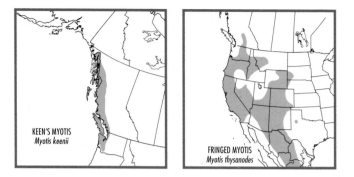

KEEN'S MYOTIS
Myotis keenii

FRINGED MYOTIS
Myotis thysanodes

cial Red List, British Columbia. **NOTE:** This bat and the Northern Myotis (*M. septentrionalis*) were formerly considered to be a single species, known as Keen's or Northern Myotis, *M. keenii*. Recent genetic work indicates that Keen's is more closely related to *M. evotis* and *M. thysanodes*.

RINGED MYOTIS   *Myotis thysanodes*   **Pl. 37**
Head and body 2 in. (45–57 mm); tail 1½ in. (35–45 mm); foot ⅜ in. (9–12 mm); ear ¾ in. (16–20 mm); forearm 1¾ in. (40–45 mm); wt. ¼ oz. (6–12 g). Fur usually yellowish, black at roots. *Dark muzzle and ears contrast with paler fur. Ears long,* extend beyond muzzle when laid forward. Calcar not keeled. *Fringe of short pale hair along the edge of tail membrane,* from tip of calcar to tip of tail. **GEOGRAPHIC VARIATION:** Fur reddish brown or dark brown (Pacific Northwest). **SIMILAR SPECIES:** Other *Myotis* lack a fringe on tail membrane. Long-eared Myotis (*M. evotis*) may have short sparse hairs on tail membrane — it has longer, darker ears (in *thysanodes* the ears are pinkish at the base). **HABITS:** Flies slowly within forest, feeding on beetles, moths, and other insects. May glean prey from the vegetation in addition to hunting flying insects. Large groups roost in caves, mines, and buildings. Young, born June–July, are raised in maternity colonies of 30–300. Hibernates in winter but may wake and be active periodically. **HABITAT:** Oak, piñon, and ponderosa pine forests, also desert scrub, usually at 4,000–9,000 ft. (1,200–2,750 m); at sea level on West Coast. **RANGE:** B.C. and Mont. to w. Tex. and Calif.; e. Wyo., sw. S.D., and w. Neb. Also Mexico south to Chiapas. **STATUS:** Uncommon.

ILVER-HAIRED BAT   **Pl. 38, Skull Pl. 1**
asionycteris noctivagans
Head and body 2½ in. (53–63 mm); tail 1⅝ in. (39–45 mm); forearm 1⅝ in. (38–45 mm); wt. ⅜ oz. (8–12 g). Fur on back *black-*

ish with silvery frosting (frosting varies from very subtle to distinct). Face dark. Ears rounded, mostly black with a pale patch at base of leading edge. *Tail membrane furred* on upper suface for about half its length. **SIMILAR SPECIES:** Hoary Bat (*Lasiurus cinereus*) is larger with yellow fur around face. **HABITS:** Emerges soon after sunset and has a characteristic very slow flight, sometimes following a repeated circuit. May fly low to the ground or at treetop level. Roosts singly or in small groups under loose bark, in woodpecker holes, and in hollow trees. In summer sexes segregate, females move north and east while males remain in wintering areas. Twins, rarely single young, are born June–July. Small nursery groups form in hollow trees. Young remain at the roost until they fly, at about 3–4 weeks of age. Mating occurs after fall migration. Hibernation sites not well known; some caves are used. **HABITAT:** Forest and forest edge, usually near waterways. Lowlands in North; to 9,000 ft. (2,750 m) in coniferous forests of the Southwest. **RANGE:** Se. Alaska to N.S., south to Calif., s. Tex., and Ga. Also ne. Mexico. **STATUS:** Locally common; uncommon in the Southeast.

WESTERN PIPISTRELLE   PI. 37
Pipistrellus hesperus

Head and body 1⅝ in. (37–47 mm); tail 1¼ in. (26–35 mm); foot ¼ in. (5–7 mm); ear ½ in. (10–14 mm); forearm 1⅛ in. (26–32 mm); wt. ⅛ oz. (3–6 g). *Tiny. Black mask and ears contrast with pale fur.* Fur on back very pale ash blond or creamy yellow. Eyes rather large. Ear medium sized, *tragus blunt and curved. Calcar unkeeled.* Wings and tail membrane black. **SIMILAR SPECIES:** This is our smallest bat; the smallest western Myotis (Western Small-footed and California) have narrow pointed tragi, smaller eyes, and keeled calcars. **HABITS:** This species is the first to appear in the evening, often becoming active before sunset. Flight is slow and

SILVER-HAIRED BAT
Lasionycteris noctivagans

WESTERN PIPISTRELLE
Pipistrellus hesperus

erratic, reminiscent of a large moth. After 1–2 hours it retires to a night roost and may not be active again until near dawn. Roosts in rock crevices and other small cracks, including outer walls of houses with swimming pools. Female gives birth to twins in June; young are raised alone or in small groups. In northern regions it hibernates in caves or mines. **HABITAT:** Desert scrub, arid grassland, canyons, and woodland, always close to water. **RANGE:** Se. Wash. to Calif. and w. Tex. Also Baja Calif., w. and e. Mexico. **STATUS:** Common to abundant.

ASTERN PIPISTRELLE
pistrellus subflavus

Head and body 1¾ in. (40–48 mm); tail 1½ in. (36–45 mm); foot ⅜ in. (7–10 mm); ear ½ in. (13–15 mm); forearm 1¼ in. (31–35 mm); wt. ⅛ oz. (3–6 g). Tiny. Fur on back brown, reddish, or pale buff gray (Florida). *Facial skin and ears pinkish brown.* Ears medium sized, tragus broad at base. Calcar unkeeled. Wing membranes dark brown with *pinkish forearms. Fur tricolor:* roots dark, midsection pale, tips brown. **SIMILAR SPECIES:** All Eastern *Myotis* have darker ears and forearms and narrow tragi. **HABITS:** Emerges at sunset; flight is slow and erratic. Feeds on tiny flies and beetles, hunting over water or at forest edge. Small groups roost in buildings or hollow trees, changing roost periodically during the summer. Twins born June–July. Young are raised in small maternity colonies of under 30 bats and are weaned at 4 weeks. In fall migrates to caves or mines and hibernates from about Nov. to April. Lone animals may become covered in droplets of water (from condensation) when hibernating. **HABITAT:** Woodland or mixed farmland.

Eastern Pipistrelle hibernating covered in dew drops. Winter cave conditions are critical: cold enough for the bat to maintain a consistent low body temperature, and moist enough to prevent desiccation.

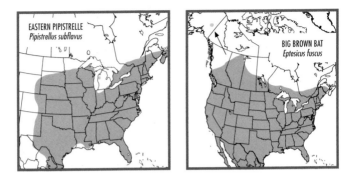

EASTERN PIPISTRELLE
Pipistrellus subflavus

BIG BROWN BAT
Eptesicus fuscus

RANGE: Se. Minn. to N.S., south to e. Tex. and n. Fla. Also e. Mexico to n. Honduras. **STATUS:** Common.

BIG BROWN BAT   *Eptesicus fuscus*   Pl. 36, Skull Pl. 1

Head and body 2⅝ in. (64–75 mm); tail 1¾ in. (42–52 mm); forearm 1⅞ in. (42–52 mm); wt. ½ oz. (13–20 g). Large. Fur on back glossy, yellowish to dark brown. Facial skin and ears blackish; ears medium sized, tips rounded. *Tragus broad and curved.* Sides of muzzle appear inflated. Tail tip extends beyond tail membrane. *Calcar keeled.* Upper tooth row has a large canine followed by a large premolar. **SIMILAR SPECIES:** Little Brown Myotis (*Myotis lucifugus*) is smaller (compare forearm lengths) and has a straight narrow tragus. All larger *Myotis* have tails fully enclosed in the tail membrane, with no more than a tiny tip protruding, and most have unkeeled calcars. In *Myotis* there appears to be a gap after the canine tooth, as the premolars are very small. Evening Bat (*Nycticeius*) is much smaller and has an unkeeled calcar. **SOUNDS:** Young chirps loudly when mother leaves roost. If a pup is dislodged, its squeaking call attracts the mother, who may retrieve it. **HABITS:** Emerges about a half hour after sunset and flies rapidly to its foraging grounds. Feeds on beetles and other insects, hunting over fields or streams or under street lamps. This species is a common house bat in the East, roosting in barns, churches, and houses. In the West it also roosts in hollow trees. Two young are born May–June after a 2-month gestation. Young are raised in maternity colonies of 20–600, usually in attics. Mating can occur in fall, winter, or spring and fertilization may be delayed. In fall it migrates short distances to hibernate in caves, mines, or attics, roosting singly or in small groups. Will awake and become active in response to temperature change — a bat seen out and about in midwinter is almost sure to be this species. **HABITAT:** Forests, farms, cities, from arid lowlands to at least 9,000 ft. (2,750 m).

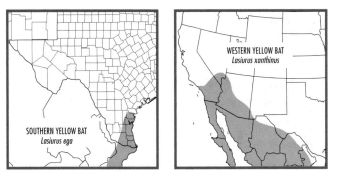

SOUTHERN YELLOW BAT
Lasiurus ega

WESTERN YELLOW BAT
Lasiurus xanthinus

RANGE: S. Canada and throughout U.S. Also Mexico and highlands of Central America to Colombia. **STATUS:** Common and widespread. Highly beneficial in providing natural control of many agricultural pests including cucumber beetle (larval form is a corn borer).

UTHERN YELLOW BAT *Lasiurus ega*   **Pl. 38**
Head and body 2½ in. (62–75 mm); tail 2 in. (40–53 mm); forearm 1¾ in. (42–48 mm); wt. ⅜ oz. (10–15 g). Female is larger than male. *Fur buff yellow.* Long pinkish ears, rounded at tips. *Upper surface of tail membrane thickly furred for about half its length.* **SIMILAR SPECIES:** Northern Yellow Bat (*L. intermedius*) is very similar but slightly larger (forearm over 50 mm in Texas). Other yellowish bats do not have furry tail membranes. **HABITS:** Not well known. Usually caught in mist nets set over water. Roosts in dead leaves or among thatched roofs. Usually 2, but up to 4, young born in June. **HABITAT:** Desert scrub to humid forest and open areas. **RANGE:** S. Tex. Also e. Mexico through Central and South America to cen. Argentina. **STATUS:** Widespread, probably fairly common.

ESTERN YELLOW BAT *Lasiurus xanthinus*
Head and body 2½ in. (61–76 mm); tail 2 in. (44–58 mm); forearm 1¾ in. (45–48 mm); wt. ⅜ oz. (10–15 g). Nearly identical to Southern Yellow Bat (*L. ega*), differing genetically. **SIMILAR SPECIES:** Range does not overlap with other yellow *Lasiurus*. Other western bats may be yellow but do not have furry tail membranes. Western Red Bat (*L. blossevillii*) has white patches at shoulder and base of thumb. **HABITS:** Has been caught in mist nets set over streams through canyons. Roosts in dead palm fronds and other trees, sometimes in urban areas. Female has 2–4 young. **HABITAT:** Deserts and canyons. **RANGE:** S. Calif to sw. N.M. Also w. and cen. Mexico. **STATUS:** Probably fairly common but not well known. **NOTE:** Recently separated from Southern Yellow Bat, *L. ega.*

NORTHERN YELLOW BAT *Lasiurus intermedius* **Pl. 38**

Head and body 3 in. (60–89 mm); tail 2½ in. (47–64 mm); forearm 2 in. (45–63 mm); wt. ¾ oz. (17–28 g). Large. *Fur dull yellow to yellowish brown.* Ears pinkish, longer than broad. *Upper surface of tail membrane furred for about half its length.* **SIMILAR SPECIES:** Southern Yellow Bat (*L. ega*) is smaller (in Texas, where the species overlap, Northern Yellow Bats have forearms of 51–56 mm; smaller animals are found in Florida). Other yellowish bats do not have furry tail membranes. **HABITS:** Feeds on flying insects 15–30 ft. (5–9 m) above the ground in open or scrubby areas. In late summer may form feeding aggregations of 100 or more. Roosts singly or in small groups under Spanish moss; in Texas roosts in palm fronds. Usually 3–4 young (less commonly twins) are born May–June. Young are left at the roost when the mother feeds, but will be taken with her if disturbed by day. **HABITAT:** Forested areas near clearings. Range is similar to range of Spanish moss. **RANGE:** Coastal S.C. through Fla. to s. Tex. Single records from Va. and N.J. Also e. and w. Mexico to Honduras. **STATUS:** Locally common.

NORTHERN YELLOW BAT
Lasiurus intermedius

EASTERN RED BAT *Lasiurus borealis* **Pl. 38, Skull Pl. 1**

Head and body 2⅛ in. (50–60 mm); tail 2 in. (45–62 mm); forearm 1½ in. (36–43 mm); wt. ⅜ oz. (9–16 g). Smaller than other tree bats. *Male is bright reddish orange, female duller,* orange-brown with white frosting. Ears short and rounded. White patches of fur at shoulder and base of thumb. *Tail membrane well furred on upper surface for most of its length.* **SIMILAR SPECIES:** This striking red or orange bat can be confused with very few species. Range of Western Red Bat (*L. blossevillii*) only overlaps in w. Texas; it is very similar but has fur only on the anterior half of the tail membrane and is usually duller in color. Seminole Bat (*L. seminolus*) is a dark mahogany brown. **SOUNDS:** Young are sometimes heard making high-pitched chirping calls when the mother leaves to forage. **HABITS:**

Eastern Red Bat male (with praying mantis) and female. The female, clinging by one foot, has wrapped her hairy tail membrane over her like a blanket.

Emerges early, flying swiftly and often following the same path each night. Has a characteristic flight silhouette, with long narrow wings and a long tail membrane held fully extended. Eats moths and other insects; roosts singly among leaves of deciduous trees. Litters of 3–4 young are born in June. Young are left at the roost unless they are disturbed during the day. Mother and young are sometimes found on the

EASTERN RED BAT
Lasiurus borealis

ground as the female may not be able to take flight with the additional weight of her young. In fall migrates south and may swarm at cave entrances, but usually hibernates among foliage. Has also been found hibernating on the ground in leaf litter. **HABITAT:** Forest and forest edge. **RANGE:** Alta. to N.S., south to N.M., Tex., and n. Fla. Also ne. Mexico. **STATUS:** Common.

ESTERN RED BAT *Lasiurus blossevillii*   **Pl. 38**

Head and body 2¼ in. (51–62 mm); tail 2 in. (45–54 mm); forearm 1½ in. (38–42 mm); wt. ½ oz. (8–19 g). Fur on back *orange to brick red*; black roots of hairs may be visible. Male slightly brighter than female. Ears short and rounded. White patches of fur at shoulder and base of thumb. *Anterior half of tail membrane well furred* on upper surface. **SIMILAR SPECIES:** Eastern Red Bat (*L. borealis*) has fully furred tail membrane and is brighter (especially male). **HABITS:** Probably similar to Eastern Red Bat. Sometimes caught in nets set over tree-lined streams through canyons. Litters of 2–3 young

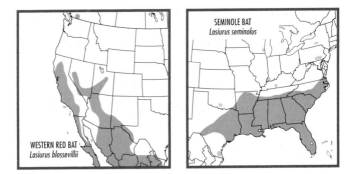

born in summer. **HABITAT:** Forested canyons and riparian zones in otherwise arid areas. **RANGE:** Calif. and Utah to w. Tex. One record for s. B.C. Also Mexico and Central America to Argentina and Chile. **STATUS:** Widespread, probably common. **NOTE:** Previously included together with Eastern Red Bat as a single species, the Red Bat, *L. borealis.*

SEMINOLE BAT   *Lasiurus seminolus*   Pl. 38

Head and body 2½ in. (60–65 mm); tail 1¾ in. (43–52 mm); forearm 1½ in. (35–45 mm); wt. ½ oz. (9–15 g). Medium sized. Fur on back rich *mahogany brown,* lightly frosted with white. White patches of fur at shoulder and at base of thumb. Upper surface of *tail membrane well furred for most of its length.* **SIMILAR SPECIES:** Eastern Red Bat female is very similar but paler and redder in color. **HABITS:** Active soon after dusk; flight is swift and direct. Usually hunts flying insects at canopy level but may also glean prey from vegetation or from the ground. Roosts singly in long clumps of Spanish moss or in foliage. Litters of 1–4 young born in June. Females with young are seldom found roosting in Spanish moss and may raise their young elsewhere. Young can fly at 3 weeks. Does not hibernate and appears to migrate southward in fall. **HABITAT:** Forest and swamp, usually associated with Spanish moss. **RANGE:** E. Tex. to N.C. and Fla.; vagrants to Wis., N.Y., and w. Tex. **STATUS:** Rare to locally common.

HOARY BAT   *Lasiurus cinereus*   Pl. 38, Skull Pl. 1

Head and body 3⅛ in. (72–84 mm); tail 2¼ in. (51–60 mm); forearm 2⅛ in. (45–57 mm); wt. 1 oz. (20–35 g). *Large.* Fur 4-banded: dark at roots, cream middle, outer layer brown *heavily frosted with white.* Nose and edge of ears black; ears rounded. *Yellow fur around face;* white patches of fur at base of thumbs and shoulders. Arms and fingers pinkish contrasting with black wing membranes.

Tail membrane thickly furred on upper surface. **SIMILAR SPECIES:** Silver-haired Bat (*Lasionycteris*) is smaller with unpatterned wings and two-tone fur. **SOUNDS:** Audible chirps and chatters may be given in flight, particularly when several bats congregate to feed. **HABITS:** Large size and fast, direct flight produce a distinctive flight pattern. Eats mainly large moths but may attack small bats and other insects. Feeds over streams and ponds, also around streetlights. Roosts near the end of branches of deciduous and evergreen trees. Usually 2 young are born in May–June. Migrates long distances; in summer, females occupy the eastern states and males the western states, with only a small area of overlap. Winter roosts include sides of buildings and tree trunks. **HABITAT:** Deciduous and coniferous forest, from dry lowlands to at least 9,000 ft. (2,750 m). **RANGE:** Most of U.S.; s. and e. Canada; Hawaii. Also Mexico to Guatemala; Brazil to Argentina. **STATUS:** Locally common in the West, uncommon in much of the East. Hawaiian Hoary Bat (*L. c. semotus*) is endangered (USFWS).

HOARY BAT
Lasiurus cinereus

VENING BAT   *Nycticeius humeralis*   Pl. 36, Skull Pl. 1

Head and body 2¼ in. (54–58 mm); tail 1½ in. (34–41 mm); forearm 1⅜ in. (34–37 mm); wt. ¼ oz. (5–10 g). Small. Fur glossy, yellow-brown to dark brown above. Ears medium sized; *tragus short and curved.* Legs short and stocky. *Calcar not keeled.* One upper incisor on each side; large tooth follows large canine in upper tooth row. **SIMILAR SPECIES:** Resembles a miniature Big Brown Bat (*Eptesicus*), but easily distinguished by size. *Myotis* have straight narrow tragi and 2 very small teeth next to the upper canine tooth. Both *Myotis* and *Eptesicus* have 2 upper incisors on each side. **HABITS:** Flies slowly and steadily over fields and open areas, feeding on beetles, moths, and other insects. In summer roosts in buildings or hollow trees. Twins are born June–July, raised in a maternity colony, usually in a building. Winter roosts poorly known.

EVENING BAT
Nycticeius humeralis

Does not enter caves but may migrate south and remain active year-round. **HABITAT:** Woodland and open areas at lower elevations. **RANGE:** S. Mich. and se. Neb. to Pa., south to cen. Tex. and Fla. Also ne. Mexico. **STATUS:** Common in the southern part of its range but declining in the northern part.

SPOTTED BAT *Euderma maculatum* Pl. 39

Head and body 2½ in. (60–75 mm); tail 2 in. (47–52 mm); forearm 2 in. (48–54 mm); wt. ⅜ oz. (16–20 g). *Huge pink ears* (almost as long as forearms), pinkish wings, and *black-and-white fur.* **SIMILAR SPECIES:** Striking color and huge ears unmistakable. **SOUNDS:** Echolocation calls are audible to humans as tinny pings or chirps that are softer and more metallic in quality than the audible calls of free-tailed bats. **HABITS:** Emerges about an hour after sunset and may travel as much as 50 mi. (80 km) to feeding grounds. Feeds over

With huge ears and relatively broad wings, the spectacular Spotted Bat might be expected to be a slow-flying, understory species. It actually flies fast, well above the treetops.

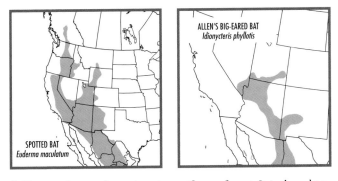

SPOTTED BAT
Euderma maculatum

ALLEN'S BIG-EARED BAT
Idionycteris phyllotis

fields, marshes, and openings in coniferous forest. It is thought to specialize on large moths that might be able to detect more typical bat echolocation calls. Its huge ears allow it to hear returning echoes of its low-frequency calls. In summer roosts in crevices in cliffs or canyon walls. Probably has a single young in June. Winter habits poorly known. **HABITAT:** Arid areas, from lowland deserts to ponderosa pines at about 9,000 ft. (2,750 m). **RANGE:** Scattered records from s. B.C. and s. Mont. to s. Calif., Ariz., and w. Tex. Also n.-cen. Mexico. **STATUS:** Long thought to be very rare, this bat has been found at many new sites in recent years and is sometimes moderately common.

LLEN'S BIG-EARED BAT   *Idionycteris phyllotis*   Pl. 39
Lappet-nosed Bat

Head and body 2⅜ in. (57–68 mm); tail 2 in. (43–54 mm); forearm 1¾ in. (43–49 mm); wt. ½ oz. (8–16 g). *Huge ears (over 35 mm); flaps of skin (lappets) project forward from base of ears.* Fur yellow-brown above, cream below. **SIMILAR SPECIES:** Townsend's Big-eared Bat has lumps on muzzle and no flaps on brow. Spotted Bat has black-and-white fur. **SOUNDS:** Audible chirps are given when flying in open areas; calls are about 1 per second and are similar to but less tinny than the calls of Spotted Bats. **HABITS:** Emerges late, an hour or more after sunset. In open areas flight is swift and direct; inside forest it moves slowly and may hover or fly vertically. Feeds on insects in clearings, over forest, or within forest. One young is born June–July. Small maternity colonies have been found in rock piles, mines, and snags. Hibernation sites not well known; lone individuals have been found in caves and mines. **HABITAT:** Coniferous and deciduous woodland, favors ponderosa and piñon-juniper woodlands. Elevation 3,000–10,000 ft. (900–3,000 m). **RANGE:** S. Nev., s. Utah, Ariz., and N.M. Also to s. Mexico. **STATUS:** Generally uncommon. **NOTE:** Previously known as *Plecotus phyllotis*.

RAFINESQUE'S BIG-EARED BAT
Corynorhinus rafinesquii

Head and body 2 in. (42–56 mm); tail 1¾ in. (42–54 mm); forearm 1⅝ in. (39–44 mm); wt. ⅓ oz. (8–12 g). Fur grayish on back, *contrasting with white belly*; hairs distinctly banded, *blackish at roots. Huge ears* (over 30 mm); *fleshy lumps on each side of snout* behind nostrils. Long hairs on toes. **SIMILAR SPECIES:** Townsend's Big-eared Bat is only comparable species in the East; it has a buff belly, indistinctly banded hairs (gray at roots), and short sparse hairs on toes. **HABITS:** Emerges later than most bats; flight is swift but highly maneuverable. Usually eats moths; as with other big-eared bats, it can hover when feeding. Groups of 1–100 roost in buildings, under culverts or bridges, in hollow trees, or behind loose bark. When roosting, hangs in partially lit areas with the ears coiled back like rams' horns. One young is born May–June. In winter hibernates in caves or mines in the northern part of its range. **HABITAT:** Wooded and riparian areas. **RANGE:** S. Mo. to Ind. and Va., south to e. Tex. and Fla. **STATUS:** Uncommon, status poorly known. **NOTE:** Previously known as *Plecotus rafinesquii*.

RAFINESQUE'S BIG-EARED BAT
Corynorhinus rafinesquii

TOWNSEND'S BIG-EARED BAT
Corynorhinus townsendii

Head and body 2⅛ in. (47–59 mm); tail 1⅞ in. (45–55 mm); forearm 1¾ in.(40–47 mm); wt. ⅓ oz. (9–12 g). Fur brownish on back, *not contrasting with buff belly*; hairs gray at roots. *Huge ears* (over 30 mm); *fleshy lumps on each side of snout* behind nostrils. Short sparse hairs on toes. **SIMILAR SPECIES:** Rafinesque's Big-eared Bat has a white belly and fur blackish at roots. Allen's Big-eared Bat (*Idionycteris*) has projections on forehead and no lumps on nose. **HABITS:** Usually emerging well after dark, this bat is a highly versatile flier not easily caught in mist nets. Eats moths and other flying

Townsend's Big-eared Bat. Exceptional fliers, these bats can avoid very small obstacles and can even hover. Their huge ears aid in echolocation and may also provide lift.

insects, foraging low over fields or high in the treetops. Roosts in caves, mines, or buildings, usually near the roost entrance. Single young born May–July. Nursery colonies of 12–1,000 are located in caves in the East; in the West it may also use buildings. Small groups cluster together in caves or mines during winter hibernation. **HABITAT:** Arid scrub, pine forest, and wooded canyons in the West; oak-hickory forest and other woodland in the East. **RANGE:** S. B.C. to Mont., south to w. Tex. and Calif. Four isolated populations: e. Okla., w. Ark., and s. Mo.; Ky.; Va. and N.C.; and W. Va. Also to s. Mexico. **STATUS:** Two eastern subspecies (*C. t. ingens* and *C. t. virginianus*) are endangered (USFWS). Generally uncommon. **NOTE:** Previously known as *Plecotus townsendii*.

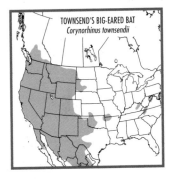

TOWNSEND'S BIG-EARED BAT
Corynorhinus townsendii

ALLID BAT *Antrozous pallidus* **Pl. 39, Skull Pl. 1**

Head and body 2¾ in. (62–79 mm); tail 1¾ in. (39–49 mm); forearm 2¼ in. (50–57 mm); wt. ⅔ oz. (14–25 g). Large, with *long, forward-pointing ears* (ears over 25 mm). *Fur pale at roots*, tipped brown on back. *Snout blunt*, openings of nostrils face forward; nose somewhat piglike. **SIMILAR SPECIES:** Most large-eared vesper bats are smaller; those of similar size have distinctive lumps or leafs on nose or strikingly colored fur. **HABITS:** Flies slowly, feeding mainly on prey captured from the ground or vegetation. Large insects,

Pallid Bat, showing its unusual piglike snout and large ears. This pale bat is a gleaner that hunts scorpions, centipedes, and large insects on the desert floor.

PALLID BAT
Antrozous pallidus

scorpions, and small vertebrates are located by noises made by prey, not through echolocation. This bat often has holes in the wings or tail membrane, probably caused by struggling prey or contact with spiny vegetation. Roosts by day in rock crevices, buildings, mines, and hollow trees. At night may rest under bridges or porches. Usually 2 young are born, May–July. Young are able to fly at 6 weeks. Hibernation sites poorly known. **HABITAT:** Desert scrub with rocky outcrops, from lowlands to oak-pines at about 6,000 ft. (1,800 m). **RANGE:** S. B.C. and Wash. to Calif. and Tex. Also Baja Calif. and south to cen. Mexico. **STATUS:** Locally common.

FREE-TAILED BATS: Molossidae

Molossids have a sturdy tail that sticks out for about half its length beyond the short tail membrane. They have stocky limbs, hairy feet, and velvety fur — features that may be useful when scurrying about in narrow crevices. These bats and their roosts have a strong and characteristic musky odor. The males have a gland on the throat that is often open and exudes a greasy musk. Free-tails have very long, narrow wings enabling fast flight but limited maneuverability. Most species select roosts that allow them to free-fall before taking flight because they are unable to gain lift from a horizontal position. They are strong fliers that often travel long distances each night, usually flying well above the ground. All are aerial insectivores, hunting moths and other flying insects. They drink at large bodies of water that are clear of surrounding vegetation and are most often captured in mist nets set across the middle of these ponds. Loud echolocation calls are given by mouth; some species produce calls that are partly audible to the human ear.

Free-tails are found in warmer climates worldwide; 7 of about 86 species occur in the U.S.

BRAZILIAN FREE-TAILED BAT   Pl. 40, Skull Pl. 1
Tadarida brasiliensis
Mexican Free-tailed Bat

Head and body 2⅜ in. (55–65 mm); tail 1⅜ in. (29–44 mm); foot ⅜ in. (8–11 mm); ear ⅝ in. (14–19 mm); forearm 1¾ in. (41–45 mm); wt. ⅜ oz. (10–14 g). Fur gray-brown, same color from root to tip. *Lips deeply creased and wrinkled.* Ears broad, not extending beyond muzzle when laid forward; ears meet on forehead but are *not joined.* Wings long and narrow; feet and legs short and stocky. *No long hairs on rump.* Tail extends beyond tail membrane for about half its length. **SIMILAR SPECIES:** See Pocketed Free-tailed Bat (*N. femorosaccus*). Other free-tails are much larger or lack wrinkled lips. **SOUNDS:** Much squeaking and chattering heard at roosts. Roaring sound as large numbers exit at dusk. **HABITS:** Soon after sunset dark, funnel-shaped clouds of these bats exit the roost, a spectacular sight, best known at Carlsbad Caverns, New Mexico. Flies at speeds of 35–60 mph (55–95 km/h) and may travel more than 60 mi. (100 km) each night. Flies in open areas and may reach altitudes of 10,000 ft. (3,000 m). Eats moths and other flying in-

Nursery roost of Brazilian Free-tailed Bats. Females leave their young in huge aggregations, returning to feed their own offspring at intervals during the day.

sects, including many agricultural pests. Roosts in large caves, under bridges, and in buildings. Huge maternity colonies form in a few caves, some of which are the largest concentration of a single species of mammal anywhere in the world. Single young, occasionally twins, are born in June or July. Births are synchronized so that all young in one maternity colony are born within 5 days of each other. Young form huge nursery groups of a million or more. Females leave the young at the roost and can recognize their own offspring among thousands when they return, based mainly on odor and voice. In fall migrates south, flying up to 800 mi. (1,300 km) to wintering grounds in Mexico. Lifespan averages about 10 years. **HABITAT:** Scrub, desert, rural areas, and towns. Not found in forested regions. **RANGE:** Many single records of wanderers in the northern states; resident from Ore. to Kans. and N.C. and throughout the South. Also Caribbean, Mexico, Central America, nw. South America, e. Brazil, Chile, and Argentina. **STATUS:** Widespread and common. Formerly abundant, numbers have declined greatly due to destruction and disturbance of roosts and poisoning by agricultural pesticides. Where huge populations still exist, these bats are major predators of many insects and play a key role in pest control.

BRAZILIAN FREE-TAILED BAT
Tadarida brasiliensis

POCKETED FREE-TAILED BAT

PL. 40

Nyctinomops femorosaccus

Head and body 2⅜ in. (58–74 mm); tail 1⅝ in. (38–45 mm); foot ⅜ in. (9–13 mm); ear ¾ in. (18–23 mm); forearm 1¾ in. (44–50 mm); wt. ½ oz. (13–17 g). Fur *gray* or dull brown, *hairs whitish at roots. Lips deeply creased and wrinkled. Ears large, joined above forehead,* extend to or just beyond tip of muzzle when laid forward. Wings long and narrow; tail free for about half its length. *Long fine hairs on rump.* The "pocket" referred to in its common name is a small fold under the leg formed by attachment of wing membrane to the upper side of the tibia. This pocket can also be found on other free-tails. **SIMILAR SPECIES:** Brazilian Free-tail (*Tadarida*) is very similar but its ears meet on, not above, the forehead, it lacks long rump hairs, and its fur is not white at roots. Other free-tails are larger or do not have wrinkled lips. **SOUNDS:** Audible, high-pitched calls given when exiting the roost, rarely heard when in flight. **HABITS:** Emerges well after dark, dropping 4–5 ft. (1.5 m) before gaining lift. As with other free-tails, flight is swift and direct. Eats moths and other insects. Roosts in small groups in rock crevices, caves, and buildings. Single young are born in July. **HABITAT:** Desert scrub and arid lowlands, not far from riparian areas. **RANGE:** S. Calif., s. Ariz., and s. N.M.; Big Bend, Tex. Also w. and cen. Mexico. **STATUS:** Local, generally uncommon. **NOTE:** Formerly *Tadarida femorosacca*.

BIG FREE-TAILED BAT *Nyctinomops macrotis* Pl. 40

Head and body 3⅛ in. (75–84 mm); tail 2 in. (40–57 mm); foot ⅜ in. (9–11 mm); ear 1 in. (25–32 mm); forearm 2⅜ in. (58–63 mm); wt. ⅞ oz. (22–30 g). Large. Fur usually *dark brown*, hairs white at roots. *Lips deeply creased and wrinkled.* Ears large, joined above forehead, extend beyond tip of muzzle when laid forward. Wings long and narrow; tail extends beyond tail membrane. *No long rump hairs.* **SIMILAR SPECIES:** Pocketed Free-tail (*N. femorosaccus*) is smaller. Other large free-tails have smooth lips. **SOUNDS:** Often gives a piercing call in flight (call is similar to that of Western Bonneted Bat). **HABITS:** Leaves the roost about an hour after sunset to feed on moths and other insects. Roosts in crevices in cliffs, in buildings, and occasionally in hollow trees. One maternity colony in Big Bend Natl. Park contained about 130 females and young. Single young are born in June. In the fall migrates to Mexico. **HABITAT:** Arid hilly regions; lowlands to about 6,000 ft. (1,800 m). **RANGE:** Colo. to s. Nev. and s. Calif. to Tex. Many single records, mainly obtained in the fall, to B.C., Iowa, and S.C. Also Mexico to Oaxaca; Greater

POCKETED FREE-TAILED BAT
Nyctinomops femorosaccus

BIG FREE-TAILED BAT
Nyctinomops macrotis

Antilles; South America to n. Argentina. **STATUS:** Widespread, fairly common. **NOTE:** Formerly *Tadarida macrotis*.

FLORIDA BONNETED BAT *Eumops floridanus* Pl. 40

Head and body 3 in. (80–108 mm); tail 2 in. (46–57 mm); foot ½ in. (12–15 mm); ear 1 in. (22–30 mm); forearm 2 in. (61–66 mm); wt. 1¼ oz. (34–47 g). Large. *Fur white at roots*, gray-brown at tip. *Lips not wrinkled; ears broad,* extend just to tip of muzzle when laid forward. Wings long and narrow. Tail extends well beyond tail membrane. Long fine hairs on rump. **SIMILAR SPECIES:** Brazilian Free-tailed Bat (*Tadarida*), the only other molossid in Florida, is much smaller. **SOUNDS:** Piercing, high-pitched chirps are given in flight. **HABITS:** Becomes active at sunset and flies high, 35 ft. (10 m) or more above the ground, traveling in a straight path. Unlike most free-tails, this bat is able to take flight from a flat surface. Feeds on moths, beetles, and other flying insects in open areas. Small groups, possibly harems, roost in hollow trees, under Spanish-tile roofs, and among palm leaves. Females may give birth twice a year, in June and Sept. **HABITAT:** Towns, open areas, and pine forests. **RANGE:** S. Fla. **STATUS:** Endangered (as *E. glaucinus floridanus*, Florida Fish and Wildlife Con. Comm.). This species was recently recognized (2004) and it is one of the most critically endangered mammals in North America. At this time it is not federally listed. Note: Previously treated as a subspecies of Wagner's Bonneted Bat, *Eumops glaucinus*.

FLORIDA BONNETED BAT
Eumops floridanus

LITTLE MASTIFF BAT
Molossus molossus

WESTERN BONNETED BAT *Eumops perotis* Pl. 40
Western or Greater Mastiff Bat

Head and body 4⅜ in. (105–125 mm); tail 2⅜ in. (55–72 mm); forearm 3 in. (73–83 mm); foot ⅝ in. (15–17 mm); ear 1½ in. (36–47 mm); wt. 2¼ oz. (50–73 g). *Our largest bat.* Fur dark brown, white at roots. Large head with *very long ears* that extend beyond tip of muzzle if pushed forward. Lips not wrinkled. Long narrow wings; tail extends well beyond tail membrane. No long hairs on rump. **SIMILAR SPECIES:** Underwood's Bonneted Bat (*E. underwoodi*) is usually smaller and almost always has smaller ears (33 mm or less, compared to 36–47 mm in *E. perotis*). Underwood's is also paler and has long hairs on the rump. All other free-tails are much smaller. **SOUNDS:** Audible high-pitched calls, a loud series of beeps, given in flight. Chatters and smacking calls given at dusk at the roost. **HABITS:** Activity starts about an hour after sunset and may continue for 6 hours or more. This large bat travels with a fast and direct flight, often 2,000 ft. (600 m) above the ground, and may travel 15 mi. (25 km) or more to foraging grounds. Feeds on large moths, crickets, beetles, and bees. Roosts in rock crevices on cliff faces and also uses crevices in buildings. Roosts are limited to those that permit at least 10 ft. (3 m) free fall. Groups of 1–100 occupy a roost. Females give birth to single young April–Aug. Northern populations do not migrate but may change roosts in winter. **HABITAT:** Deserts and canyons, also found in cities. **RANGE:** Calif., s. Nev., Ariz., and sw. N.M. Also n. Mexico; much of South America. **STATUS:** Widespread but uncommon.

WESTERN BONNETED BAT
Eumops perotis

NDERWOOD'S BONNETED BAT

PL. 40

mops underwoodi
Underwood's Mastiff Bat

Head and body 4⅜ in. (95–112 mm); tail 2¼ in. (48–66 mm); foot ⅝ in. (15–19 mm); ear 1⅛ in. (26–33 mm); forearm 2⅝ in. (66–74 mm); wt. 2 oz. (40–60 g). *Very large.* Fur white at roots, tips *gray-brown* on back. Face pinkish, *lips smooth. Ears broad but not long,* do not reach tip of nose when pushed forward. Wings long and narrow. Tail extends beyond tail membrane. Long fine hairs on rump. **SIMILAR SPECIES:** Western Bonneted Bat (*E. perotis*) is larger with much longer ears and darker fur and face. Big Free-tailed Bat (*N. macrotis*) is smaller with wrinkled lips. **SOUNDS:** Audible high-pitched peeps sometimes given in flight, especially when flying over ponds. **HABITS:** Flight is swift and direct, usually well above the ground. Feeds on beetles, grasshoppers, and other hard-bodied insects. Recorded in the U.S. only from mist net captures over a few ponds in s. Arizona, it may roost in Mexico and cross the border only to drink. Roosts are poorly known: it has been found in hollow trees and below a palm leaf, and more recently in a hollow cactus. Females give birth to single young in June or July. Habits and distribution in winter remain a mystery. **HABITAT:** Desert scrub, pine-oak forest, and deciduous forest. **RANGE:** Pima Co., Ariz. Also w. Mexico to Belize and Nicaragua. **STATUS:** Generally uncommon or rare. Fairly common at Quitobaquito Tank, Organ Pipe Cactus Natl. Monument.

UNDERWOOD'S BONNETED BAT
Eumops underwoodi

LITTLE MASTIFF BAT *Molossus molossus* Pl. 40

Head and body 2½ in. (59–65 mm); tail 1⅜ in. (30–39 mm); foot ⅜ in. (8–11 mm); ear ½ in. (12–14 mm); forearm 1½ in. (36–40 mm); wt. ⅜ oz. (10–14 g). Smaller than other free-tails. Fur brown, hairs white at roots. Lips smooth; muzzle narrow and steeply ridged. Ears rather short, joined over forehead, do not extend to nose if pushed forward. Wings long and narrow; tail free for about half its length. **SIMILAR SPECIES:** Brazilian Free-tailed Bat (*Tadarida*) is larger and has wrinkled lips and bigger ears. **SOUNDS:** May be heard scurrying and squeaking in walls or attics, especially near dusk. **HABITS:** Emerges early and can be clearly seen taking flight. Eats mainly beetles. Colonies of 300 or more occupy gaps between corrugated roofs and eaves, where they tolerate very high temperatures. Hollow trees and palm leaves are also used as roost sites, but all known roosts in Florida are in roofs. **HABITAT:** Towns and wooded areas. **RANGE:** Known in the U.S. from Fla. Keys only (Boca Chica, Stock I., and Marathon). Also Caribbean; s. Mexico through Central and South America to n. Argentina and Peru. **STATUS:** Locally common. Three colonies, ranging in size from about 70 to 300, occupy the Florida Keys.

Carnivores: Carnivora

Carnivores are adapted to catch and kill animal prey and have teeth designed for tearing and slicing. Not all carnivores are strict meat-eaters; many include fruit, nuts, berries, and other vegetation in the diet. Carnivores range in size from the largest land mammal in North America, the Brown Bear, weighing up to 2,100 lbs. (950 kg), to the diminutive Least Weasel, a mere 2 oz. (57 g).

Carnivores eat whatever prey is most common or most easily obtained. They are almost always less common than herbivorous prey species, but their generalist diet allows them to occupy a variety of habitats, and most species have extensive geographic ranges.

Most carnivores are terrestrial or arboreal, but some are aquatic. The seals and sea lions were previously classified in a separate order, Pinnipedia. However, recent research indicates that these species arose from the same ancestral group that gave rise to the terrestrial carnivores, and they are now included within the Carnivora.

There are 11 families of carnivores and about 270 species worldwide. Eight families and 54 species occur in the U.S. and Canada.

CATS: Felidae

Most cats are similar in body form. They have lithe bodies, short faces, and rather small ears. They are digitigrade (walk on their toes) and have 4 weight-bearing toes on each foot. Their claws are retractile and very seldom leave an impression in tracks.

Cats are secretive, move silently, and are seldom seen. They do leave signs of their presence: they travel long distances and may leave tracks on trails, in snow, or on muddy banks; they scratch on logs and trees and often mark the same area with strong-smelling urine; some cats cover large kills with sticks and other debris.

There are 37 species of cats worldwide, with 6 species in the U.S. and Canada.

OUGAR *Puma concolor*

Mountain Lion, Puma, Florida Panther

Pl. 48, Skull Pl. 7

Head and body 3–5 ft. (0.9–1.5 m); tail 24–40 in. (0.6–1.0 m); wt. 66–265 lb. (30–120 kg). Large and *long-tailed, with a small head. Uniform sandy brown* to reddish brown above, whitish below. Tail often tipped black. Eyeshine bright yellow. *Young* marked with *circular dark brown spots.* **SIMILAR SPECIES:** Jaguarundi is smaller with short legs. Jaguar silhouette is big-headed with shorter legs and tail. **SOUNDS:** Reputed to make an eerie wailing cry but usually silent. May growl or purr. Female whistles to young and yowls when in heat. **HABITS:** Active night or day, but mainly nocturnal in areas of human habitation. Travels long distances, often on dirt roads or trails. Usually avoids water (but sometimes crosses rivers) and deep mud. Mainly terrestrial but climbs well. Hunts mostly large mammals such as deer, Elk, and Wild Boar. Covers uneaten portions of kill with dirt and sticks. Home range may be 300 sq. mi. (800 km²). Solitary, retiring, and seldom seen. Although there are occasional cases of Cougar attacks (especially in California and British Columbia), they usually avoid contact with humans. Litters of 1–6 young (normally 3) are born

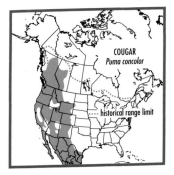

COUGAR
Puma concolor

···· historical range limit

The Cougar is the most widely distributed cat in the Western Hemisphere, found from Chile to British Columbia. It occurs in a variety of habitats, from snow-covered slopes to the swamps of the Everglades.

at any time of year in well-concealed dens, usually in dense vegetation. **HABITAT:** Wilderness areas: forests, mountains, or deserts. **RANGE:** Sw. Canada and w. U.S.; s. Fla. South through Mexico to s. Argentina and s. Chile. **STATUS:** Florida Panther (*P. c. coryi*) and Eastern Cougar (*P. c. cougar*) are endangered; all western subspecies are threatened (USFWS). Extirpated from cen. and e. U.S. Widespread but seldom common.

OCELOT *Leopardus pardalis*   **Pl. 48**

Head and body 25–33 in. (64–84 cm); tail 12–17 in. (30–42 cm); wt. 20–35 lb. (9–16 kg). Medium sized; long narrow tail. S*potted*; spots in form of rosettes with tawny centers on rump, more elongate *ovals or stripes on neck and back*; solid black spots on tail and lower limbs. Front feet broader than hind feet. Eyeshine bright yellow. **SIMILAR SPECIES:** Bobcat has a short tail. Jaguar is much larger with rosettes on neck and back. Jaguarundi silhouette is long and low. **SOUNDS:** Usually silent in wild. Captives meow, purr, and growl. **HABITS:** Mainly nocturnal or crepuscular; sometimes active on overcast days. Climbs well but hunts on the ground and may travel 2–4 mi. (3–6 km) each night in search of food. Eats mostly small to medium-sized mammals, also reptiles, birds, and land crabs. Sleeps on a tree branch or in a hollow tree, or in dense cover on the ground. Solitary. Litters of 1–2 young are born after a 2½-month gestation. **HABITAT:** Forests and dense thickets. Sometimes hunts in open areas. **RANGE:** Extreme s. Tex., e. and w. Mexico south to n. Argentina. **STATUS:** Endangered (USFWS, CITES Appendix I). Population is about 100 in s. Texas (about 40 in Laguna Atascosa N.W.R.); many are killed annually by collision with vehicles. Greatest threat throughout its range is habitat loss. Although protected in Latin America, still suffers from illegal hunting for fur and for the pet trade. **NOTE:** Margay (*Leopardus wiedii*) was reported from Eagle Pass, Texas, in 1852. There have been no subsequent records of this cat in the U.S., and there is some question as to whether

historical range limit

OCELOT
Leopardus pardalis

this single specimen was actually caught in Texas or in Mexico. Margay is smaller (wt. 7–15 lb. [3–7 kg]) than Ocelot, with a proportionally longer tail.

JAGUARUNDI *Herpailurus yagouaroundi* Pl. 48

Head and body 20–33 in. (52–83 cm); tail 13–23 in. (33–59 cm); wt. 7–17 lb. (3–8 kg). *Long body and tail; short legs.* Head small, with short rounded ears. *Uniformly colored,* with two color phases and variants: gray (gray-brown, blue-gray, or dark charcoal gray) and red (tawny yellow, reddish orange, or chestnut). Gray and red kittens possible in single litter. Eyeshine dull, reddish. **SIMILAR SPECIES:** Cougar is much larger and has longer legs. Other cats are spotted. **SOUNDS:** Birdlike whistles, chitters, and purrs in captivity. Female screams loudly during mating. **HABITS:** Mainly active by day. Travels and hunts on the ground, feeding on small mammals, birds, and reptiles. Dens in thickets or under fallen trees. Solitary or in pairs. May breed twice a year; litter size is 1–4 (usually 2). **HABITAT:** Dense thickets, desert scrub, and forest edge. **RANGE:** Rio Grande, Tex., possibly extreme s. Ariz. and Big Bend, Tex. Records from Fla. are probably escapes. South to Brazil and n. Argentina. **STATUS:** Endangered (USFWS, CITES Appendix I) in U.S., Mexico, and Central America. Suffers from habitat loss but is not hunted for fur.

JAGUARUNDI
Herpailurus yagouaroundi

BOBCAT *Lynx rufus* Pl. 47, Skull Pl. 7

Head and body 20–39 in. (50–100 cm); tail 4–8 in. (9–20 cm); wt. 11–40 lb. (5–18 kg). Males larger than females. Smallest in Appalachian Mts., largest in Northeast. *Tail bobbed; tip of tail black above, white below.* Color and spotting pattern variable (variation is both geographic and nongeographic): pale tawny brown, gray brown, or deep reddish brown, marked with diffuse spots or unspotted on back; chest, belly, and inside legs white or cream with black spots. Can be all-black (Florida). **SIMILAR SPECIES:** Canada Lynx

A Bobcat in its winter coat. Note the short ear tufts and prominent black spots on the underparts of this species.

BOBCAT
Lynx rufus

tail is entirely black at tip; it has very long legs and big feet. Lynx is usually slightly larger (on Cape Breton I. and some other locales, Bobcat is larger than Lynx). Other cats have long tails. **SOUNDS:** Caterwauls in breeding season; spits, growls, and hisses if threatened. **HABITS:** Mainly nocturnal, but can be active at any time of day. Swims well. Climbs trees to escape predators; travels and hunts on the ground. Eats mainly rabbits and rodents; also preys on deer, birds, and other vertebrates. Sneaks up on prey, then pounces and strikes. Attacks deer when they are bedded down. Usually dens among rocks or in caves on craggy hills, sometimes in woodchuck burrows or brush piles. Mainly solitary. Young are born in spring or summer; litter size is 1–6. Young are weaned at 2 months but travel with the mother until 6 months old. Young disperse before the next litter is born. Maximum lifespan in the wild is 10–14 years, usually less. **HABITAT:** Highly variable: coniferous and deciduous forest, swamps, thickets, arid rocky areas, and mountains. **RANGE:** S. Canada and much of U.S. to cen. Mexico. **STATUS:** This is the wild cat most likely to be seen in North America. Although it is generally common in the South and West, it has been extirpated in much of the n. Midwest and parts of the East. A Mexican subspecies (*L. r. escuinapae*) is endangered (CITES Appendix I).

CANADA LYNX   *Lynx canadensis*   **Pl. 47**
Head and body 24–37 in. (60–95 cm); tail 3–5 in. (7–13 cm); wt. 11–37 lb. (5–17 kg). *Very long legs* and *large feet. Tail bobbed, tip entirely black.* Fur on back grayish, mottled but not clearly spotted.

CARNIVORA

Canada Lynx. Even in its summer coat, shown here, this cat has much longer ear tufts than the Bobcat. Its huge feet help it travel and hunt in deep snow.

CANADA LYNX
Lynx canadensis

Legs and belly usually marked with black or brown spots. *Long black tufts on ears.* Coat gray and very thick in winter, shorter and browner in summer. **SIMILAR SPECIES:** Bobcat has shorter legs and smaller feet, tip of tail white below; shorter tufts on ears. Cougar has a long tail. **SOUNDS:** During the breeding season male makes a loud bass meow, female a whining purr. **HABITS:** Most active at dusk or dawn. Large feet and long legs aid in travel through deep snow in winter. Hunts by stalking close, then pouncing in one or two bounds onto prey. Feeds mainly on Snowshoe Hares. Lynx populations follow a cyclical pattern with highs every 10 years, lagging behind a similar cycle of Snowshoe Hare abundance. Dens under rocks, in hollow trees, or in dense brush. Mainly solitary. Litters of 1–5 (usually 3) are born in spring or summer. Young are weaned at 3 months but remain with the mother for about 9 months. **HABITAT:** Northern coniferous forest. Favors areas with dense vegetation, swamps, and rocks. **RANGE:** Alaska and much of Canada; also Pacific Northwest, Rocky Mts., and n. Minn. Local in Northeast. **STATUS:** Threatened (USFWS). Fairly common in some northern regions. Southern part of range reduced due to habitat loss and overexploitation for fur.

JAGUAR *Panthera onca*   **Pl. 48**
Head and body 3½–6 ft. (1.1–1.8 m); tail 16–27 in. (0.4–0.7 m); wt. 66–350 lb. (30–160 kg). *Spotted; large* and powerful with a *big head*

and broad feet. Tail narrow, less than half head and body length. Upperparts pale yellow-brown, marked with black rosettes. Spots solid black on belly and legs. All-black animals are known from South America only. Eyeshine golden. **SIMILAR SPECIES:** Ocelot is much smaller and has elongated spots on neck and back. Cougar, in distant silhouette, has small head and long legs and tail. **SOUNDS:** Occasionally gives a series of deep, resonant grunting roars, *uh, uh, uh . . . ,* of increasing volume and duration. **HABITS:** Mainly nocturnal, sometimes active by day. Climbs well but usually travels on the ground. Swims very well and often hunts in or near water. Eats medium-sized and large mammals, also reptiles, birds, and fish. Can kill animals of 3–4 times its own weight and may drag prey for ½ mi. (1 km) or more before eating. Home range is 4–65 sq. mi. (10–170 km²). Marks territory by urinating or defecating in prominent areas and scratching trees. Litter size is 1–4; breeding may occur year-round. **HABITAT:** Dry forest, desert scrub, and mountains in U.S.; elsewhere in wet and dry forest, mangroves, and flooded grasslands. **RANGE:** Extreme se. Ariz. and sw. N.M. through e. and w. Mexico south to n. Argentina. **STATUS:** Endangered (USFWS, CITES Appendix I). Probably does not breed in U.S.; recent records thought to represent wanderers from Mexico. Uncommon and patchily distributed throughout much of its extensive range.

historical range limit

JAGUAR
Panthera onca

WOLVES AND FOXES: CANIDAE

Canids in North America are similar in form to the domestic dog. They have long narrow muzzles, erect triangular ears, flat backs, and bushy tails. They have 5 toes on the front foot and 4 on the hind foot. All tracks are 4-toed, however, as the 5th front toe does not bear weight. Their claws are nonretractile and show in the tracks.

Canids have an acute sense of smell and use odor cues both when hunting and in territorial marking. Most canids lack the jaw strength to overcome very large prey unless they are hunting in packs. Wolves, the most social canids, frequently hunt larger prey in packs but are also capable of bringing down and killing large prey individually. The smaller species usually hunt alone and feed on small prey. Canids generally chase down their prey, but foxes may stalk and pounce, hunting in a more catlike manner. Wolves have suffered from centuries of persecution; the Red Wolf is essentially extinct in the wild and the range of the Gray Wolf has been pushed drastically northward.

There are 34 species of canids worldwide, and 9 species (excluding domestic dogs) in the U.S. and Canada.

OYOTE *Canis latrans*   **Pl. 49, Skull Pl. 9**

Head and body 28–31 in. (0.7–0.8 m); tail 12–16 in. (0.3–0.4 m); shoulder ht. 21–24 in. (0.5–0.6 m); wt. 20–50 lb. (9–22 kg). Long legs and *large ears; long narrow muzzle*. Body color variable, grayish in North, pale tawny in South; legs and muzzle rusty. Tail bushy, usually tipped black. Eyeshine greenish yellow. Usually runs with tail held down. **SIMILAR SPECIES:** Gray Wolf (much larger) has relatively larger feet and shorter ears; nosepad more than 1 in. (25 mm) wide (less than 1 in. in Coyote). See Red Wolf and Eastern Timber Wolf. Domestic dogs have less bushy tails and shorter muzzles. **SOUNDS:** Long-range, howling calls consisting of short high yips from one or more animals, followed by a series of loud eerie howls, ending with short sharp yaps (given mainly at night). At close range individuals communicate with growls, barks, and whimpers. **HABITS:** Widespread and highly adaptable; habits vary from one region to another. Most active at dawn or dusk in East. May be nocturnal or diurnal in West, depending on human disturbance and prey activity. Sleeps by day in dense vegetation where

Coyote howling. Coyotes have recently expanded their range in the East and are now often found in urban settings.

persecuted, but may sleep in open areas if undisturbed. Eats a variety of foods including small mammals, birds, snakes, insects, fruit, berries, and vegetable matter. Feeds on deer, often as carrion, but occasionally hunts big game cooperatively. Small groups can bring down an Elk or deer, especially in deep snow or if prey is weak or sick. May travel alone or in pairs. Packs of 3–7 consist of a mated pair and offspring of different ages. Larger groups are less stable associations of nonbreeding animals. Packs defend a territory of about 4–8 sq. mi. (10–24 km²), scent-marking boundaries with urine. Breeds once a year, Jan.–March. Maternal dens may be under rocks or in hollow logs but are usually in burrows (existing burrows may be modified or new burrows excavated). Litters of 2–17 (usually 4–6) are born after a 2-month gestation. Pups are tended by both parents and by older siblings. They eat regurgitated meat at 3 weeks and are weaned at 6 weeks. **HABITAT:** Grassland, deserts, woodlands, mountains, agricultural areas, and urban areas. Most common in mixed habitats; less common in large tracts of unbroken forest. **RANGE:** Alaska, much of mainland Canada, and throughout the U.S., south through Mexico and Central America to w. Panama. **STATUS:** Formerly heavily trapped for fur; presently trapped, hunted, and poisoned for reputed attacks on livestock or pets (Wildlife Services, a U.S. federal agency, kills some 90,000–100,000 Coyotes per year). Despite ongoing human persecution, this species has expanded its range greatly and is common and widespread. **NOTE:** Coydogs (crosses between dogs and Coyotes) are often reported in the Northeast. Such crosses are possible and do result in viable offspring, but most pups die early. Close analysis of 200 animals suspected to be Coydogs showed that most were either dogs or Coyotes, only a very few were hybrids. The reproductive cycles of the two species are somewhat incompatible: male Coyotes seldom mate with female dogs; female Coyotes can mate with male dogs, but these females are left to raise the pups alone.

COYOTE
Canis latrans

RAY WOLF *Canis lupus*

Timber Wolf

Head and body 35–52 in. (0.9–1.3 m); tail 14–20 in. (0.3–0.5 m); shoulder ht. 28–31 in. (0.7–0.8 m); wt. 60–154 lb. (25–70 kg). Male is slightly larger than female. Large and *long-legged*, with big feet and relatively small ears. Muzzle long but *not greatly tapered*. Color variable: most commonly *grayish* on back (heavily grizzled black and white with some tawny underfur visible, often with a whitish saddle line); muzzle cream, gray, or orange-brown; legs and undersides off-white, cream, or pale orange. Sometimes pure white or pale gray (mostly in Arctic regions), entirely black, or blackish brown. Tail held up or straight out when running. **SIMILAR SPECIES:** See Red Wolf and Eastern Timber Wolf. Coyote is smaller with proportionally longer ears and more tapered muzzle. Domestic dog usually smaller and shorter-legged; tail longer and less bushy. **SOUNDS:** Howls often start with bark of lone animal or yapping of pups, followed by long mournful cries made by several pack members, then ending with several short barks. Howls may rise in pitch and die away, be at a constant pitch and volume, or be punctuated by barks. Howls are much deeper and lower in pitch than Coyote howls. Whines, whimpers, barks, and growls are also used. **HABITS:** Mainly crepuscular, but may be active by day. Eats mostly large mammals such as Moose, White-tailed Deer, Elk, Caribou, and Dall Sheep, also Beaver and Snowshoe Hare. The most social of the canids; lives in packs of 2–15 (usually about 6), composed of family members and relatives. The pack has a well-defined social heirarchy with a linear system of dominance among males and females. One male is dominant over other males; the lead female dominates all females and the low-ranking males (male or female may be dominant over entire pack). Packs occupy

The Gray Wolf varies in color from white to black. A single pack, made up mainly of close relatives, may exhibit more than one color, as shown here.

an annual home range of 56–1,000 sq. mi. (146–2,600 km²) and live at densities of about 1–4 wolves per 40 sq. mi. (100 km²). Breeds Jan.–April; litters of 1–11 (usually about 6) pups born after a 2-month gestation. Maternity dens are located in burrows or depressions on the ground. Mother remains with the pups for about 2 months; pack members bring food and tend pups. Young are mature at 2 years but usually do not breed until age 3. Males and females form long-lasting pair bonds. Lifespan is 10–18 years. **HABITAT:** Forest and tundra. Presently limited to areas of extensive wilderness. **RANGE:** Alaska, w. and ne. Canada, and Arctic islands; w. Mont., w. Wyo., and cen. and n. Idaho. Also e. Europe, China, n. India, and parts of former Soviet Union. **STATUS:** Endangered in U.S. except in Alaska (USFWS). Not at risk in Canada. Range and numbers greatly reduced by human persecution. Reintroductions have met with mixed success; individuals sometimes shot by ranchers for perceived threats to livestock. Successful reintroductions in Yellowstone area and parts of Idaho.

GRAY WOLF
Canis lupus

historical range limit

EASTERN TIMBER WOLF
Canis lycaon

EASTERN TIMBER WOLF *Canis lycaon* Pl. 49, Skull Pl. 9

Head and body 34–42 in. (1.0–1.3 m); tail 13–17 in. (0.3–0.4 m); shoulder ht. 26–32 in. (0.7 m); wt. 50–115 lb. (23–52 kg). Long-legged and *rangy*. *Ears large*. Muzzle slightly tapered but not as narrow as in Coyote, slightly broader than in Red Wolf. Coloration variable: back gray-brown, blackish, or *reddish brown* with a paler saddle; lower sides, legs, top of muzzle, and ears tawny; chest and belly grayish white. Dark shadow inside upper part of forelegs. Tail tipped black. **SIMILAR SPECIES:** Red Wolf is very similar but tends to be slightly more colorful. See Red Wolf for comparison with Coyote. Gray Wolf is larger with a stockier muzzle, relatively shorter ears, and bigger feet. Color varies in both species, but Eastern Timber Wolf is usually redder, especially on legs. **SOUNDS:** Howl is similar to

Gray Wolf. **HABITS:** Similar to Gray Wolf. Many studies of Gray Wolf (e.g., in Michigan and Minnesota) may pertain to this species. **HABITAT:** Favors heavily forested areas but travels widely and may be found in a variety of habitats. **RANGE:** Ne. Minn. and se. Man. to Que. (but see Note). **STATUS:** Endangered (as *C. lupus*, USFWS). Special concern (as *C. lupus lycaon*, COSEWIC). **NOTE:** This species was formerly included as a subspecies of Gray Wolf (*C. lupus*). It appears to be much more closely related to Red Wolf (*C. rufus*) than to Gray Wolf, based on genetic data and morphology. Some authorities include Eastern Timber Wolf as a subspecies of Red Wolf, while others continue to list it as a subspecies of Gray Wolf. Others include *C. rufus* and *C. lycaon* as subspecies of *C. lupus*. The above range was the circumscribed range of the former subspecies *C. lupus lycaon*. Recent work indicates that the Eastern Timber Wolf does not occur in the U.S. or Manitoba and that those wolves may be more closely related to Gray Wolf. If that is indeed the case, this species only occurs in Ontario and Quebec and should probably be known as Eastern Canadian Wolf.

~~R~~ED WOLF *Canis rufus* Pl. 49

Head and body 32–40 in. (0.8–1.2 m); tail 13–17 in. (0.3–0.4 m); shoulder ht. 28 in. (0.7 m); wt. 44–90 lb. (20–41 kg). Long-legged and *rangy. Ears large.* Coloration variable: back gray-brown, blackish, or *reddish brown* with a paler saddle; *lower sides, legs, top of muzzle, and ears tawny;* belly, chest, throat, and sides of muzzle white. Runs with tail held out or up. **SIMILAR SPECIES:** Coat color can be indistinguishable from Coyote. In Coyote, sides of muzzle grayish with a thin line of white around lips and on sides of nosepad (white extends higher on muzzle on Red Wolf). Nosepad more than 1 in. (25 mm) wide in Red Wolf, less than 1 in. in Coyote. Coyote runs with tail held down. See Eastern Timber Wolf. **SOUNDS:** Howl is similar to Coyote but deeper; long smooth howl usually ends on a high note. **HABITS:** Mainly nocturnal, but may be active by day in winter. Eats rabbits, deer, and other small to medium-sized mammals and birds. Moves with a bounding motion and may stand up on hind legs to investigate surroundings. Travels in mated pairs or small packs. Mates from late Dec. to March; litters of 2–10 young (usually 6 or 7) born April–June. **HABITAT:** Formerly in pine and broadleaf forest, coastal prairies, and other densely vegetated regions in the Southeast. **RANGE:** Formerly throughout the Southeast from e. Tex. and Okla. to s. Ind. and s. N.J. Reintroduced to islands off S.C., Miss., and Fla. and in Alligator River N.W.R. (N.C.) and Great Smoky Mt. Natl. Park (Tenn.). **STATUS:** Endangered (USFWS); critically endangered (IUCN). Extirpated

RED WOLF
Canis rufus

in the wild by 1980 as a result of overtrapping, habitat loss, and in-breeding with Coyotes. Captive animals obtained in 1970s were released in the areas listed above, with small islands being used for breeding purposes only. In 1997 the Red Wolf population numbered about 80 in the wild or semiwild (including 30 in North Carolina), along with 160 in captivity.

ARCTIC FOX *Alopex lagopus* Pl. 50, Skull Pl. 9

Head and body 18–26 in. (46–67 cm); tail 10–17 in. (25–42 cm); shoulder ht. 12 in. (30 cm); wt. 5–15 lb. (2.2–7 kg). *Short muzzle and short legs; furred feet. Ears short and rounded.* **GEOGRAPHIC VARIATION:** Mainland form: *entirely white* in winter; gray-brown above and cream below in summer. Coastal and island form (rare): pale *blue-gray* in winter; dark chocolate brown or dark blue-gray in summer. **SIMILAR SPECIES:** Red Fox has long legs and muzzle; it is nor-

Arctic Foxes are well adapted for cold climates, with compact bodies and short ears and legs. Their long dense fur insulates them so well they can withstand temperatures below −70°F in relative comfort.

ARCTIC FOX
Alopex lagopus

mally orange-brown in color (silver form has a white-tipped tail). Coyote is much larger. **SOUNDS:** High-pitched barks, mainly heard during the breeding season. **HABITS:** Mainly nocturnal; hunts in daylight during Arctic summer. Active year-round. Not shy of humans; may enter campsites and steal food at night, also raids garbage dumps. Eats small rodents, Arctic Hares, and birds and their eggs. Scavenges kills of Polar Bears and other carrion in winter. Travels alone or in pairs, but may congregate at rich feeding areas. Pairs seek out a den in spring for birth of young. Throughout most of its range, dens cannot be dug in spring and den sites are limited by permafrost. Previously excavated dens are therefore used for centuries. Each generation adds new entrance holes and old dens may have as many as 80 entrances. Litters of 3–25 pups (usually 6–10) are cared for by both parents. Most pups do not survive more than 6 months; adults may live 3–4 years in the wild. **HABITAT:** Tundra, coastal areas, and shifting sea ice. **RANGE:** Circumpolar in Arctic. **STATUS:** Fairly common in most areas. Introduced to Aleutian Is., where it has had serious impact on nesting seabirds. Efforts to eradicate the fox are under way on these islands. Very rare in Scandinavia.

WIFT FOX   *Vulpes velox*   **Pl. 50**
Head and body 19–21 in. (48–53 cm); tail 9–12 in. (24–30 cm); shoulder ht. 12 in. (30 cm); wt. 4–7 lb. (2–3 kg). Small. Back finely grizzled *pale yellowish gray;* ears, sides of neck, and legs yellow-orange. Throat and belly white. Dark spots on sides of muzzle. Ears medium sized, well separated on forehead. Tail bushy, gray above with a *black tip.* **SIMILAR SPECIES:** Kit Fox is slightly smaller with a relatively long tail and large ears that almost meet on forehead. Gray Fox has a black line on top of tail and more heavily grizzled fur. Red Fox has a white-tipped tail. Coyote is much larger. **SOUNDS:**

High-pitched yaps, growls, and a burping or bubbling call. High-pitched *whar-whar-whar* given as a contact call by lone animals. **HABITS:** Mainly nocturnal. Sleeps by day in underground dens but sometimes rests outside den in warm weather. Curious and less wary than other foxes. Eats small mammals, rabbits, birds, insects, and lizards. Each fox uses several dens, and each den has multiple entrances. Entrances are 8 in. (20 cm) wide, often keyhole-shaped. Adults pair up for the year but hunt singly. Litters of 3–6 young are born Feb.–April. Young stay in the den for a month; after 3 months they start to hunt, and are fully independent by Sept. **HABITAT:** Short-grass prairies and shrub grassland. **RANGE:** S. Sask., s. Alta., and Wyo. to Tex. **STATUS:** Range much reduced due to habitat loss and trapping for fur. Northern Swift Fox (*V. v. hebes*) was extirpated in Canada in 1928 but has been reintroduced. It is presently listed as endangered (COSEWIC).

KIT FOX *Vulpes macrotis*   Pl. 50

Head and body 17–20 in. (44–52 cm); tail 10–14 in. (25–36 cm); shoulder ht. 11 in. (28 cm); wt. 3–6 lb. (1.4–2.7 kg). Smallest fox on mainland U.S. Back finely grizzled *pale yellowish gray;* ears, sides of neck, and legs pale orange. Throat and belly white. Dark spots on sides of muzzle. *Ears large, almost meet on forehead. Tail long* and bushy, gray above with a *black tip.* **SIMILAR SPECIES:** See Swift Fox. Gray Fox has a black line on top of tail and more heavily grizzled fur. Red Fox has a white-tipped tail. Coyote is much larger. **SOUNDS:** Similar to those of Swift Fox. **HABITS:** Mainly nocturnal, sometimes seen by day. Diet consists mostly of small rodents, especially kangaroo rats; also eats rabbits, lizards, insects, and berries. Dens are similar to those of Swift Fox. Litters of 3–5 young are born in Feb. or March. **HABITAT:** Arid open areas, shrub grassland, and desert. **RANGE:** S. Ore. and s. Calif. to w. Colo. and sw. Tex.; also n. Mexico. **STATUS:** Range much reduced due to habitat loss, trapping for fur, and possibly predation by Coyotes. San Joaquin Kit Fox (*V.*

An adult Kit Fox (foreground) and three offspring near their den. This small, slender fox usually mates for life. Insects make up the bulk of their diet.

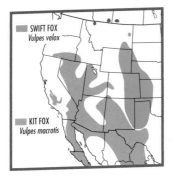

SWIFT FOX
Vulpes velox

KIT FOX
Vulpes macrotis

macrotis mutica) is endangered (USFWS). **NOTE:** Kit Fox has often been treated as a subspecies of Swift Fox, *V. velox*, but recent genetic data indicate that the two should be regarded as separate species.

ED FOX   *Vulpes vulpes*   p. 98, Pl. 50, Skull Pl. 9

Head and body 20–26 in. (52–65 cm); tail 14–18 in. (35–45 cm); shoulder ht. 16 in. (41 cm); wt. 8–15 lb. (3.5–7 kg). Medium sized. Long legs and *long bushy tail*. Color variable, most commonly *orange-red with black stockings* and black ears; belly and *tip of tail white*. "Silver phase" blackish with variable amounts of silvery frosting. "Cross phase" gray or orange-brown with a dark cross on shoulders. Silver and cross phases occur mainly in Canada and Alaska. In high mountains (Rockies, Cascades, and Sierras) can be very pale yellow, or gray, or front half reddish with rear half gray. *Tip of tail is white* in all color phases in North America. Juvenile is brown with white-tipped tail. **SIMILAR SPECIES:** No other fox has a contrasting white-tipped tail. **SOUNDS:** High-pitched barks, whines, and yaps. Parents chortle to young when bringing food to

Red Fox, caught mid-bound, appears rangy and long-legged in its summer coat. In all seasons and color phases it has a distinctive white-tipped tail.

RED FOX
Vulpes vulpes

den. **HABITS:** Mainly nocturnal or crepuscular, but may hunt by day, especially in winter. Feeds on small rodents, rabbits, birds (including poultry), insects, fruit, and berries. Also raids garbage and feeds on carrion. Hearing is sensitive to low-frequency rustling or gnawing sounds made by prey. Hunts by stalking close, then lunging up into air, landing on and pinning down prey with forefeet. Caches excess food, covering it with dirt and leaves. Adults form long-term pair bonds but are usually seen singly, as each fox forages alone. Pairs occupy and defend a territory year-round; territory size varies from 150 to 1,500 acres (60 to 600 ha). Breeds Jan.–March; litters of 4–10 (usually 5) young are born after an 8-week gestation. Young are born in underground dens with several entrances. Both parents tend the young. Young are weaned at about 2 months but stay with the parents until fall. Males disperse widely; young females may stay with the parents for several years and "help" with the next litter. Lifespan is 3–7 years. **HABITAT:** Favors mixed habitats of brushland and fields; also edges of forest and farmland, marshy areas, suburbs, and wooded ravines in urban areas. **RANGE:** Throughout mainland Canada, Alaska, and most of U.S. except southwestern deserts. Also Europe, continental Asia, n. India, China, Japan, and n. Africa. Introduced to Australia. **STATUS:** Common. Historical range (1600s) did not include New England, the East, or south of Wyoming. A combination of factors, including introduction of European Red Fox, fragmentation of eastern forests for agriculture, and extirpation of Gray Wolf and Red Wolf, is thought to have resulted in its large range increase. Formerly hunted intensively for fur and sport. This species is one of the main vectors of rabies.

COMMON GRAY FOX
Urocyon cinereoargenteus   p. 98, Pl. 50, Skull Pl. 9

Head and body 19–28 in. (48–72 cm); tail 11–17 in. (28–43 cm);

COMMON GRAY FOX
Urocyon cinereoargenteus

ISLAND GRAY FOX
Urocyon littoralis

shoulder ht. 14½ in. (37 cm); wt. 7–15 lb. (3–7 kg). Medium sized, relatively *short-legged*. Back *grizzled gray*; ears, neck, line on sides, and legs rusty-orange; belly and throat white. *Bushy tail black on upper surface and at tip.* Young is dark brown. **SIMILAR SPECIES:** Red Fox has longer legs with "dark stockings" and a white-tipped tail. Swift and Kit Foxes are smaller with less grizzled fur and black only at tip of tail. **SOUNDS:** Usually silent in the wild; may bark and whine. **HABITS:** Mainly nocturnal or crepuscular. Usually seen on the ground but can climb to the tops of trees to feed on fruit or escape predators. More omnivorous than other foxes; feeds mostly on small mammals in winter, may eat large quantities of insects and fruit in summer. Home range size is 0.8–2 sq. mi. (2–5 km²). Sleeps by day in dense vegetation, among rocks, in burrows, or in hollow logs. Seen alone or in pairs. Litters of 1–7 (usually 4) young are born March–May after a 2-month gestation. Young leave the den at 2–3 months and stay with the mother for about 7 months. Lifespan in the wild is usually 4–5 years. **HABITAT:** Deciduous forest and oldfields in East, brushy areas and riparian forest in rugged terrain in West. **RANGE:** S. Ont. and s. Man.; w., cen., and e. U.S. Also through Mexico to n. Colombia and Venezuela. **STATUS:** Common in U.S. Threatened in Canada (COSEWIC). Hunted and trapped for fur throughout its range.

ISLAND GRAY FOX   *Urocyon littoralis*
Head and body 13–20 in. (34–50 cm); tail 6–13 in. (14–32 cm); wt. 2.2–6 lb. (1–2.7 kg). *Very small*; short tail and rather short legs. Upperparts grizzled grayish; ears, legs, and line on sides rusty orange; belly whitish. *Tail black on midline and at tip.* **SIMILAR SPECIES:** Common Gray Fox is very similar but larger (ranges do not overlap). **SOUNDS:** Sharp, terrier-like barks; growls and hisses. **HABITS:** Active by day or night; approachable, not shy of people. Eats deer mice, insects, fruit, berries, and ground-nesting birds. Uses any

sheltered site as a den and usually does not excavate a burrow. Breeds in Feb. or March; litter size is 1–5, usually 2. **HABITAT:** Occupies all terrestrial habitats within its limited range. **RANGE:** San Miguel, Santa Rosa, Santa Cruz, Santa Catalina, San Clemente, and San Nicolas Is., Calif. **STATUS:** Threatened (California Dept. Game and Fish); 4 of 6 island subspecies endangered (USFWS). Suffers from habitat loss, competition with feral cats, and collisions with vehicles.

BEARS: URSIDAE

Bears are the largest living terrestrial carnivores. They have stocky bodies with small, inconspicuous tails. Bears have 5 toes on each foot and walk on the entire sole.

Bears rely more on their sense of smell than on vision. Most bears are omnivorous, eating fruits, nuts, grasses and forbs, small mammals, and carrion. Polar Bears are largely carnivorous, as there is little else for them to eat in their Arctic habitat, although they also eat some plant material when available.

Bears use dens during the winter and enter a deep sleep for up to 6 months. The form of hibernation employed by bears is different from that of small mammals, as bears do not eat, drink, urinate, or defecate during hibernation. Bears mate in summer, but implantation of the embryo is delayed until Nov. Young are born in Jan. in the den and are very small at birth, weighing 7–24 oz. (200–700 g).

There are 8 species of bears in 6 genera worldwide. The 3 North American species belong to 1 genus.

BLACK BEAR *Ursus americanus*   Pl. 51, Skull Pl. 9

Head and body 4–6 ft. (1.2–2 m); shoulder ht. 2½–3½ ft. (0.8–1 m); wt. 100–900 lb. (45–400 kg). Male is larger than female. *Snout straight or convex in profile.* Almost all color forms have a *buff brown muzzle.* **GEOGRAPHIC VARIATION:** *Body black,* sometimes with a white "V" on chest (East and parts of West); cinnamon (Alberta, Saskatchewan, Wyoming, w. Montana, Idaho, and e. Colorado) or blond (parts of West); bluish gray (coastal Alaska) or yellow-white (Kermode phase, islands off British Columbia). **SIMILAR SPECIES:** Brown Bear is larger, with a concave facial profile and a humped shoulder. A distant silhouette of Black Bear is highest at rump, Brown Bear is highest at shoulder. **SOUNDS:** Series of huffs if threatened; growls, grunts, moans, and screams; female calls cubs with *uh-uh*'s; cubs squeal and purr. **HABITS:** Usually active by day in wilderness areas; may be nocturnal near human habitation or if frequently disturbed. Walks with a shuffling gait but can gallop at speeds of up to 35 mph (56 km/h). Climbs well. Eats mainly nuts,

Black Bear female suckling cubs outside their winter den. Most winter dens are in hollow trees or logs, but shallow caves, brush piles, or holes in banks may also be used.

BLACK BEAR
Ursus americanus

berries, and vegetation, also takes insects, birds' eggs, young mammals, and carrion. Mostly solitary but may congregate and form a social heirarchy at a rich feeding area (e.g., rural garbage dump). Male occupies a large range (about 850 sq. mi. or 1,500 km² in Ontario) that encompasses the range of several females. Dens under fallen trees, in hollow logs, under roots, or in rock caves or crevasses. In North, males and females hibernate for up to 7 months. In South, only pregnant females hibernate. Litters of 1–3 cubs, commonly twins, are born in winter den Jan.–Feb. Cubs tiny at birth, 7–14 oz. (200–400 g). Cubs weaned late summer but remain with mother for 1 year. Females breed every 2 years. Maximum lifespan more than 30 years. **HABITAT:** Forests and swamps in East; mountains, tundra, and rain forest in West. **RANGE:** Alaska, Canada, and Northwest south through Rocky Mts. and into n. Mexico; patchy in East. **STATUS:** Louisiana Black Bear (*U. a. luteolus*) is threatened (USFWS). Range much reduced in East. Over 90 percent of adult mortality is due to human factors (shooting, trapping, collisions with motor vehicles, etc.). Many are killed in misguided belief that they pose a threat to humans. Black Bears are usually shy and retiring and very seldom dangerous.

BROWN BEAR *Ursus arctos*   Pl. 51, Skull Pl. 9
Grizzly Bear, Kodiak Bear
Head and body 5½–9 ft. (1.7–2.8 m); shoulder ht. 3–5 ft. (0.9–1.5 m); wt. 180–2,100 lb. (80–950 kg). Very large and robust. *Promi-*

Grizzly Bear and playful young. Note the pronounced shoulder hump. This subspecies of Brown Bear is relatively small and has paler, more grizzled fur than coastal forms.

BROWN BEAR
Ursus arctos

--- historical range limit

nent hump on shoulder. Dished face in profile. Fur usually *warm brown,* may be blond or almost black. Front claws very long (3–4 in.), twice length of hind claws. **GEOGRAPHIC VARIATION:** Grizzly Bear (Rocky Mts., interior Alaska and Canada) is smaller, with pale tips to fur giving a grizzled appearance. Kodiak Bear (*U. a. middendorffi,* s. Alaska) is the largest subspecies. **SIMILAR SPECIES:** Brown-phase Black Bear is smaller, with face flat or Roman in profile and shoulder lower than rump. **SOUNDS:** Lone bears usually silent; cubs bark and whine; adults growl on feeding grounds. **HABITS:** Mainly crepuscular, but often active by day, especially prior to hibernation. Moves with a swinging walk or loping gallop. Swims well; cubs climb well but adults very seldom climb. Eats fruit, green vegetation, tubers, carrion, and fish; also excavates small mammals from their burrows and may hunt young or sick ungulates. Sometimes caches food in a shallow depression and covers loosely with sticks or earth. Solitary or in small family groups of female and cubs. May congregate along salmon runs and form a dominance hierarchy, with females subordinate to males. Mother sends her young up a tree if a male appears, as males sometimes attack and eat cubs. Male occupies a larger range than female; range size also varies greatly with habitat and food availability. Not territorial. In winter, dens in cave, under rocks or base of tree, or in hollow tree. Pregnant female may line den with moss. Remains in den for 5–7 months. Female gives birth to 1–4 cubs from Jan. to March. Cubs tiny at birth, about 1 lb. (500 g); weaned at 18–30 months. Females reach breeding age at 5–10 years and breed every 2–4 years. Behavior toward humans is unpredictable; female with cubs or bear defending carcass especially dangerous. **HABITAT:** Mountains, coasts, rivers, and tundra, in open country and coastal forests. **RANGE:** Alaska and w. Canada south through Rocky Mts. to Wyo. Also widely distributed in Palearctic. **STATUS:** Range greatly reduced by human activity. Great Plains Grizzly (*U. a. horribilis*) is threatened (USFWS). Normally avoids humans and requires large wilderness areas to survive.

POLAR BEAR *Ursus maritimus* Pl. 51, Skull Pl. 9

Head and body 6–8½ ft. (1.8–2.6 m); shoulder ht. 4¼–5¼ ft. (1.3–1.6 m); wt. 330–1,600 lb. (150–730 kg). Male is larger than female. *Very large and long-necked, with a small head. White or yellowish* with black eyes and nose. Familiar and unmistakable. **SOUNDS:** Usually silent; growls in aggression. **HABITS:** Swims well, with head and neck above water. Eats mostly Ringed Seals, taking adults from winter breathing holes or on ice, digging young out of lairs in snow. Also feeds on Bearded and Harp Seals, Walrus, Beluga, Narwhal, and sea ducks. Most occupy large ranges and may travel distances of over 600 mi. (1,000 km). Usually solitary except when breeding or with cubs. May fast for long periods when ice has melted in summer; in fall, pregnant female moves to winter den and may not eat for up to 8 months. Dens in areas of deep snow. Litters of 1–4 young, commonly twins, are born in dens Dec.–Jan. Cubs weigh about 1½ lb. (700 g) at birth. Family emerges in late March. Cubs stay with the mother 2–3 years. Females mature at 5–6 years and breed every 2–4 years. **HABITAT:** Pack ice, rocky shores,

Polar Bears are marine mammals that are fully dependent on the ocean for seals, their preferred prey, and they are excellent swimmers. Nonetheless, this cub is attempting a dry crossing.

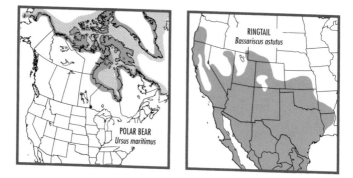

and islands. **RANGE:** Circumpolar in Arctic, on coasts and islands. **STATUS:** World population thought to be stable. Subsistence hunting permitted in most of its range.

RACCOONS AND RELATIVES: PROCYONIDAE

Procyonids have 5 toes on each foot, and most walk with soles flat on the ground, although the Ringtail walks on its toes. They are omnivorous, consuming large amounts of fruit when available. This family is restricted to the New World, and most species are tropical.

RINGTAIL *Bassariscus astutus*   **Pl. 52, Skull Pl. 7**
Cacomistle, Ring-tailed Cat

Head and body 13–15 in. (34–38 cm); tail 13–16 in. (33–41 cm); wt. 1¾–2½ lb. (0.8–1.1 kg). Slim and *catlike*. Short pointed snout; large eyes with whitish eye-rings. Body grayish. *Long bushy tail with very distinct black and white bands.* Eyeshine bright reddish orange. **SIMILAR SPECIES:** Northern Raccoon is larger with a much shorter tail. White-nosed Coati has a long snout and an indistinctly banded tail. **SOUNDS:** Generally quiet. Sharp barks, growls, and undulating howls sometimes given. **HABITS:** Nocturnal. Seldom seen, but not very shy when encountered. Dens among rock crevices or in burrows, hollow trees, or attics by day; seldom emerges before dark. Lithe and agile; seems to glide along canyon walls and can travel rapidly on tree branches. Can rotate wrists 180° for climbing down rock walls and trees. Varied diet includes small mammals, invertebrates, carrion, fruit, and acorns. Usually solitary and territorial; pairs sometimes remain together after mating. Breeds March–April; 1–4 young are born after 7 weeks' gestation. Young start hunting at 2–3 months. **HABITAT:** Dry, rocky, or moun-

The Ringtail is strictly nocturnal. At night it moves with great agility through treetops or in rocky canyons. By day it is sometimes encountered resting on a tree branch.

tainous areas with scattered oaks and conifers. **RANGE:** S. Ore., Colo., and Tex. to Baja Calif. and Isthmus of Tehuantepec, Mexico. **STATUS:** Fairly common.

NORTHERN RACCOON *Procyon lotor* PI. 52, Skull PI. 7

Head and body 16–24 in. (40–60 cm); tail 6–16 in. (15–40 cm); wt. 5–33 lb. (2.3–15 kg). The familiar "masked bandit." *Black nose and mask contrasts with white sides of muzzle* and white above eyes. Fur long, grizzled grayish. *Tail rather short, banded* cream or orange and black. Eyeshine yellowish. **GEOGRAPHIC VARIATION:** North: large, dark, and short-tailed. South: paler, smaller-bodied, and long-tailed. Florida Keys: smallest (wt. 5–8 lb.), very pale with an indistinct mask. Mainland Florida: small, long-legged, often orange-brown on shoulders. **SIMILAR SPECIES:** Ringtail and White-nosed Coati have relatively longer tails. **SOUNDS:** Generally quiet. High-pitched squeals, growls, and screams in aggression or courtship. Mother trills to young. **HABITS:** Mainly nocturnal, but sometimes seen by day. Moves with a characteristic bouncing gait, back arched and head held low. Lopes off or retreats up a tree when caught in a light. Sleeps by day on a branch or in a tree hollow, sometimes in a burrow or building. Eats a wide variety of plant and animal food and often hunts along streams or marshes. Dabbles in water for prey and manipulates items with front paws, but does not wash food. Does not hibernate but may stay in den for several days in bad weather. Usually solitary; groups of up to 20 may share a den, and young remain with the mother for 6–9 months. Adult females stay in the same area; males travel more widely in search of mates. Breeding takes place in early spring, and 2–7 young are born April–May. Juveniles disperse in fall or stay with mother over winter. **HABITAT:** Varied. Most common in wetlands, damp woods, and suburban areas. **RANGE:** S. Canada and

Northern Raccoon dabbling in water. This familiar carnivore does not wash its food, but it often hunts aquatic prey along the shores of ponds and rivers.

NORTHERN RACCOON
Procyon lotor

most of U.S., through Mexico and Central America to cen. Panama. **STATUS:** Abundant. Hunted in some areas for fur or sport. Can carry rabies and other parasites; raids cornfields and henhouses.

WHITE-NOSED COATI   *Nasua narica*   **Pl. 52, Skull Pl. 7**
Coatimundi

Head and body 17–27 in. (44–68 cm); tail 16–27 in. (40–68 cm); wt. 6–14 lb. (2.7–6.5 kg). *Long mobile snout;* white muzzle and white spots above and below eyes. Mainly brown, shoulders grizzled with cream. *Long, indistinctly banded tail* often held erect. Eyeshine bluish white. **SIMILAR SPECIES:** Northern Raccoon has a shorter tail. Ringtail is smaller and short-nosed, with a more distinctly banded tail. **SOUNDS:** Short sharp barks in alarm; whines, chatters, and chirps used for group contact. **HABITS:** Diurnal, unlike other procyonids. Travels and feeds mainly on the ground but can climb well. Sleeps on a tree branch at night and during the heat of the day. Feeds on invertebrates in the leaf litter, small vertebrates, and fruit. Erect, slowly waving tails are often one's first sight of a group parading through the woods. Females, subadults, and young live in stable groups of up to about 40. Males are solitary except during the breeding season ("Coatimundi" is a South American term for a lone male). Mating takes place in April, with 2–5 young born in June. **HABITAT:** Canyons and mountains, mainly in oak-sycamore woods near water, sometimes in coniferous forest or desert scrub. **RANGE:** Se. Ariz., sw. N.M., and s. Tex. Also throughout Mexico and Central America to n. Colombia. **STATUS:** Threatened in Texas (Texas Parks and Wildlife), uncommon and local in Arizona and New Mexico. Common south of the U.S. border.

WHITE-NOSED COATI
Nasua narica

SKUNKS: MEPHITIDAE

Skunks are familiar to everyone in North America for their distinctive black-and-white color and their habit of spraying noxious musk if provoked. Most skunks provide some warning before spraying: they may rise up on their hind feet for a few steps, then drop down and stamp their front feet or hiss; finally they turn their body into a U-shape (spotted skunks "handstand" onto front feet) so that their anal glands and eyes are facing the opponent. Musk is sprayed from the anal glands and can travel 12 ft. (3.7 m). The musk causes temporary blindness if it enters the eyes. It is very difficult to remove the odor from fur or clothing; soaking in tomato juice or dilute chlorine bleach or plain water may be somewhat effective.

Skunks were formerly included as members of the weasel family, Mustelidae, but recent research suggests that they should be classified as their own family. Not all authors agree with this familial split. There are 9 species of skunks in 3 genera, found only in the Americas. Also included in this family are the stink-badgers from Java and the Philippines.

WESTERN SPOTTED SKUNK *Spilogale gracilis* Pl. 53
Head and body 8–11 in. (20–29 cm); tail 4½–6¼ in. (11–16 cm); wt. 7–31 oz. (200–900 g). *Small.* Strikingly marked with 4–6 rows of *white spots and stripes* on a black background. *Large triangle of*

The beautifully marked Western Spotted Skunk is shy and seldom seen. Spotted skunks sometimes climb trees to avoid predators or to feed.

white between eyes and broad white stripe behind eye through base of ear to midback. Tail relatively short and bushy, black at base and white at tip. **SIMILAR SPECIES:** Eastern Spotted Skunk is slightly larger, with a smaller triangle of white between eyes and a narrow stripe from behind eye to midback. Other skunks are larger and are not spotted. **HABITS:** Nocturnal and secretive; seldom seen even where common. Faster and more agile than the larger skunks. Can climb trees to escape predators or to feed, but is usually found on the ground. If alarmed, will run toward attacker, stop abruptly, then turn and "handstand" onto front feet, displaying white-tipped tail and anal glands. Will spray if further provoked. Eats small mammals, birds, insects, carrion, and some vegetable matter. Makes dens under rocks or buildings, or may use burrows of other mammals. Each skunk has several dens and may share its dens with neighbors. Breeds in fall, although implantation of embryo is delayed until March; litters of 2–6 young born April–May. **HABITAT:** Open woods, canyons, and farmland. **RANGE:** Sw. B.C. to Colo., w. Tex., and n. Mexico. **STATUS:** Generally uncommon; may be declining in some areas.

WESTERN SPOTTED SKUNK
Spilogale gracilis
EASTERN SPOTTED SKUNK
Spilogale putorius

Pl. 53, Skull Pl. 8
ilogale putorius

Head and body 8–17 in. (20–44 cm); tail 5–11 in. (13–28 cm); wt. 9–31 oz. (250–885 g). *Small.* Strikingly marked with 4–6 rows of *white spots and stripes* on a black background. *Small triangle of white between eyes* and *narrow white stripe behind eye* and below ear to midback. Tail relatively short and bushy, black at base and white at tip. **SIMILAR SPECIES:** See Western Spotted Skunk. **HABITS:** Similar to Western Spotted Skunk. **HABITAT:** Rocky and brushy areas, farmland, open woods. **RANGE:** Much of East and Midwest to s. Tex. and Tamaulipas, Mexico. **STATUS:** Declining in Midwest and parts of East, common in s. Florida.

STRIPED SKUNK *Mephitis mephitis* Pl. 53, Skull Pl. 8

Head and body 12–20 in. (30–50 cm); tail 9–14 in. (23–36 cm); wt. 2–11 lb. (1–5 kg). Larger in North than in South; male larger than female. Medium sized and stocky-bodied. Tail (including long hair at tip) equal to or shorter than head and body length. Strikingly marked with black and white, pattern variable; always has narrow white stripe down center of face. Usually has *2 broad white stripes that meet on shoulder and crown of head and extend to sides of rump.* Stripes sometimes very broad, separated only by a thin black line down center of lower back; or stripes narrow, more widely spaced, extending to flank. Stripes may be broken and the skunk may appear spotted, but does not have rows of spots as in spotted skunks. Tail mostly white, all-black, or mixed. **SIMILAR SPECIES:** See Hooded Skunk and White-backed Hog-nosed Skunk. **SOUNDS:** Rummages and moves noisily through leaf litter; growls, purrs, or hisses in warning; stamps front feet before spraying. **HABITS:** Mainly nocturnal, occasionally abroad by day. This common and well-known skunk is often seen shuffling along roadsides at night or emerging from under the porch of a house at dusk. Eats mainly insects, also small mammals, birds and birds' eggs, fruit, carrion, and plant matter. Usually solitary, but several may share a winter den or aggregate at a good feeding area. Dens in hollow logs, burrows, under buildings, or in rock piles. Fattens up in fall and spends much of winter in den in North. Does not hibernate and may emerge on warm days. Remains active year-round in South. Litters of 3–10 young are born in May. Lifespan is about 2–3 years in the wild. Principal predators are Great Horned Owls and hawks. **HABITAT:** Brushy fields, farmland, open woods, deserts, and suburbs, usually not far from water. **RANGE:** Throughout s. Canada and U.S. to n. Mexico. **STATUS:** Common to abundant. Many are killed on roads.

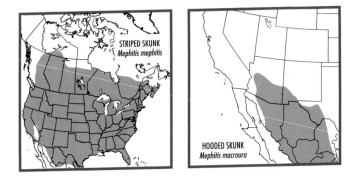

HOODED SKUNK *Mephitis macroura* Pl. 53

Head and body 11–14 in. (28–36 cm); tail 13–17 in. (33–43 cm); wt. 1–4½ lb. (0.5–2.0 kg). Medium sized and *long-tailed.* Strikingly marked with black and white, pattern variable; nearly always has a *narrow white stripe down center of face.* Stripe patterns: (a) 1 broad white stripe down back, most of tail white, white stripe grizzled on rump and tail; (b) 2 narrow white stripes on sides of body and sides of tail; (c) 3 stripes on back, center stripe broad and grizzled gray, side stripes narrow, tail mainly white (combination of a and b); (d) mostly black with a white hood on back of neck and some white hairs in tail. **SIMILAR SPECIES:** Striped Skunk typically has 2 stripes placed higher on back than in 2-striped form of Hooded Skunk. Striped Skunk tail is proportionally shorter. White-backed Hog-nosed Skunk has a shorter tail, no stripe on face, and a long snout that is bare near the tip. **HABITS:** Nocturnal; more secretive than Striped Skunk. Snuffles among leaf litter for beetles and other insects but does not dig deep into the soil. Also feeds on fruit and small mammals and may visit garbage dumps. Mainly solitary, but several may feed together without aggression. Dens in rock crevices or burrows. Litters of 3–5 young are born May–June. **HABITAT:** In dense vegetation along streams or canyons, brushy areas, and desert washes. **RANGE:** S. Ariz. to w. Tex., south to sw. Costa Rica. **STATUS:** Uncommon in the U.S., locally common in Mexico and Central America.

WHITE-BACKED HOG-NOSED SKUNK Pl. 53, Skull Pl. 8
Conepatus leuconotus
Rooter Skunk

Head and body 13–21 in. (32–55 cm); tail 8–16 in. (20–41 cm); wt. 2½–10 lb. (1.1–4.5 kg). Our largest skunk. *Pure white stripe from crown of head to rump, rest of body black. Snout long, naked*

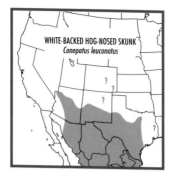

White-backed hog-nosed skunk
Conepatus leuconotus

near tip, rest of head black to crown. *Tail relatively short,* all-white or underside black at base. **SIMILAR SPECIES:** Striped and Hooded Skunks sometimes have all-white backs, but both have proportionally longer tails and usually have a white blaze on the forehead. **HABITS:** Mainly nocturnal, but may be active by day in winter. Known in Texas as "Rooter Skunk" for its habit of turning the soil in search of food, leaving large plowed areas in its wake. Feeds on insects and other invertebrates, small mammals, roots, fruit, and vegetable matter. If disturbed, usually runs for cover, but if cornered will threaten by standing on hind legs, advancing, then dropping to the ground and hissing, tail held up over back. It may then spray and bite the attacker. Mainly solitary; dens alone in crevices among rocks. Litters of 2–4 are born April–May. **HABITAT:** Thorn brush and mesquite brush; dry rocky slopes and canyonlands; also found in agricultural areas. **RANGE:** S. Ariz., N.M., and Tex. to Nicaragua. **STATUS:** Rare and local; appears to be declining. Formerly occurred in Colorado and Oklahoma. **NOTE:** Formerly considered to be 2 species, Eastern and Western Hog-nosed Skunk.

EASELS, OTTERS, AND RELATIVES:
USTELIDAE

This family includes a diversity of shapes and sizes, although most North American mustelids have long slender bodies and short legs. Mustelids have 5 toes on each foot, all of which leave an impression in the track. They have well-developed anal scent glands and usually have a musky odor. (Skunks were formerly included in this family but are now placed in their own family, Mephitidae.)

The 56 species in 22 genera of mustelids are found almost worldwide except in Australia and some oceanic islands. There are 11 species in the U.S. and Canada.

The American Marten usually feeds on squirrels and other arboreal prey, but it is also attracted to carrion such as this deer carcass.

AMERICAN MARTEN *Martes americana*   Pl. 55, Skull Pl. 8

Head and body 13–17 in. (33–43 cm); tail 5½–7¾ in. (14–20 cm); wt. 1–2 lb. (0.4–0.8 kg). Male is larger than female. *Long-bodied and bushy-tailed.* Body usually *dark chocolate brown,* sometimes pale tan or straw-colored; head paler than back; chin brown, *throat white, cream, or orange.* Legs, feet, and tail darker than back, usually blackish brown (paler in straw-colored animals). Feet relatively large. Variation in coat color is not geographic. **SIMILAR SPECIES:** Fisher is larger and stockier, grizzled on head and neck, with no throat patch. Mink is more uniformly colored with a shorter, less bushy tail. **SOUNDS:** Usually silent in the wild. Trapped animals chuckle, growl, scream, or whine. **HABITS:** Active by day or night but seldom seen. Agile and semi-arboreal, often escapes by climbing high into trees. Swims well. Usually hunts on the ground and may travel under snow in winter, using tunnels made by other animals. Feeds on voles, Snowshoe Hares, Ruffed Grouse, and squirrels.

.... historical range

AMERICAN MARTEN
Martes americana

Also takes birds' eggs, amphibians, nuts and berries, and carrion. Diet varies with food availability and season. Sleeps on branches or in hollow logs; may den under snow in winter. Does not hibernate. Litters of 1–5 young are born March–April. **HABITAT:** Mature coniferous or deciduous-coniferous forest. **RANGE:** Alaska and much of Canada, local in U.S., mainly in mts. of West. **STATUS:** Newfoundland subspecies (*M. a. atrata*) is endangered (COSEWIC). Range reduced due to habitat loss in East and parts of West. Reintroduced in some areas and can be locally common. Trapped for fur.

SHER *Martes pennanti* Pl. 55, Skull Pl. 8

Head and body 17–31 in. (45–78 cm); tail 12–16 in. (31–41 cm); wt. 4½–12 lb. (2–5.5 kg). Male is about twice as heavy as female. Large, long-bodied, and *bushy-tailed. Head, neck, and shoulders grizzled yellow-brown* or grayish yellow; *body dark brown* with long dark guard hairs; legs, feet, and tail blackish. **SIMILAR SPECIES:** See American Marten. Wolverine is larger with yellowish bands from shoulder to rump. **SOUNDS:** Usually silent; may hiss, growl, or make a low throaty call if disturbed. **HABITS:** Active day or night. Climbs well but usually hunts on the ground. Eats a variety of small mammals, especially Snowshoe Hares, also fruit, nuts, and fungi; is attracted to carrion. Well known as one of the few predators of adult porcupines, which it attacks on the ground, biting at the face and eventually flipping the animal to open its unarmored belly. Usually sleeps on tree branches in summer and in hollow trees or belowground in winter. Does not hibernate, but its movements are hindered by deep soft snow. Litters of 1–6 are born March–April. Breeding takes place soon after young are born; implantation of the embryo is delayed for about 11 months. **HABITAT:** Mature coniferous or deciduous-coniferous forest with plentiful

The Fisher travels widely in winter, moving along fallen logs, tree branches, or on well-established trails through its extensive home range in the north woods.

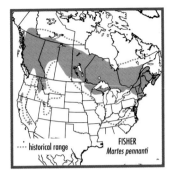

historical range

FISHER
Martes pennanti

fallen trees. **RANGE:** S. Canada and mts. of West. Local in New England and Mid-Atlantic States. **STATUS:** Range and numbers greatly reduced in 1900s by overtrapping for fur and habitat loss. Reintroduced widely, recovering in suitable habitat.

LEAST WEASEL *Mustela nivalis*   Pl. 54

Head and body 4¾–6¾ in. (12–17 cm); tail ¾–1⅜ in. (2–4 cm); wt. 1–2 oz. (31–57 g). Male is slightly larger than female. Smallest of all carnivores. *Diminutive; long-bodied and very short-tailed.* Summer: back warm brown; underparts white or off-white (occasionally brown with white only on throat and lower abdomen); forefeet often white, sometimes brown, hind feet usually brown, sometimes white. Winter (in North): entirely white or off-white, seldom yellowish; tail same color as back with a *few black hairs at tip.* **SIMILAR SPECIES:** Other weasels are larger with much longer, black-tipped tails. **SOUNDS:** Shrill squeaks or hisses in alarm. Female calls young with a trilling note. **HABITS:** Alternates periods of activity and rest throughout the day and night. Frenetically active when awake, darting in and out of runways and burrows, pausing momentarily to stand up and look around. Feeds on voles and mice; narrow body allows it to pursue prey into small burrows. Also eats birds and birds' eggs, insects, shrews, and moles. Eats almost half its body weight daily, and caches excess prey in chambers in burrow. Dens in abandoned burrow of mouse or ground squirrel, lines nest with mouse fur. Male home range includes ranges of several females; strong-smelling musk is used to mark territory. Female may have 2–3 litters of 1–6 young per year. **HABITAT:** Open areas: meadows, brush, and marshland. Occasionally in coniferous or highland forest. **RANGE:** Throughout Alaska and mainland Canada to Mont., Kans., and Va. Also most of Palearctic; Japan. Introduced to New Zealand. **STATUS:** Generally uncommon or rare, but can be locally abundant.

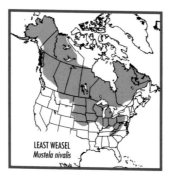

LEAST WEASEL
Mustela nivalis

RMINE   *Mustela erminea*   **Pl. 54**
Short-tailed Weasel

Head and body: males 6–9 in. (15–24 cm), females 5–8 in. (13–21 cm); tail: males 2⅜–3⅝ in. (6–9 cm), females 2–2⅝ in. (5–7 cm); wt.: males 2½–6 oz. (70–172 g), females 1½–2½ oz. (47–73 g). Long, low form; *tail less than half head and body length.* Summer: back reddish brown to dark brown; *belly whitish, cream, or yellow;* feet usually brown with some white on toes, front feet sometimes all-white; tail same color as back with a *black tip.* Winter: head and upper body white, grading to yellow on midback or rump; tail usually yellow at base (may be white) with a long black tip. Eyeshine bright blue-green. **SIMILAR SPECIES:** Long-tailed Weasel is slightly larger. If sex is known, species can usually be identified by size, but male Ermine is same size as female Long-tailed, therefore animals seen in the wild are best distinguished by relative tail length. In Long-tailed Weasel, tail (including brush at tip) is more than half head and body length, in Ermine it is less. Long-tailed has an orange belly in West. See Least Weasel. **SOUNDS:** Usually silent in wild. Screeches or squeals if alarmed; trills in social interactions. **HABITS:** Active for short periods, followed by 3- to 5-hour rests throughout the day and night. Travels with a flat-backed trot or speeds to a bounding gallop with back arched. Busily investigates its surroundings, stopping periodically to stand up and scan the area. Swims well and can climb high into trees. Can be attracted to squeaking calls imitating a young bird. Eats small rodents, rabbits, shrews, insects, and other animal prey. Sometimes kills prey larger than itself. Dens in the burrow of a chipmunk or other small mammal, lines nest with fur and feathers of prey. Usually has several nests in different parts of its territory. Active year-round; hunts and travels in rodent tunnels under snow in North. Mates in summer but embryonic development is delayed for about 9 months. Litters of 4–9 young are born the following

ERMINE
Mustela erminea

spring. Young are naked and tiny at birth, their eyes and ears closed. At 2–3 months of age, young leave the nest and learn hunting skills from the mother. **HABITAT:** Mainly coniferous forest or mixed conifer-hardwood forest; also brushy fields, tundra, hedgerows, and dense vegetation around swamps and marshes. **RANGE:** Alaska and Canada; w. U.S. to Calif. and N.M.; Northeast and n. Midwest. Circumboreal in Northern Hemisphere. Introduced to New Zealand. **STATUS:** Widespread and common. Subspecies on Queen Charlotte Is. (*M. e. haidarum*) is threatened (COSEWIC).

LONG-TAILED WEASEL *Mustela frenata* **Pl. 54, Skull Pl. 8**
Head and body: males 9–11½ in. (23–29 cm), females 7–9 in. (18–23 cm); tail: males 4½–6⅝ in. (11–17 cm), females 3–5¼ in. (7–13 cm); wt.: males 4⅝–10 oz. (132–284 g), females 3–4 oz. (85–115 g). *Largest weasel; tail more than half head and body length* (including black fur at tip). Coloration highly variable, generally *brown above, white or orange below* in summer, white or yellowish in winter in North. In South remains brown year-round. Eyeshine greenish. **GEOGRAPHIC VARIATION:** Summer coats. East: dark to medium brown above, throat white, belly whitish or creamy yellow; feet usually all-brown or tipped white. W. Canada and nw. U.S.: upperparts reddish brown to orange-brown, throat white or cream, belly yellow to orange; tops of feet usually same color as belly, sometimes brown. S. California: back pale orange-brown; throat white, belly bright orange, toes whitish or orange; head marked with a pale orange triangle between eyes and pale orange vertical band between eye and ear. Southwest (N.M., Tex.): "bridled" form — back rich orange-brown, throat white, belly and feet bright orange; head blackish with white markings between and behind eyes. Intermediate forms also occur. **SIMILAR SPECIES:** See Ermine. Mink is larger with a dark belly. **SOUNDS:** Usually silent, but may trill

Long-tailed Weasel in partial molt. Its pure white winter coat changes to mostly brown in spring. The extremities (legs, tail, and top of the head) are the last parts of the body to change color.

LONG-TAILED WEASEL
Mustela frenata

when hunting; also screeches or squeals when disturbed. **HABITS:** Active day or night. Gallops with back arched and tail held up. Hunts for prey on the ground, in trees, and in underground burrows. Swims well. Feeds on small and medium-sized mammals such as mice, voles, pocket gophers, Sewellel, muskrats, young rabbits, and hares. Also eats birds and birds' eggs, snakes, insects, and carrion. Nests in a burrow or in rock piles or brush piles. As in Ermine, breeding takes place in summer but young are not born until the following spring. Litter size is 4–9. **HABITAT:** Forests, meadows, and fields; favors open areas with dense vegetation near water. **RANGE:** S. Canada and U.S. through Mexico and Central America to Venezuela and Bolivia. **STATUS:** Widespread but generally uncommon or rare.

AMERICAN MINK   *Mustela vison*   Pl. 55, Skull Pl. 8
Head and body 12–16 in. (30–42 cm); tail 5¾–8 in. (14–20 cm); wt. 1–2¼ lb. (0.4–1 kg). Male is larger than female. Medium sized; long low body. Back and belly dark chocolate brown; small white patches on chin and sometimes on throat and chest. Tail well furred, dark brown at base, blackish at tip. Eyeshine yellow-green. **SIMILAR SPECIES:** Weasels are smaller with white or orange bellies. American Marten has a pale throat and a long bushy tail. **SOUNDS:** Hisses, snarls, or screams if alarmed; purrs when content; chuckles during breeding season. **HABITS:** Mainly nocturnal or crepuscu-

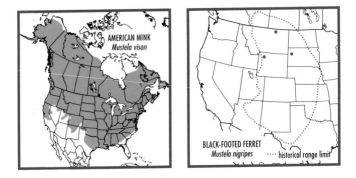

AMERICAN MINK
Mustela vison

BLACK-FOOTED FERRET
Mustela nigripes   ····· historical range limit

lar, but can be seen by day. An excellent swimmer; pursues mainly
aquatic prey in summer, hunts on land in winter. Feeds on small to
medium-sized mammals, crayfish, frogs, snakes, and birds. Dens
near water among tree roots, in muskrat houses, or in burrows on
banks; may use several different dens. Males occupy a larger range
than females (up to 1,900 acres or 760 ha). Breeds early in the year;
litters of 1–10, normally 4, are born April–May. Young hunt with
the mother at about 2 months, and they remain together until fall.
Lifespan is usually less than 3 years. **HABITAT:** Along streams, lakes,
swamps, and marshes, usually in wooded areas. **RANGE:** Throughout Canada and U.S. except Canadian Arctic and southwestern
deserts. **STATUS:** Widespread, common in suitable habitat.

BLACK-FOOTED FERRET   *Mustela nigripes*   **Pl. 54**
Head and body 14–18 in. (36–46 cm); tail 4⅜–5½ in. (11–14 cm);
wt. 1½–2½ lb. (0.6–1.1 kg). Male is larger than female. *Weasel-like
body,* about size of Mink. Mostly *yellowish brown,* with contrasting *black mask, feet, and tip of tail.* **SIMILAR SPECIES:** Desert foxes
have longer legs and bushier tails. Long-tailed Weasel smaller and
darker, without contrasting black feet. **SOUNDS:** Mother calls young
with a low plaintive cry. May chatter or hiss in alarm. **HABITS:** Mainly
nocturnal and crepuscular, occasionally abroad during the day.
Eats prairie dogs and other animals that live in prairie dog towns.
Catches prey at burrow entrance or inside burrow. Takes over burrows of prairie dogs and enlarges entrance and interior. Makes
characteristic diggings when excavating prey (especially in winter
when prey is hibernating), throwing out large mounds of dirt.
These mounds are not tamped down like those made by prairie
dogs and often have a trough down the middle. Breeds in early
spring; litters of 1–5 are born in May. Young are weaned in July, but
the mother continues to bring food for them until Sept. Young

The Black-footed Ferret is our most endangered mammal. A concerted captive breeding program in the U.S. and Canada may bring it back from the brink of extinction.

reach breeding age at 1 year. **HABITAT:** Arid prairies, associated with prairie dog towns. **RANGE:** Formerly throughout Great Plains. Reintroduced to ne. Mont., w. S.D., and se. Wyo. **STATUS:** Endangered (USFWS). Extirpated in Canada (COSEWIC). Thought to have become extinct in the wild by 1987; maintained by captive breeding programs and reintroduced into wild. Suffered mainly from eradication of prairie dog towns by ranchers. Small remnant populations are susceptible to canine distemper and problems resulting from inbreeding.

WOLVERINE *Gulo gulo*   Pl. 56, Skull Pl. 8
Glutton, Skunk Bear

Head and body 2–3 ft. (60–85 cm); tail 8–10 in. (21–26 cm); wt. 18–44 lb. (8–20 kg). *Powerful,* somewhat bearlike. Short dark limbs and very large feet; short bushy tail. Body *dark brown with broad yellowish band on side from shoulder to base of tail.* Muzzle blackish, forehead and ears yellowish. **SIMILAR SPECIES:** Fisher is smaller

Wolverine. This powerful carnivore eats all kinds of animal prey, including carrion, and may even drive a Cougar or bear from its kill. It is a denizen of the northern wilderness.

and lacks pale band on side. **HABITS:** Active night or day, traveling long distances at a loping gallop. Swims and climbs well. Diet includes all kinds of meat, especially carrion; also eggs, roots, and berries. Reputed to rob traplines and raid trappers' food caches; may drive other predators off their kills. Male occupies an area of more than 770 sq. mi. (2,000 km²) in a year (Idaho); 2–3 females occupy smaller ranges within this area. Mates April–Aug.; female digs den in snow or under rocks where 1–5 young are born Feb.–April. Average life expectancy is 4–6 years; captives have survived 17 years. **HABITAT:** Tundra, taiga, and montane regions. **RANGE:** Alaska and n. Canada; parts of n. Rocky Mts.; Scandinavia through Siberia and Asia. **STATUS:** Endangered in e. Canada (COSEWIC). Vulnerable (IUCN). Never common; found only in large tracts of undisturbed wilderness. Most populations in U.S. and s. Canada have been reduced or extirpated.

···· historical range

WOLVERINE
Gulo gulo

AMERICAN BADGER *Taxidea taxus*   **Pl. 52, Skull Pl. 8**

Head and body 20–26 in. (50–66 cm); tail 4–6 in. (10–14 cm); wt. 11–26 lb. (5–12 kg). Stocky and *very short-legged.* Very long, powerful front claws. Back grizzled yellow-gray; belly yellowish buff. *White stripe on top of head* (sometimes extending down back), white cheeks and ears. *Sides of muzzle and spot in front of ears black.* No other mammal has the same broad low shape and patterned head. **SOUNDS:** Usually quiet. Snarls, hisses, and squeals in aggression. **HABITS:** Mainly nocturnal, but sometimes seen early or late in the day. Proficient digger, constructs and uses burrows for resting, rearing young, and food storage. Burrow entrances are low broad ellipses, 8–12 in. (20–30 cm) wide, with a large mound of dirt in front. Digs up and feeds mainly on rodents; also takes invertebrates, birds, snakes, and carrion. In bad weather may stay in burrow and become torpid for brief periods but does not hibernate. Solitary except when breeding; males hold large territories

American Badger emerging from its den. Each den has several low, broad burrow entrances that are marked with a large mound of dirt.

and may mate with more than one female. Mates in summer or fall; implantation is delayed and young are born March–April. Litter size is 2–5. **HABITAT:** Plains, prairies, deserts, open valleys, woodland edge, and alpine meadows. **RANGE:** Sw. Canada, w. and cen. U.S., to s. Mexico. **STATUS:** Locally common to rare. Endangered in British Columbia and Ontario (COSEWIC). Protected in Illinois, Wisconsin, and Michigan.

AMERICAN BADGER
Taxidea taxus

NORTHERN RIVER OTTER

Pl. 56, Skull Pl. 8

Lontra canadensis

Head and body 26–31 in. (66–79 cm); tail 12–20 in. (30–51 cm); wt. 10–24 lb. (4.5–11 kg). Large, sleek, and short-legged; *semiaquatic.* Tail very thick at base, tapering at tip. Feet broad and *webbed.* Upperparts rich brown, belly silvery. Eyeshine bright; pale orange in color. **SIMILAR SPECIES:** Beaver has a flat scaled tail. Muskrat is smaller with a thin naked tail. Mink is much smaller. See Sea Otter. **SOUNDS:** High-pitched chirps, barks, and low growls. **HABITS:** Mainly crepuscular, but also active by night or day. Strong swimmer; moves with head exposed, body underwater. May travel long distances on land when dispersing or in search of open water in winter. Moves over hard snow or ice by alternately galloping and sliding. Makes slides on muddy banks or on steep icy slopes. Eats mainly fish, frogs, crayfish, and shellfish. Leaves piles of shells, crayfish claws, and fish scales on rocks in streams and in haul-out areas on banks, a clear indication of its presence in an area. Dens on banks in burrows or under roots or brush, sometimes in the lodge of a beaver or muskrat. The entrance may be above or

A Northern River Otter trots across a frozen lake, displaying its streamlined form and thickened tail. This playful mammal enjoys sliding on snow or mud slopes and bodysurfing in river currents.

NORTHERN RIVER OTTER
Lontra canadensis

historical range limit

below water level. Most groups are a female and her young; males are usually solitary but may form bachelor groups. Litters of 1–6, usually 2–4, are born in early spring. Mating takes place soon after young are born; implantation of the embryo is delayed 8–9 months. **HABITAT:** Lakes, streams, rivers, swamps, and coastal areas. **RANGE:** Alaska, much of Canada, Northwest, Rocky Mts., and parts of East. **STATUS:** Extirpated from much of former range due to overhunting. Now protected and reintroduced successfully in 7 states and in Alberta. Suffers from water pollution and habitat loss (CITES Appendix II).

SEA OTTER *Enhydra lutris*   Pl. 56

Head and body 29–44 in. (70–110 cm); tail 10–14 in. (26–36 cm); wt. 35–100 lb. (16–45 kg). Male is larger than female. *Aquatic, floats on back. Head pale yellow or grayish,* contrasting with *dark brown body.* Feet completely webbed to toes. Tail rather short and thick, flattened from above. **SIMILAR SPECIES:** Seals and sea lions have very short tails. Northern River Otter has a dark head and a longer tail. **SOUNDS:** Pup cries like a gull; adult coos and grunts in satisfaction, screams or growls in alarm. **HABITS:** Usually seen near shore, floating on back in water. Hauls out onto land only in bad storms. When undisturbed, swims slowly on back, propelled by hind flippers. If pursued, swims "right side up" underwater, moving lower body, tail, and hind legs up and down. Sleeps at night on back in kelp beds. Feeds mainly on clams, sea urchins, abalone, and crabs. Takes prey from the sea floor to the surface and uses chest as table; may collect a rock to break open hard-shelled animals. Fairly social, rests in sexually segregated groups; usually disperses to feed. Does not migrate, but subadult males may wander widely. Female gives birth to 1 young each year, in winter or spring in California, in early summer in Alaska. Young stays with the mother for a year or more. **HABITAT:** Coastal waters with kelp beds and rocky bottoms. **RANGE:** Coast of Calif. to s. Alaska. **STATUS:** Southern Sea Otter (*E. l. nereis*) is threatened (USFWS). Heavily hunted for fur and driven close to extinction in early 1900s. Some populations have recovered, but where common it is resented by abalone fishermen. Plays a key role in controlling herbivores (especially sea urchins) in kelp beds. Without Sea Otters, kelp becomes overgrazed and an entire ecosystem is affected.

SEA OTTER
Enhydra lutris

WALRUS: Odobenidae

The Walrus is the only species in this family. Hind flippers can be turned forward and used when walking on land. Both sexes have a pair of long tusks.

WALRUS *Odobenus rosmarus*   **Pl. 59, Skull Pl. 14**
Length: male 9–12 ft. (2.7–3.6 m), female 7–10 ft. (2–3 m); wt.: male 1,640–3,400 lb. (795–1,560 kg), female 1,250–2,300 lb. (565–1,040 kg). *A huge seal with long white tusks* (longer and stouter in male) and short whiskers on broad snout. Skin wrinkled and folded, usually *warm pinkish brown;* becomes paler when in water. Familiar and unmistakable. **SOUNDS:** Male produces bell-like sounds and clicks underwater and sharp clucks and whistles above water during the breeding season. Groups bellow and grunt. **HABITS:** Moves slowly on land using front and back flippers. On ice uses foreflippers only. Dives to feed on sea floor, rooting with the

The Atlantic Walrus, shown, is smaller and has shorter tusks than the Pacific Walrus. The tusks are used for defense against predators and male-male disputes, for hauling out on ice, and for searching for bottom-dwelling prey.

snout for mollusks and other invertebrates. Shelled prey are sucked out of the shell before they are swallowed. Highly gregarious; groups of up to several thousand haul out together and stay in close contact. Most populations migrate north and south, remaining close to the pack ice. Tusks are used mainly for displaying and fighting, also for hauling out, cutting through ice to make breathing holes, and as defense against predators. Breeds in winter; females congregate on ice and males display in the water in "mobile leks." Mating takes place in water. Implantation is delayed for 4 months; gestation is about 11 months, with young born in May. Females breed every 2–4 years and give birth to single young. **HABITAT:** Moving pack ice over shallow continental shelf waters. Also coastal beaches and rocky islets. **RANGE:** Arctic Ocean and islands. **STATUS:** Greatly depleted by commercial hunting in 18th and 19th centuries. Largest remaining population in the Pacific. Walrus in North America are used for subsistence hunting and face a number of other challenges, including competition with fisheries, noise pollution, and increased ecotourism.

WALRUS
Odobenus rosmarus

Fur seals and sea lions have small, triangular external ears. Eared seals have well-developed front flippers and hind flippers that can be turned forward for walking on land. They sit with head and chest raised, supported by front flippers. Males are much larger than females. There are 16 species in 7 genera worldwide, with 4 species occurring off the West Coast.

ORTHERN FUR SEAL *Callorhinus ursinus* PL. 57
Alaska Fur Seal

Length: male 6–7 ft. (1.8–2.1 m), female 3½–5 ft. (1–1.5 m); wt.: male 400–615 lb. (180–280 kg), female 95–110 lb. (43–50 kg). *Small head with short pointed snout.* Fur ends abruptly at top of front flippers. Long hind flippers. Male dark brown or blackish with a *long thick neck* and short "Roman nose"; female gray-brown, belly reddish; young pup black. **SIMILAR SPECIES:** Sea lions have longer, rounded snouts and are slightly larger. **SOUNDS:** Males roar and bark on breeding grounds. **HABITS:** Spends most of the year out to sea, sleeping on its back or side in the water during the day and hunting at night. Feeds mainly on small schooling fish, caught at depths of 160–750 ft. (50–230 m). In fall and winter it migrates up to 6,200 mi. (10,000 km) each year, returning north in May. Usually seen alone or in small groups at sea. Comes to shore only during the breeding season, May–July; huge numbers congregate on the Pribilof Is. Males defend territories but do not control specific females or form a harem. Single young, rarely twins, are born in June or July. Females mate a few days after giving birth and may breed every year. **HABITAT:** Offshore waters and rocky islets. **RANGE:** North Pacific Ocean, west to Sea of Okhotsk and Japan. **STATUS:** In 1786 the population numbered 2.5 million on the Pribilofs. By 1910 the herd was reduced through hunting to under 300,000. Regulations

Northern Fur Seals. Note the huge size difference between the two black males (left of center, back) and the numerous pale-colored females (foreground).

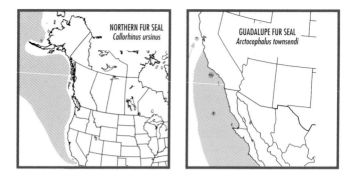

on take allowed numbers to increase to about 1.5 million by 1950. The herd declined again by about 50 percent, but in 1993 it was estimated at 1.2 million. Threats include overfishing, entanglement in plastic net scraps, and subsistence hunting.

GUADALUPE FUR SEAL   *Arctocephalus townsendi*   **Pl. 57**
Length: male 6–7½ ft. (1.8–2.2 m), female 4½–6 ft. (1.4–1.9 m); wt.: male 220–485 lb. (100–220 kg), female 110 lb. (50 kg). *Muzzle pointed and slightly upcurved.* Flippers large, fur extends onto top of foreflippers. Male has a thick neck with a *silvery mane* and blackish brown body; female dark gray-brown. **SIMILAR SPECIES:** Sea lions are larger with rounded snouts. Males of all eared seals are distinctive; females may be indistinguishable in water. **SOUNDS:** Male produces different sounds in response to different situations. Calls include whimpers, barks, puffs, and growls. Female bawls and calf whines. **HABITS:** Can be found on shore year-round and remains near breeding areas. Feeds on fish and squid. Does not land on sandy beaches, but chooses rocky areas near tall cliffs. These fur seals are unusual in using caves and recesses as breeding sites. Males take up territories before the arrival of females. Young are born May–July and may remain with the mother on the breeding territory for a year. **HABITAT:** Warm water and rocky coastal islands. **RANGE:** Cen. Calif. to Cedros I. off Baja Calif. Breeds on Guadalupe I. and Islas San Benito. Also seen hauled out on San Miguel, San Nicolas, and San Clemente Is. **STATUS:** Threatened (USFWS). Overexploited for fur and thought extinct in 1928. Population now numbers about 7,000 and is thought to be increasing.

STELLER'S SEA LION   *Eumetopias jubatus*   **Pl. 57**
Northern Sea Lion
Length: male 9–10½ ft. (2.7–3.2 m), female 7–9½ ft. (2.2–2.9 m); wt.: male 1,200–2,400 lb. (540–1,100 kg), female 600–770 lb. (270–

summer only
above dash line

STELLER'S SEA LION
Eumetopias jubatus

historical range limit

350 kg). Broad rounded muzzle. Male huge with relatively flat forehead and *massive neck. Pale orange-brown,* darker on flippers and belly. Appears blond when wet. **SIMILAR SPECIES:** Male California Sea Lion is blackish with a high forehead and narrower muzzle. Females are easily confused — California appears blackish in water and has a narrower muzzle. **SOUNDS:** Male gives deep bellows, female barks, and young bleats. Outside the breeding season usually quiet. **HABITS:** Spends much time hauled out on isolated rocky shores and islands. Avoids people and may enter water if approached by boats. Feeds on fish, squid, octopi, clams, and crabs in coastal water, and sometimes enters rivers to hunt. Breeds on rocky islets in summer; males establish and defend territories against other males. Females mate 1–2 weeks after giving birth. Single young suckle for about a year. **HABITAT:** Coastal waters and rocky shores. **RANGE:** Pacific Ocean, west to Japan. **STATUS:** Endangered in Alaska and Russia (west of 144° longitude), threatened elsewhere (USFWS). Population in Alaska declined about 90 percent in last 20 years, for unknown reasons.

ALIFORNIA SEA LION
lophus californianus

Pl. 57, Skull Pl. 14

Length: male 6½–8 ft. (2–2.5 m), female 5–6 ft. (1.5–1.8 m); wt.: male 440–900 lb. (200–400 kg), female 110–260 lb. (50–120 kg). Male much larger than female. Long, *relatively narrow, rounded muzzle.* Male *blackish with pale domed crown;* female yellow-brown. Both appear *blackish when wet.* This is the familiar "seal" of live animal acts. **SIMILAR SPECIES:** Steller's Sea Lion is larger and paler, male has a broad muzzle and flatter forehead. Guadalupe Fur Seal is smaller with a pointed snout, male has a silvery neck. **SOUNDS:** Honking barks given by bulls on breeding grounds. Wails and bleats given by females and young. Generally noisy. **HABITS:** Gallops on land, using front and back flippers. Fast and acrobatic in water, can dive to 450 ft. (135 m) and stay underwater for 20 minutes. Usually feeds in shallower water, taking mainly schooling fish and squid. Males migrate north as far as Vancouver I. in autumn and winter. Females and young remain in breeding areas year-round. Breeds on remote islands off California. In early summer males set up and defend a territory for 1 to 1½ months. They do not feed during this time but patrol and bark constantly. Mating takes place in shallow water. A single pup is born about 11 months later. **HABITAT:** Coastal waters and small protected islands. **RANGE:** South to Gulf of Calif. and Nayarit, Mexico; Galápagos Is. **STATUS:** Fairly common. Previously killed for meat and oil, now protected. Suffers from entanglement in gill nets and plastic materials.

CALIFORNIA SEA LION
Zalophus californianus

HAIR SEALS: Phocidae

These seals do not have external ears. The hind flippers always face back and the front flippers are small. On land hair seals move like large caterpillars. They are usually seen lying down with the head slightly raised. Males and females are usually similar in size; in some species the males are larger than females. There are 19 species in 10 to 13 genera worldwide, with 9 species occurring in North American waters.

HARBOR SEAL   *Phoca vitulina*   Pl. 58, Skull Pl. 14
Common Seal (Europe)
Length 4–6 ft. (1.2–1.9 m); wt. 100–370 lb. (45–170 kg). Male is larger than female. *Short muzzle,* nostrils close together forming a "V." Color highly variable: whitish or yellowish with *dark spots,* sometimes dark with pale rings. Belly spotted. *Young usually dark gray and spotted at birth;* a few are born white. **SIMILAR SPECIES:** Gray

HARBOR SEAL
Phoca vitulina

extralimital

Seal has longer "Roman nose" with parallel nostrils. Largha Seal is very similar but it is usually darker on the back and head (Harbor Seal can be dark also); it is found near pack ice and young are always white at birth. See Harp Seal. **SOUNDS:** Generally quiet. May grunt in alarm before entering water if disturbed. **HABITS:** Usually seen basking on rocks in small groups. Remains alert and will enter water if approached. Dives to depths of 660 ft. (200 m) and can remain underwater for 30 minutes. Feeds on a variety of fish and invertebrates. Stays in the same area year-round and routinely uses the same haul-out areas. Large groups breed on rocky shores or beaches. Female gives birth to a single young each year, in summer in northern populations, in early spring in the South. Most young molt the white lanugo (coat of downy hairs) before birth; in a few it is shed soon after birth. **HABITAT:** Rocky shores and coastal waters, also rivers, estuaries, and some northern freshwater lakes. **RANGE:** Widely distributed in North Pacific and North Atlantic Oceans. **STATUS:** Common. Some populations much decreased through hunting, pollution, or disturbance.

Harbor Seal. This rather common seal often holds up its rear flippers and adopts a banana-shaped pose on land.

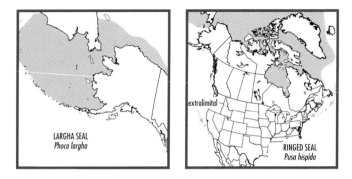

LARGHA SEAL *Phoca largha* Pl. 58
Spotted Seal

Length 4½–5½ ft. (1.4–1.7 m); wt. 140–265 lb. (65–120 kg). Very similar to Harbor Seal. Color variable: *always spotted, back and top of head dark, usually whitish below. Young is white for 2 to 3 weeks after birth.* **HABITS:** Usually found close to pack ice except in summer, when it moves closer to the coast. In fall, migrates offshore to the edge of the pack ice and hauls out on ice floes. Unlike most seals, this species appears to be serially monogamous. Pairs space themselves about 660 ft. (200 m) from other pairs on ice and give birth to single, white-coated young in April or May. Young do not enter the water until they are weaned at about 1 month. **HABITAT:** Polar pack ice in winter and spring, coastal waters in summer. **RANGE:** North Pacific Ocean, west to Siberia and Japan. **STATUS:** Fairly common.

RINGED SEAL *Pusa hispida* Pl. 58
Jar, Silver Jar

Length 3½–5¼ ft. (1.1–1.6 m); wt. 65–300 lb. (30–140 kg). Size varies geographically. Male is slightly larger than female. *Small and stocky.* Short muzzle. Back *dark gray with pale rings; belly silvery white.* Young white for about 3 weeks after birth, then silvery gray without rings. **SIMILAR SPECIES:** Harbor and Largha Seals are larger, usually with dark spots on sides and belly and spots (not rings) on back. **SOUNDS:** Gives a variety of calls underwater and may call year-round. **HABITS:** Stays mainly in water under thick ice from late summer to early spring. Follows the permanent ice pack and may wander long distances. Feeds on fish and crustaceans. Finds a breathing hole or keeps a hole open with its front claws. In early spring, forms a lair in the snow above the breathing hole. Females, adult males, and some nonreproductive animals make lairs. Young are born March–April and remain in the birth lair until weaning,

1–2 months later. **HABITAT:** Stable landfast ice near shore in spring, open water or shifting polar ice in summer. Rarely hauls out on land. **RANGE:** Arctic waters, including fresh water (Nettiling Lake). **STATUS:** Most common Arctic seal. Some populations considered vulnerable or endangered (IUCN). **NOTE:** Sometimes placed in the genus *Phoca*.

ARP SEAL *Pagophilus groenlandicus* PL. 58
Saddleback Seal, Greenland Seal, Ragged Jacket, Bedlamer, Beater

Length 5–6½ ft. (1.5–2.0 m); wt. 240–310 lb. (110–140 kg). Short muzzle. Color variable: adult male *silver with a black face and black harp- or horseshoe-shaped patch on back.* Adult female similar to male but dark markings are paler and *often broken up into spots.* Subadult and juvenile dark gray above, paler below, with indistinct dark spots on back and belly. *Young is white* for 2–4 weeks after birth. **SIMILAR SPECIES:** Adult is distinctively marked. Harbor Seal is more heavily spotted than subadult Harp Seal. Ringed Seal has pale rings on back. **SOUNDS:** Makes a variety of underwater calls. On land adults grunt *uurh,* and pups wail and cry. **HABITS:** Travels in lively herds of a few to several hundred, porpoising and churning the water surface. Groups may use communal breathing holes in the ice. Feeds on schooling fish and invertebrates and can dive to depths of 900 ft. (275 m). Makes extensive migrations, traveling up to 6,000 mi. (9,600 km) each year, following an established route. In Feb. large numbers haul out onto pack ice near the Magdalen Is. and off the coast of Newfoundland and Labrador to breed. Single young are born and nurse for 2–3 weeks. After weaning, the young remain on land until they have molted their white coat. **HABITAT:** Shifting pack ice, open sea in summer. **RANGE:** North Atlantic Ocean. **STATUS:** Population stable at present. Young are the famous "whitecoat" seals that aroused public outcry against the annual hunt for fur. This industry has been in operation for 200 years and formerly killed up to 687,000 seals per year (maximum take in

A subadult Harp Seal. This pelage stage, known as a Beater or Bedlamer, usually exhibits fewer, larger spots than that of a Harbor Seal, but the two species can be confused.

1831). Presently the annual take is controlled. In some areas, ecotourism has taken the place of hunting. **NOTE:** Sometimes placed in the genus *Phoca.*

HARP SEAL
Pagophilus groenlandicus

RIBBON SEAL
Histriophoca fasciata

RIBBON SEAL   *Histriophoca fasciata*   PL. 58
Banded Seal

Length 4½–6 ft. (1.4–1.8 m); wt. 150–220 lb. (70–100 kg). Relatively slim-bodied. Short muzzle. Adult male *distinctively marked, dark brown with pale bands* around head, front flippers, and lower body. Female has similar markings but background color is pale brown and bands are much less distinct. Young white at birth for 4–5 weeks, then gray above, whitish below (unspotted) for 1 year. Bands develop after molt at age 1. **SIMILAR SPECIES:** Adult distinctive; immature Largha Seal is spotted. **HABITS:** Thought to spend part of the year entirely at sea. In spring, hauls out onto offshore ice to breed and molt. More easily approached than other seals when resting. Often lies for long periods with head down, but can move very rapidly over ice. Generally solitary; individuals remain well spaced on ice floes. Young are born April–May and nurse for 3–4 weeks. **HABITAT:** Sea ice and offshore water. Seldom hauls out on shorefast ice. **RANGE:** North Pacific Ocean, west to Sea of Japan. **STATUS:** Appears to be uncommon, difficult to survey. **NOTE:** Sometimes placed in the genus *Phoca.*

GRAY SEAL   *Halichoerus grypus*   PL. 58

Length 6½–8 ft. (2–2.4 m); wt. 330–770 lb. (150–350 kg). Male is larger than female. *Long muzzle, especially pronounced in male,* which appears "Roman-nosed." *Nostrils widely spaced, almost parallel.* Color variable: usually *gray with brown mottling;* male darker, can be solid black. Young whitish for about 3 weeks after birth. **SIMILAR SPECIES:** Harbor Seal has a short muzzle with nostrils almost touching at base to form a "V." Hooded Seal is usually more boldly spotted and looks bluish, not gray-brown. **SOUNDS:** Male gives long calls and hoots, female barks and hisses, young whine and yap. **HABITS:** Lone animals or small groups may be seen bobbing in the water with head up. Feeds mainly on bottom-dwelling fish, also takes salmon in some areas. May spend some time ashore in summer when molting. Some subadults wander widely, and some populations may migrate from Sable I. to Gulf of St. Lawrence. Breeds in isolated coves, sandy beaches, and on ice floes. Moves well on land and may travel some distance from shore to give birth. Young are born Jan.–March. Females usually stay on land while nursing and are aggressive if threatened. Young are weaned after about 2½ weeks; females then come into heat and males compete for mating. **HABITAT:** Rocky or sandy shores and around islands, sometimes in estuaries. Seldom far from land. **RANGE:** North Atlantic Ocean and Baltic Sea. **STATUS:** Fairly common, population increasing. Unpopular with fisherman since it eats game fish and damages nets; also acts as a host for codworm, a fish parasite. Protected in the U.S., hunted in Canada.

GRAY SEAL
Halichoerus grypus

HOODED SEAL   *Cystophora cristata*   **Pl. 58**
Bladdernose Seal, Crested Seal

Length 6½–9½ ft. (2.0–2.8 m); wt. 320–960 lb. (145–435 kg). Male is larger than female. Rather long muzzle. Male has an *inflatable sac on the top of the snout* that forms a 2-lobed dark "hood." Male can also inflate the lining of one nostril and extrude a *red balloon-like structure.* Both sexes *blackish on face* and flippers, *silvery with blackish splotches on body.* At birth, young is *dark blue-gray above, whitish below,* with a black face. Spots appear at 1 year of age. **SIMILAR SPECIES:** Gray Seal is browner in color and male lacks inflatable structures on head. Harbor Seal is smaller and has a

Hooded Seal male, its hood fully extended. The male can also eject and inflate its nostrils into a large red "bladder."

shorter muzzle. **HABITS:** The hood and balloon of the male are probably used during breeding, but it is not clear if they function mainly to attract females or in male-male competition. Feeds on fish in deep offshore waters. Migrates to Denmark Strait and e. Greenland to molt in summer, hauling out on pack ice. The entire population is thought to use these two areas and may stay for 1–2 months without eating. After the molt, disperses widely to feed, congregating again in Feb. or March to breed. Breeding grounds are off Labrador, in the Gulf of St. Lawrence, and in the Davis Strait, on thick sea ice. Female gives birth to a single young, which feeds on very rich milk for only 4 days, during which time it gains about 65 lb. (30 kg). Male stays with one female and her calf until weaning; mating subsequently takes place in water and female leaves. The male may then find another mate. **HABITAT:** Thick offshore ice and deep waters. **RANGE:** North Atlantic Ocean, east to Spitsbergen, Norway. Occasionally strays south to Fla. **STATUS:** Generally uncommon; w. Atlantic population numbers about 300,000. Hunted in Canadian waters.

HOODED SEAL
Cystophora cristata

BEARDED SEAL
Erignathus barbatus

Length 6½–8 ft. (2.0–2.5 m); wt. 450–800 lb. (200–360 kg). Female is slightly larger than male. *Small head;* thick *stiff whiskers* (beard) on broad muzzle. Front flippers squared off. *Uniformly brown to silver-gray.* At birth, young is dark brown with a pale mask and pale bands on back; molts to adult color after weaning. **SIMILAR SPECIES:** Other seals are spotted or patterned. **SOUNDS:** Produces a long warbling song underwater followed by a short moan. These songs may be heard over long distances underwater and are given most often during the breeding season. **HABITS:** Swims with head and back exposed and may sleep hanging vertically in the water. Rolls as it dives. Hauls out on ice year-round, resting with head very close to an escape hole. Feeds mainly on benthic crustaceans and mollusks and may dive to depths of 660 ft. (200 m). Generally solitary except when breeding. Single young are born on ice March–May. Young are nursed for 2–3 weeks and learn to swim and hunt during this period. **HABITAT:** Sea ice and relatively shallow water. **RANGE:** Circumpolar in Arctic waters. **STATUS:** Uncommon but widespread.

ORTHERN ELEPHANT SEAL Pl. 59
irounga angustirostris

Length: male 13–16 ft. (4–5 m), female 6½–10 ft. (2–3 m); wt.: male 4,000–5,950 lb. (1,800–2,700 kg), female 770–2,000 lb. (350–900 kg). *Male huge;* long, *massive, wrinkled neck;* inflatable, *pendulous proboscis.* Female large, *relatively long snout; uniformly blond* or buff. Young blackish at birth. Unlikely to be confused with other species in its range. **SOUNDS:** Male snorts and gives a series of guttural pulses in threat. Female gives a loud low bark in threat. Pup makes shrill squeals if separated from mother. **HABITS:**

Two male Northern Elephant Seals in an aggressive display. The smaller females are visible in the background.

Spends 9–10 months of the year at sea. Feeds on deep-water squid and fish and can dive to depths of 5,000 ft. (1,500 m). Hauls out on sandy beaches in Dec. to breed. Males fight to establish dominance by rearing and threatening, and sometimes lunge at each other. A dominant male may control a group of 25–50 females. Females give birth to single pups that are nursed for about a month. Females mate with the dominant male after weaning their young, then return to sea. Pups stay on the beach for another month without feeding. **HABITAT:** Warm sandy beaches and temperate waters. **RANGE:** Pacific Ocean, west to Japan and Hawaii. Males range north to Gulf of Alaska and Aleutians. **STATUS:** Stable. Population is increasing and presently numbers about 125,000. Driven almost to extinction in late 1800s. A tiny remnant population on Guadalupe I. was protected and increased to recolonize former breeding areas.

NORTHERN ELEPHANT SEAL
Mirounga angustirostris

breeding range

Even-toed Ungulates:
Artiodactyla

This order of mammals includes deer, goats, sheep, antelopes, pigs, and relatives. These hoofed mammals have 2 functional toes. The bones of the hands and feet have been elongated and raised, so these mammals walk on "tiptoes." Artiodactyls are large, fast-moving herbivores that occur almost worldwide.

LD WORLD SWINE: Suidae

Native to Africa and Eurasia, Old World swine comprise 8 species. One of these, the domestic pig, has been introduced worldwide. Domestic pigs that escape and form wild breeding populations are known as Feral Hogs. Domestic pigs were derived from and are the same species as the European Wild Boar. Wild Boars were introduced as game animals in several states and subsequently established breeding populations. Feral Hogs are also established breeders in many areas.

ILD BOAR *Sus scrofa* (introduced) **Pl. 44, Skull Pl. 12**
Feral Hog, Feral Pig

Shoulder ht. 2–3½ ft. (0.6–1.1 m); wt. 100–350 lb. (50–150 kg). Large head with *upward-curving tusks*; stocky body. Fur coarse, variable in color: commonly blackish or gray-brown, can be black and white. *Medium-sized tail.* Four toes on each foot. Young striped and spotted. **SIMILAR SPECIES:** Collared Peccary is much smaller and has a collar and almost no tail. It has 3 toes on the hind foot. Domestic pig is stockier and usually almost naked. **SOUNDS:** Loud snuffles when rooting through soil; snorts when disturbed. **HABITS:** Mainly active by day in winter; nocturnal or crepuscular in summer. Males are usually solitary, females and young travel in small groups. Omnivorous; eats acorns, roots, fruit, small vertebrates, and birds' eggs. Shelters in thickets or makes a bed of vegetation and crawls under it. Females have litters of 3–12 young and may breed twice a year. **HABITAT:** Forested slopes and low-lying areas, also dry brush. **RANGE:** Wild Boar introduced to N.H., N.C., Tenn., Calif., and Hawaiian Is.; Feral Hogs found in much of Southeast from Va. to Fla. and west to Tex.; also scattered populations (mostly Feral Hogs) in N.M., Ariz., and possibly sw. Ore. **STATUS:** Fairly common. Causes considerable environmental damage (destroys native plants, eats amphibians and eggs of ground-nesting birds) in some areas such as Great Smoky Mts. Natl. Park, Tennesee, and in the Hawaiian Is.

WILD BOAR
Sus scrofa

PECCARIES: Tayassuidae

Peccaries are piglike mammals, but they are not closely related to true pigs. Three species are native to the New World, with 1 ranging into the U.S.

COLLARED PECCARY *Tayassu tajacu* **Pl. 44, Skull Pl. 12**
Javelina
Shoulder ht. 15–20 in. (0.4–0.5 m); wt. 25–57 lb. (12–26 kg). Piglike, with a *large triangular head*, stocky body, and slim legs. Small tusks point downward. Fur coarse and grizzled with a *pale yellow collar from shoulder to chest. Tiny tail is concealed in fur.* Four toes on forelegs, 3 toes on hind legs. Young reddish or pinkish, paler than adult, with a faint collar. **SIMILAR SPECIES:** Wild Boar is larger, lacks a collar, and has a conspicuous tail. **SOUNDS:** Sharp barks given in alarm; grunts and purrs used to maintain group contact. **HABITS:** Active night or day, but usually inactive in hot weather. Social; travels in herds of up to 50, although smaller feeding groups of 2–5 are most often encountered. Frequents dust baths and mud wallows, permeating these areas with a characteristic and obvious "old cheese" odor produced from a musk gland

Collared Peccary and young differ in color but both exhibit the characteristic pale collar. Young stand behind, not alongside, the mother when nursing.

on its back. Eats cacti, mesquite beans, fruit, and nuts. Shelters in caves, abandoned burrows, or under logs. Breeding can take place year-round, although most births are in summer. The dominant male of the group fathers most of the young. After a 4-month gestation, 2–6 young, usually twins, are born. **HABITAT:** Desert scrub, canyons, and oak-pine forest. **RANGE:** Sw. U.S., e. and w. Mexico, Central and South America south to Peru and n. Argentina. **STATUS:** Widespread and generally common. **NOTE:** Sometimes placed in the genus *Pecari* or *Dicotyles*.

COLLARED PECCARY
Tayassu tajacu

￼EER: Cervidae

Cervids, as deer and their kin are called, have antlers, not horns. Antlers are bony outgrowths of the skull that grow and are shed each year. Antlers grow only on the male or buck in most deer; Caribou are unusual in that both sexes possess antlers. Occasionally females of other species such as White-tailed Deer may sport antlers. Antlers start to grow in spring, covered in skin and fine hair or velvet. In fall the velvet is shed and rubbed off, and the antlers cease to grow. After the mating season or rut, males shed their antlers. Young males have antlers with a single point or tine, but with age they develop branching antlers with multiple tines.

Most young deer are spotted. Deer are ruminants with a multi-chambered stomach that harbors bacteria to aid in digestion of plant material. Deer lack upper incisors; the lower incisors close against a rough pad on the upper jaw. They therefore do not neatly "snip" at vegetation but often tear it: ragged and ripped plants indicate previous deer activity.

There are about 51 species of deer worldwide, 5 of which are native to the U.S. and Canada. In addition, 4 nonnative deer have established wild breeding populations in the U.S.

ELK *Cervus elaphus* Pl. 42, Skull Pls. 10, 11
Wapiti

Shoulder ht. 4–5 ft. (1.3–1.5 m); wt. 400–1,100 lb. (200–500 kg). One of our largest deer; male is larger than female. Head, neck, and legs dark brown; body paler; *rump patch and short tail pale buff.* Shaggy fur under neck in winter. Antlers of male have *one main beam* and typically 6 points. Young is spotted. **GEOGRAPHIC VARIATION:** Tule Elk (isolated populations in California) is small and pale in color. Roosevelt Elk (Pacific Northwest) is large; body color is rich orange-brown. Rocky Mountain Elk (widespread, Rockies and plains) is large with pale cream body and dark head, neck, and legs. **SIMILAR SPECIES:** Moose has palmate (flattened) antlers and lacks pale rump patch. Mule Deer is smaller and more uniformly

A majestic bull Rocky Mountain Elk throws back its head to bugle during the fall rut.

ELK
Cervus elaphus

···· historical range-

colored. Sika Deer is smaller and may be spotted. **SOUNDS:** During rutting season male gives a high whistling bugle that starts and ends with low grunts. Cow barks and calf squeals when alarmed. **HABITS:** Mainly nocturnal, but also active at dawn and dusk. Feeds on grass, herbs, and woody plants. Fires and other disturbance in forested areas create good forage for this species — it was one of the first large mammals to colonize Mt. St. Helens after the 1980 eruption. Highly social; travels in herds of 200–400 in open areas; herds are smaller in forested regions. Adult bulls join herds of females and young during the rut, in Sept. or Oct. Single young are born in June. Moves up to mountain meadows to forage in summer, migrates to wooded slopes and valleys in winter. **HABITAT:** Variable: dense woodland, young conifer stands, meadows, and plains, from hot dry lowlands to high mountains. **RANGE:** Sw. Canada and w. U.S. Small populations in Okla. and Tex. Introduced or reintroduced in many areas including n. Mich., n. Pa., and Fla. European Red Deer (a subspecies of *Cervus elaphus*) has been introduced in Ky., Tex., and Calif. **STATUS:** Suffered in 19th century from overhunting; present range is much smaller than historical range. Population now appears to be stable, primarily in mountains or protected areas.

▌KA DEER *Cervus nippon* (introduced) **Pl. 42, Skull Pls. 10, 11**
Shoulder ht. 2½–3½ ft. (0.75–1.0 m); wt. 100–240 lb. (45–110 kg). Stocky, with a *small triangular head.* Coat usually reddish brown and spotted in summer, dark brown and unspotted in winter, but can be dark brown or blackish year-round. *Midline of back black. Rump patch and tail mostly white;* white rump hairs erected in alarm; rump bordered with black. Thin black line down tail. Buck has narrow antlers with 2–5 points. Young are spotted. **SIMILAR SPECIES:** Larger and more conspicuous white patch on rump than in other spotted deer. Elk is much larger. **SOUNDS:** Whistled heehaws,

SIKA DEER
Cervus nippon

howls, and whines given by rutting bucks; shrill alarm whistles; bleats and neighs between mother and young. **HABITS:** Crepuscular or nocturnal. Eats grass and browse in summer, mainly acorns and twigs in winter. Solitary or in small herds; males fight for territory and defend a harem of females in summer. Single young are born in spring. **HABITAT:** Woodland with dense undergrowth, thickets, and swamps. **RANGE:** Introduced to Md., Kans., Okla., Wisc., and Tex. Native to Japan, Manchuria, Taiwan, Korea, and China. **STATUS:** Largest populations in Texas Hill Country and Assateague I., Maryland.

SAMBAR DEER *Cervus unicolor* (introduced)

Shoulder ht. 3¾–5 ft. (1.1–1.5 m); wt. 400–700 lb. (180–320 kg). Large. Coat mostly *warm brown*, slightly grayer in winter; paler on belly, inside legs, and on chin. *Adult and young unspotted.* Ruff of fur on neck and chest in winter. Tail long, whitish below. Buck has heavy antlers with 3 points. **SIMILAR SPECIES:** Elk has pale rump patch. White-tailed Deer is smaller (especially in Florida and Texas). Other exotic deer are smaller, and most are spotted in summer. **SOUNDS:** Metallic bellows given by rutting stags. **HABITS:** Mainly nocturnal and solitary, but sometimes forms small groups. **HABITAT:** Forested areas with dense brush and clearings. **RANGE:** Introduced to St. Vincent I., Fla., and in Tex. and cen. Calif. Native to India, Sri Lanka, Malay Pen., and East Indies. **STATUS:** Population on St. Vincent I. is 50–90; some are found in Texas and California on large ranches.

AXIS DEER *Axis axis* (introduced)   PL. 42
Chital, Spotted Deer

Shoulder ht. 2⅓–3⅓ ft. (0.7–1.0 m); wt. 100–250 lb. (45–115 kg). *Male, female, and young reddish brown with white spots; spotted year-round.* White patch on throat. Dark stripe on midline of back;

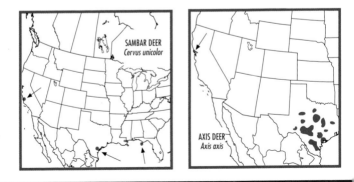

---

rump and *tail brown* thinly edged with white. Three points on each antler of buck. **SIMILAR SPECIES:** White-tailed Deer fawn lacks dark stripe on back. Fallow and Sika Deer have black tails. **SOUNDS:** Loud bellows (often in a series of 3 calls) given by rutting bucks. **HABITS:** Diurnal, but often inactive in the heat of the day. Feeds on grass and forbs, with some browse. More social than most deer, in herds of 5–50. Young males form separate herds. Single young born in spring. **HABITAT:** Open woodland. **RANGE:** Introduced in Tex. and Calif. Native to India, Nepal, Sikkim, and Sri Lanka. **STATUS:** The most abundant Texas exotic.

ALLOW DEER *Dama dama* (introduced) **Pl. 42, Skull Pl. 10**
Shoulder ht. 3–3½ ft. (0.9–1.1 m); wt. 80–225 lb. (35–100 kg). Rangy, rather long tail. *Color highly variable:* usually brown with white spots in summer; dark gray-brown, unspotted or faintly spotted in winter. May be entirely blond or whitish, reddish brown, or dark brown-black, spotted or unspotted. Spots merge on lower sides to form a white stripe. Midline of back, *tail, and edge of rump black.* Prominent larynx (Adam's apple) in both sexes. Sheath of penis has *tuft of fur at tip.* Adult male has *palmate antlers.* **SIMILAR SPECIES:** Axis and Sika Deer stockier, lack Adam's apple. Young White-tail has tail brown above, white below. **SOUNDS:** Deep bellows and belching roars given by rutting bucks; short barks in alarm; females bleat and whicker. **HABITS:** Mainly crepuscular, sometimes active by day. Eats grass and some browse. Usually in herds of 5–7 with bucks separate from does and young; may form large feeding groups. Single young or twins born in spring. **HABITAT:** Woodlands bordering open areas. **RANGE:** Introduced in Md., Ga., Ala., Ky., Neb., Tex., Calif., and B.C. Native to Europe and Asia Minor. **STATUS:** Widespread. Adapts well to a semiwild existence in parks and reserves.

FALLOW DEER
Dama dama

WHITE-TAILED DEER

Odocoileus virginianus
Key Deer

Shoulder ht. 1¾–3½ ft. (0.5–1.1 m); wt. 50–300 lb. (23–135 kg). Highly variable in size, male about 20 percent larger than female. Coat usually grayish in winter, reddish brown in summer. Belly white. Ears medium sized, about ⅓ length of head. *Tail relatively long*, edge of rump and *underside of tail white*. Metatarsal gland (on hind leg) short, less than 2 in. (3 cm) long, whitish. Antlers of male have small brow tines and *one main beam, with several vertically directed points* branching off the main beam. Fawn reddish brown with white spots. Spots fade after 3–4 months. **GEOGRAPHIC VARIATION:** Numerous subspecies occur in the U.S., the most distinctive being Key Deer, Coues's White-tail, Carmen Mountain White-tail, and Columbian White-tail. Key Deer (Florida Keys) is very small (wt. 50–77 lb., 23–35 kg), coat reddish brown to yellow-brown. (Deer in mainland Florida are slightly larger than Key Deer but much smaller than more northerly races.) Coues's White-tail (Arizona and w. New Mexico) and Carmen Mountain White-tail (Big Bend, Texas) are small with relatively long ears and grayish fur (gray-yellow in summer, slightly grayer in winter). Columbian White-tail (Pacific Northwest) is moderately small and dark with compact antlers. Largest subspecies are found in Canada and n. U.S. **SIMILAR SPECIES:** Mule Deer has longer ears and a shorter white tail tipped with black. Male Mule Deer has antlers with more than one main branch. **SOUNDS:** Sharply exhaled nasal snort in alarm, also foot-stamping. Buck may grunt when fighting. **HABITS:** Mainly nocturnal or crepuscular, but where not hunted may be seen at any time of day. Makes a bed in grass, leaves, or snow when resting. When encountered, this familiar species may snort and raise

Key Deer, adult male. This diminutive, endangered subspecies of White-tailed Deer is fully protected in the National Key Deer Refuge in Florida.

Buck and doe White-tailed Deer. Note the branching pattern of the male's antlers: single tines arise individually from the main, forward-directed beam.

WHITE-TAILED DEER
Odocoileus virginianus

its "white flag" as it bounds off, only to drop the flag when nearly out of sight. Feeds on leaves, twigs, nuts, berries, and fungi; also grazes on grass or crops such as corn and soybeans. Usually seen in small groups of females and young or in groups of bachelor males. In winter, groups may join up in "deer yards" of up to 150. In North requires conifer stands for overwintering. Groups are not territorial but maintain a fixed home range that may be long and narrow, allowing access to a variety of habitats. During the breeding season, mature buck rubs forehead and antlers on saplings and makes scrapes that are marked with urine. These areas are visited repeatedly by bucks and does. Mating takes place in fall in North, midwinter in South. Females are mature at 1 year but usually first breed at age 2. Two-year-old females usually have a single fawn, then twins each year thereafter. For the first month of life the fawn is left in a well-concealed place when the mother forages. If disturbed, fawn remains motionless, relying on its spotted coat for camouflage. As the fawn matures it travels with the mother, using speed to avoid predators. Maximum lifespan is 20 years, but commonly less than 10 years in the wild. **HABITAT:** Variable; main requirements are some woodland for cover and open areas for foraging. Most abundant in low-lying, fragmented, eastern deciduous forest and in mesquite brushland or thorn scrub. Also occurs in arid areas and montane forest, where it uses riparian corridors for water and cover. **RANGE:** S. Canada and most of U.S. south through Mexico and Central America to n. South America. **STATUS:** Key Deer (*O. v. clavium*) and Columbian White-tail (*O. v. leucurus*) are endangered (USFWS). Elsewhere generally common to abundant. This deer has benefited from human activity and is thriving in suburban and agricultural areas.

MULE DEER *Odocoileus hemionus* Pl. 41, Skull Pl. 11
Black-tailed Deer

Shoulder ht. 3–3½ ft. (0.9–1.1 m); wt. 70–330 lb. (30–150 kg). Male is 20 percent larger than female. Coat usually gray in winter, brown in summer. *Ears large*, about half length of head. Rump patch white. *Tail short, usually narrow and mainly white with a black tip.* Metatarsal gland (on hind leg) more than 2 in. (5 cm) long, brown. *Antlers of male are dichotomously branched, each branch dividing to form 2 points.* Fawn dark gray-brown with white spots and white rump patch. **GEOGRAPHIC VARIATION:** Black-tailed Deer (Pacific Northwest) is rather small with *a thicker tail that is black above, white below.* Summer coat is reddish brown and ears relatively small. Black-tailed fawn is reddish with white spots. Mule Deer of Southwest deserts is grayish in summer and winter with very large ears. **SIMILAR SPECIES:** White-tailed Deer has smaller ears and a longer, fuller tail (without a black tip) that it raises in alarm; male has antlers with a single main beam. Mule Deer is usually found in drier habitats. **SOUNDS:** Usually silent but may snort during rut; uses odor from glands on the leg to communicate alarm. **HABITS:** Mainly nocturnal or crepuscular; beds down during the heat of the day and for part of the night. When disturbed, this attractive deer springs away with all four feet leaving the ground at the same time. This bouncing gait is called "stotting" and is not seen in the White-tailed. Eats herbaceous plants, berries, acorns,

Buck Mule Deer with antlers shedding velvet. Note the complex antler branching pattern, white rump patch, and narrow white tail in this species.

and fruit in summer; buds and twigs in winter. Buck is often solitary in summer, does are usually seen with young of the year and yearlings. Mule Deer that live in mountainous regions migrate to lower elevations in winter, using an established migratory pathway. In other areas this species is nonmigratory and occupies a fixed home range of 0.8–2 sq. mi. (2–5 km²). Breeding season is Oct.–Nov. Dominant bucks mate with several does. Young doe has single offspring, older doe may have twins. **HABITAT:** Desert, brushland, forest, and mountains. In the Southwest it occupies the desert and dry highland coniferous forest, while the White-tailed occurs in the wetter canyons and oak-pine zone. **RANGE:** Sw. Canada and w. U.S. to Wisc. and w. Tex., south to Baja Calif. and n. Mexico. **STATUS:** Generally common and widespread.

MULE DEER
Odocoileus hemionus

1OOSE *Alces alces* Pl. 43, Skull Pls. 10, 11
Shoulder ht. 6½–7½ ft. (1.9–2.3 m); wt. 660–1,300 lb. (300–600 kg). Our largest deer; male is larger than female. Pronounced *"Roman nose" overhangs mouth;* long *"bell"* or *dewlap on chin.* Ears very long. Shoulder higher than rump. Head and body mainly blackish; long legs whitish. Very large, widely spread, and *palmate (flattened) antlers on male.* Young unspotted, orange-brown. **SIMILAR SPECIES:** Much taller than other deer; appears to be on stilts. Male unmistakable, female recognizable by size and long bulbous nose. **SOUNDS:** Loud bellows and barks given by rutting male; cow may moan, moo, or grunt. **HABITS:** Most active at night, but also abroad by day; often encountered in or near water. Feeds on leaves, twigs (particularly willows and aspens), and aquatic plants. Generally solitary; several may gather at good feeding areas. In fall, bulls fight for cows but do not retain a harem. Females give birth every other year to 1 or 2 young. Young stay with the mother for a year or until she gives birth again. Lifespan is up to 20 years,

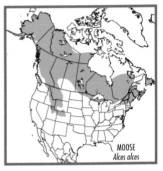

The Moose is the largest cervid in the world. The bull, shown here, has very broad, palmate antlers.

MOOSE
Alces alces

usually less for bulls. **HABITAT:** Tundra, willow thickets, swamps, and northern forests. **RANGE:** Alaska, much of Canada to n. New England and n. Rockies. Also found in Scandinavia (local name: Elk). **STATUS:** Locally common.

CARIBOU   *Rangifer tarandus*   **Pl. 43, Skull Pls. 10, 11**
Shoulder ht. 2¼–4½ ft. (0.7–1.4 m); wt. 145–660 lb. (65–300 kg). Male weighs about twice as much as female. Usually has *pale neck contrasting with darker head,* legs, and body. *Very large, curved, and much-branched antlers* with 1 or 2 flattened, *forward-projecting brow tines* on male. Unlike other deer, *female also has antlers* that are smaller and much thinner than those of male (female sheds antlers in June, male sheds in winter). Young not spotted. **GEOGRAPHIC VARIATION:** Peary Caribou (High Arctic Is.) — very small and almost white, with spindly antlers. Barren Ground Caribou (tundra of Canada and Alaska) — medium sized, with very long, gracefully curved antlers; head and legs dark brown, neck cream white, maned below; body gray-brown. Woodland Caribou (boreal forest of Canada) — largest, coloration similar to Barren Ground Caribou but antlers heavier, more compact, and flattened in cross-section. **SIMILAR SPECIES:** Moose is larger and darker, with a long pendulous nose. White-tailed Deer is more uniformly colored and has a longer tail. **SOUNDS:** Usually quiet but may snort in

Barren Ground Caribou male in early fall. Easily recognized by its contrasting white neck and mane, the bull also has a forward-facing flattened brow tine that is not found in other deer.

CARIBOU
Rangifer tarandus

alarm; rutting male gives a grunting roar. **HABITS:** Mainly diurnal; usually alert and restless all day. In summer feeds on shrubs and grass, in winter eats lichen dug out from under snow or taken from the bark of trees. Caribou are very gregarious, traveling in large herds. There are about 100 discrete herds in North America that use the same migration paths and keep to the same general range. The largest herds occur in n. Alaska and n. Canada and may number 50,000–500,000. The herd is usually broken up into groups of 10–1,000, but comes together for spring and fall migration and after calving. Barren Ground Caribou are famed for their long-distance migration; herds may travel over 600 mi. (1,000 km) from summer feeding grounds on the tundra to winter in boreal forest with extensive beds of lichen. Males compete for females in fall; some males hold harems while others attempt to mate with as many females as possible. Mating occurs in Oct. and single young are born in late May or June. Young are highly precocial and travel with the mother soon after birth. **HABITAT:** Tundra and boreal coniferous forest. **RANGE:** Alaska and much of Canada, extreme ne. Wash., and n. Idaho. Also Scandinavia and Siberia. **STATUS:** Peary Caribou (*R. t. pearyi*) is endangered (COSEWIC). Woodland Caribou is endangered in e. Canada (USFWS) and boreal and mountain populations are considered threatened (COSEWIC). Woodland Caribou numbers have declined greatly due to overhunting and habitat disturbance — the lichen on which they depend in winter will only grow on or under mature trees and is very slow to regenerate after logging. Barren Ground Caribou still exist in large numbers but are threatened by oil and gas exploration and other changes in habitat and land use. **NOTE:** Reindeer are domestic stock of this species. Wild Caribou in the Old World are also known as Reindeer.

PRONGHORNS: Antilocapridae

There is a single species in this family, which despite its scientific name (*antilo* = antelope, *capra* = goat) is neither an antelope nor a goat. The Pronghorn has horns that are branched in males (unlike the unbranched horns of sheep and goats). In antelopes, goats, and other mammals with true horns, the horns grow throughout life; the Pronghorn is unique in that the sheath of the horn is shed each year but the bony core is retained.

PRONGHORN *Antilocapra americana*   Pl. 44, Skull Pl. 13

Shoulder ht. 2½–3½ ft. (0.8–1.0 m); wt. 75–140 lb. (34–64 kg). Male is 10 percent larger than female. Both sexes mainly sandy brown to tan; *cheeks, two bands on neck, chest, belly, and lower sides white.* Prominent *white rump patch.* Male has a distinctive pattern of black and white markings on head and a black mane. *Horns black.* Horns of male are branched and curved, with one prong jutting forward and one angled back. Female has short simple horns with a single point. **SIMILAR SPECIES:** Deer lack white markings on neck and lower sides; male deer have antlers, not horns. Female Blackbuck has a pale eye-ring and no white bands on neck. **SOUNDS:** Male roars and snorts and may caw like a crow;

Pronghorn, 4 females and a male (upper left). A remnant species of an ancient lineage, it has unique pronged horns that shed their keratin sheath annually.

mothers and calves grunt and bleat. **HABITS:** Active night or day; remains alert and watchful, using great speed (up to 70 mph, 110 km/h) to avoid predators. Long white rump hairs can be fanned and flashed in warning when alarmed. Grazes on grass, forbs, and cacti in summer, browses in winter. In summer, small groups of females and young travel separately from male herds. Older males set up territories in spring and defend females in their territory. One or 2 young are born in spring or early summer. **HABITAT:** Open grassland and sagebrush deserts. **RANGE:** Sw. Canada and w. U.S. south to Baja Calif. and cen. Mexico. **STATUS:** Formerly abundant; suffered serious declines in the early 1900s. Reintroductions and herd management have resulted in increased population size and mixing of genetic stocks, although distribution is still patchy. Sonoran Pronghorn (*A. a. sonoriensis*) is endangered (USFWS).

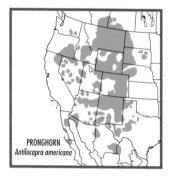

PRONGHORN
Antilocapra americana

ATTLE, ANTELOPES, SHEEP, AND GOATS:
OVIDAE

Members of the Bovidae have true horns (bony outgrowths from the skull) that are never shed and are unbranched. Horns are always present in males and usually in females. Bovids are related to antilocaprids, and some authors include them in the same family.

Included among our bovids is the Mountain Goat — not a true goat but a member of the rupicaprines, or rock-goats. Other members of this group occur in Europe and Asia Minor and include the Chamois. The Muskox, although somewhat cowlike in appearance, is not a true ox but is more closely allied with goats and sheep.

There are 5 native bovids in the U.S. and Canada as well as 4 nonnative species that are now established and breeding in the wild.

NILGAI *Boselaphus tragocamelus* (introduced)   **p. 90**
Bluebuck
Shoulder ht. 4–5 ft. (1.2–1.5 m); wt. 240–670 lb. (110–300 kg). Male
is larger than female. Cowlike, with a *small head* and *high shoulders.* Male iron gray to blackish with a tuft of hair on underside of
neck and a pair of short straight horns; female warm brown, hornless. Both sexes have a white band on cheek and patch on throat;
2 *white bands on ankles.* **SIMILAR SPECIES:** High shoulders and coloration of male is distinctive. Female could be mistaken for domestic cow, but note white patches on head, neck, and legs. **HABITS:**
Usually active by day, sometimes travels long distances at night
and does not maintain a fixed territory. Feeds on grass and also
browses on fruit or beans. Females form herds of 10–15, bachelor
males travel in smaller groups. One or 2 young are born Sept.–
Oct. in Texas. **HABITAT:** Mixed grassland-woodland in Texas. Prefers
areas with some cover. **RANGE:** Introduced in s. Tex. Native to India
and Pakistan. **STATUS:** There may be as many free-ranging animals
along the s. Gulf Coast of Texas (about 37,000) as in their native
range.

AMERICAN BISON *Bos bison*   **Pl. 45, Skull Pl. 13**
Buffalo
Shoulder ht. 5–6½ ft. (1.5–2.0 m); wt. 770–2,200 lb. (350–1,000 kg).
Male is larger than female. Very large, *cowlike,* with a *massive head
and large humped shoulders.* Adult dark brown or blackish. Woolly
fur on head and shoulders extends onto forelegs. Short curved
horns in both sexes. Young calf reddish orange, darkens after 2–3
months. **GEOGRAPHIC VARIATION:** Wood Bison (Canada) — large and
dark; horns long, extend beyond crown; thick hair on forehead extends below level of eye; front legs lack "chaps" of fur; tail long
and heavily furred. Plains Bison (w. U.S.) — smaller than Wood

American Bison formerly roamed the Plains in vast herds. Decimated by 1900, its numbers have since increased, but only a few large free-ranging populations exist.

Bison, shoulders yellow-brown; horns short, concealed in fur; thick hair on forehead only well above level of eye; thick chaps on forelegs and thick tuft of fur on penis sheath; tail short, thinly furred. **SIMILAR SPECIES:** Domestic cattle smaller, not woolly, seldom dark brown. **SOUNDS:** Deep roaring bellow and loud snorts given by rutting bull; snorts and wails between cow and calf. **HABITS:** Most active early or late in the

AMERICAN BISON
Bos bison

---- historical range

day. Feeds on grass and some browse. Makes wallows of dust or mud, rolling to relieve itches or to cover coat with mud as protection from insects. Large herds formerly migrated 200 mi. (320 km) or more in spring and fall. Some Wood Bison still travel over 100 mi. (160 km) from wooded areas to valleys. Usually found in herds of 5–20, with male herds separate from females and young except during the breeding season. Single calves are born in spring, young join the herd a few days after birth. **HABITAT:** Plains and prairies, also woodland. **RANGE:** Free-ranging only in N.W.T., ne. B.C., Wyo., and Alaska. **STATUS:** Wood Bison (*B. b. athabascae*) is endangered (USFWS). All Bison are listed as threatened in Canada (COSEWIC). Prior to European settlement, Bison numbered 30–70 million. Slaughtered for food, skins, "sport," and in efforts to lay siege to Native Peoples; herds were so drastically reduced that by 1900 fewer than 1,000 Bison remained. Management and rescue efforts have brought numbers up to 65,000, but few of these are free-ranging. **NOTE:** Sometimes placed in the genus *Bison*.

BLACKBUCK   *Antilope cervicapra* (introduced)   **p. 88**
  Shoulder ht. 27–30 in. (0.7–0.8 m); wt. 40–125 lb. (18–57 kg). Adult *male strikingly marked black and white* with long *spiraling horns*. Female brown, pale eye-ring, *pale stripe high on sides*; white chest and belly. Young male dark brown. **SIMILAR SPECIES:** Adult male Blackbuck unmistakable. Female Pronghorn has white markings on face, small horns, and no stripe on sides. **HABITS:** Mainly diurnal. Feeds on short grass. Usually travels in herds of 5–50, with bachelors traveling separately. Adult males maintain territories, females are more nomadic. Single young may be born at any time of year. **HABITAT:** Grassland with brushy cover, or open woodland. **RANGE:** Introduced to Tex. and Calif. Native to India, Pakistan, and Nepal. **STATUS:** Population in Texas (centered on Edward's Plateau) is larger than in its native range.

MOUNTAIN GOAT   *Oreamnos americanus*   **Pl. 46, Skull Pl. 13**
  Shoulder ht. 3–4 ft. (0.9–1.2 m); wt. 100–300 lb. (46–136 kg). Male larger than female. Male and female horned, *horns narrow and erect,* slightly curved back. Nose, eyes, hooves, and *horns black,* contrasting with *cream white fur.* Fur long and thick in winter, especially on shoulders and legs. *Bearded year-round.* **SIMILAR SPECIES:** Dall's Sheep has heavy, yellowish, curved horns and short fur. **HABITS:** Mainly diurnal. Traveling on precipitous slopes and narrow ledges, it has specialized hooves that can grip like pincers or be spread out to act as brakes. The undersides of the hooves are rough-textured and rubbery, providing traction. Moves easily in areas where predators cannot follow, suffering greater mortality from avalanches and rockslides than from predation. Feeds on

BLACKBUCK
Antilope cervicapra

MOUNTAIN GOAT
Oreamnos americanus

Mountain Goat female with young. The kid can walk and climb soon after birth and remains with its mother for about a year. Both sexes have narrow erect horns.

pockets of vegetation among rocks and in alpine meadows. Seen alone or in small groups; sexes travel separately except during the mating season (Nov.–Dec.). One or 2 young, occasionally 3, are born in late May or June. In winter, moves to slightly lower elevations but usually stays on steep slopes where the wind blows the snow off and food is more easily obtained than in snow-covered meadows. **HABITAT:** Steep rocky mountains and talus slopes, usually above the tree line. **RANGE:** S. Alaska and s. Yukon to Alta., n. Idaho, Mont., and Wash. Introduced in mts. of Wash., Ore., Wyo., S.D., Nev., Utah, and Colo. **STATUS:** Fairly common. On the Olympic Pen., Washington, introduced Mountain Goats have become very common and have had a negative impact on alpine plants, including several endemic species.

MUSKOX *Ovibos moschatus*   Pl. 45, Skull Pl. 13

Shoulder ht. 3–5 ft. (0.9–1.5 m); wt. 400–900 lb. (180–410 kg). Male larger than female. *Large, shaggy, and cowlike. Fur very long and thick, hangs at least to knees.* Lower legs pale gray. Humped shoulders and rump. *Massive down-curved horns* in both sexes. **SIMILAR SPECIES:** Unmistakable; few large hoofed mammals in its range. Caribou have antlers and shorter fur. **SOUNDS:** Male bellows during breeding season; both sexes snort and stamp feet in alarm. **HABITS:** Feeds on sedges, grass, and dwarf willows in summer, woody vegetation in winter. Social; females and subadults form herds of 10–20, males travel alone or in bachelor herds. When threatened by wolves, their chief predator, the group forms a tight circle or crescent around the young, with horned heads held low, facing outward. An individual may rush at a wolf and hook it with its horns. As the name suggests, has a musky odor, most pronounced in

A small herd of Muskoxen in a defensive ring, encircling their young to protect them from wolves, their main predator.

breeding males. This odor is from urine, not musk glands. During the breeding season a dominant male defends his harem from other males by scent-marking, bellowing, and head-butting. Females breed every 2 years and have single young in April or May. Herds travel short distances (50 mi., 80 km) from summer ranges in meadows and valleys to winter on windswept slopes. **HABITAT:** Arctic tundra. **RANGE:** Arctic Ocean is. and mainland N.W.T. Reintroduced in parts of Alaska and n. Quebec. Also ne. Greenland. **STATUS:** Hunted to extinction in the U.S. and almost eliminated in Canada in the 19th century. Presently protected in Canada, where it has largely recovered; some populations reestablished in Alaska.

BARBARY SHEEP
p. 92, Skull Pl. 13

Ammotragus lervia (introduced)
Aoudad

Shoulder ht. 30–44 in. (0.7–1.1 m); wt. 110–320 lb. (50–145 kg). Male is larger than female. Fur sandy brown, palest on mane and inside legs. Long *mane on underside of neck;* fur forms "chaps" on

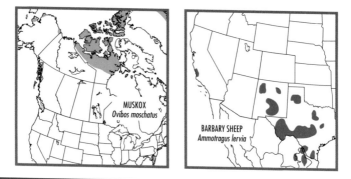

MUSKOX
Ovibos moschatus

BARBARY SHEEP
Ammotragus lervia

forelegs (mane and chaps shorter on female). *Long tufted tail.* Large horns, flared out and back, pronounced in both male and female. **SIMILAR SPECIES:** Bighorn has a very short tail, lacks mane and chaps. **HABITS:** Active early and late in the day. Eats forbs and grass and can survive long periods without access to water. Groups number 5–40 and may include several breeding males. Single young are born in spring. **HABITAT:** Dry rocky slopes. **RANGE:** Introduced in the Southwest in Tex., N.M., Calif., and n. Mexico. Native to North Africa. **STATUS:** Populations increasing in some areas, may have a negative impact on Desert Bighorn.

BIGHORN SHEEP *Ovis canadensis* Pl. 46, Skull Pl. 13

Mountain Sheep, Rocky Mountain Sheep

Shoulder ht. 3–3½ ft.; wt. 75–275 lb. (34–124 kg). Male is much larger than female. Muzzle, belly, backs of legs, and *rump patch white*, rest of coat, including tiny tail, pale to dark brown. Horns on both sexes. Ram's *horns massive, strongly curved.* Horns on ewe smaller, narrow, slightly curved. **GEOGRAPHIC VARIATION:** Desert and Nelson's Bighorns (Southwest deserts and California) — relatively small, rangy; pale tan or sandy brown; horns of ram curve back and flare out away from the head. Rocky Mountain Bighorn — larger, stocky; tan to dark chocolate brown; horns of ram massive, tightly curled in almost full circle close to head. **SIMILAR SPECIES:** Dall's Sheep white or gray, found farther north. Barbary Sheep lacks white rump patch, has mane under neck. **SOUNDS:** Loud clashes as rams butt heads; snorts in alarm. **HABITS:** Active by day; periods of feeding interspersed with lying down and chewing cud. At night scrapes out a bed and may sleep in the same spot repeatedly, leaving a characteristic odor and piles of droppings around the bed. Eats grasses and sedges in summer, woody plants in winter. Occupies open mountainous terrain and requires steep cliffs and rock faces as "escape routes" to avoid predators. Social; travels in

Rocky Mountain Bighorn Sheep. Two males spar for females.

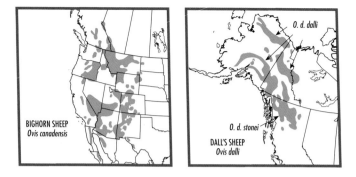

BIGHORN SHEEP
Ovis canadensis

O. d. dalli

O. d. stonei

DALL'S SHEEP
Ovis dalli

groups of 5–80, with females and young separated from bachelor herds. In rutting season (Nov.–Dec.), rams fight for females, rearing up and running at high speed toward each other and slamming foreheads. The skull contains air spaces to absorb impact, but rams can be injured or even die during these contests. Single young are born May–June. In winter, northern populations move to areas where snow will be blown off the slopes. In the desert, movements may be related to availability of water. **HABITAT:** Open, rugged, mountainous areas. High meadows to deserts, but always near steep slopes. **RANGE:** Sw. Canada to se. Calif. and w. Tex.; also south to Baja Calif. and n. Mexico. **STATUS:** Endangered (USFWS). Many U.S. populations were extirpated, but some reintroduction efforts have been successful. Desert populations are very rare and declining in many areas. Barbary Sheep may compete with Desert Bighorn in w. Texas.

DALL'S SHEEP   *Ovis dalli*   PI. 46
Thinhorn Sheep, White Sheep

Shoulder ht. 30–40 in. (0.7–1.0 m); wt. 100–200 lb. (45–90 kg). Male is much larger than female. Male has *massive, yellowish, strongly curved horns*; female has small, narrow, slightly curved horns. **GEOGRAPHIC VARIATION:** Dall's Sheep (*O. d. dalli*), typical form, Alaska, Yukon, and extreme nw. British Columbia — coat *pure white.* Stone Sheep (*O. d. stonei*), n. British Columbia and s.-cen. Yukon — *dark gray to black* with blaze, muzzle, rump patch, belly, and backs of legs white. In the area of contact between black- and white-phase sheep, intermediates occur, with a pale gray body and whitish head and neck. (Formerly known as Fannin's Sheep, this gray phase is now considered to be the same subspecies as Stone Sheep.) **SIMILAR SPECIES:** Mountain Goat has shaggy fur and erect black horns. Range does not overlap with Bighorn Sheep. **SOUNDS:**

Loud clashes as rams butt heads. **HABITS:** Diurnal. Feeds on grass, forbs, and sedges in summer, low woody plants in winter. Usually seen from a distance as patches of white dotted across the side of a slope — a group of females and young fanned out to graze. From Nov. to Dec. males fight for access to females, rearing up and racing toward each other with heads lowered, slamming horns. Single young, rarely twins, are born in May. In winter, herds move to bare windswept slopes. **HABITAT:** Rugged mountainous regions. **RANGE:** Alaska, Yukon, w. N.W.T., and n. B.C. **STATUS:** Populations disjunct but locally common.

EUROPEAN MOUFLON *Ovis musimon* (introduced)   p. 92

Shoulder ht. 2–3 ft. (0.6–0.9 m); wt. 77–110 lb. (30–50 kg). Male is larger than female. Male *dark brown* with white socks and *pale saddle.* Female sandy brown with *dark line on lower sides,* white belly, and pale socks. Large curled horns on male, *female hornless.* **SIMILAR SPECIES:** Desert Bighorn has a white rump patch and uniform sandy brown color extending onto legs; doe is horned. **HABITS:** Feeds on grass in the morning and afternoon, inactive at midday. Travels in small groups in spring and summer, larger groups in winter. In fall rams fight, rearing up before running at each other and clashing horns. Dominant rams mate with most of the females. Single lambs are born in spring. **HABITAT:** Upland regions with pastureland and scrub. **RANGE:** Introduced to Tex. Native to Corsica and Sardinia. **STATUS:** Common in Texas Hill Country. **NOTE:** Some authors consider all mouflon conspecific with domestic sheep, *Ovis aries;* others include this species with Asiatic Mouflon, *Ovis orientalis.*

EUROPEAN MOUFLON
Ovis musimon

WHALES, DOLPHINS, AND PORPOISES: CETACEA

Cetaceans are the most fully aquatic of all mammals; those found in North American waters are all marine species. They have forelimbs modified into paddlelike flippers, no external hind limbs, and a fishlike form. The flukes (tail fins) of a whale are flattened horizontally, whereas a fish's tail is flattened vertically. Like other mammals, cetaceans suckle their young and breathe air. As they rise to the surface they expel moisture-laden air from blowholes (nostrils) on top of the head, often creating a distinct "blow" of fine spray. Some of the large whales can be identified by the shape and form of the blow. The smaller dolphins are often active and may be seen leaping clear of the water, allowing identification in the field. Some of the deep-sea species are difficult to see and identify alive; a few species are known primarily from stranded individuals.

Although whales and dolphins do not resemble most other mammals, they are known to be closely related to the even-toed hoofed mammals (Artiodactyla) based on similarities in DNA and on fossil evidence (unique characteristics of the ankle joint are shared by fossil amphibious whales and artiodactyls). There are 2 living suborders of cetaceans: the Mysticeti, or baleen whales, and the Odontoceti, or toothed whales. Baleen whales have 2 blowholes and have baleen plates in place of teeth. There are 13–14 species of baleen whales, 10 of which occur in North American waters. Toothed whales have a single blowhole and have 2–100 teeth. There are about 70 species of toothed whales, 39 of which are found off North America. **CONSERVATION OF WHALES:** In the past, whaling was a huge and unregulated industry. The large baleen whales were the primary target of whaling ships, but as their numbers were depleted, other species were also exploited. The International Whaling Commission (IWC) now controls the number, size, and species of large whales that can be hunted, and many of these whales are fully protected. Not all countries respect the spirit of the IWC restrictions. The Northern Right Whale, hunted almost to extinction, remains critically endangered, and the small remnant populations are not showing signs of recovery. Other whales have recovered well, and some populations are growing even with continued subsistence hunting. Whales also suffer from entanglement in fish nets and from collisions with vessels. They are thought to be adversely affected by overfishing of prey species, global warming, pollution, underwater noise, and military exercises. All cetaceans are listed by the Convention on International Trade in Endangered Species (CITES). All the baleen whales along with the Sperm Whale, Baird's Beaked Whale, and Northern Bottlenose Whale are on Appendix I; the others are all on Appendix II.

TOOTHED WHALES, DOLPHINS, AND PORPOISES: Odontoceti

Toothed whales range in size from the smallest cetaceans — the porpoises and small dolphins — to one of the largest species, the Sperm Whale. All toothed whales do have teeth, but the teeth may not emerge from the jaw or may be visible in one sex only. There is great variation in the size, shape, and number of teeth. Toothed whales have a single blowhole on the top of the head. All toothed whales may echolocate, although this has been established for only a few species. Most toothed whales eat fish and squid.

NARWHAL AND BELUGA: Monodontidae

The Narwhal and Beluga are the only species in the family Monodontidae. They have almost no beak and lack a dorsal fin. They are found in cold Arctic waters; Belugas also enter subarctic waters.

NARWHAL *Monodon monoceros* **Pl. 63**
Length 13–19 ft. (4–6 m); wt. 1–1.5 tons (900–1,600 kg). Male is larger than female. Male and some females have 1 (rarely 2) *very long, spiraled tusk* (to 10 ft./3 m). Adult *speckled blackish with white* above, mainly white below with some dark flecks; young blue-gray or dark gray; old adult whitish with dark spots on head and dorsal ridge. *Head rounded;* body spindle-shaped. Short flippers with upturned tips. Trailing *edge of tail convex.* **SIMILAR SPECIES:** Only cetacean of similar size in same range is Beluga. Beluga is whitish and lacks a tusk. Beached young Narwhal has no visible teeth, young Beluga has 32 or more teeth. **HABITS:** When breathing or "spy-hopping" the long tusk may be exposed, an unmistakable and striking feature of this "unicorn whale." A deep diver, it can

NARWHAL
Monodon monoceros

remain underwater for 20 minutes and reaches depths of over 3,300 ft. (1,000 m). Feeds on squid, fish, shrimp, and octopus, sucking up prey and swallowing it whole. In summer moves into deep sounds and fjords, in fall migrates to offshore pack ice. Travels in groups of 3–8, occasionally up to 20, but may form large aggregations at times. Tusks may be used for sparring between males during the breeding season. Single young are born after a 14-month gestation and are nursed for about 20 months. Females probably breed every 3 years. **HABITAT:** Usually in deep water, but may be found in shallow waters in summer. **RANGE:** High Arctic seas of w. North Atlantic. Also Soviet Arctic. **STATUS:** Seasonally common. Seen regularly near Pond Inlet and Arctic Bay, e. Canada, in summer. Hunted in Canada and Greenland for its skin ("maqtak") and meat, which are eaten by the Inuit. The ivory tusk is a valuable commodity.

BELUGA   *Delphinapterus leucas*   Pl. 63, Skull Pl. 14
White Whale

Length 11–16 ft. (3.3–5 m); wt. 0.3–1.5 tons (300–1,400 kg). Male is slightly larger than female. Adult is *entirely white* or cream; young is blue-gray or brown (becomes white after about 6 years). *Head rounded with a short beak.* Stocky body, *no dorsal fin.* **SIMILAR SPECIES:** Young Narwhal has no visible teeth, young Beluga has 32 or more teeth. **SOUNDS:** Loud chirps and squeals sometimes audible to humans. **HABITS:** May roll and twitter when surfacing to breathe. Unlike most whales, the Beluga has a flexible neck and can rotate its head. It is not acrobatic, but it does "spy-hop" and can peer from side to side. Feeds on fish, shrimp, squid, and benthic organisms. Social; travels in small to large groups, and thousands may aggregate in summer and fall. Some populations are migratory, others are year-round residents. Many enter relatively warm estuaries and rivers in summer. Young are born from spring to late summer after a gestation of 14–15 months and nurse for about 1½ years. Females usually breed every 3 years. **HABITAT:** Coastal, estuarine, and offshore waters. **RANGE:** Arctic and subarctic waters, south to Gulf of St. Lawrence in East and se. Alaska in West. **STATUS:** Populations in Ungava Bay and e. Hudson Bay are endangered, popula-

A Beluga surfaces to scan its surroundings. Note the small conical teeth in the upper and lower jaws.

BELUGA
Delphinapterus leucas

tions in Cumberland Sound and St. Lawrence Estuary are threatened (COSEWIC). Subsistence hunting, habitat alteration, and pollution are ongoing threats. Population in St. Lawrence R. suffers from numerous illnesses apparently caused by industrial pollutants such as PCBs and DDT.

OCEANIC DOLPHINS: Delphinidae

The Delphinidae include the typical beaked dolphins and also the larger blunt-headed killer whales and pilot whales. All delphinids have rows of conical teeth on the upper and lower jaws, and most species have a prominent dorsal fin. They have a single blowhole on the top of the head. There are at least 33 species in 17 genera in this family worldwide; 19 species are known from North American waters.

Most species have complex social behavior, well-developed auditory communication (many can be heard squeaking and chirping as they travel), and long-term mother-infant bonds. Highly intelligent and trainable, Common Bottlenose Dolphins and Killer Whales have been exploited by aquariums and animal parks for live animal shows. Impressive as these shows may be, they do not compare to the sight of a wild group of Spinner Dolphins leaping and spinning apparently for the sheer joy of it.

ROUGH-TOOTHED DOLPHIN *Steno bredanensis* **Pl. 61**

Length 6½–9 ft. (2–2.7 m); wt. 265–350 lb. (120–160 kg). Back dark brown, sides paler, marked with *whitish spots and scratches. Narrow beak gradually rises to melon with no distinct crease. Lips and belly white.* Dorsal fin tall, erect. **SIMILAR SPECIES:** Conical head and white lips are distinctive at close range. **HABITS:** Sometimes seen skimming the water with beak near the surface, dorsal fin exposed. Sometimes bow-rides. Usually travels in schools of 10–20, may form larger groups. **HABITAT:** Warm offshore waters. **RANGE:** Mainly tropical but can venture north to Wash. in Pacific and to Va. in Atlantic. Occurs worldwide. **STATUS:** Uncommon and poorly known.

COMMON BOTTLENOSE DOLPHIN **Pl. 61, Skull Pl. 14**
Tursiops truncatus

Length 6–13 ft. (2–3.9 m); wt. 440–600 lb. (200–275 kg). Stocky with a *short but distinct beak. Grayish, with an indistinct dark cape and pale belly.* Dorsal fin large, usually falcate. Familiar to many as "Flipper" and other captive performers. **SIMILAR SPECIES:** Rough-toothed Dolphin has no crease between beak and forehead. Risso's Dolphin has a taller fin that usually appears darker than the back, and has no beak. Atlantic Spotted Dolphin (immature and some adults are unspotted) has a longer beak and a more clearly marked cape. **HABITS:** Usually travels sedately, showing only the back and dorsal fin. The "smiling" face is seldom seen at sea. Attracted to boats and often bow-rides or travels at the stern. Sometimes acrobatic when feeding; captives can be trained to perform impressive leaps. Eats a wide variety of bottom-dwelling and water-column prey. Usually seen in groups of 10–25, sometimes in larger assemblages, and may associate with other species. Fe-

Two Common Bottlenose Dolphins leap in unison. This is one of the most widespread and well-known dolphin species, often seen close to shore.

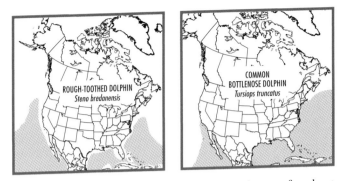

ROUGH-TOOTHED DOLPHIN
Steno bredanensis

COMMON
BOTTLENOSE DOLPHIN
Tursiops truncatus

males bear a single young every 2–3 years and nurse for about a year. Calf may be tended by other adults when mother hunts. **HABITAT:** Coastal, shelf, and offshore waters. Separate populations occur in inshore and pelagic waters. A dolphin seen from land in warmer waters is most likely to be this species, as the coastal form will enter bays, estuaries, and shallow water. **RANGE:** North to cen. Calif. in Pacific and to R.I. in Atlantic. Coastal form more common in Gulf of Mexico, but offshore form also enters these waters. Found in tropical and temperate waters worldwide. **STATUS:** Common and widespread. Hunted in some areas. Coastal populations suffer from pesticide poisoning and pollution.

ANTROPICAL SPOTTED DOLPHIN

PL. 61

tenella attenuata
Bridled Dolphin

Length 5–8½ ft. (1.6–2.6 m); wt. 220–265 lb. (100–120 kg). Slender body. Adult marked with small *whitish spots*. Young unspotted. *Long narrow beak*, white at tip. Dark line from eye to beak and mouth to flipper. *Well-defined dark cape rises high above eye and dips down on flank* in front of dorsal fin. Tail stock dark above, pale below. Has 35–48 pairs of teeth in each jaw. **SIMILAR SPECIES:** Atlantic Spotted Dolphin stockier, lacks dark mask, and has indistinct cape with a pale blaze from flank toward dorsal fin. Common Bottlenose Dolphin has a shorter beak. **HABITS:** Fast and active; leaps high out of the water and may bow-ride. Diet includes flying

PANTROPICAL
SPOTTED DOLPHIN
Stenella attenuata

fish and squid. Travels in groups of 100–1,000 or more, often in association with Spinner Dolphins and tuna. **HABITAT:** Mainly offshore waters. A coastal subspecies occurs off w. Mexico. **RANGE:** Gulf of Mexico to R.I. Worldwide in tropical and warm temperate waters. **STATUS:** Common and widespread. Some populations have been depleted by incidental kills in purse-seine fishing for tuna.

ATLANTIC SPOTTED DOLPHIN   *Stenella frontalis*   **PL. 61**

Length 6–7½ ft. (1.8–2.3 m); wt. 220–310 lb. (100–140 kg). Robust. Adult marked with large *white spots above, black spots below*; spotting very prominent to faint or absent. Young unspotted. *Beak moderately long with white lips and tip.* Faint stripe from eye to flipper. Indistinct dark cape with *pale blaze from shoulder toward dorsal fin.* Tail stock entirely gray. Has 30–42 pairs of teeth in each jaw. **GEOGRAPHIC VARIATION:** Large, heavily spotted (coastal form, Carolinas southward). Smaller, lightly spotted or unspotted (Gulf Stream, off New England). **SIMILAR SPECIES:** Pantropical Spotted Dolphin has dark mask and line from flipper to mouth, not to eye, and a two-toned tail stock. Common Bottlenose Dolphin (easily confused with unspotted form) has a slightly shorter, gray beak and is more uniformly gray in color. **HABITS:** Fast and agile; bow-rides and leaps out of the water. Eats fish, squid, and bottom invertebrates. Coastal groups may number 1–15; offshore groups may be larger. **HABITAT:** Coastal and offshore in tropical and warm temperate waters. **RANGE:** New England to Fla. and Gulf of Mexico. Widespread in Atlantic Ocean. **STATUS:** This is the most common shallow-water dolphin of se. U.S. and Gulf of Mexico. Status of offshore populations is not well known.

ATLANTIC
SPOTTED DOLPHIN
Stenella frontalis

SPINNER DOLPHIN   *Stenella longirostris*   **PL. 61**

Length 5–7 ft. (1.6–2.2 m); wt. 110–165 lb. (50–75 kg). Small and slender. Dark cape, pale gray sides, white belly; *bands of color are roughly parallel. Very long, narrow beak.* Nearly triangular dorsal fin. Has 42–62 pairs of teeth in each jaw. **SIMILAR SPECIES:** Clymene Dolphin has shorter beak and cape dipping down below dorsal fin. Common Bottlenose Dolphin is stockier with a much shorter beak. Other dolphins have more complex coloration. **HABITS:** Extremely agile and acrobatic; sprints and leaps out of the water, dashes forward and aft of boats, and, most notably, spins on the

The Spinner Dolphin is highly acrobatic, sometimes leaping vertically from the water and spinning on its long axis. Note the long slim body and narrow beak of this species.

long axis during a high leap and reenters the water with a huge splash. Feeds on small fish and squid caught at middle depths. Travels in small to very large herds and frequently associates with other dolphins or whales. Female gives birth after 10½ months' gestation and nurse for 1–2 years. **HABITAT:** Mainly found offshore (beyond the continental shelf) in tropical and warm temperate waters. May ap-

SPINNER DOLPHIN
Stenella longirostris

proach the coast and rest near shore in some areas, such as Hawaii. **RANGE:** R.I. to Tex. Tropical seas worldwide. **STATUS:** Common and widespread. Some populations depleted by incidental catches of tuna industry.

LYMENE DOLPHIN   PL. 61
enella clymene

Length 6–6½ ft. (1.8–2 m); wt. 165–190 lb. (75–85 kg). *Small and rather stocky. Dark gray saddle dips below dorsal fin, sides pale gray, belly white. Beak relatively short,* black "moustache" on top of beak, tip and lips also black. Has 38–49 pairs of teeth in each jaw. **SIMILAR SPECIES:** Spinner Dolphin is slimmer with a longer beak,

CLYMENE DOLPHIN
Stenella clymene

lacks dark saddle and dark "moustache." **HABITS:** Fast, agile swimmer; sometimes spins on long axis. Little known; occasionally seen in groups of 50 or fewer. **HABITAT:** Deep offshore tropical and subtropical waters. **RANGE:** Atlantic only: N.J. through Gulf of Mexico. Also to w. Africa and s. Brazil. **STATUS:** Poorly known. May be rare in some areas but is moderately common in Gulf of Mexico.

STRIPED DOLPHIN *Stenella coeruleoalba* PL. 61

Length 7½–9 ft. (2.3–2.7 m); wt. 220–330 lb. (100–150 kg). Stocky. *Strikingly marked:* back black, sides pale gray with *blaze from shoulder to dorsal fin; black lines from eye to anus* and from eye to flipper. Beak moderately long. **SIMILAR SPECIES:** Fraser's Dolphin

is only other species with dark line from eye to anus; it has a small beak and dorsal fin and lacks a pale shoulder blaze. **HABITS:** Some are shy and wary of boats, others may bow-ride occasionally. Makes long low leaps and can be acrobatic, leaping high out of the water. Travels in large groups of 30–500 that segregate by age and breeding condition. **HABITAT:** Cool temperate to tropical offshore waters. Sometimes enters continental shelf waters. **RANGE:** North to Wash. in Pacific, to N.S. in Atlantic. More abundant in waters off Calif. and se. U.S. Found worldwide. **STATUS:** Common and widespread. Hunted in Japanese waters.

FRASER'S DOLPHIN *Lagenodelphis hosei* PL. 60

Length 7–9 ft. (2.1–2.7 m); wt. 220–460 lb. (100–210 kg). *Stocky and short-beaked* with *very small appendages.* Back blackish, sides gray; *broad black stripe from eye to anus.* Belly white or pinkish. Dorsal fin small and upright, usually triangular. **SIMILAR SPECIES:** Striped Dolphin has a pale blaze from eye to dorsal fin. It and other dolphins have longer flippers and flukes and larger dorsal fins. **HABITS:** Fast and active; creates a spray from the head when surfacing. Generally avoids boats and seldom bow-rides. Feeds on deep-water fish, shrimp, and squid. Found in large groups of 100–1,000, often in association with other species. **HABITAT:** Deep tropical waters. **RANGE:** Gulf of Mexico to Caribbean. Patchily distributed worldwide. **STATUS:** Uncommon to rare. One of the dolphins occasionally caught in purse-seine nets for yellow-fin tuna; also taken by harpoon fisheries in Lesser Antilles.

FRASER'S DOLPHIN
Lagenodelphis hosei

HORT-BEAKED COMMON DOLPHIN

Pl. 61

elphinus delphis

Short-beaked Saddleback Dolphin, Common Dolphin

Length 6½–8½ ft. (2–2.6 m); wt. 155–240 lb. (70–110 kg). Slim-bodied. Distinctive *hourglass pattern of pale gray and tan on sides, below dark, pointed saddle. Relatively long beak.* Dark line from beak to eye, *pale area below eye to flipper.* Prominent dorsal fin, triangular or falcate. **SIMILAR SPECIES:** Long-beaked Common Dolphin is slightly slimmer and shows less contrast in facial stripes (no white streak below eye) but can be difficult to distinguish at sea. Other dolphins lack an hourglass pattern on sides. **HABITS:** Bouncy and acrobatic; often leaps high out of the water. May bow-ride for extended periods and will follow the bow waves of large whales. Feeds on deep-water squid and fish. Highly social; group size averages about 100 but can number several thousand. Groups sometimes feed with Pacific White-sided Dolphins. **HABITAT:** Mainly in deep continental shelf and offshore waters, occasionally near shore. **RANGE:** Lab. to s. Fla. in Atlantic; Vancouver I. to Baja Calif. in Pacific. Found in warm temperate and tropical waters world-

Short-beaked Common Dolphin. Note the unusual tan color on the flanks, visible as this species leaps out of the water.

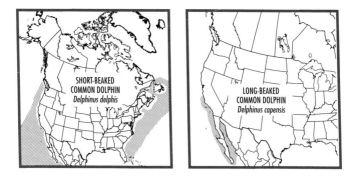

SHORT-BEAKED
COMMON DOLPHIN
Delphinus delphis

LONG-BEAKED
COMMON DOLPHIN
Delphinus capensis

wide. **STATUS:** Common and widespread. One of the species ravaged by purse-seine fishing for tuna.

LONG-BEAKED COMMON DOLPHIN   Pl. 61
Delphinus capensis
Long-beaked Saddleback Dolphin
Length 6–8¼ ft. (1.9–2.5 m); wt. to 300 lb. (135 kg). Slim-bodied. Distinctive *hourglass pattern of gray and tan on sides,* below dark, pointed saddle. *Very long beak and rather flat head.* Dark line from beak to eye; *gray below eye to flipper.* Prominent dorsal fin, triangular or falcate. **SIMILAR SPECIES:** See Short-beaked Common Dolphin. **HABITS:** Similar to Short-beaked Common Dolphin, although average group size is close to 200 in this species. **HABITAT:** Nearshore tropical and warm temperate waters. **RANGE:** Cen. Calif. to s. Baja Calif. Also scattered populations near tropical coasts worldwide. **STATUS:** Fairly common in s. California waters. **NOTE:** Formerly included in Common Short-beaked Dolphin, *D. delphis.*

WHITE-BEAKED DOLPHIN   Pl. 60
Lagenorhynchus albirostris
Length 6–10 ft. (1.8–3.1 m); wt. 400–770 lb. (180–350 kg). Stocky. Mostly *dark gray with a diffuse pale gray patch below dorsal fin extending back to form a saddle* over flank. *Small, thick, white beak* (beak may be dark in some individuals). Tall, falcate dorsal fin. Has 22–28 pairs of teeth in each jaw. **SIMILAR SPECIES:** Atlantic White-sided Dolphin has sharply defined pale patches that do not form a saddle on flank. **HABITS:** Less acrobatic than White-sided Dolphin, but may leap or tail-slap. Group size is typically 5–50 but may be as large as 1,500; groups may associate with whales or other dolphins. **HABITAT:** Continental shelf and deep offshore waters. **RANGE:** Atlantic from Cape Cod to Lab. and Davis Strait. Also east to Norway,

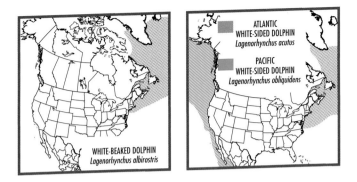

ATLANTIC
WHITE-SIDED DOLPHIN
Lagenorhynchus acutus

PACIFIC
WHITE-SIDED DOLPHIN
Lagenorhynchus obliquidens

WHITE-BEAKED DOLPHIN
Lagenorhynchus albirostris

Sweden, and Europe. **STATUS:** Common, but numbers off ne. U.S. have declined in recent years.

ATLANTIC WHITE-SIDED DOLPHIN

Pl. 60

Lagenorhynchus acutus

Length 6–9 ft. (1.9–2.8 m); wt. 400–500 lb. (180–230 kg). Rather stocky. Upper back, flippers, and dorsal fin black. *Narrow white patch on flanks; yellowish stripe above white patch* extends toward tail. Sides mainly gray, belly white. *Short stocky beak,* upper lip black, lower lip white. Dorsal fin tall, falcate. Has 30–40 pairs of teeth in each jaw. **SIMILAR SPECIES:** White and yellow flank patches diagnostic and usually visible at sea. **HABITS:** Acrobatic and energetic; often leaps high above the water. Eats mainly squid and schooling fish. Found in small to large groups, sometimes in association with Fin, Humpback, or Pilot Whales. Single young are born in summer; females probably breed every 3 years. **HABITAT:** Continental shelf and offshore waters. May move inshore in summer and offshore in winter. **RANGE:** Atlantic from Chesapeake Bay to Nfld. and Davis Strait. Also east to Iceland and France. **STATUS:** Locally abundant.

PACIFIC WHITE-SIDED DOLPHIN

Pl. 60

Lagenorhynchus obliquidens

Length 6–9 ft. (1.7–2.7 m); wt. 165–440 lb. (75–200 kg). Stocky, with a *very short beak* and *sharply falcate, bicolor dorsal fin.* Back dark with pale stripes from head to tail. **SIMILAR SPECIES:** Short-beaked Common Dolphin has a longer beak, a dark dorsal fin that is not sharply hooked, and an hourglass pattern on sides. Dall's Porpoise is chunky and small-headed with a smaller dorsal fin. **HABITS:** Travels in herds of 200–1,000, moving with acrobatic leaps. Feeds on fish and squid, mainly at night. A single calf is born in early fall, after a 10-month gestation. **HABITAT:** Cold temperate continental shelf and offshore waters. **RANGE:** Pacific from Alaska to s. Gulf of Calif. Also west to Japan. **STATUS:** Very common.

NORTHERN RIGHT WHALE DOLPHIN Pl. 60
Lissodelphis borealis

Length 6½–10 ft. (2–3 m); wt. to 250 lb. (113 kg). Male is larger than female. Very *long and slender. Almost entirely black.* Young is grayish. Short but distinct beak and *no dorsal fin.* **SIMILAR SPECIES:** All other beaked dolphins have a dorsal fin. **HABITS:** Shy; groups flee from boats by swimming just below the surface or by making a series of long low leaps as they rapidly move off, disturbing a large body of water. Feeds on deep-sea fish and squid, and can dive 650 ft. (200 m) or more. Travels in herds of 100 to over 1,000. A single calf is born after a 12-month gestation. **HABITAT:** Cool offshore waters. May enter continental shelf waters in winter. **RANGE:** Pacific from s. B.C. to n. Baja Calif. Also west to Japan. **STATUS:** Common to abundant. Occasionally caught in gill nets and seines.

RISSO'S DOLPHIN *Grampus griseus* Pl. 62
Grampus

Length 11–12½ ft. (3.3–3.8 m); wt. 880–1,300 lb. (400–600 kg). Large, *stocky, and blunt-headed.* Vertical crease on forehead. Body gray above, *palest on head,* darker on appendages; belly white. Adult often *heavily scarred. Tall, falcate dorsal fin;* long sickle-shaped flippers. Newborn is pale gray, changes to chocolate brown or gray; pales and becomes scarred with age. Has 7 pairs of teeth in lower jaw, no upper teeth. **SIMILAR SPECIES:** Squared-off, beakless head in combination with tall narrow dorsal fin and heavy white scars distinctive. **HABITS:** May move slowly, showing only dorsal fin, but can be active, leaping and slapping with flippers or flukes.

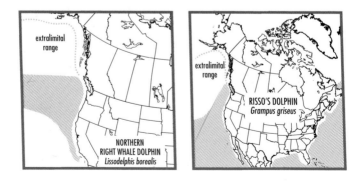

Found in groups of 25–200 or more; may associate with other dolphins. Eats squid. **HABITAT:** Deep tropical and warm temperate waters. **RANGE:** S. Alaska southward in Pacific; Nfld. southward in Atlantic. Worldwide. **STATUS:** Common and widespread.

MELON-HEADED WHALE *Peponocephala electra* PL. 62
Many-toothed Blackfish

Length 6½–9 ft. (2–2.7 m); wt. 330–600 lb. (150–275 kg). *Mainly dark gray-black with a black cape. Almost no beak;* head somewhat pointed when viewed from above; *lips white. Flippers long, with pointed tips.* Dorsal fin tall, falcate, located at midpoint of back. Has 20–25 pairs of teeth in upper and lower jaw. **SIMILAR SPECIES:** Pygmy Killer Whale is very similar, distinguishable only at close range. It has a shorter head that is rounded from above, and flippers with rounded tips. False Killer Whale is larger and slimmer and has a hump on the leading edge of the flipper. **HABITS:** Fast swimmer, moving with frequent changes in course. Large groups of 150–1,500 travel bunched tightly together and may form mixed associations with other species such as Fraser's Dolphin. **HABITAT:** Deep tropical and subtropical waters. **RANGE:** Gulf of Mexico and Fla.; one record from Md. Tropical waters worldwide. **STATUS:** Generally uncommon and poorly known.

PYGMY KILLER WHALE *Feresa attenuata* PL. 62

Length 6½–8½ ft. (2–2.6 m); wt. 330–500 lb. (150–225 kg). *Mainly dark gray-black with a black cape. No beak; head short and rounded* when viewed from above. *Lips white,* color often extending onto chin as white "goatee." Flippers long with *rounded tips.* Dorsal fin tall, falcate, located near midpoint of back. Has 8–13 pairs of teeth in upper and lower jaws. **SIMILAR SPECIES:** Melon-headed Whale has a longer head that is almost pointed from above and flippers with

MELON-HEADED WHALE
~ *Peponocephala electra*

PYGMY KILLER WHALE
Feresa attenuata

pointed tips. False Killer Whale is longer and slimmer, lacks white lips. **HABITS:** Sometimes lolls at the surface but also swims quickly if disturbed. Average group size is about 25. **HABITAT:** Deep tropical and subtropical waters. **RANGE:** Fla. and Gulf of Mexico. Found in tropical oceans worldwide but is more common in Southern Hemisphere. **STATUS:** Uncommon.

FALSE KILLER WHALE *Pseudorca crassidens*   PL. 63

Length 15–20 ft. (4.5–6 m); wt. 1.3 tons (1,360 kg). *Very long and slender.* Uniformly grayish black. No beak; upper lip overhangs lower lip. *Flippers long with a hump on leading edge.* Dorsal fin narrow, falcate, sometimes rounded at tip. Upper and lower jaws have 7–12 pairs of large teeth. **SIMILAR SPECIES:** Melon-headed and Pygmy Killer Whales are smaller with white lips and relatively larger dorsal fins. Killer Whale has white markings and is larger. **HABITS:** Agile and acrobatic; leaps out of the water and makes high-speed turns. May approach ships and bow-ride. Usually found in groups of 10–60 or more. Sometimes steals fish from line fishermen and may attack porpoises caught in seine nets. **HABITAT:** In deep warm temperate and tropical waters. **RANGE:** Mainly in warmer waters off Calif. in Pacific and Gulf of Mexico and Fla. in Atlantic, but also recorded north to s. Alaska and New England. Found worldwide. **STATUS:** Fairly common and widespread. Several mass strandings reported; the largest consisted of 835 individuals.

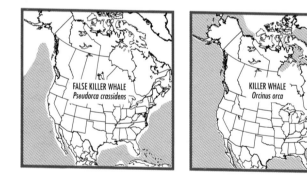

FALSE KILLER WHALE
Pseudorca crassidens

KILLER WHALE
Orcinus orca

KILLER WHALE *Orcinus orca*   PL. 63
Orca

Length 20–32 ft. (6–9.8 m); wt. 3–5.5 tons (3,000–5,600 kg). Male is larger than female. *Striking black-and-white coloration:* white patch behind eye and white of belly extending onto rear flank.

Killer Whale. The dorsal fin of the female, foreground, is shorter and curved, unlike the tall, erect fins of the two males behind her.

Gray saddle behind dorsal fin. Flippers large and rounded. Dorsal fin *very tall, narrow, and erect in male,* smaller and falcate in female and immature. Well known and unmistakable. **SOUNDS:** Clicks are thought to be used in echolocation, screams for communication. Calls range from 4 to 5 kHz. **HABITS:** Often cruises with tall fin clearly visible; also breaches, spy-hops, and flipper-slaps; is not wary of boats. Takes a wide variety of prey including fish, seals, baleen whales, seabirds, and sea turtles. Lives in stable pods of 3–30. In the Northwest some pods are migratory and eat mainly marine mammals, others are resident and eat mainly fish. Larger prey is hunted in a coordinated, cooperative manner. Females give birth to single young at any time of year. Young are nursed for about 2 years; females reproduce about every 5 years. Nonreproductive adults have been known to care for the older calf of a female with a young baby. **HABITAT:** Widely distributed in coastal and offshore waters. Most common in cold nearshore waters, especially in the Northwest. **RANGE:** Worldwide in all oceans, from Arctic pack ice to tropics. **STATUS:** Common to rare. Some populations suffer from pollution, hunting, and other human disturbance. Some are taken for use in zoos and aquariums, where they are easily trained but have a life expectancy about a quarter of that in the wild.

HORT-FINNED PILOT WHALE PL. 63

lobicephala macrorhynchus

Length 13–23 ft. (4–7 m); wt. 1–3 tons (1,000–3,000 kg). Mainly black with a pale saddle behind the dorsal fin. *Bulbous forehead* (most pronounced in male) and almost no beak. *Dorsal fin low and very broad, tip rounded, set well forward on back.* Flippers sickle-shaped, about ⅙ body length. Has 7–9 pairs of teeth in each jaw. **SIMILAR SPECIES:** Very easily confused with Long-finned Pilot Whale, usually indistinguishable at sea. Compare fin lengths. Ranges overlap but Short-fin is generally tropical and Long-fin is temperate. Other black whales with rounded heads have narrow upright dorsal fins. **HABITS:** Lolls at surface or travels at slow speed and is easily approached by boat. Does not bow-ride and rarely breaches, but may spy-hop or "lob-tail" (slap water repeatedly with tail flukes). Eats mainly squid and will follow prey to feeding or spawning grounds, at times entering inshore waters. Social; travels in cohesive pods of about 25 that often join with other pods to form groups of several hundred. Distress calls from one stranded animal may cause an entire school to strand. Groups often associate with other dolphins. Females give birth every 3 years and may breed at any time of year. **HABITAT:** Tropical and warm temperate regions, mainly in deep offshore waters. **RANGE:** North to s. Alaska in Pacific, to N.J. in Atlantic. Found worldwide. **STATUS:** Common to abundant.

LONG-FINNED PILOT WHALE *Globicephala melas* **Pl. 63**
Pothead, Northern Pilot Whale

Length 13–20 ft. (4–6.2 m); wt. 1.3–2.3 tons (1,300–2,300 kg). Mainly black, sometimes with a pale saddle behind the dorsal fin. *Bulbous forehead* (most pronounced in male) and almost no beak. *Dorsal fin low and very broad, tip rounded, set far forward on back.* Flippers sickle-shaped, about ⅕ body length. Has 8–11 pairs of teeth in each jaw. **SIMILAR SPECIES:** Short-finned Pilot Whale is usually indistinguishable at sea. **HABITS:** Similar to Short-finned Pilot Whale. Pods usually number 10–15 and often combine with other pods. Breeds every 5 years, mating in spring and giving birth the following summer. Females nurse the young for at least 3 years. **HABITAT:** Cool temperate waters of the continental shelf and slope. **RANGE:**

North Atlantic from Baffin Bay to Cape Hatteras; also to Iceland and North Africa. A separate population is widespread in the Southern Hemisphere. **STATUS:** Abundant. Hunted off Faeroe Is. and Greenland.

PORPOISES: Phocoenidae

Porpoises are diminutive cetaceans with small rounded heads and almost no beak. They have spade-shaped teeth, unlike the cone-shaped teeth of dolphins. Most porpoises are found in coastal waters. There are 4 genera and 6 species worldwide, with 2 species occurring in U.S. and Canadian waters.

HARBOR PORPOISE   *Phocoena phocoena*   PL. 62
Common Porpoise, Puffing Pig, Puffer

Length 4½–6 ft. (1.4–1.8 m); wt. 120–143 lb. (54–65 kg). *Our smallest cetacean.* Stocky body; *small head, flippers, and flukes.* Dark gray above, grading to whitish below and on sides above flippers. No beak. *Low triangular dorsal fin.* **SIMILAR SPECIES:** Dall's Porpoise has striking black-and-white coloration; dolphins are larger with tall curved dorsal fins. **SOUNDS:** Soft puffing exhalation may be heard within about 300 ft. (100 m), hence local names "Puffer" or "Puffing Pig." **HABITS:** Shy and often difficult to approach; does not bow-ride. Seldom breaches but may arc and splash when pursuing prey. Makes short dives lasting 2–3 minutes. Travels singly or in small groups of 2–10.

HARBOR PORPOISE
Phocoena phocoena

Larger numbers may aggregate during migration or at feeding areas. Young are born May–July and females may breed annually or every other year. **HABITAT:** Cold coastal waters. **RANGE:** Alaska to s. Calif. in Pacific; Baffin I. to S.C. and occasionally Fla. in Atlantic. Nearly circumpolar in Northern Hemisphere. **STATUS:** Widespread and locally common. Some populations depleted by accidental catches in gill nets and by subsistence hunting.

DALL'S PORPOISE   *Phocoenoides dalli*   PL. 62

Length 6–7 ft. (1.8–2.2 m); wt. 300–485 lb. (135–220 kg). One of the smallest cetaceans. *Very stocky body,* small head, flippers, and flukes. *Striking black-and-white coloration:* mostly black with ex-

Dall's Porpoise is usually easy to identify, as it is an energetic swimmer that frequently shows its bicolored dorsal fin and white belly as it races alongside a boat.

tensive *white belly patch* and *white trailing edges on dorsal fin and flukes*. Rarely all-gray, all-black, or all-white. Young dark gray with a pale gray belly patch. Dorsal fin almost triangular. **SIMILAR SPECIES:** Often confused with Killer Whale, which is much larger and has a tall black dorsal fin. Pacific White-sided Dolphin has a taller, falcate dorsal fin and gray pattern on body. **HABITS:** A fast, energetic swimmer; creates a curved tail of spray from dorsal fin when surfacing. Usually surfaces about 4 times, exposing the characteristically marked dorsal fin and sometimes showing the white belly patch, but very seldom leaps out of the water. May surface slowly; appears to pause momentarily with the back and keeled tail stock exposed. After a dive it can travel some distance before surfacing again. Groups, usually numbering 2–12, often bow-ride or accompany boats, darting from side to side in an erratic and unpredictable path. Females breed every year, producing a single calf in June and mating July–Aug. **HABITAT:** Coastal and offshore waters. **RANGE:** North Pacific: s. Bering Sea to n. Baja Calif.; also west to Sea of Japan and Sea of Okhotsk. **STATUS:** Common to abundant. Often seen by whale watchers in the Northwest.

DALL'S PORPOISE
Phocoenoides dalli

As the name suggests, beaked whales usually have a pronounced beak. They have a pair of grooves on the throat forming an inverted "V" and no notch in the tail. Their small flippers fit into depressions (flipper pockets) when pressed against the body. The dorsal fin is relatively small, set about ⅔ of the way back from the head, and is usually triangular or slightly falcate. Adult males have 2–4 functional teeth in the lower jaw that sometimes develop into large tusks. The tusks are probably used for intraspecific fighting — in most species adult males are often heavily scratched and scarred while juveniles and females are largely unmarked.

Beaked whales are pelagic (offshore) species, and most are poorly known. They are thought to feed on deep-water squid and fish, remaining submerged for up to 2 hours. They capture prey by suction, as they do not possess functional teeth. The mesoplodonts (*Mesoplodon* spp.) are very difficult to distinguish; females and subadults in particular are almost certainly indistinguishable at sea, and even stranded individuals may be distinguishable only by experts. Stranded adult males can usually be identified by the shape and position of the tusks; it is unlikely that the tusks would be clearly visible at sea. The offshore habitat and retiring habits of these whales result in few live sightings, and much of our limited knowledge of this group is from stranded animals.

There are about 20 species in 6 genera of beaked whales worldwide, with 13 species entering North American waters.

CUVIER'S BEAKED WHALE   *Ziphius cavirostris*   PL. 64
Goose-beaked Whale

Length 16–23 ft. (5–7 m); wt. 2.5 tons (2,500 kg). Female is slightly larger than male. Color variable: dark brown or gray above, usually paler below. Males become whiter and more scarred with age; old males can appear all-white. Head small; adults have a bulging melon with a stubby beak and a distinctive "smile." Two small pointed teeth at tip of lower jaw in male. Body robust, cigar-shaped. **BLOW:** Low and inconspicuous, projects forward and to the left. **SIMILAR SPECIES:** Northern Bottlenose Whale (Atlantic only) has a bul-

CUVIER'S BEAKED WHALE
Ziphius cavirostris

bous forehead and well-defined beak. Beaked whales (*Mesoplodon* spp.) usually have longer beaks and flatter heads. **HABITS:** Wary of boats and seldom seen. Breaches occasionally. Makes deep dives to feed on squid and deep-water fish. Usually seen as singles or pairs, occasionally more. **RANGE:** North to Aleutian Is. in Pacific and N.S. in Atlantic. Found in deep waters worldwide. **STATUS:** Insufficient information available.

BAIRD'S BEAKED WHALE   *Berardius bairdii*   PL. 64

Length 36–43 ft. (11–13 m); wt. 7–14 tons (7,000–14,000 kg). Female is slightly larger than male. *Largest beaked whale.* Body dark, marked with many pale scratches. Bulbous *forehead clearly demarked from tubular beak*; lower jaw extends slightly beyond upper jaw. Four teeth on lower jaw, 2 visible at tip of jaw. *Small rounded dorsal fin is set more than ⅔ of the way back* from head to tail. **BLOW:** Low and bushy. **SIMILAR SPECIES:** Northern Bottlenose Whale has a more bulbous forehead, a shorter beak, and a longer dorsal fin. Beaked whales (*Mesoplodon* spp.) are generally smaller with flatter foreheads and usually no visible blow. **HABITS:** Wary and poorly known; occasionally breaches or spy-hops. Can stay underwater for an hour and dive to depths of 6,600 ft. (2,000 m). Eats deep-sea fish and squid. Very gregarious; travels in groups of up to 50 or more. **RANGE:** E. Pacific from Aleutian Is. to Gulf of Calif. and w. Mexico. Also nw. Pacific and Sea of Japan. **STATUS:** Poorly known. Only about 400 occur off the West Coast.

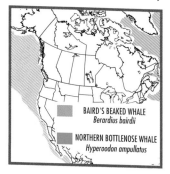

BAIRD'S BEAKED WHALE
Berardius bairdii

NORTHERN BOTTLENOSE WHALE
Hyperoodon ampullatus

NORTHERN BOTTLENOSE WHALE   PL. 64
Hyperoodon ampullatus
North Atlantic Bottle-nosed Whale

Length 23–32 ft. (7–9.8 m); wt. 7–10 tons (7,500–10,000 kg). Male is slightly larger than female. Older male has white beak and forehead. Young uniform chocolate brown, becoming paler and grayer with age. *Bulbous forehead*, most pronounced in adult male; *dolphinlike beak*. Two teeth at tip of lower jaw in males. Body robust; *dorsal fin prominent*, set well back. **BLOW:** Bushy, angled slightly forward, to about 6½ ft. (2 m) high. **SIMILAR SPECIES:** Superficially similar to Common Bottlenose Dolphin but much larger. Other beaked whales have less bulbous foreheads, are usually smaller, and lack a conspicuous blow. **HABITS:** After a long dive, remains near the surface for about 10 minutes and may show distinctive melon and beak. Flukes are sometimes raised before a dive. May stay underwater for up to 2 hours and reach depths of more than 3,300 ft. (1,000 m). Eats mainly squid, also some pelagic fish, shrimp, and sea stars. Social; usually travels in groups of 2–10 but may migrate in schools of several hundred. Female matures at 9 years and gives birth every other year. **RANGE:** W. North Atlantic. Winters from N.Y. to Grand Bank, Nfld.; some migrate as far as Baffin I. in summer. Also found in e. North Atlantic. **STATUS:** Commercial whaling for this species ceased in 1972, but stocks thought to be critically depleted.

LONGMAN'S BEAKED WHALE   *Indopacetus pacificus*   Pl. 64
Tropical Bottlenose Whale

Length 23–26 ft. (7–8 m). Brownish above, paler below. Bulbous melon and moderately long beak. Two teeth near tip of lower jaw in male. Dorsal fin prominent, set well back. **BLOW:** Low, bushy. **SIMILAR SPECIES:** Beaked whales (*Mesoplodon* spp.) are smaller. Northern Bottlenose Whale has a more pronounced melon (ranges do not overlap). Cuvier's Beaked Whale has a shorter beak and sloping forehead. **HABITS:** Dives for 18–25 minutes. Has been seen breaching. Travels in large groups of up to 100. **RANGE:** Deep tropical waters, in Pacific off Baja Calif. and southward. Possible sighting off Ore. Not confirmed in Atlantic, possible sighting in Gulf of Mexico. **STATUS:** Very poorly known, thought to be rare.

LONGMAN'S BEAKED WHALE
Indopacetus pacificus

PERRIN'S BEAKED WHALE   *Mesoplodon perrini*   Pl. 64

Length about 14 ft. (4 m). Dark above, paler below. Mouthline straight, beak rather short. Male has a *narrow tooth on each side of the lower jaw about ½ in. (1–2 cm) back from the tip of the snout*. **SIMILAR SPECIES:** Straight mouth line and teeth at tip of jaw separate this from other n. Pacific mesoplodonts; Cuvier's Beaked Whale has a stubby beak and adult male is often white. **RANGE:** Known only from 5 strandings on s. Calif. coast. **STATUS:** This species was recently described and its status is unknown. The stranded animals were initially identified as Hector's Beaked Whale (*M. hectori*), a species now considered to be restricted to the Southern Hemisphere.

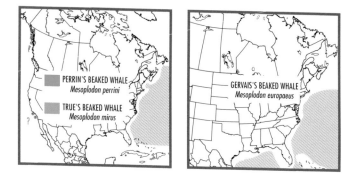

TRUE'S BEAKED WHALE *Mesoplodon mirus* Pl. 64

Length 16½–17½ ft. (5–5.3 m); wt. about 1.4 tons (1,400 kg). Gray above, pale gray below. *Mouthline nearly straight, beak relatively long and narrow, melon rounded.* Male has 2 *teeth at tip of lower jaw.* **SIMILAR SPECIES:** Other *Mesoplodon* males have teeth placed farther back on jaw (although male Gervais's Beaked Whale is very similar and probably indistinguishable at sea, and females or young of this species are virtually indistinguishable both at sea and stranded). Cuvier's Beaked Whale has a much shorter, stockier beak. **RANGE:** W. North Atlantic from N.S. to se. Fla. Also e. Atlantic from Scotland to France; South Africa; Australia. **STATUS:** Uncommon. Known from 16 strandings on the East Coast.

GERVAIS'S BEAKED WHALE Pl. 64
Mesoplodon europaeus

Length 15–17 ft. (4.5–5.2 m); wt. about 1.7 tons (1,700 kg). Dark gray above, pale gray below. *Lower jaw almost straight in both male and female;* beak relatively short. Male has 1 *small tooth on each lower jaw about ⅓ of the way up mouth from tip of beak.* **SIMILAR SPECIES:** Male recognized by position of teeth near tip of snout. See True's Beaked Whale. Sowerby's Beaked Whale has a much longer beak and usually occurs farther north. **RANGE:** Warm temperate and tropical Atlantic waters from N.Y. to Fla. and Gulf of Mexico; also through Caribbean region to n. South America; a few records from Europe and w. Africa. **STATUS:** The most commonly stranded *Mesoplodon* on the East Coast (around 50 strandings).

SOWERBY'S BEAKED WHALE *Mesoplodon bidens* Pl. 64
North Sea Beaked Whale

Length 15½–18 ft. (4.7–5.5 m). Dark gray above, usually paler below. Adult often marked with pale streaks and splotches. Lower jaw slightly arched; *beak long and narrow.* Male has *1 tooth about halfway along each lower jaw.* **SIMILAR SPECIES:** Male recognized by medial position of teeth; female and young have long beaks but may be indistinguishable from other beaked whales. **HABITS:** Has been seen in groups of 8–10. Can dive for at least 28 minutes. **RANGE:** W. North Atlantic from Lab. to Mass.; one record from Gulf of Mexico, Fla. More common in North Sea and e. North Atlantic. Mainly in cold temperate waters. **STATUS:** Uncommon. May be vulnerable in Canada (COSEWIC).

PYGMY BEAKED WHALE *Mesoplodon peruvianus* Pl. 64

Length about 5 ft. (1.6 m). Dark gray above, paler below. *Lower jaw sharply arched in male, curved in female.* Beak relatively short. One tooth on each side of jaw of male, more than halfway up mouth from tip of beak. Tail flukes unusually broad (¼ body length). **SIMILAR SPECIES:** Other beaked whales are much larger. **RANGE:** Known in U.S. only from strandings off Calif.; ranges from Baja Calif. to Chile; one recent stranding from New Zealand. **STATUS:** Recently described and very poorly known. Some are killed in drift gill nets off South America.

HUBBS'S BEAKED WHALE *Mesoplodon carlhubbsi* Pl. 64
Arch-beaked Whale

Length 17½ ft. (5.3 m); wt. 1.4 tons (1,400 kg). *Striking white cap and white beak on male.* Male mainly blackish, heavily scarred. Female and young gray above, whitish below. *Lower jaw sharply arched in male, beak rather short. Large tooth* on each side of lower jaw near highest point of arch. **SIMILAR SPECIES:** Stejneger's Beaked Whale male lacks white cap and beak. Female and young similar to other *Mesoplodon* spp. **RANGE:** North Pacific. Prince Rupert, B.C., to s. Calif.; also Japan. **STATUS:** Some are killed in drift gill nets off California.

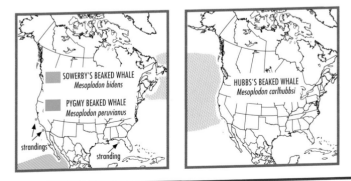

SOWERBY'S BEAKED WHALE
Mesoplodon bidens

PYGMY BEAKED WHALE
Mesoplodon peruvianus

strandings

stranding

HUBBS'S BEAKED WHALE
Mesoplodon carlhubbsi

GINKGO-TOOTHED BEAKED WHALE
Mesoplodon ginkgodens

Pl. 64

Length 15–16 ft. (4.7–4.9 m); wt. unknown. Adult male is mostly dark gray with some white spots on lower belly (usually not scarred); female and subadult are gray above, paler below. Beak moderately long. *Mouthline curves up sharply about halfway from tip of beak in male.* Male has a *broad flat tooth on each side of lower jaw, about halfway down beak.* Shape of male tooth resembles

gingko leaf and is broadest of all beaked whales, 4 in. (100–120 mm) wide, but does not project above beak. **SIMILAR SPECIES:** Broad low tooth of male distinctive. Female and subadult are indistinguishable from other *Mesoplodon* spp. **RANGE:** E. North Pacific off s. Calif. and Baja Calif.; also w. North Pacific and Indian Oceans. **STATUS:** Very few records from West Coast. Poorly known worldwide.

BLAINVILLE'S BEAKED WHALE
Mesoplodon densirostris
Dense-beaked Whale

Pl. 64

Length to 15½ ft. (4.7 m); wt. about 1 ton (1,000 kg). *Male entirely gray,* usually *heavily scarred and blotched;* female and young dark above, paler below. *Lower jaw arched;* in male extends over upper jaw with a *large broad tusk at highest point.* **SIMILAR SPECIES:** Male recognized by flat head with highly arched jaw and exposed tusklike tooth; female and subadult easily confused with other beaked whales. **HABITS:** Seen in groups of 3–7. **RANGE:** N.S. to Fla. and Gulf of Mexico in Atlantic; north to n. Calif. in Pacific. Worldwide in tropical and temperate waters. **STATUS:** The most widely distributed *Mesoplodon*.

STEJNEGER'S BEAKED WHALE
Mesoplodon stejnegeri
Bering Sea Beaked Whale

Pl. 64

Length to 18 ft. (5.5 m); wt. about 1.4 tons (1,500 kg). Gray or blackish, sometimes with pale areas on head and mouth. Adult male often heavily scarred. *Mouthline sharply arched in male, beak rather short.* Large *tusklike tooth on each side of lower jaw, just in front of highest part of arch.* **SIMILAR SPECIES:** Hubbs's Beaked Whale

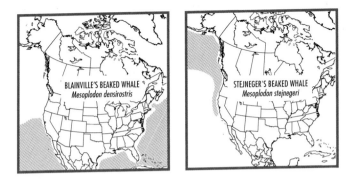

BLAINVILLE'S BEAKED WHALE
Mesoplodon densirostris

STEJNEGER'S BEAKED WHALE
Mesoplodon stejnegeri

is similar but has a white cap on melon and white-tipped beak. Female and young indistinguishable from other *Mesoplodon* spp. **HABITS:** Travels in groups of 3–15. Feeds on deep-sea squid. **RANGE:** S. Bering Sea and Aleutians to s. Calif. Also Commander Is. (Russia) to Japan. Found in deep continental slope waters. **STATUS:** Poorly known.

SPERM WHALES: Physeteridae, Kogiidae

Sperm whales usually have teeth only in the narrow, underslung lower jaw. They are specialized for deep diving and have reached depths of over 1 mi. (2 km) below the surface. Their name is derived from the large spermaceti organ on the head. This oil-filled organ is thought to play some role in deep diving: it may aid in nitrogen removal or buoyancy, or it may function as an acoustic lens in echolocation. Sperm whales produce series of intense clicks that are probably used for echolocating in deep unlit waters. The Pygmy and Dwarf Sperm Whales appear to be only distantly related to the Sperm Whale and are placed in their own family, Kogiidae.

SPERM WHALE *Physeter macrocephalus*   **Pl. 66**
Length 33–60 ft. (10–18 m); wt. 7–56 tons (7,000–57,000 kg). Male is almost twice as large as female. *Head huge, rectangular;* single blowhole placed far forward on head and offset to left. *Underslung jaw with whitish lips;* peglike teeth on lower jaw only. Head often marked with scratches and circular scars; *body appears wrinkled.* Dorsal fin replaced by low hump followed by series of bumps along tail stock. Tail flukes dark above and below, straight-edged, and deeply notched. **BLOW:** Bushy, about 8 ft. (2.5 m) high, *directed sharply forward and to the left.* **SIMILAR SPECIES:** Squared-off head and

SPERM WHALE
Physeter macrocephalus

angled blow distinctive. Back and tail could resemble Humpback, but tail of Humpback is concave and irregular along the edge and white below. **HABITS:** A deep diver; emerges and blows sharply, then stays near the surface for up to an hour, blowing as many as 50 times before diving again. Flukes are raised vertically well above the water before a dive. Dives to depths of over a mile (2,000 m) and can stay underwater for 1–2 hours. Feeds mainly on squid and octopi. Seen singly or in groups of up to 50. Females and young form stable groups that are joined by an adult male during the breeding season. Large males venture toward polar regions in summer, females and subadults stay in temperate waters; all move into warmer water in winter. Females mature at 7–13 years and breed every 3–6 years. Calves are born after a 14- to 15-month gestation and nurse for 2 years. **HABITAT:** Deep waters, especially along the edge of the continental shelf. **RANGE:** North to Aleutian Is. in Pacific and Baffin I. in Atlantic. Found worldwide. **STATUS:** Endangered (USFWS, CITES Appendix I). Hunted until 1979 but still one of the most abundant great whales, with a world population of about 1.5 million.

A group of four Sperm Whales underwater, displaying many characteristics of this species: a massive squared-off head, small underslung lower jaw, and wrinkly skin on the body.

PYGMY SPERM WHALE   *Kogia breviceps*   Pl. 62
Length 9–11 ft. (2.7–3.4 m); wt. 660–880 lb. (300–400 kg). *Squared-off head, false gill on side of head. Underslung, sharklike lower jaw*

with 12–16 (rarely 10–11) pairs of teeth; no teeth in upper jaw. No throat creases. *Small (less than 8 in./20 cm high) dorsal fin set almost ⅔ of the way back from head.* **BLOW:** Inconspicuous, low. **SIMILAR SPECIES:** Dwarf Sperm Whale is smaller with a larger dorsal fin and fewer lower teeth. **HABITS:** Seldom seen; rises slowly to the surface and produces a slight blow. Sometimes rests near the surface with back of head above water and tail hanging down. If alarmed it may excrete reddish feces before diving. Feeds on squid and deep-sea fish. Seen in small groups of 1–6. Known mainly from strandings. **HABITAT:** Warm temperate and tropical regions, mostly in deep offshore waters. **RANGE:** To Wash. in Pacific; north to N.S. in Atlantic. Worldwide to about 40° in both northern and southern latitudes. **STATUS:** Uncommon or rare in most areas. Sometimes caught in gill nets.

PYGMY SPERM WHALE
Kogia breviceps

DWARF SPERM WHALE   *Kogia simus*   Pl. 62

Length 7–9 ft. (2.1–2.7 m); wt. 300–600 lb. (135–270 kg). *Squarish head, false gill on side of head. Underslung, sharklike lower jaw* with 8–11 (rarely 12–13) pairs of teeth; up to 3 pairs of teeth in upper jaw. Pair of *short creases in the throat. Dorsal fin erect, relatively large (over 8 in./20 cm high)*, positioned slightly more than halfway down back. **BLOW:** Inconspicuous, low. **SIMILAR SPECIES:** Pygmy Sperm Whale is slightly larger with a smaller dorsal fin set farther back. Dolphins have more rounded heads and are more active. **HABITS:** Similar to Pygmy Sperm Whale. When resting near the surface, less of the head is exposed. Seen in small groups of 1–10. Known mainly from strandings. **HABITAT:** Warm temperate and tropical waters, mainly on the continental slope or deeper water. **RANGE:** To Vancouver I. in Pacific; north to Chesapeake Bay in Atlantic. Worldwide to about 40° in both northern and southern latitudes. **STATUS:** Uncommon. Not recognized

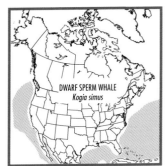

DWARF SPERM WHALE
Kogia simus

as a distinct species until 1966 and difficult to identify at sea, thus information on population size and range scanty.

BALEEN WHALES: Mysticeti

Baleen whales are toothless. They have plates of baleen, a keratinous material, that hang from the roof of the mouth. The inner edges of the baleen plates are fringed and overlapping, forming a fine mesh. These whales feed by taking in large mouthfuls of water and forcing the water out through the sievelike baleen. Prey, mainly small crustaceans, are trapped on the baleen and swallowed. Baleen whales have 2 blowholes placed well back on the top of the head.

Baleen whales include the largest of all whales, the Blue Whale. Most species are large, but Minke Whales and Pygmy Right Whales (found only in the Southern Hemisphere) are smaller than some of the toothed whales.

RIGHT WHALES: Balaenidae

Northern Hemisphere right whales are huge baleen whales with massive heads and arched jaws. These whales have robust bodies and no dorsal fin. The baleen plates can be up to 13 ft. (4 m) long and are finely fringed for filtering small plankton. They usually feed by skimming open-mouthed near the water surface. Three of 4 species occur in North American waters.

NORTH ATLANTIC RIGHT WHALE   PL. 66
Eubalaena glacialis

Length 50–60 ft. (15–18 m); wt. 59–98 tons (60,000–100,000 kg). Female is larger than male. Body rotund, tapering to narrow tail stock. Body mottled *blackish*, white patch on belly. *Head very large*, about ⅓ body length, marked with *whitish growths* (callosities). Flippers very broad. Back smooth with *no dorsal fin*. Flukes large, black, with smooth margins and a deep cleft. **BLOW:** V-shaped, low and bushy. **SIMILAR SPECIES:** Bowhead lacks callosities on head (where ranges overlap, Bowhead is present in winter, Right Whale in summer). Humpback and Gray Whales have ridges on lower back. **SOUNDS:** Low-pitched moans and belches. **HABITS:** Surfaces to blow about every 5–20 minutes. Blows about twice a minute 5–10 times before diving and usually raises flukes as it descends. May breach or flipper-slap noisily. Eats small crustaceans including krill, feeding at the surface or at depths of up to 900 ft. (275 m). Usually seen singly or in small groups of 2–12. Summers in the Gulf of Maine and Scotian Shelf. Courtship takes place here in fall; groups of adults splash and roll but do not fight, and a female may mate with several males. Migrates south in late fall. Some females spend the winter in the waters off Georgia and Florida where they give birth after a 1-year gestation. Mother and calf stay together for a year, moving north in March or April.

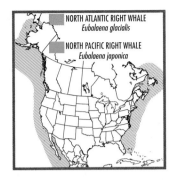

HABITAT: Temperate waters, often close to shore. RANGE: W. North Atlantic from s. Fla. to Lab.; also European waters from Iceland and Norway to Spain. STATUS: Endangered (USFWS). Previously common, this whale became known as the "right whale" to hunt because it swims close to shore, swims slowly enough to be approached by sailboats, floats when killed, and yields long pieces of baleen and much oil from the thick blubber. Once the whale most familiar to people, the two northern right whales are now the rarest baleen whales in the world. Hunting right whales was banned in 1937, but the population has not recovered — North Atlantic Right Whales presently number only about 300. Entanglement and collision with ships still account for about 30 percent of annual mortalities.

NORTH PACIFIC RIGHT WHALE *Eubalaena japonica*
Very similar to North Atlantic Right Whale in appearance and habits, but genetically distinct. HABITS: As for North Atlantic Right Whale. Summer movements of the remnant population in the North Pacific are poorly known. It has been reported occasionally off the West Coast and Baja California, but calving grounds are unknown and no calves have been seen in e. North Pacific in over 100 years. RANGE: E. North Pacific from Baja Calif. to n. Alaska; also w. North Pacific from Taiwan to Sea of Okhotsk. STATUS: Critically endangered. Probably only about 100 remain in e. North Pacific.

BOWHEAD WHALE *Balaena mysticetus*   Pl. 66
Length 46–60 ft. (14–18 m); wt. 60–98 tons (61,000–100,000 kg). Female larger than male. Body almost entirely black though may have white scars; rotund, tapering to narrow tail stock. *Head very large* (⅓ or more of body length). *Lower lips and chin often white;*

lower jaw massive; *arched upper jaw.* Back smooth with *no dorsal fin.* **BLOW:** V-shaped. **SIMILAR SPECIES:** Other large whales are usually not seen as far north. Gray Whale has ridges on the spine and knobby skin. Blue Whale is paler and has a small dorsal fin. **SOUNDS:** Low-frequency grunts and moans. **HABITS:** Can remain underwater for 40 minutes or more. Sometimes hangs vertically in water with head exposed. May breach or slap water with flipper or tail. Feeding on zooplankton, this huge-mouthed whale has longer baleen than all other whales, enabling it to process enormous quantities of water. Skims at the surface and may also feed near the bottom in shallow waters. Usually travels alone or in small groups but may congregate at feeding areas. Winters near the southern limits of pack ice, moving north in spring as the ice breaks up. Females probably calve every 3–4 years; most young are born in spring. **HABITAT:** Close to polar pack ice. **RANGE:** Previously circumpolar in Arctic; present distribution patchy. **STATUS:** Endangered (USFWS). Heavily depleted by whaling in the past two centuries. Presently numbers about 9,000. The largest population (Beaufort Sea and n. Alaska) is still subject to subsistence hunting by indigenous groups but is healthy and appears to be growing. All other populations are very small.

BOWHEAD WHALE
Balaena mysticetus

GRAY WHALE: Eschrichtiidae

The Gray Whale is the only species in the family Eschrichtiidae. This is the only baleen whale that habitually feeds on the sea bottom.

GRAY WHALE *Eschrichtius robustus*   **Pl. 66**
Length 36–50 ft. (11–15 m); wt. 16–33 tons (16,000–34,000 kg). Female slightly larger than male. Body *mottled gray with patches of*

Gray Whale and calf. With its mottled gray skin and low dorsal hump, this is the focal species of the huge California and Baja whale-watching industry.

whitish barnacles. Baleen short, yellowish, with coarse fringes. Head narrow, V-shaped from above, slightly down-curved in profile. Dorsal fin replaced by *low hump and followed by humps or ridges along the tail stock.* **BLOW:** Low (10 ft./3 m) and puffy; may appear heart-shaped. **SIMILAR SPECIES:** Humpback has long flippers. Sperm Whale is not mottled. **HABITS:** Typically blows 3–5 times at intervals of 15–30 seconds, then dives for 3–5 minutes when traveling; may dive for up to 15 minutes when feeding. Flukes often raised above the water before a dive. Raises head vertically out of the water (spy-hops), and sometimes breaches. Feeds by sucking up amphipods and other invertebrates from the sea floor. Seen alone or in groups of up to 16. Feeds in northern seas May–Nov., then migrates south to breeding grounds off Mexico. Female matures at 5–11 years; mates Nov.–Jan. and gives birth 13 months later. Calving takes place in shallow lagoons; young travels north with its mother and is weaned at 7 months. **HABITAT:** Coastal waters. **RANGE:** Pacific Ocean. Summers in Bering, Chukchi, and w. Beaufort Seas; winters off Baja Calif. and mainland Mexico. Also found in w. North Pacific. **STATUS:** Previously listed as endangered, it was delisted in 1994 when population reached about 20,000. Gray Whales are a key species in the large whale-watching industry. Became extinct in Atlantic in 1700s; very rare in w. Pacific.

GRAY WHALE
Eschrichtius robustus

Rorquals are baleen whales with a small dorsal fin and grooves or pleats on the throat and chest. These whales feed by actively lunging and gulping or by passively skimming at the surface. As water enters the mouth, the throat pleats open to form a huge pouch (the whale assumes the form of a giant tadpole) and an enormous volume of water is taken in. When the mouth closes the pleats are contracted and the tongue is pushed up against the roof of the mouth, forcing water out through the baleen. Prey — mainly krill but also small schooling fish for all but Blue Whales — is trapped on the fringes of the baleen.

Most rorquals are migratory, spending the summer feeding in cold high-latitude waters and wintering at low latitudes. Mating and calving take place on wintering grounds, where they feed little if at all.

BLUE WHALE *Balaenoptera musculus*   Pl. 65

Length 72–92 ft. (22–28 m); wt. 60–170 tons (61,000–173,000 kg). *Largest animal that has ever lived.* Female larger than male. *Skin bluish, mottled with pale gray.* Baleen black. *Head broad, U-shaped* when viewed from above. Body very long; *small dorsal fin* positioned on last ¼ of back. **BLOW:** Narrow, vertical, and tall (up to 30 ft./9 m in still air). **SIMILAR SPECIES:** Fin Whale is darker and not mottled, head V-shaped from above and asymmetrically colored, dorsal fin larger. **SOUNDS:** Makes loud but very-low-frequency calls (inaudible to humans) that can travel thousands of miles in deep water. **HABITS:** Blow is followed by view of long back; after 3–4 seconds the small dorsal fin appears. Usually resurfaces to breathe up to 20 times at 20-second intervals. On the last breath before diving, the tail flukes may appear just above the water. One of the fastest whales, it can travel at 30 mph (48 km/hr) if pursued. Feeds almost exclusively on krill. Usually seen alone or in small groups. In fall, travels south from feeding grounds and probably does not feed until the next spring. A single calf is born in late fall or winter. Calves are nursed for 7–8 months and gain up to 200 lb. (90 kg) per day. Females are sexually mature at 5 years and breed every 2–3 years thereafter. **HABITAT:** All oceans, often on the edge of continental shelves but also in deep water and in shallow inshore water. **RANGE:** North to n. Alaska in Pacific and to Baffin I. in Atlantic. Found worldwide. **STATUS:** Endangered (USFWS). About 2,000 remain in the North Pacific and a few hundred in the North Atlantic. Numbers have not increased greatly since whaling was halted in 1965.

Blue Whale, from above. Note its very large rounded head and the small dorsal fin positioned far back on the body.

BLUE WHALE
Balaenoptera musculus

IN WHALE *Balaenoptera physalus*

Finback, Finner, Common Rorqual

Length 59–79 ft. (18–24 m); wt. 44–69 tons (45,000–70,000 kg). Female is larger than male. Mainly dark gray, often with a pale chevron behind head. *Head narrow, V-shaped* from above. Asymmetrical color on head: *right lower jaw and right front baleen white, left lower jaw gray* and remainder of baleen striped yellowish and blue-gray. Dorsal fin small but prominent, positioned on last ⅓ of back. **BLOW:** Tall (to 20 ft./6 m), bushy, and cone-shaped. **SIMILAR SPECIES:** Blue Whale is mottled blue-gray and has a smaller dorsal fin that appears well after the blow. Sei and Bryde's Whales (easily confused) are uniformly colored on lower jaws. **SOUNDS:** Makes high-volume, very-low-frequency calls (inaudible to humans) that can travel thousands of miles in deep water. **HABITS:** This is one of the more commonly seen large whales in the w. North Atlantic. Blow is followed by view of back for 1–2 seconds before dorsal fin ap-

FIN WHALE
Balaenoptera physalus

pears. Usually surfaces to breathe about 10 times at intervals of 15–20 seconds. On the last dive, the tail stock behind the dorsal fin appears, but flukes are not raised. Dives last 5–10 minutes. One of the fastest whales, it can travel at 20 mph (32 km/hr). Feeds on krill and small schooling fish. Lunges into massed prey and often rolls onto its side while gulping water or when pursuing prey. Commonly seen alone or in small groups but may form temporary large aggregations. Most populations move northward in spring and south in fall, others may remain in tropical areas year-round. Mating takes place midwinter, single calves are born a year later. **HABITAT:** Favors continental shelf waters (but also found in coastal and offshore waters) at temperate and cold latitudes; less common in tropical waters. **RANGE:** North to w. Alaska in Pacific and to Baffin I. in Atlantic. Occurs worldwide. **STATUS:** Endangered (USFWS). Some populations appear to be recovering from earlier whaling.

SEI WHALE *Balaenoptera borealis* **PL. 65**

Length 43–62 ft. (13–19 m); wt. 8.4–15 tons (8,500–15,500 kg). Female is larger than male. Dark gray above, *marked with oval scars* (appears to be spotted). Baleen blackish with *very fine, curly white fringes.* Head somewhat pointed and V-shaped from above. *Both lower jaws dark.* Single ridge from blowholes to snout. Dorsal fin

small but prominent, *usually falcate,* positioned on last ⅓ of body. **BLOW:** Inverted cone, to 15 ft. (4.5 m). **SIMILAR SPECIES:** Fin Whale has asymmetrically colored lower jaws and an unspotted back. It shows back after blow, before appearance of dorsal fin. Bryde's Whale (easily confused, only distinguishable at close range) has 3 ridges on rostrum. **HABITS:** Rises to breathe at a shallow angle so that blow, back, and dorsal fin are visible almost simultaneously. Usually does not dive deeply after breathing, instead slips under the water without raising lower back or tail. Feeds on copepods, krill, squid, and small fish by skimming near the surface and by gulping. Usually found alone or in small groups but may aggregate at feeding areas. Migrates south in fall and northward in spring. Also may suddenly appear in an area and subsequently disappear. Single young are born in winter. **HABITAT:** Temperate coastal and offshore waters. **RANGE:** North to w. Alaska in Pacific and to Baffin I. in Atlantic. Occurs worldwide. **STATUS:** Endangered (USFWS).

RYDE'S WHALE   *Balaenoptera brydei*   **Pl. 65**

Length 39–46 ft. (12–14 m); wt. 11–16 tons (11,300–16,200 kg). Female is larger than male. Dark gray above, sometimes marked with oval scars. Baleen dark gray or black with *coarse gray fringes*. Head not sharply pointed. *Three ridges on rostrum* in most individuals. Dorsal fin small but prominent, *usually falcate* and often with a frayed rear margin, positioned on last ⅓ of body. **BLOW:** Similar to Sei Whale. **SIMILAR SPECIES:** Sei Whale (very easily confused) has a single ridge on the rostrum. **HABITS:** Surfaces at a steep angle, exposing part of head, then rolling sharply and humping the back before diving. Does not raise flukes above the water before a dive. When chased, responds by making frequent changes in direction rather than increasing speed. Feeds by actively lunging and favors schooling fish as prey. Some populations are resident year-round in shallow waters; those that occupy deep waters migrate north in spring and south in fall. Young are usually born in winter; some nonmigrant populations may breed at any time of year. **HABITAT:** Tropical and subtropical waters, both coastal and offshore. **RANGE:** Chesapeake Bay and southward in Atlantic. Usually not north of Baja Calif. in Pacific (2 strays seen off s. Calif.). Equator to about 40° in both hemispheres. **STATUS:** Status poorly known due to earlier confusion with Sei Whale. **NOTE:** The smaller form from Indian and w. Pacific Oceans is considered to be a distinct species, *B. edeni*. (Some authors consider both forms to be a single species under the name *B. edeni*.)

BRYDE'S WHALE
Balaenoptera brydei

MINKE WHALE   *Balaenoptera acutorostrata*   **Pl. 65, Skull Pl. 14**
Lesser Rorqual, Piked Whale

Length 23–33 ft. (7–10 m); wt. 14,000–20,000 lb. (6,300–9,200 kg). Female is slightly larger than male. *Head narrow and sharply pointed.* Baleen yellowish white with fine white fringes. Single ridge on rostrum. *Band of white on flippers.* Relatively *tall, falcate dorsal fin*. **BLOW:** Low and inconspicuous, often exhales underwater. **SIMILAR SPECIES:** Other baleen whales are larger. Sei and Bryde's Whales lack white bands on flippers. **HABITS:** When breathing, back and dorsal fin appear at the same time; blow is seldom visible. Before a dive, raises tail stock above the water but usually does not expose flukes. Often raises the pointed snout when surfacing and occasionally breaches. Feeds on small fish, krill, and copepods.

Minke Whale. This small rorqual has a pointed head when viewed from above, and bright white patches on its flippers that are visible below the water.

Mainly seen alone or in pairs but may congregate in groups of 100 or more at feeding areas. Some migrate north in spring and south in fall; others move little. Young may be born in summer or winter; mature females give birth every year. **HABITAT:** Coastal and offshore waters. **RANGE:** North to Point Barrow in Pacific and to Davis Strait and Baffin Bay in Atlantic. Widely distributed in both North Atlantic and North Pacific. **STATUS:** Relatively common. Hunted by fisheries in Korea and Japan.

HUMPBACK WHALE   *Megaptera novaeangliae*   Pl. 66

Length 36–49 ft. (11–15 m); wt. 25–44 tons (25,000–45,000 kg). Head broad and rounded, *snout and lips marked with fleshy knobs.* Baleen black with coarse fringes. *Flippers very long, bumpy on leading edge,* white above and below (in North Atlantic) or black above, white below (in North Pacific). Dorsal fin humped or stepped, followed by a series of *bumps on the tail stock.* Tail flukes broad, deeply notched, white below. **BLOW:** Short (10 ft./3 m), broad, and bushy. **SIMILAR SPECIES:** Very long flippers are unique among large whales. **SOUNDS:** Long complex songs (audible to humans) given by

MINKE WHALE
Balaenoptera acutorostrata

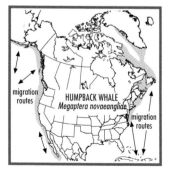

migration routes

HUMPBACK WHALE
Megaptera novaeangliae

migration routes

Breaching Humpback Whale displays the extremely long, knobby flippers that characterize this species. It is more acrobatic than other large whales.

males during the winter breeding season. Grunts and whoops or song fragments may be given in summer. **HABITS:** Blows 2–8 times before raising flukes high into the air and diving for up to 20 minutes. Acrobatic; can leap clear of the water when breaching, also frequently slaps water with long flippers or tail. Feeds on schooling fish or krill, using several different feeding methods. Groups may cooperate to produce a curtain or cloud of bubbles to trap and concentrate prey. Also lunge-feeds. Most commonly seen alone or in small groups but may congregate in feeding and wintering grounds. Feeds in summer at high latitudes, in fall moves south to tropical waters to mate or give birth. Single young are born every 2 years. **HABITAT:** In winter and summer found in coastal areas or near islands; migrates through open oceans. **RANGE:** W. Alaska and Aleutian Is. to Baja Calif. in Pacific, Baffin I. to N.Y. in Atlantic. Occurs worldwide. **STATUS:** Endangered (USFWS). Populations reduced by overexploitation are presently recovering only in the w. North Atlantic.

GLOSSARY

altricial. Young born relatively helpless (usually hairless, blind, and unable to walk) and requiring a long period of parental care.

antitragus. Flap of skin at the base of the ear (in front of the tragus in some bats).

baculum. Penis bone.

baleen. A series of comblike, keratinous plates hanging in rows from the upper jaws of mysticete (baleen) whales.

blowhole. Nostril of a cetacean, located on the top of the head.

breaching. Term used to describe a whale or dolphin leaping out of the water.

bow-ride. Swimming immediately ahead of a boat or large whale.

buff, buffy. Pale yellowish brown.

calcar. Cartilage or bone projecting from the ankle, along the leading edge of the tail membrane of a bat.

continental shelf. Submerged, relatively flat part of a continent, from shore to a depth of about 600 ft. (180 m).

crepuscular. Active at dawn or dusk.

cusp. A pointed or rounded projection on the biting surface of a tooth.

dental formula. A shorthand enumeration of the type and number of teeth on one side of the jaw (see skull plates).

dentition. The number and kind of teeth.

diurnal. Active by day.

dormancy. A resting condition characterized by reduced body temperature and slowed breathing and heartbeat. Also called torpor.

echolocation. Using sound echoes (in air, usually at high frequency) to determine the position of an object.

estivation. A period of dormancy in the summer.

falcate. Sickle-shaped (as in the dorsal fin of some dolphins).

fenestrated. Having windows or perforations (as in the skulls of rabbits).

feral. Domestic animals that have established breeding populations in the wild.

flukes. The two horizontally flattened halves of a whale's tail.

foramen, foramina. An opening or orifice in a bone.

forb. An herb that is not a grass.

fossorial. Living underground.

gestation. Pregnancy.

gill net. A net that is suspended vertically in the water.

guard hairs. Long, stiff hairs that extend beyond the underfur.

hibernation. A state of winter dormancy in which body temperature drops for an extended period and all bodily functions are greatly slowed.

home range. Area used by an animal in its normal daily activities. Not defended.

lanugo. Soft downy coat of fur, as on some newborn seals.

lek. A display area in which several males aggregate to attract females for mating.

mammae. Milk-producing organs (mammary glands).

melanistic. Dark or black.

melon. The bulging forehead of a toothed whale.

metatarsal gland. Bare patch of thickened skin on the lower part of the hind leg of a deer.

migration. Movement from one area to another, usually on a seasonal basis.

montane. Inhabiting or pertaining to mountainous regions.

noseleaf. Triangular flap of skin on the nose of a bat.

nocturnal. Active at night.

oldfield. A pasture or field that has not been cultivated or mown and has some early-succession shrub growth.

palmate. Flattened and branching, as in some antlers.

pelagic. Living in offshore waters, not coastal.

pinna, pinnae. Outer part of the ear or ears.

precocial. Young born relatively well developed, fully furred, with eyes open, and usually able to walk at birth.

prehensile tail. Tail with a gripping tip that can support all or part of an animal's weight.

recurved. To curve or bend back, as in the shape of the incisor teeth of some rodents.

riparian. Along the banks of a river or water course.

rostrum. The forward extension of the nasal region of the face and upper jaw.

sagittal crest. Ridge of bone along the midline of the top of the skull.

spy-hopping. Term used for whales and dolphins raising vertically out of the water and scanning their surroundings.

tail stock. Base of the tail of a whale or dolphin.

tines. Branches of a deer's antlers.

tragus. Fleshy projection inside the external ear of most bats.

ultrasonic. Sound waves above the range of hearing of most humans.

ungulate. Hoofed mammal.

unicuspid. Tooth with a single projecting surface or cusp, used to describe the small teeth of shrews between the first incisor and the molar teeth.

zygomatic arch. Arch of bone between the rostrum and braincase below the eye.

REFERENCES

TECHNICAL WORKS AND REFERENCES NOTED IN THE INTRODUCTION

Hall, E. Raymond. *The mammals of North America,* second edition. 1981. New York: John Wiley and Sons.

Nowak, Ronald M. *Walker's mammals of the world,* sixth edition. 1999. Baltimore: Johns Hopkins University Press.

Springer, Mark S., Michael J. Stanhope, Ole Madsen, and Wilfred W. de Jong. "Molecules consolidate the placental mammal key." 2004. *Trends in Ecology and Evolution* 19, no. 8.

Wilson, Don E., and DeeAnn M. Reeder, eds. *Mammal species of the world: A taxonomic and geographic reference,* third edition. 2005. Baltimore: Johns Hopkins University Press.

REGIONAL GUIDES

The books listed below are a selection of the numerous federal, state, and provincial guides that are available. Many other regional guides can be found via the Web.

Banfield, A.W.F. *The mammals of Canada.* 1974. Toronto: University of Toronto Press.

Dalquest, Walter W. *Mammals of Washington.* 1948. Lawrence, KS: University of Kansas.

Davis, William B., and David J. Schmidly. *The mammals of Texas.* 1994. Austin, TX: Texas Parks and Wildlife Press.

Feldhamer, George A., Bruce C. Thompson, and Joseph A. Chapman, eds. *Wild mammals of North America: Biology, management, and conservation,* second edition. 2003. Baltimore: Johns Hopkins University Press.

Hoffmeister, Donald F. *Mammals of Arizona.* 1986. Tucson: University of Arizona Press.

Jameson, E. W., Jr., and Hans J. Peeters. *California mammals.* 1988. Berkeley: University of California Press.

Merritt, Joseph F. *Guide to the mammals of Pennsylvania.* 1987. Pittsburgh, PA: University of Pittsburgh Press.

Peterson, Randolph L. *The mammals of eastern Canada.* 1966. Toronto: Oxford University Press.

Schwartz, Charles W., and Elizabeth R. Schwartz. *The wild mammals of Missouri.* 1981. Columbia: University of Missouri Press.

Verts, B. J., and Leslie N. Carraway. *Land mammals of Oregon.* 1998. Berkeley: University of California Press.

Whitaker, John O., Jr., and William J. Hamilton, Jr. *Mammals of the eastern United States,* third edition. 1998. Ithaca, NY: Comstock Publishing Associates.

Wilson, Don E., and Sue Ruff. *The Smithsonian book of North American mammals.* 1999. Washington, DC: Smithsonian Institution.

GUIDES TO MAMMAL TRACKS

Elbroch, Mark. *Mammal tracks and sign: A guide to North American species.* 2003. Mechanicsburg, PA: Stackpole Books.

Murie, Olaus J., and Mark Elbroch. *Peterson field guide to animal tracks,* third edition. 2005. Boston: Houghton Mifflin.

GUIDES TO MARINE MAMMALS

Reeves, Randall R., Brent S. Stewart, Phillip J. Clapham, and James A. Powell. *National Audubon Society guide to marine mammals of the world.* 2002. New York: Alfred. A. Knopf.

WEB SITES AND ORGANIZATIONS

American Society of Mammalogists, available on the Web at www.mammalsociety.org, has checklists for many states and publishes both the technical *Journal of Mammalogy* and *Mammalian Species,* a detailed source of information for single species.

Animal Diversity Web: http://animaldiversity.ummz.umich.edu.

Bat Conservation International: www.batcon.org.

Mammal Species of the World: http://nmnhgoph.si.edu/msw.

Photo Credits

Dr. J. Scott Altenbach: 394, 396, 408, 420, 423, 425
Ronn Altig: 385, 458
Jessica L. Blois: 313
Craig Brandt: ii–iii, 169, 197, 309
Robin Brandt: 181, 436, 499, 547
Marvin Cattoor/The Image Finders: 505
Brandon Cole/Visuals Unlimited: 517, 528, 543
Susan Day/Daybreak Imagery: xxii–1
Patrick J. Endres/Alaska PhotoGraphics.com: 180, 452, 479
W. K. Fletcher/Photo Researchers: 185
Mark E. Gibson/The Image Finders: 513
Francois Gohier/Photo Researchers: 484, 541, 546
Barry Griffiths: 453, 474
Dan Guravich/Photo Researchers: 481
Dave Haas/The Image Finders: 175
Jeff Henry/Roche Jaune Pictures, Inc.: 134
Tom and Pat Leeson: 178, 206, 444, 469 (top), 469 (bottom), 472, 489, 494, 503, 514, 525, 536
George Lepp/Photo Researchers: 519
Craig Lorenz/Photo Researchers: 358
Maslowski Productions: 183, 210, 230, 345, 347, 389, 446, 447, 495
Steve Maslowski/Visuals Unlimited: 203
Joe McDonald/Visuals Unlimited: 269
Tom McHugh/Photo Researchers: 243, 259, 329
Robert McKemie/Daybreak Imagery: 441
Anthony Mercieca/Photo Researchers: 251, 384
Michael Patrikeev: 173, 234, 238, 241, 256, 261, 279, 285, 293, 296, 304, 314, 322, 334, 366, 369, 381, 388, 390, 409, 417, 424, 462, 467
B. Moose Peterson/WRP: 364
Len Rue Jr.: 171, 186, 338, 439, 456, 471, 496, 500, 507
Leonard Lee Rue III: 198, 433, 437, 548–49

Ischi Rue: 485

Ivin Staffan/Photo Researchers: 292

om J. Ulrich: 184, 204, 342, 413, 463, 475, 490, 498, 506

Mark S. Werner/The Image Finders: 451

Mark and Sue Werner/The Image Finders: 356

David T. Wyatt: 455

INDEX

Numbers in **bold** refer to illustrations and photographs.

THE PETERSON SERIES®

PETERSON FIELD GUIDES®

BIRDS

ADVANCED BIRDING North America
BIRDS OF BRITAIN AND EUROPE
BIRDS OF TEXAS Texas and adjacent states
BIRDS OF THE WEST INDIES
EASTERN BIRDS Eastern and central North America
EASTERN BIRDS' NESTS U.S. east of Mississippi River
HAWKS North America
HUMMINGBIRDS North America
MEXICAN BIRDS Mexico, Guatemala, Belize, El Salvador
WARBLERS North America
WESTERN BIRDS North America west of 100th meridian and north of Mexico
WESTERN BIRDS' NESTS U.S. west of Mississippi River

FISHES

ATLANTIC COAST FISHES North American Atlantic coast
FRESHWATER FISHES North America north of Mexico
PACIFIC COAST FISHES Gulf of Alaska to Baja California

INSECTS

BEETLES North America
EASTERN BUTTERFLIES Eastern and central North America
INSECTS North America north of Mexico
WESTERN BUTTERFLIES U.S. and Canada west of 100th meridian, part of northern Mexico

MAMMALS

ANIMAL TRACKS North America
MAMMALS North America north of Mexico

PETERSON FIELD GUIDES® continued

ECOLOGY

PLANTS

EARTH AND SKY

REPTILES AND AMPHIBIANS

EASTERN REPTILES AND AMPHIBIANS Eastern
and central North America

WESTERN REPTILES AND AMPHIBIANS
Western North America, including
Baja California

SEASHORE

ATLANTIC SEASHORE Bay of Fundy to Cape Hatteras

CORAL REEFS Caribbean and Florida

PACIFIC COAST SHELLS North American Pacific coast, including
Hawaii and the Gulf of California

SHELLS OF THE ATLANTIC Atlantic and Gulf coasts and the West
Indies

SOUTHEAST AND CARIBBEAN SEASHORES Cape Hatteras to the Gulf
Coast, Florida, and the Caribbean

PETERSON FIRST GUIDES®

ASTRONOMY

BIRDS

BUTTERFLIES AND MOTHS

CATERPILLARS

CLOUDS AND WEATHER

DINOSAURS

FISHES

FORESTS

INSECTS

MAMMALS

REPTILES AND AMPHIBIANS

ROCKS AND MINERALS

SEASHORES

SHELLS

SOLAR SYSTEM

TREES

URBAN WILDLIFE

WILDFLOWERS

PETERSON FIELD GUIDE AUDIOS

BACKYARD BIRD SONG
    cassettes
    CD

BIRDING BY EAR Eastern North
    America
        cassettes
        CD

BIRDING BY EAR Western North
    America
        cassettes
        CD

BIRD SONGS Eastern and central
    North America, revised
        CD

BIRD SONGS Western North
    America, revised
        CD

MORE BIRDING BY EAR Eastern and
    central North America
        cassettes
        CD

PETERSON FIELD GUIDE COLOR-IN BOOKS

BIRDS

BUTTERFLIES

DINOSAURS

MAMMALS

REPTILES AND AMPHIBIANS

SEASHORES

SHELLS

WILDFLOWERS

PETERSON FLASHGUIDES®

ANIMAL TRACKS
ATLANTIC COASTAL BIRDS
BACKYARD BIRDS
BIRDS OF THE MIDWEST
BUTTERFLIES
EASTERN TRAILSIDE BIRDS

HAWKS
TREES
ROADSIDE WILDFLOWERS
WATERFOWL
WESTERN TRAILSIDE BIRDS

PETERSON FIELD GUIDES can be purchased at your local
    bookstore or by calling our toll-free number, (800) 225-3362.
    Visit **www.petersononline.com** for more information.